AF574531

Snapshots

Snapshots

CHRISTIAN SKREIN — THE EYE OF THE CENTURY

With contributions by Mit Beiträgen von

CARL AIGNER
FRITS GIERSTBERG
PETER NOEVER
CHRISTIAN SKREIN

HATJE CANTZ

Contents Inhalt

SNAPSHOTS SCHNAPPSCHÜSSE

PETER NOEVER

Der Blick des Reporters

Ich glaube, es war der 23. Februar 1968, als ich zum ersten Mal Christian Raoul Skrein von Bumbala – so sein Name in voller Länge – getroffen habe. In seinem Fotoatelier in der Lainzer Straße 71 in Wien hatte der damals 23-jährige Skrein zum »Sehen und Gesehenwerden« geladen. Allein, zu sehen war kaum jemand, denn die Massen und insbesondere die wichtigsten Proponenten der Wiener Kunstszene ertranken buchstäblich in einem Meer aus Styroporkugeln. Skrein war der Shootingstar unter den Fotografen, und er bekam (fast) alle vor sein Objektiv, die in den sechziger Jahren die neuesten Tendenzen zeitgenössischer Kunstproduktion bestimmten oder am besten Weg dazu waren. Seine unkonventionelle Herangehensweise, ein Anflug von Wahnsinn und seine Aufmachung, wie David Hemmings als Starfotograf und Held in Michelangelo Antonionis *Blow-Up,* haben es Skrein ermöglicht, vom 17-jährigen Fotoreporter zu einem der gefragtesten Künstlerporträtisten und Modefotografen aufzusteigen. Seine Aufnahmen von der Wiener Kunstszene sind legendär, Fotografien von Joseph Beuys, Christo oder den Beatles gingen um die Welt, aber auch seine Experimente mit Weitwinkelaufnahmen waren maßgeblich für die Trendentwicklung der Modefotografie in den siebziger Jahren. Im Alter von 25 Jahren legte er die Kamera von einem Tag auf den anderen aus der Hand und hat sie seither nie wieder angerührt, hat berufliche Ausflüge in den Werbefilm und, später, in die so genannte New Economy unternommen. Tatsächlich losgelassen hat ihn die Fotografie jedoch nie. Nur kann er sich heute voll und ganz auf die Passionen seines Lebens konzentrieren: das Rauchen kubanischer Zigarren, die Pflege einer großbürgerlichen Villa im Salzkammergut und, mit der Hingabe eines Privatgelehrten, seine vor 35 Jahren begonnene Sammlung an Schnappschüssen, zusammengetragen von allen möglichen Plätzen aus allen Teilen der Welt. Skreins Sammlung konzentriert sich ausschließlich und mit philanthropischem Genuss auf Bilder von Amateuren, zeigt die Genialität der Unbekümmertheit und vertreibt die dem Medium innewohnende Trivialität. Dies gelingt jedoch nur durch eine akribische Auswahl der Fotografien, wofür Skrein wiederum sein professionell fotografisch geschultes Auge einsetzt. Als Sammler und Dokumentarist bleibt er seinem Selbstverständnis als Reporter treu, einer Profession, deren ureigenster Wesenszug die Faszination für das Alltägliche und die Neugier als treibende Kraft ist. Mit der Offenlegung der Sammlung bleibt er auf gewohntem Terrain, verlässt sich auf das, was er kennt, was er selbst gesehen hat, kennen lernen möchte, was ihn fasziniert – die Darstellung des Alltags, dauerhaft gültige Bilder des Unbestimmten und nicht zu Bestimmenden und dennoch unbestechlich das fließende Wesen der Zeit ausdrückend. Der Zeit, die wir gerade noch begreifen, die aber dennoch nicht unsere ist.

PETER NOEVER

The Reporter's View

I think it was February 23, 1968, when I met Christian Raoul Skrein von Bumbala—this being his name in full length—for the first time. In his photo studio at 71 Lainzer Strasse in Vienna the then twenty-three-year-old Skrein had invited us over "to see and to be seen." But nobody could be seen because the masses, especially the most important proponents of the Viennese art scene literally drowned in a sea of Styrofoam balls. Skrein was the shooting star of the photographers, and he got (nearly) everybody in front of his lens who defined the newest tendencies in contemporary art production in the sixties or who were well on their way to defining it. His unconventional approach, a touch of madness, and his appearance—akin to David Hemmings as a star photographer and hero in Michelangelo Antonioni's *Blow-Up*—made it possible for Skrein to work his way up from a seventeen-year-old photo reporter to one of the most sought-after portraitists of artists and fashion photographers. His photographs of the Viennese art scene are legendary—photographs of Joseph Beuys, Christo, and the Beatles went around the world—and his experiments with wide-angle shots were also influential in the development of trends in fashion photography in the seventies. One day, at the age of twenty-five, he put the camera away and has not touched it since. He made professional forays into advertising, film, and, later, into the so-called New Economy. Yet photography never left him completely. Today he is fully able to focus on the passions of his life: smoking Cuban cigars, looking after his villa in the Salzkammergut region of Austria, and tending, with the devotion of a private scholar, his collection of snapshots which he initiated thirty-five years ago, compiled from all possible places in all parts of the world. Skrein's collection focuses on amateur shots exclusively and with philanthropic pleasure, showing the ingeniousness of being carefree and dispersing the intrinsic triviality of the medium. But this only succeeds through meticulous selection of the photographs for which Skrein in turn utilizes his professionally schooled eye. As collector and documentary he stays faithful to his self-conception as a reporter, a profession with the special characteristic trait of a fascination for the ordinary and for curiosity as its driving force. By publishing the collection he stays on known terrain: he relies on what he knows, what he has seen for himself, what he wants to get to know, what fascinates him—the representation of everyday life, permanently valid images of the uncertain and of what cannot be defined, nevertheless expressing unerringly the flowing essence of time. Of a time we can just grasp but which yet is not ours.

CHRISTIAN SKREIN

Das Auge des Jahrhunderts

Es war 1969, als ich eine Entdeckungsreise in das Innere der feinkörnigen Fotokunst begann – eine scheinbar beiläufige Forschungsreise, die gleichzeitig das Sehen lernen mit bewusst geschärften Augen zum Ziel hatte. Anstelle von Arbeiten verehrter Meister fand ich weggelegte, vergessene, nicht mehr beachtete, abgegriffene Alben und aus dem Leim gegangene Fotoschachteln, Motive einst mit kolonialer Fantasie geschaffen. Aus Passion nahm ich diese bedeutungslosen, anonymen Abzüge mit nach Hause, um sie einfach nur aufzuheben – man weiß ja nie, was sich da an Schätzen verbirgt –, hier in einem chinesischen Schrank, dort in einer Zigarrenkiste mit der Beschriftung »verpatzte Schnappschüsse«. Diese, wie sich herausstellte, nur vermeintlich unwesentlichen Dinge, denen ich, als ich herumreiste, maßvolles Gewicht gab, wurden mir im Verlauf von 33 Jahren die leichteste Sache der Welt. Sie stillten die Sehnsucht nach Zeichen der Zeit, indem sie losgelassen wurden.

Beide sind untrennbar miteinander verbunden: Sehnsucht und Ziel – der sichtbarste Ausdruck unbegreiflicher, hoher Macht gepaart mit zufälliger Schöpferkraft als Zeugnis schlichter, empfindungsvoller Augenblicke. Mit dem Leben, wie immer es auch ausfiel, eng verbunden, mit offenen Augen, manches Mal mit einer banalen Weltverbundenheit ist es nun ein sehr reicher Schatz an Lebensmomenten.

Diese dargestellten Zeugnisse des Lebens sind nun durchaus geeignet, neue Bedeutung zu erlangen, zwar wurden sie aus ihrem eigentlichen Kontext herausgerissen, doch konnte dadurch ihr Charakter nicht beschädigt werden.

Von Jahr zu Jahr sind weitere überraschende Lichtblicke hinzugekommen, die genauso wenig mit dem kühnen Anspruch in die Welt treten, als beispielhaft gelten zu wollen, wohl aber den bescheidenen Wunsch haben, dass Einzelne einzig sein mögen, da sie doch ihrem trivialen Inhalt nach alles in natürlicher Weise anschauen und erfassen.

Licht, theatralische Regungen des Herzens, aufbrausende Leidenschaft, Nacktheit ohne Scheu und Schminke, Freude und Schmerz, Lust und Trauer, Schatten, Übermut und Niedergeschlagenheit, Wirklichkeit und Traum in einfacher Harmonie – das sind meine »Kinder«. Reine Erzeugnisse natürlicher Anschauungsweise, manchmal mit einem übertriebenen, manchmal mit einem spielerischen Streben nach Kunst, dennoch auch Abfall und Zufall.

Unter ihnen befinden sich so manche, die so gewohnt, vertraut und sogar heimisch geworden sind, dass sie durch die Hintertür unsterblich wurden und in Publikationen, Ausstellungen und Museen – Zufluchtsorten gleich – notlandeten, nur um den Geschmack an einfacher Sehfreude und Fantasie zu befriedigen.

Erzählt wird das Märchen von ein paar seltsamen Schnappschüssen, zusammengetragen mit dem Empfinden, ein scheinbares Lebenswerk lebendig zum Leben zu bringen. Denn: Abnormal ist normal, weil Unsinn Sinn ergibt.

CHRISTIAN SKREIN

The Eye of the Century

It was 1969 when I began an expedition into the heart of the fine-grained art of photography—an expedition that only appeared to be incidental, yet was undertaken with a simultaneous purpose of learning to see with consciously sharpened eyes. Instead of works of admired masters, I found photo albums put away, forgotten, ignored, worn out; photo boxes fallen apart; motifs which had once been created by colonial fantasy. Nevertheless, out of passion I took home these meaningless, anonymous prints, to simply preserve them—one never knows what treasures could be hidden inside—here in a Chinese cupboard, there in a cigar box labeled "botched snapshots." These, as it turned out later, only seemingly insignificant things, which I gave measured weight while traveling about, became the easiest thing in the world for me over the course of thirty-three years. By setting them free, they satisfied the yearning for signs of the time.

Both are connected inseparably: yearning and purpose—the most visible expression of a higher power beyond comprehension, paired with random creative power as a reference of simple moments filled with sensations. Closely knit with life, whatever way it turned out to be, with open eyes, and sometimes relating to the world in a banal way, these images now constitute a very rich treasure of life's moments.

These depicted testimonials of life are definitely capable of gaining a new significance. Although removed from their original context, their character could not be harmed by this.

More surprising rays of light have been added to this from year to year. These do not step into the world under the bold pretense of serving as examples but are an expression of the modest wish to be unique as individuals. Because of their trivial content, they behold and touch everything in a natural way.

Light, theatrical emotions of the heart, erupting passion, nudity without shyness and makeup, pleasure and pain, lust and mourning, shadow, high spirits and disheartenment, reality and dream in simple harmony—these are my "children." They are pure works of a natural point of view, striving towards being art, sometimes in an exaggerated way, sometimes in a playful way. They are as much an expression of chance as well as they are detritus.

Among them are many which have become familiar, intimate, and even homelike, thereby gaining immortality through the back door. They are performing emergency landings in publications, exhibitions, and museums—akin to places of refuge—just to satisfy a taste in simple viewing pleasure and fantasy.

This is the tale of a couple of odd snapshots, compiled while experiencing the sensation of bringing to life an apparent life's work in a lively way. Because: Abnormal is normal, since nonsense does make sense.

FRITS GIERSTBERG

Das Auftauchen und Verschwinden der Privat-(Amateur-)Fotografie im Museum

In den Privatfotos von anderen erkennen wir unsere eigenen Fotos. Es ist sogar noch mehr als das: In diesen Bildern erkennen wir spezifische Situationen, Ereignisse, Familienrituale und sogar Emotionen. Ein Geburtstag, der Urlaub, das neue Auto, der Hund, unterm Weihnachtsbaum, mit Freunden, die neue Freundin, am Strand.

Die Macher sind anonym, die fotografierten Personen ebenfalls. Wir kennen ihre Namen nicht, wissen nicht, wie alt sie waren, als das Foto gemacht wurde, wo sie herkamen, welchen Beruf oder welche gesellschaftliche Stellung sie hatten. Auch die Fotos selbst sind »anonym«: Ort und Zeitpunkt ihres Entstehens sind oft unbekannt; wir wissen nichts über die Motive des Machers noch derjenigen, die diese Fotos weggaben. Wir wissen nichts als: Diesen Ort, an dem diese Menschen zu sehen sind, gab es einmal, und sie sahen genauso aus. Wir können uns nur darüber wundern.

Die hier präsentierten Fotos wurden in der ersten Hälfte des 20. Jahrhunderts aufgenommen. Die meisten Menschen auf diesen Bildern sind inzwischen tot. Ihr Foto ist unsere einzige Verbindung zu ihrer Geschichte, einer Geschichte, die einst Teil der »großen« Geschichte der Welt und der Menschheit gewesen ist. Die ungeschriebenen, individuellen Geschichten, die »kleinen Geschichten«, verblassen im festlichen Licht des Erkennens, das unter unseren Augen zu leuchten beginnt. Sie verschwinden hinter den mentalen Projektionen unserer eigenen Erinnerungen und Fantasien auf dem Raster, das wir im Leben dieser anderen Menschen zu entdecken glauben: Ja, so sieht unser Leben auch aus, dieselben Rituale, dieselben Augenblicke, dieselben Gefühlsregungen. Fest steht, dass diese Fotos nie Kunst sein wollten. Sie sind ohne ein künstlerisches Konzept entstanden. Wenn es außer der Technik ein gemeinsames Merkmal gibt, dann ist es die Tatsache, dass die Amateurfotografen wahrscheinlich ihre Freude dabei hatten: beim Knipsen, beim Zeigen, beim Aufbewahren, beim immer wieder von neuem Betrachten. Jetzt sind diese Bilder aus dem privaten Bereich und der intimen Atmosphäre, in die sie gehören, herausgelöst. Uns stört das wenig. Es sind »interessante«, »schöne«, »faszinierende« Bilder. Wem sie gehört haben, ist eigentlich ziemlich einerlei. Auch durch sie wird unser moderner Hunger nach Privatbildern gestillt. Sie nähren unser Verlangen nach Authentizität, nach authentischen Bildern. Die Menschen auf den Fotos hatten ja noch nicht ein so starkes »Medienbewusstsein« wie wir heute. Ihre Haltung gegenüber dem Fotoapparat war unbefangen und ohne Argwohn, ihre Posen ehrlich und naiv. Zumindest denken wir das gern.

Inzwischen steht fest, dass diese Form der Fotografie, mit ihren verschiedenen Formaten und Farbtönen, den gezackten Rändern, den Leimresten und den handschriftlichen Kommentaren auf der Rückseite, auf einem Papierabzug mit einer silberhaltigen Emulsion und in ein Album eingeklebt, sicher bezeichnend für das 20. Jahrhundert ist. Das gilt auch für die Art, diese Fotografien *zu sammeln*. Es ist ziemlich unwahrscheinlich, dass wir in fünfzig oder hundert Jahren digitale Fotodateien auf dem Flohmarkt finden werden. Oder finden wir sie dann im World Wide Web?

FRITS GIERSTBERG

The Appearance and Disappearance of Private (Amateur) Photography in the Museum

We recognize our own photos in the private photographs of others. It is even more than that: in these pictures we recognize specific situations, events, family rituals, and even emotions. Births, birthday celebrations, vacations, new cars, dogs, under the Christmas tree, with friends, new girlfriend, on the beach.

The makers are anonymous, as are the photographed persons. We do not know their names, we do not know how old they were when the photo was made, where they came from, what their profession was, or what their social position was. Even the photos themselves are "anonymous": the location and the time of their creation often are unknown; we know nothing about the motives of the maker or about those who gave these photos away. The only thing we know is: the place in which these people can be seen existed once, and this is exactly what they looked like. We can only wonder at this and be amazed. The photographs presented here were made in the first half of the twentieth century. Most of the people in these pictures are dead by now. Their photo portrait is our only connection to their personal story, a story that once was part of the "big" story of the world and of mankind. The unwritten, individual stories—the "small stories"—fade under the festive light of recognition which begins to shine in our eyes. They disappear behind the mental projections of our own memories and fantasies on the pattern that we seem to discover in the life of these other people: yes, this is what our life looks like, too, the same rituals, the same moments, the same emotions. Certainly these photographs never wanted to be art. They came into existence without an artistic program or concept. If there is a common attribute beside the technology connecting them then it is the fact that the amateur photographers probably had their fun: making snapshots, showing them around, preserving them, looking at them again and again. Now these images have been removed from the private sphere and the intimate atmosphere where they belong. This does not bother us much, we are not embarrassed by this when we look at them. They are "interesting," "beautiful," "fascinating" images. It really does not matter to whom they belonged. Through them, too, our modern hunger for private images is satisfied. They feed our desire for authenticity, for authentic images. The people in those photos did not have such a strong "media consciousness" as we have today. Their attitude towards the camera was unbiased and without distrust, their posing honest and naive. At least that is what we like to think.

In the meantime it has been established that this form of photography, with its different formats and colorings, the zigzag edges, the residue of glue and scotch tape and the comments scribbled by hand onto the backside, on a paper print pasted with an emulsion containing silver and glued into an album, surely is representative of the twentieth century. The same is true of the way these photographs *are being collected.* It is rather unlikely that we will find digital photo files on the flee market in fifty or a hundred years from now. Or will we then find them on the World Wide Web?

Künstler und Berufsfotografen lassen sich von diesen anonymen Schnappschüssen inspirieren. Gleichzeitig finden wir in jeder Sammlung solcher Amateurfotos Bilder, die dem Werk berühmter Fotografen sehr ähnlich sind. Jacques-Henri Lartigue, Walker Evans, Eugène Atget, Robert Frank, Diane Arbus, Garry Winogrand, August Sander, Man Ray: Allesamt sind sie dort zu finden. Ihre Versuche, einen eigenen Stil zu entwickeln oder einzigartige Fotos zu machen, erscheinen rückwirkend überflüssig und sinnlos: Alles ist nicht nur schon einmal fotografiert, alles ist auch schon einmal in jedem erdenkbaren Stil fotografiert.

Das führt uns zur Frage nach dem Kunststatus dieser Fotos. Sie waren sicher nicht als Kunst gedacht. Vielleicht versuchte sich der eine oder andere Amateurfotograf zu profilieren, indem er eine »künstlerische Perspektive« wählte, und vielleicht ist das dem einen oder anderen auch einmal gelungen. Aber meistens entstehen diese Bilder aus Zufall oder Unwissenheit: Der Horizont ist aus Versehen schief geraten, die doppelte Belichtung ist einem schlecht funktionierenden Apparat zu verdanken, die abgeschnittene Figur wurde nicht bemerkt. Oft wurde das betreffende Foto vom Fotografen selbst als nicht besonders gelungen angesehen. Dass wir diese »lookalikes« überhaupt finden, geschieht nicht *trotz*, sondern *dank* der Werke bekannter Fotografen. Sie haben uns ja das Sehen gelehrt, und wir haben uns ihre Lektionen bewusst oder unbewusst gelernt. Der Zufall, der dem Entstehen dieser Fotos zugrunde liegt, ist also ein scheinbarer Zufall; unser Staunen über diese »Funde« wirkt gespielt. Anno 2004 schaut niemand mehr unbefangen, unser Blick hat eine umfassende Schulung hinter sich. Die erste Hälfte des 20. Jahrhunderts ist die Ära der Moderne und der Modernität. Mit zwei Weltkriegen und dem Holocaust handelt es sich um eine der traumatischsten Zeitabschnitte der Menschheitsgeschichte. Es ist auch die Zeit, in dem die Massenmedien, wie Fotografie und Film, die Welt zum ersten Mal für jedermann sichtbar machen – und zwar vor allem innerhalb der verschiedenen ästhetischen Bezüge, die von den damaligen Avantgardebewegungen in der bildenden Kunst (und in der Fotografie, im Film, in den grafischen Künsten) propagiert wurden. Die Schulung unseres Blicks auf die Welt durch die Massenmedien setzt also in dieser Zeit ein. Im Grunde beginnt damit auch die Verästhetisierung unseres Weltbildes, die in der zweiten Jahrhunderthälfte, in der Postmoderne, ihren vorläufigen Höhepunkt finden sollte.

Die Postmoderne lehrte uns, »die großen Geschichten« zu vergessen. Sie lehrte uns zu sehen, ohne wissen zu müssen. Sie lehrte uns, Privatfotos ohne besonderen Grund zu betrachten, und machte damit den Weg frei für ein wertfreies Interesse an ihrer Qualität als *Bild*. Heute sind wir imstande, sie an die Wand zu hängen, ohne dass wir auch nur das Geringste über das Leben der Menschen wissen, die darauf zu sehen sind. So kommt es zu diesem merkwürdigen Paradox: In dem Moment, in dem diese von passionierten Sammlern zusammengetragenen Amateurbilder en masse aus der Geschichte auftauchen und ihren Weg in unsere Museen finden, verschwinden ihre Einzelgeschichten endgültig in der Vergessenheit.

Artists and professional photographers find inspiration in these anonymous snapshots. At the same time we find images in every collection of such amateur photographs very similar to the work of famous photographers. Jacques-Henri Lartigue, Walker Evans, Eugène Atget, Robert Frank, Diane Arbus, Garry Winogrand, August Sander, Man Ray: all of them can be found there. Their attempts at developing a style of their own or at making unique photos seem redundant and useless in hindsight: not only has everything been photographed once, everything has been photographed already in every conceivable style. This leads us to the question of the art status of these photos. They surely were not intended to be art. Maybe the one or the other amateur photograph tried to distinguish themselves as an artist by choosing an "artistic perspective," and maybe the one or the other succeeded on occasion (the chance is small, we know that through our own experience). But mostly these pictures come into being through chance or ignorance: through an oversight the horizon ended up lopsided, the double exposure was caused by a malfunctioning camera, the cut-off figure simply was not noticed. Often the photo at hand was not regarded as very successful by the photographer himself. The fact that we are discovering these "look-alikes" at all is not happening *in spite of* but *thanks to* the works of known photographers. Since they taught us seeing we embraced their lessons either consciously or subconsciously. The coincidence which, according to our opinion, underlies the production of these images, thus is a seeming coincidence; our amazement in the face of these "finds" seems acted. In the year 2004 nobody looks unconsciously, our gaze has gone through an extensive training. The first half of the twentieth century was the era of Modernism and of modernity. With two world wars and the Holocaust it was one of the most traumatic periods in the history of mankind. It was also the time when mass media such as photography and film made the world visible for everyone for the first time–and especially within the different aesthetical references being propagated by the then avant-garde movements in the fine arts (and in photography, in film, in the graphic arts). The training of our gaze onto the world through mass media started at that time. Essentially, what began as well was the over-aestheticization of our world view that would peak in the Postmodernism of the second half of the century. Postmodernism taught us to forget "the big stories." It taught us to see without having to know. It taught us to look at private photos without any special reason and therefore paved the way for an unbiased interest in their quality as an image. Today we are able to hang them on the wall full of admiration without knowing even the very least about the life of the people who are depicted in them. That way we arrive at this odd paradox: at the moment, at which these amateur pictures compiled by passionate collectors in collections appear from history finding their way onto the walls of our museums, their individual stories disappear into oblivion forever.

CARL AIGNER Im Bilde sein oder das Phantasma der Fotografie

Um wirklich zu sehen, muss man das, was man sieht, mit dem vergleichen, was man gesehen hat.
OCTAVIO PAZ

Die Fotografie hat nur einen Sinn, wenn sie alle Möglichkeiten von Bildern erschöpft.
ITALO CALVINO

Claude Lévi-Strauss unterscheidet in seiner strukturalen Anthropologie grundlegend zwischen »kalten«, sich kaum verändernden und »heißen«, auf dem Prinzip der Dynamik basierenden Gesellschaften. Auffallend dabei ist, dass die »heißen« Gesellschaften Bilder-Gesellschaften sind, dass Bilder Teil gesellschaftlicher Dynamiken, mehr noch: selbst Basis dieser Dynamiken implizieren. In der Geschichte der Bilder ist dafür der wohl signifikanteste Part die Erfindung der Fotografie (und des Films), die, wie Roland Barthes einmal bemerkenswert schrieb, die Geschichte der Welt in zwei Hälften teilt.

Wenn wir davon ausgehen, dass eine auf Bildern basierende Gesellschaft auf einem anthropologischen Verhältnis zu diesen beruht, so können wir daraus schließen, dass das Erscheinen der Fotografie im 19. Jahrhundert eine elementare kulturelle, soziale und ästhetische Transformation kokonstituiert und darstellt. Zunächst und vor allem ist es das Moment der gesellschaftlichen Beschleunigung. Die Fotografie ist dabei sowohl Teil (sie ist das schnellste Bildmedium des vorletzten Jahrhunderts) dieser Beschleunigung als auch Kontrapunkt, indem sie sie quasi dialektisch fixiert und piktural zum Stillstand bringt: Sie hält (einen Augenblick) fest. Es ist die daraus resultierende Ambivalenz, die ein wesentliches Faszinosum dieses ersten, apparativen Bildmediums in der Geschichte der Bilder ist (in seiner Dromologie schreibt Paul Virilio einmal zutreffend vom »rasenden Stillstand«, in dem wir uns seit langem befinden). Wie überhaupt die Fotografie die Ambivalenz von »noch/ aber schon« produziert, die gleichsam die gesamte europäische Gesellschaft des 19. und frühen 20. Jahrhunderts charakterisiert: noch Handwerk, aber schon Apparat, noch Original, aber schon Reproduktion, authentisch, aber schon Kopie, noch Bild, aber schon Fragment, noch Abbildung, aber schon Weltbild, noch singuläre Bildmöglichkeit, aber schon Massenbildmedium.

Die fotografischen Bilder – und darauf gilt es den Blick zu richten – erzeugen und illustrieren ein Begehren, das unmittelbar mit der angesprochenen sozialen, gesellschaftlichen und kulturellen Dynamisierung verknüpft ist. Die damit einhergehende Auflösung jahrzehnte- und jahrhundertelanger existenzieller Konstanten (die Humanwissenschaften sprechen vom Säkularisierungsprozess) evoziert in einer elaborierten Bildergesellschaft einen Transfer: Die Bilder werden zu neuen Orten einer Seinsvergewisserung. Kein anderes Bildmedium vermag dies so existenziell zu formulieren und zu gewähren wie die Fotografie: Sie ist, wie als erster Roland Barthes im Hinblick auf ihre mediale Spezifik feststellte, die erste und einzige Bildform, die eine zertifikatorische Kraft bezüglich des Gezeigten besitzt – die analoge, chemische Fotografie kann nur das zeigen, was physikalisch existiert und referiert wird.

CARL AIGNER

Being in the Picture, or The Phantasm of Photography

In order to really see, one has to compare what one sees with that which one has seen.
OCTAVIO PAZ

Photography has meaning only when it exhausts all possibilities of images.
ITALO CALVINO

Claude Lévi-Strauss differentiates in his structural anthropology fundamentally between "cold" societies hardly changing and "hot" societies based on the principle of dynamics. It is striking that the "hot" societies are image-societies, that images are part of the dynamics of the society, and even more: implicate the basis of these dynamics. In the history of images arguably the most significant part for this is the invention of photography (and of film), which, as Roland Barthes wrote, divides the history of the world into two halves.

Assuming that a society based on images depends on an anthropological relationship with these, we can conclude that the appearance of photography in the nineteenth century co-constitutes and represents an elemental cultural, social, and aesthetical transformation. Firstly and foremost, it triggers social acceleration. In doing so, photography is part of this acceleration (it is the fastest image medium of the nineteenth century, as well as a counterpoint in that it virtually freezes it in a dialectical way, bringing it to a halt pictorially: it makes a record (of a moment). It is the ambivalence resulting from this which represents an essential fascination of this first, apparatus-based image medium in the history of images (in "dromology" Paul Virilio wrote of the "speeding standstill" we have been experiencing for a long time). As photography generally produces the ambivalence of "still/but already" which characterizes more or less the whole European society of the nineteenth and early twentieth century: still handicraft but already apparatus, still an original but already a reproduction, authentic but already a copy, still an image but already a fragment, still a picture but already a view of the world, still singular possibility of an image but already a mass medium of images.

The photographic images—and this is where we should direct our gaze—produce and illustrate a desire directly connected to the said social and cultural dynamic sampling. The accompanying dissolution of decade- and century-long existential constants (the humanities speak of the secularization process) refer to it as a transfer within an elaborated image society: the images become new places of an ascertainment of being. No other image medium can express and guarantee this in such an existential way as photography can: it is, as Roland Barthes was the first to assert with regard to its medial specificity, the first and only image form featuring a certifying power with regard to that which is shown—analogue, chemical photography can only show what exists physically and what is being reported.

So only up to a point is it a matter of a new, more efficient possibility of reproduction (the idea of and the desire for a representable visual world itself is part of the secularization process),

Es geht also nur bedingt um eine neue, effizientere Abbildungsmöglichkeit (die Vorstellung und das Verlangen nach einer abbildbaren visuellen Welt ist selbst Teil des Säkularisierungsprozesses), sondern um die einzigartige neue Möglichkeit über sich selbst und die Welt eine existenzielle (Selbst-)Vergewisserung zu gewinnen. Das fotografische Verlangen, der fotografische Bilderrausch kompensiert den Verlust des transzendentalen Weltbildes und versöhnt ihn mit und durch die neue, fotografische Bilderflut. Darin verbirgt sich auch das Verlangen nach Unvergänglichkeit. Insofern ist es kein Zufall, dass die Fotografie auch das erste Zeit-Bild in der Geschichte der Bilder ist: Durch das Licht unmittelbar an die Zeit der Belichtung gebunden, vermag sie uns das Moment der Aufgehobenheit, der Unvergänglichkeit zu suggerieren, indem sie scheinbar das Gezeigte einbalsamiert, wie es immer wieder heißt.

Jetzt, am Ende des Zeitalters der Fotografie können wir das in erstaunlicher Nachdrücklichkeit und Eindringlichkeit sehen. Die gut einhundertfünfzig Jahre währende Epoche der Fotografie ist der pikturale Herzschlag der Gesellschaft in ihrem Verhältnis von Subjekt, Bild und Gesellschaft. Die Fotografie wurde zum Traum und zum Trauma des Begehrens nach Unsterblichkeit. »Eine illegitime Kunst« nennt Pierre Bourdieu eine grundlegende soziologische Studie über die sozialen Gebrauchsweisen der Fotografie, die er in den sechziger Jahren des vorigen Jahrhunderts realisierte. Die Illegitimität, von der er spricht, markiert eine weitere fotografische Ambivalenz im Spannungsfeld von Kunst und Nichtkunst, indem durch die Fotografie auch die Grenzen der damaligen gesellschaftlichen Definition von Kunst überschritten und neu formuliert werden. Seit dem 18. Jahrhundert, seit dem Entstehen einer Ästhetik wurde die Kunst immer wieder als Ort des Wahren, Schönen und Ewigen charakterisiert, dies sind nichts anderes als Synonyme für Unvergänglichkeit. Wenn aber die Kunst jene Möglichkeit ist, mittels derer eine Gesellschaft oder ein Individuum Unvergänglichkeit imaginiert, wird die ambivalente gesellschaftliche Haltung gegenüber der Fotografie als Kunst nachvollziehbar, weil sie, die Fotografie, ein absolut neues Verhältnis von Bild zu Kunst, Zeit und Gesellschaft evozierte.

Im fotografischen Bilde sein meint also eine Teilhabe an diesem fotografischen Moment der Aufgehobenheit. Wenn die Fotografie eine Kongruenz und Identität von Bild und Welt hergestellt hat (und sie hat es tatsächlich), ist auch nachvollziehbar, warum fotografische Bildwerdung Subjektwerdung bedeutet. Im fotografischen Bild aufscheinen heißt, eine Identität mit der Welt zu postulieren: Seht, ich bin da im Bild, ich bin da in der Welt, ich bin also da! Jede Fotografie bestätigt das Dasein und macht es scheinbar ewig. Ihre Serialität und Multiplizität in der pikturalen Gestion endloser Abziehbarkeit vom Negativ akzentuiert dies weiter: Die Fotografie schaffte eine einzigartige visuelle und räumliche Ubiquität. Und jederzeit und immer zumindest visuell sein zu können, ist eine andere Form der Aufhebung von Raum und Zeit.

Es ist kein Zufall, dass seit den siebziger Jahren des letzten Jahrhunderts die anonymen Fotogra-

but rather about the unique new possibility to gain an existential ascertainment (of the self) about oneself and the world. The desire to photograph, the thrill of photographic images compensates for the loss of the transcendental world view and reconciles it with the new flood of photographic images. Therein also lies the desire for immortality. Insofar it is no coincidence that photography is also the first time-image in the history of images: bound directly to the time of exposure through light, it can suggest to us the moment of abolishment, of immortality by its apparent embalming of the visible, as it is called repeatedly.

Now, at the end of the age of photography we can see this with astonishing emphasis and forcefulness. The era of photography, which has lasted some 150 years, is the pictorial heartbeat of society in its relationship to subject, image, and society. Photography became the dream and the trauma of the desire for immortality. Pierre Bourdieu titled his seminal sociological study on the social uses of photography, written in the nineteen-sixties, "An Illegitimate Art." The illegitimacy he discusses marks another photographic ambivalence in the conflict field of art and non-art by way of photography transgressing and formulating anew the boundaries of the social definition of art at that time. Since the eighteenth century, since the development of aesthetics, art has been characterized as the place of the true, the beautiful, and the eternal time and again. These are nothing but synonyms for immortality. But if art is that possibility by which a society or an individual imagines immortality, the ambivalent social attitude towards photography as an art becomes comprehensible because it, photography, evoked an absolutely new relationship of the image to art, time, and society.

Thus, being in the picture means a participation in this photographic moment of abolishment. If photography created a congruency and identity (and it really has), it is also comprehensible why, photographically, the becoming of image stands for the becoming of subject: to appear in the photographic image means to postulate an identity with the world: look, there I am in the picture, there I am in the world, therefore I am! Every photograph confirms existence and seemingly immortalizes it. Its seriality and multiplicity in the pictorial administration of endless printability from the negative further accentuates this: photography created a unique visual and spatial ubiquity. And the ability to at least be visual every time and all of the time is another form of the reversal of space and time.

It is no coincidence that anonymous photographs have come into the field of vision of contemporary discourses of art since the nineteen-seventies (and in the mean time have also become an indispensable phenomenon of the art market and the museum). Photography (and especially the so-called snapshot) is able to transport in a pure way the here just briefly outlined context to a certain extent: carried by a single intention of capturing something without an explicit aesthetical or artistic strategy that is already passing in the moment of capturing it, the anonymous pho-

fien ins Blickfeld gegenwärtiger Kunstdiskurse geraten (und inzwischen auch ein nicht unwesentliches Kunstmarkt- und Museumsphänomen geworden) ist. Gerade sie (und insbesondere der so genannte Schnappschuss) vermag gewissermaßen in purer Weise diese hier nur kurz skizzierten Zusammenhänge zu transportieren. Getragen von einer einzigen Intention, nämlich etwas ohne explizite ästhetische oder künstlerische Strategie festzuhalten, was im Moment des Festhaltens schon im Vergehen ist, offenbaren die anonymen Fotografien Arsenale des Erinnerns und des Gedächtnisses: »Und das Leben, das ihr lebt, um es zu fotografieren, ist schon im Anfang Erinnerung an sich selbst«, formuliert es Italo Calvino in seiner schönen Erzählung »Abenteuer eines Fotografen«.

tographers disclose arsenals of remembering and of memory: as Italo Calvino put it in his beautiful tale "Adventures of a Photographer," "And the life that you live in order to photograph it is already a memory of itself at its beginning."

1)

Moments Augenblicke

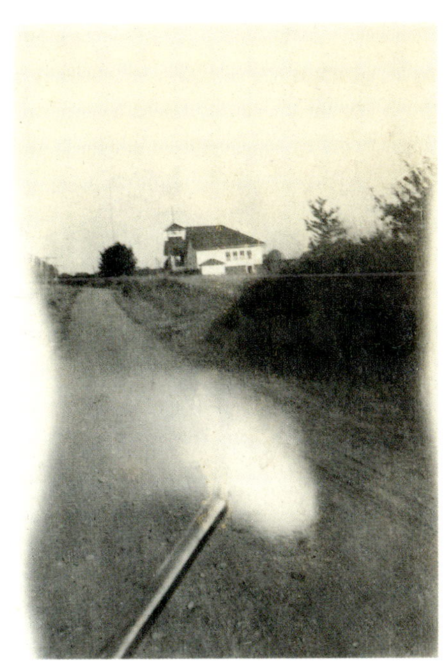

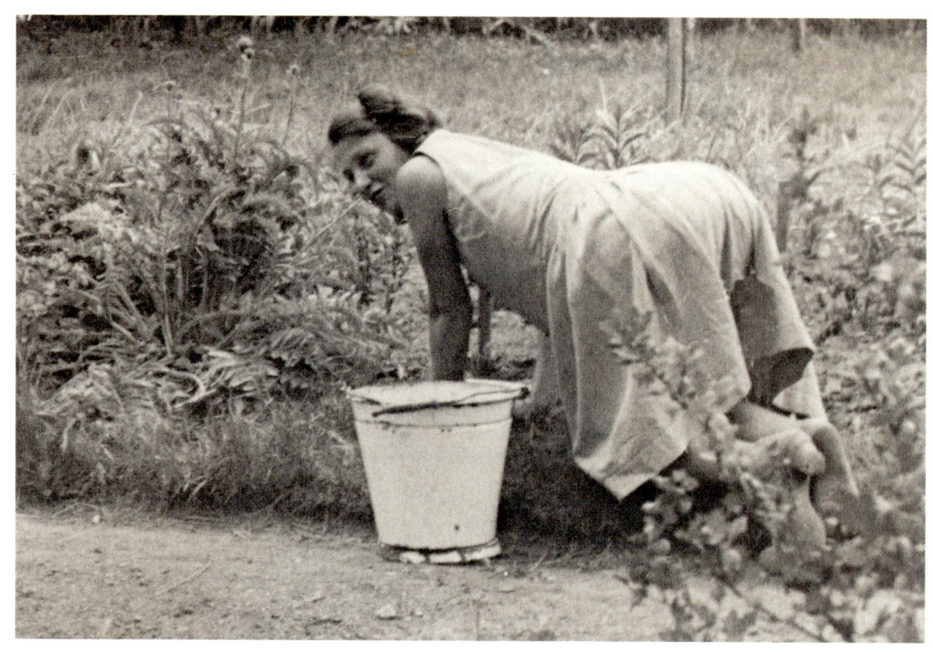

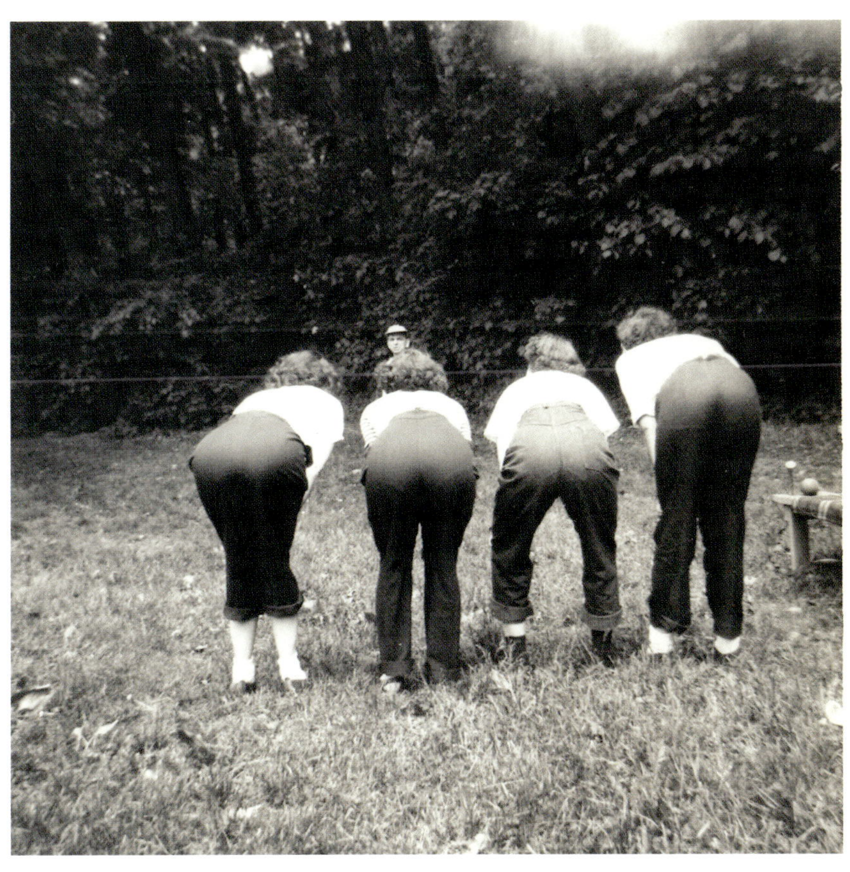

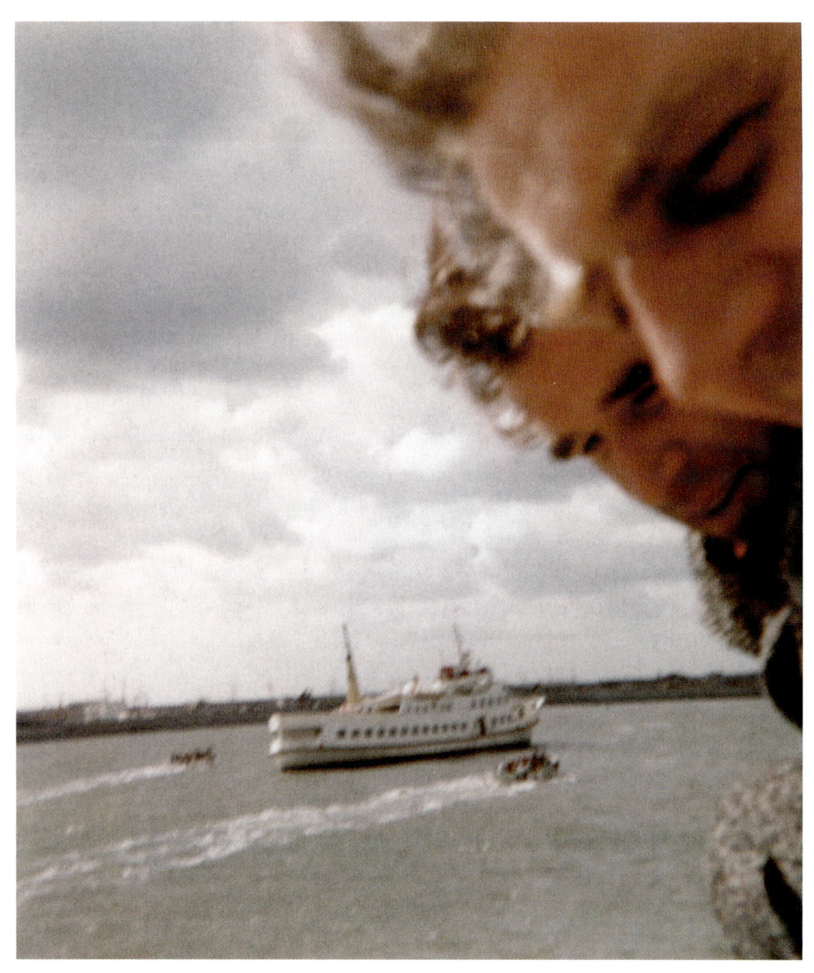

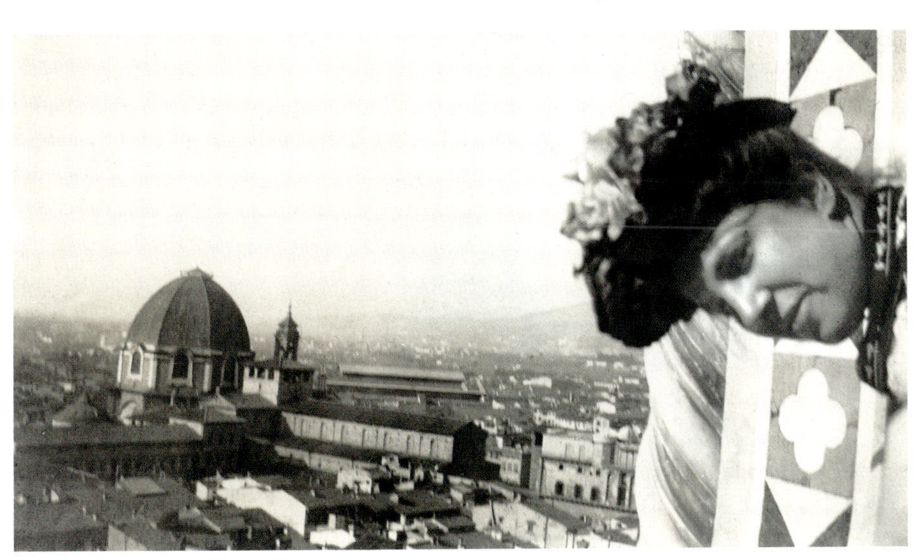

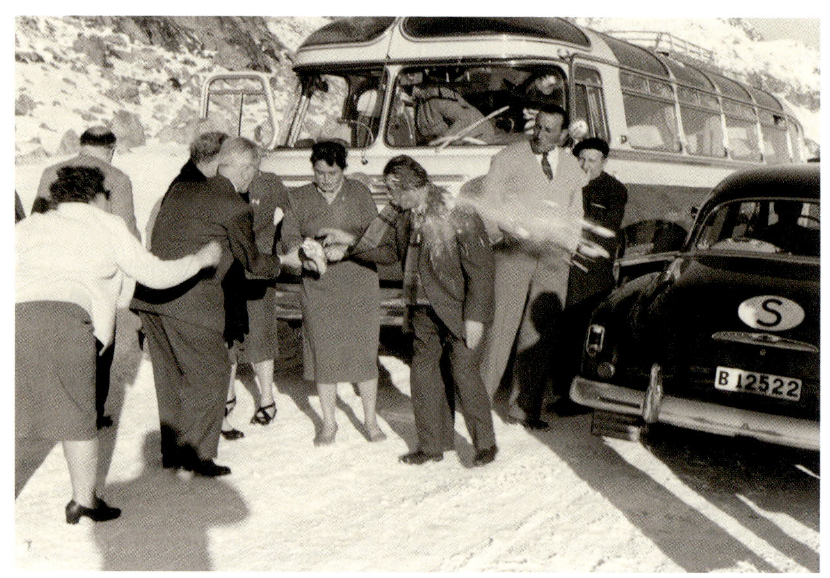
S
B 12522

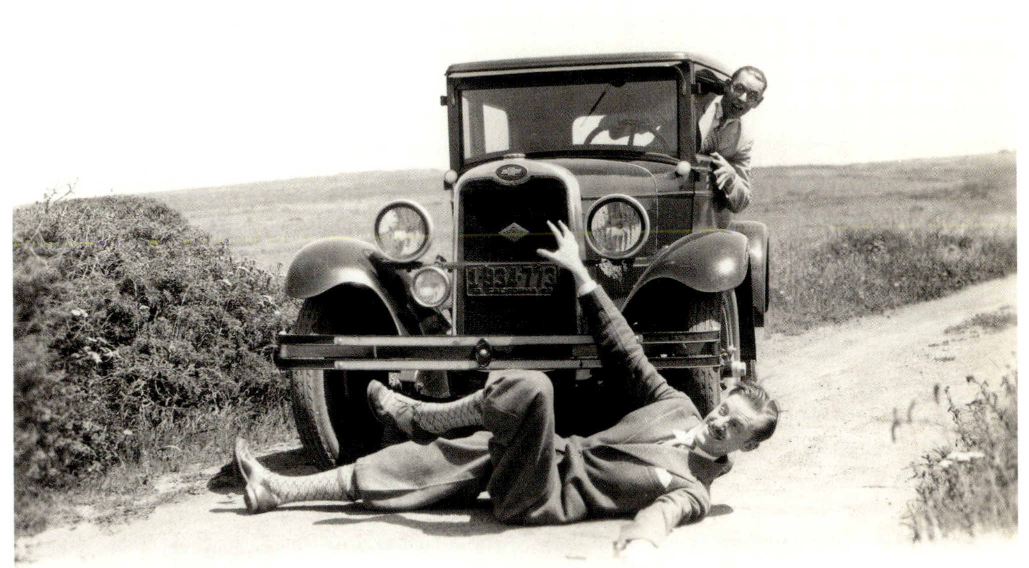

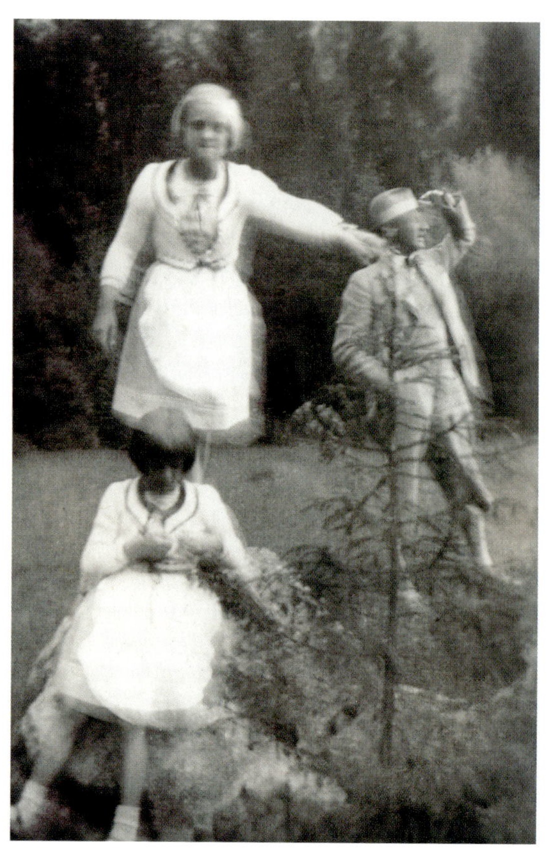

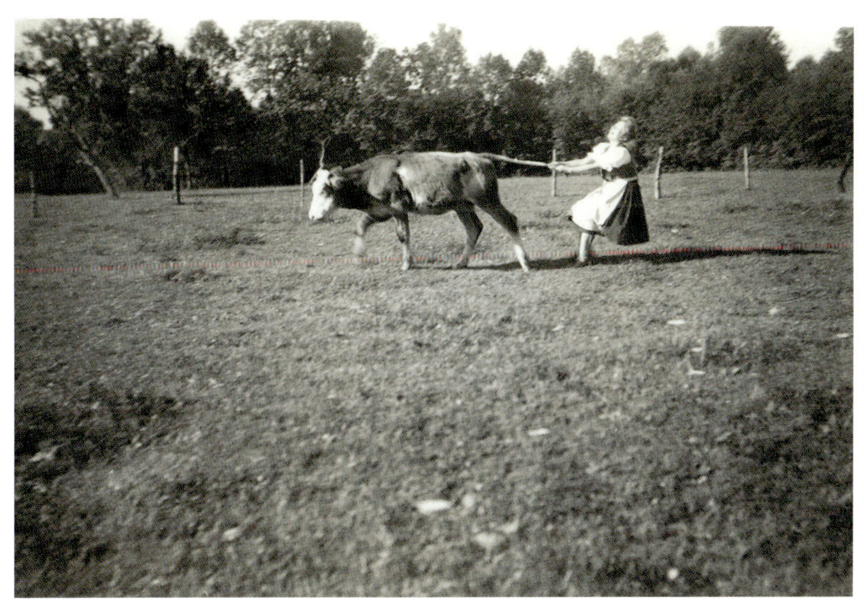

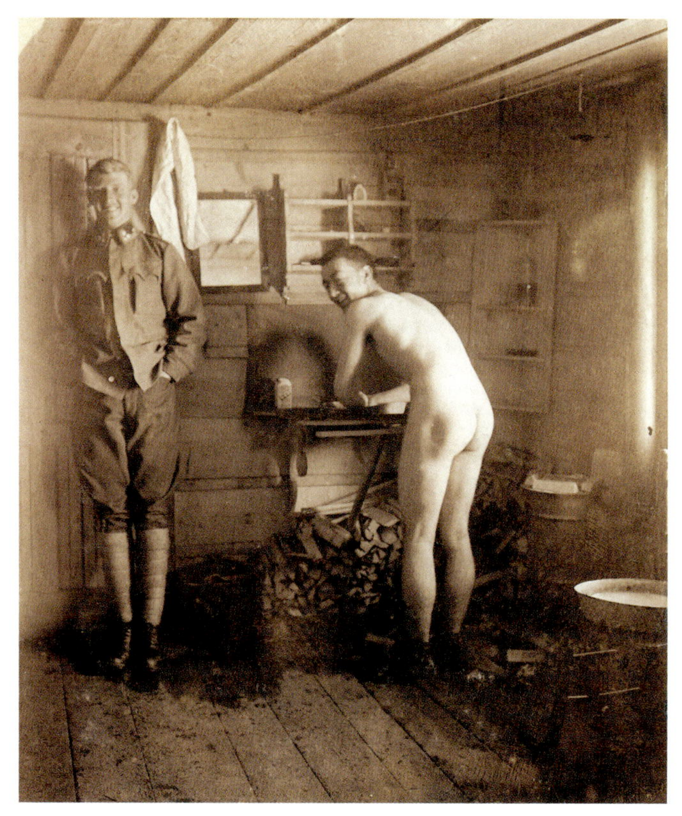

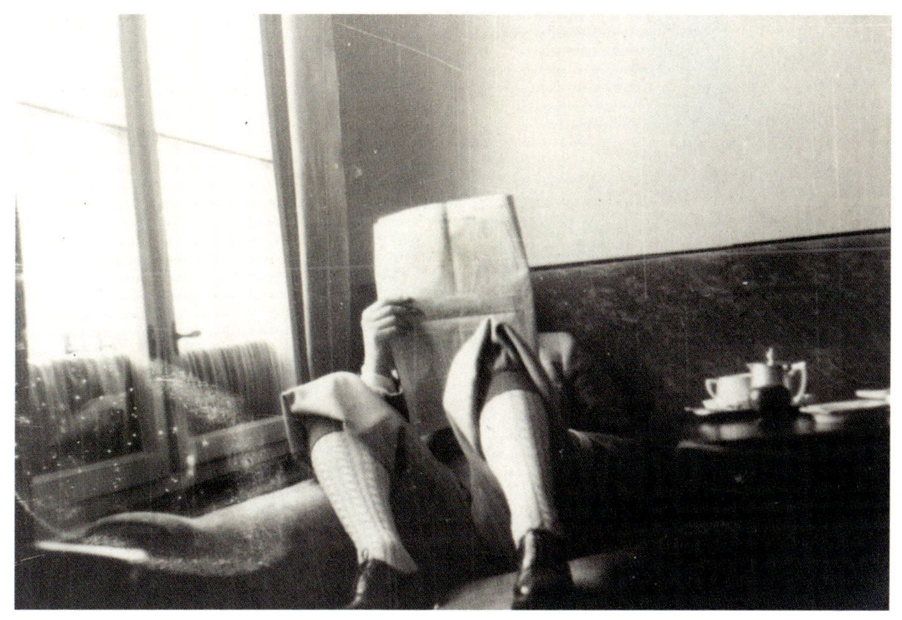

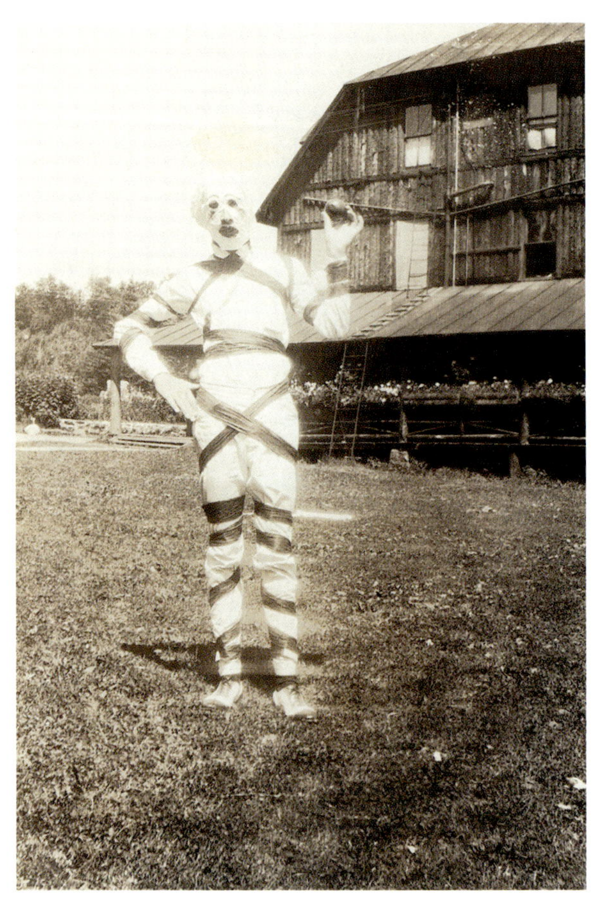

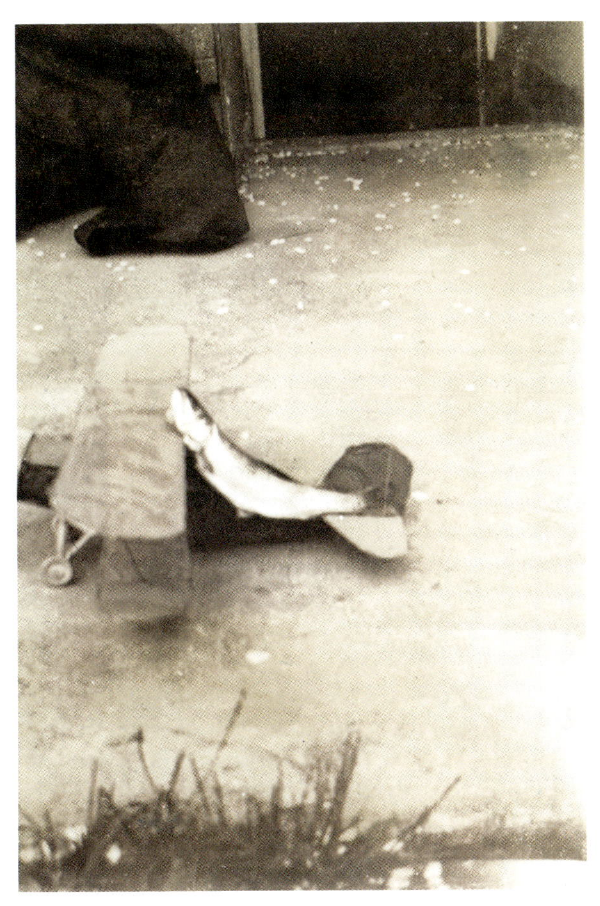

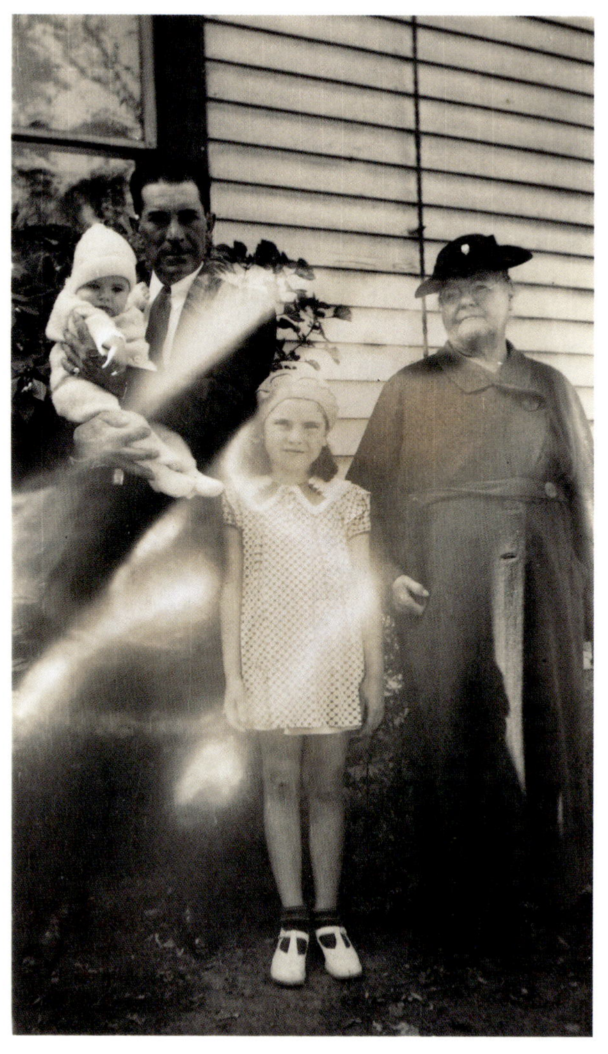

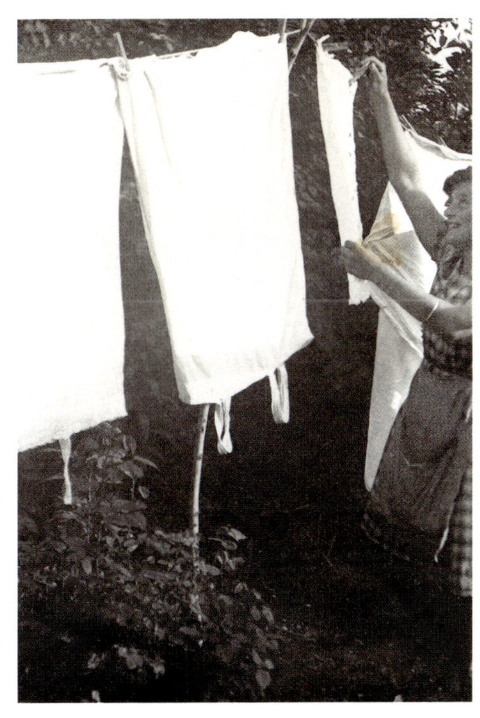

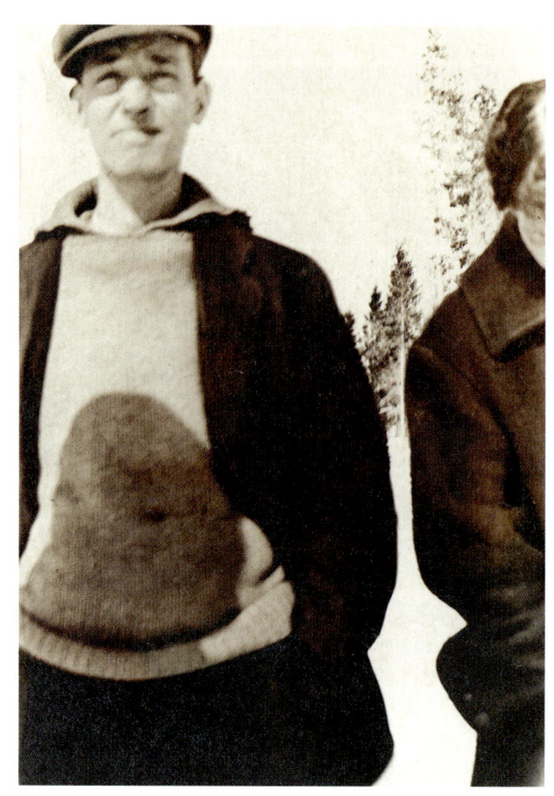

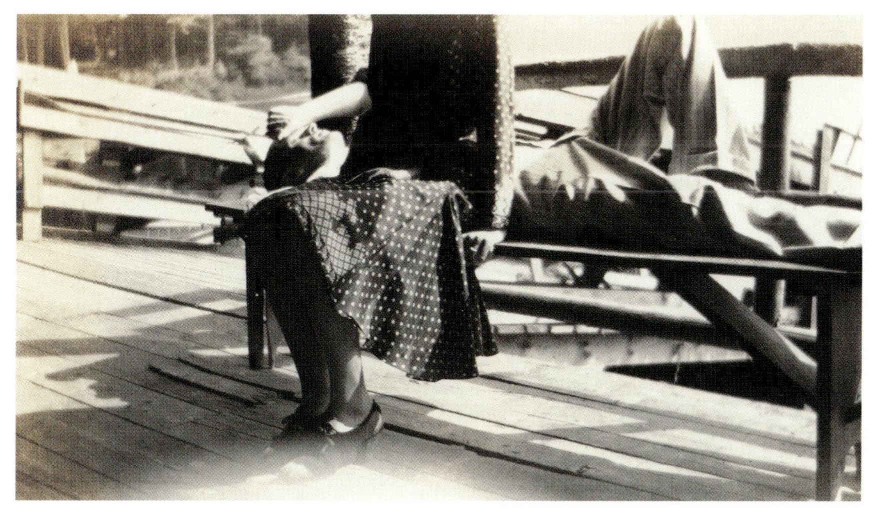

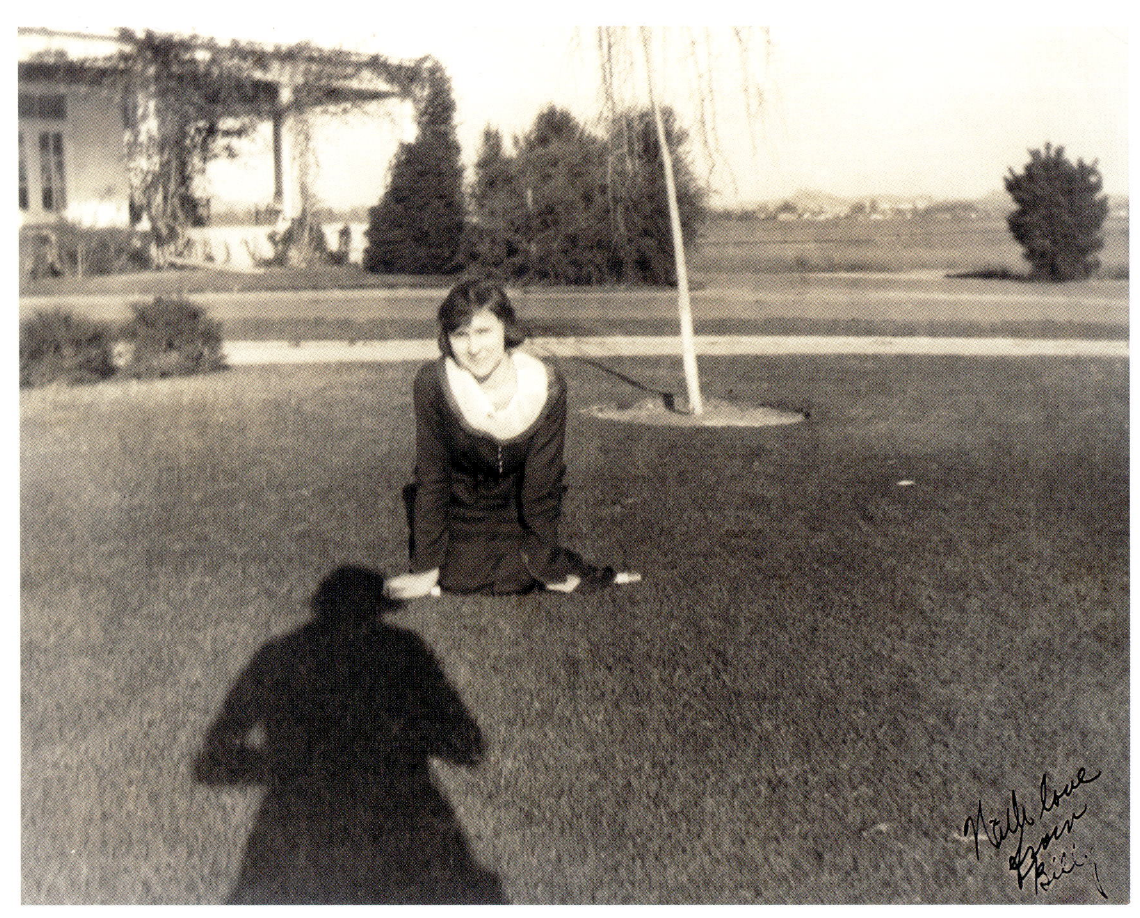
With love
from

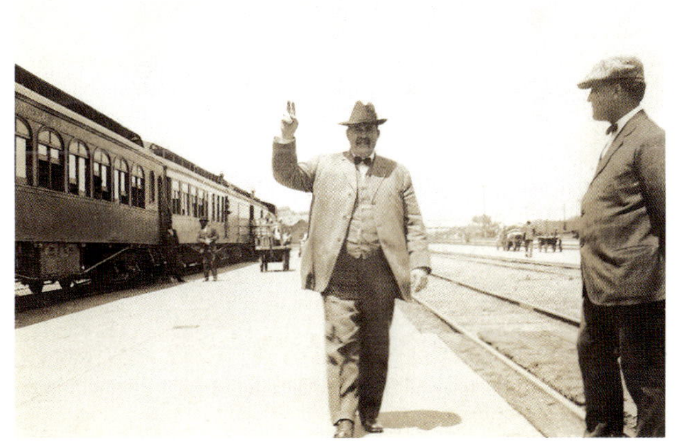

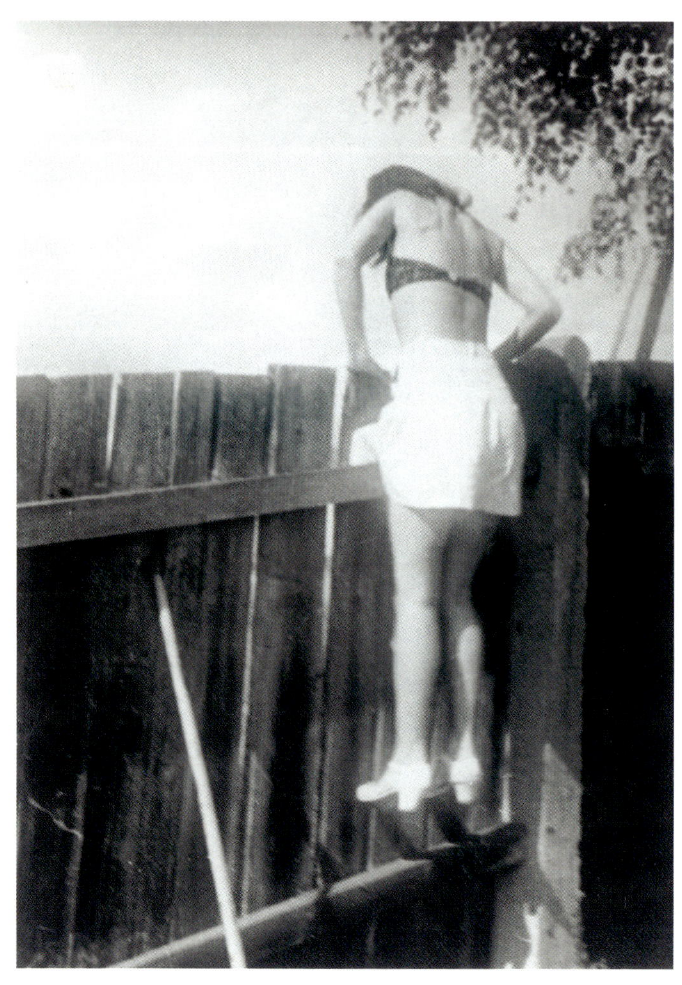

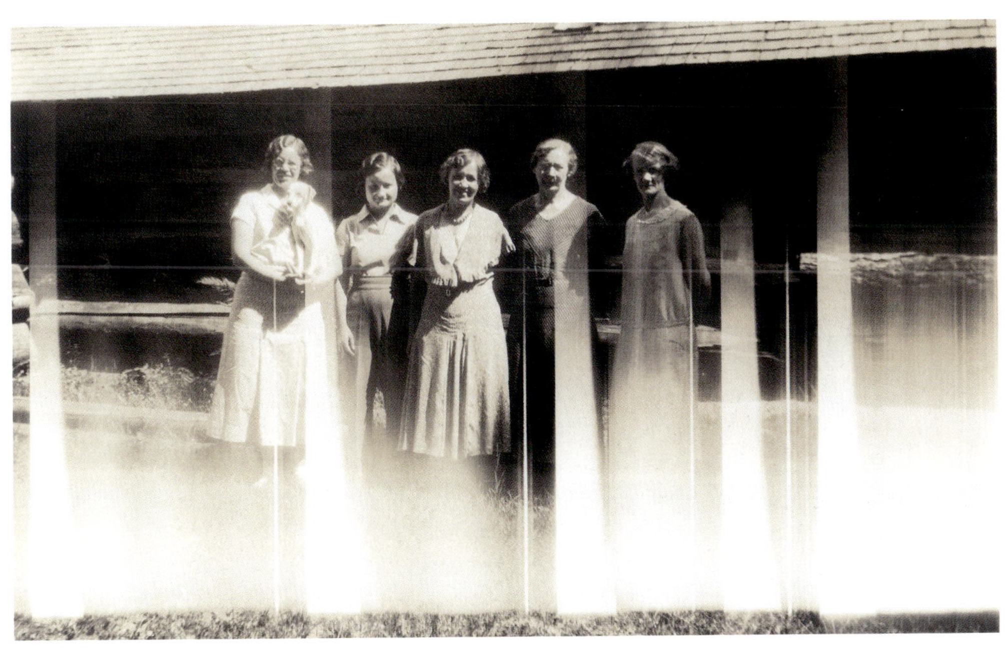

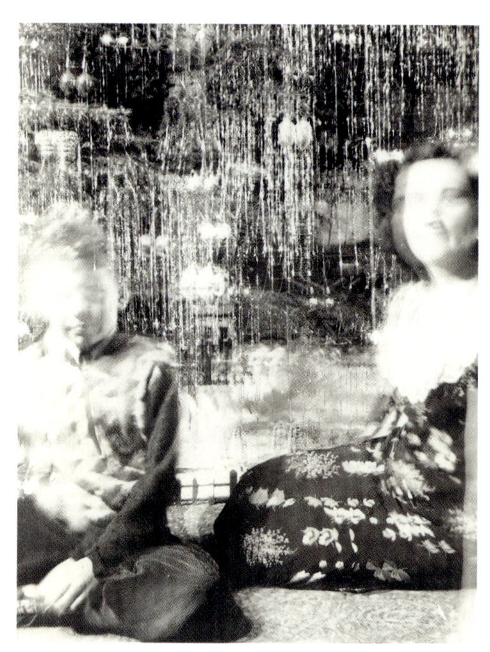

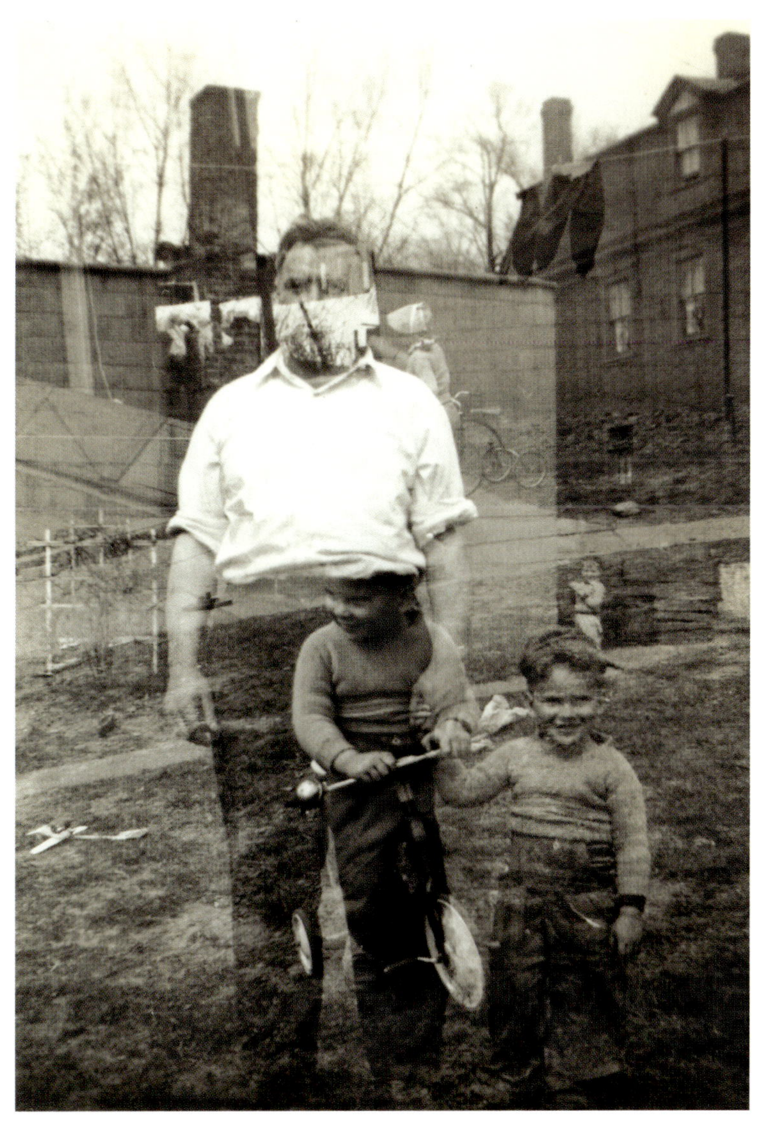

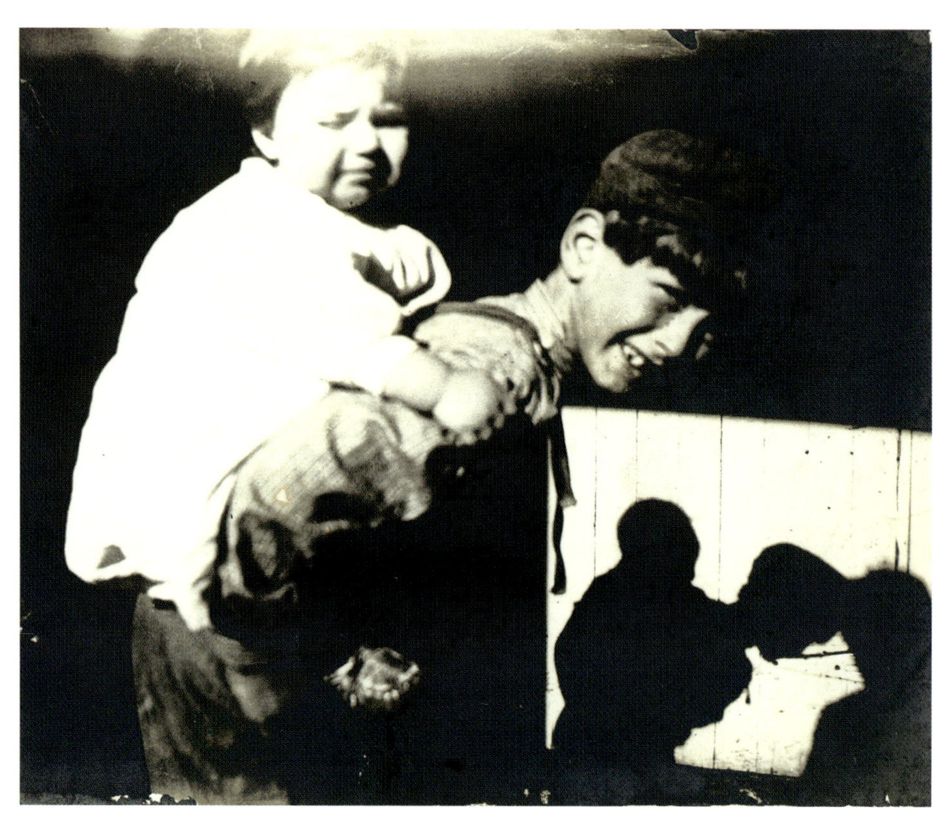

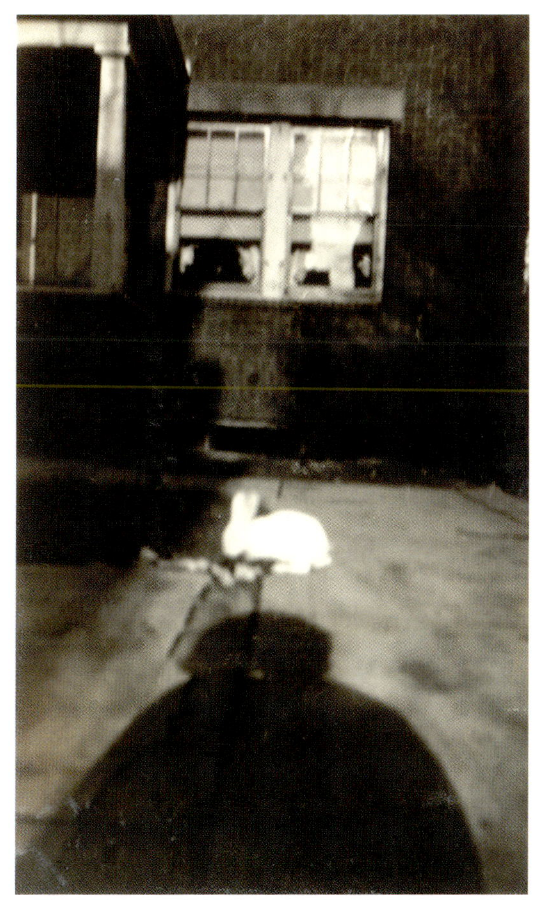

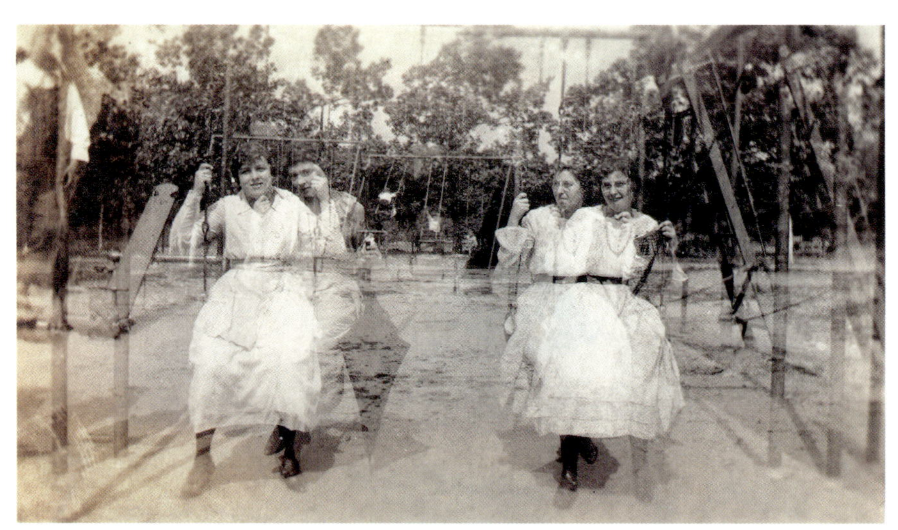

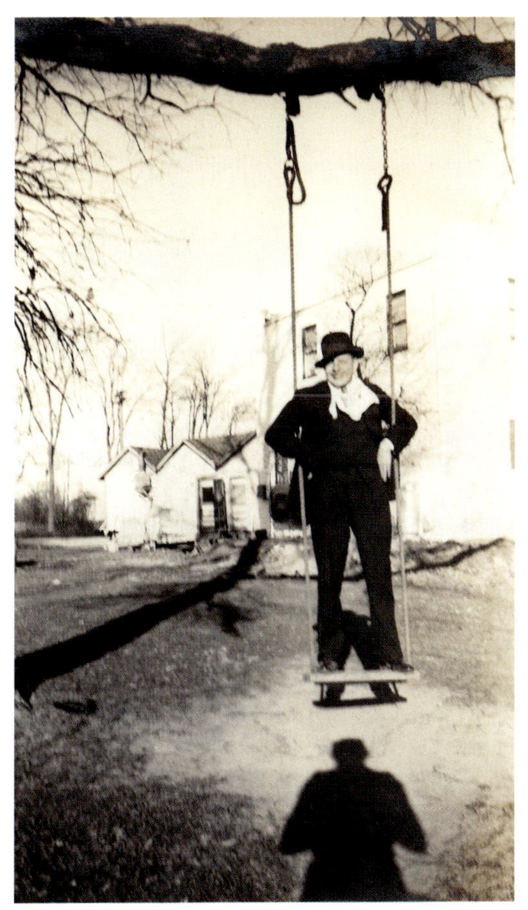

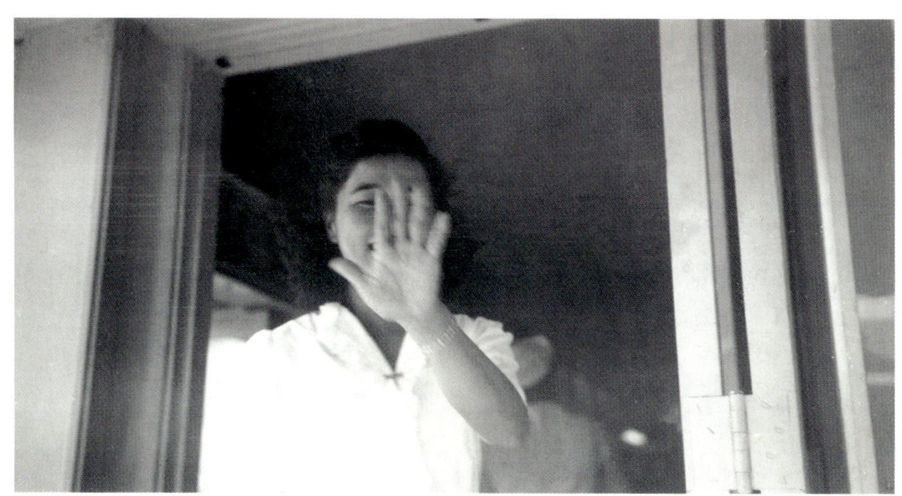

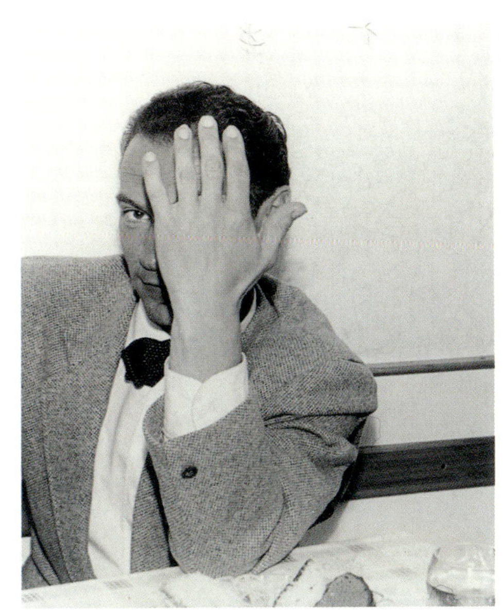

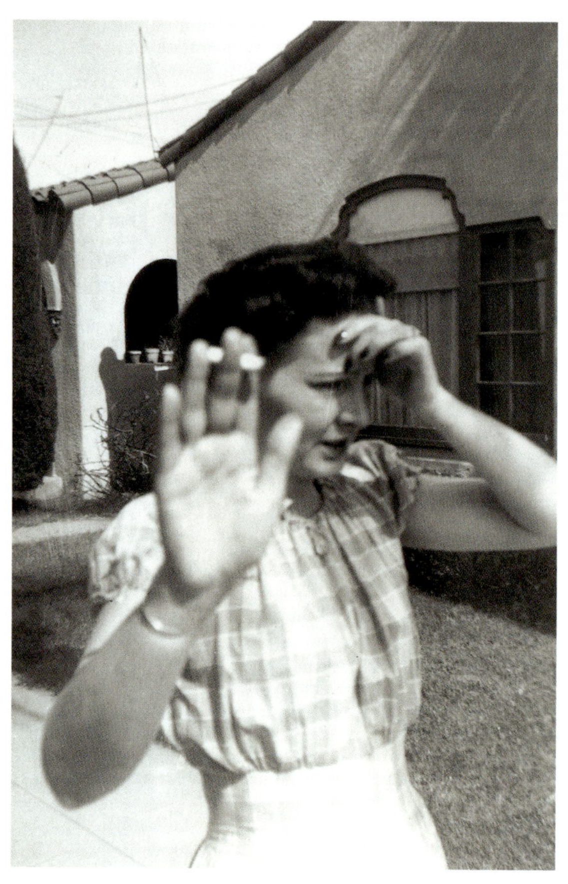

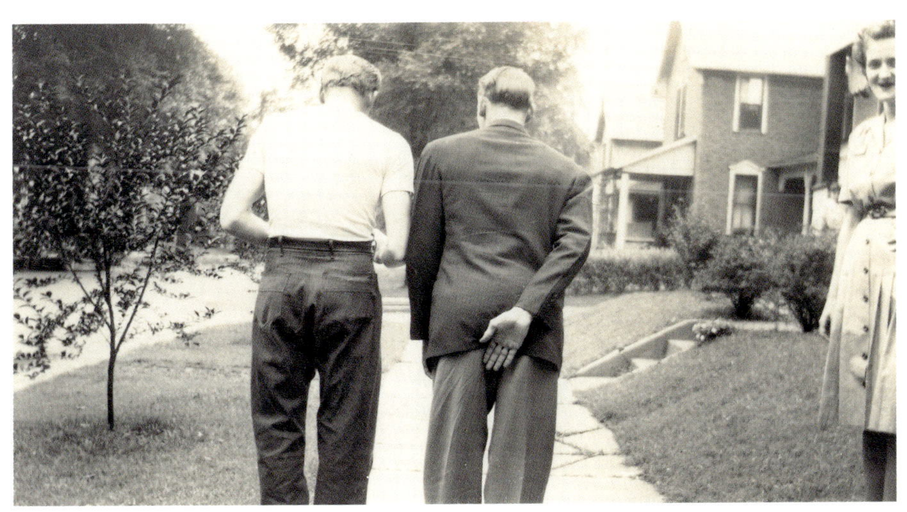

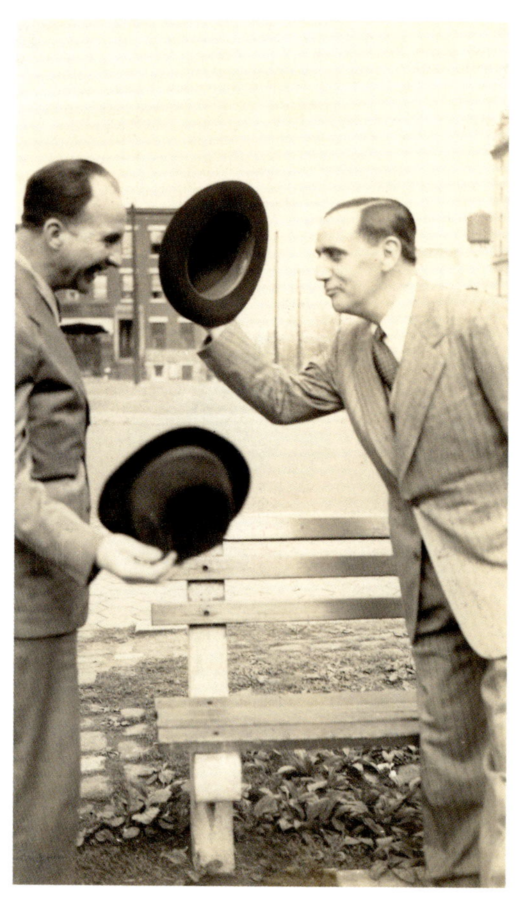

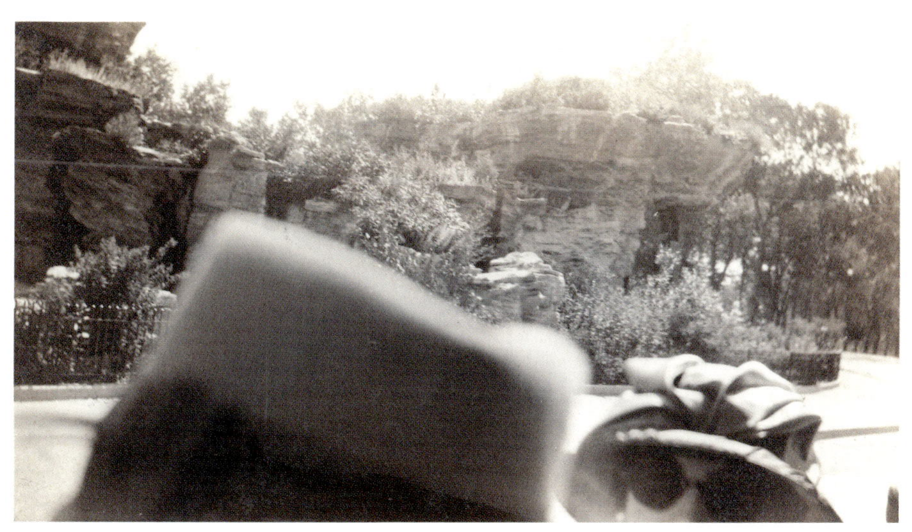

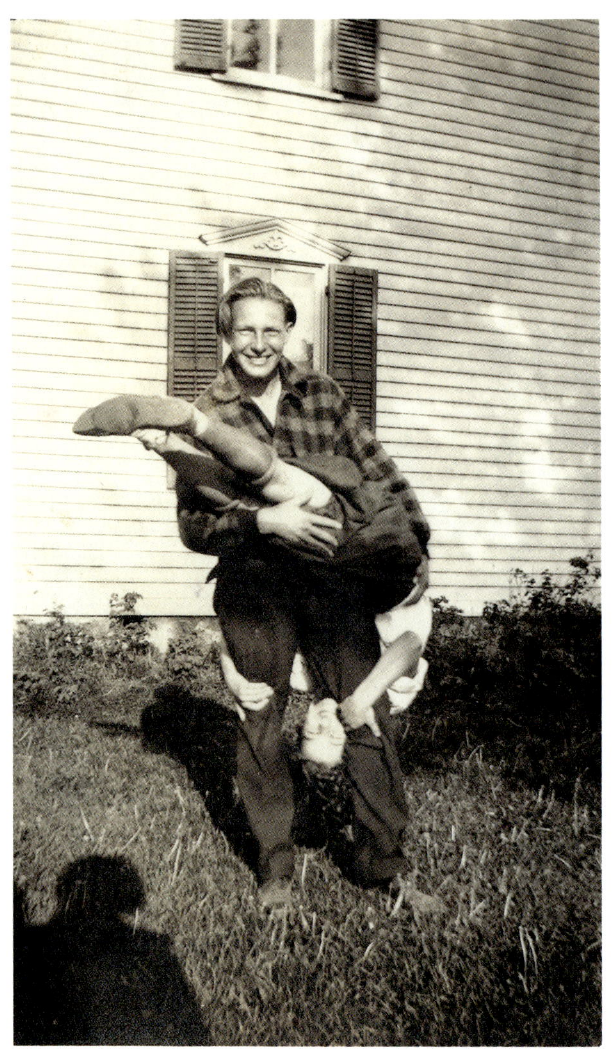

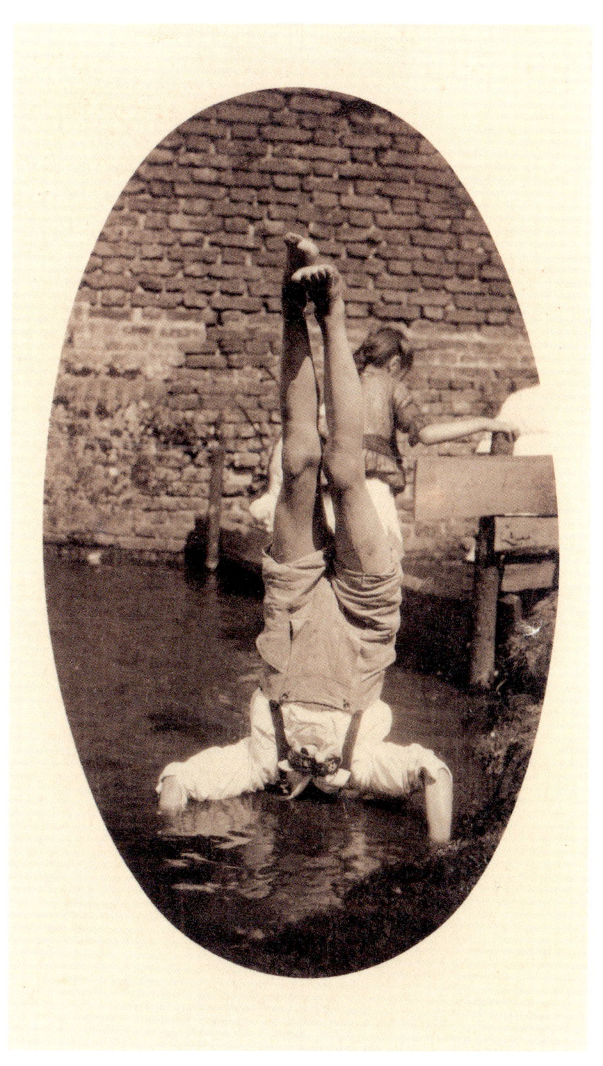

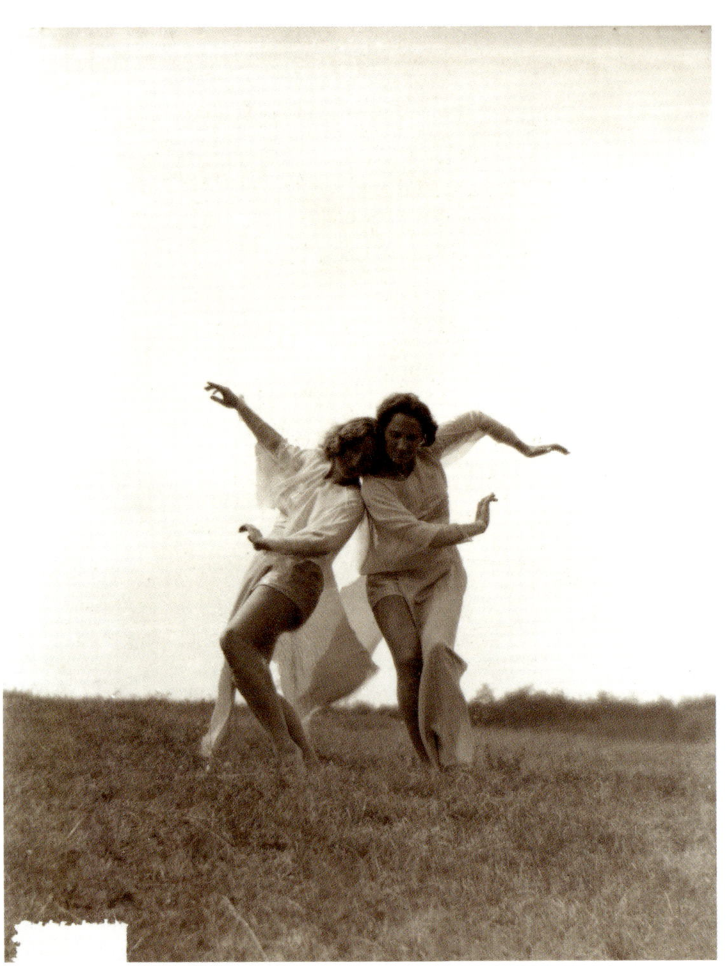

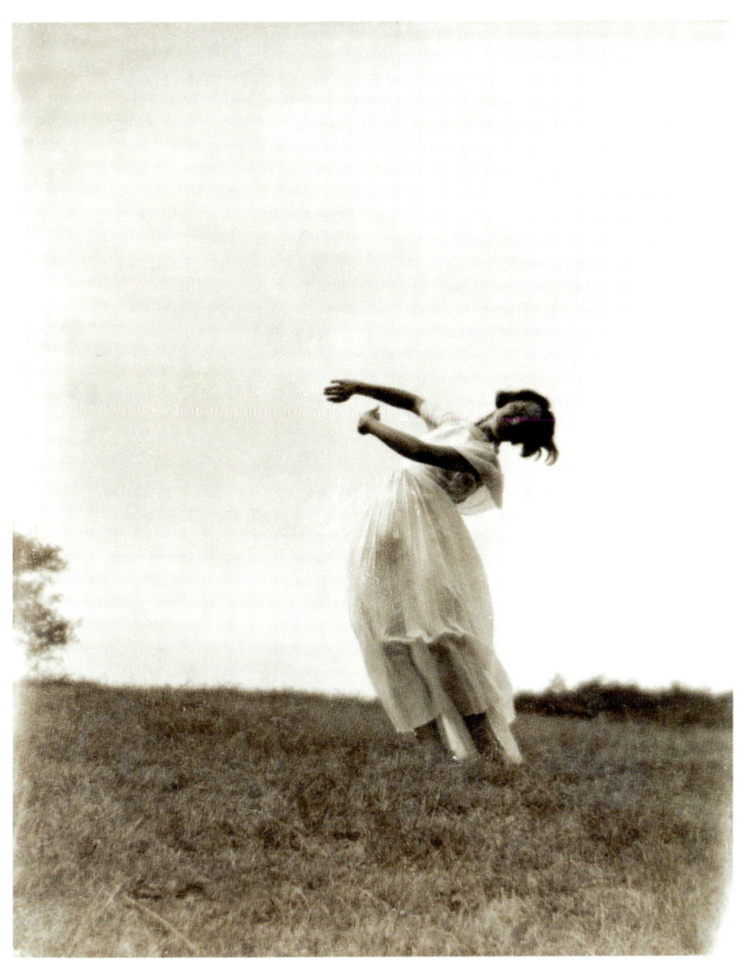

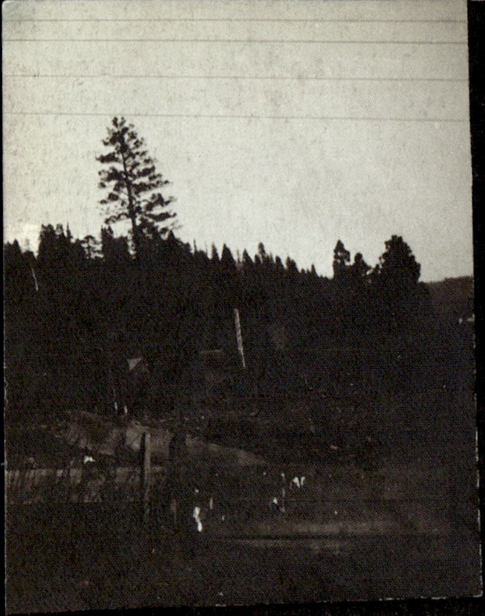

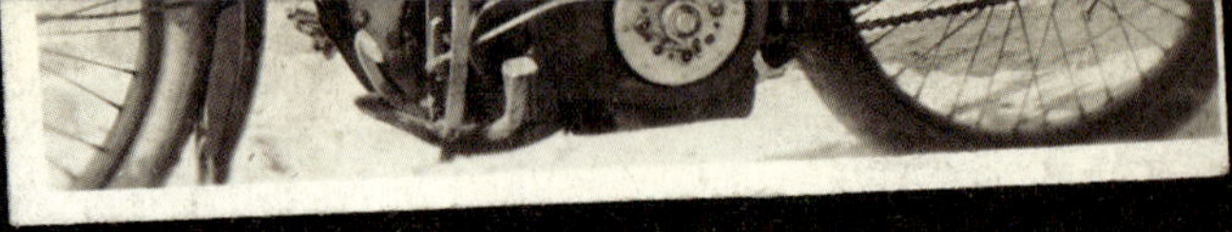

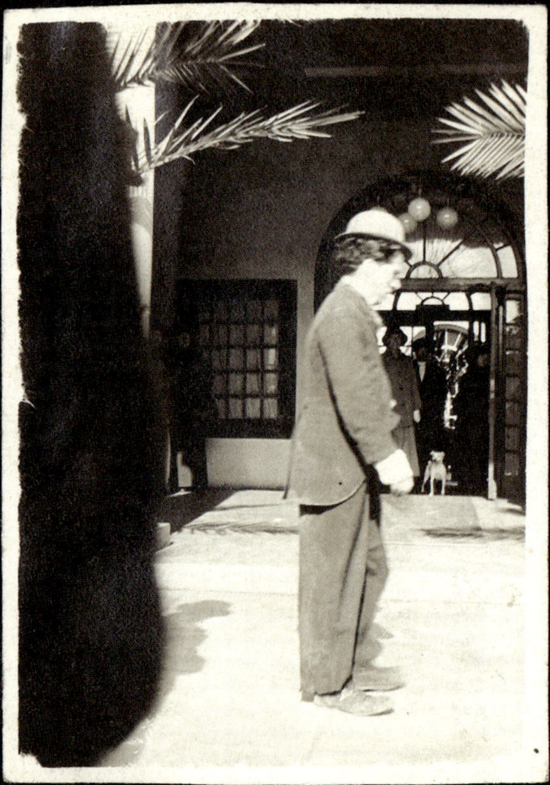

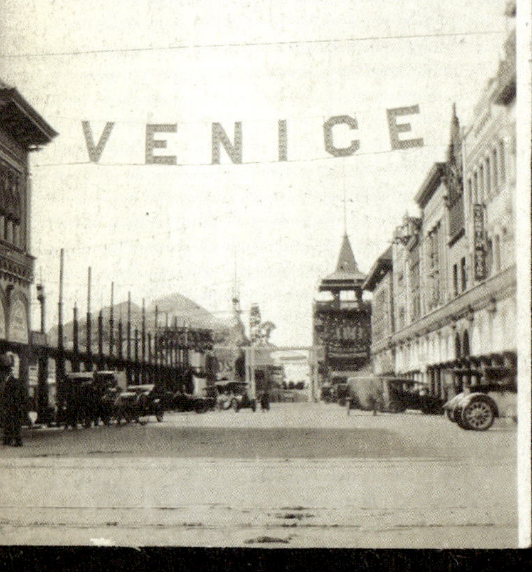
VENICE

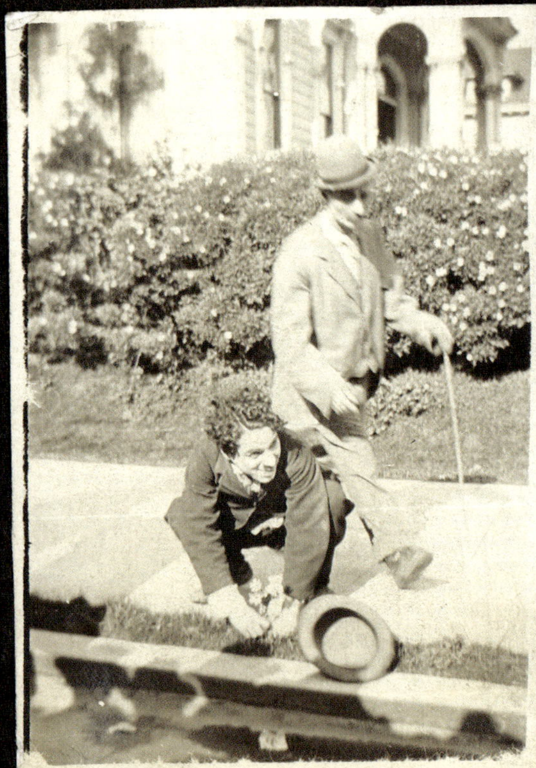

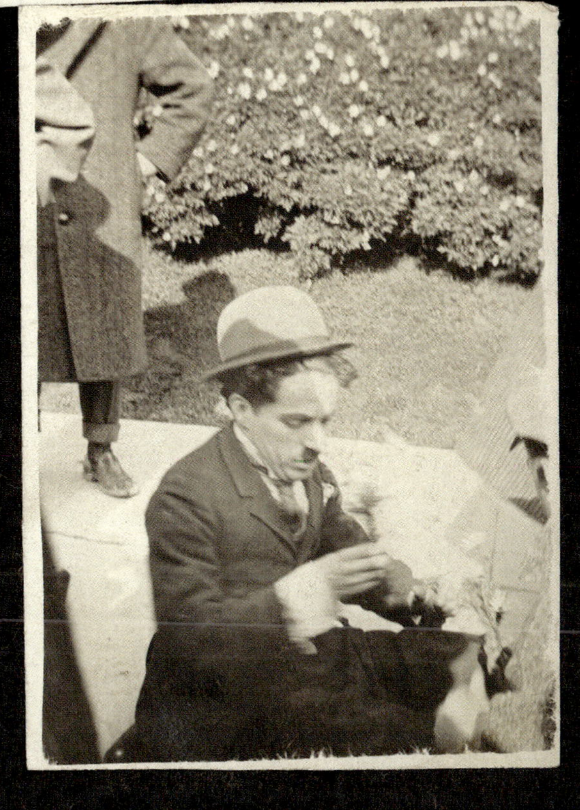

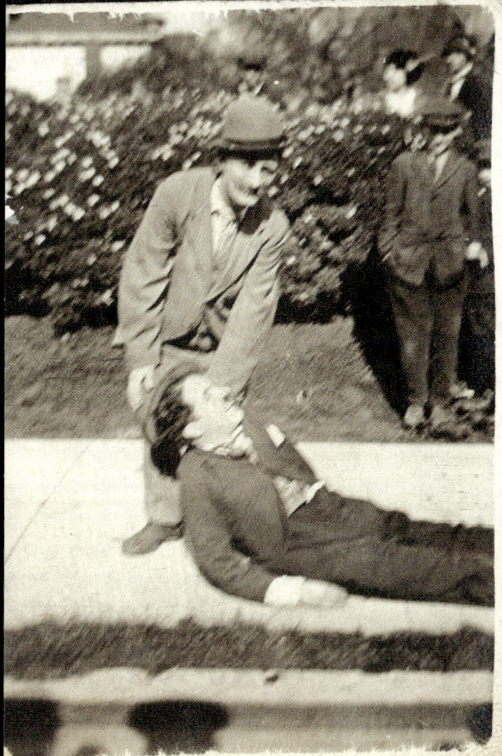

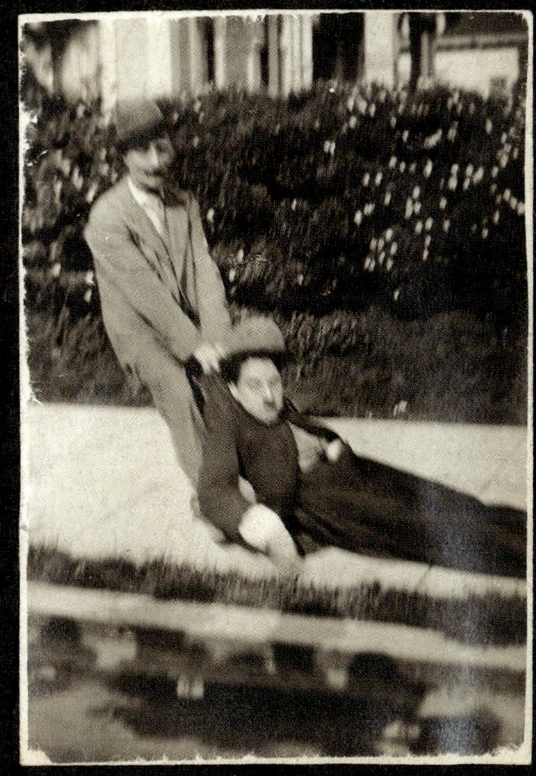

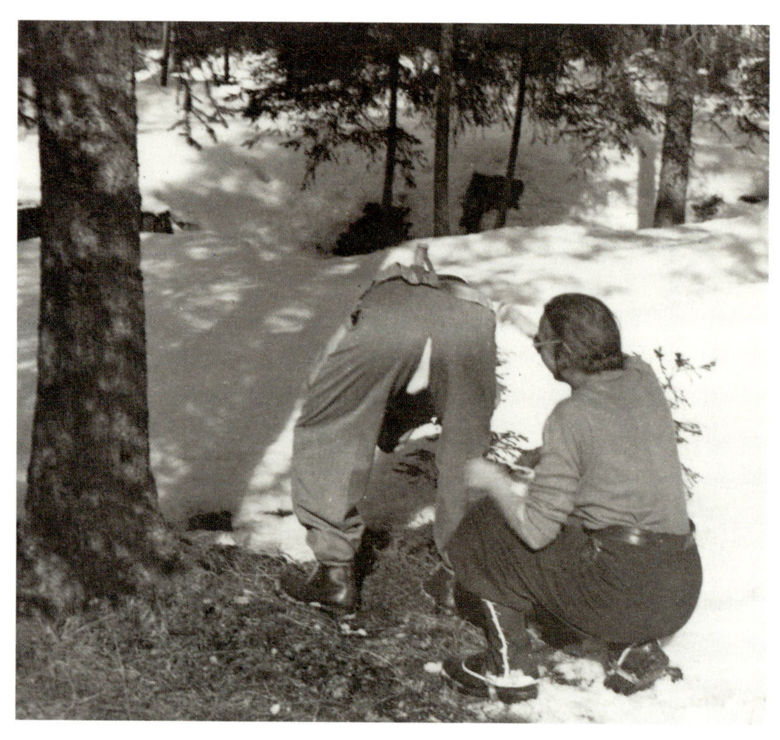

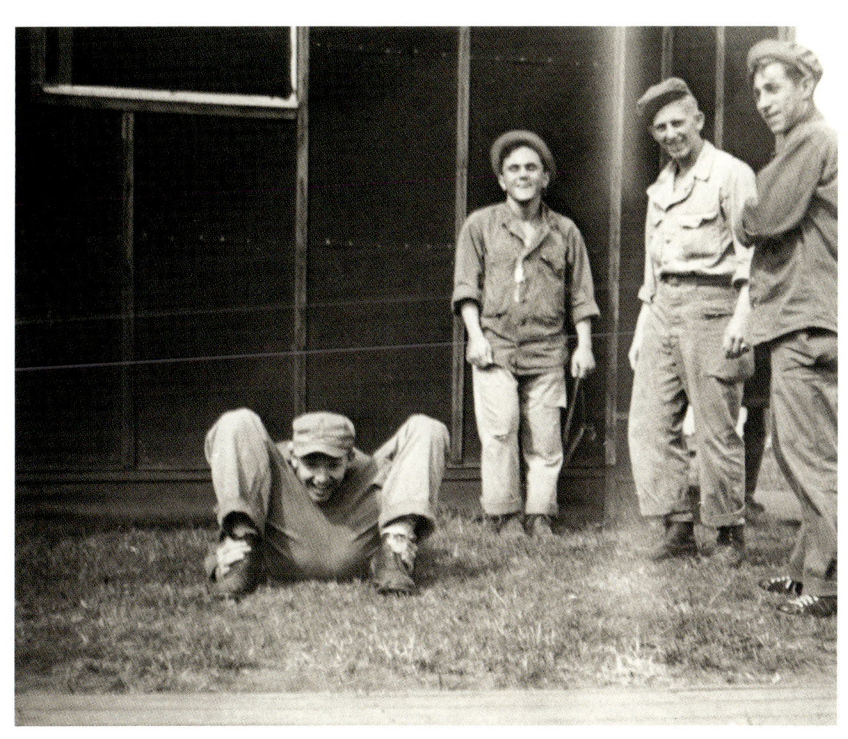

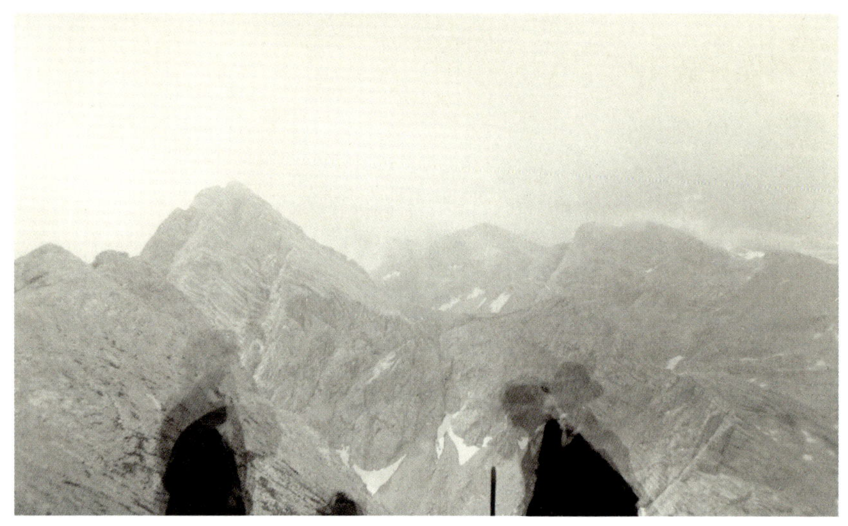

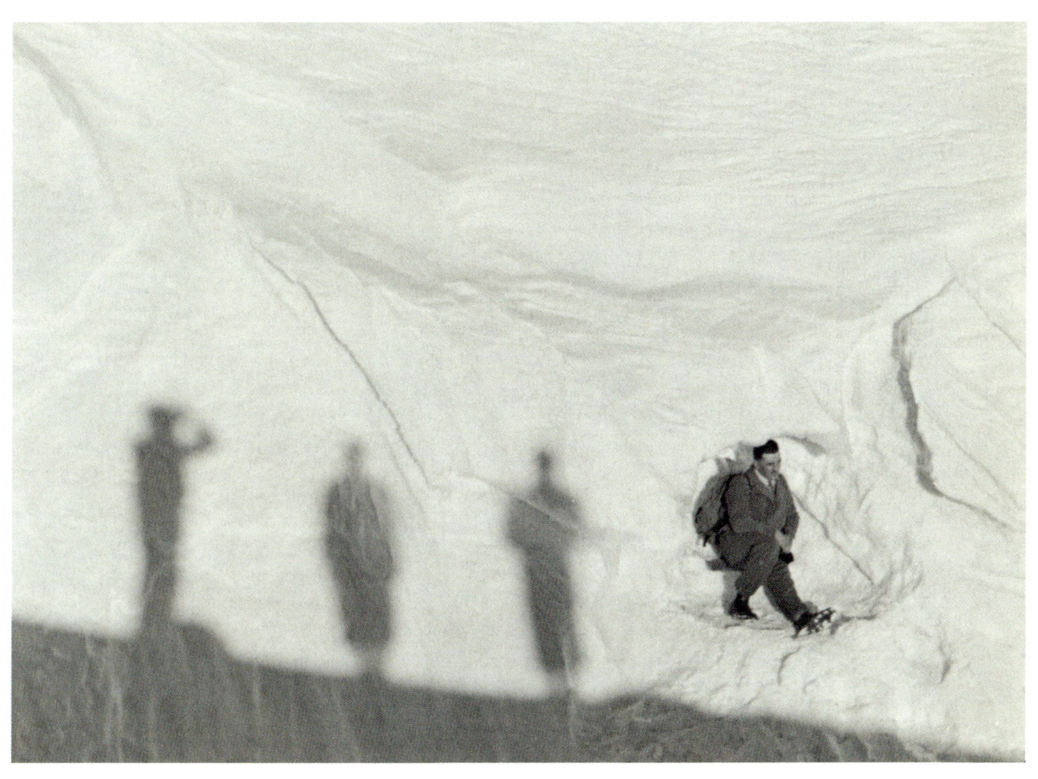

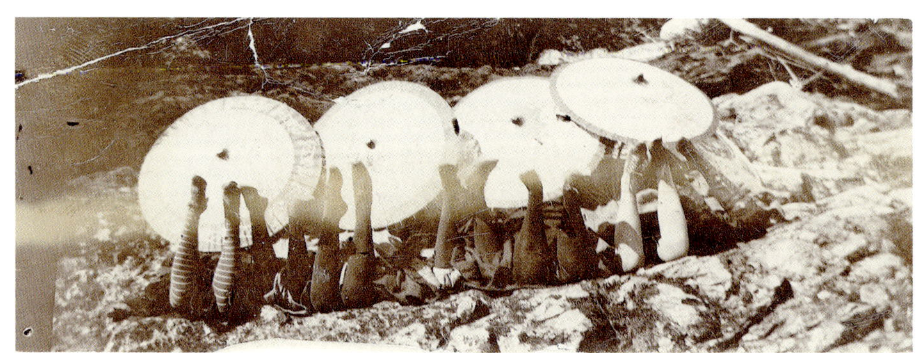

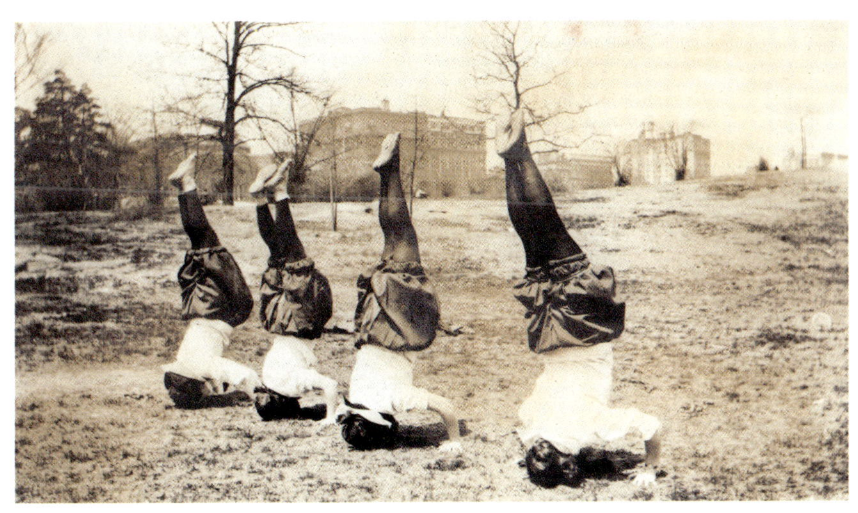

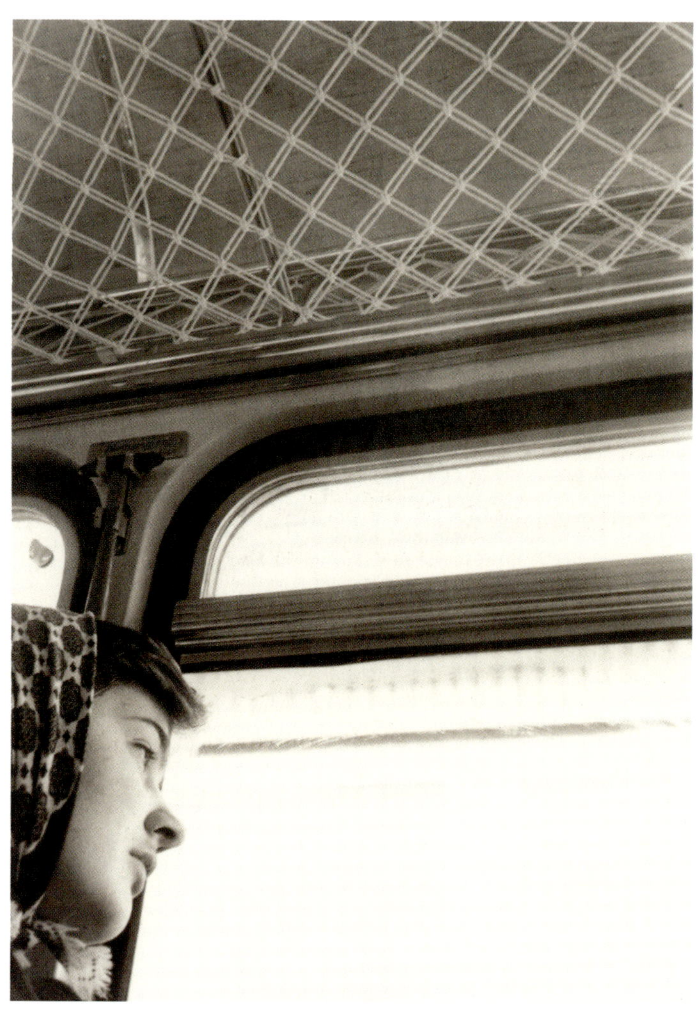

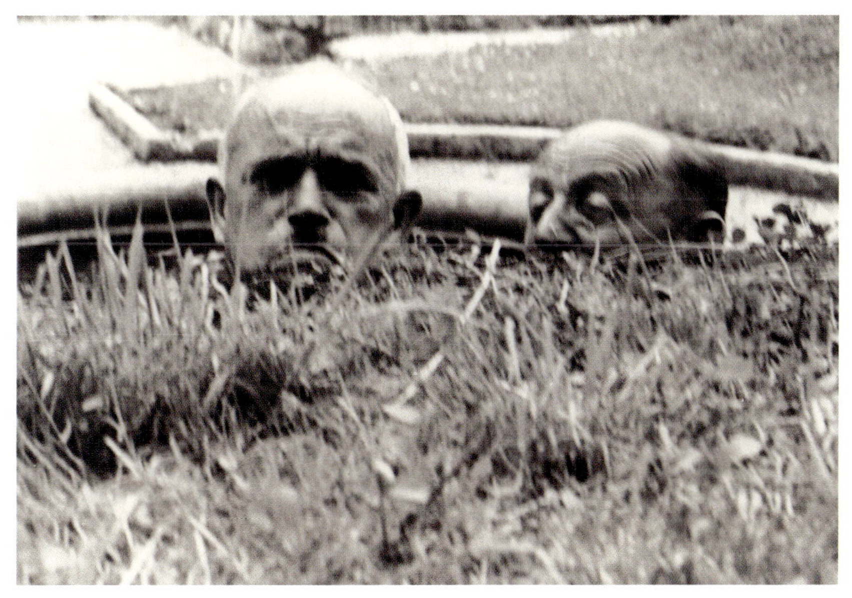

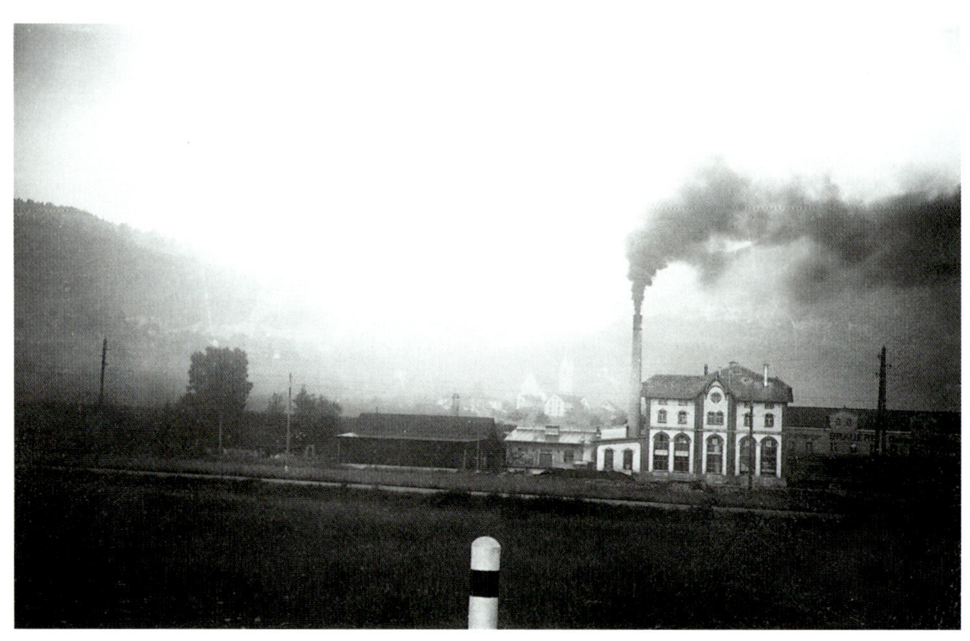

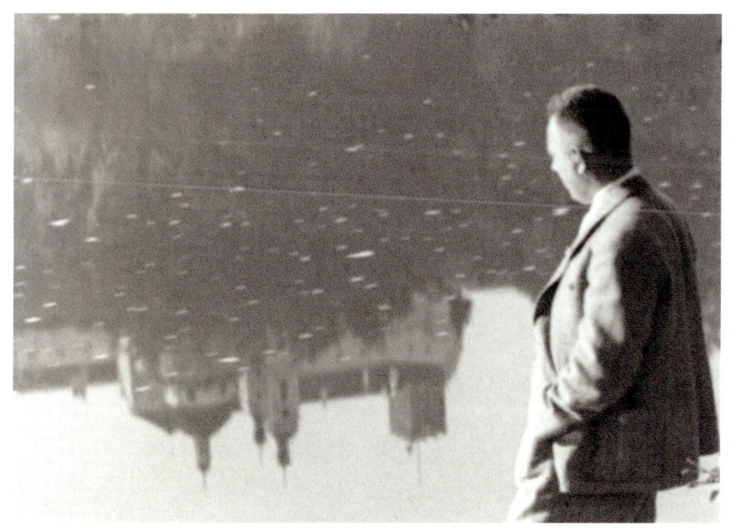

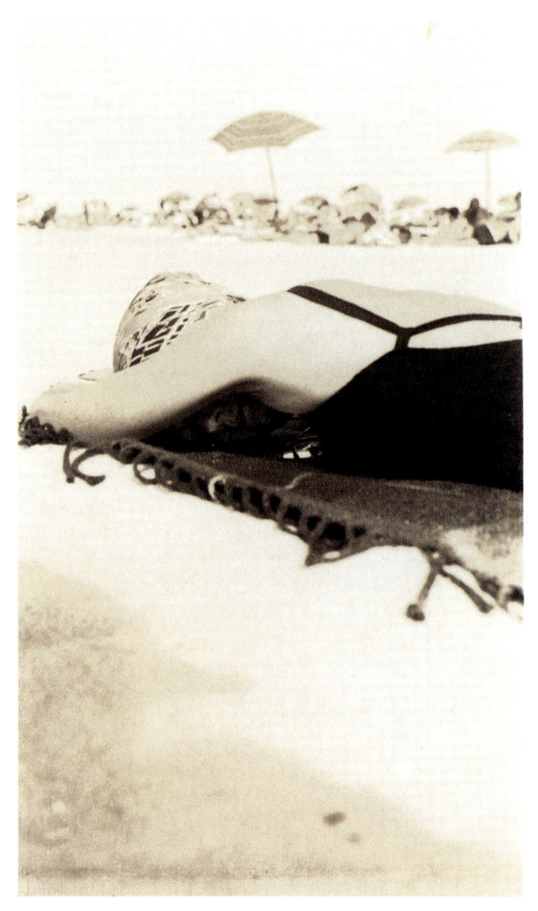

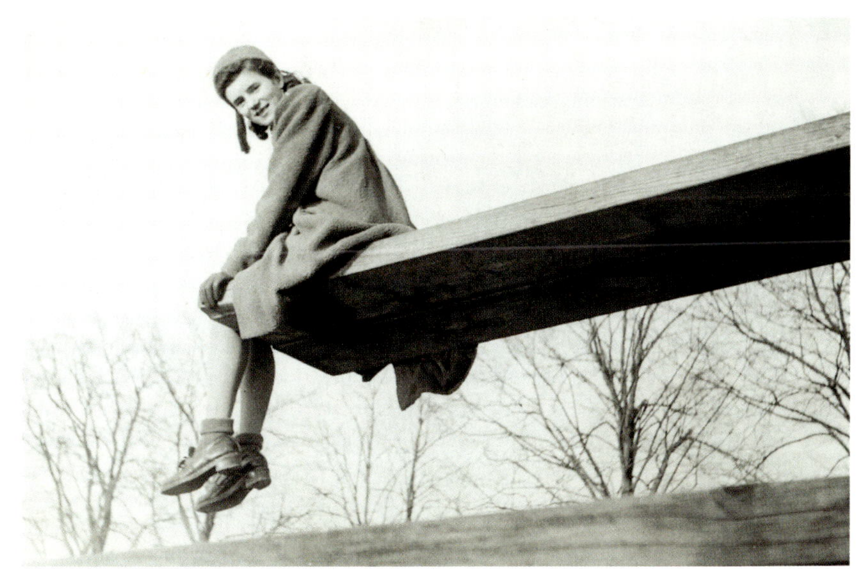

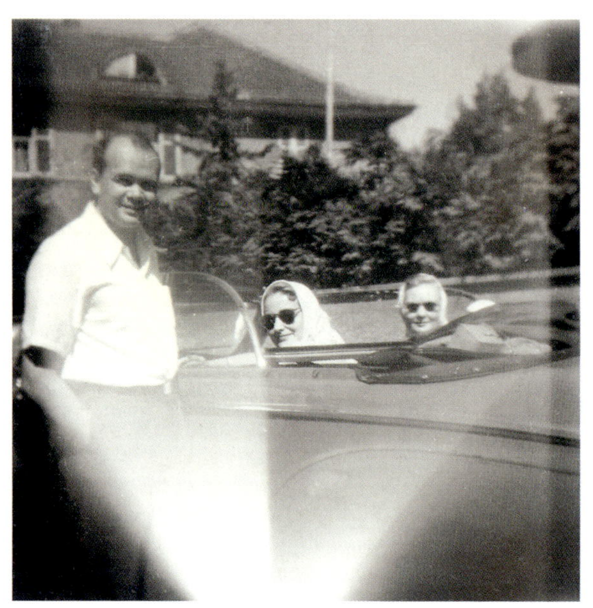

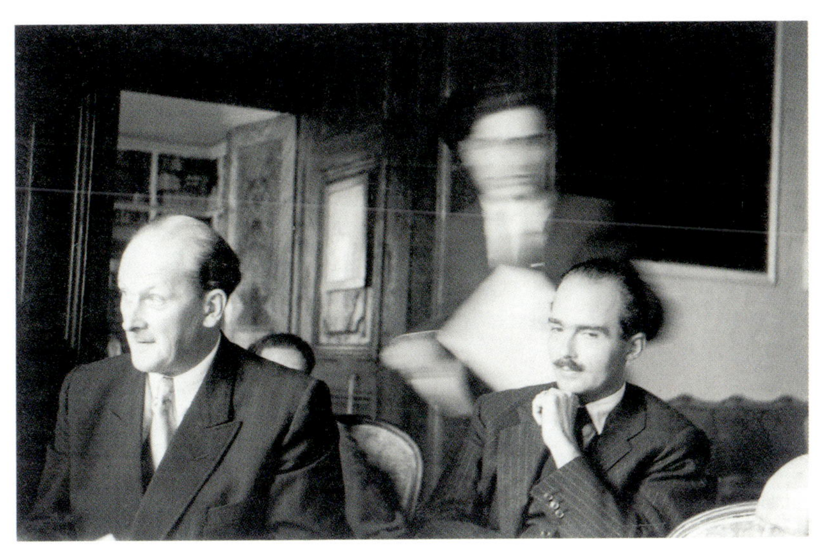

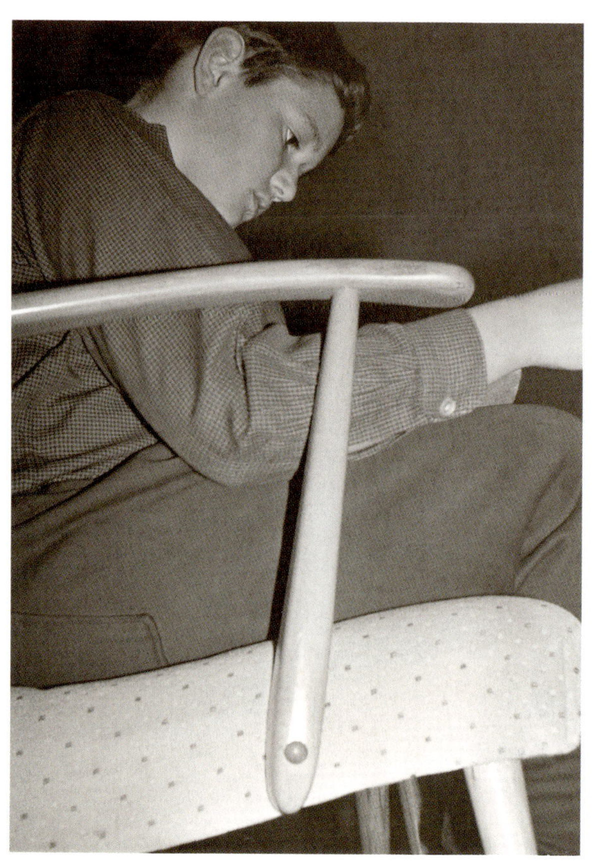

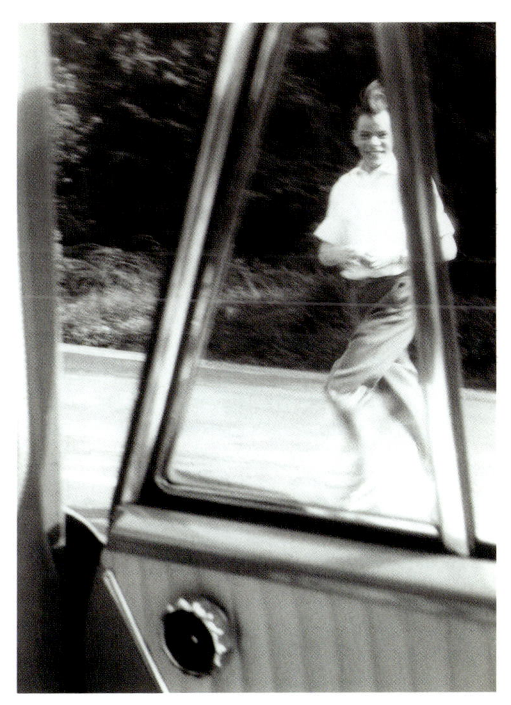

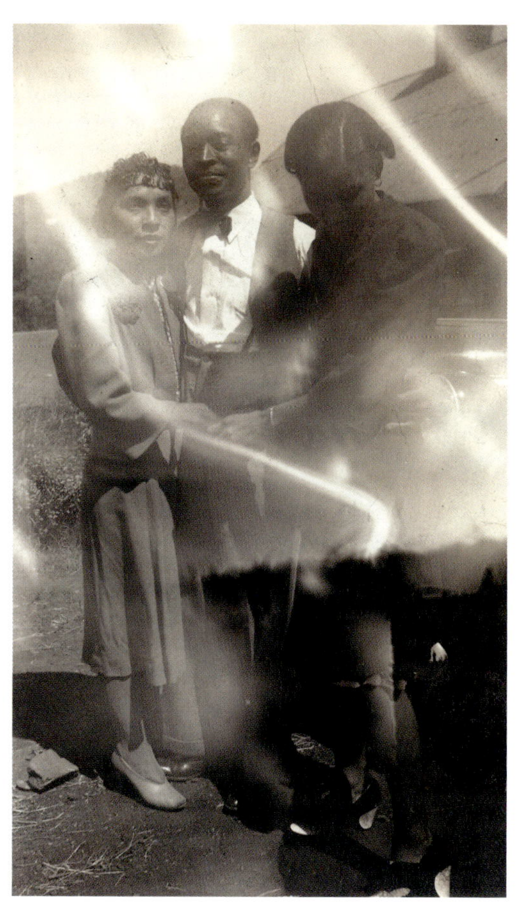

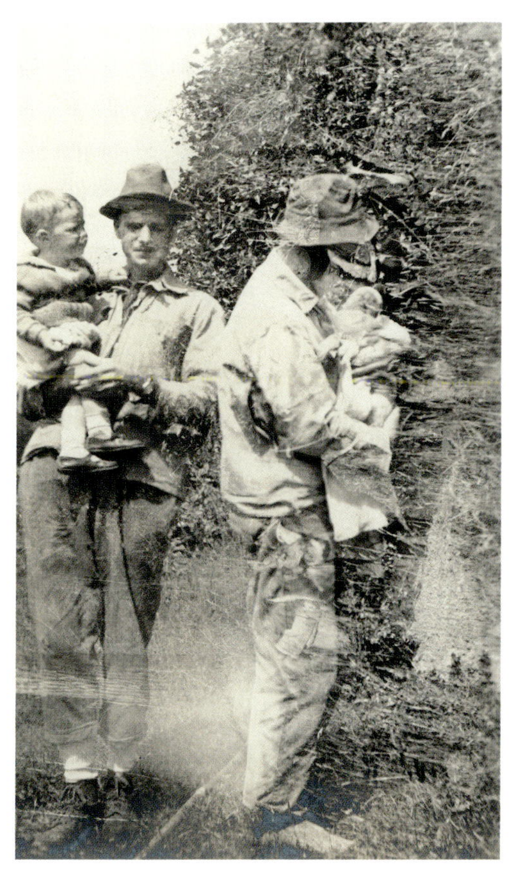

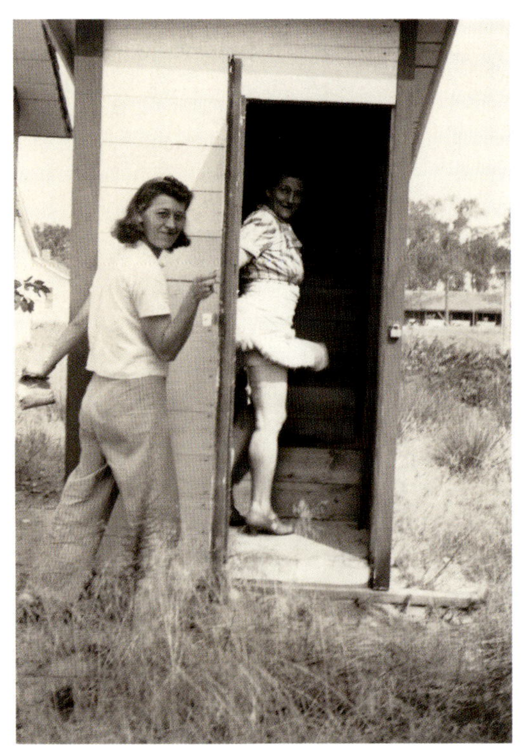

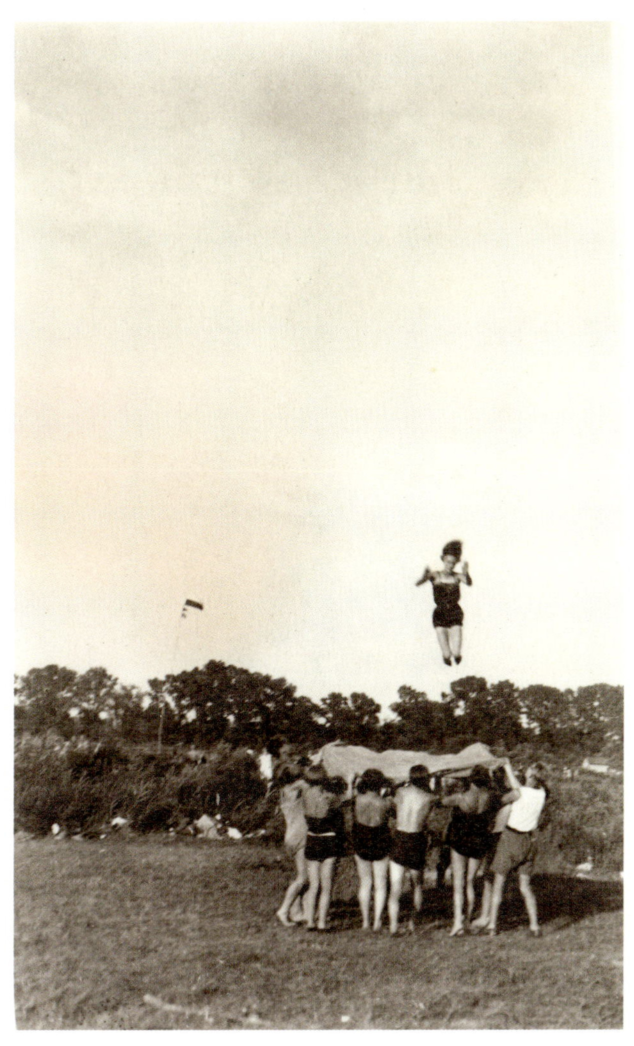

2)

Women Frauen

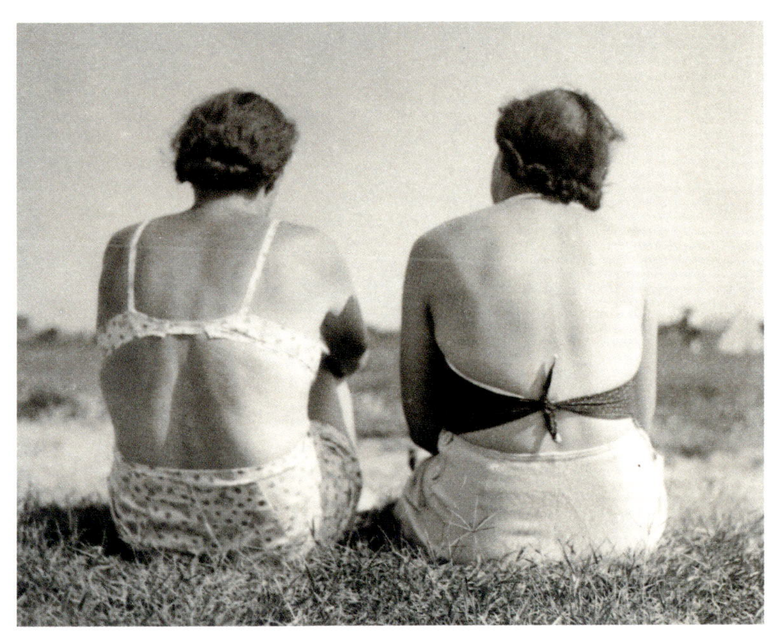

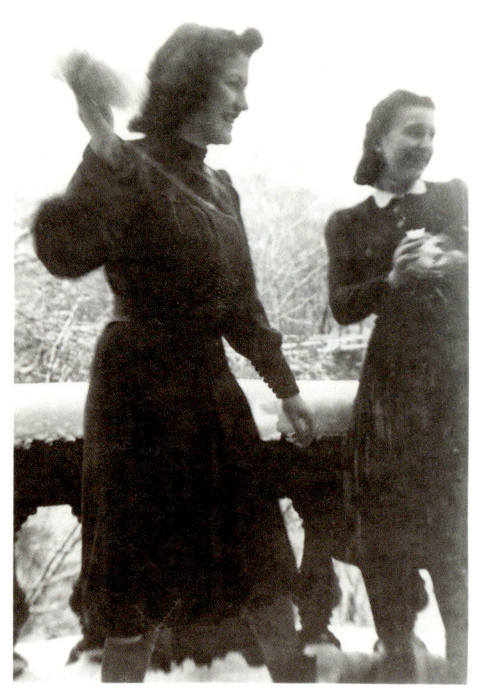

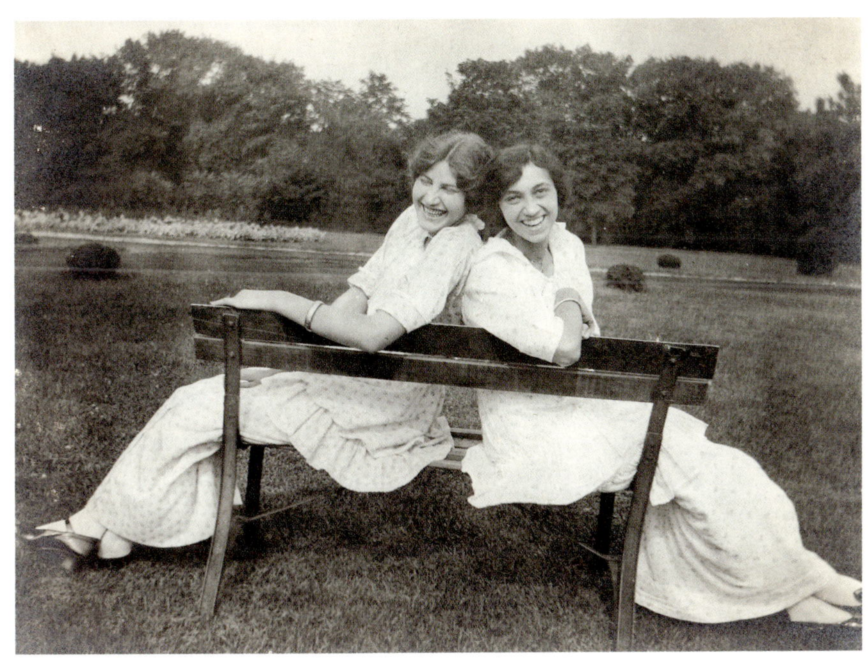

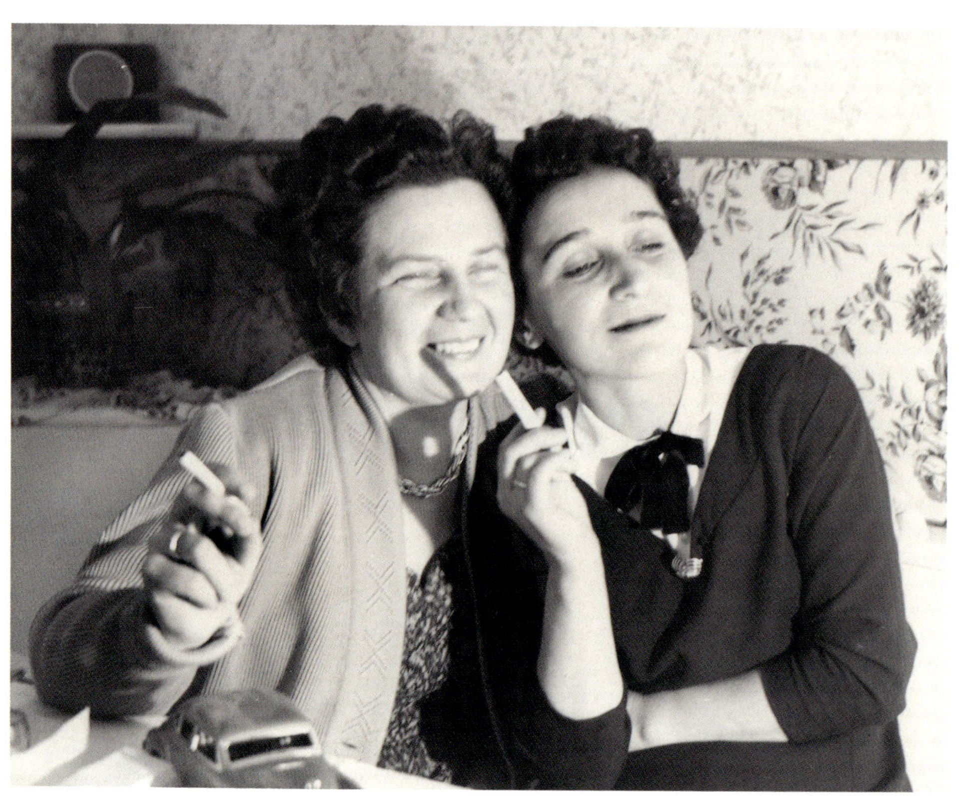

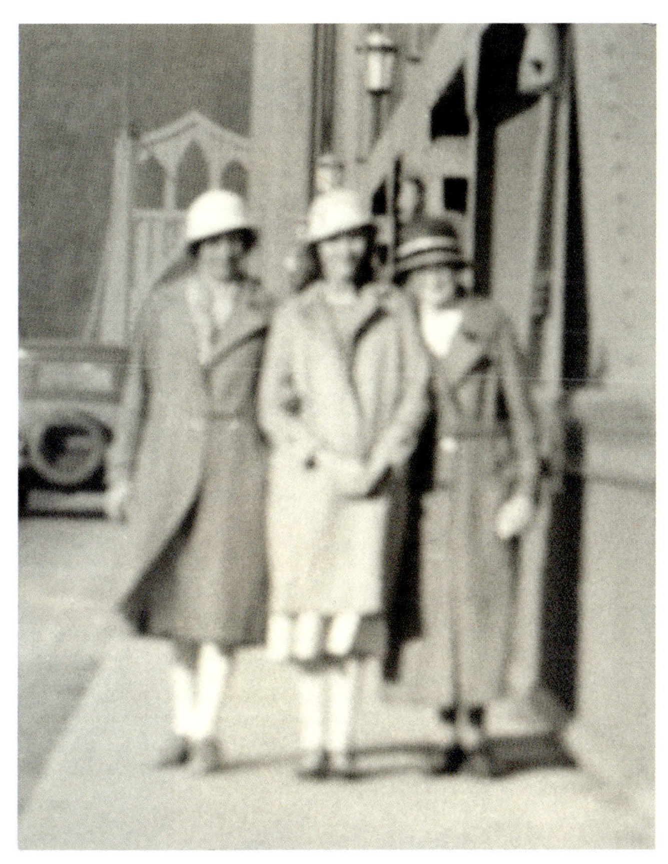

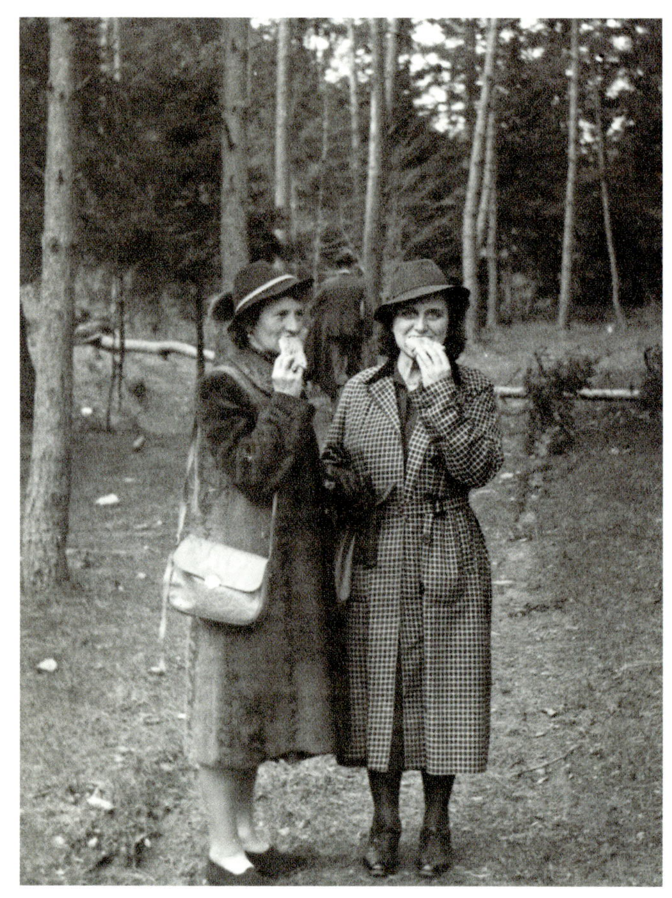

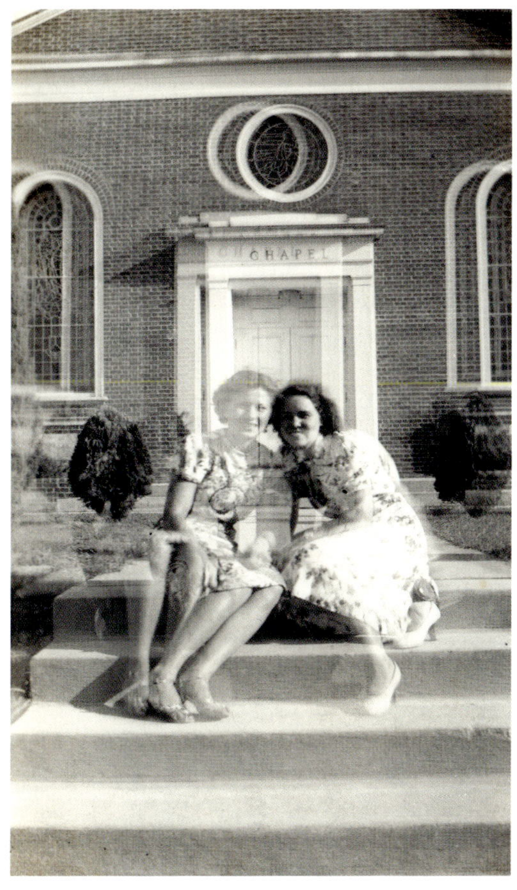
CHAPEL

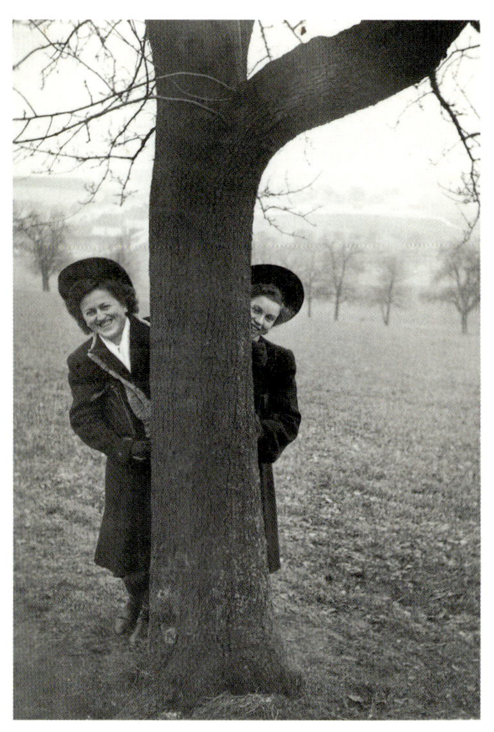

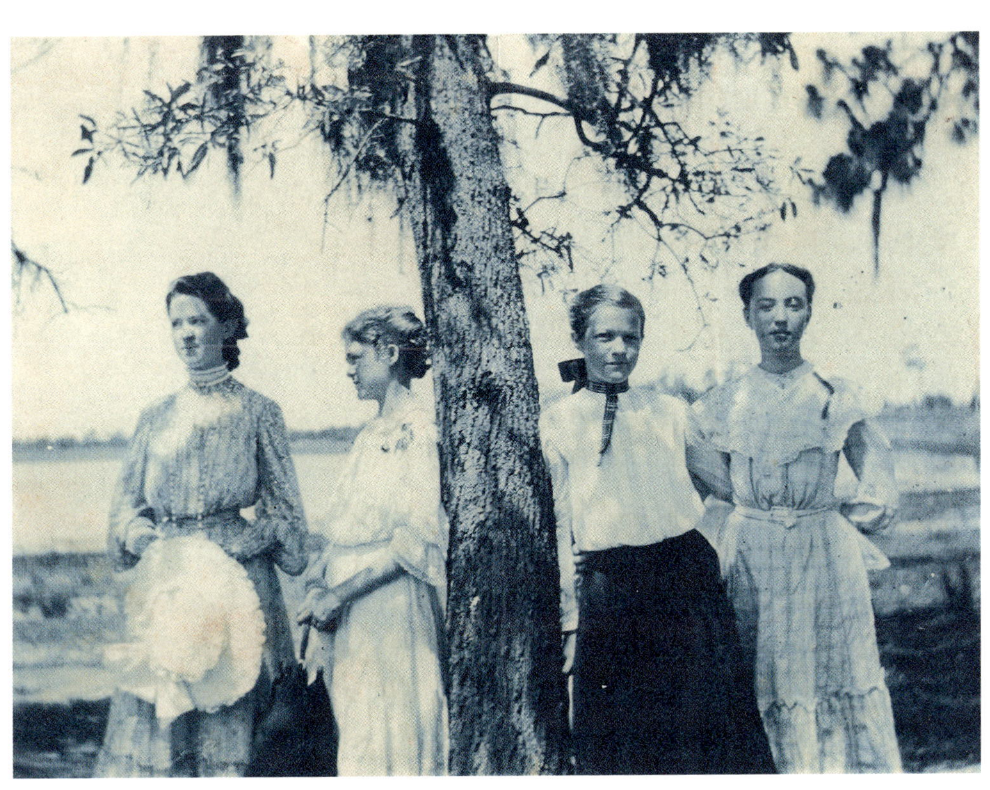

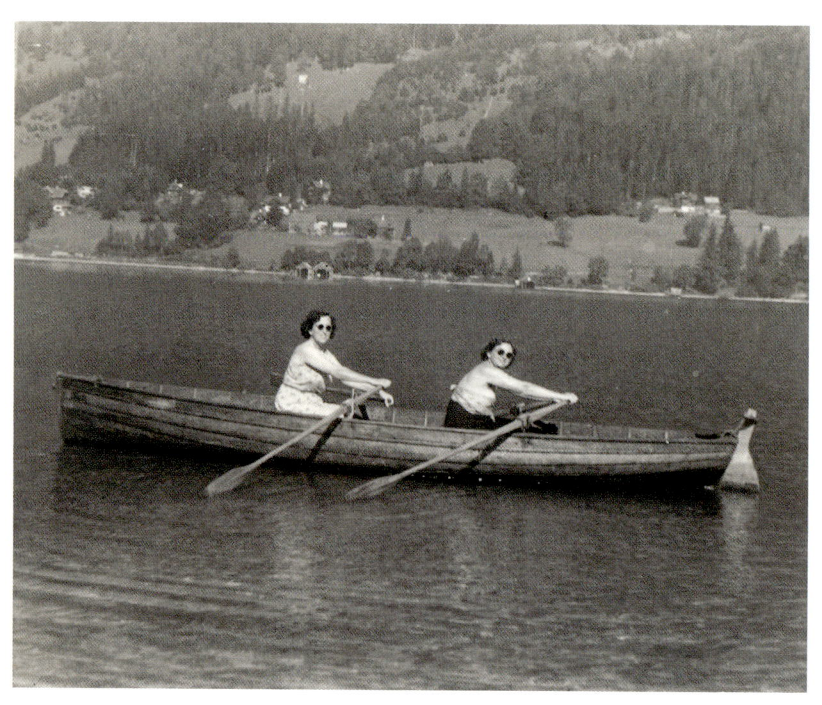

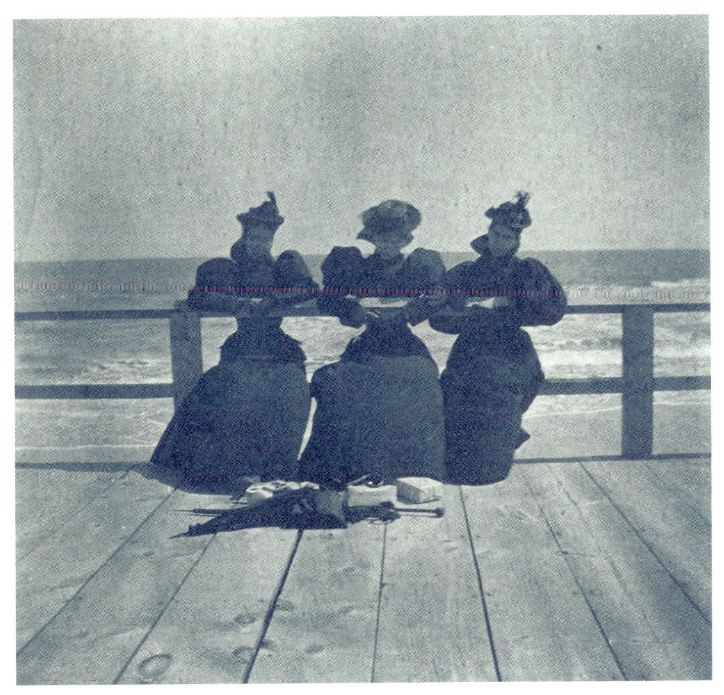

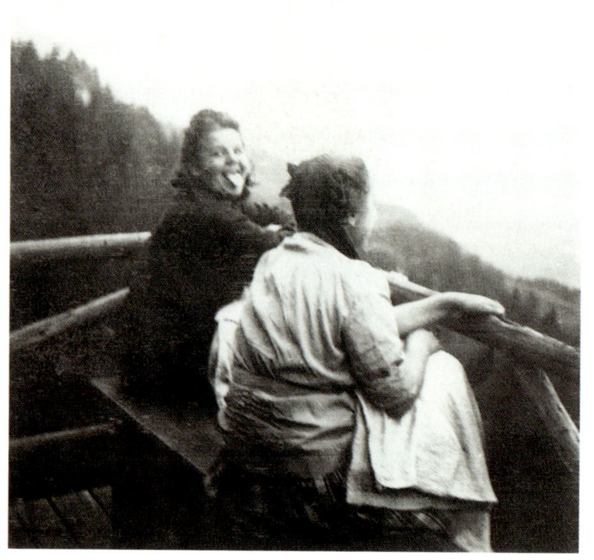

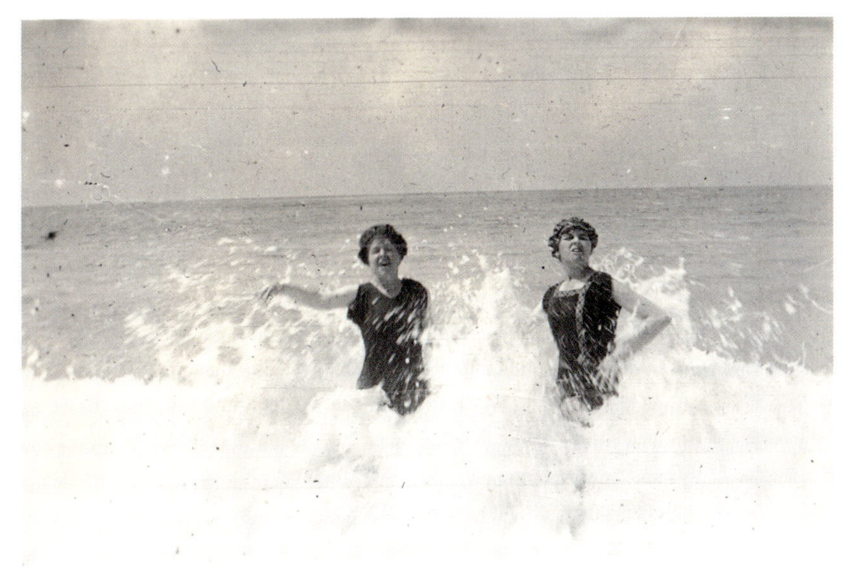

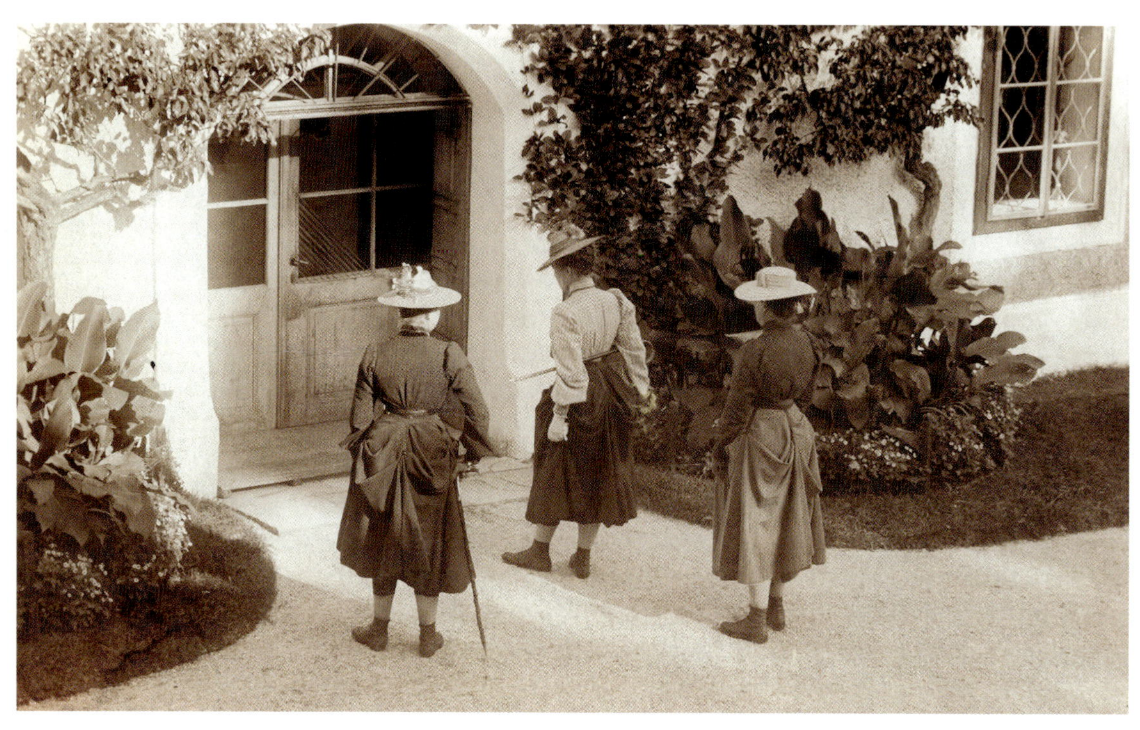

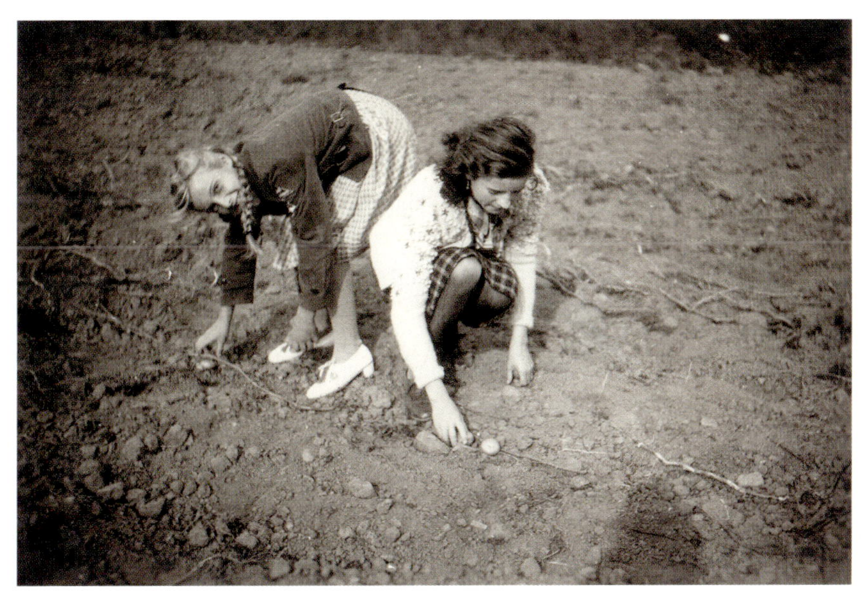

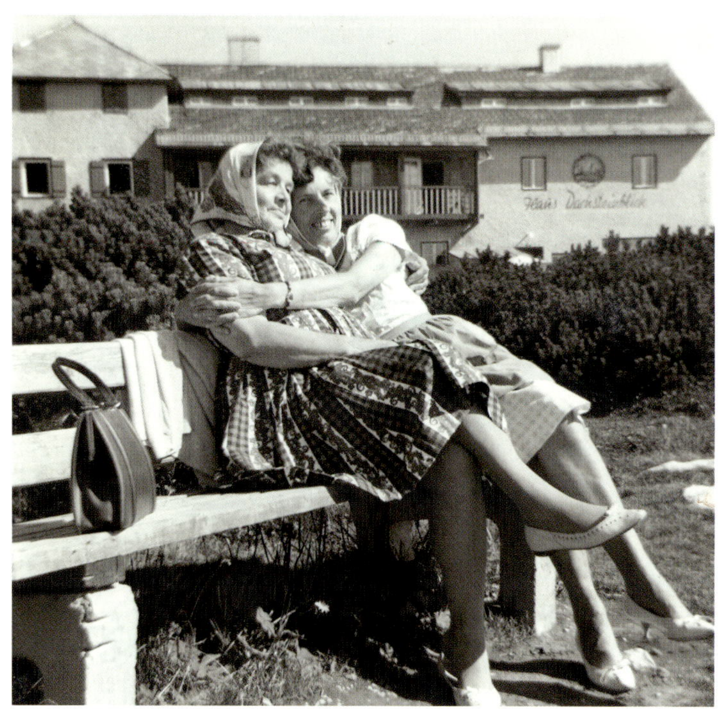

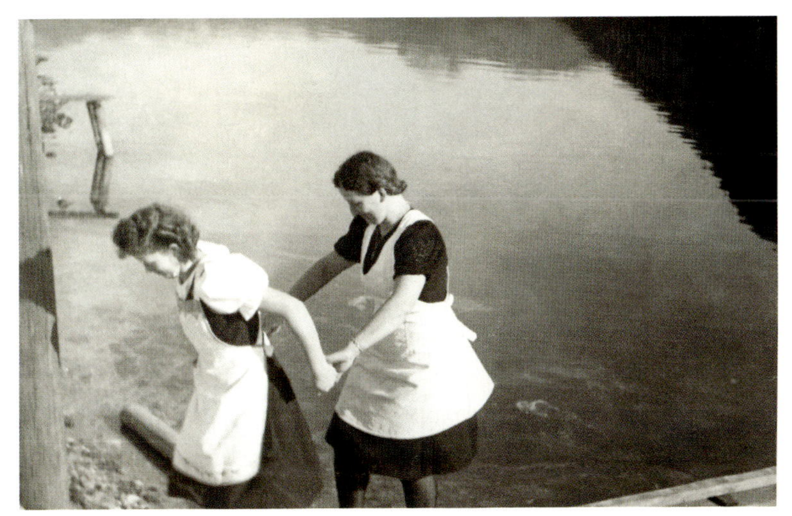

3)

Men Männer

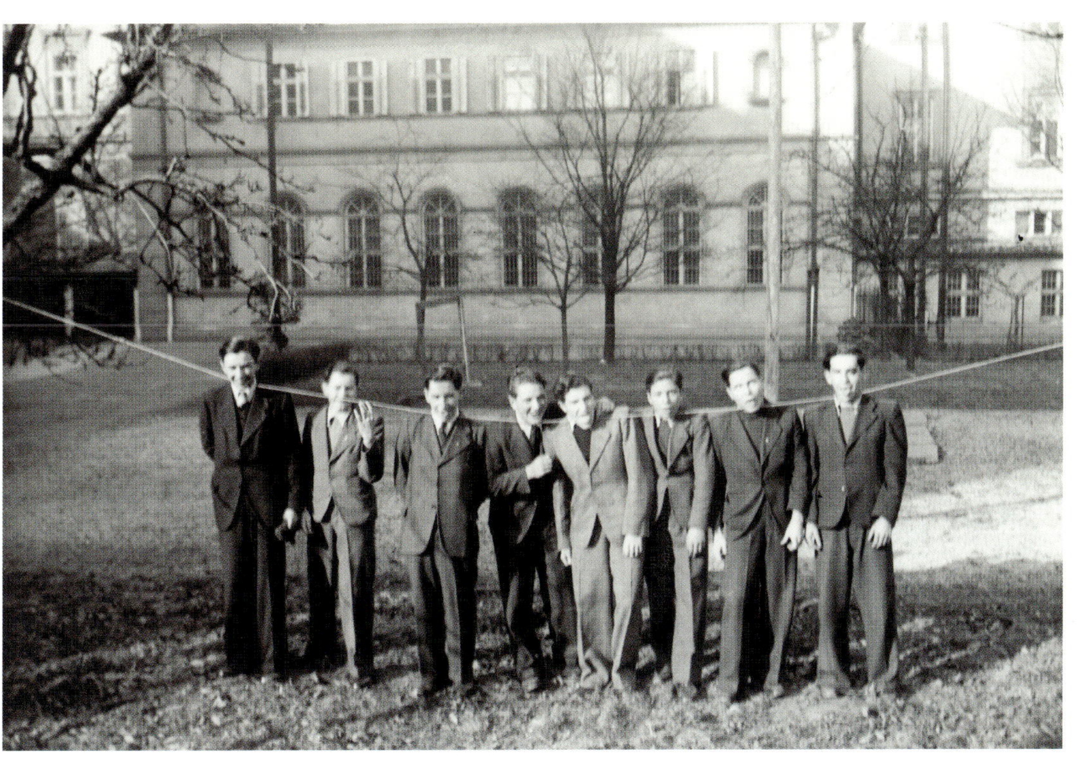

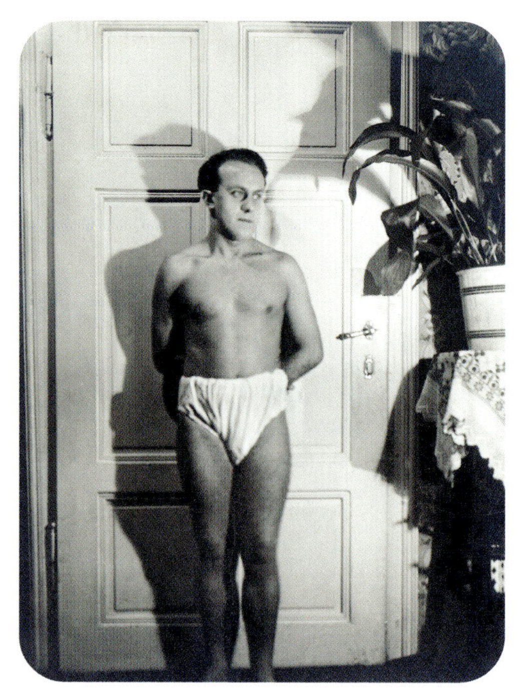

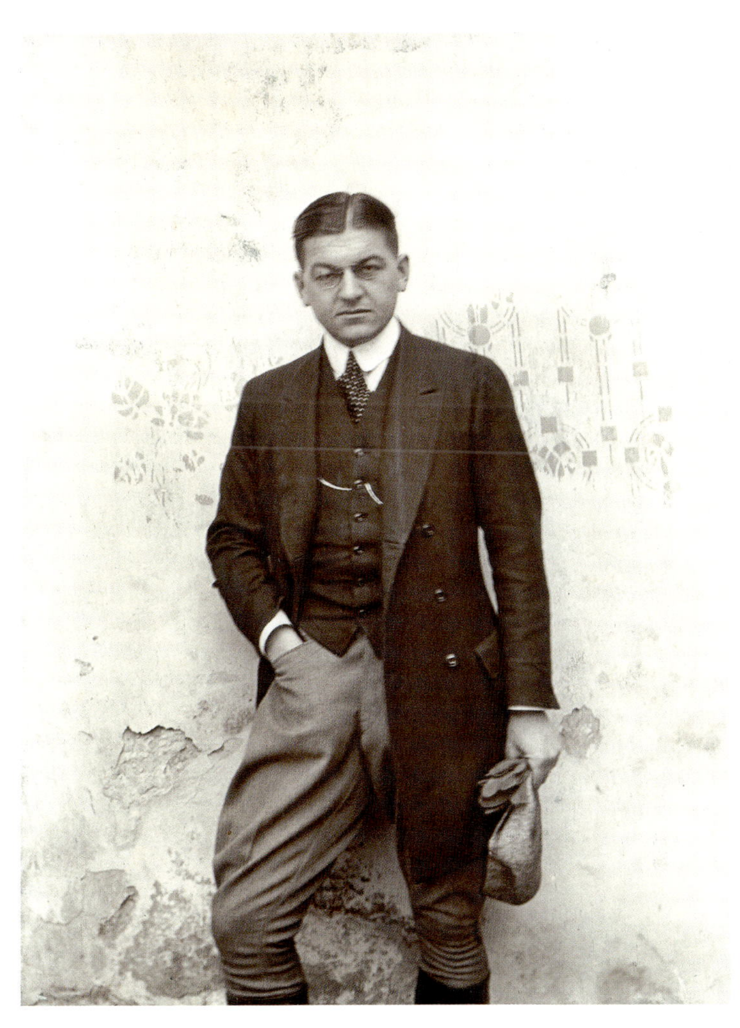

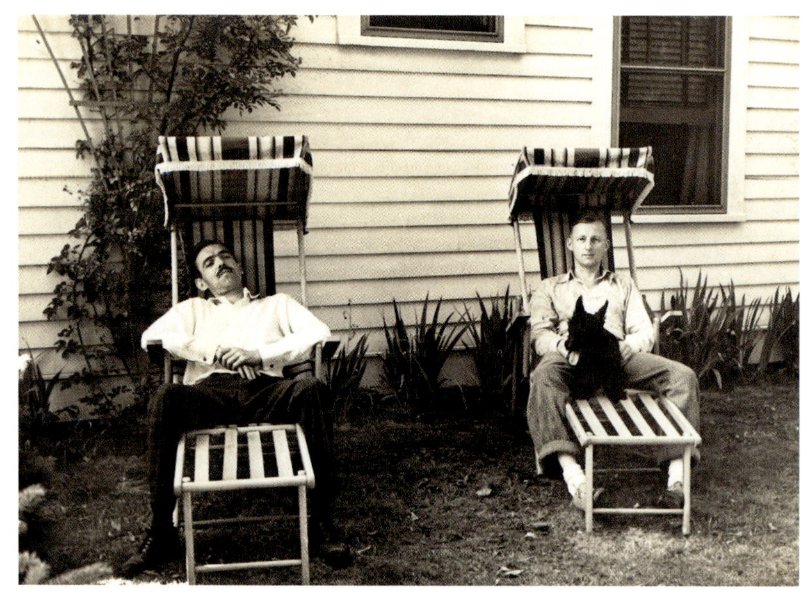

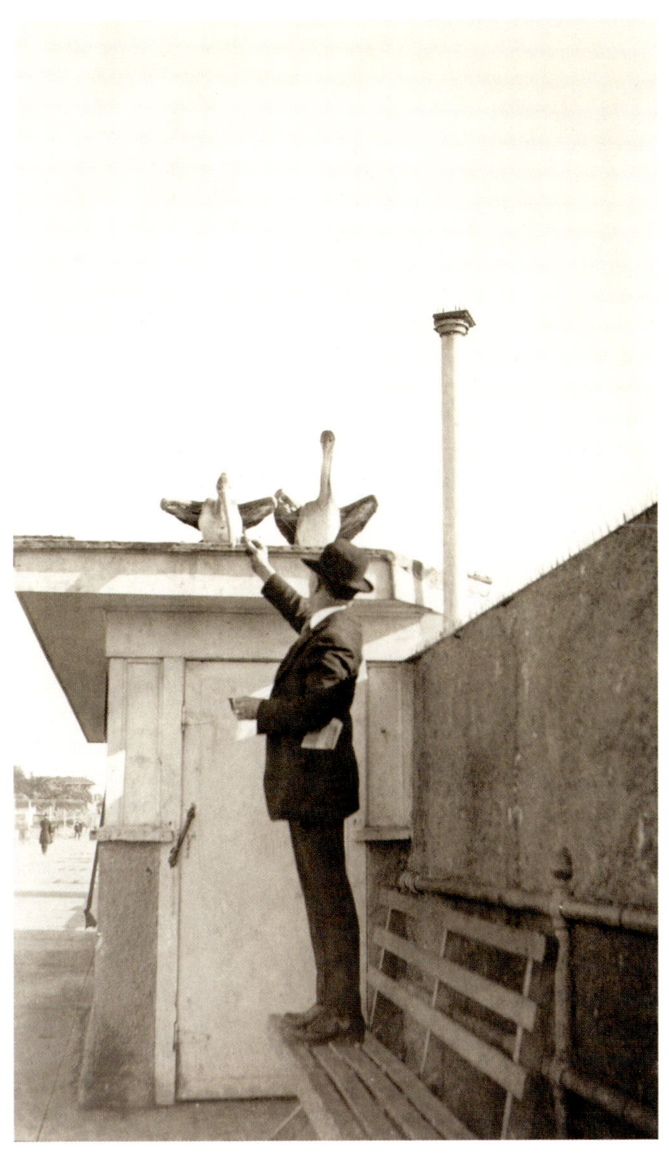

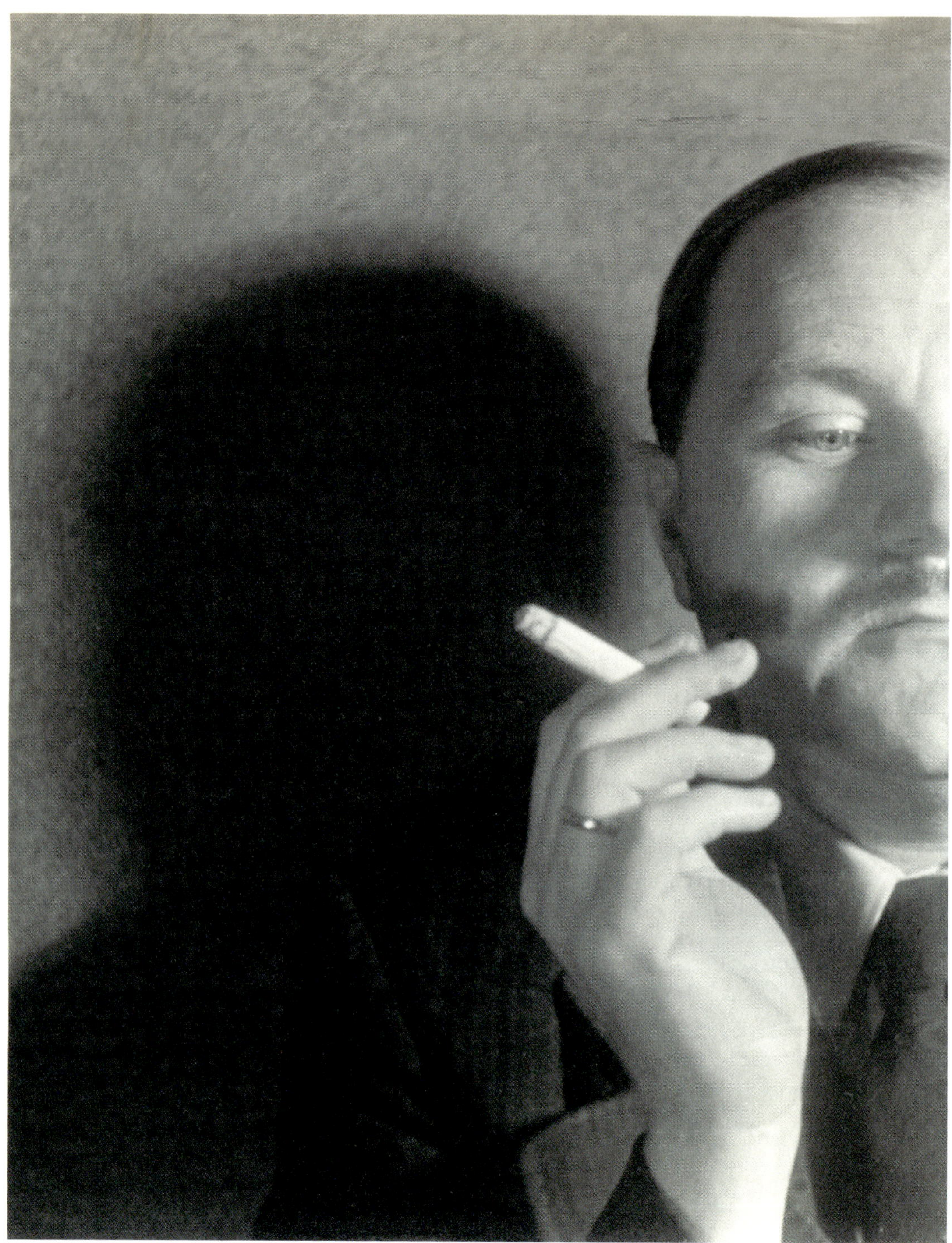

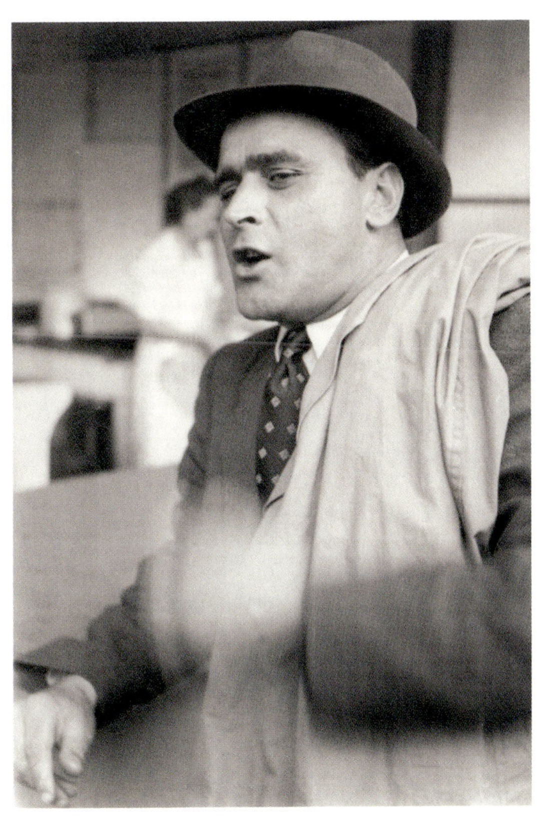

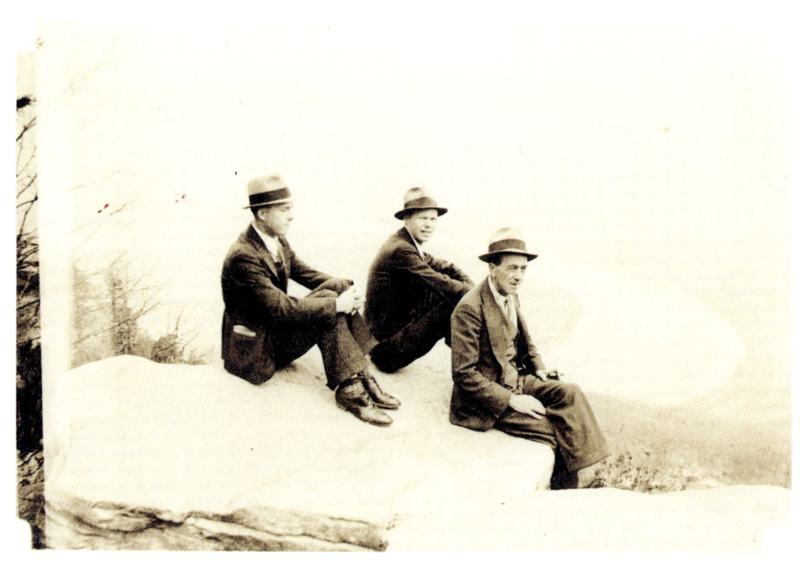

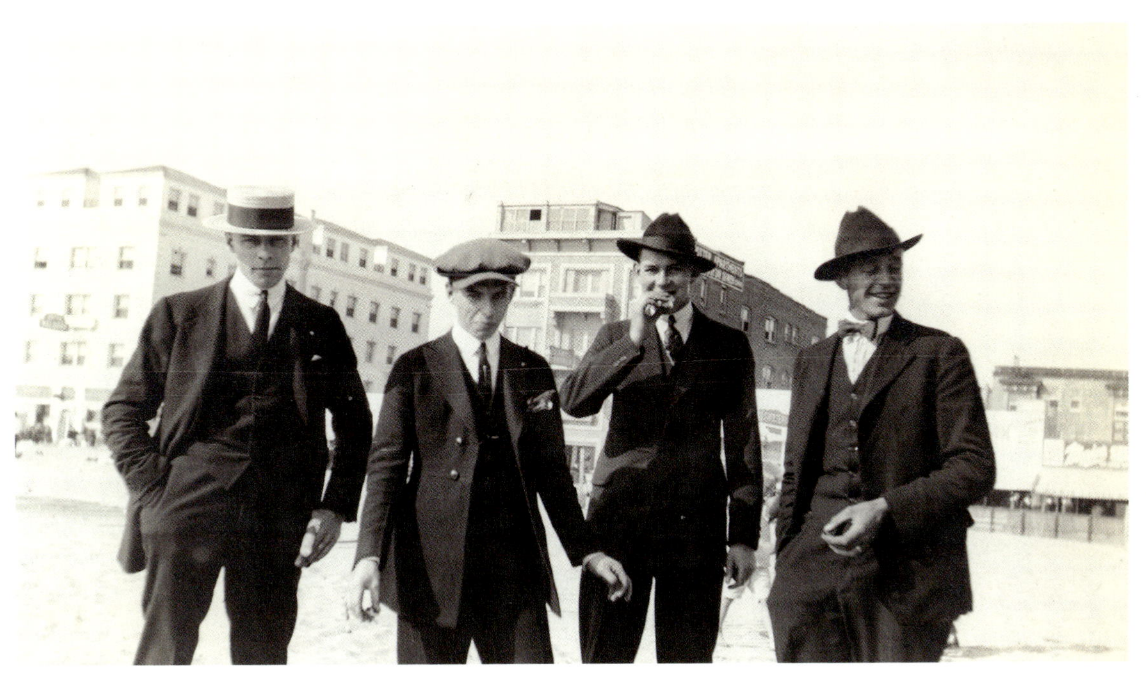

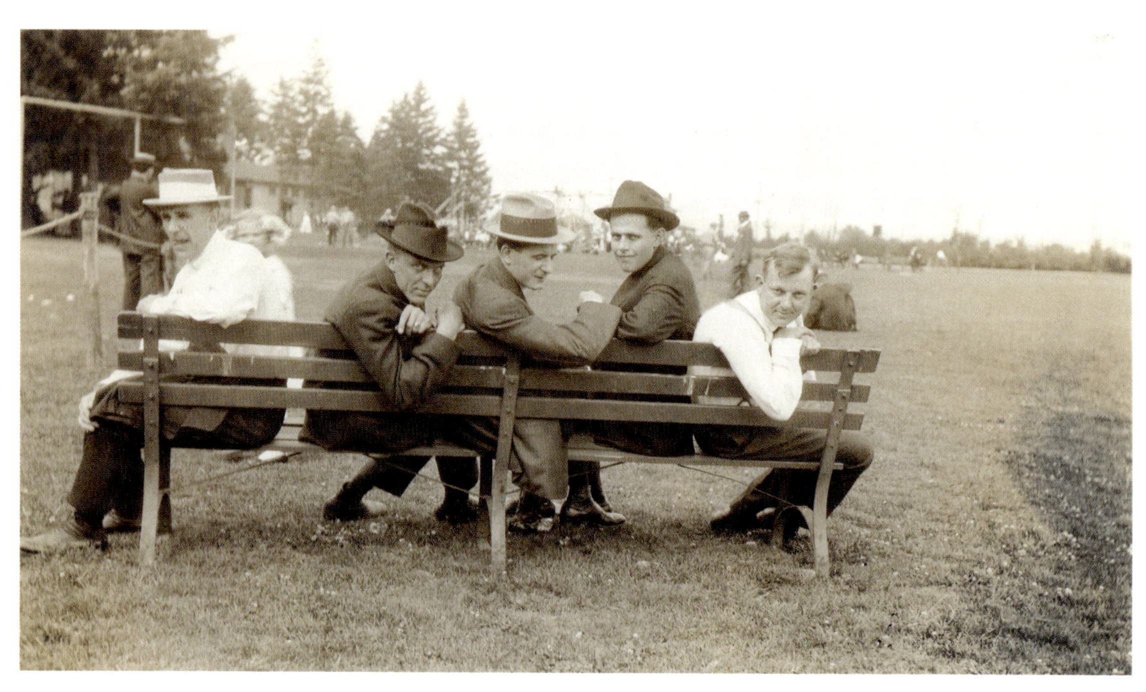

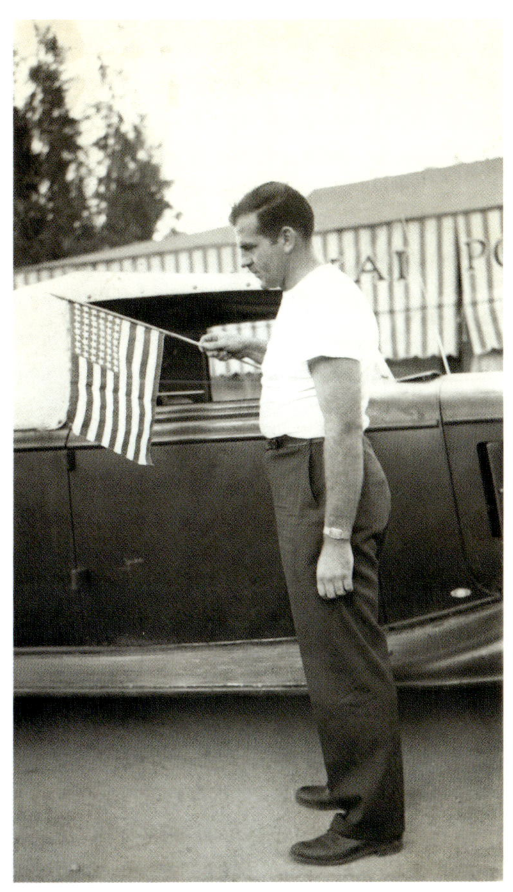

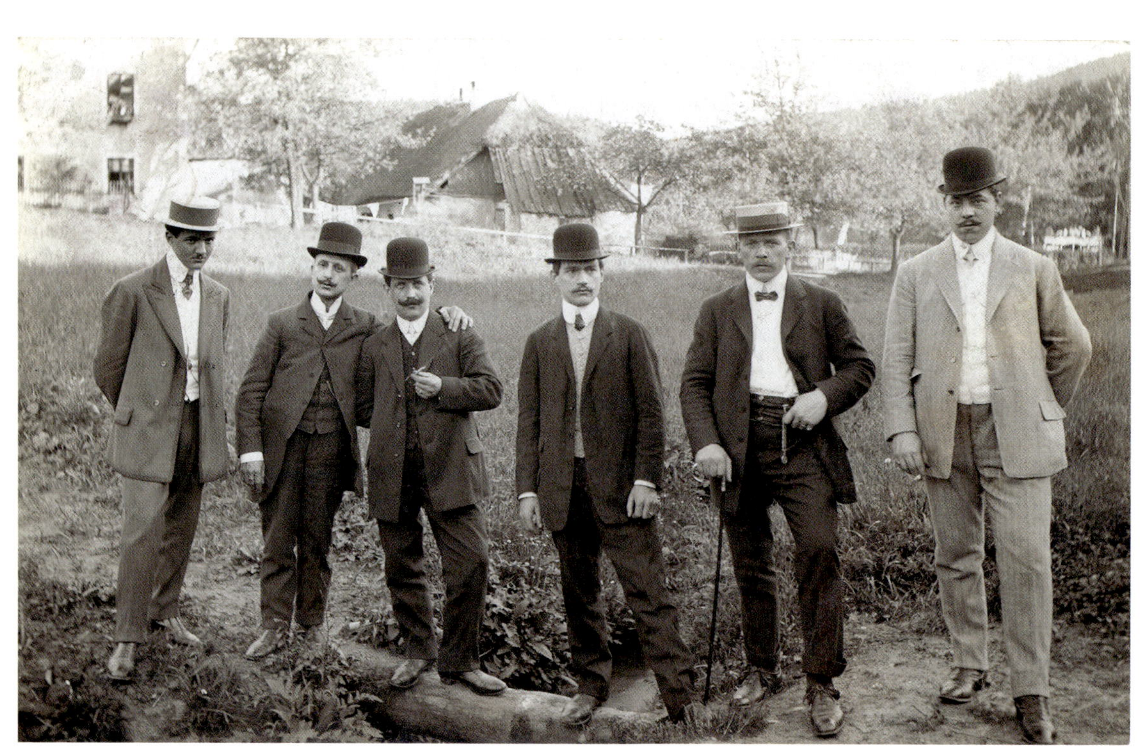

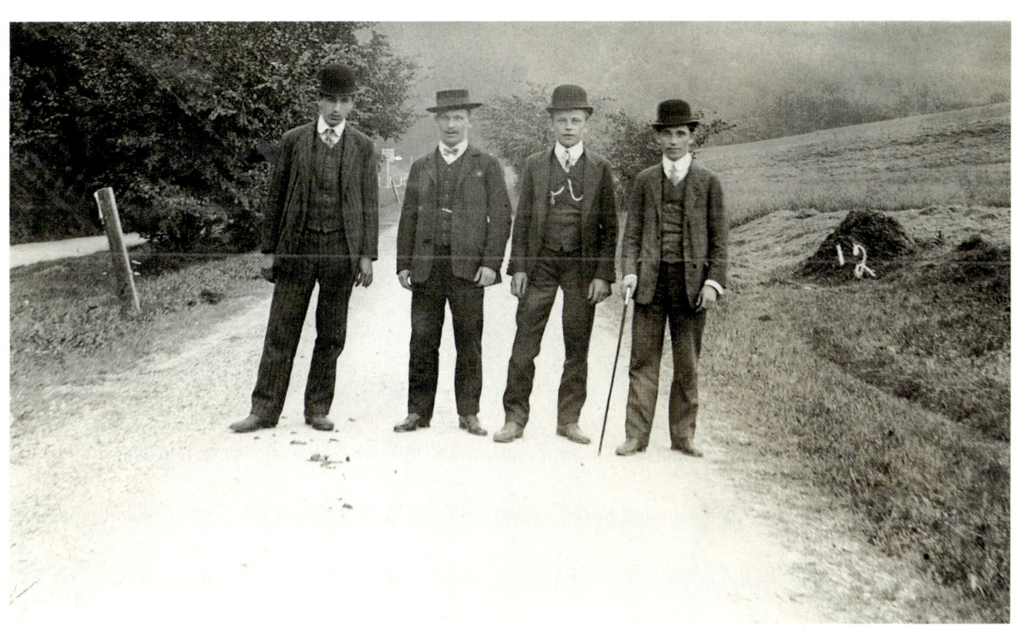

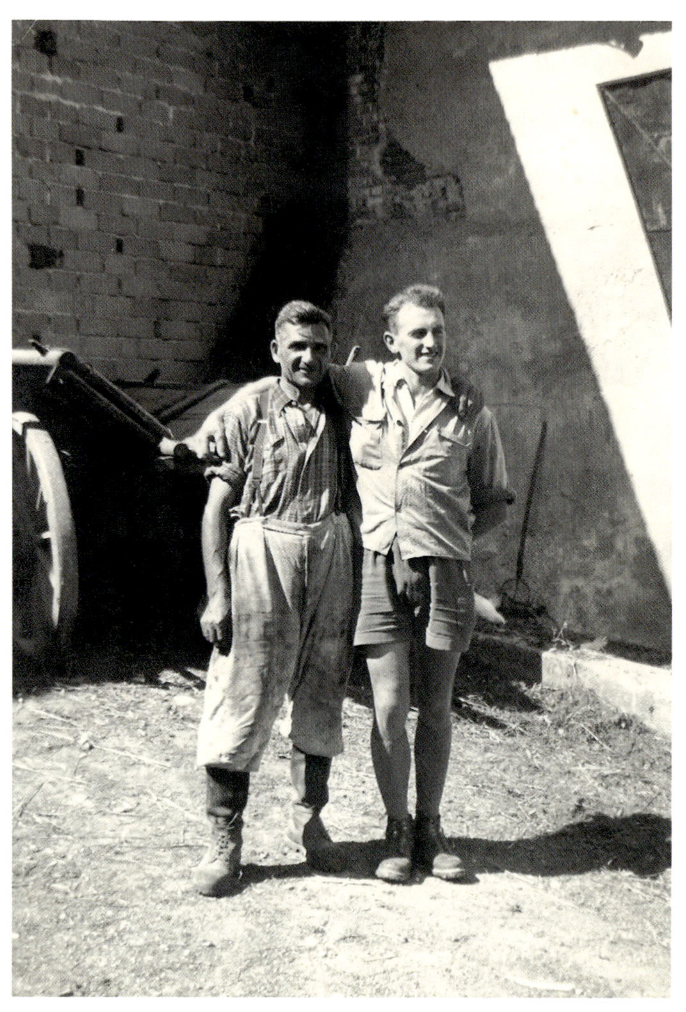

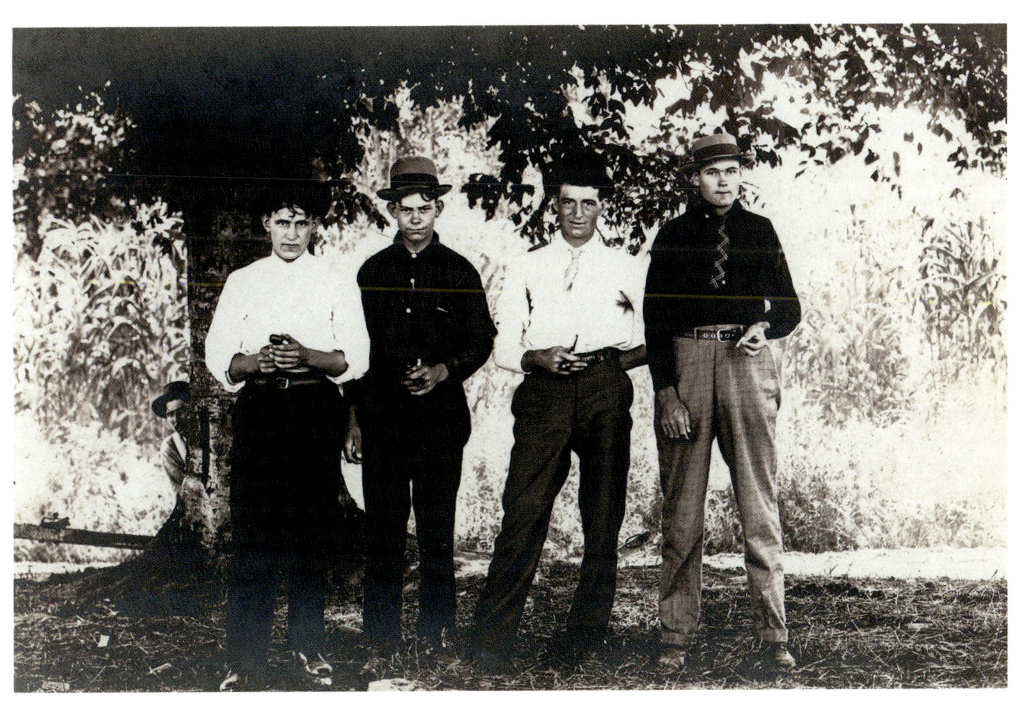

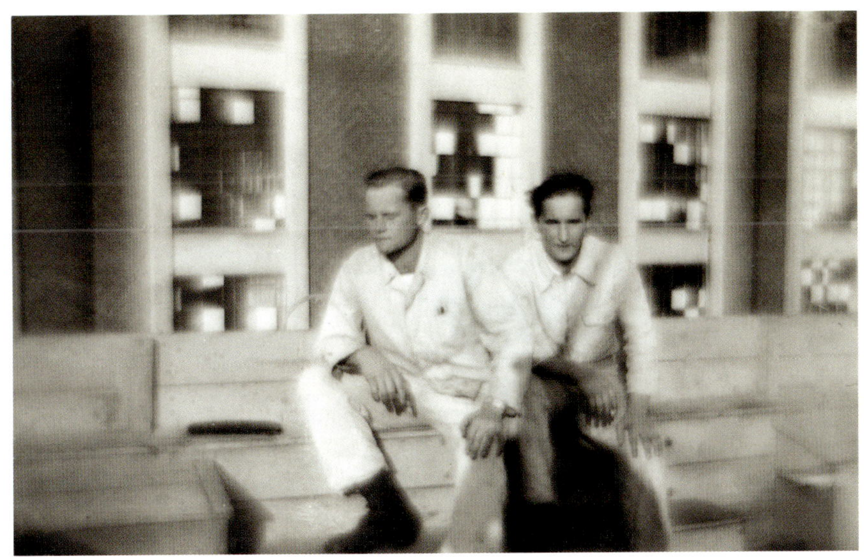

4)

Posing Posen

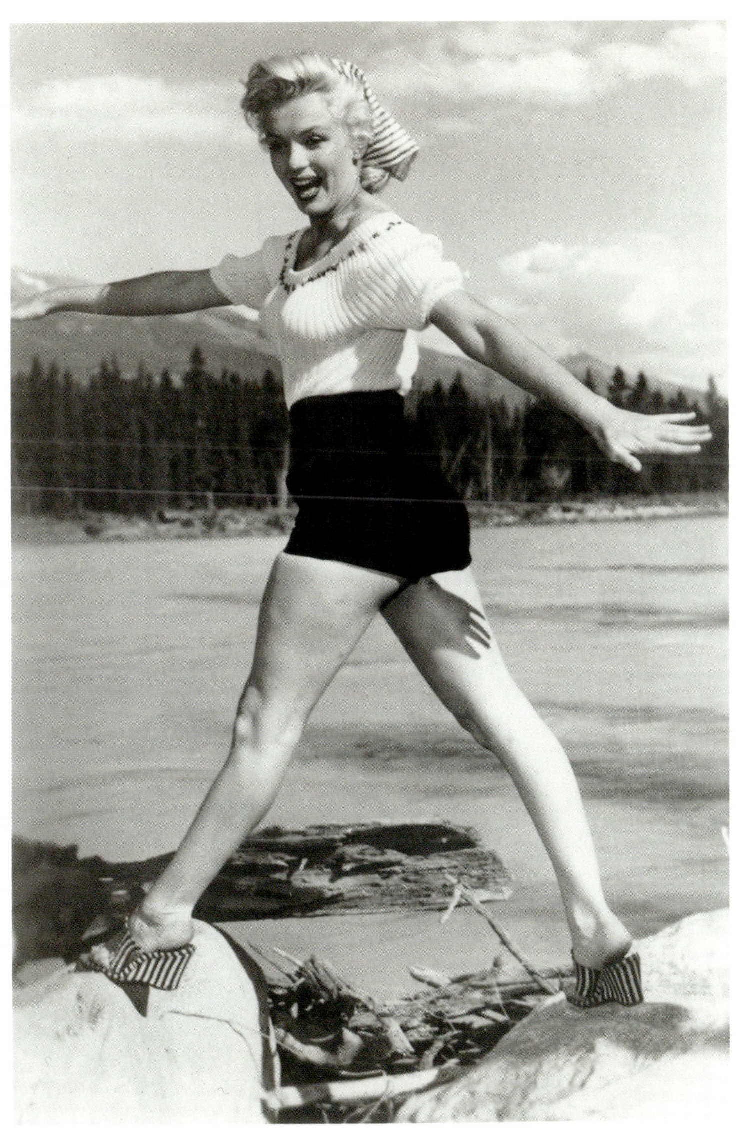

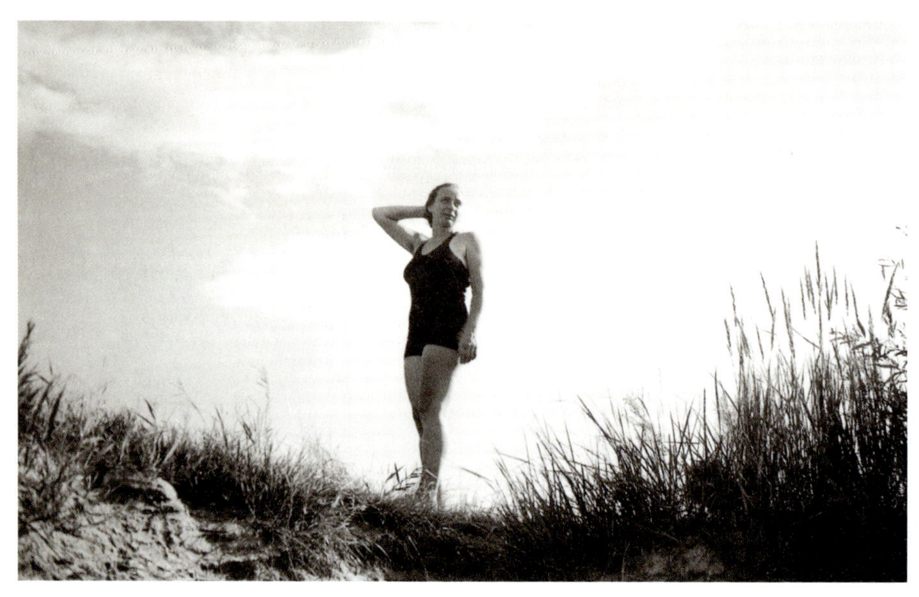

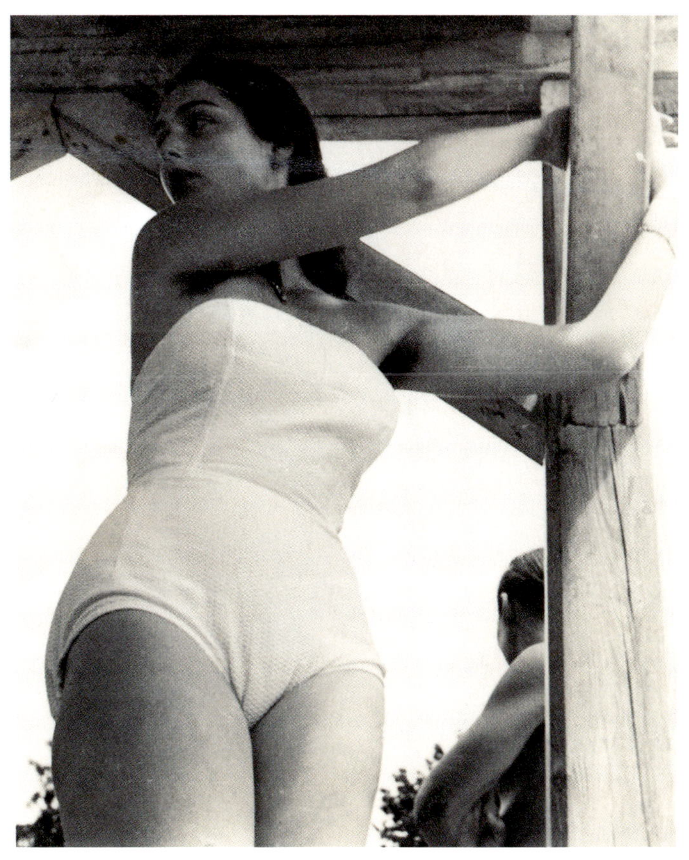

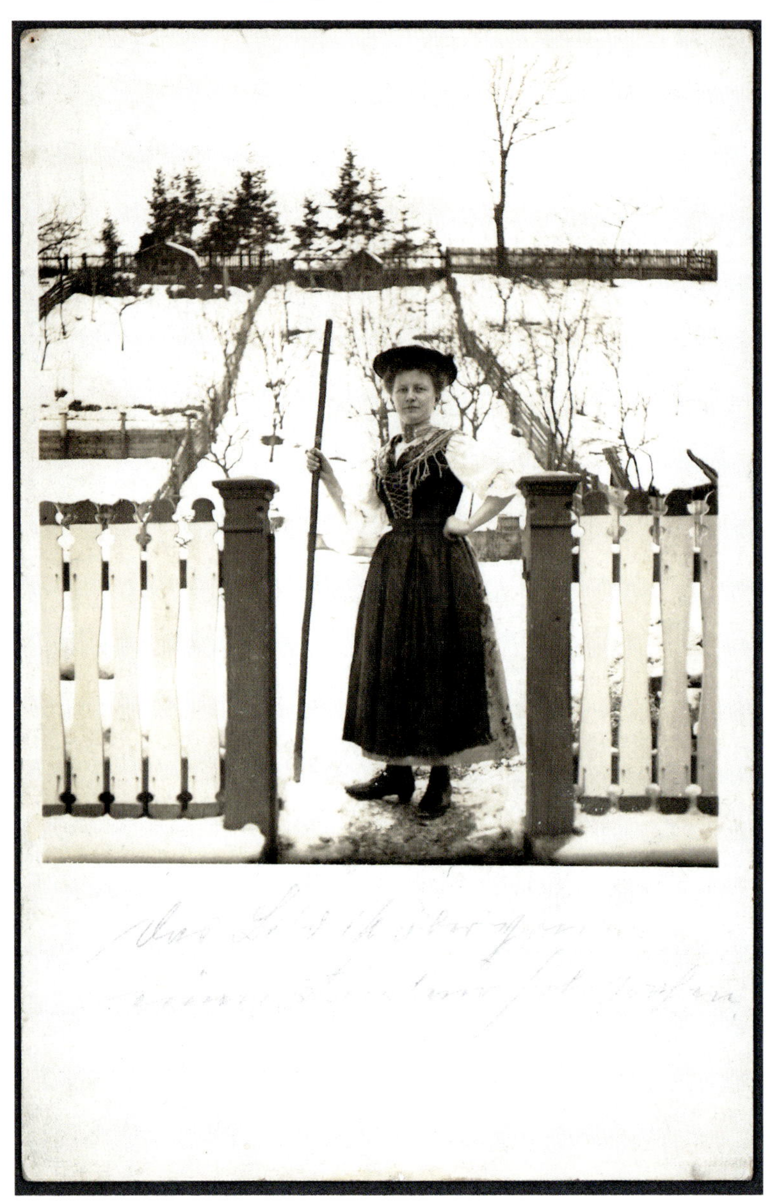

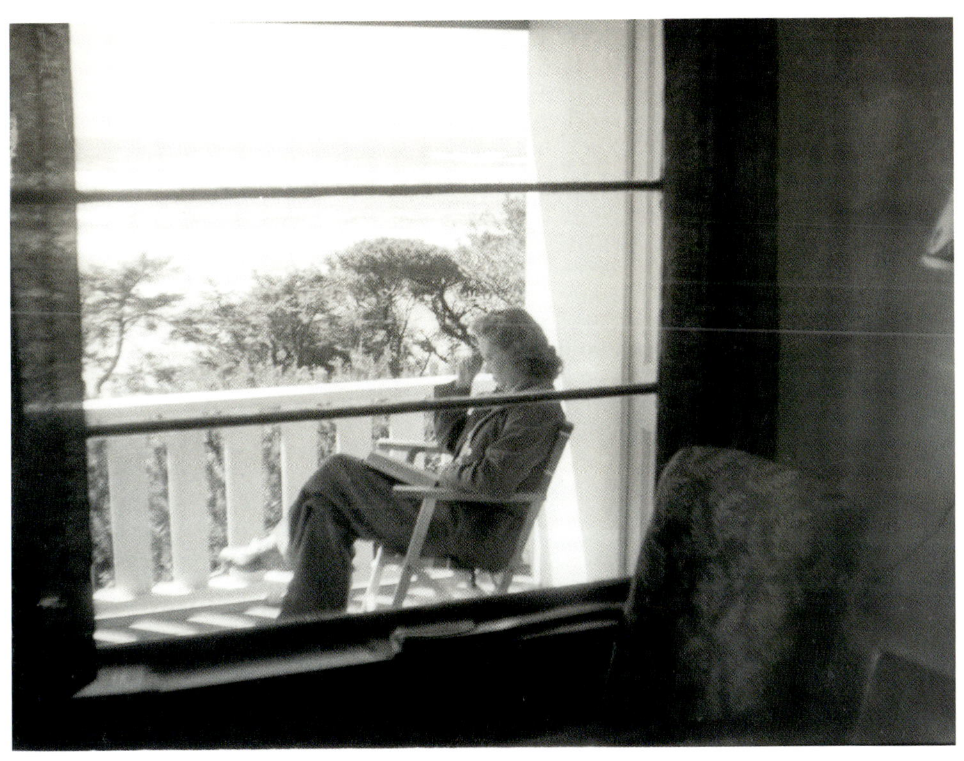

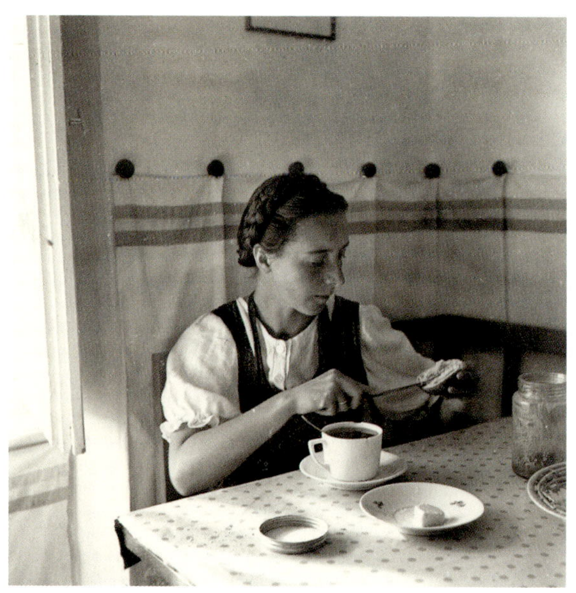

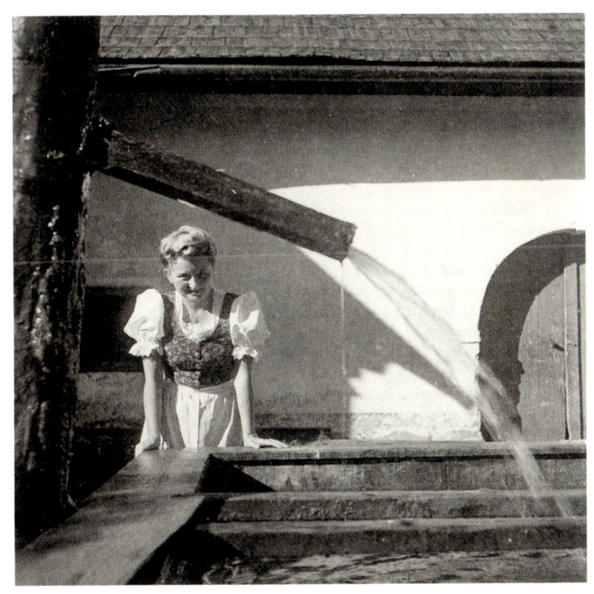

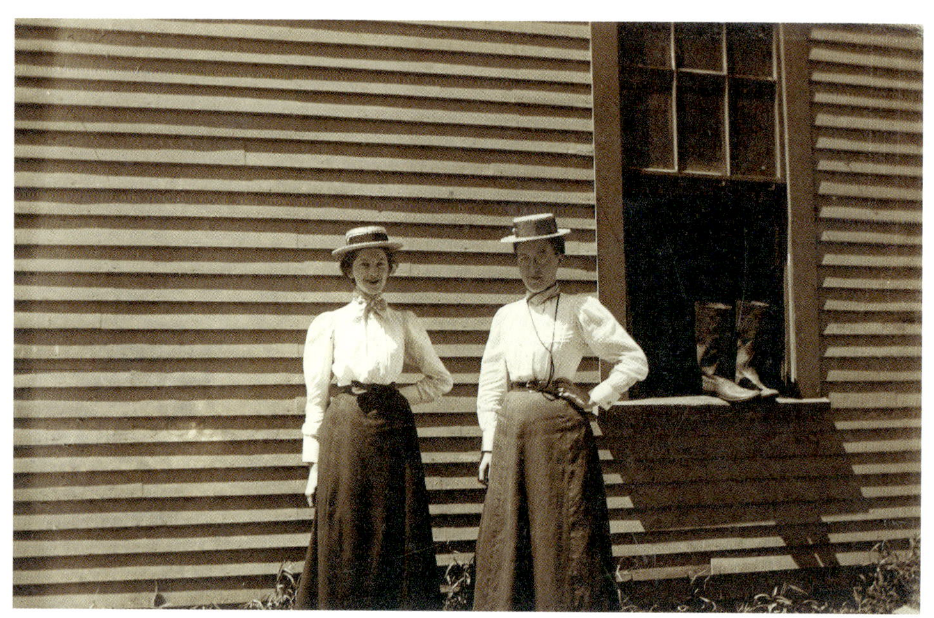

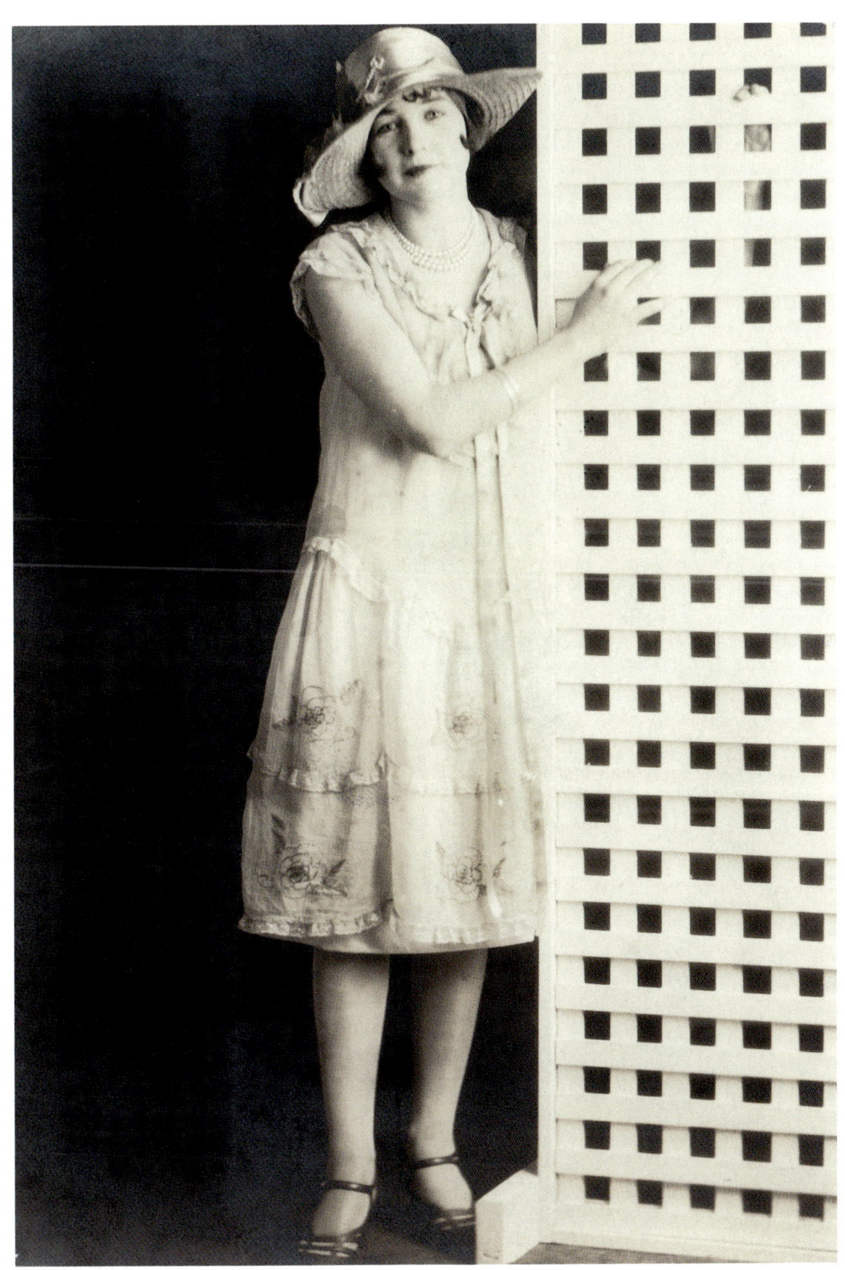

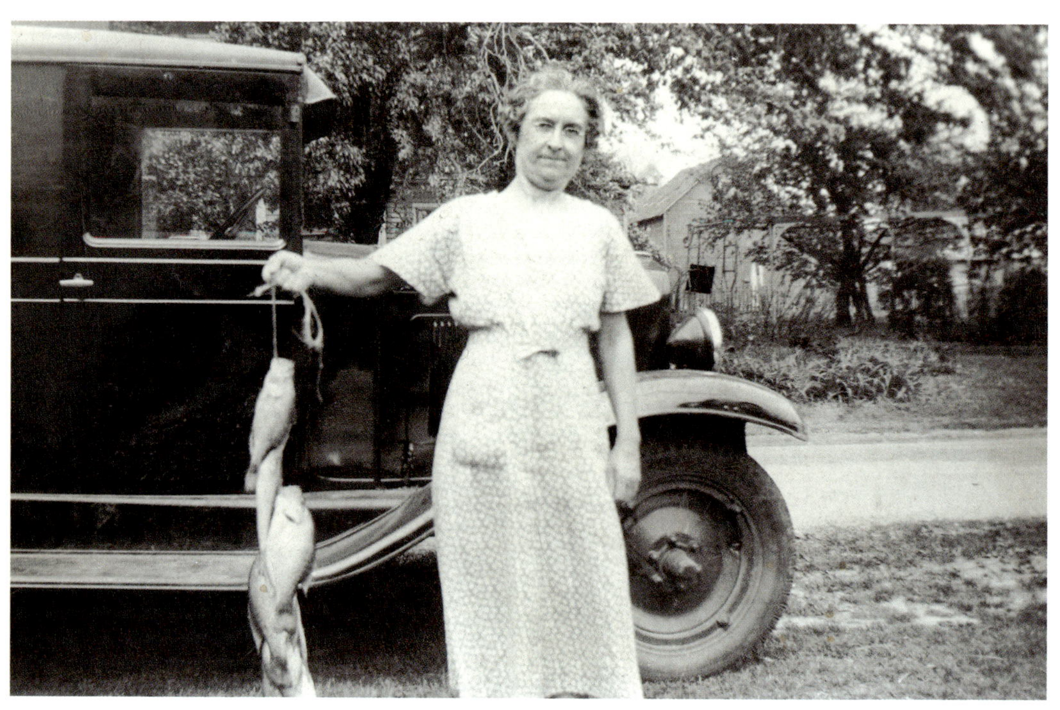

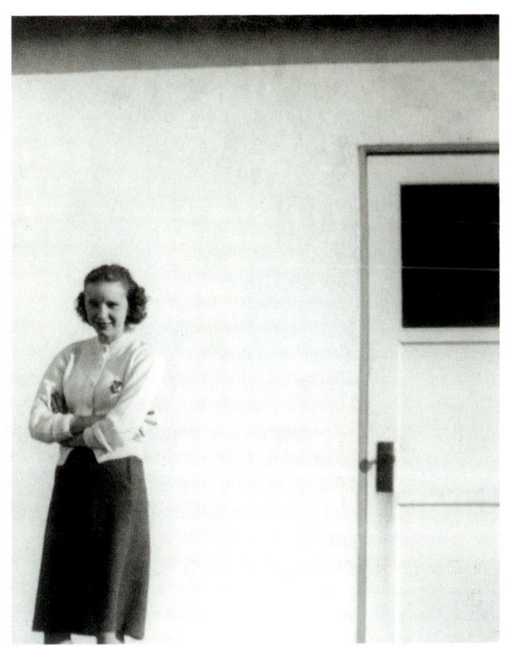

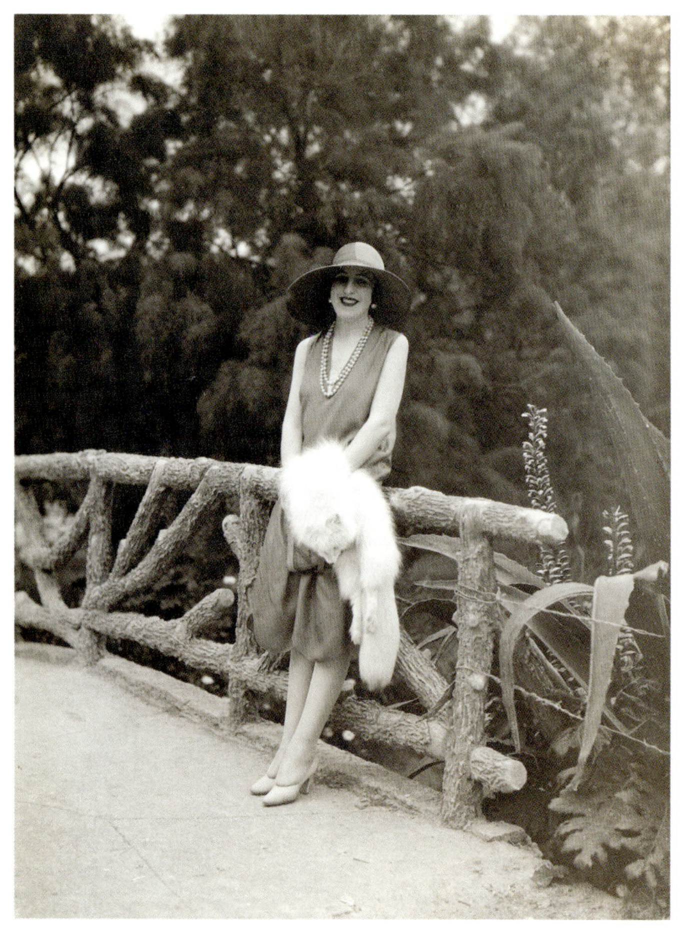

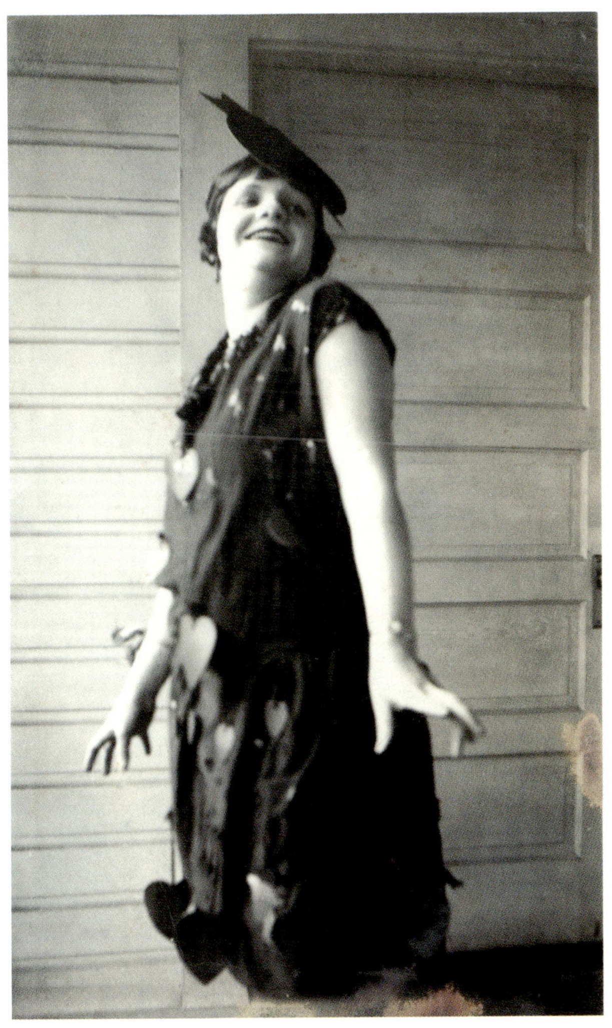

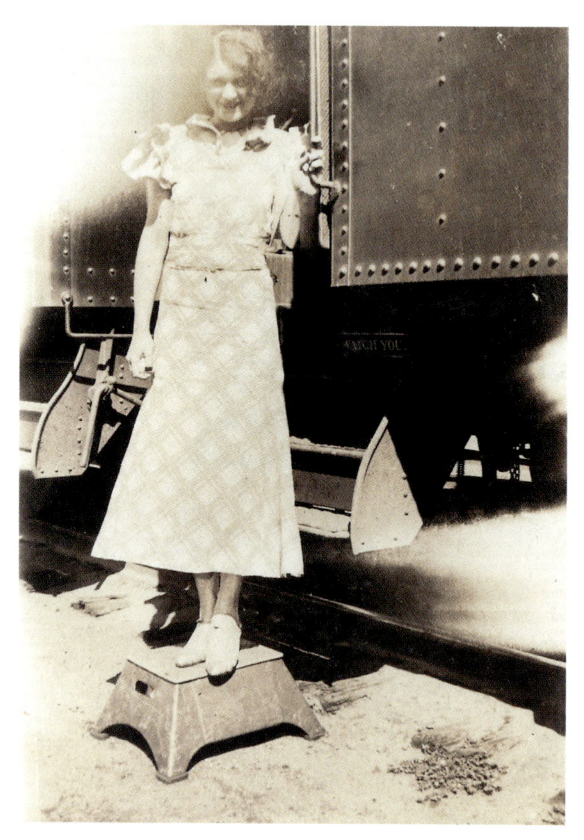

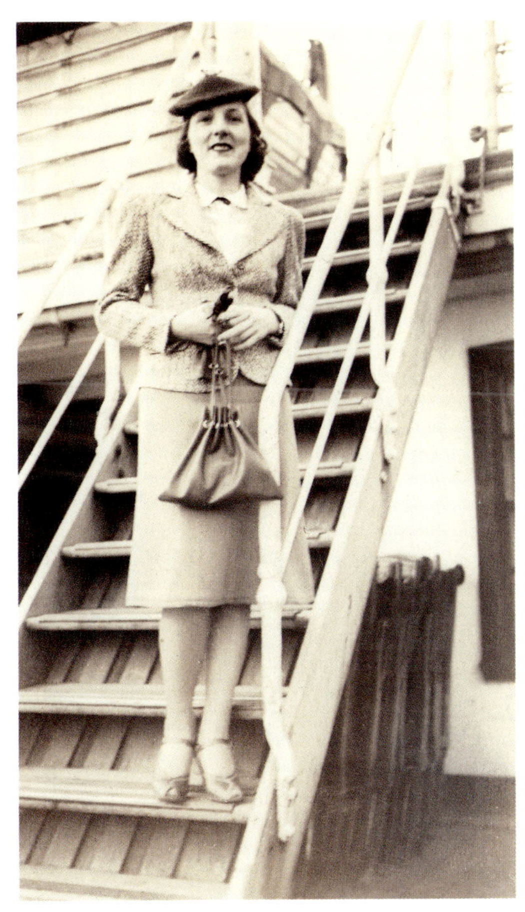

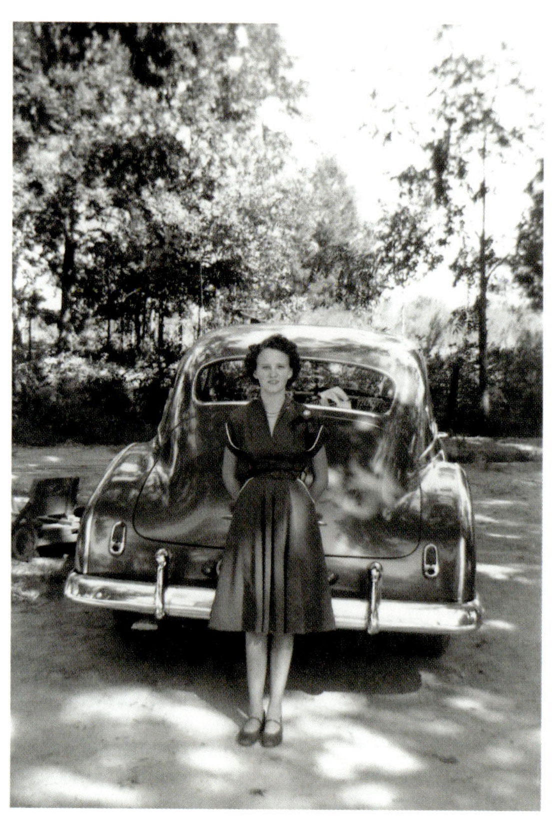

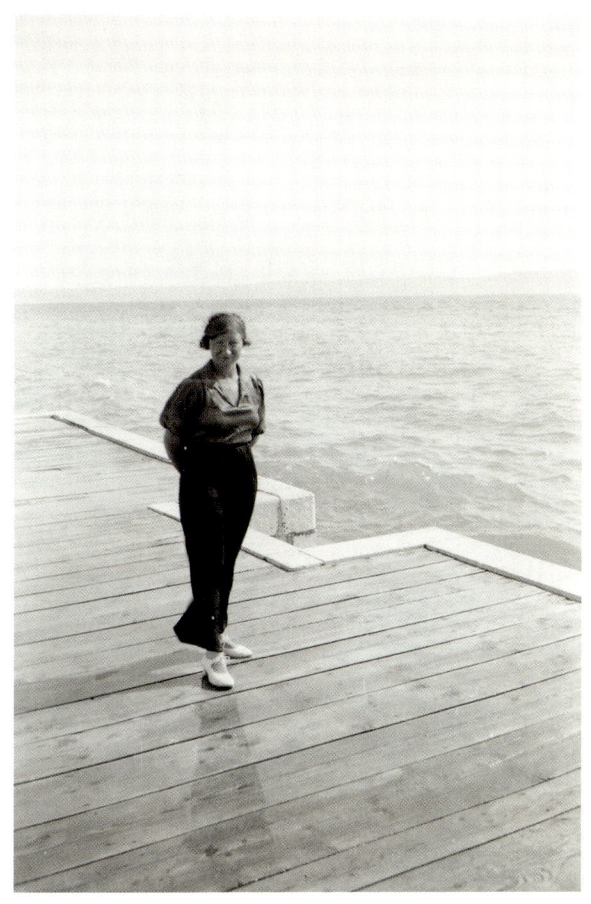

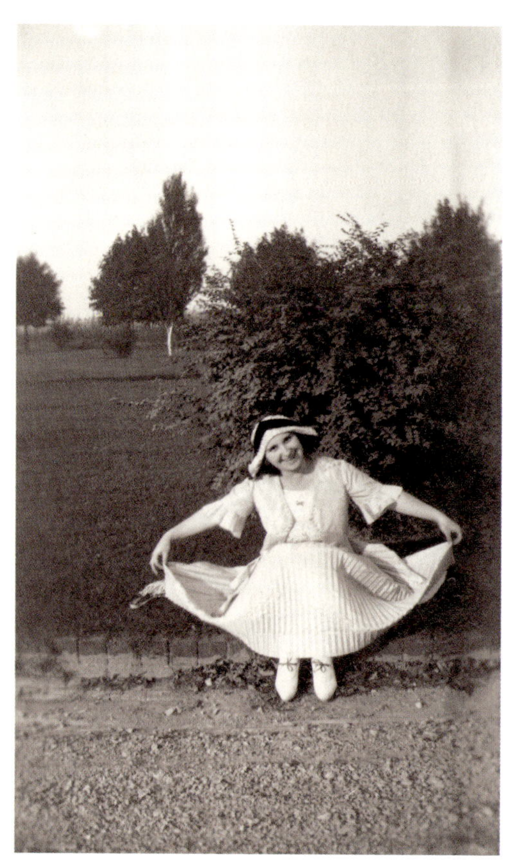

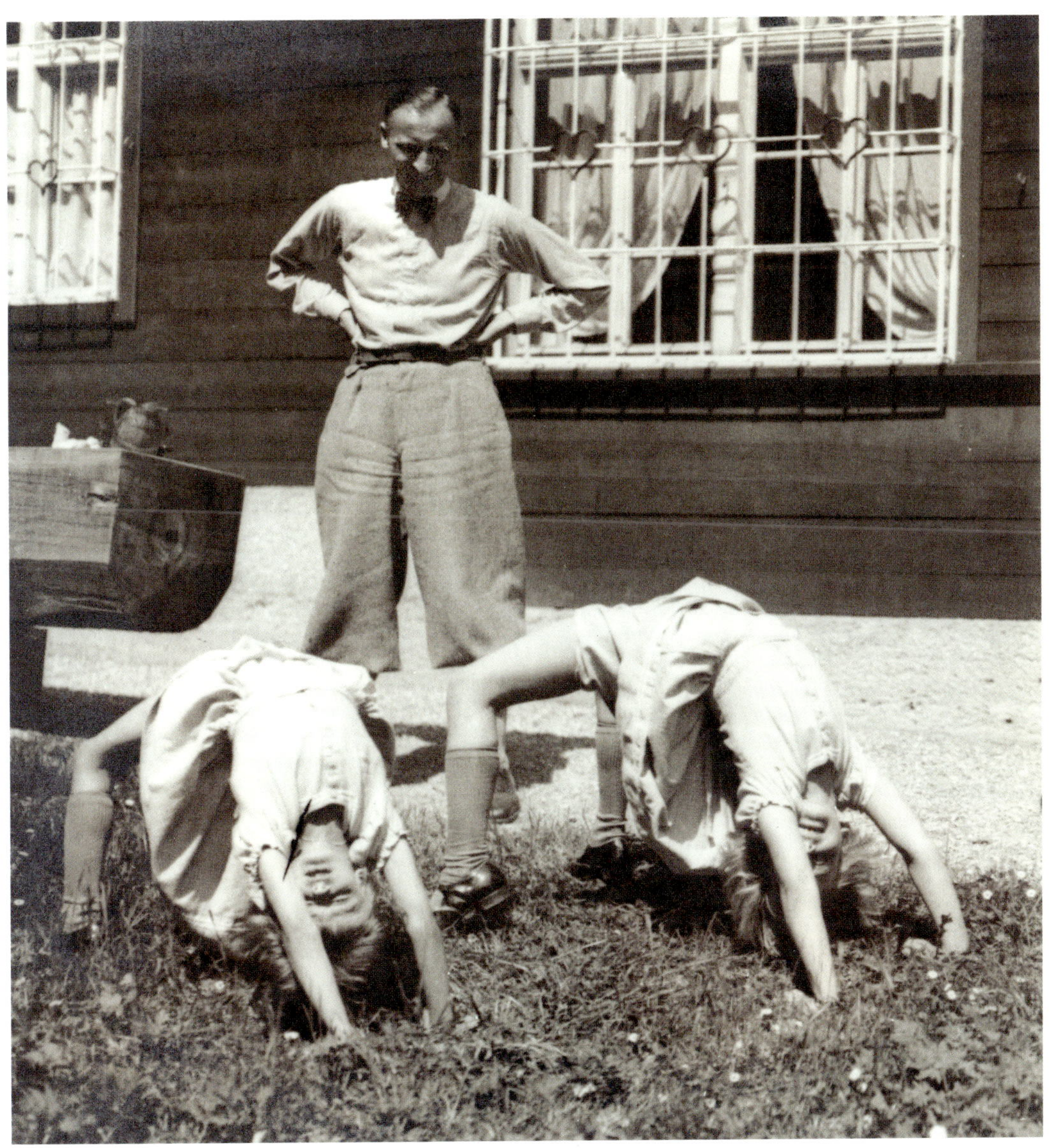

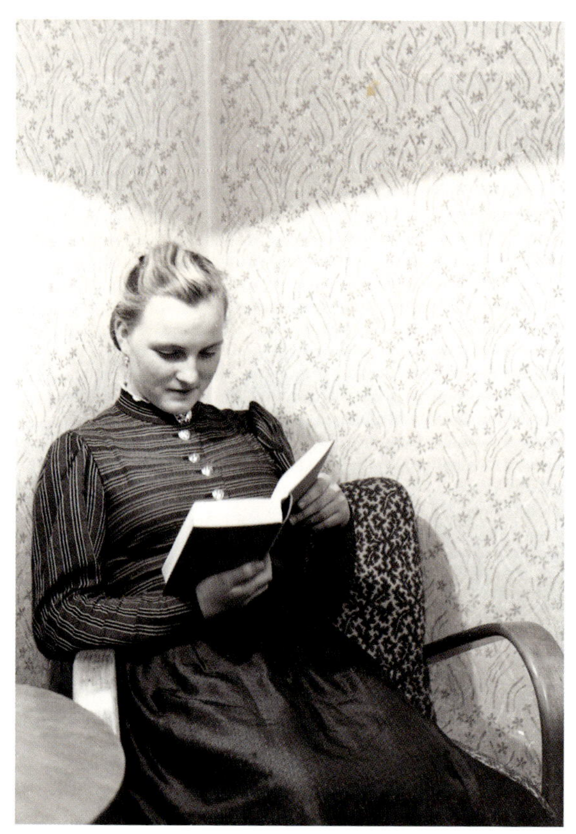

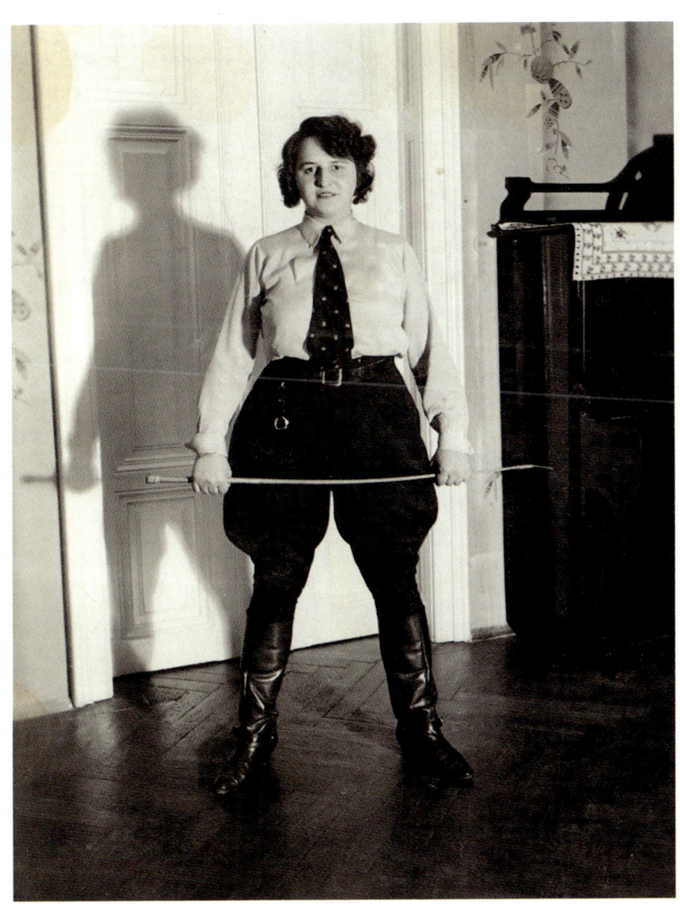

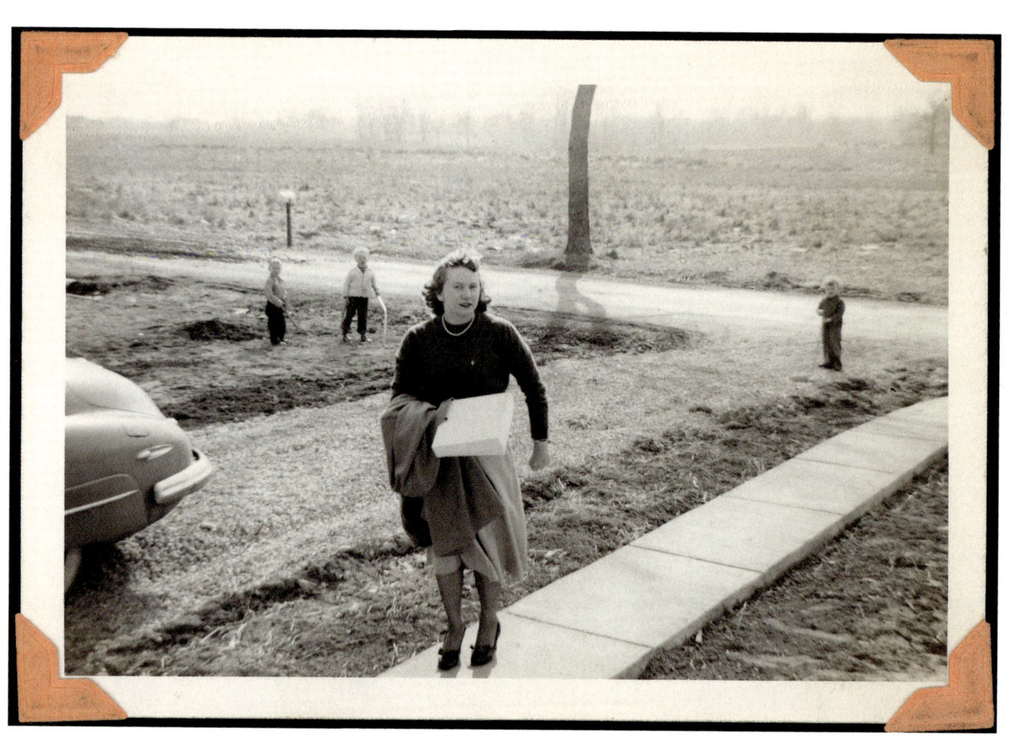

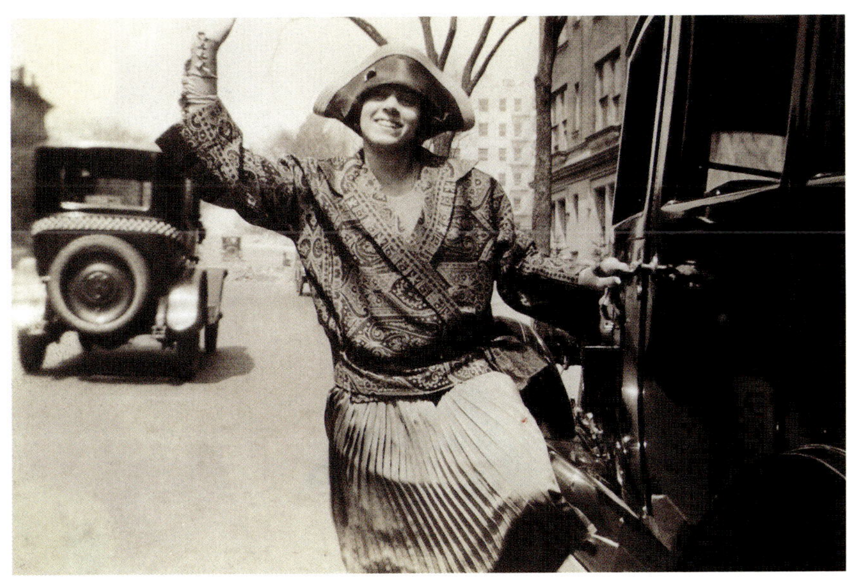

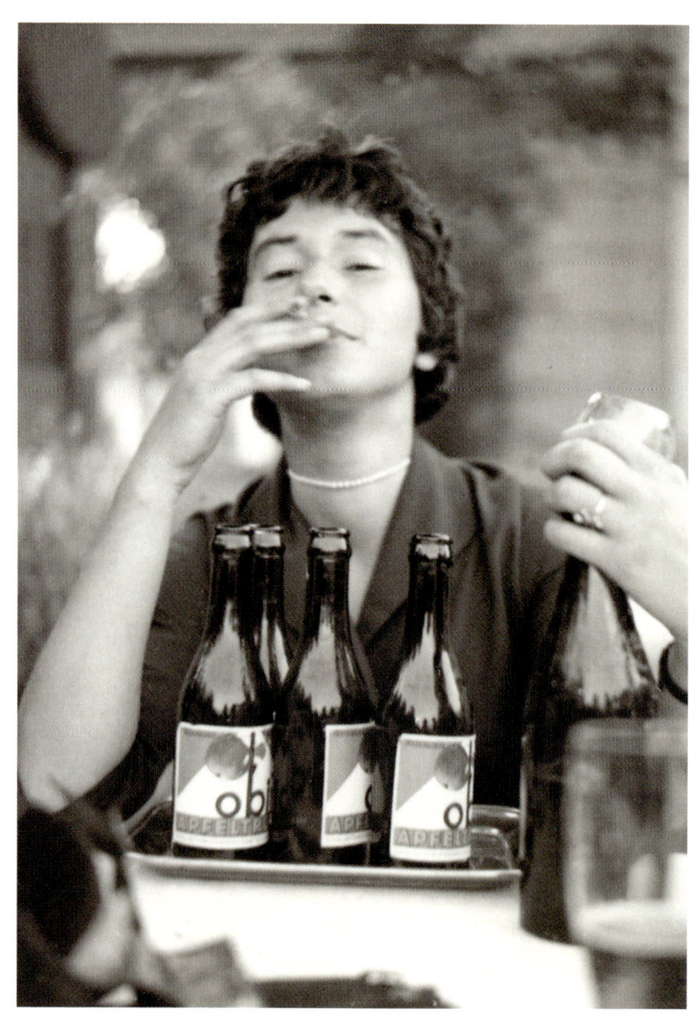
obi

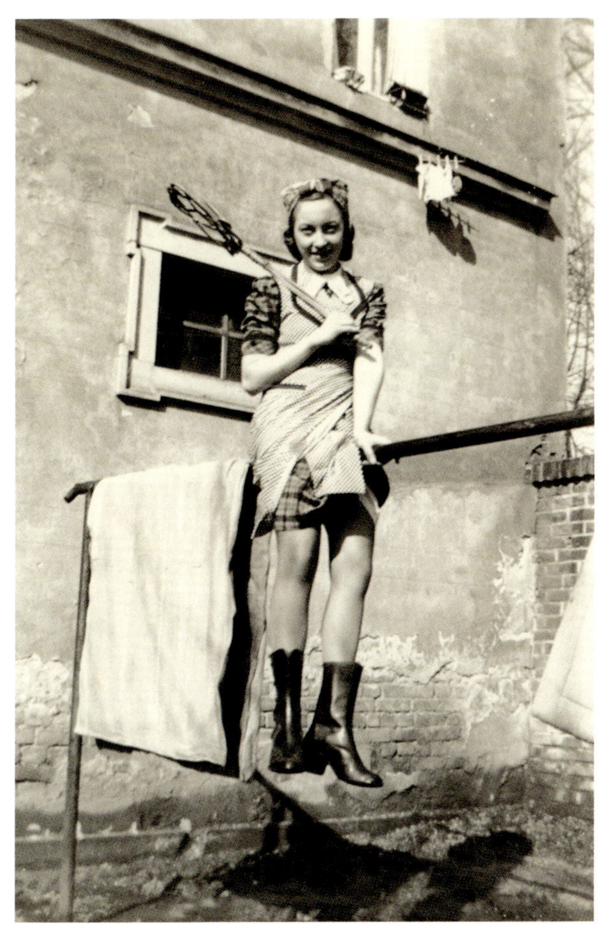

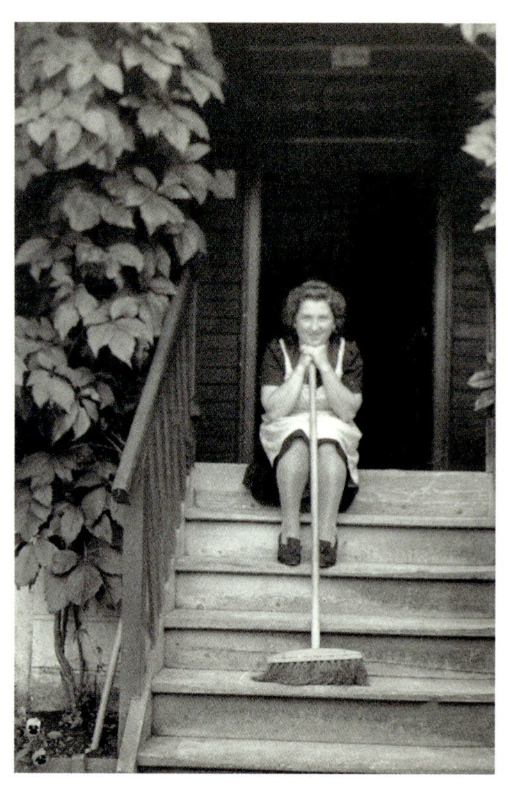

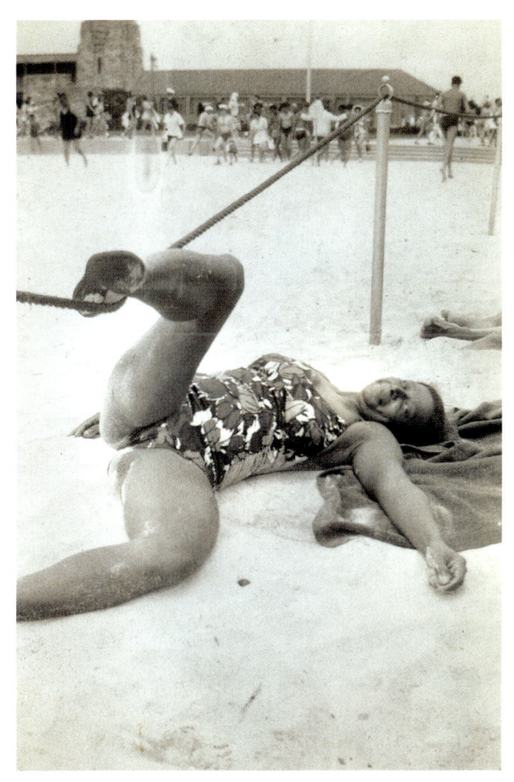

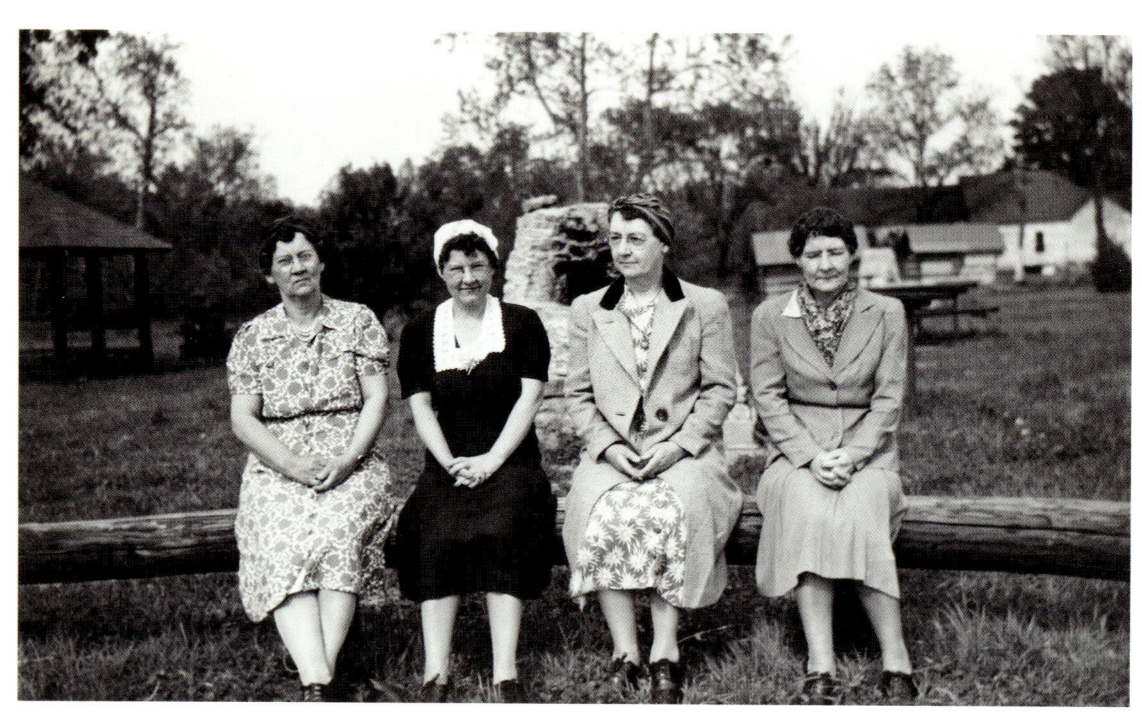

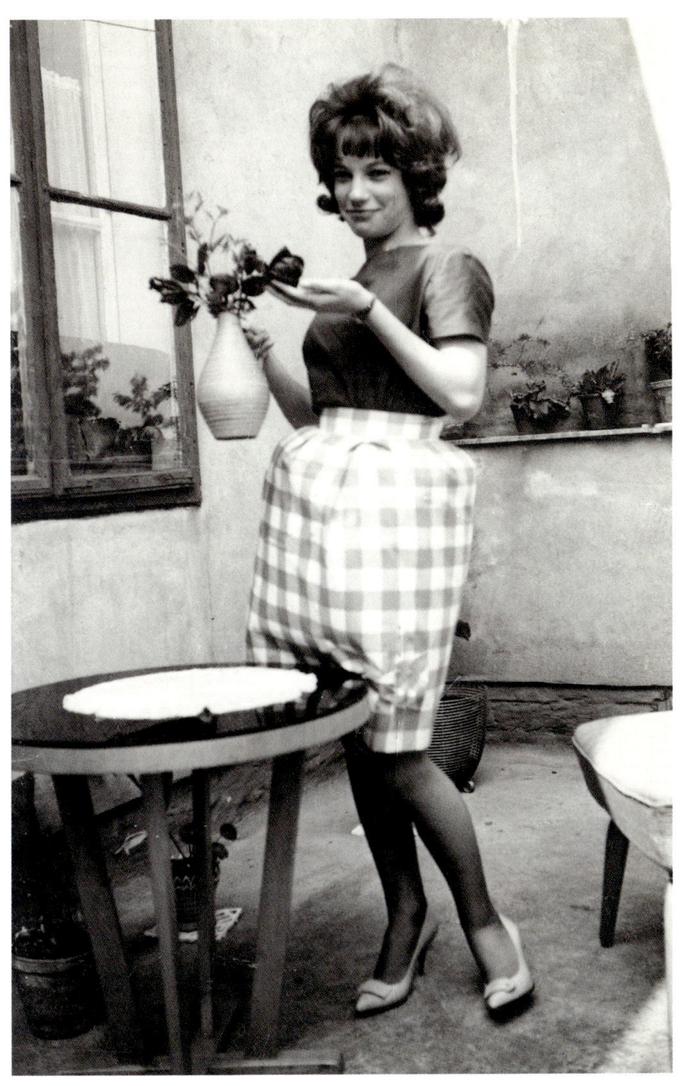

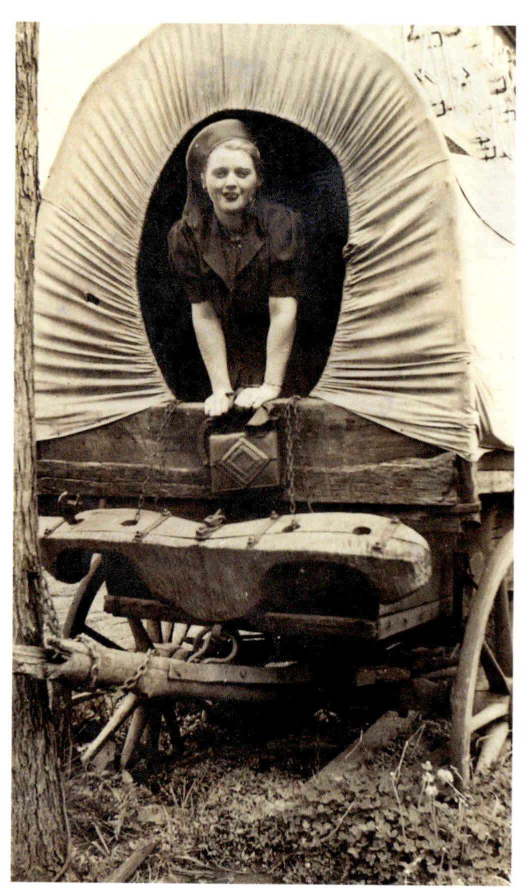

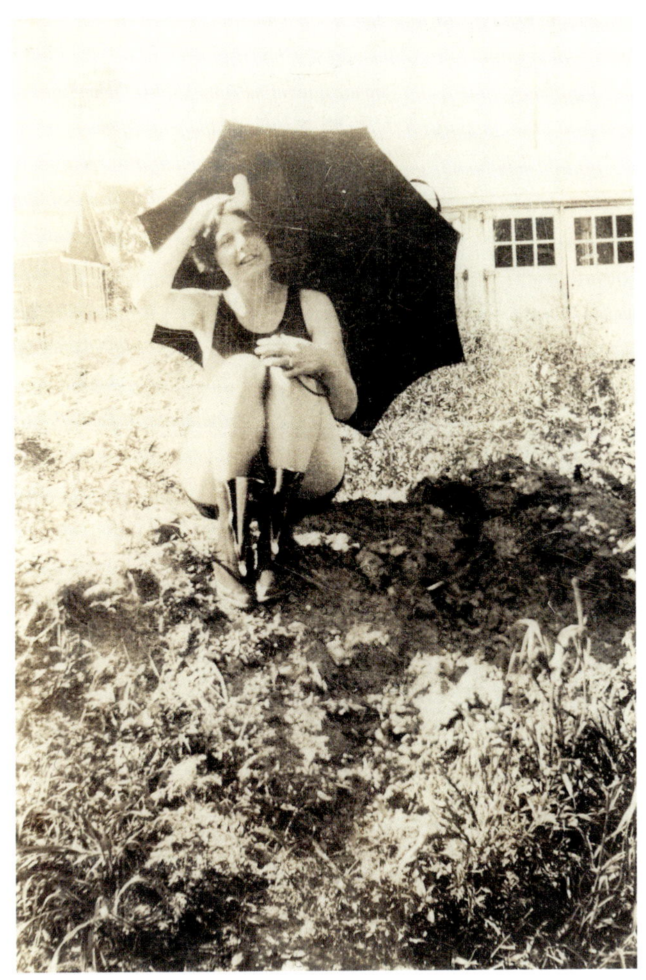

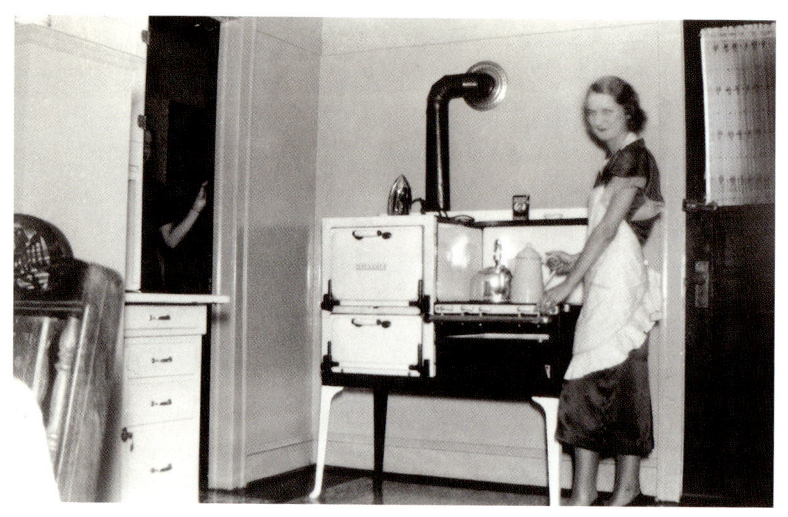

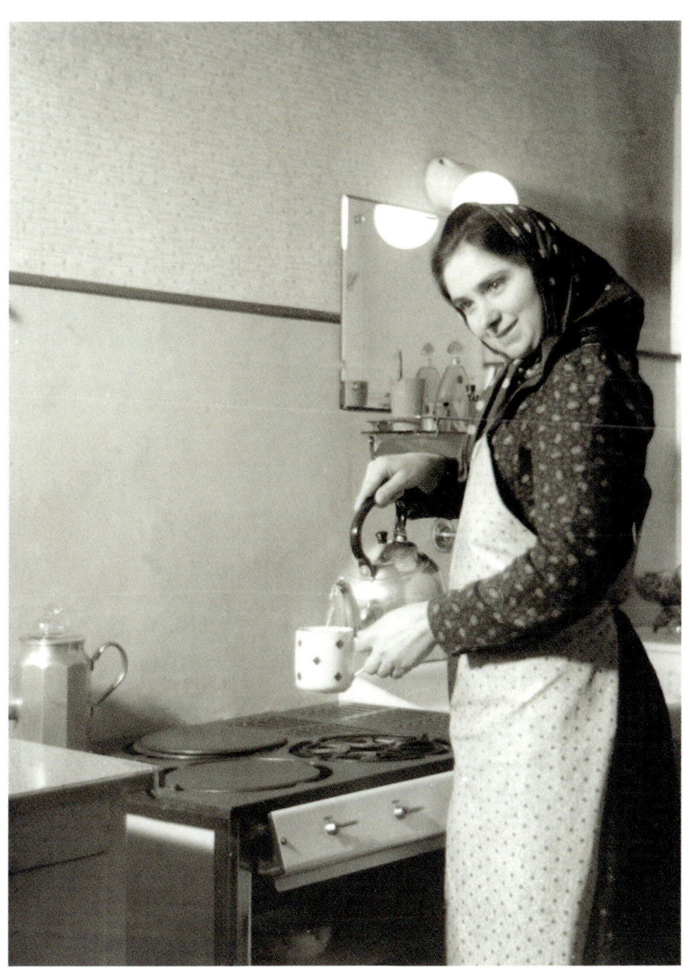

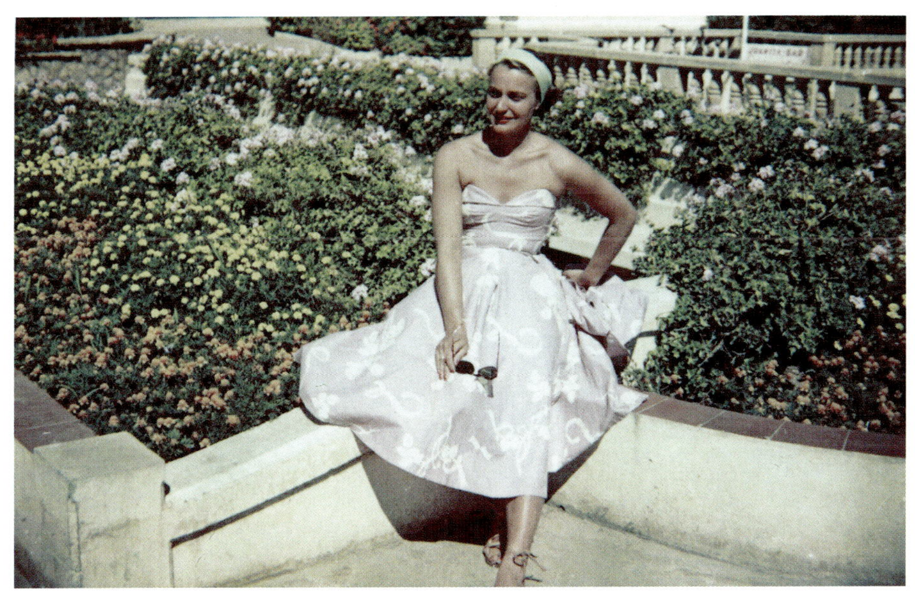

5)

Kids Kinder

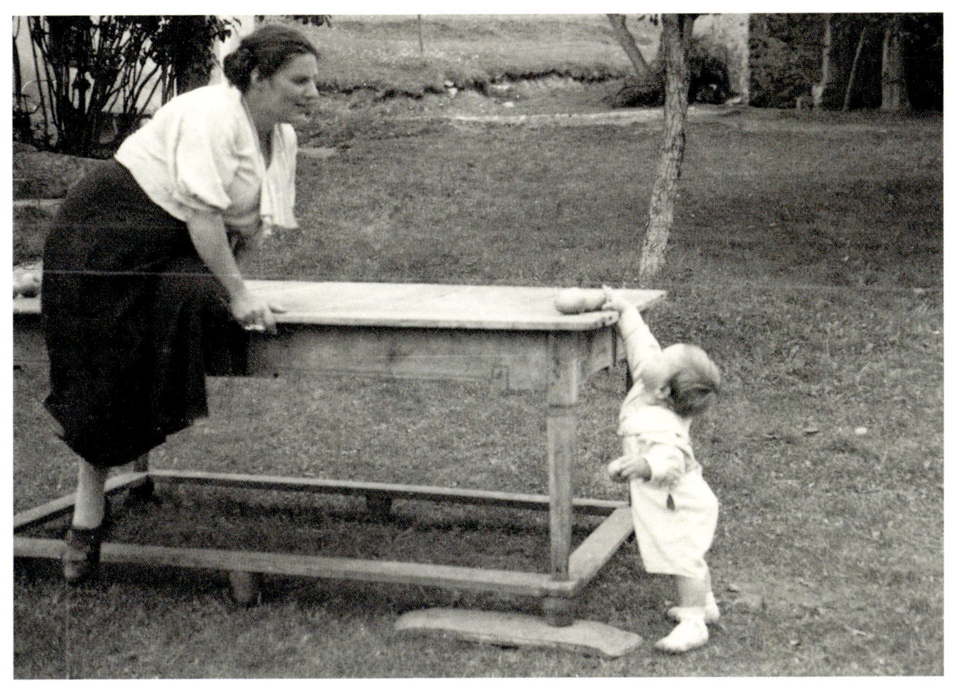

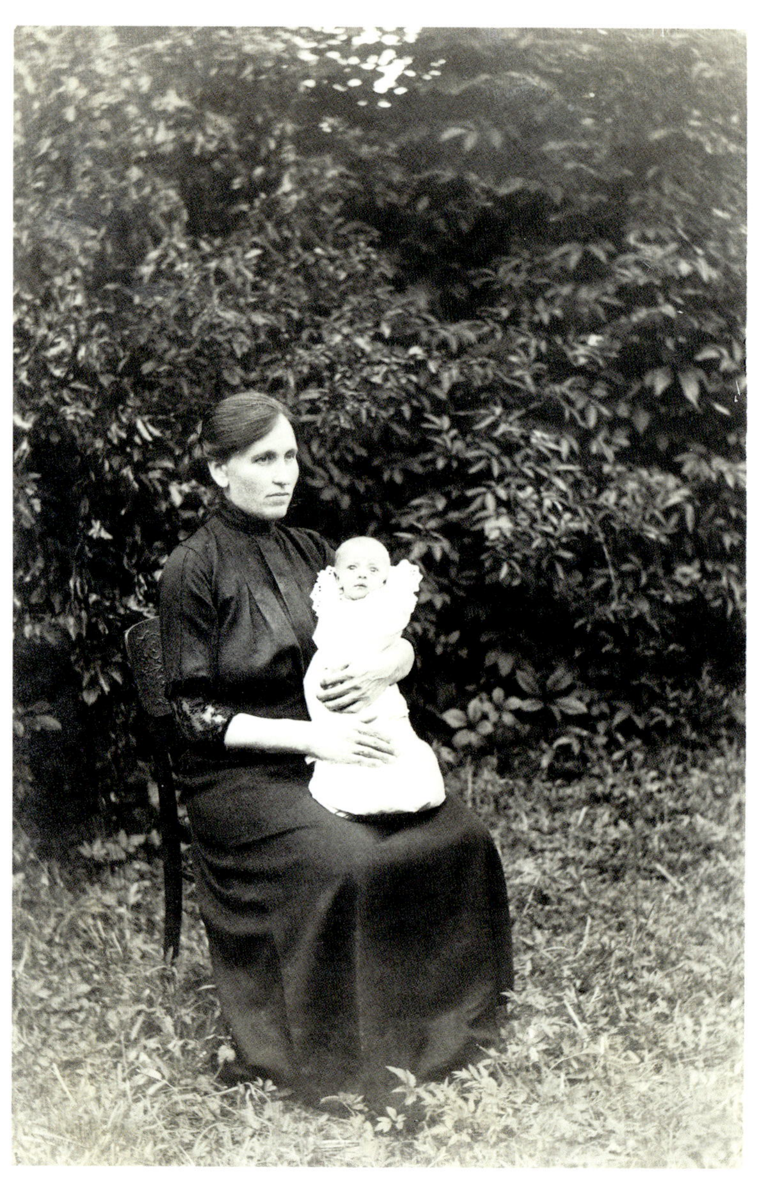

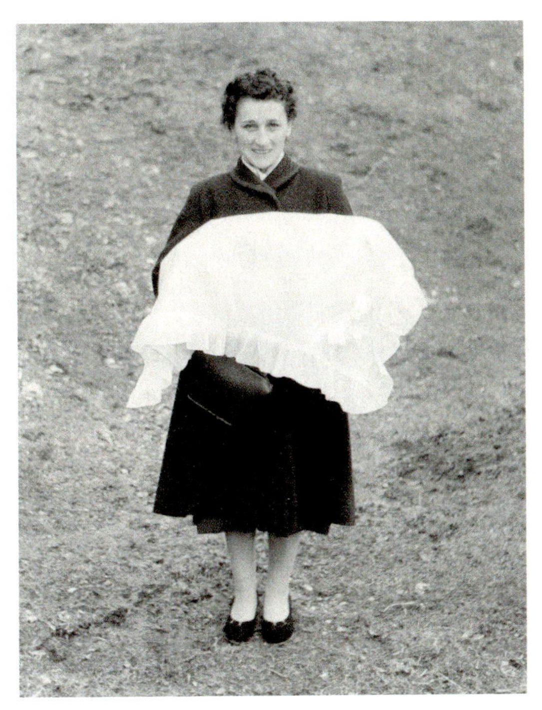

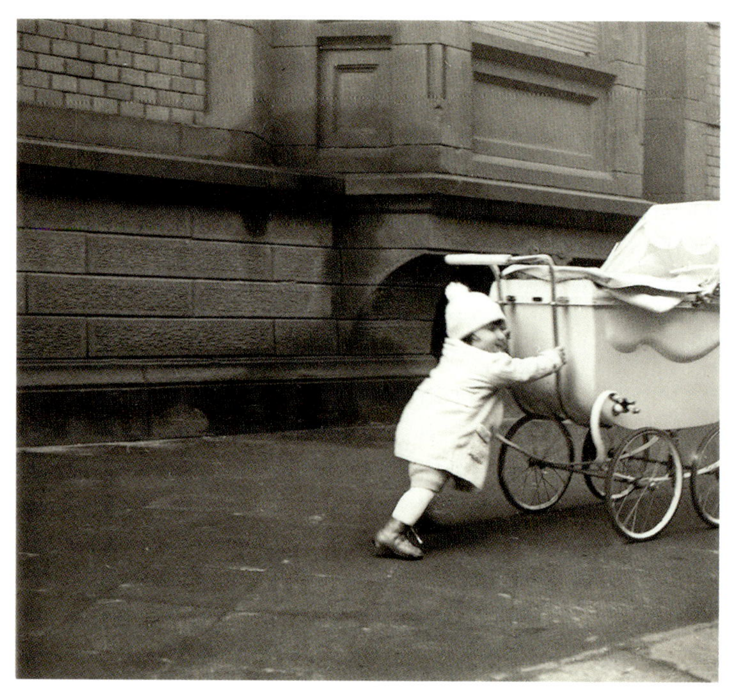

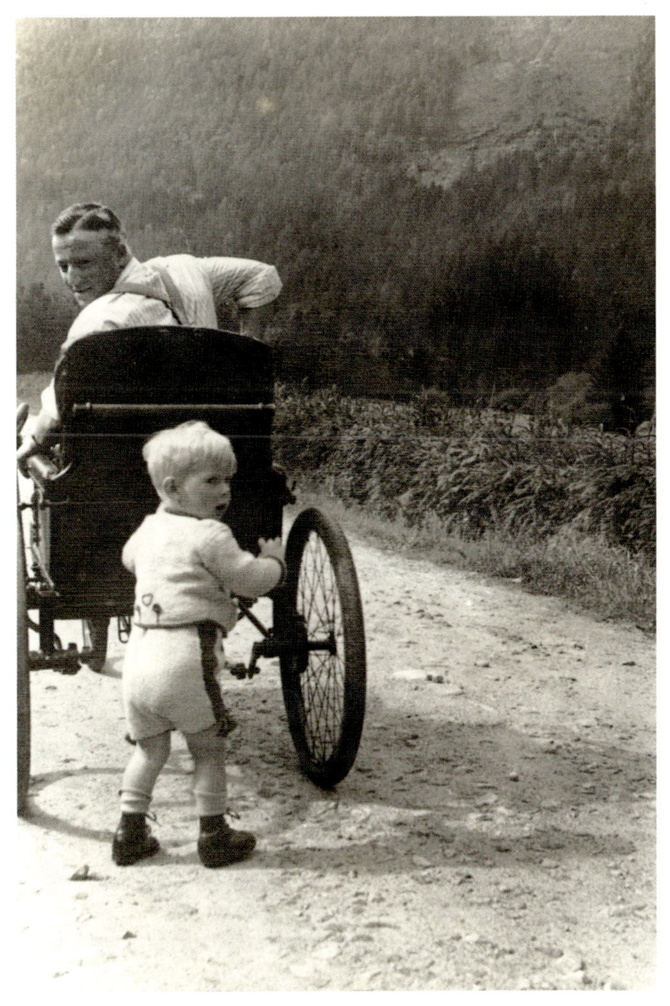

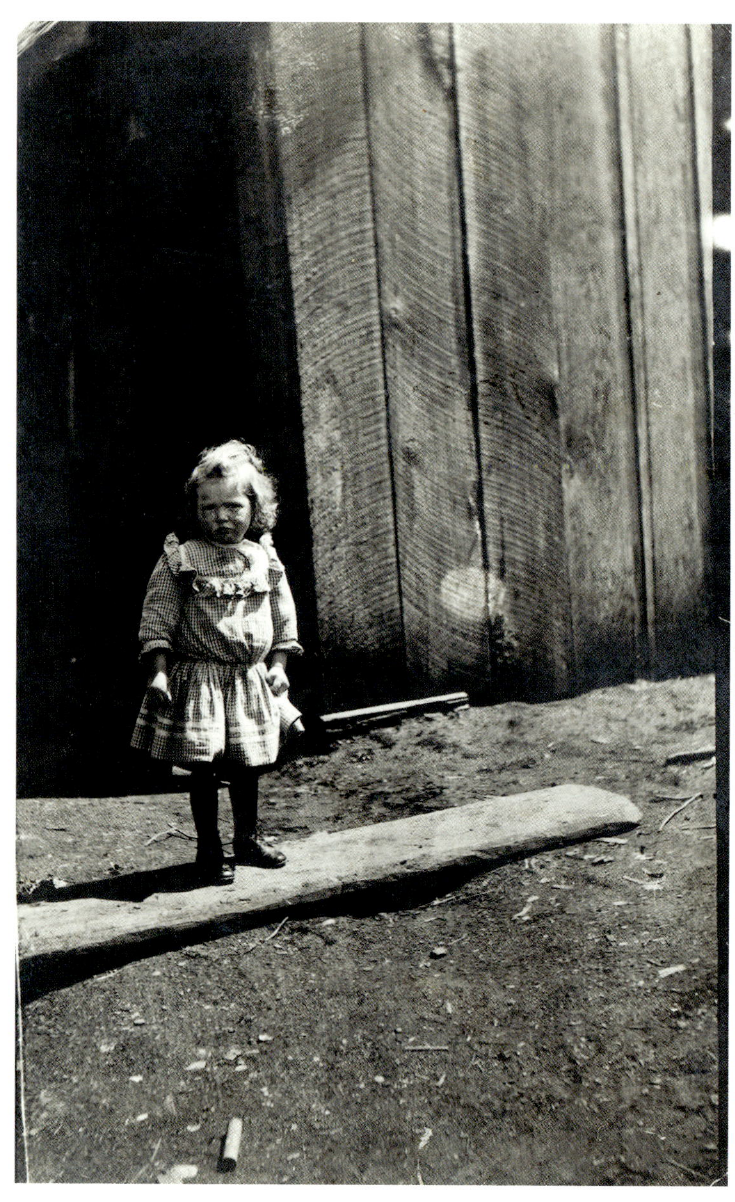

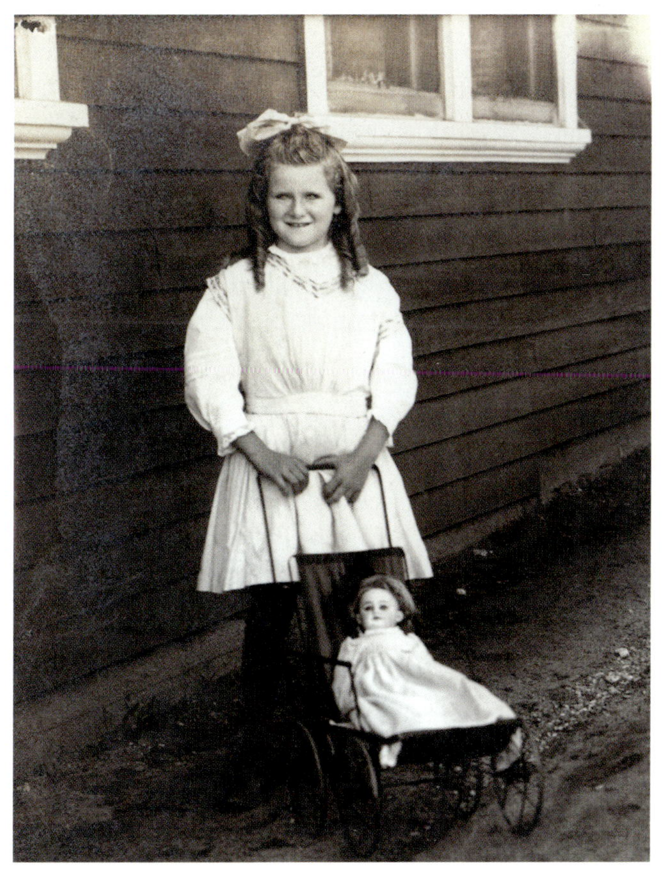

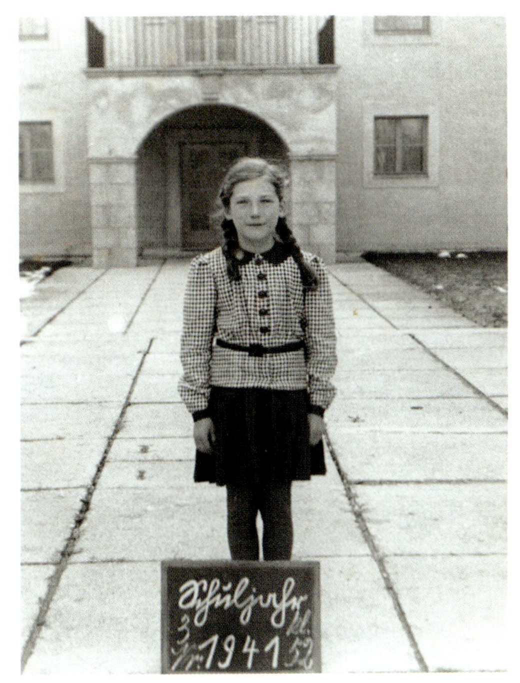
1941

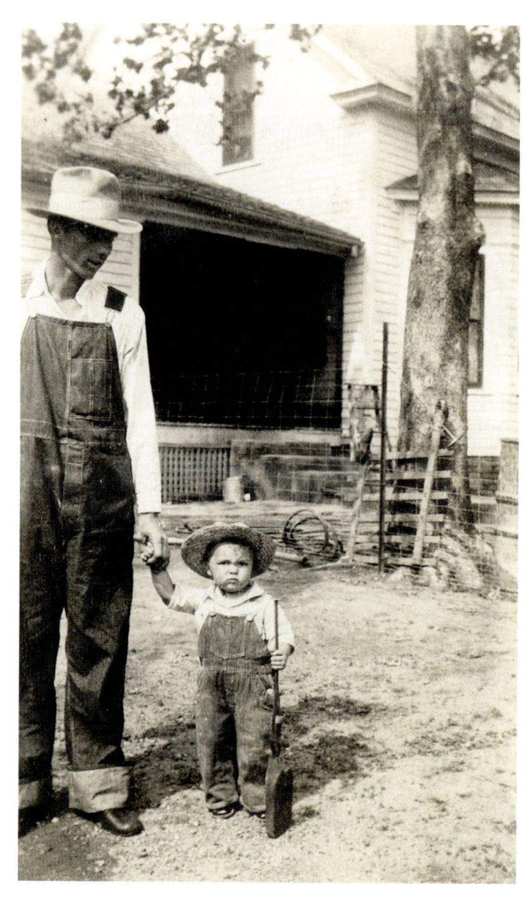

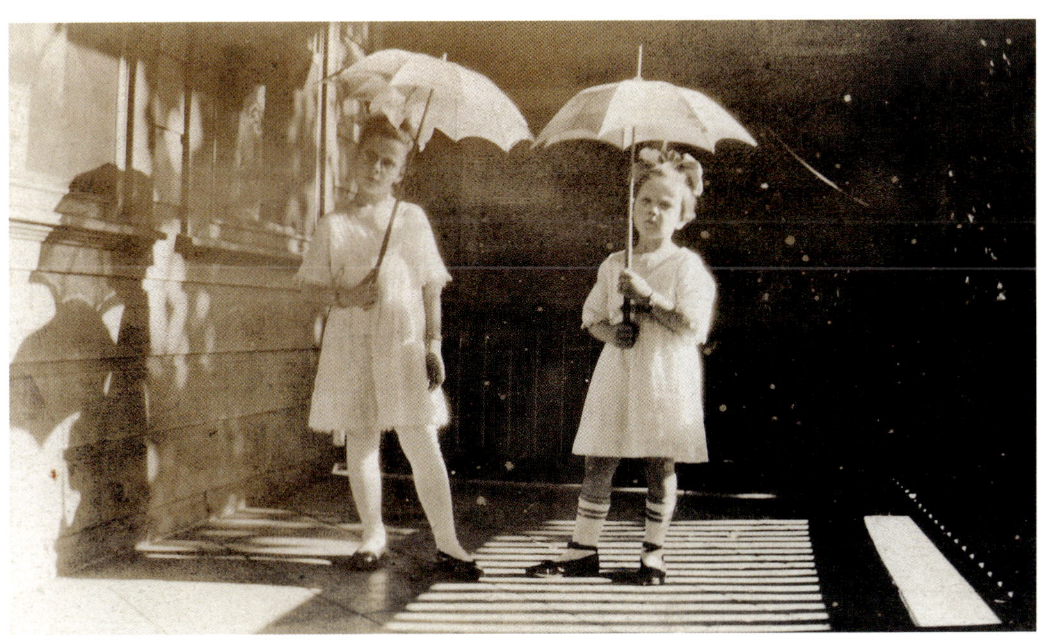

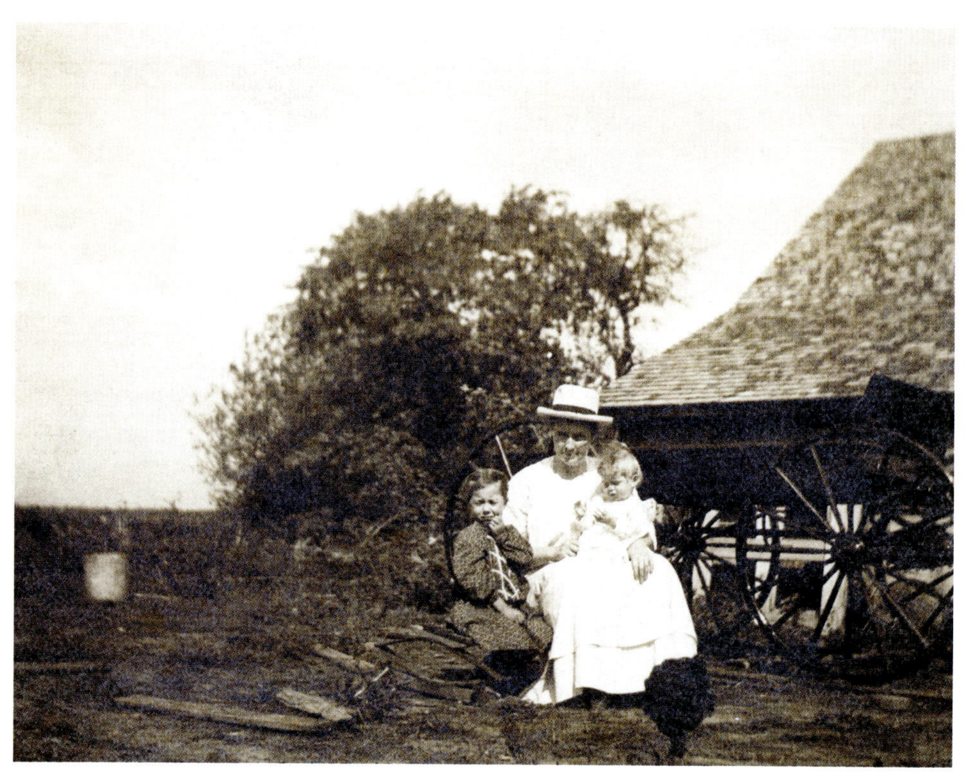

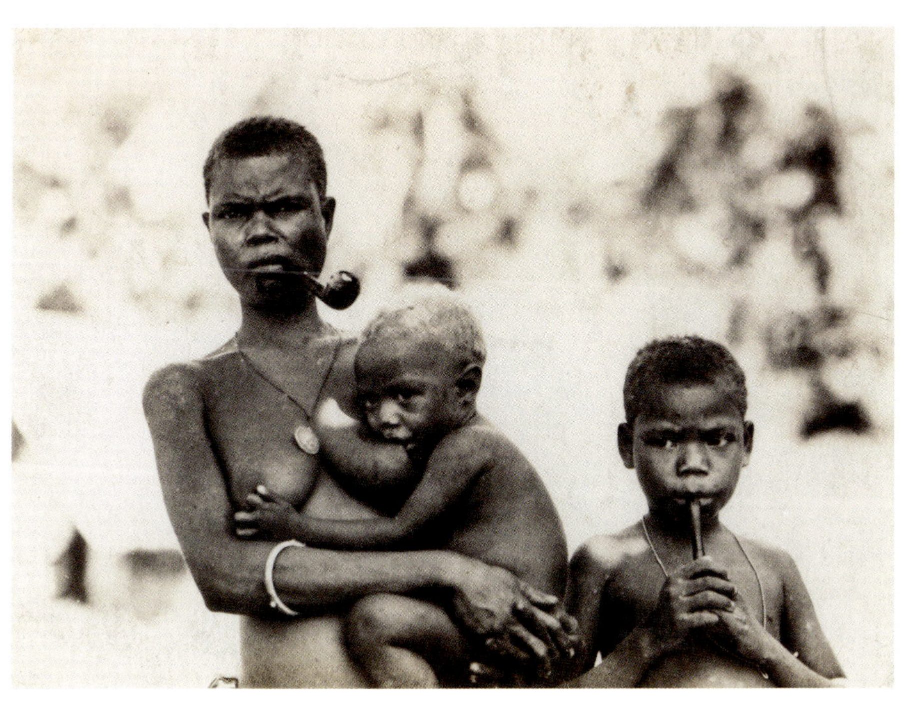

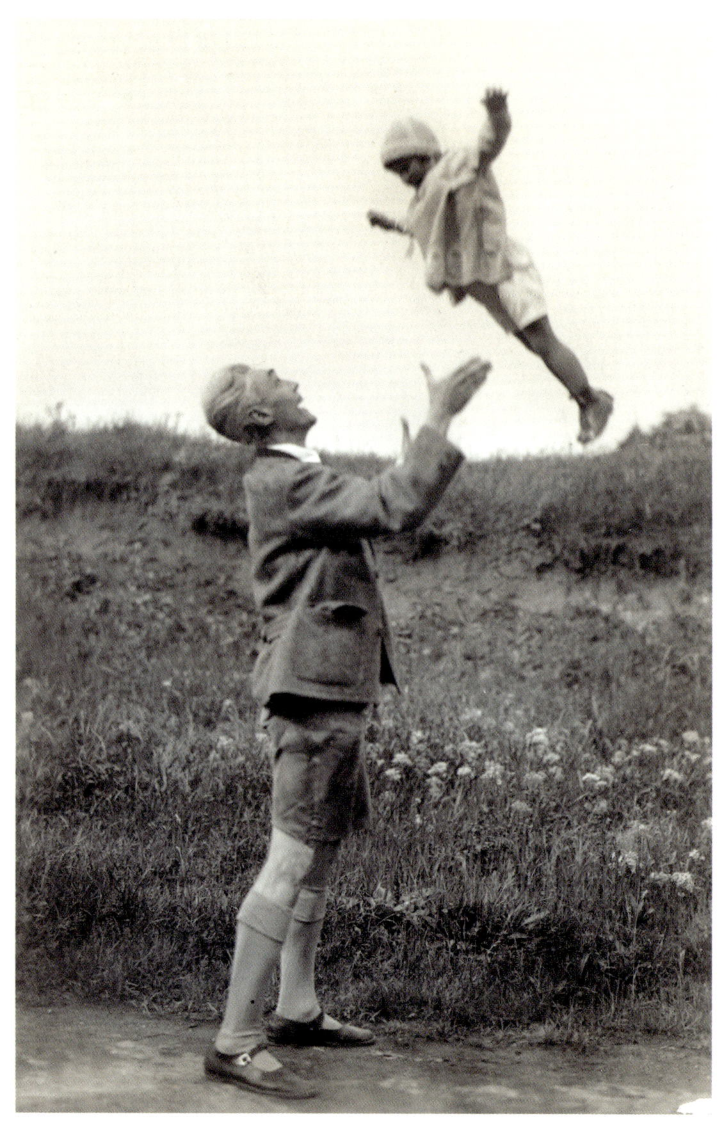

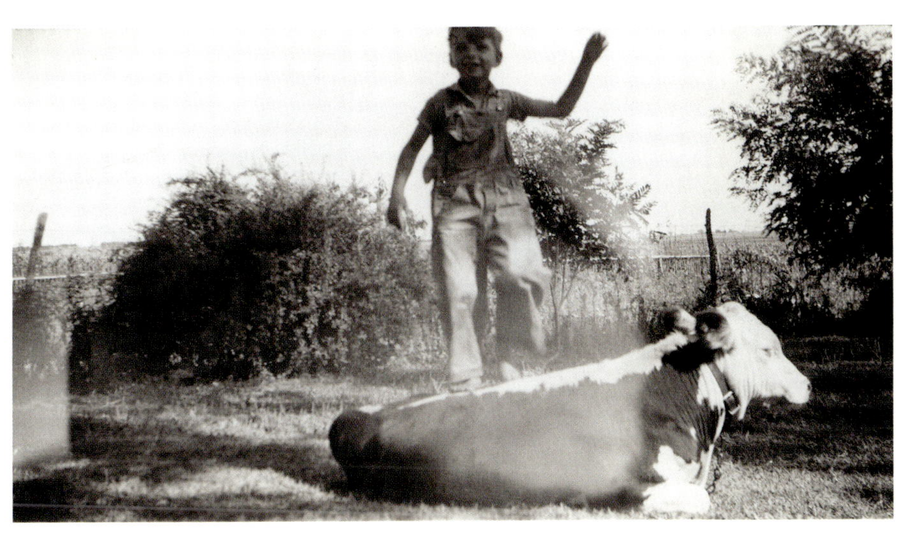

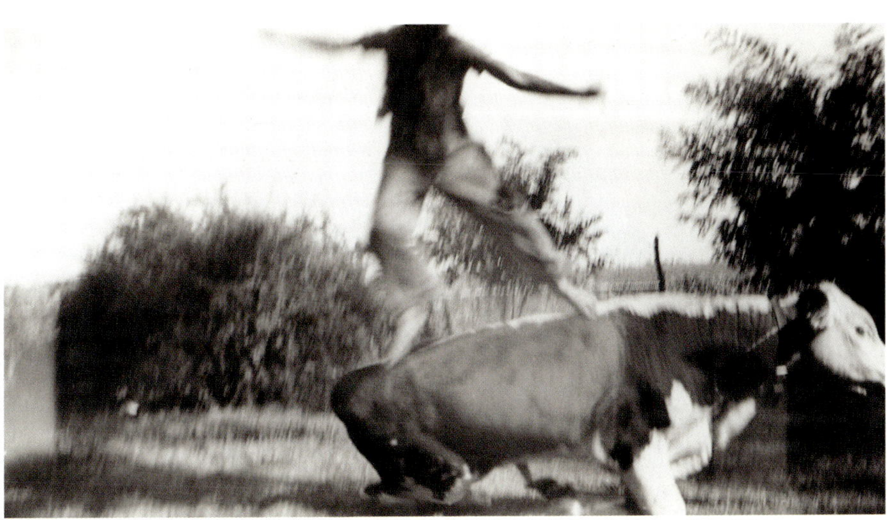

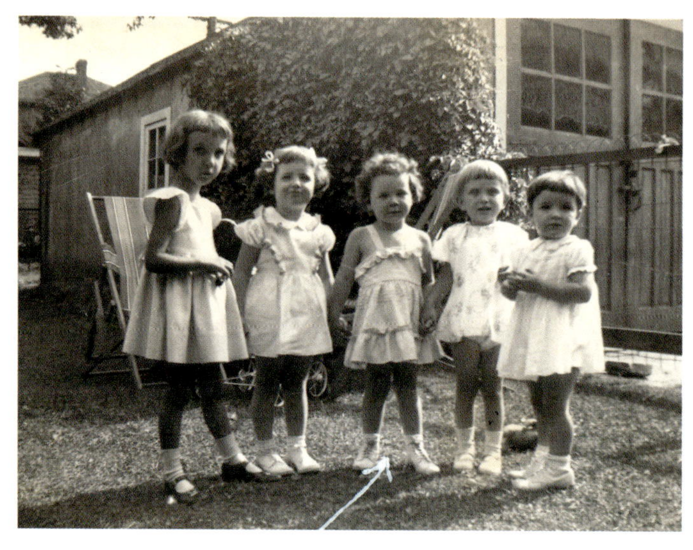

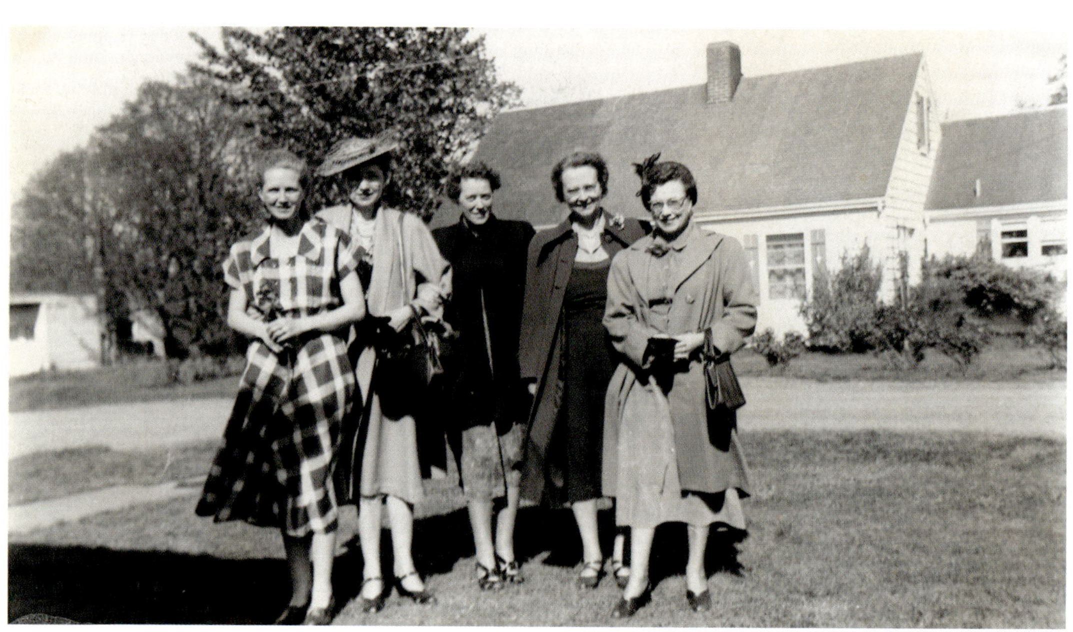

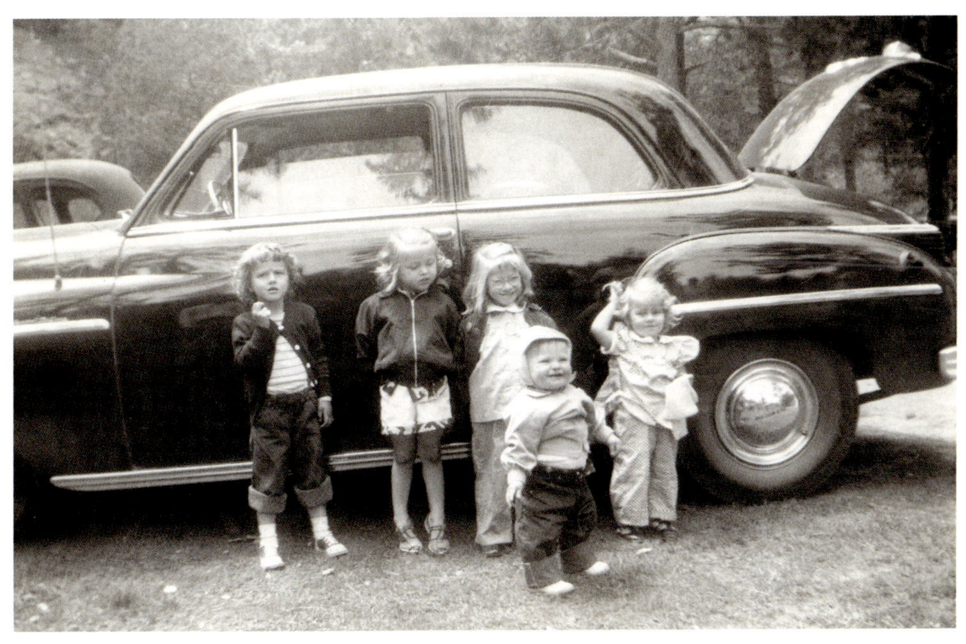

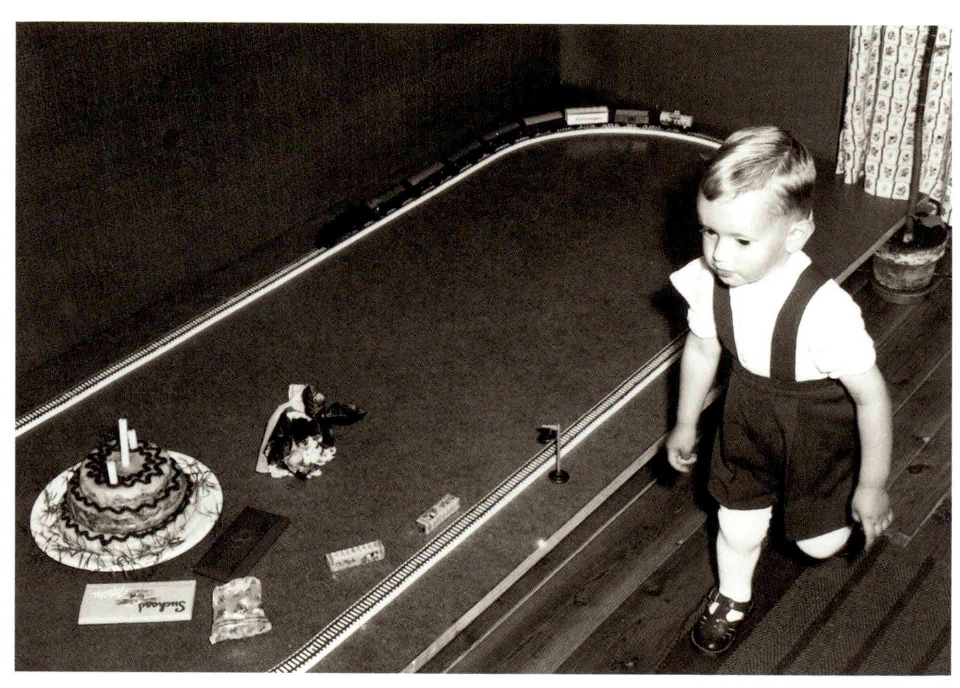

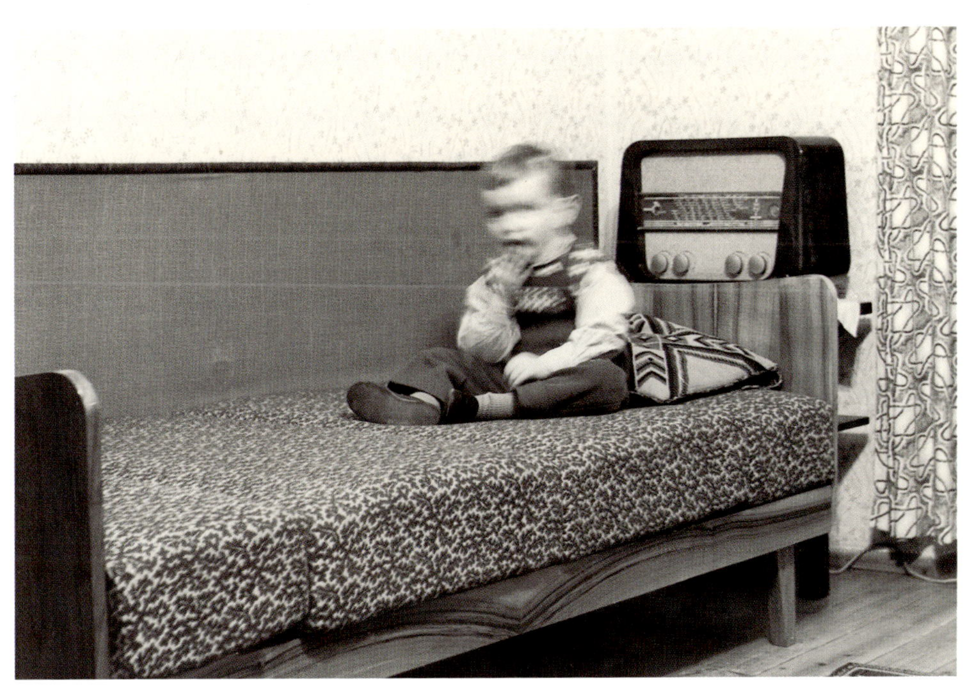

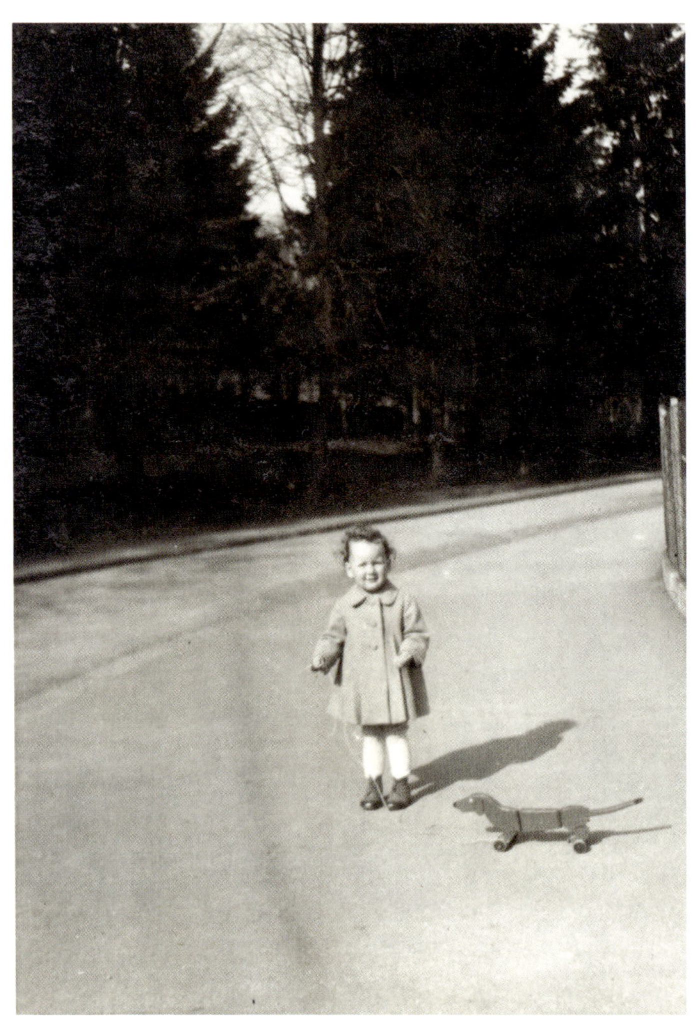

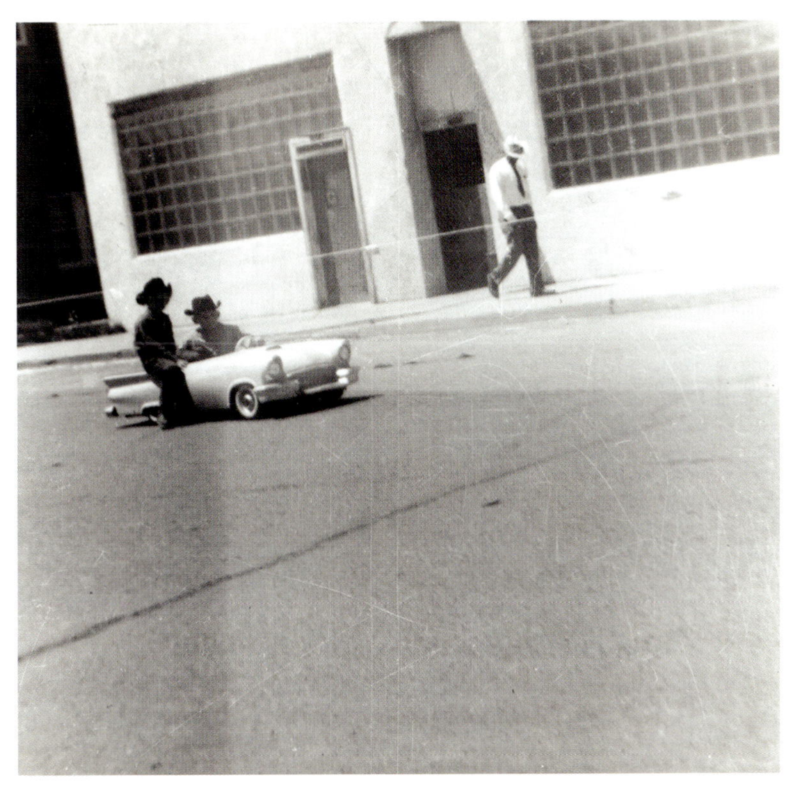

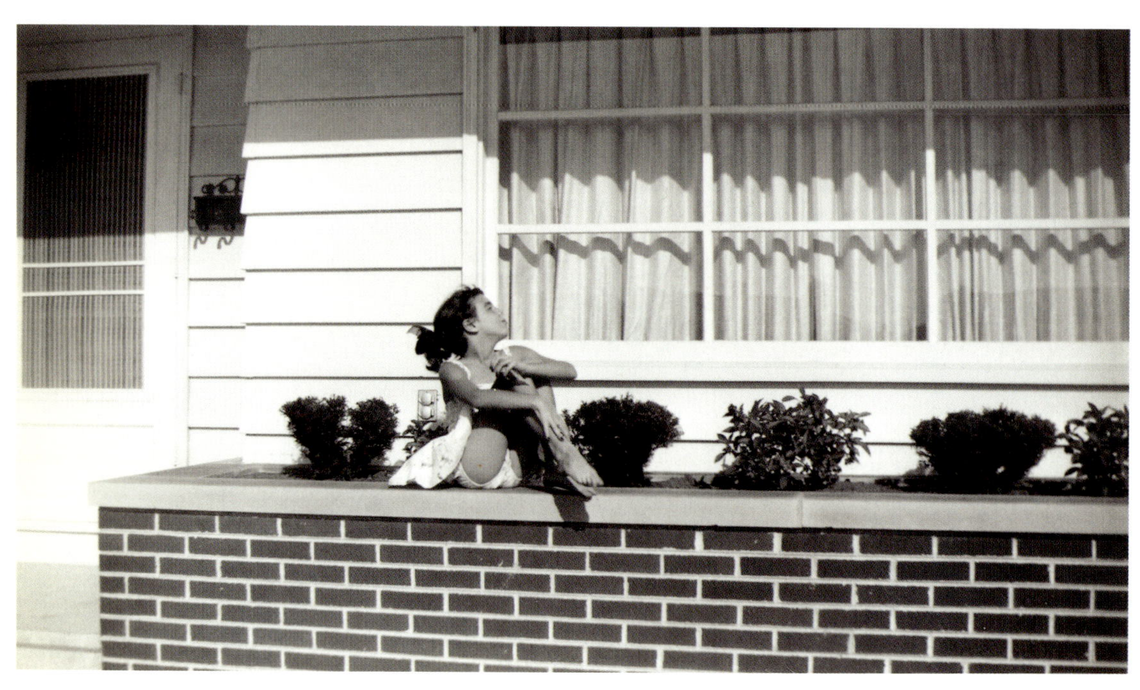

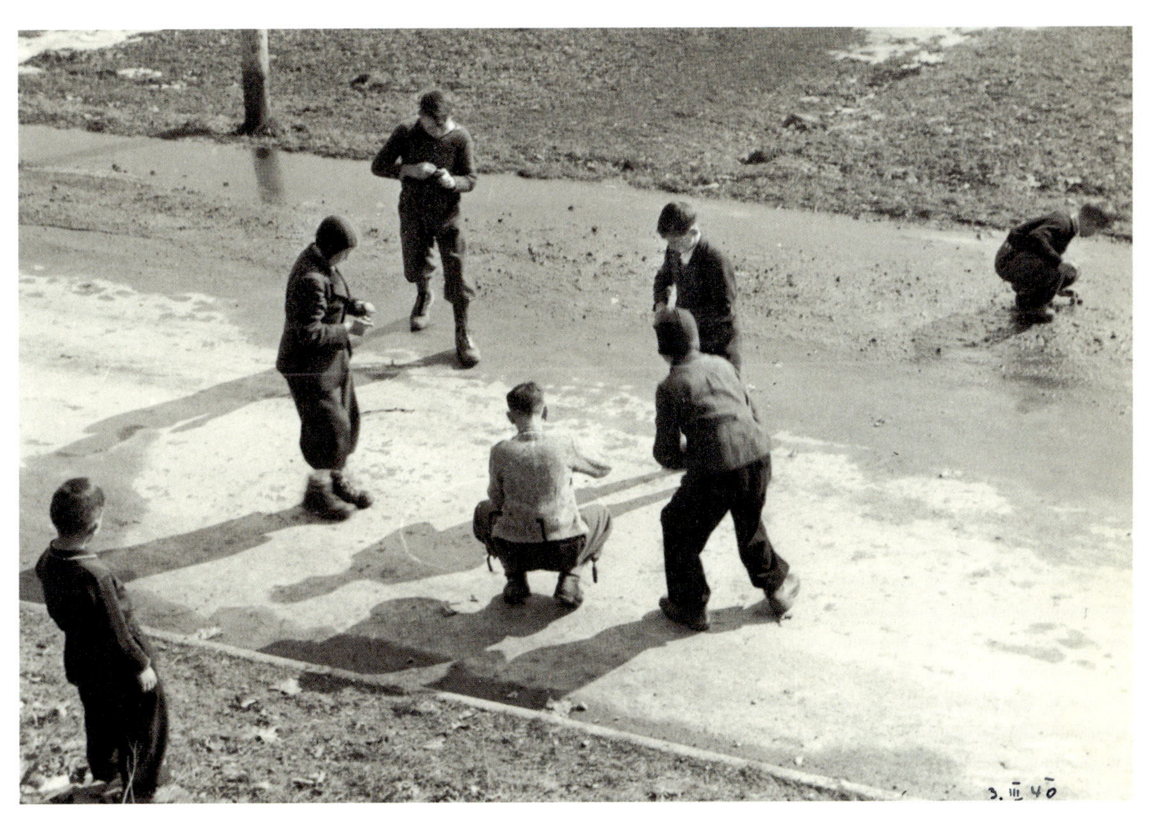
3. III 40

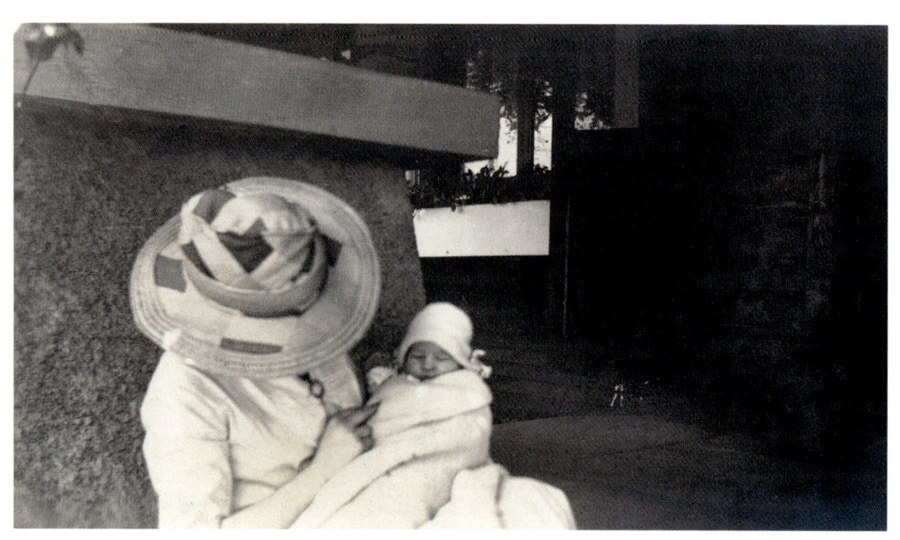

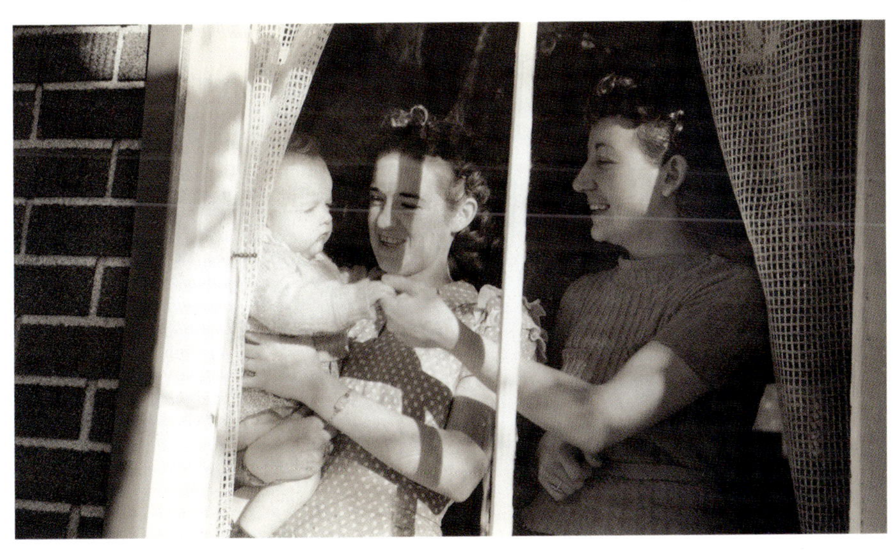

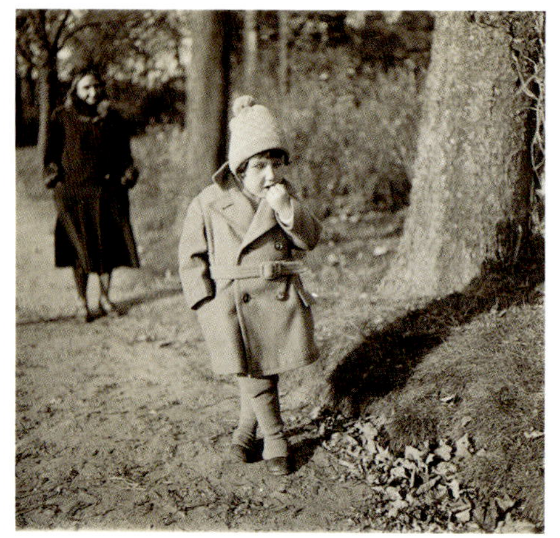
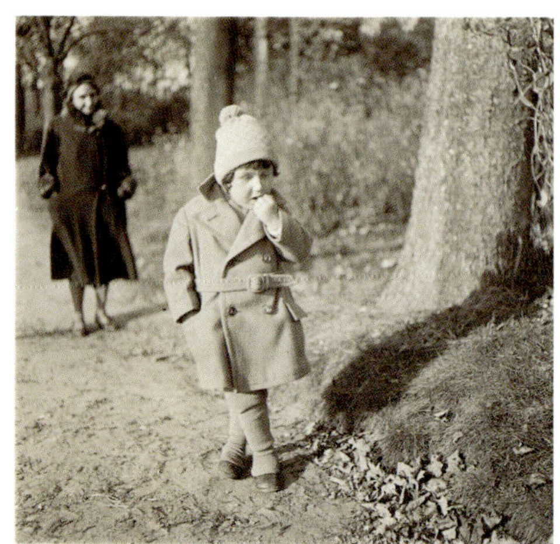
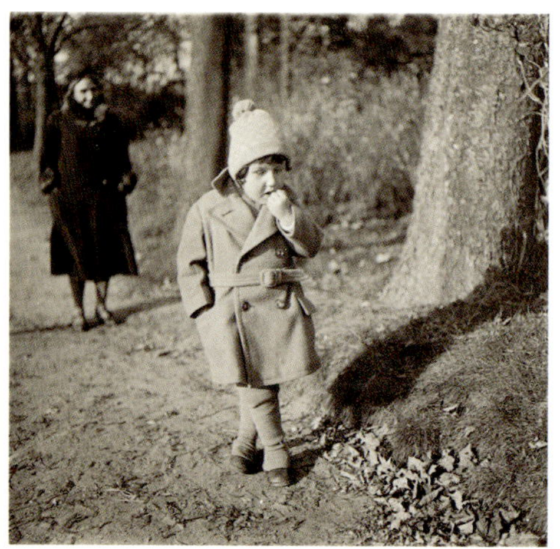
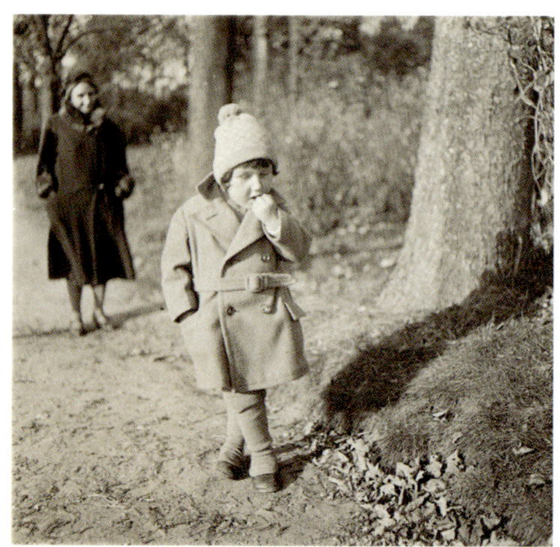

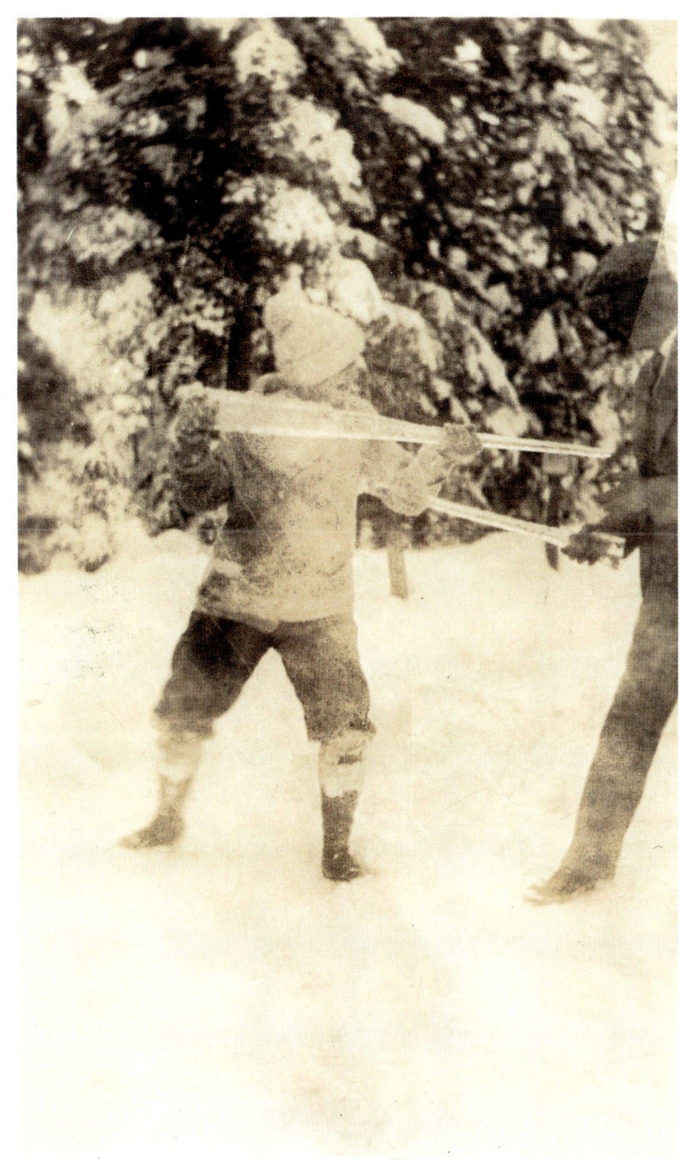

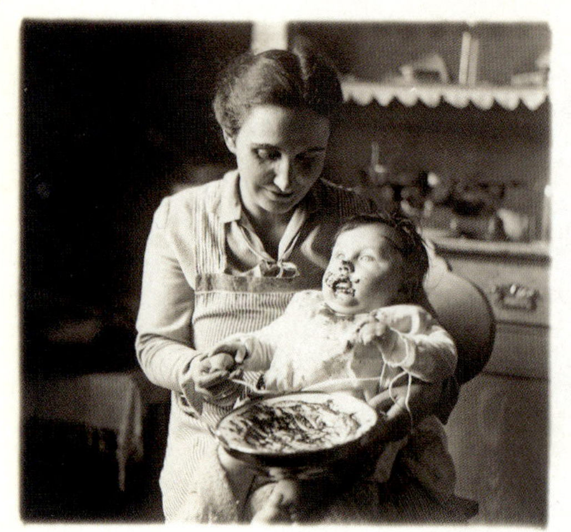
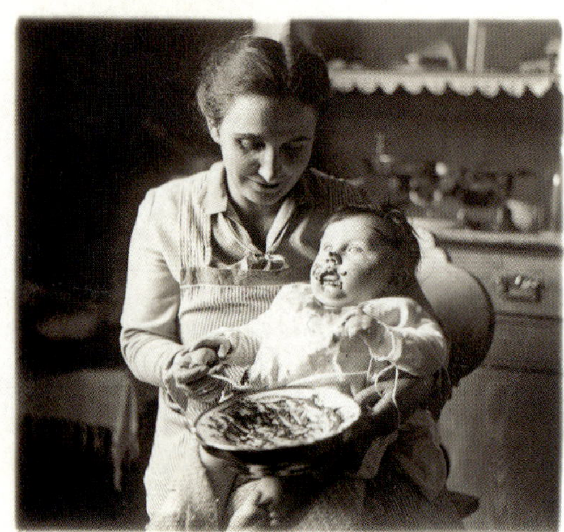

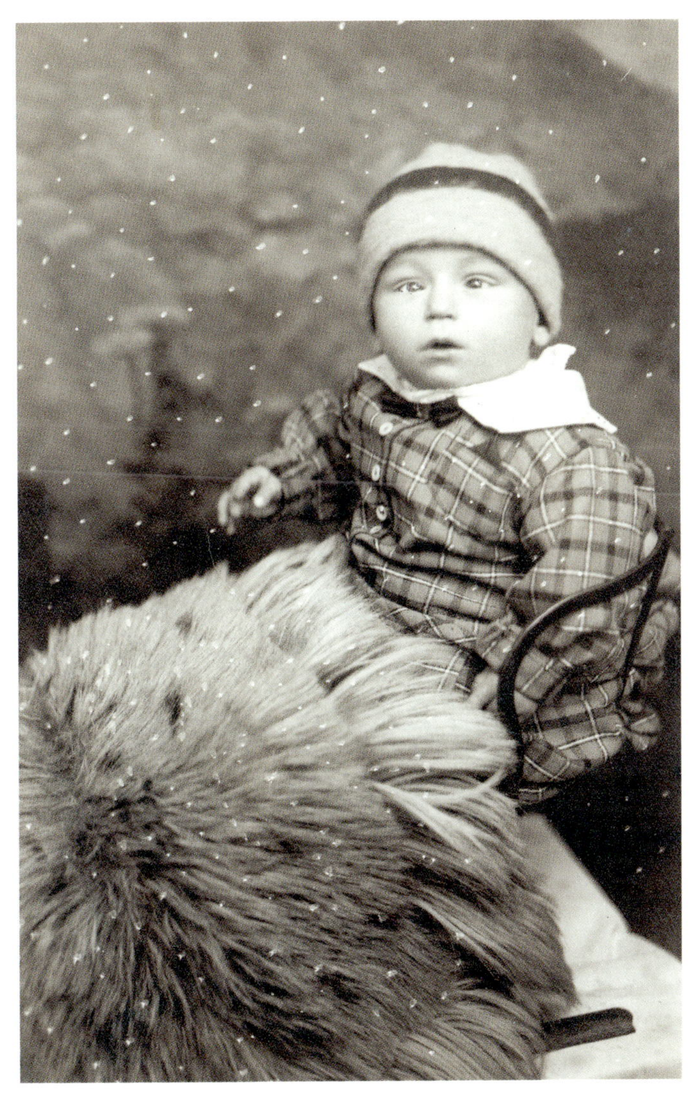

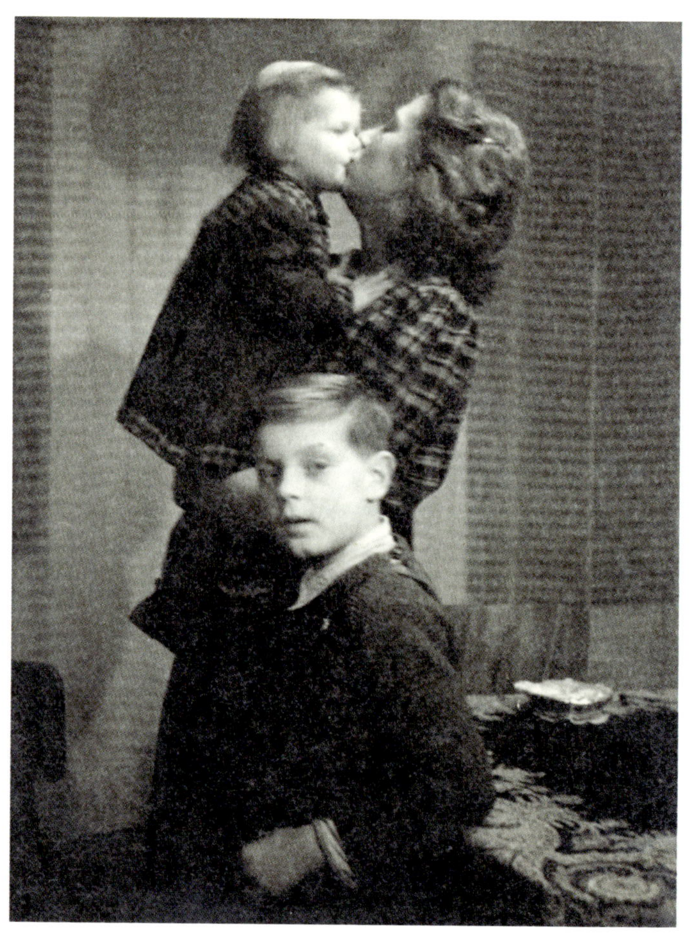

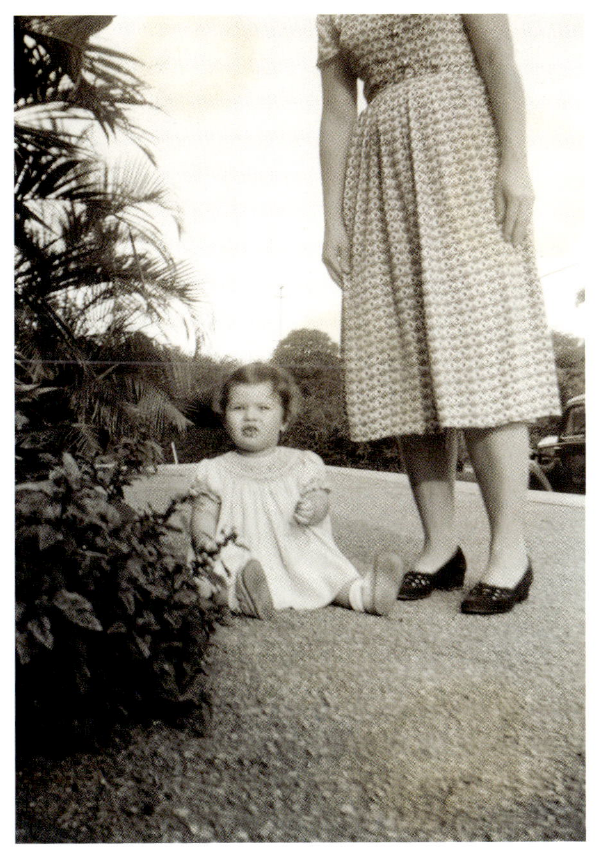

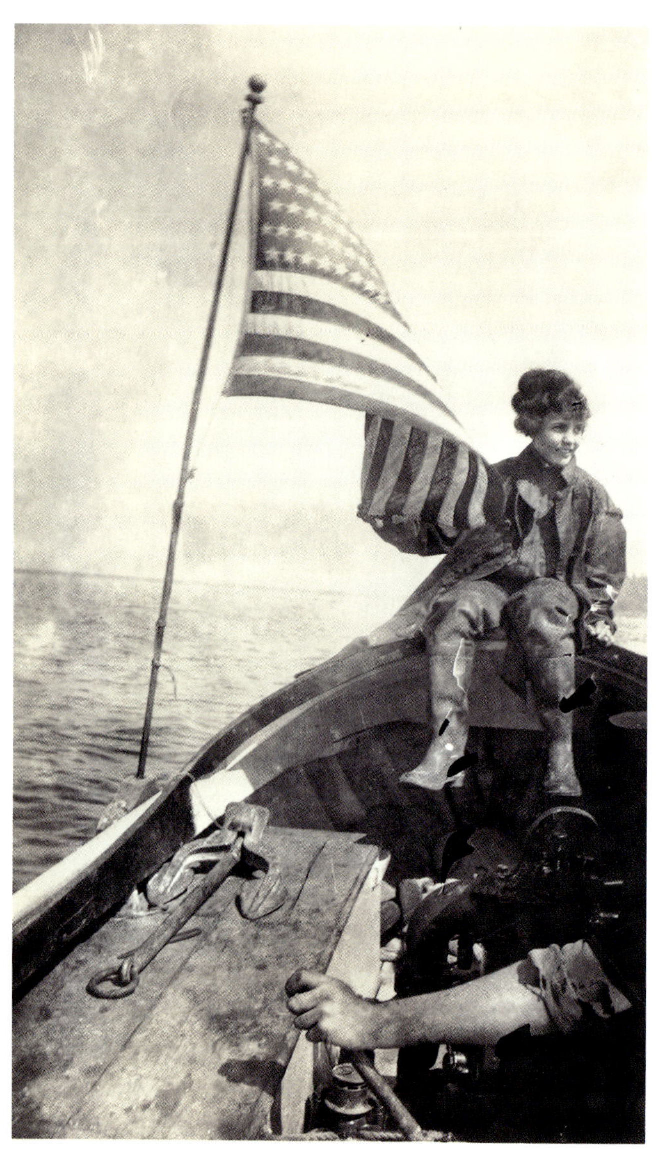

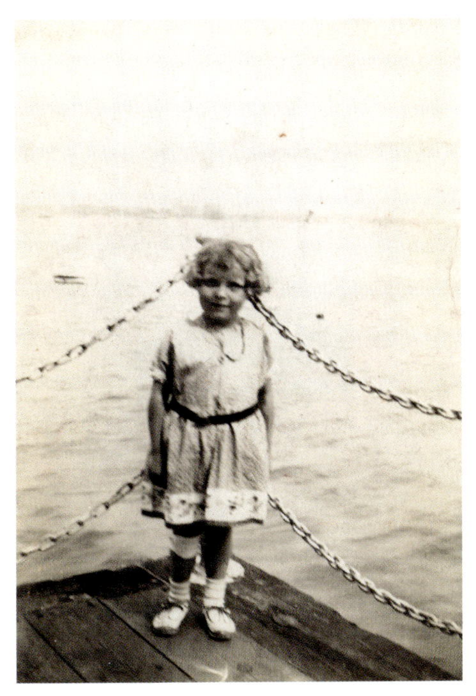

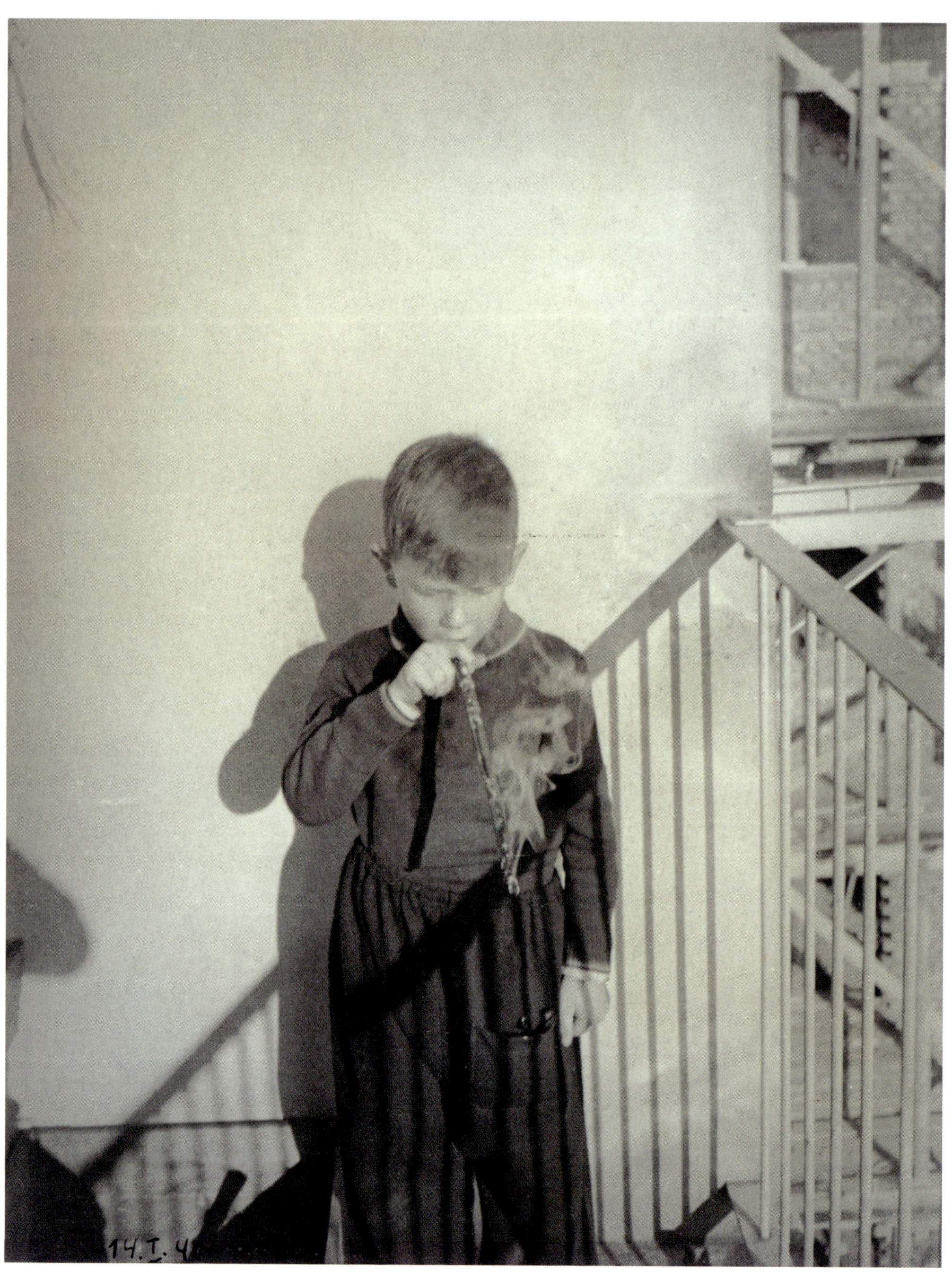
14.I.4

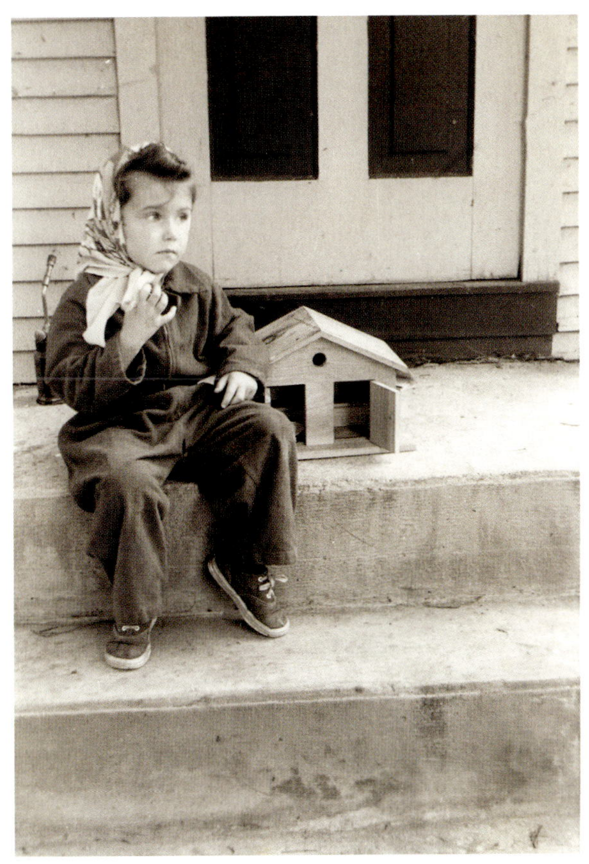

6)

Together Beisammen

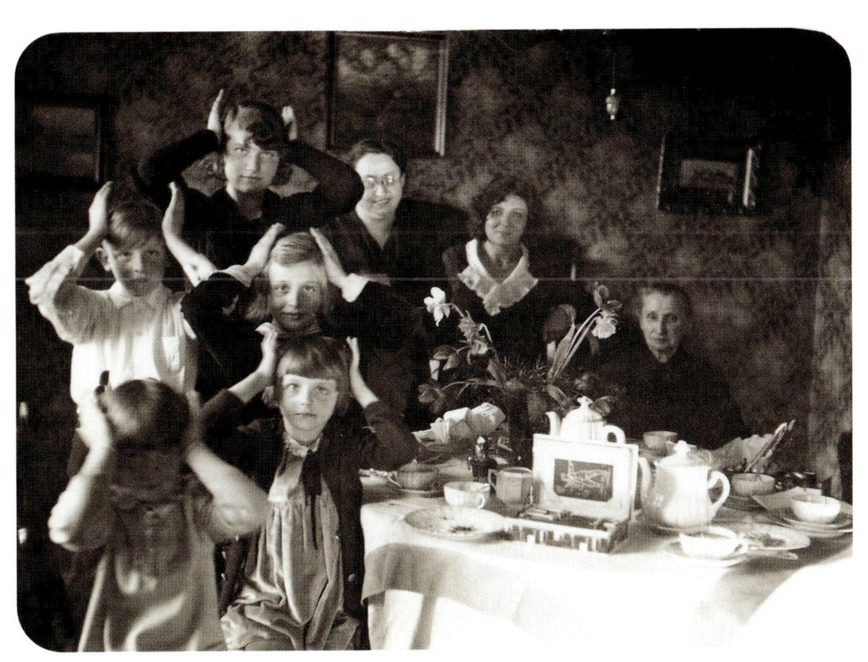

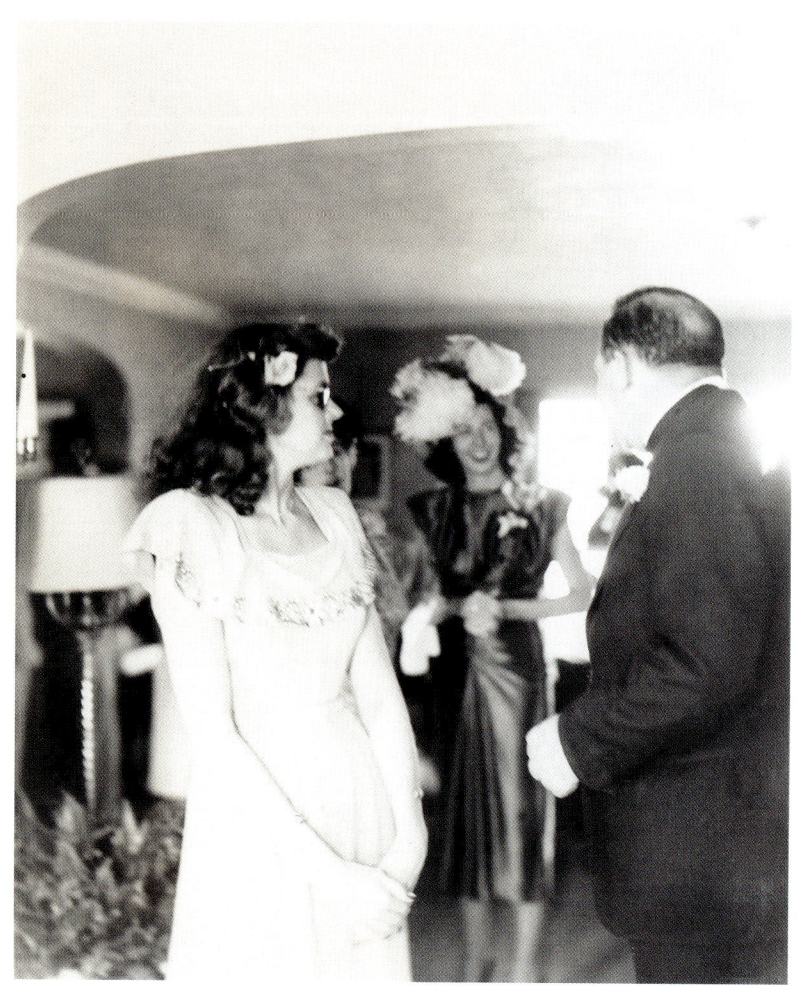

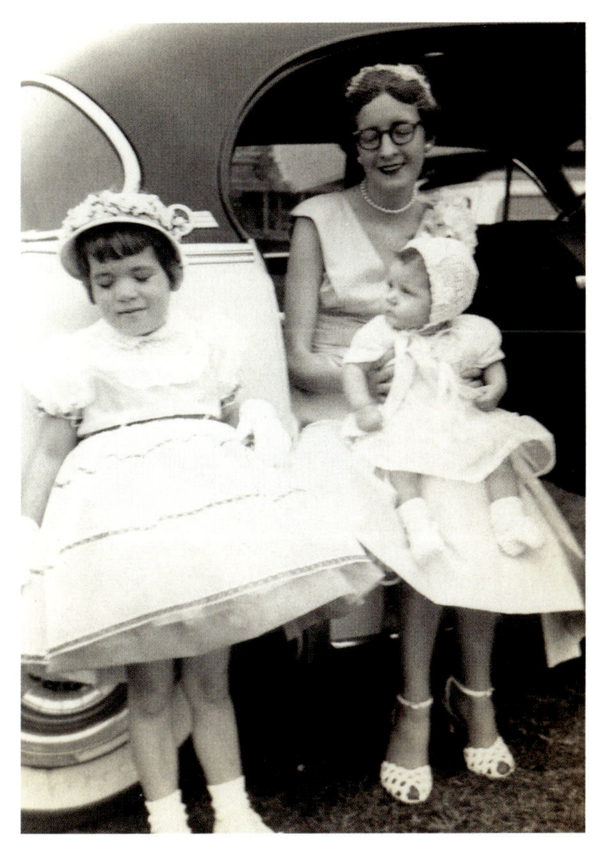

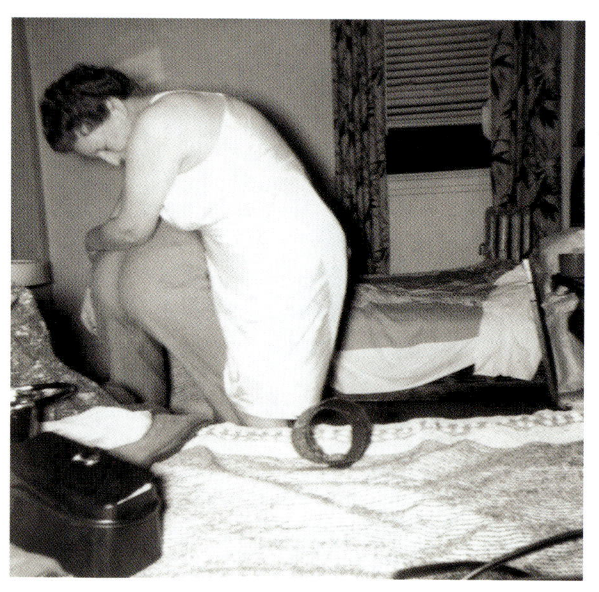

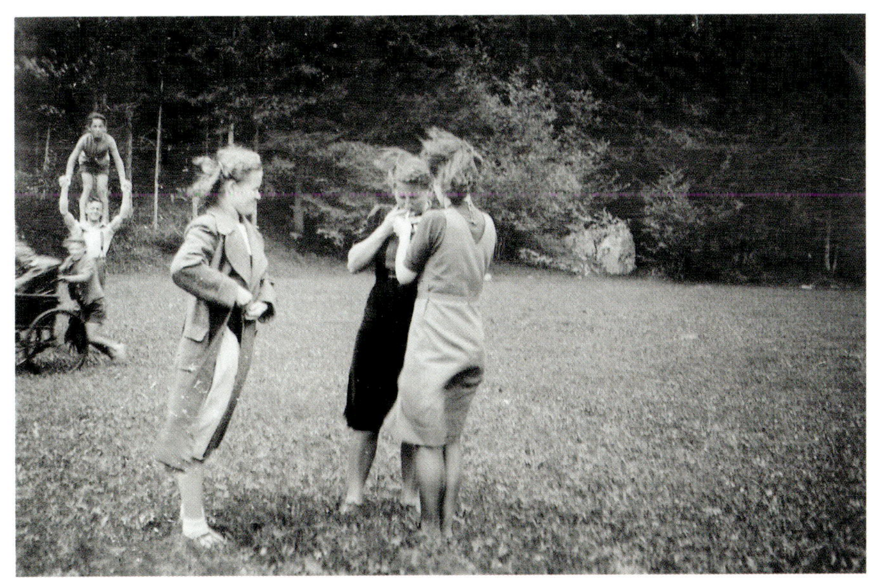

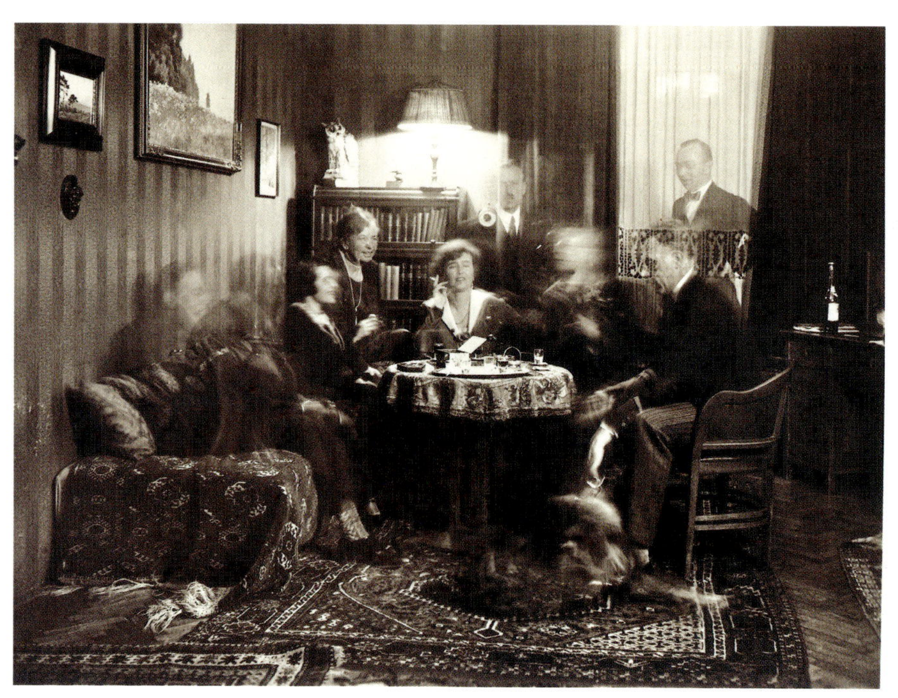

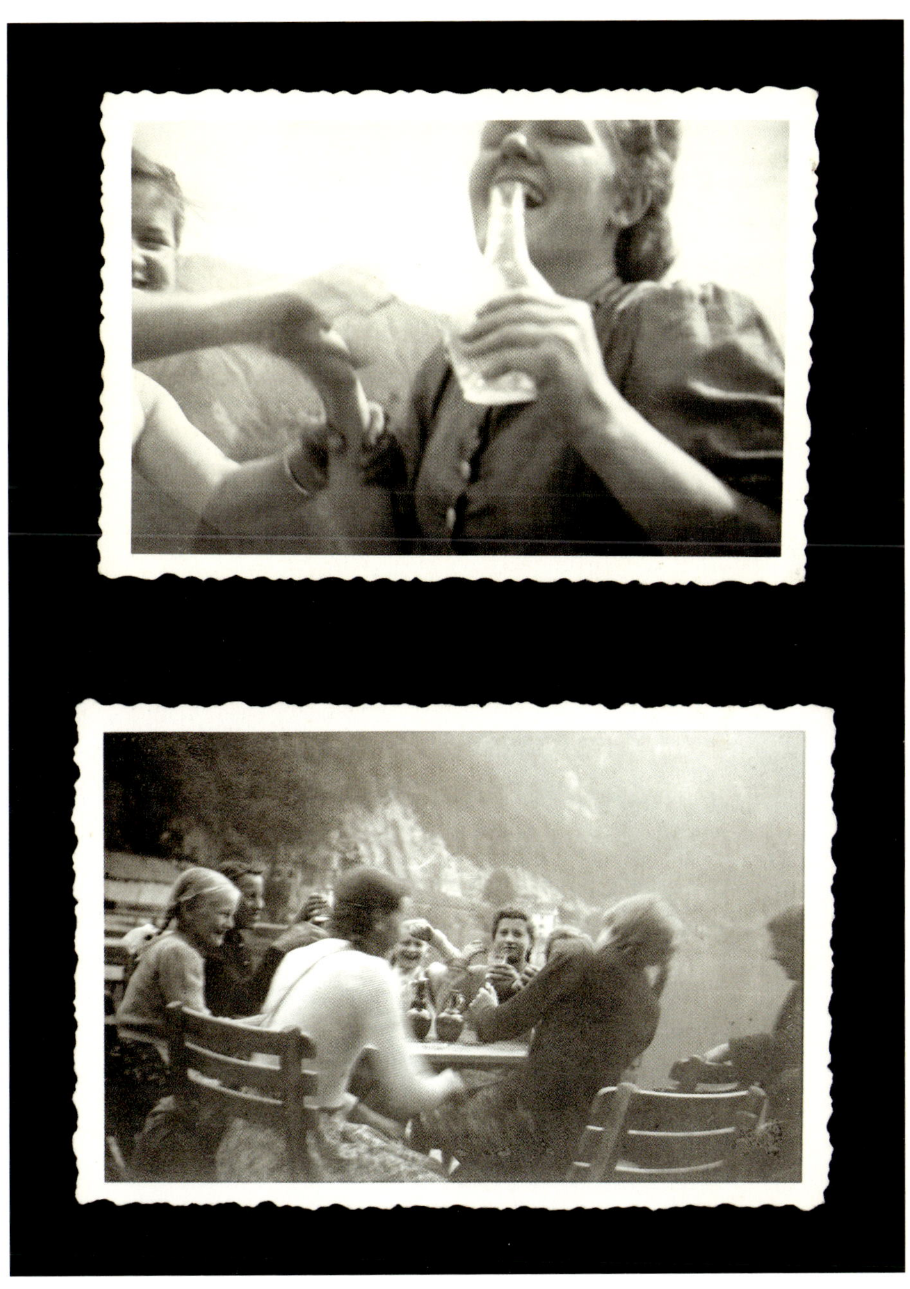

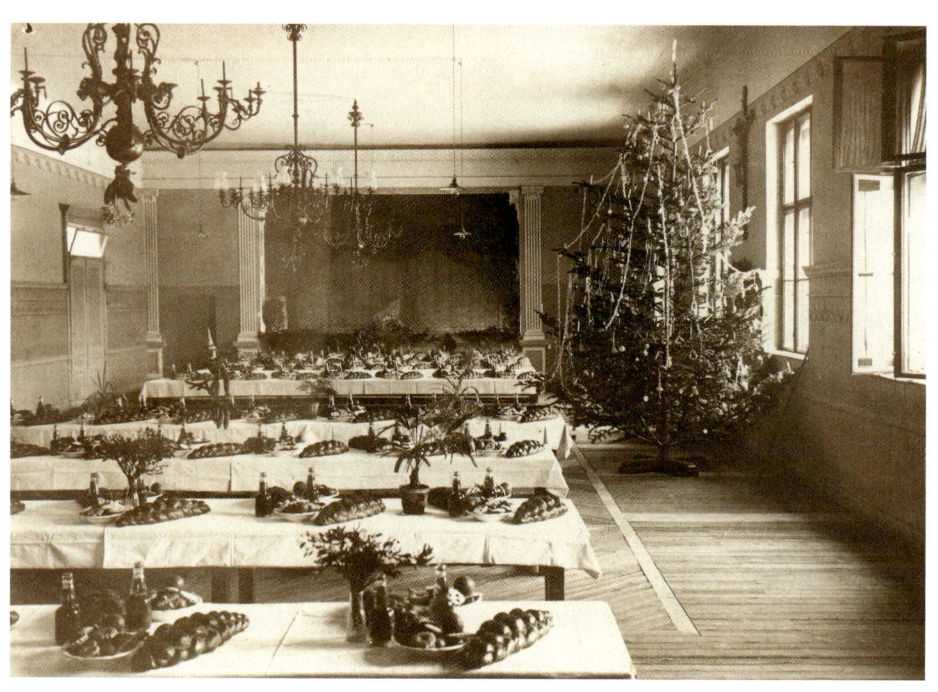

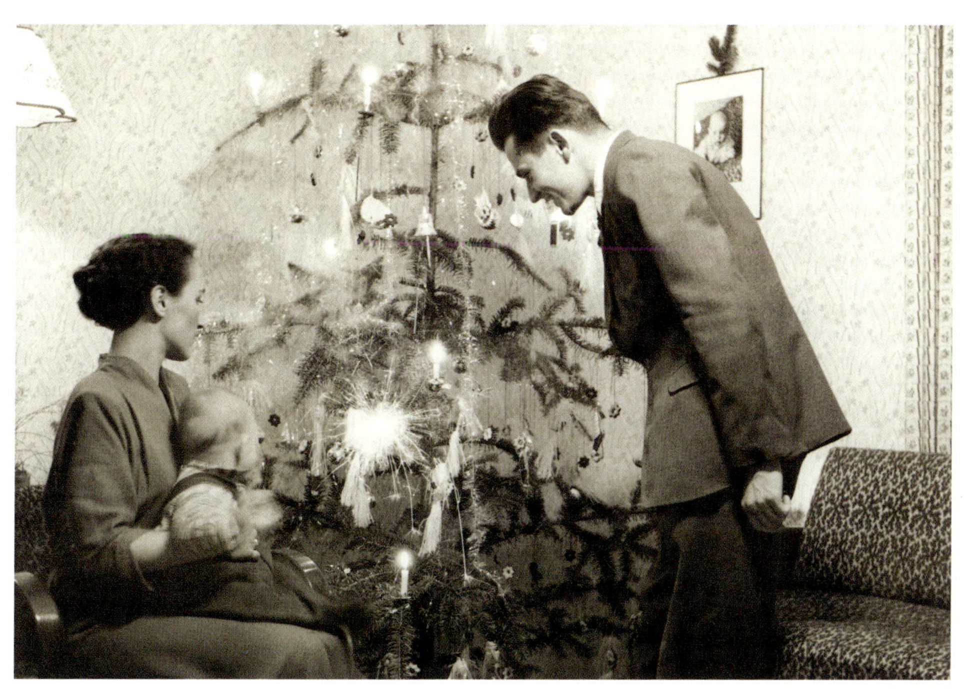

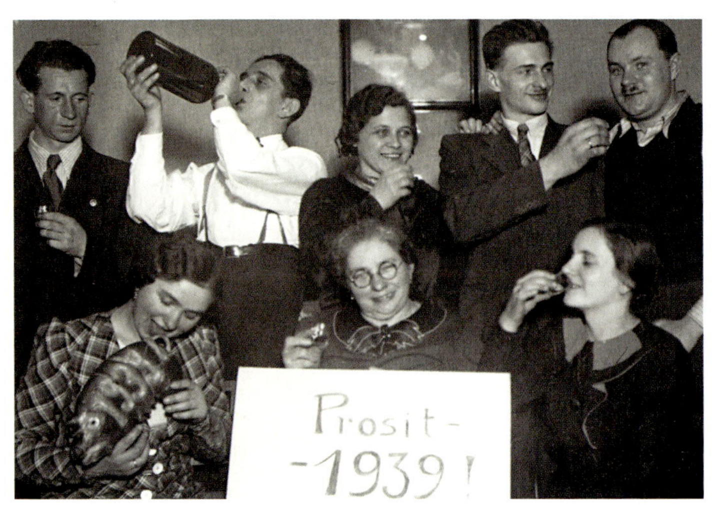
Prosit-
-1939!

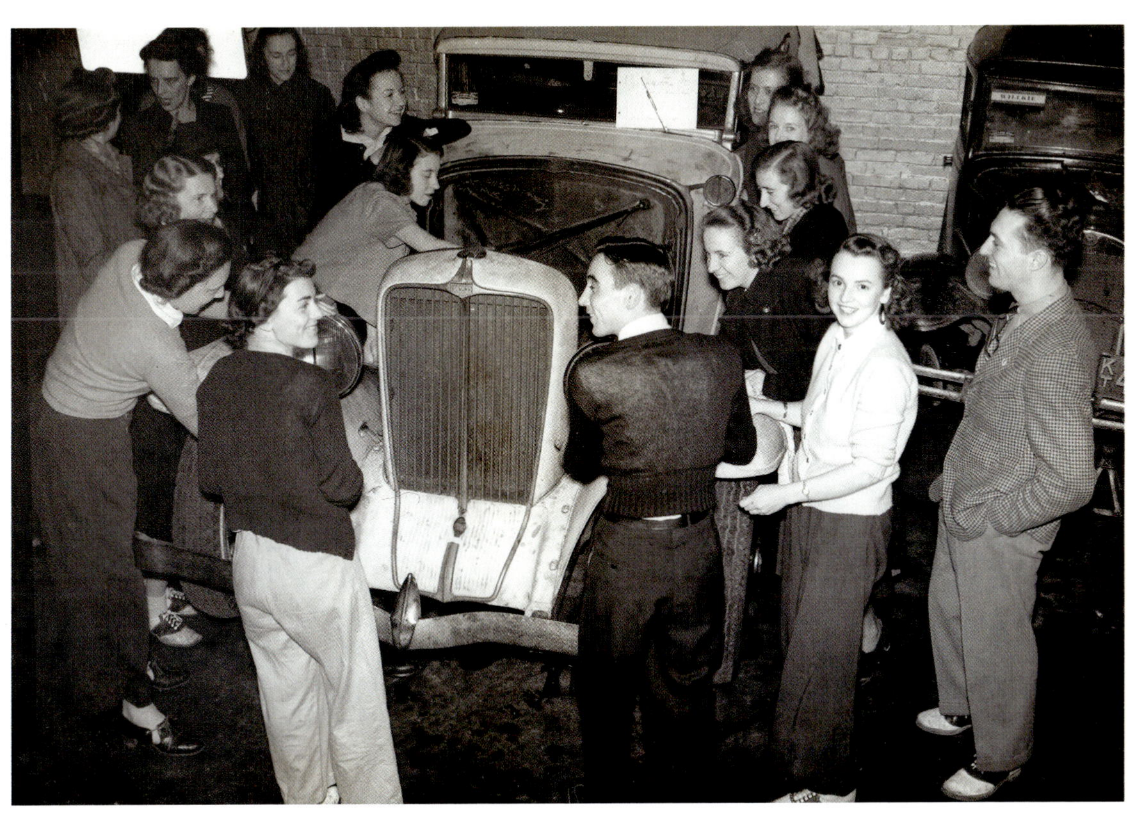

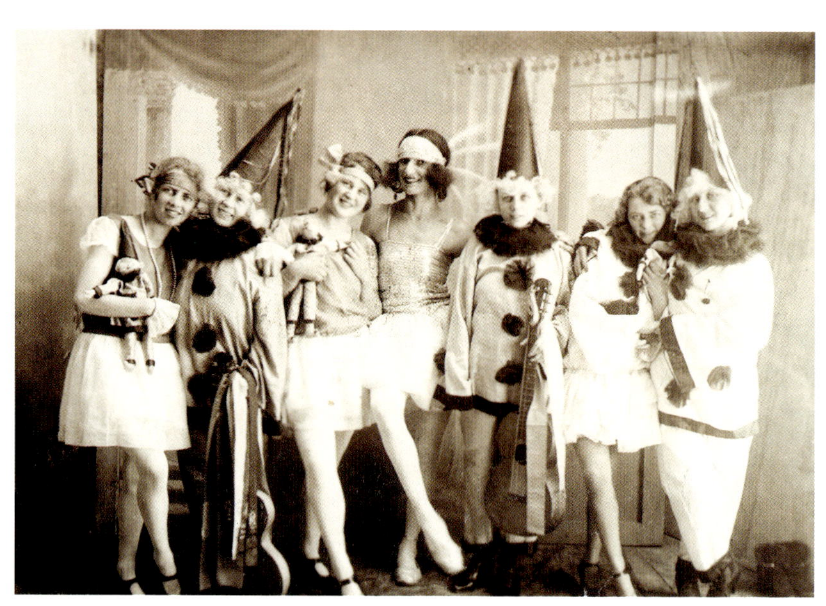

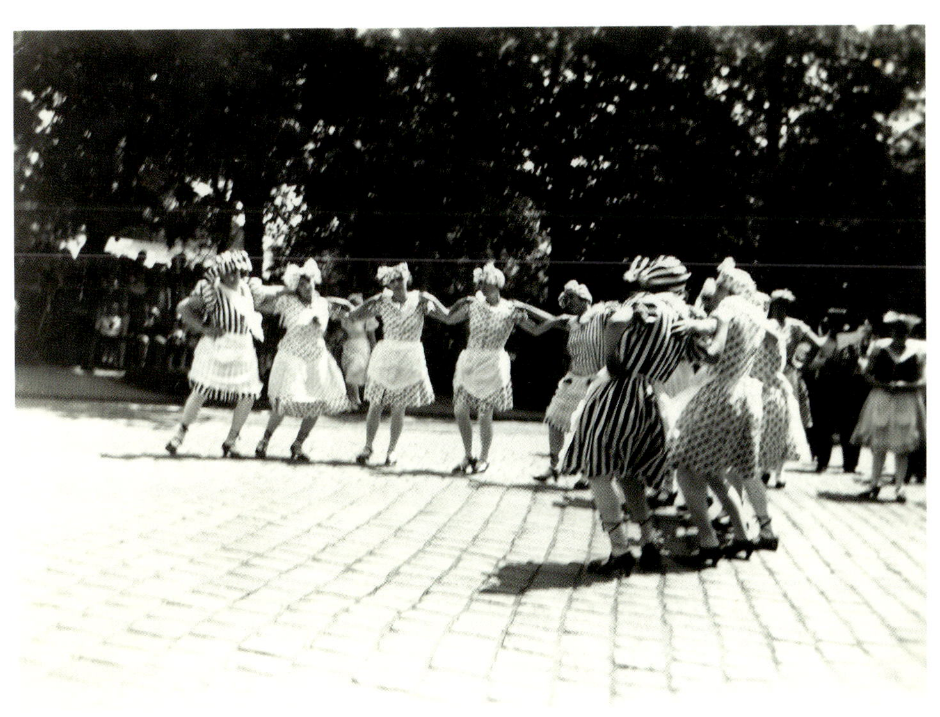

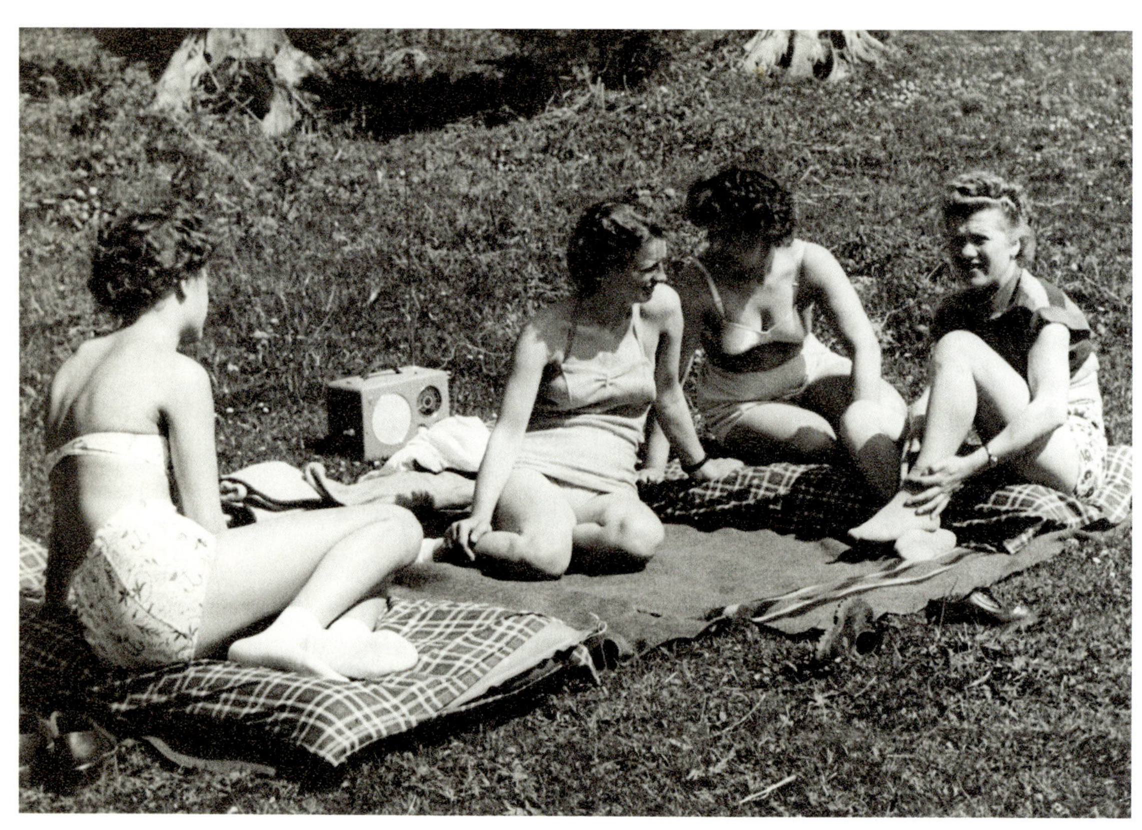

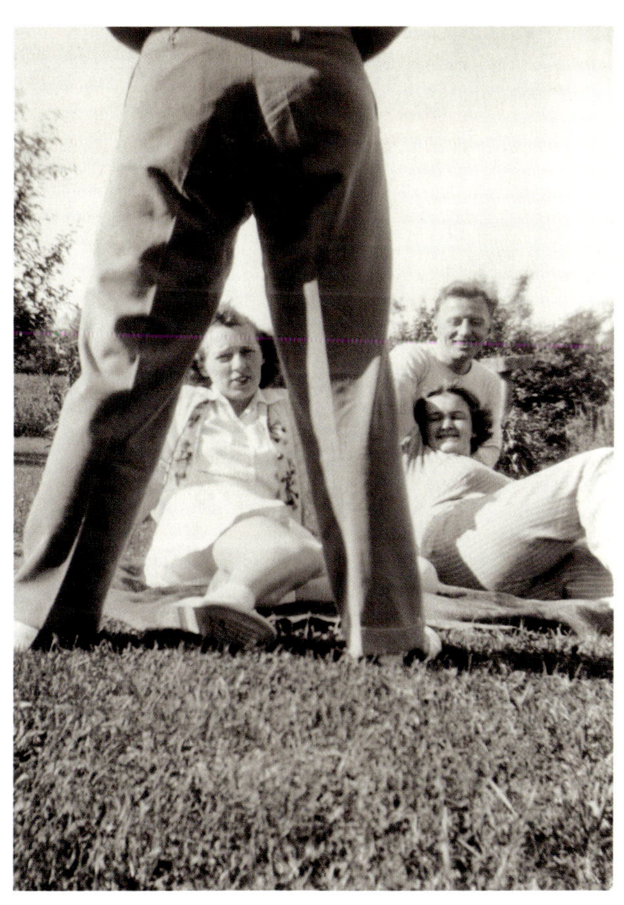

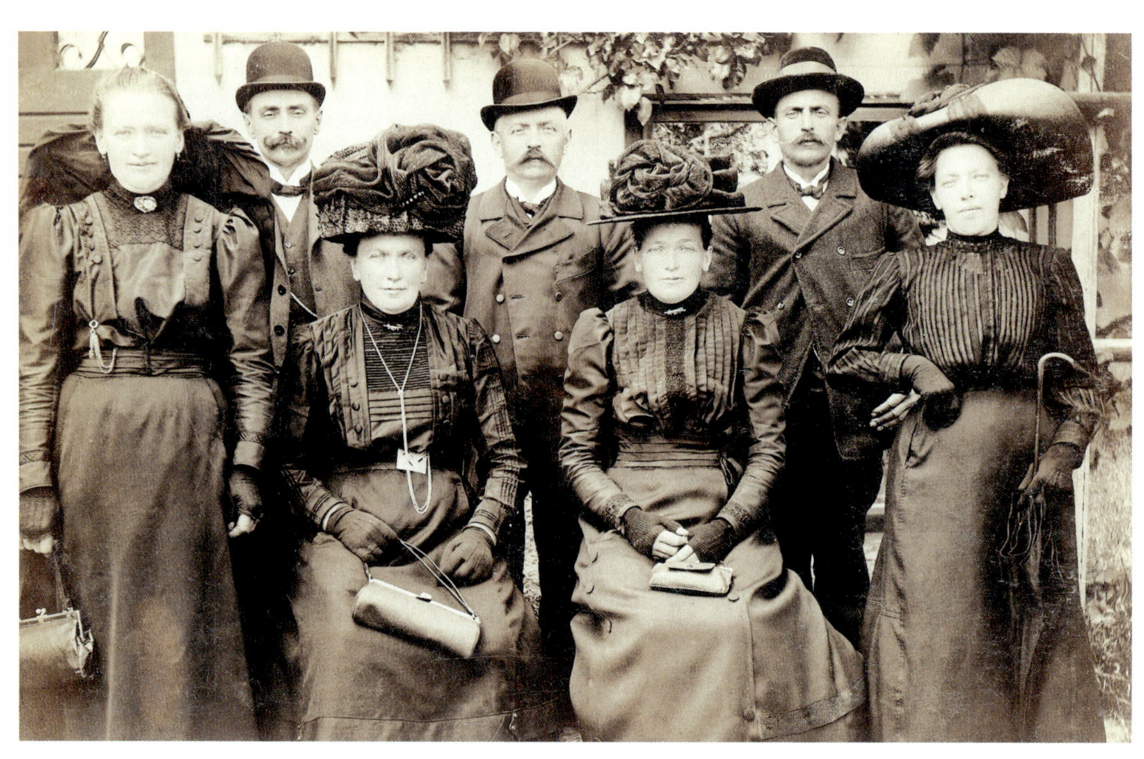

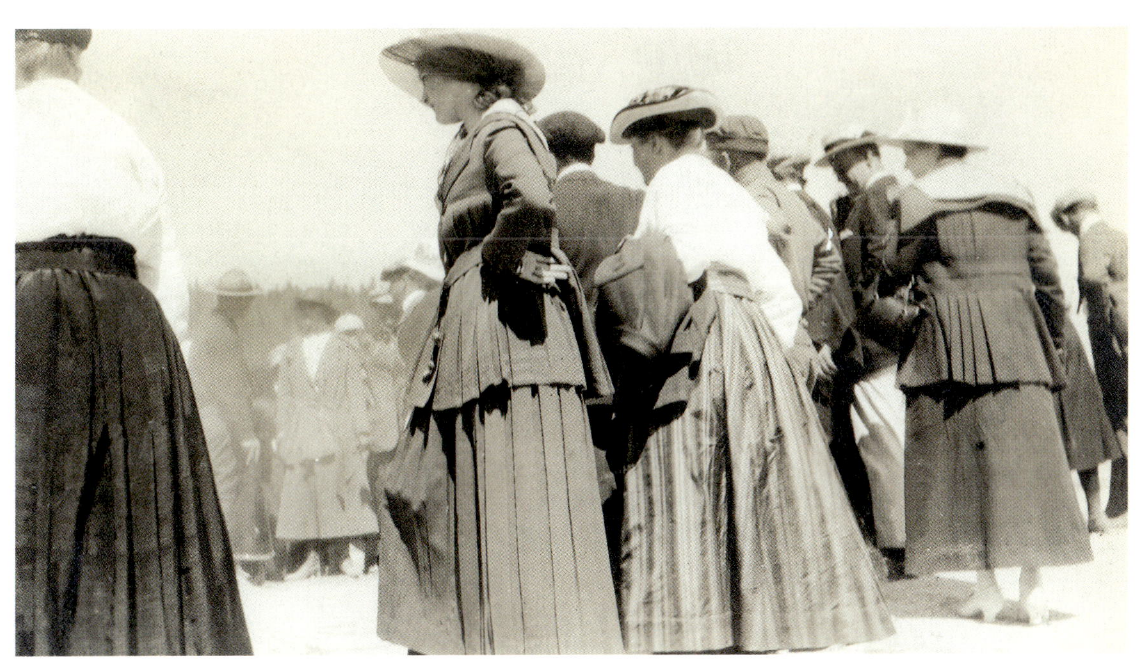

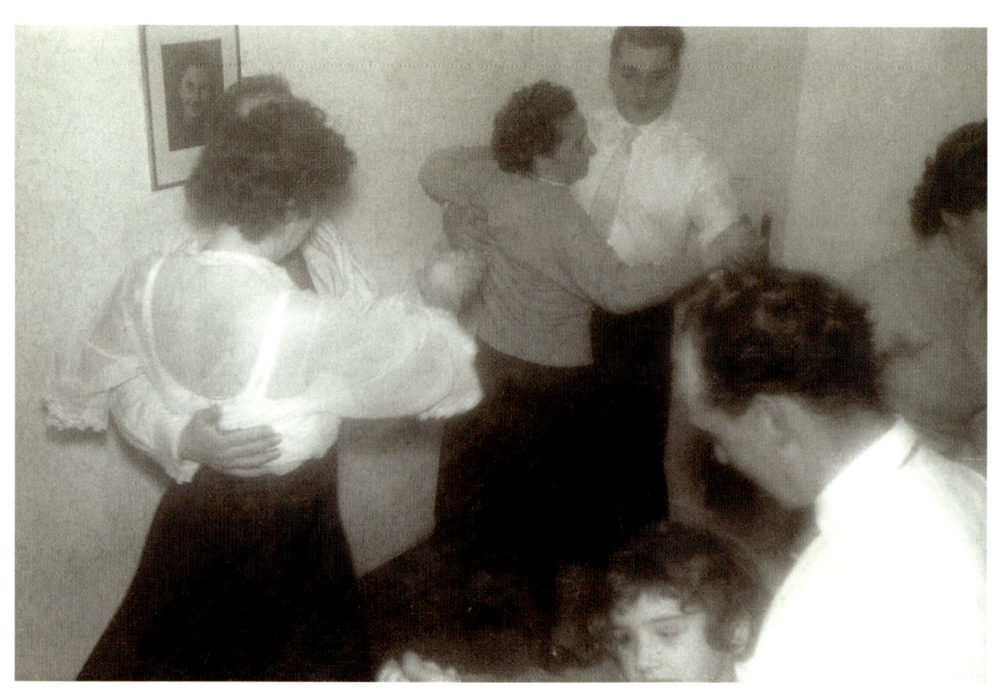

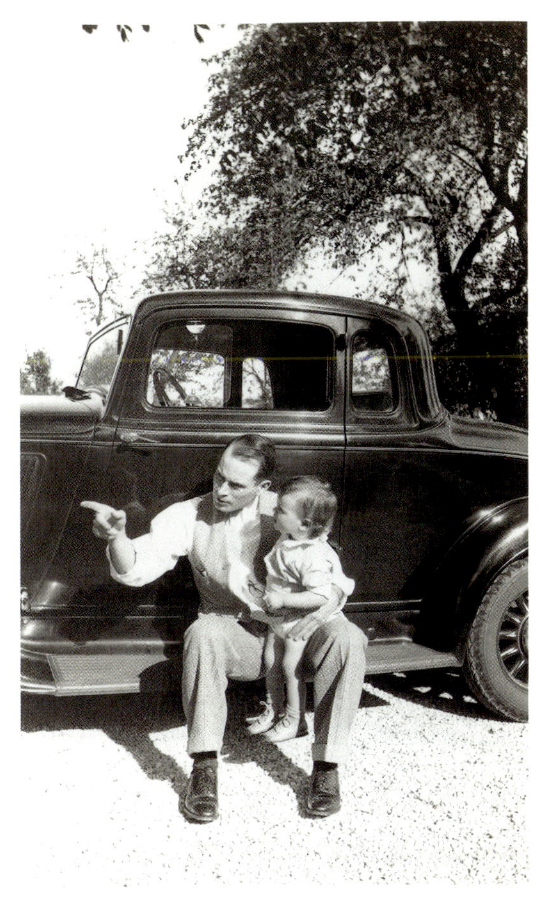

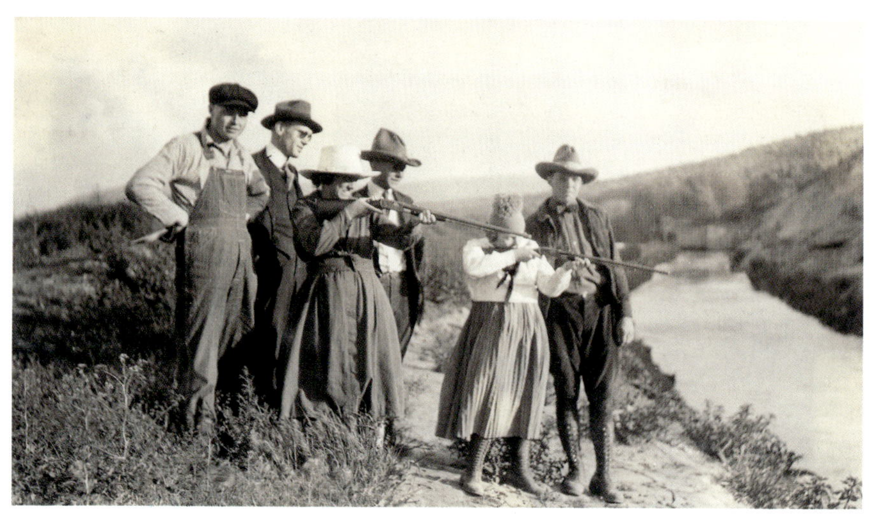

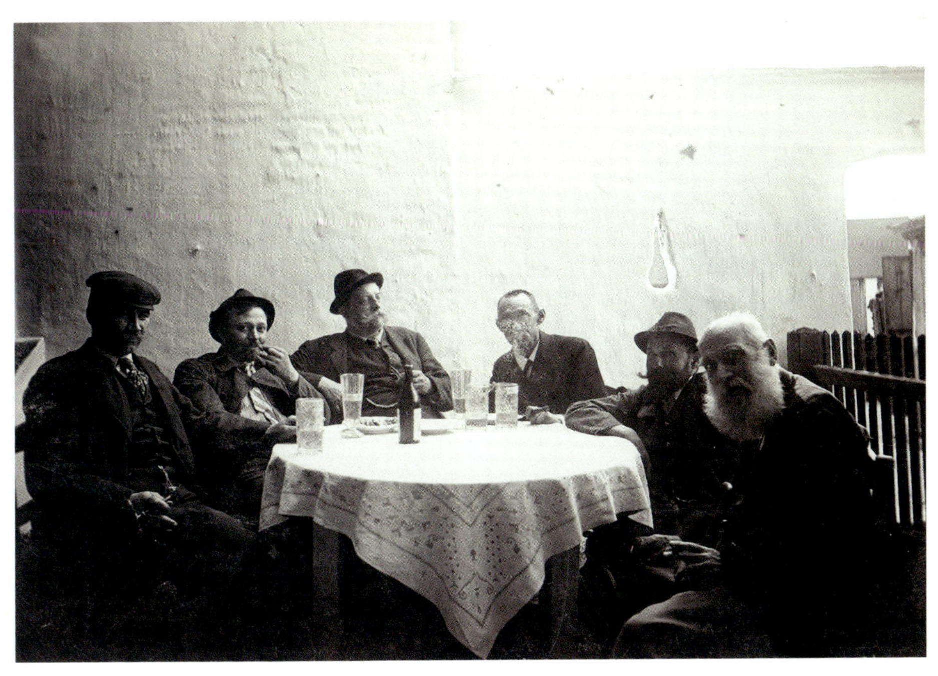

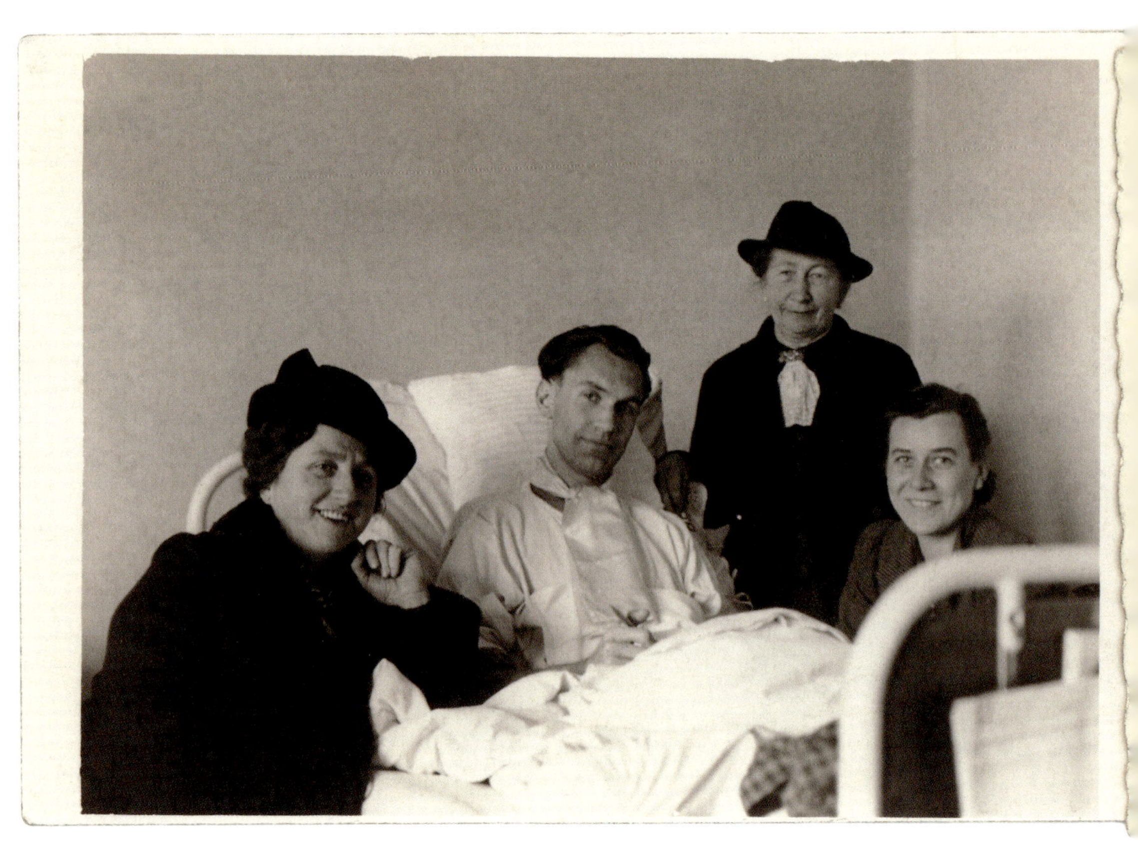

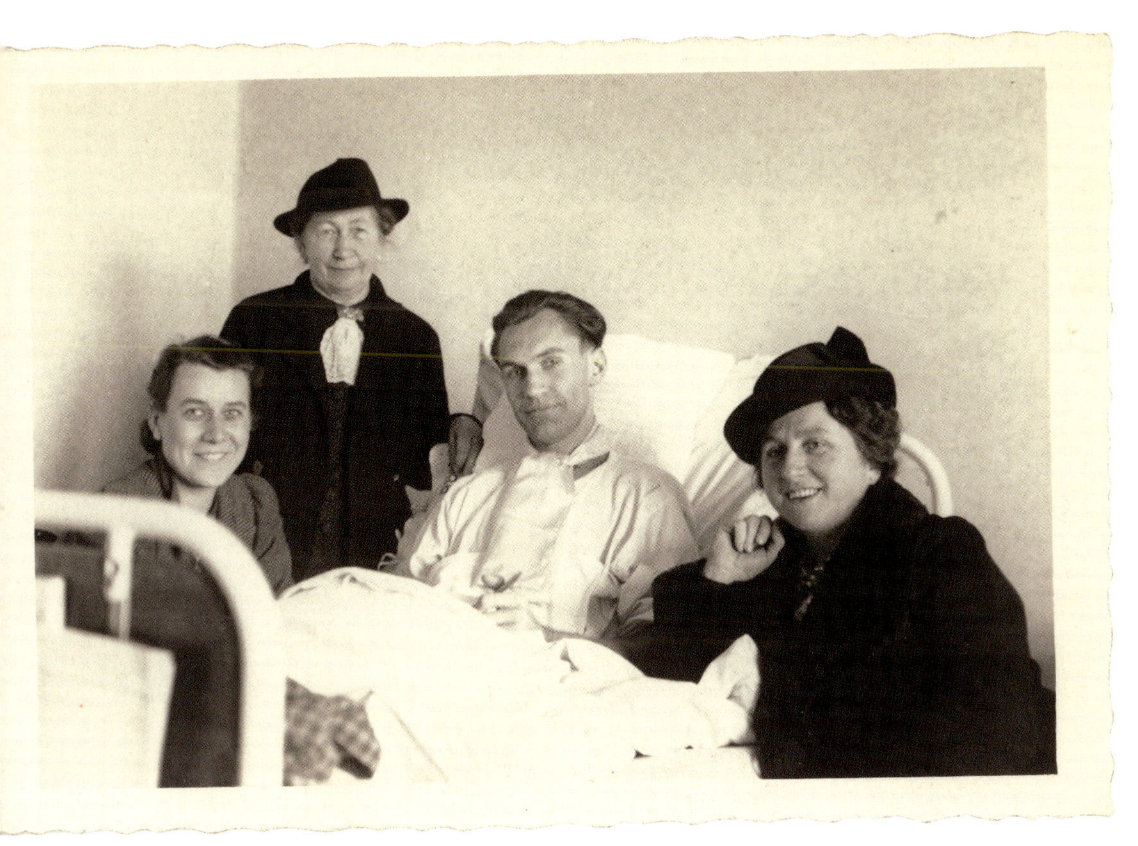

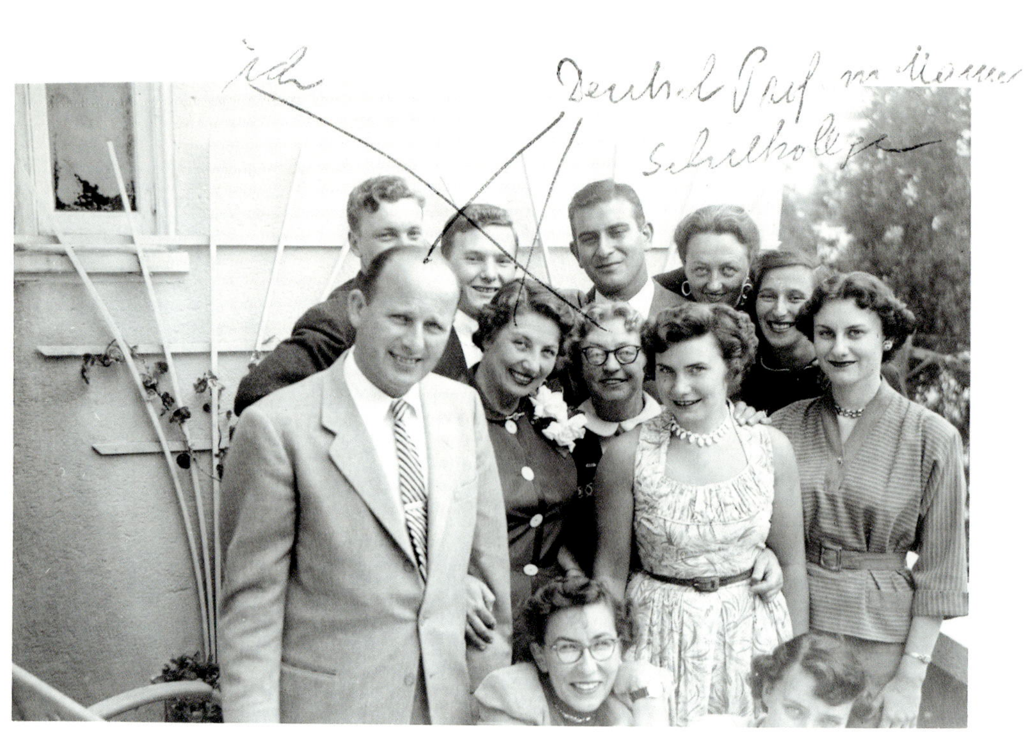

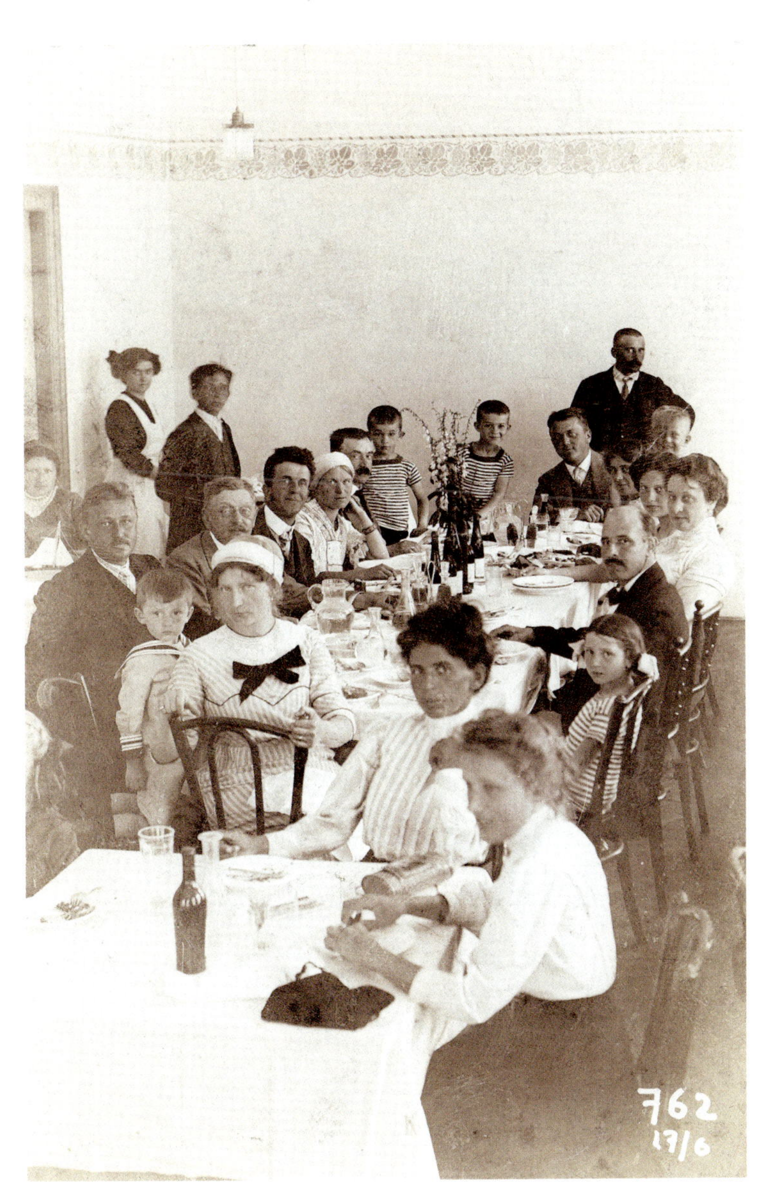
762
17/6

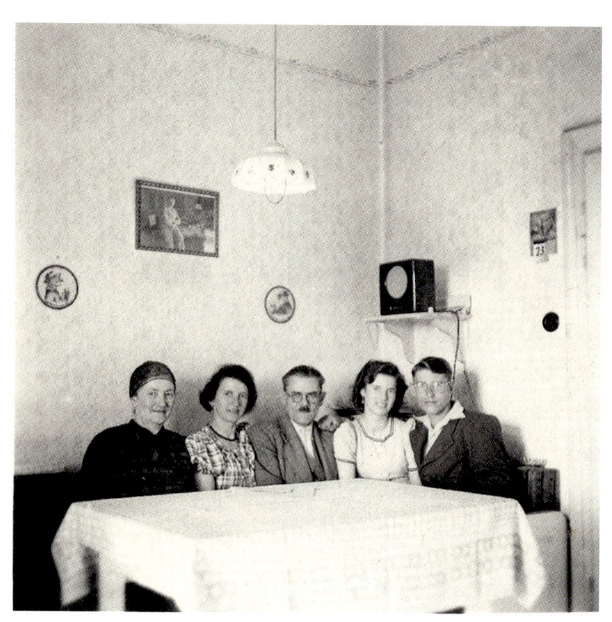

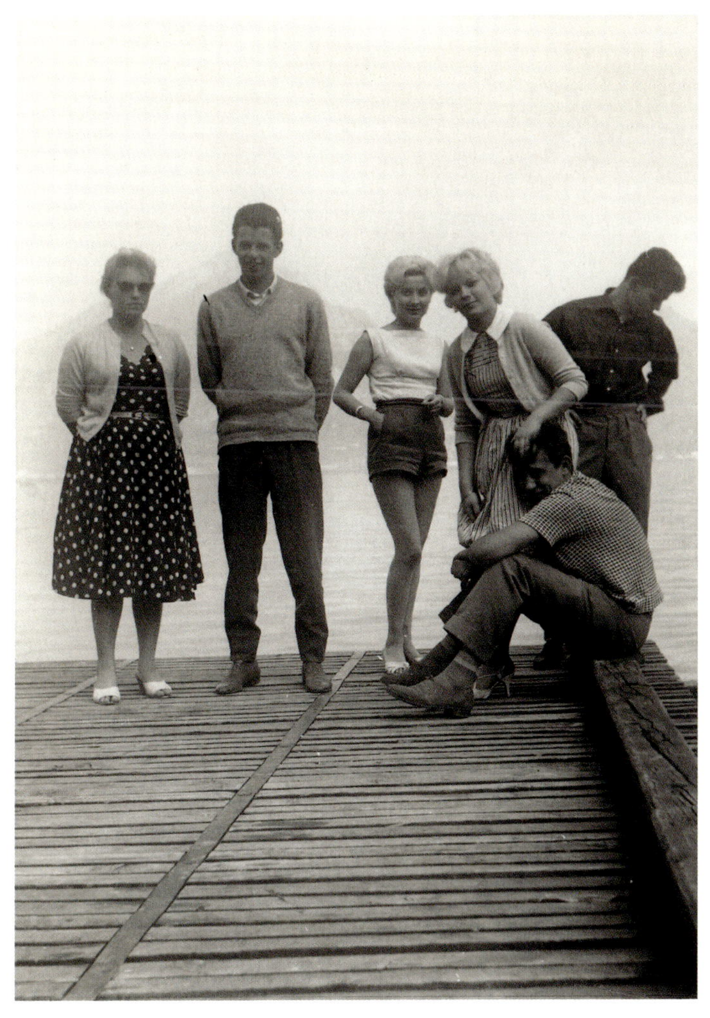

7)

Love Liebe

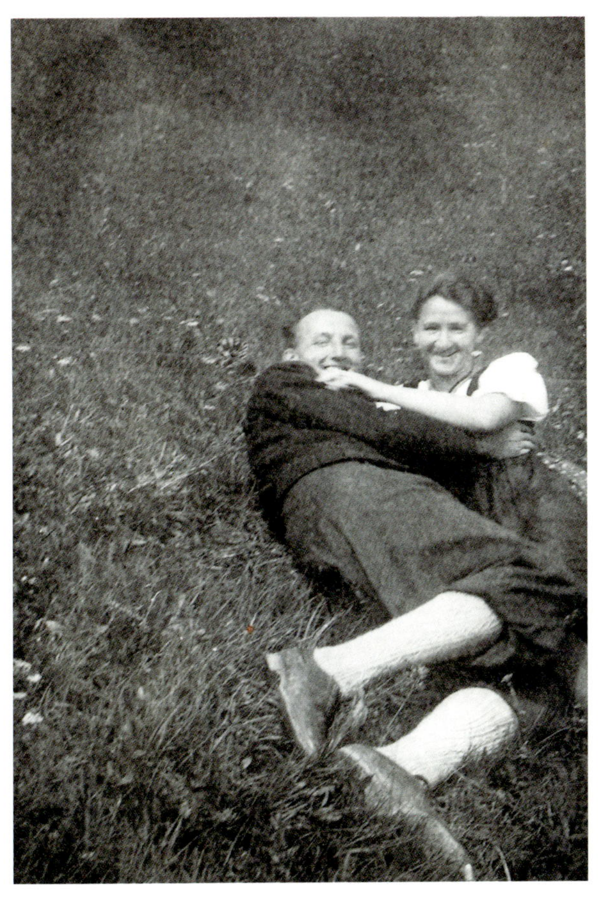

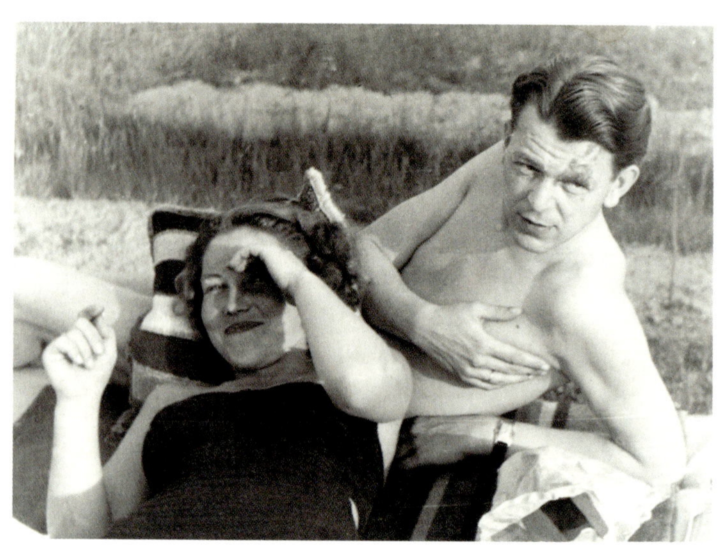

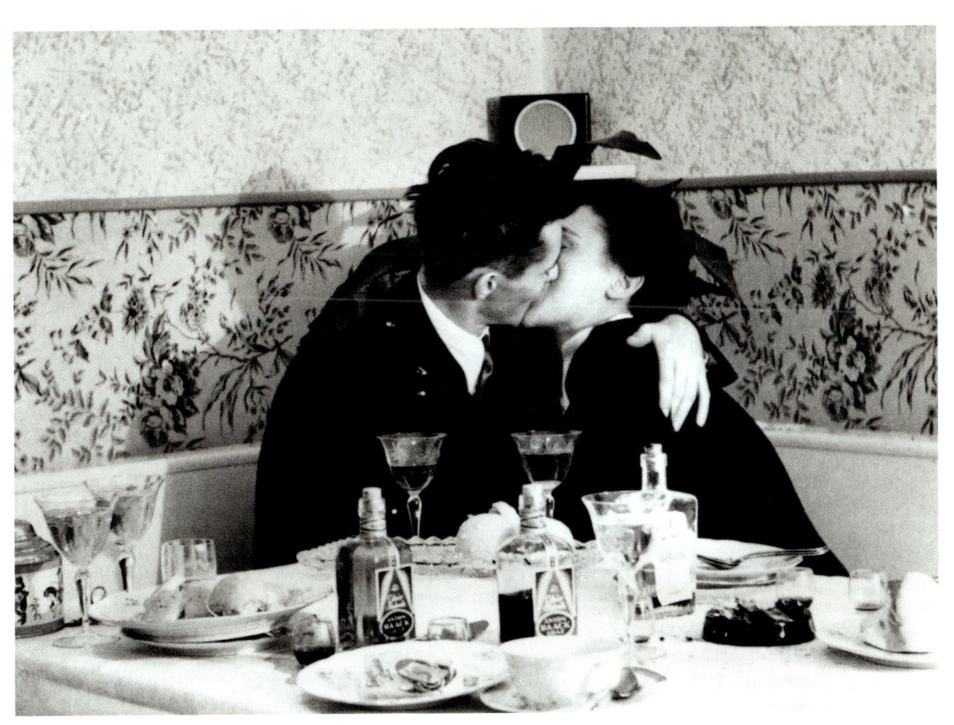

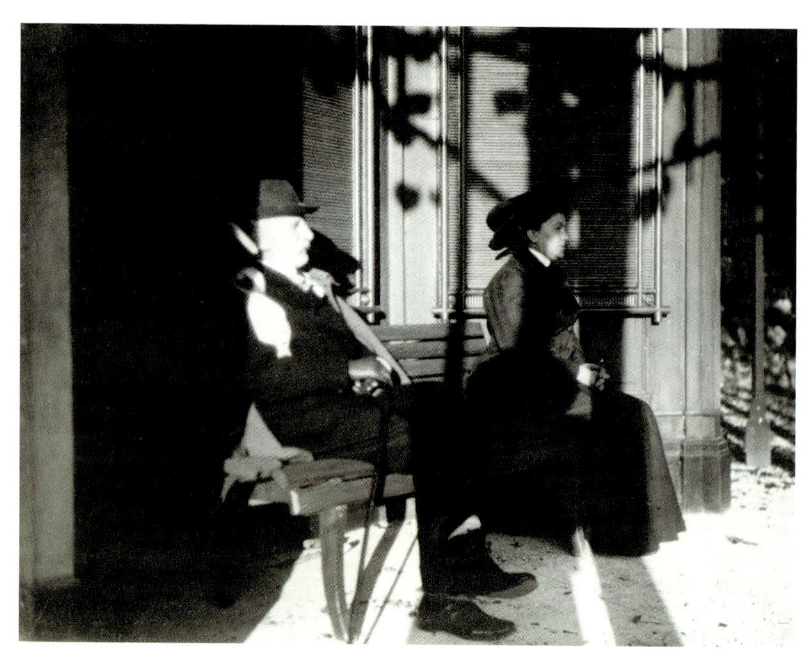

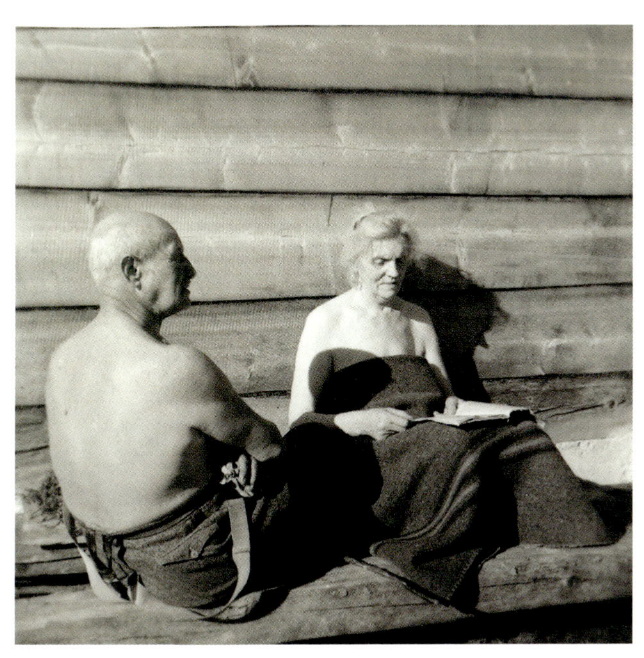

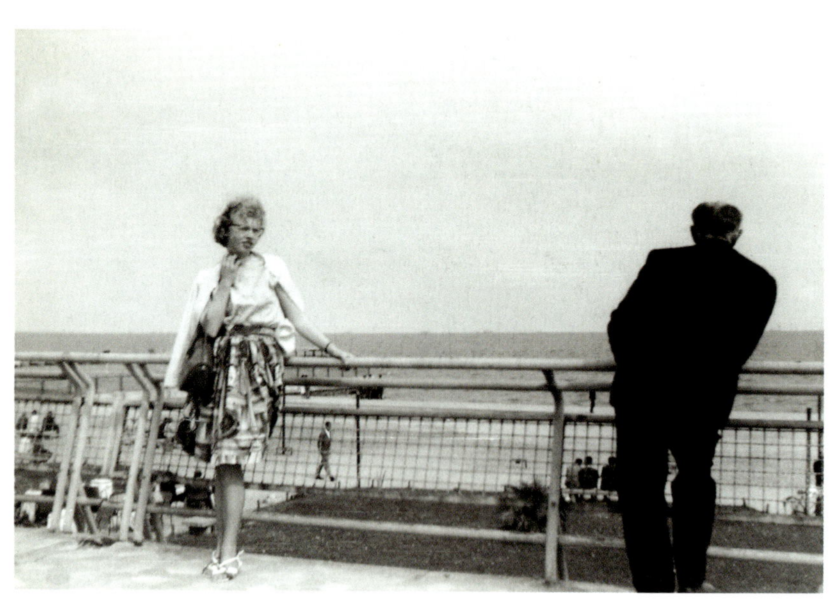

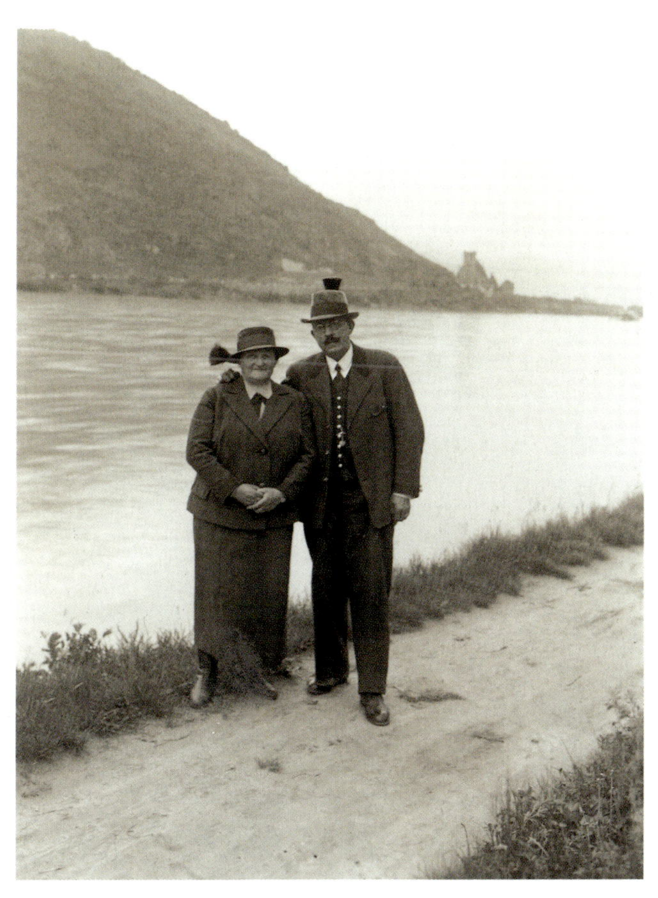

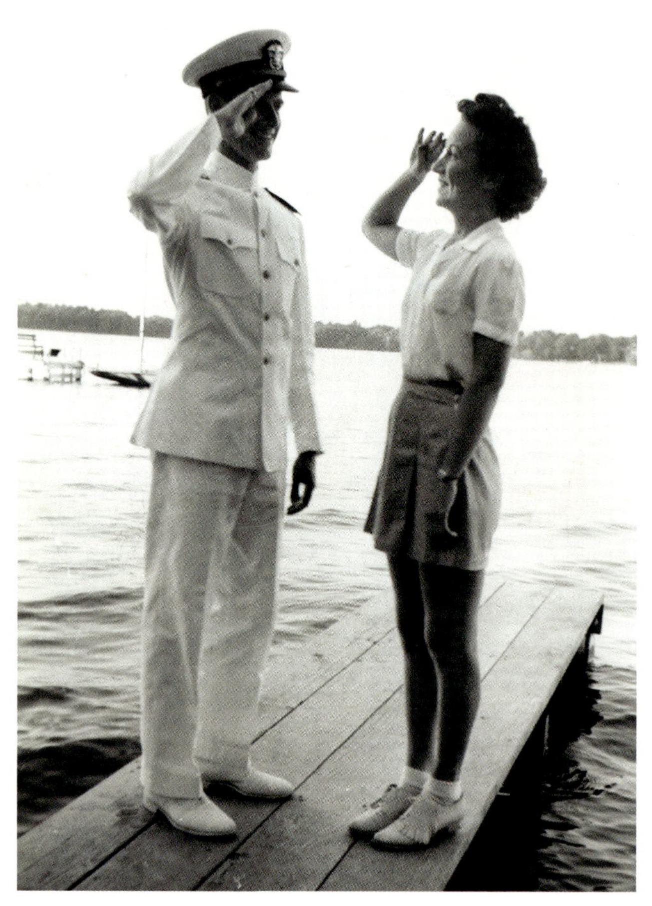

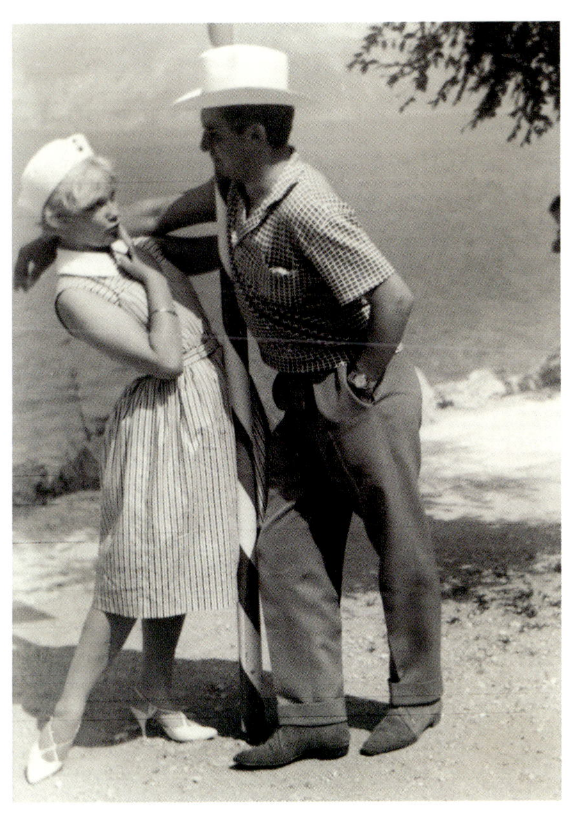

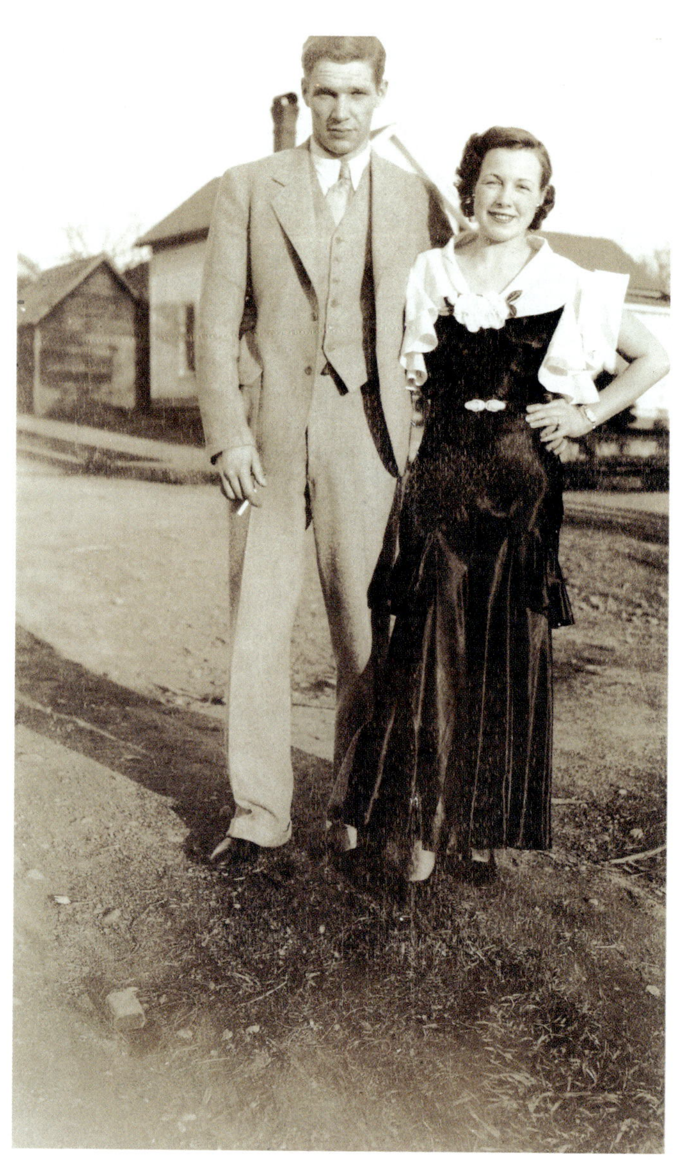

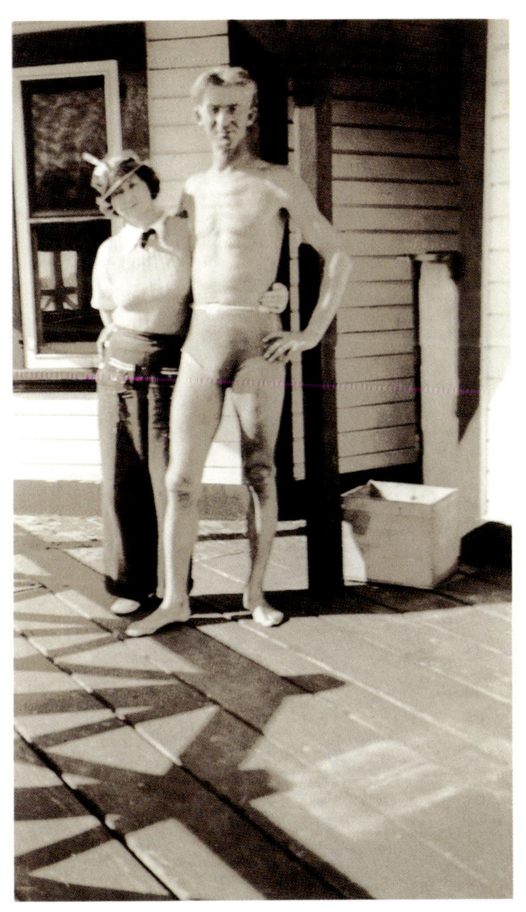

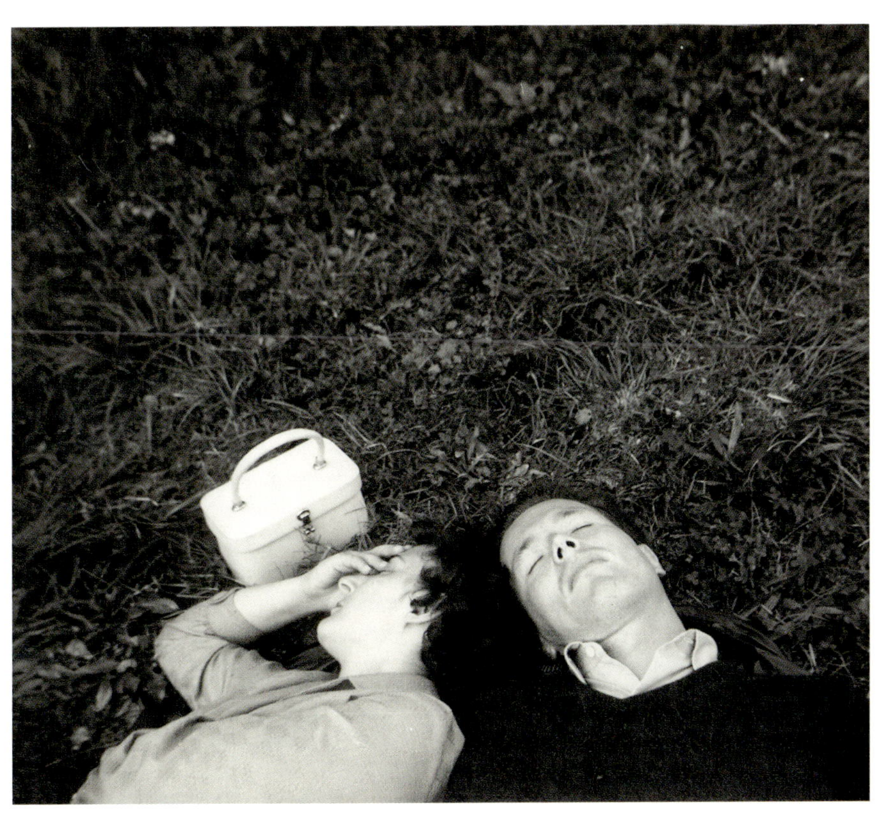

8)

Nudes Akte

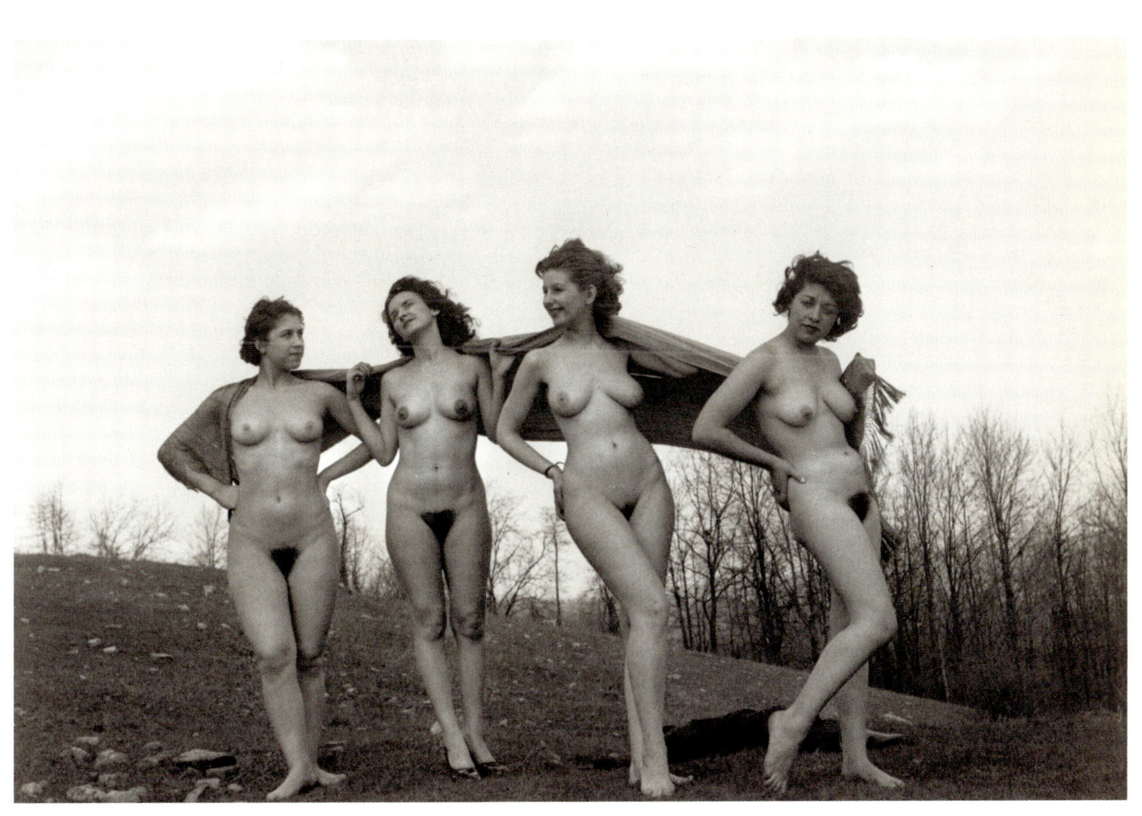

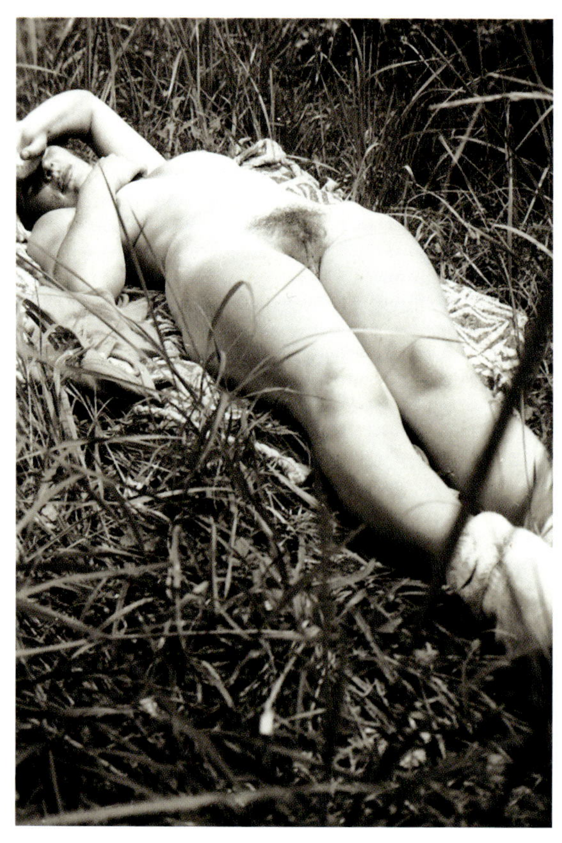

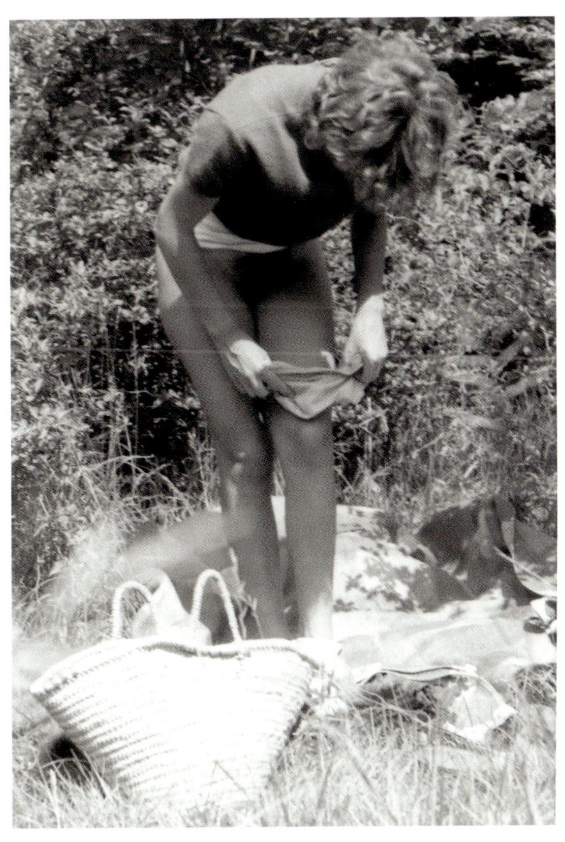

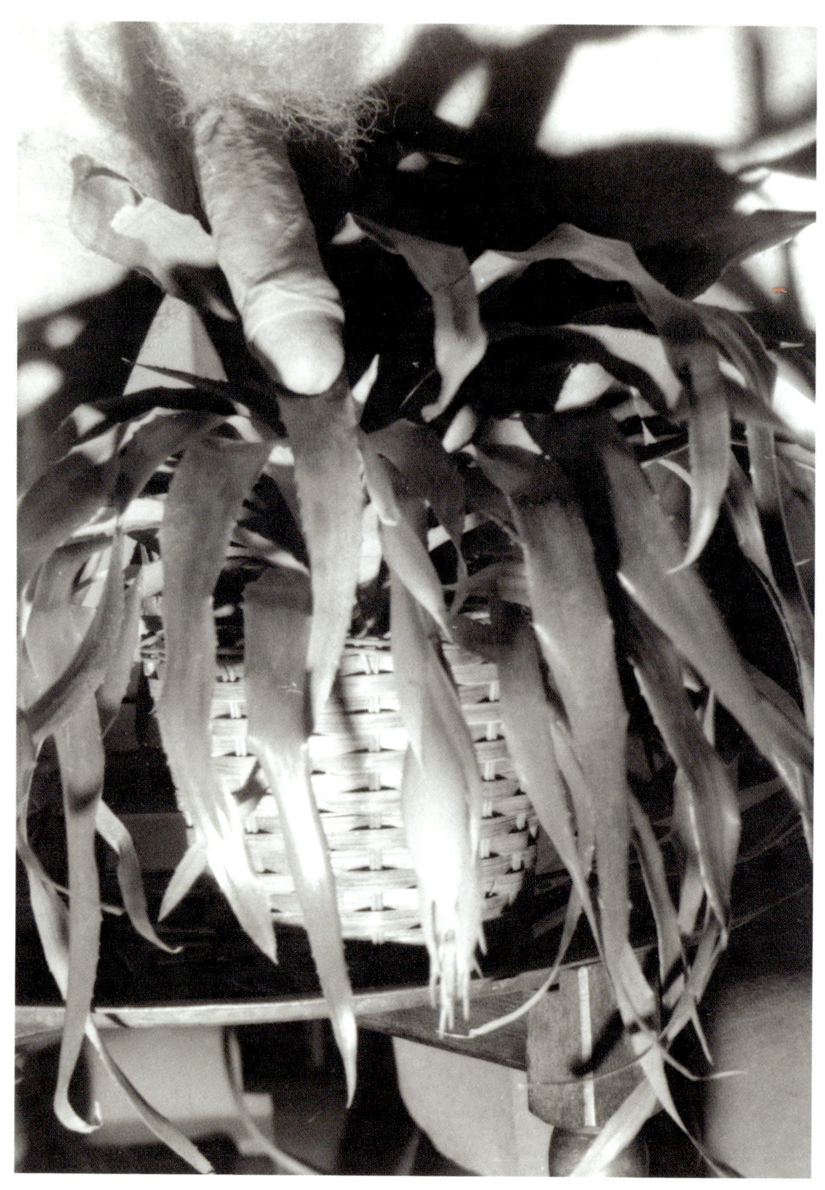

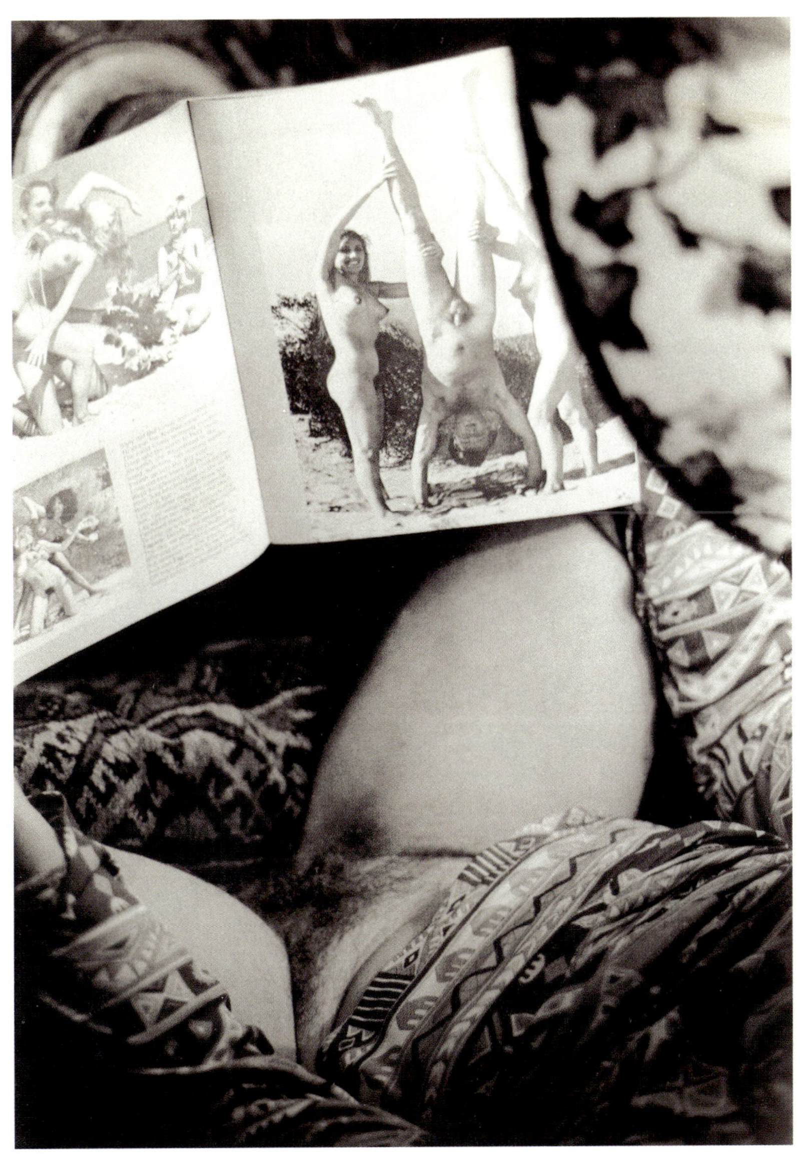

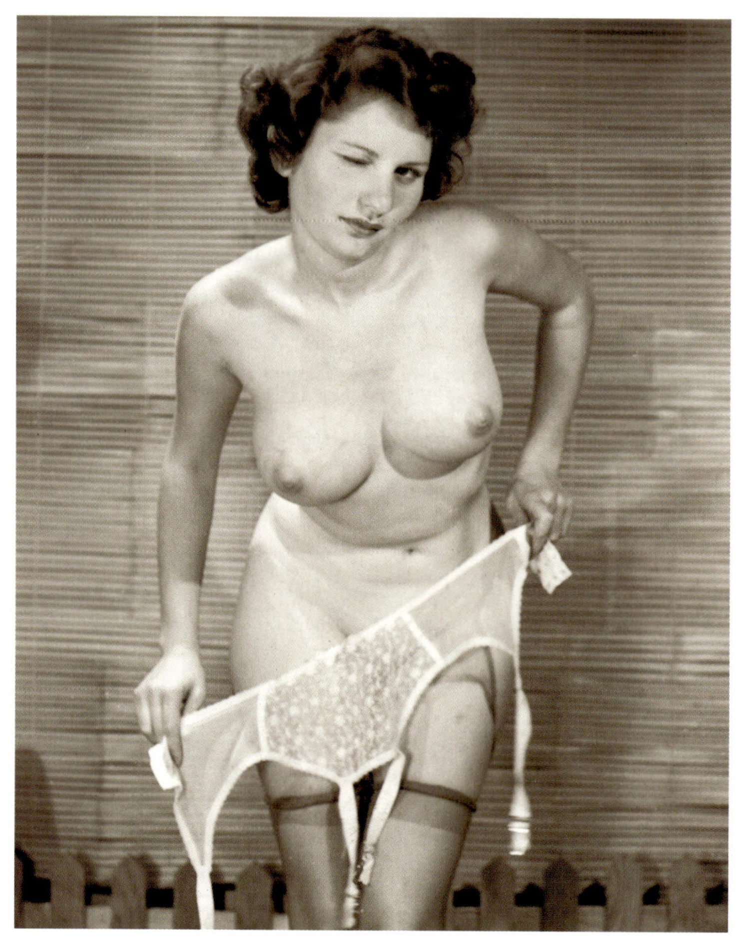

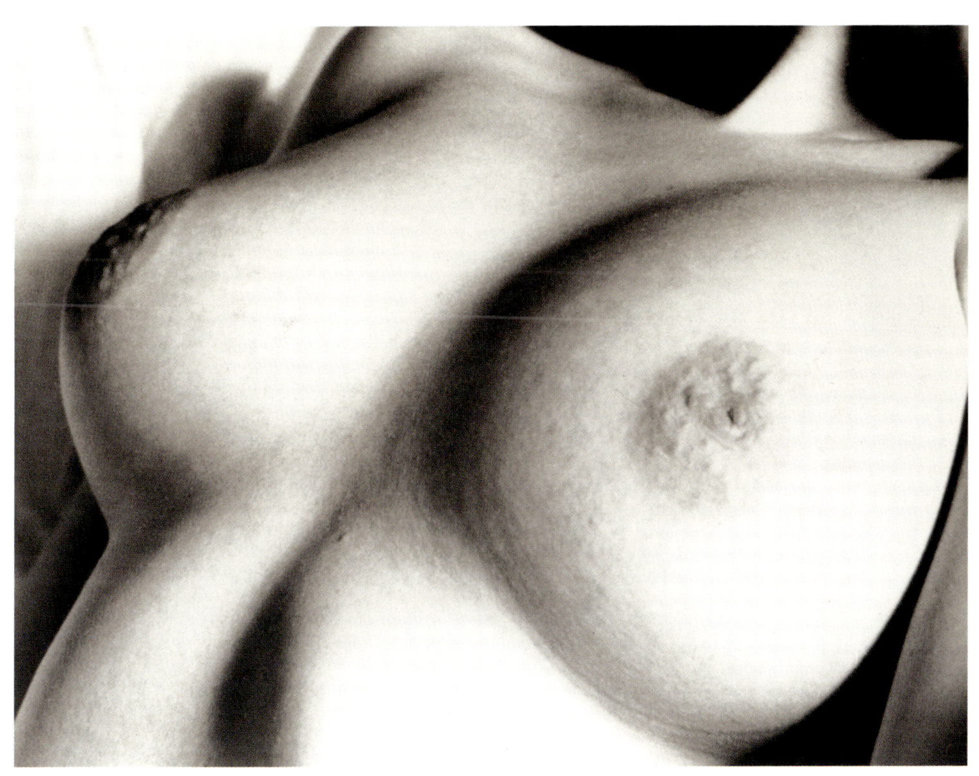

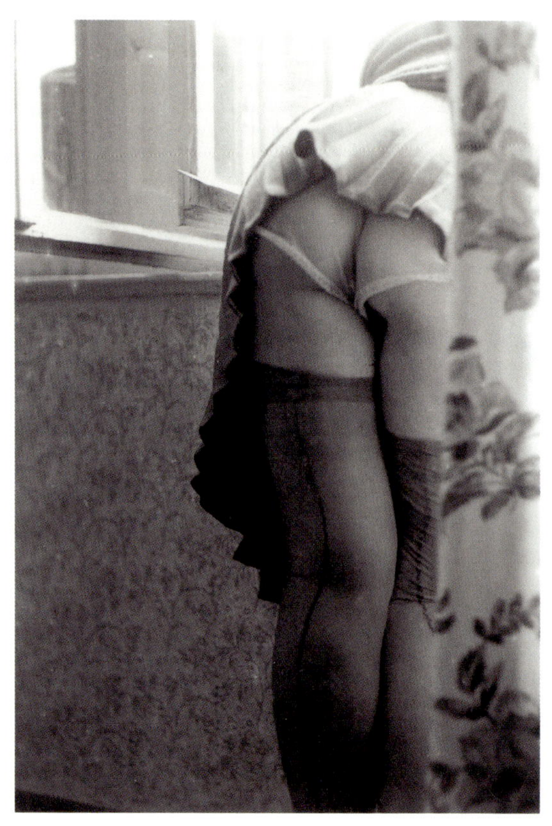

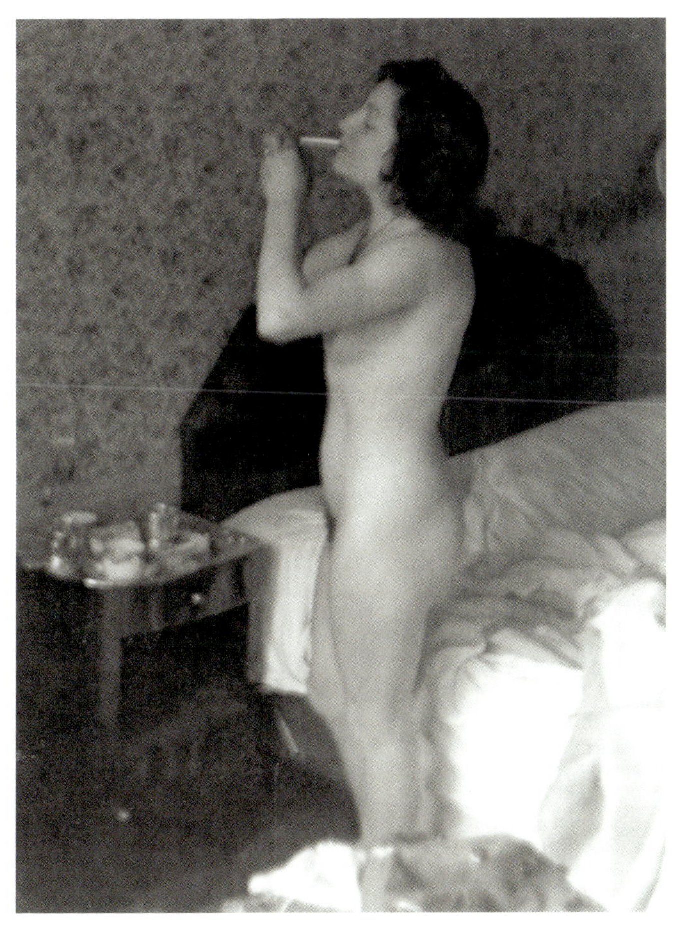

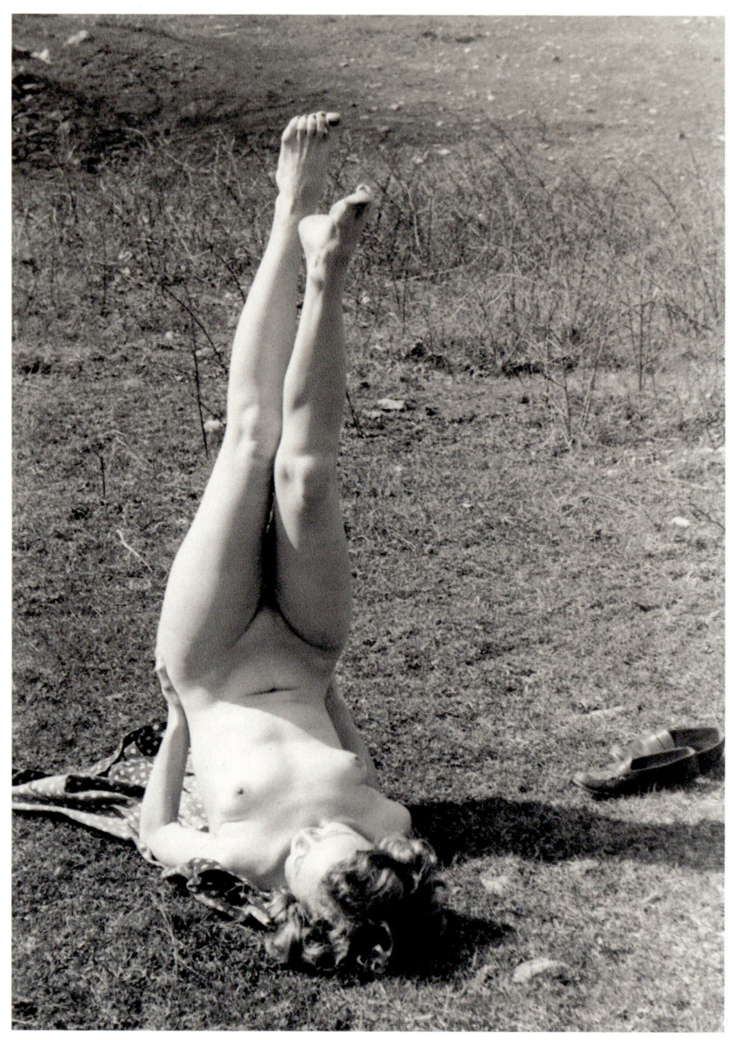

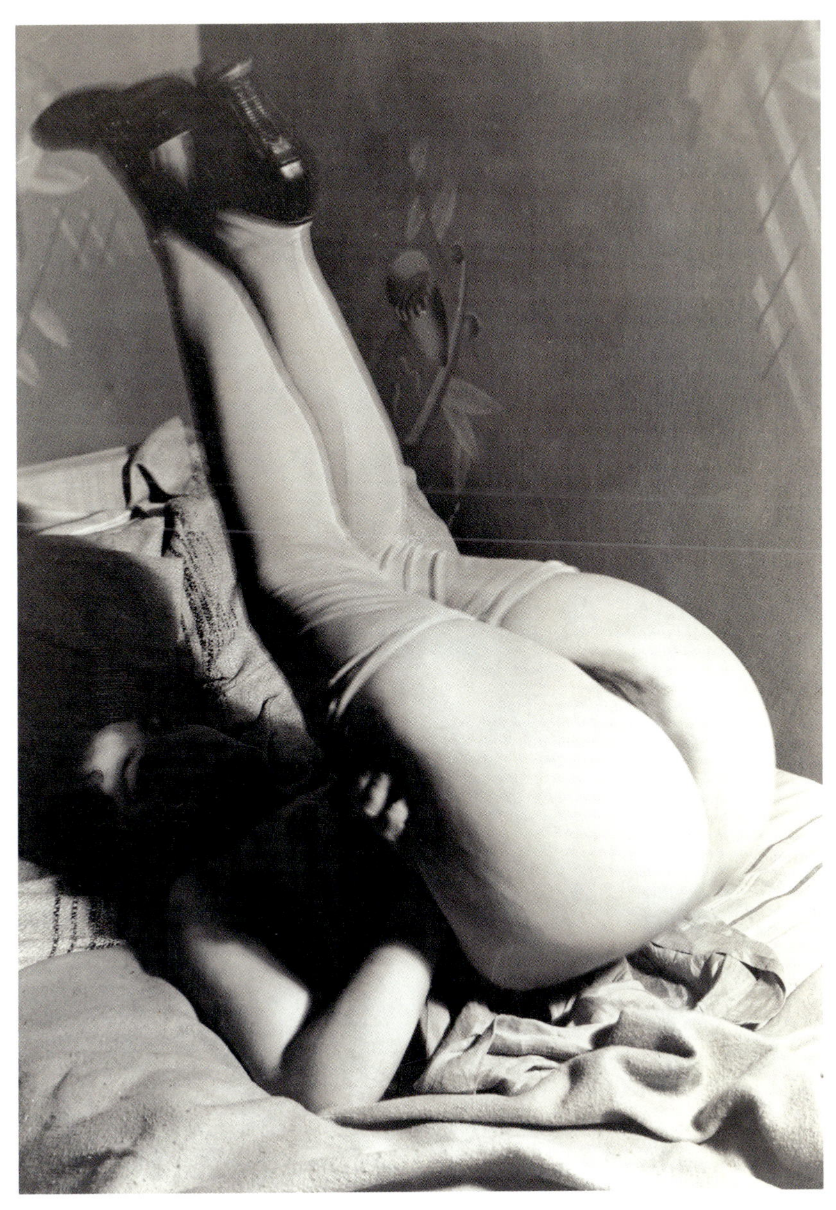

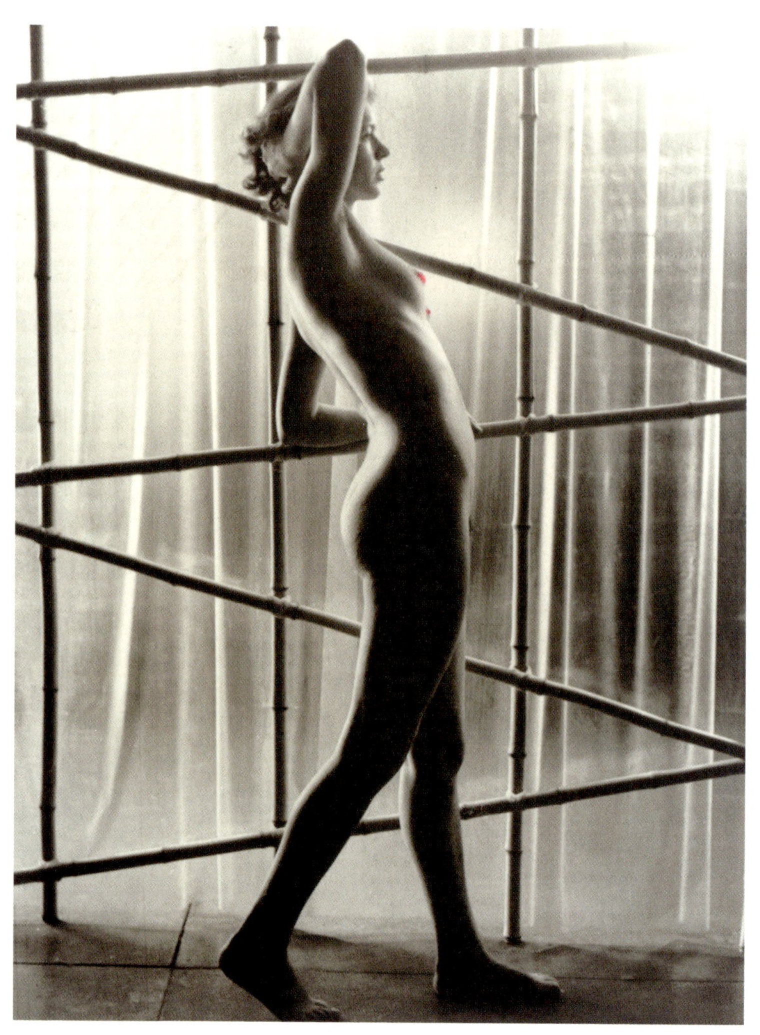

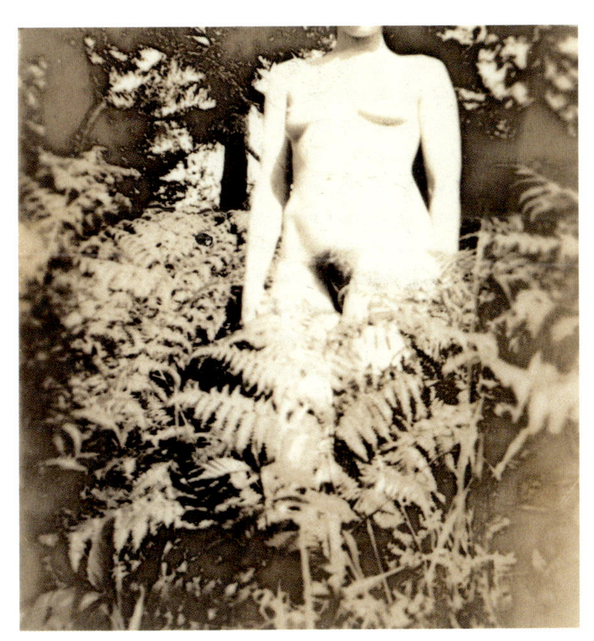

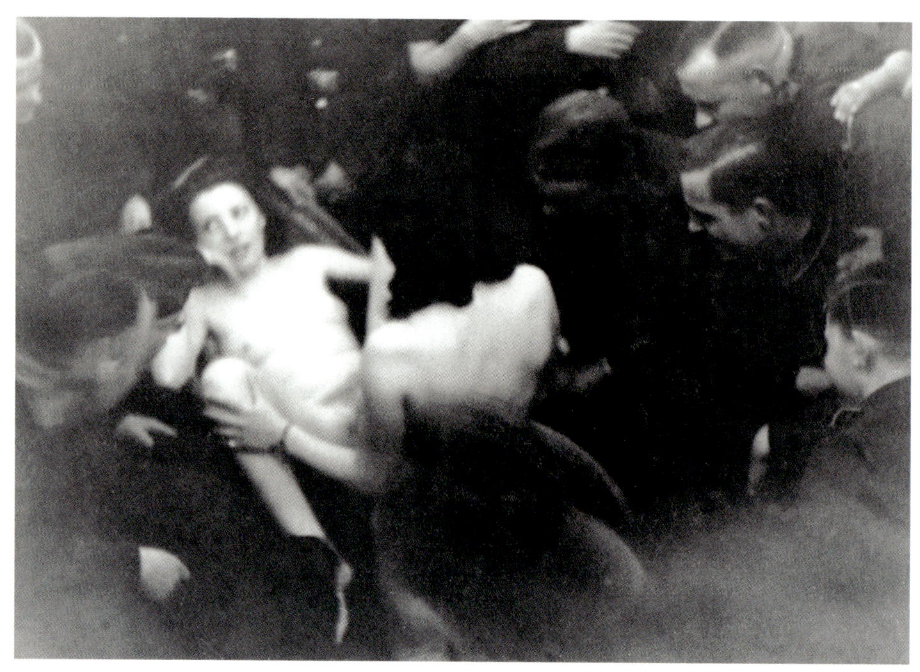

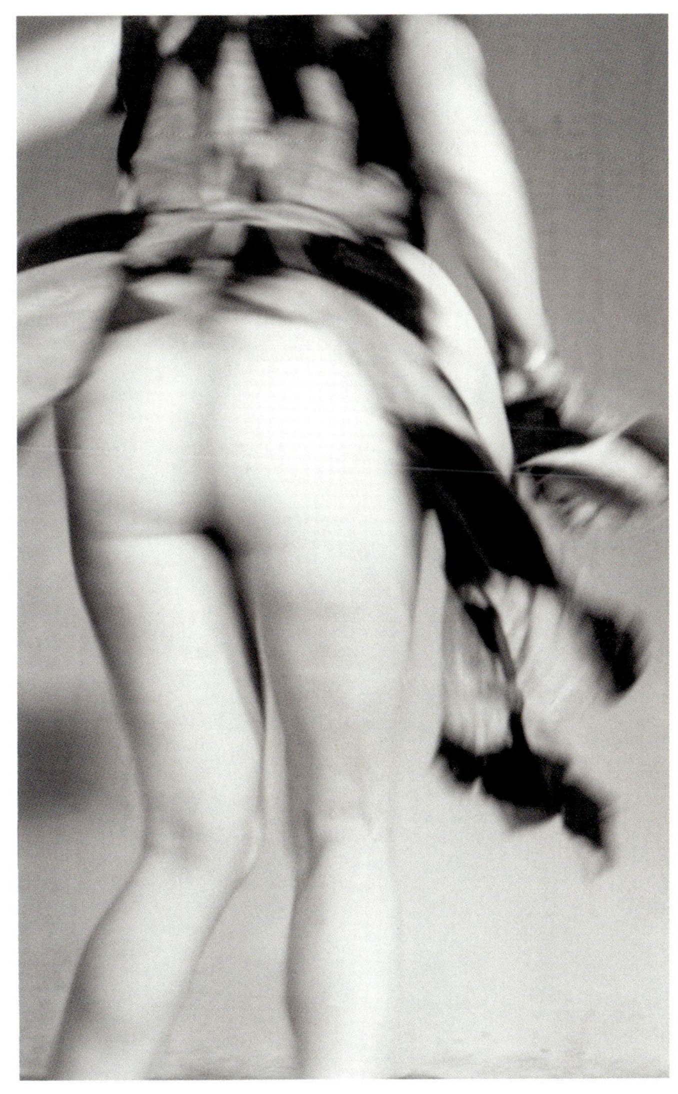

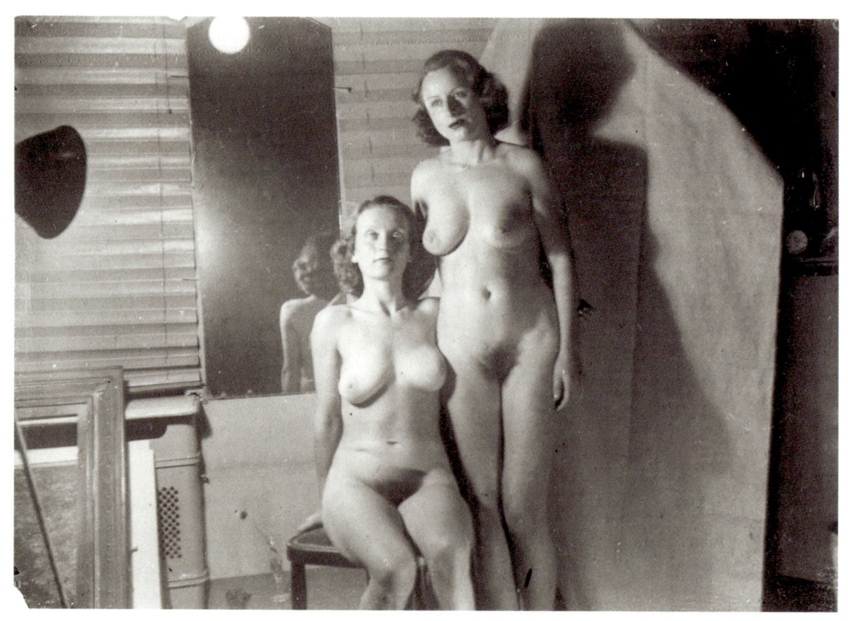

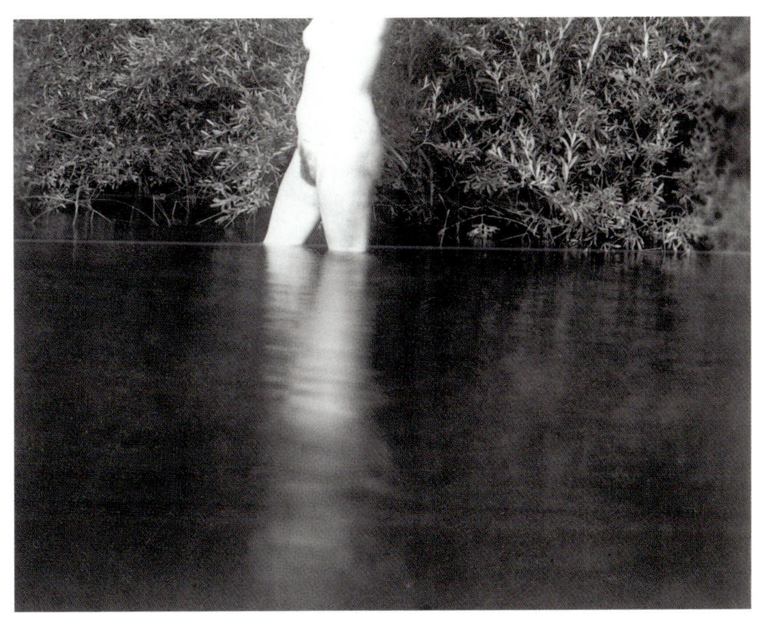

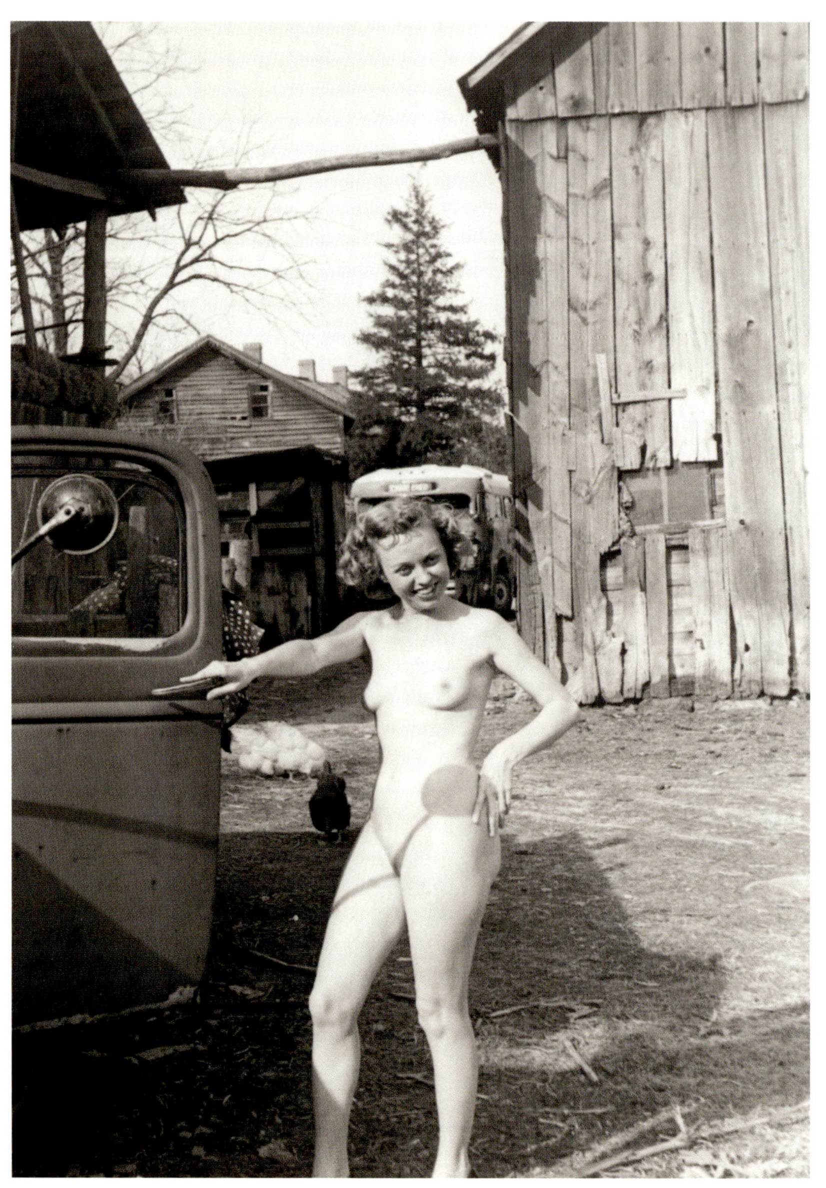

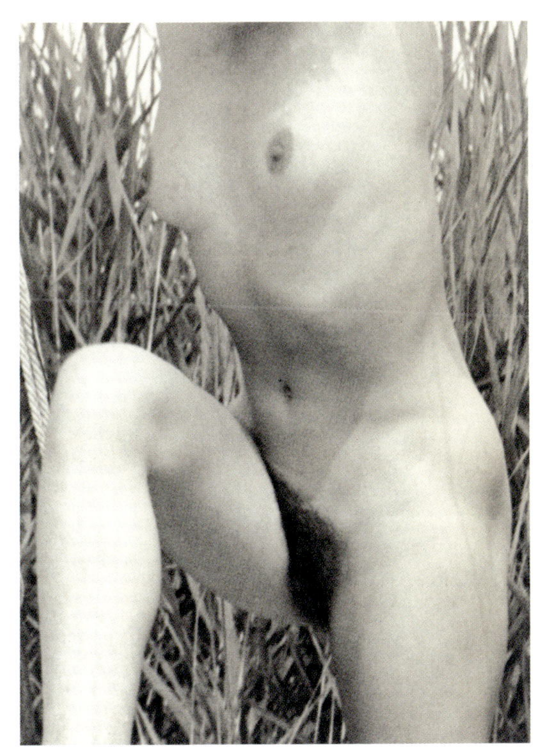

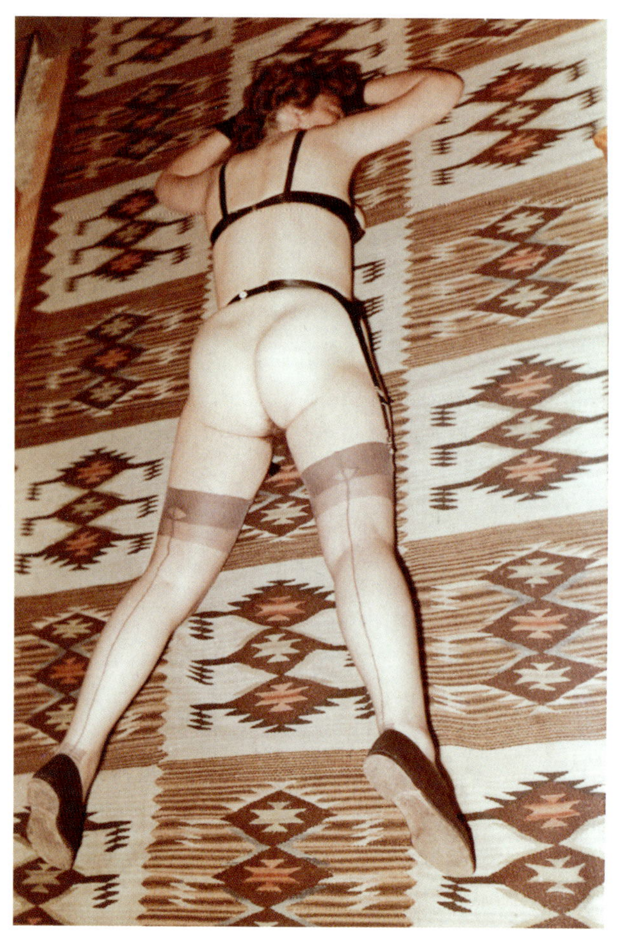

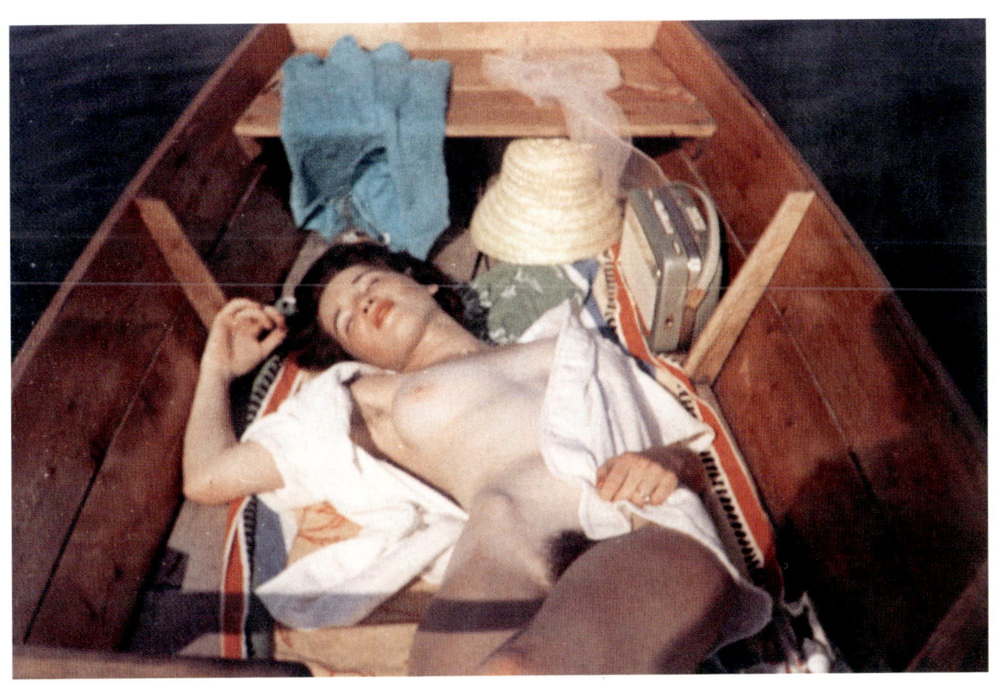

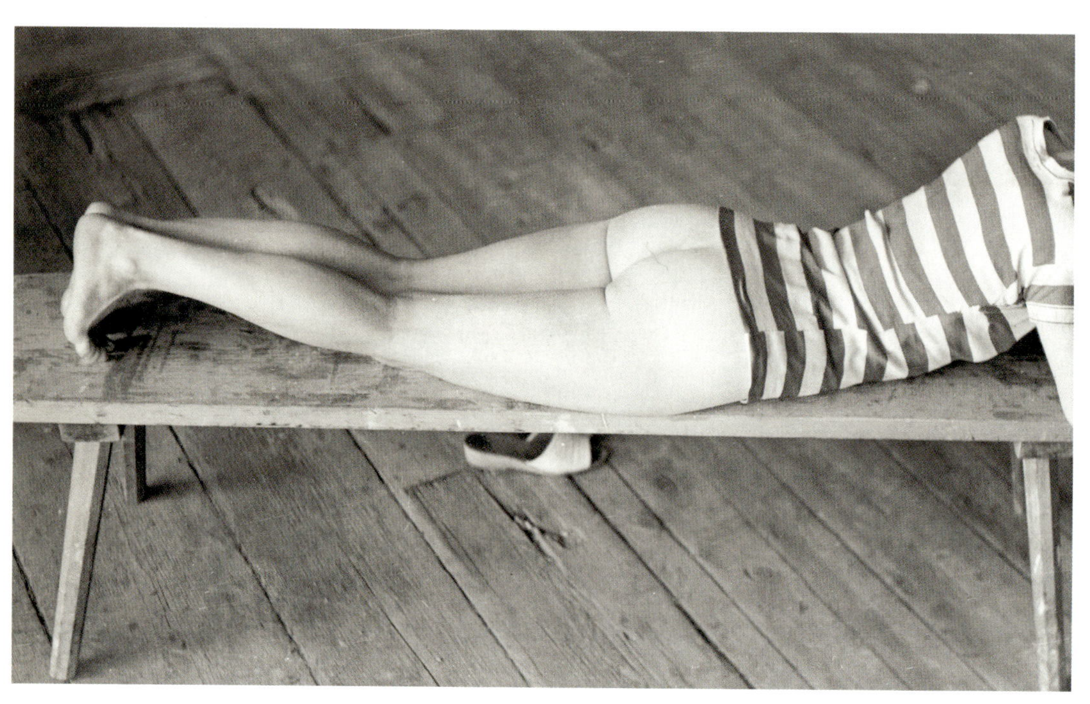

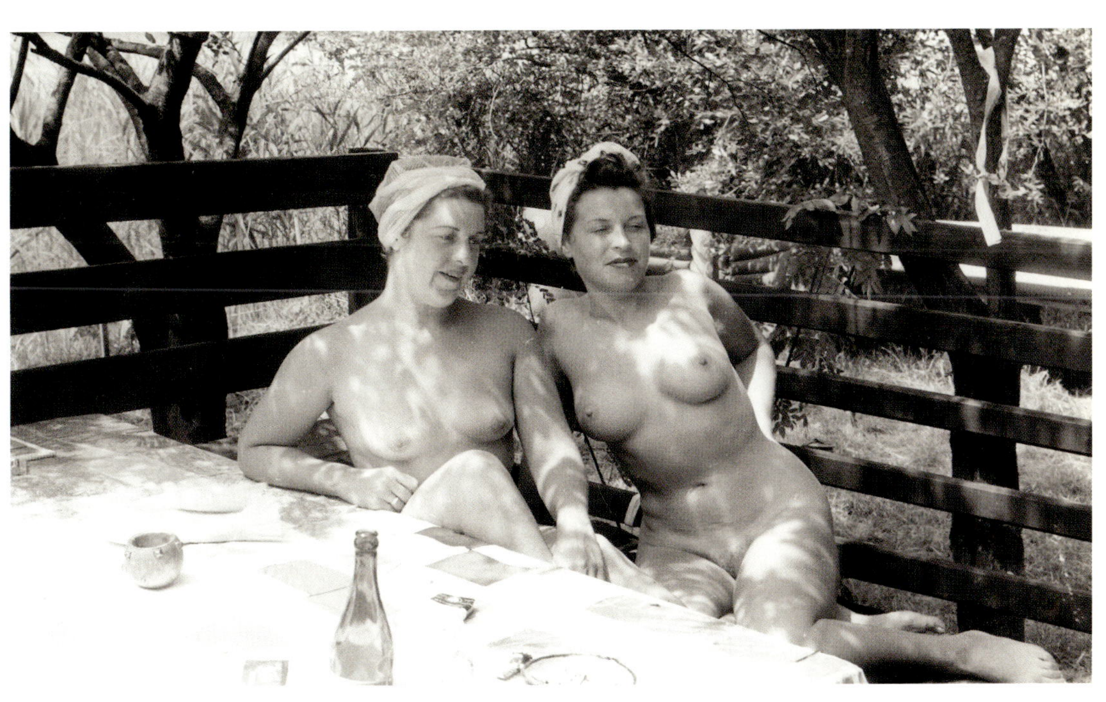

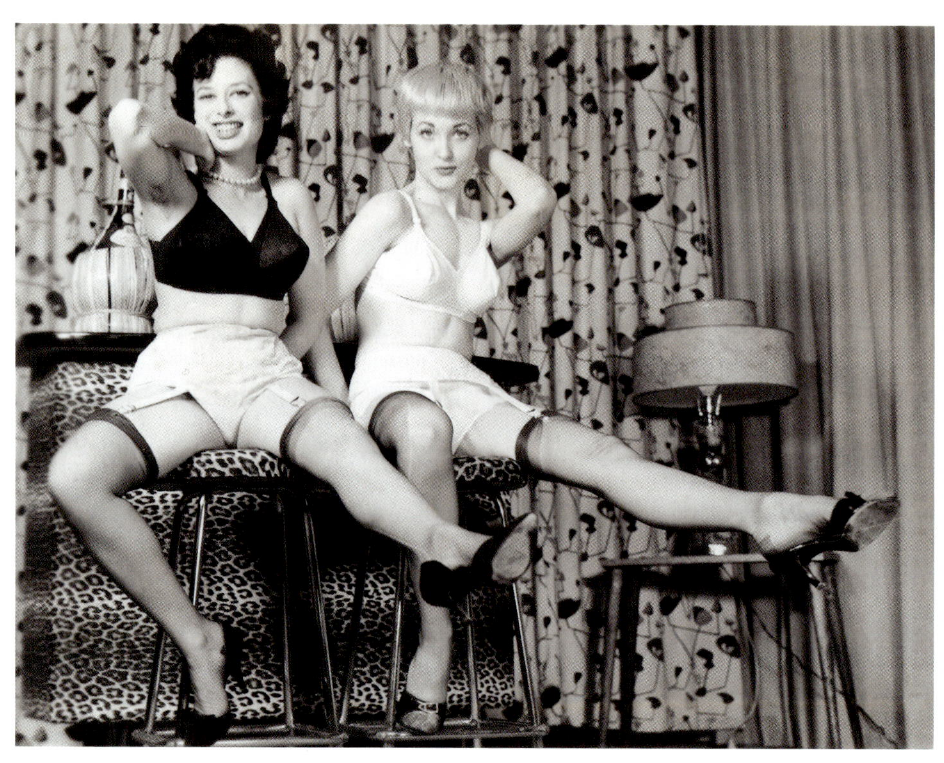

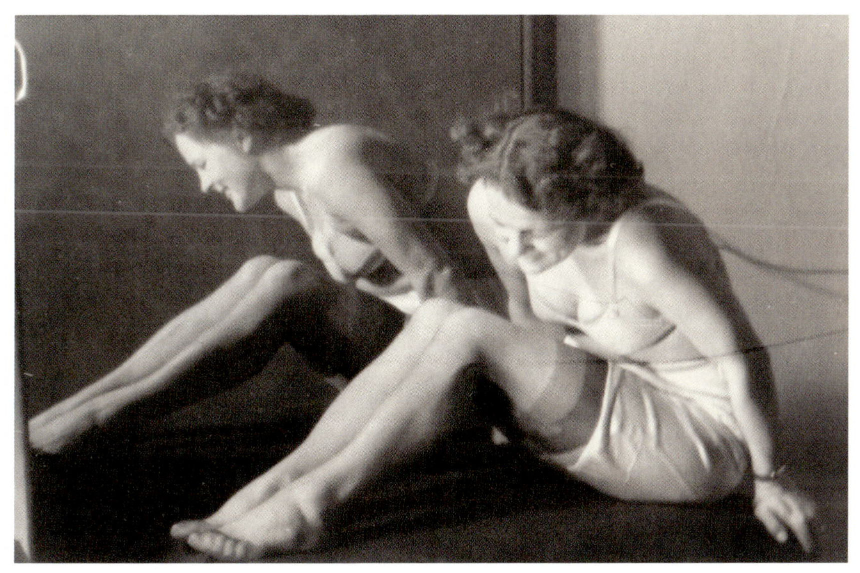

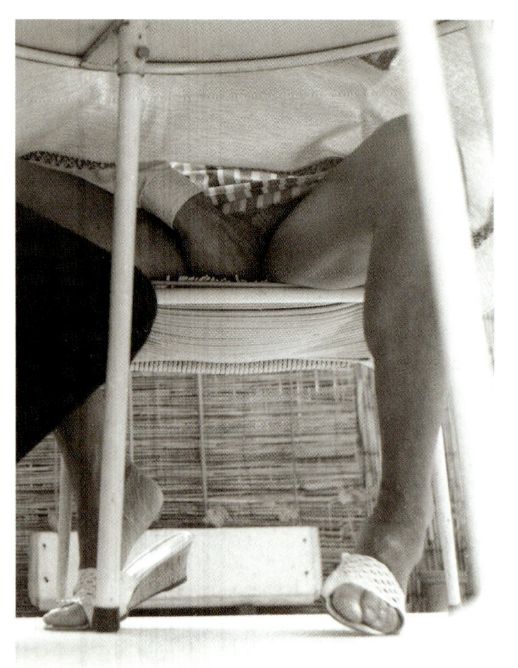

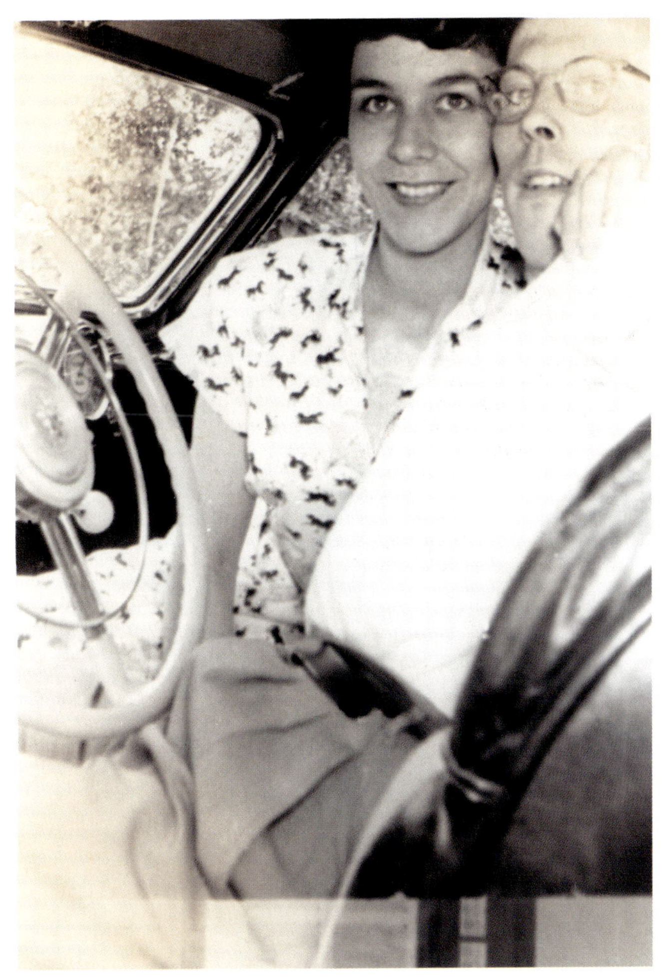

9)

Nature Natur

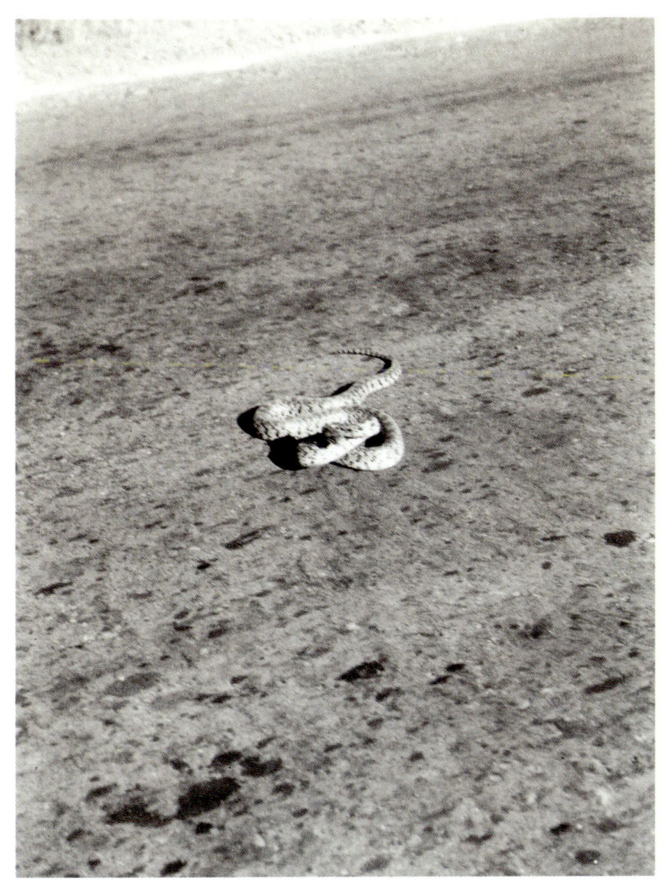

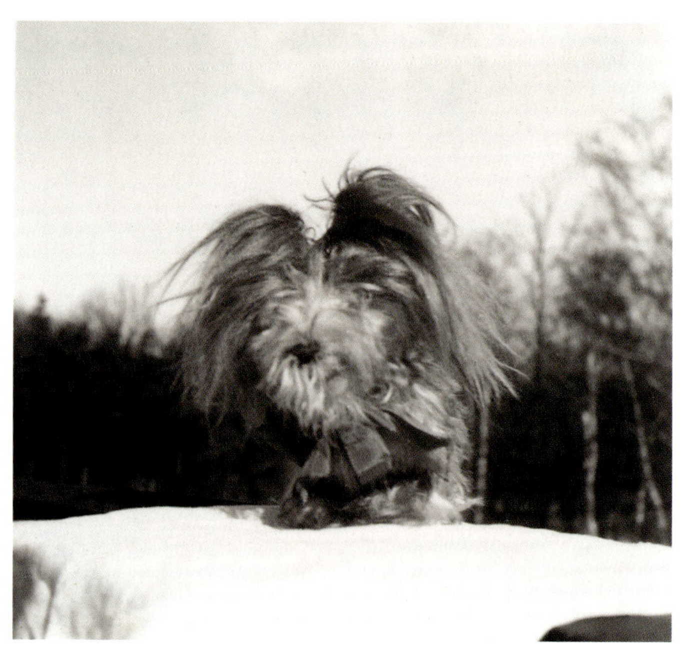

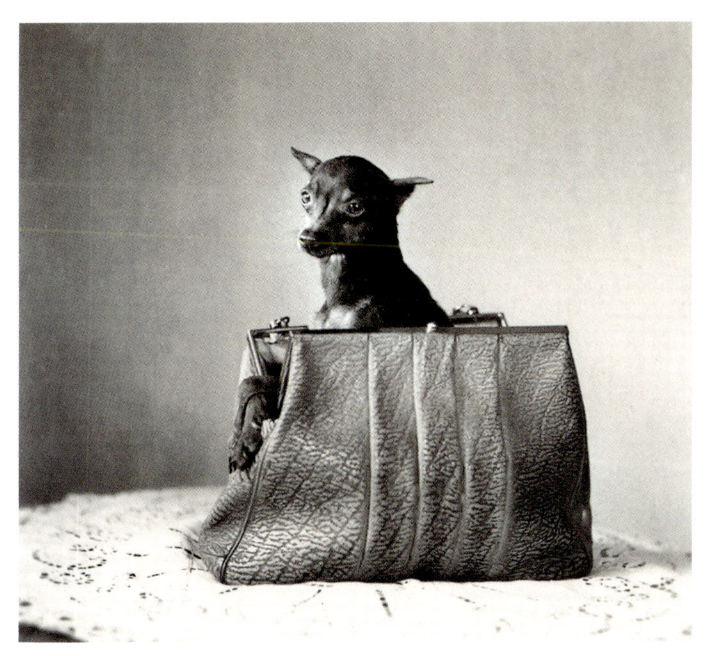

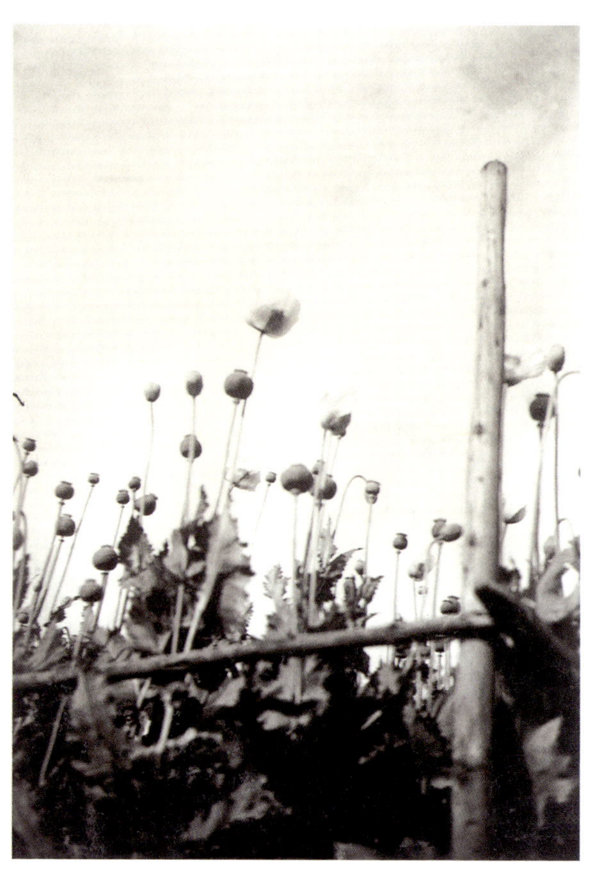

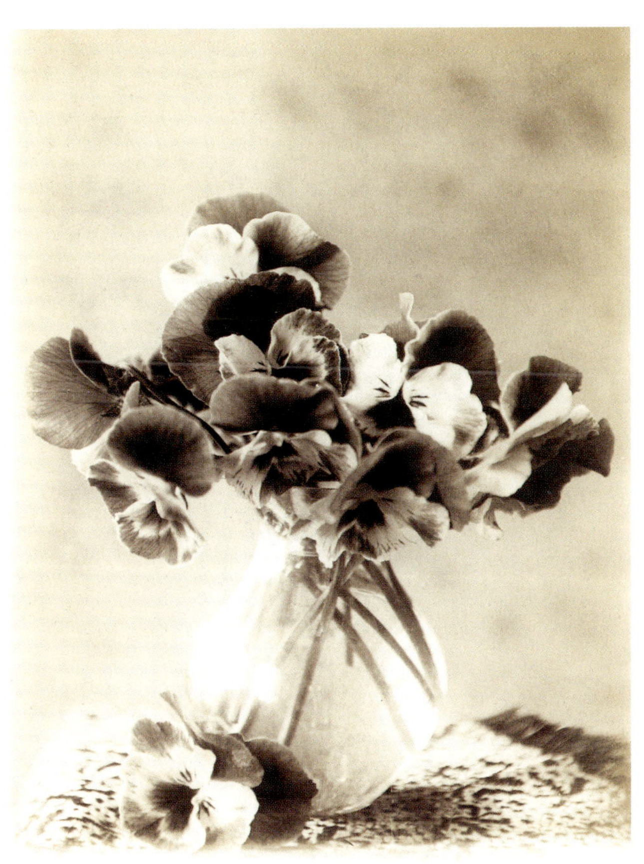

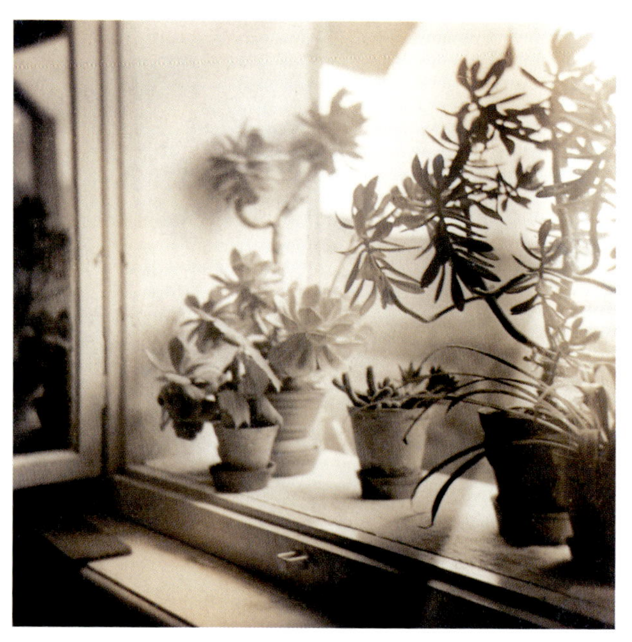

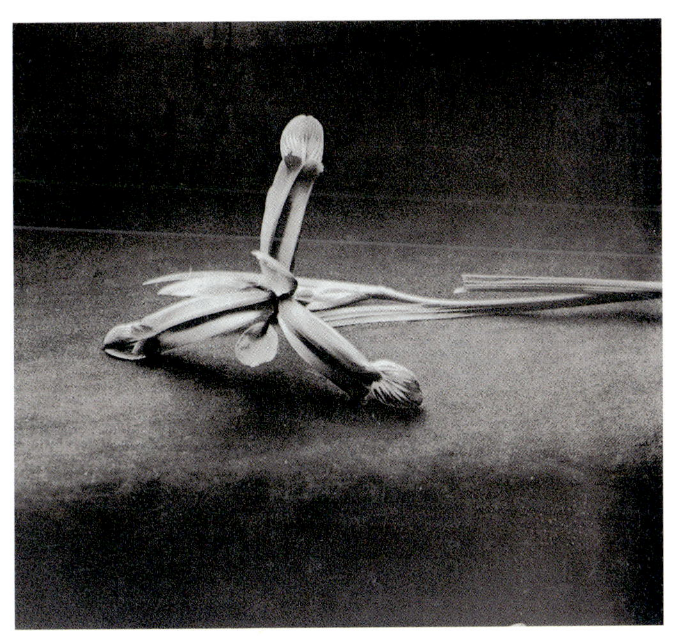

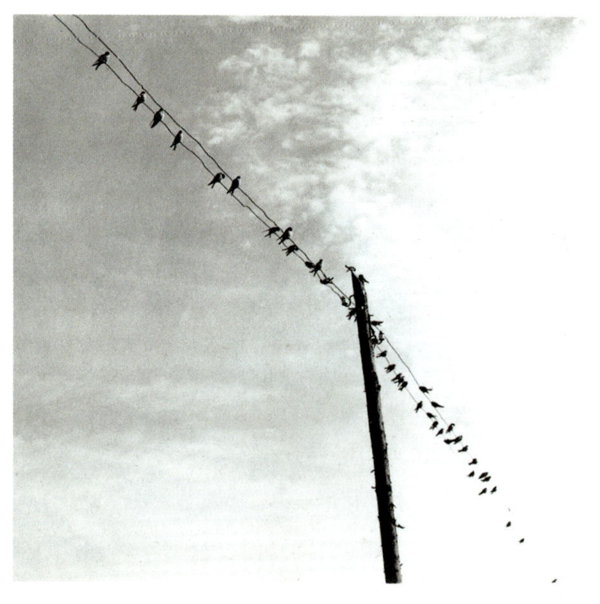

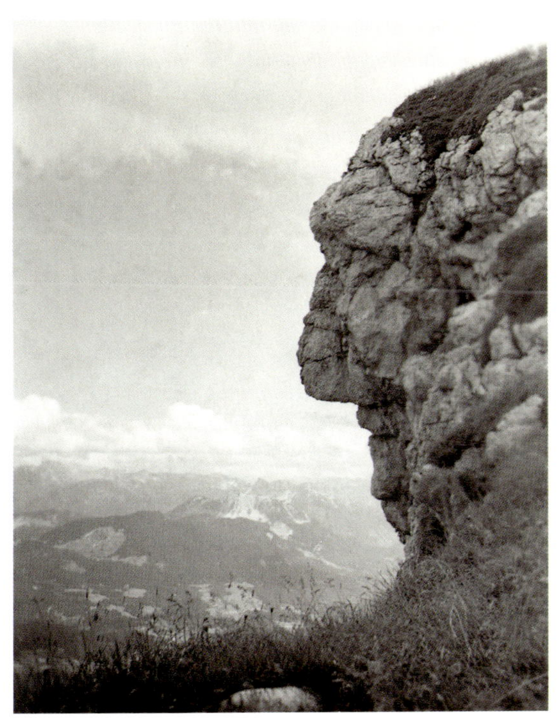

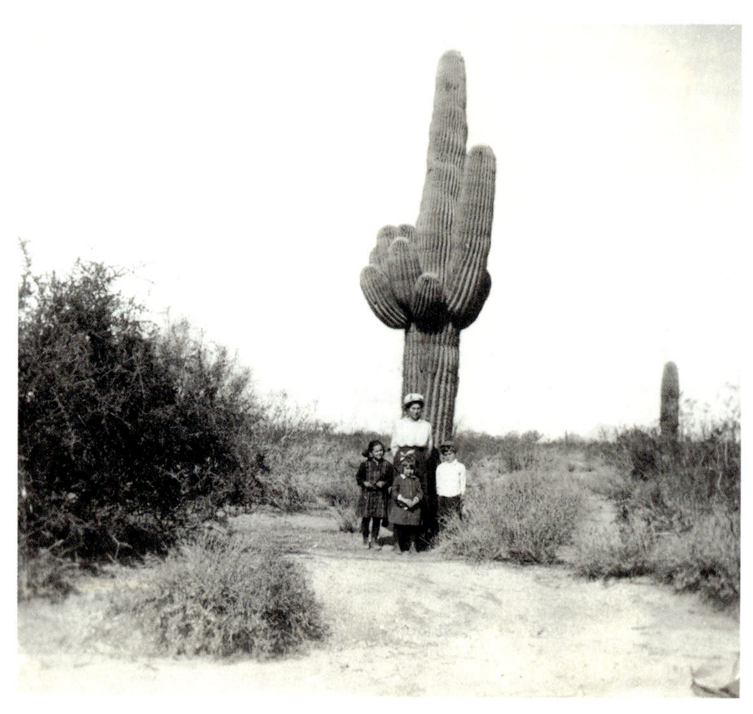

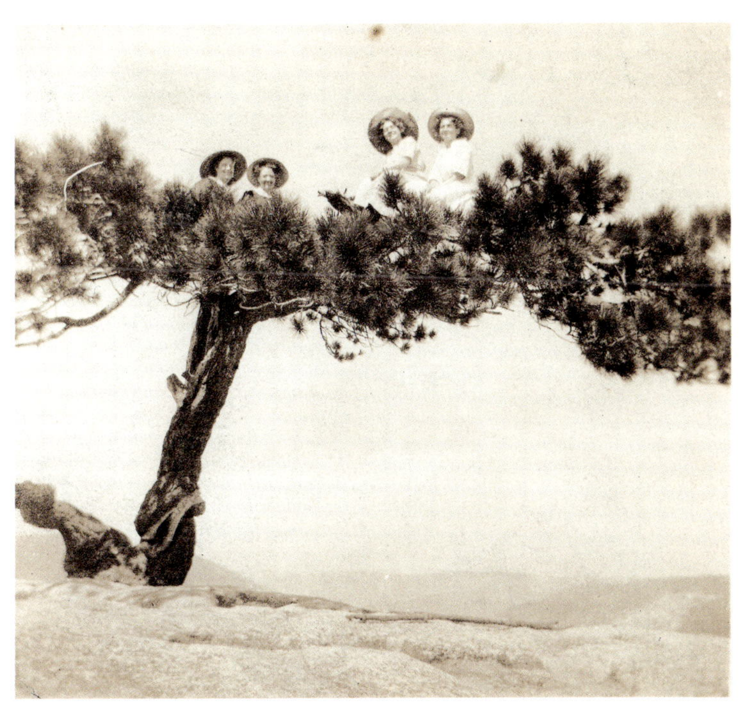

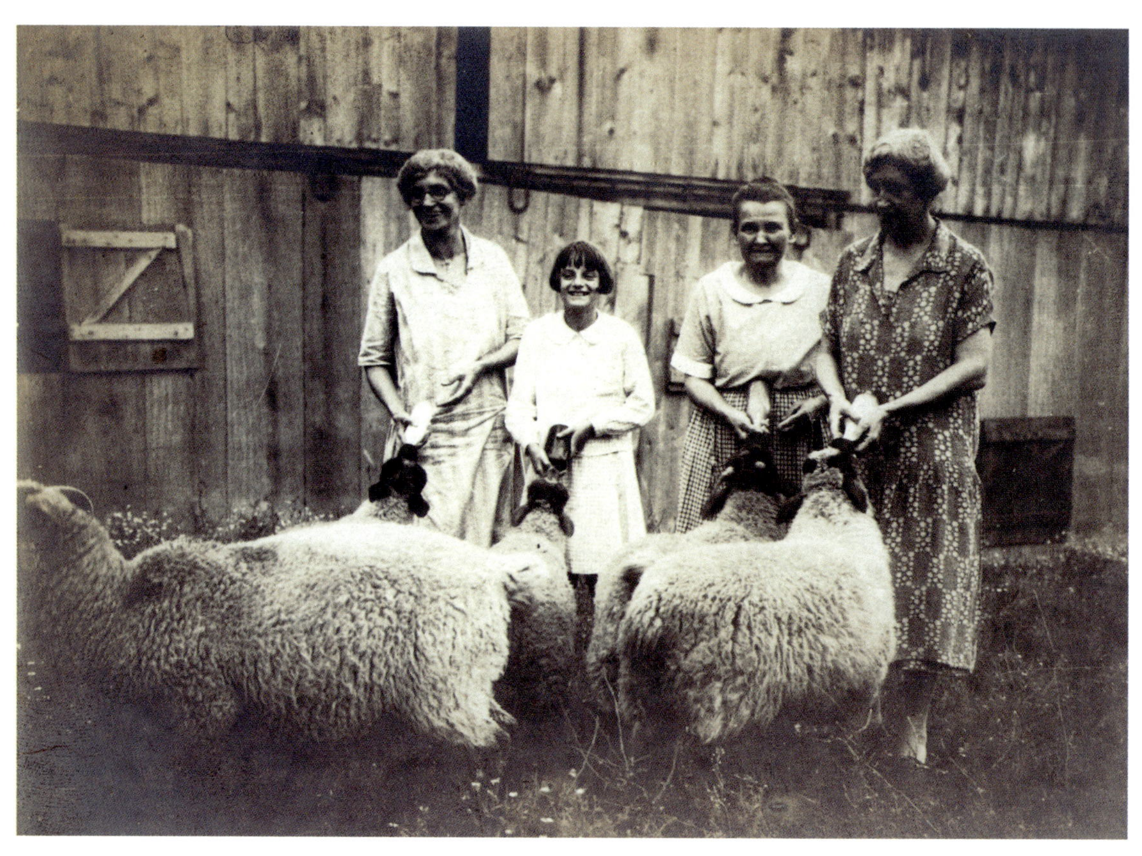

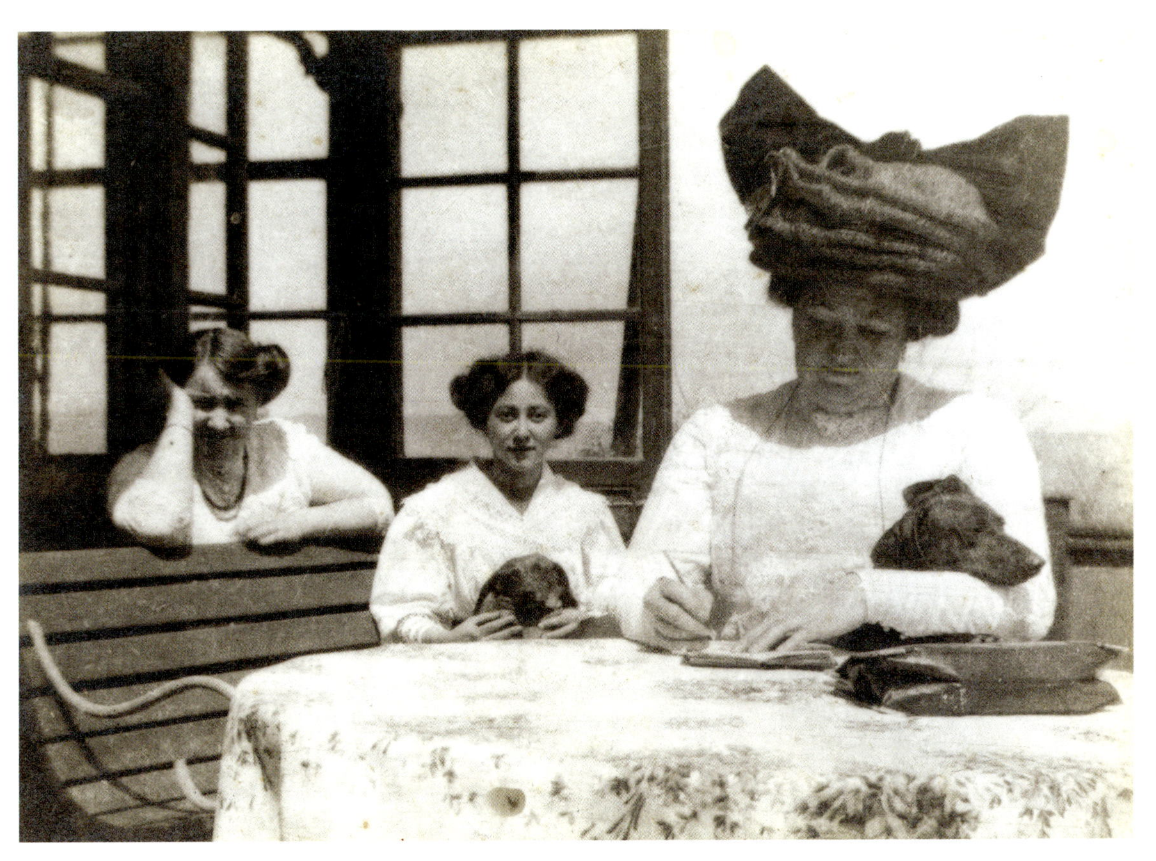

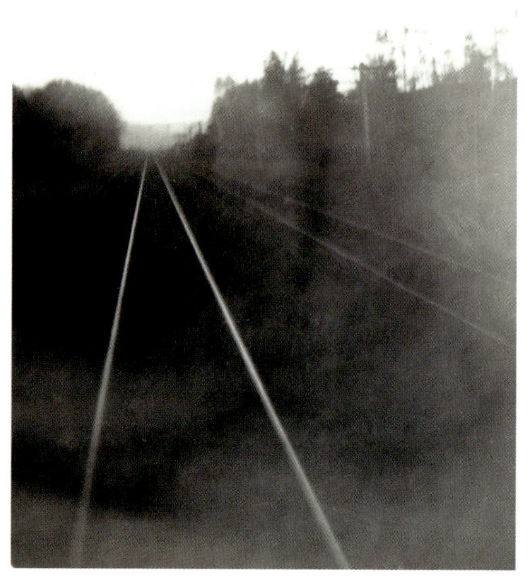

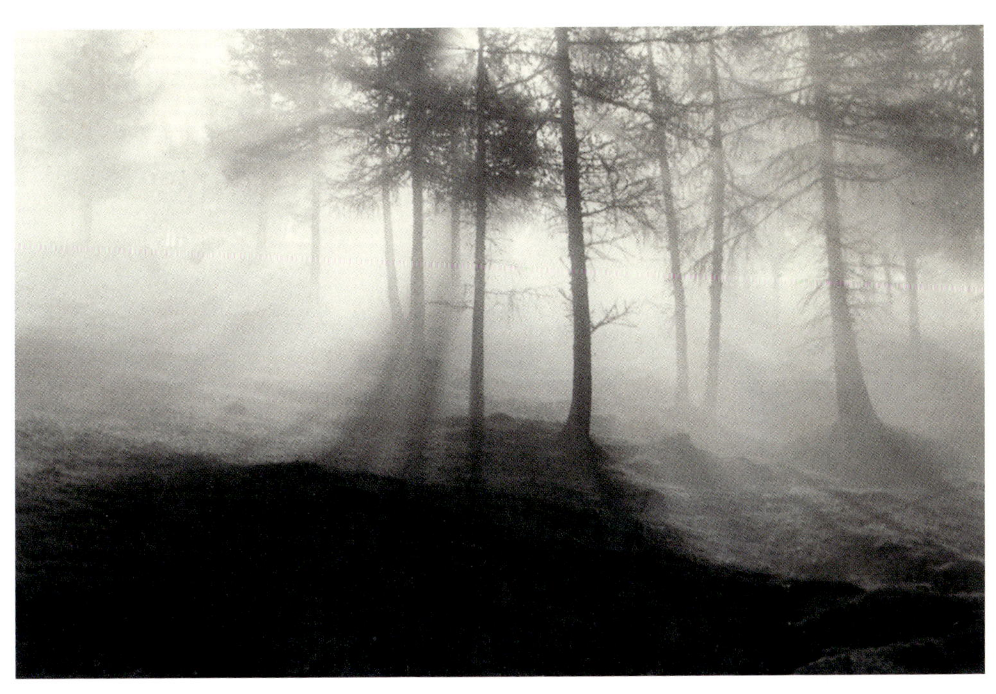

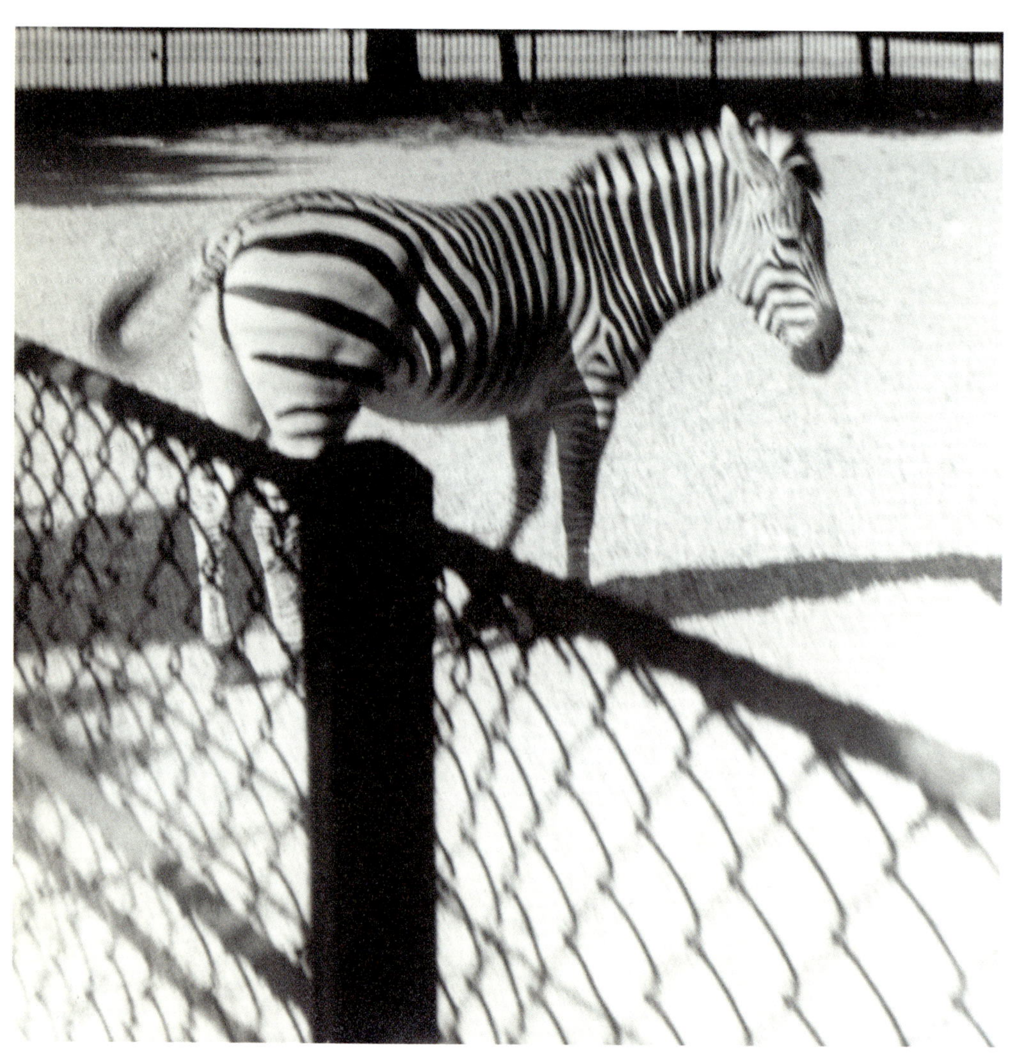

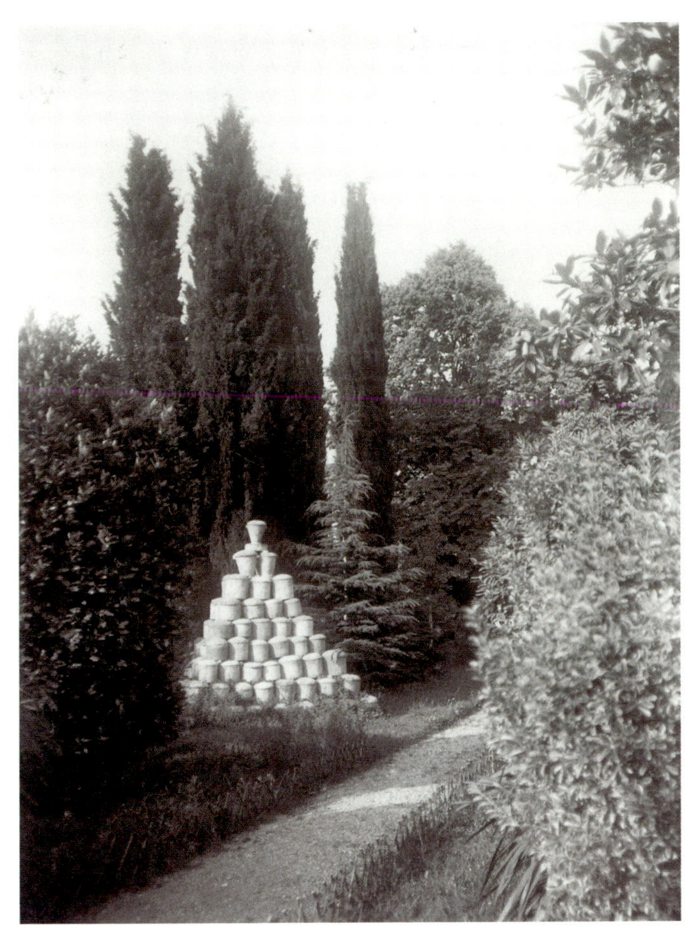

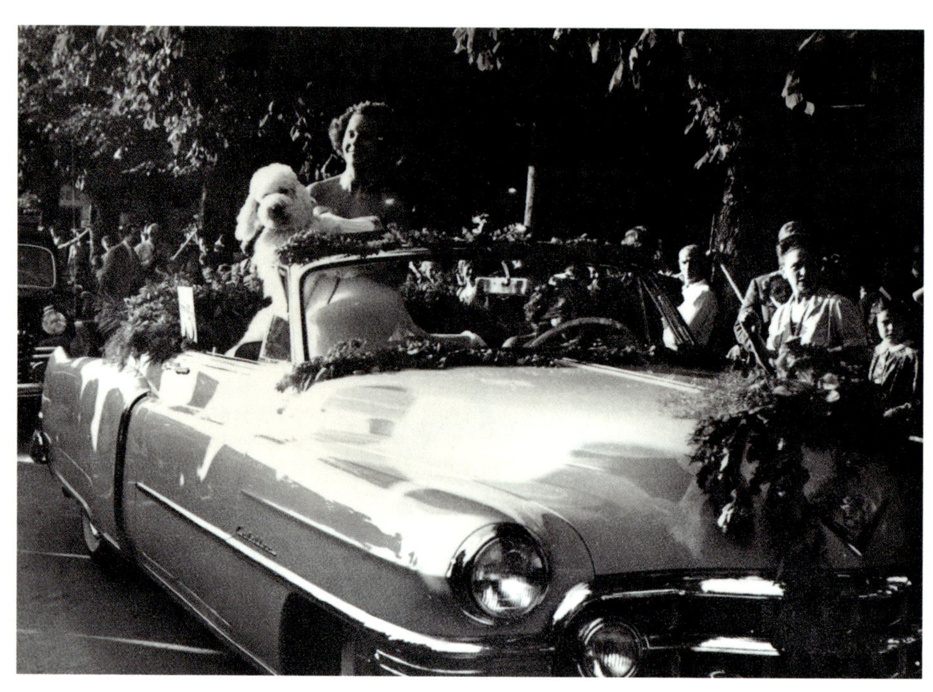

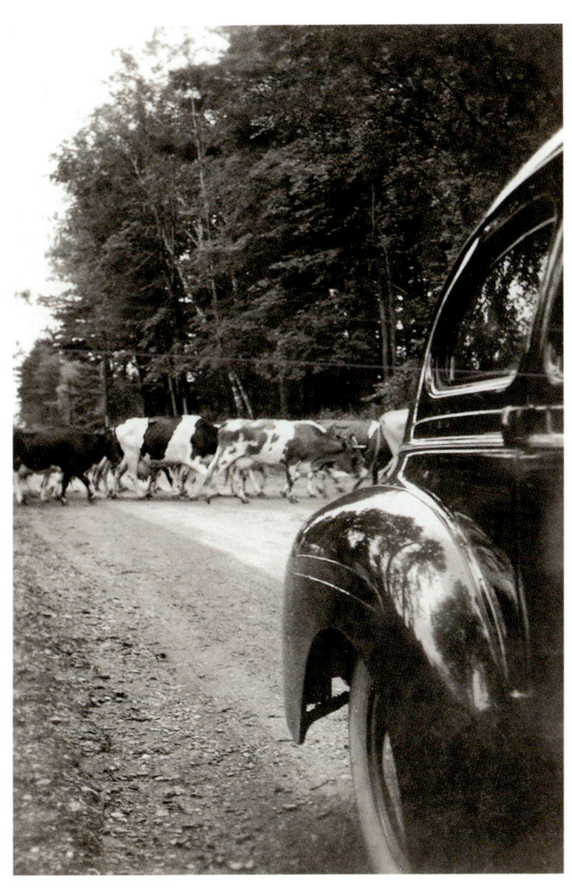

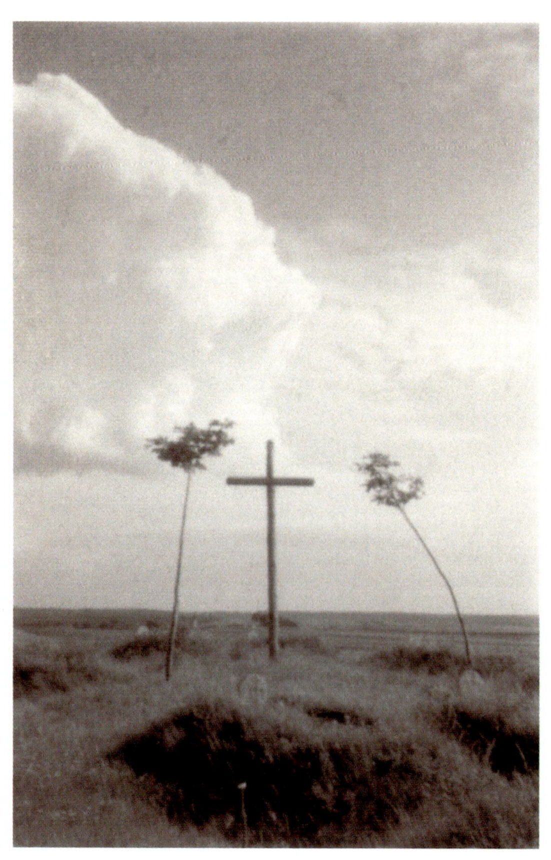

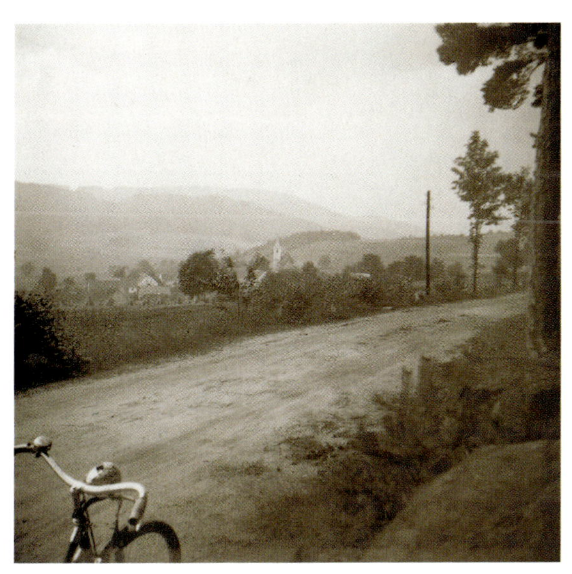

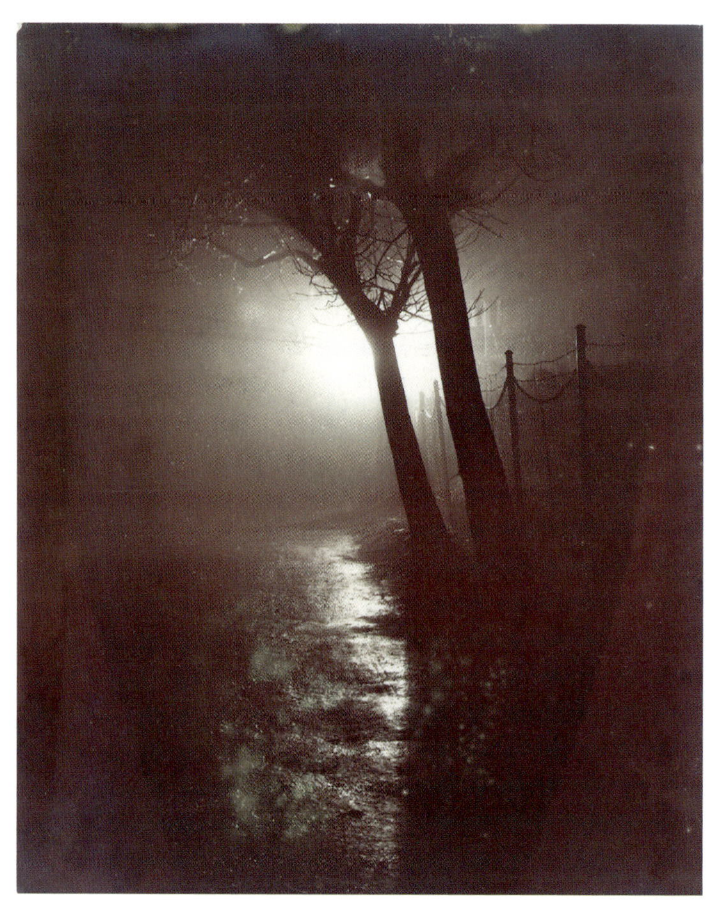

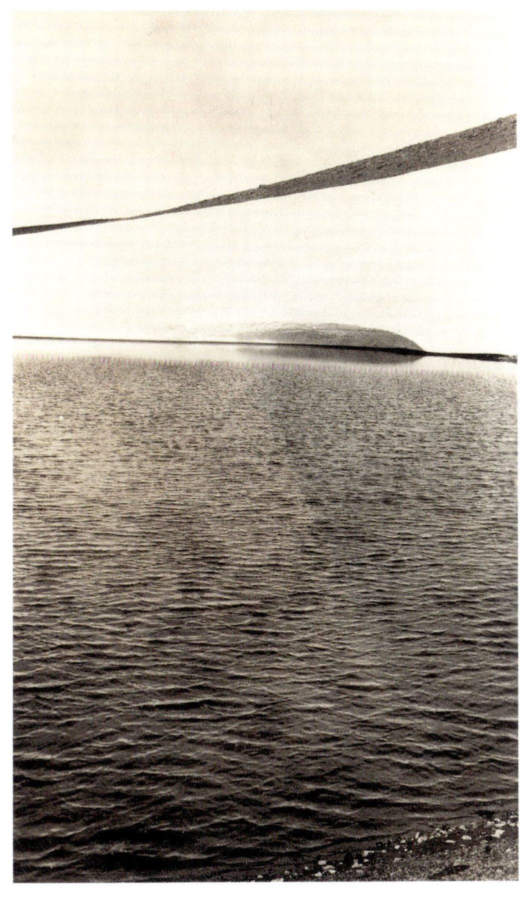

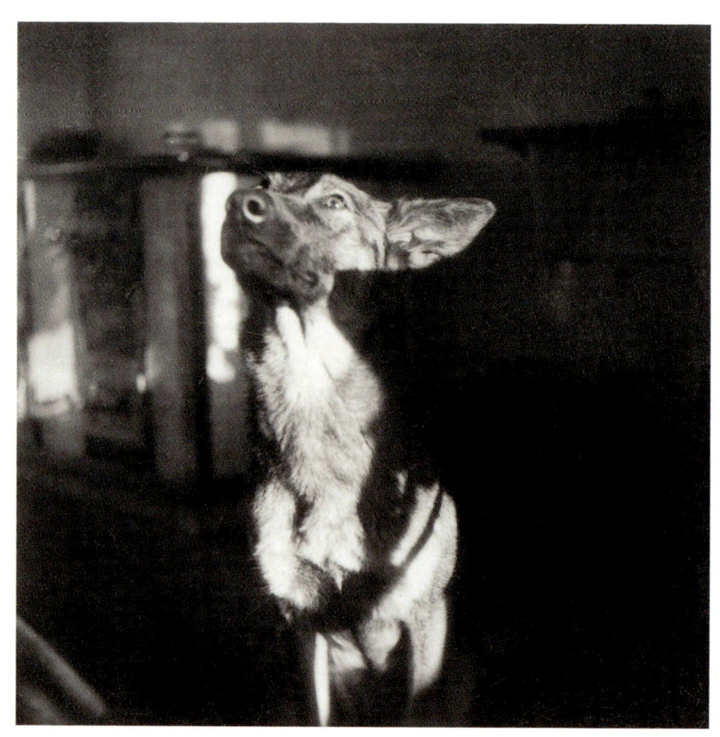

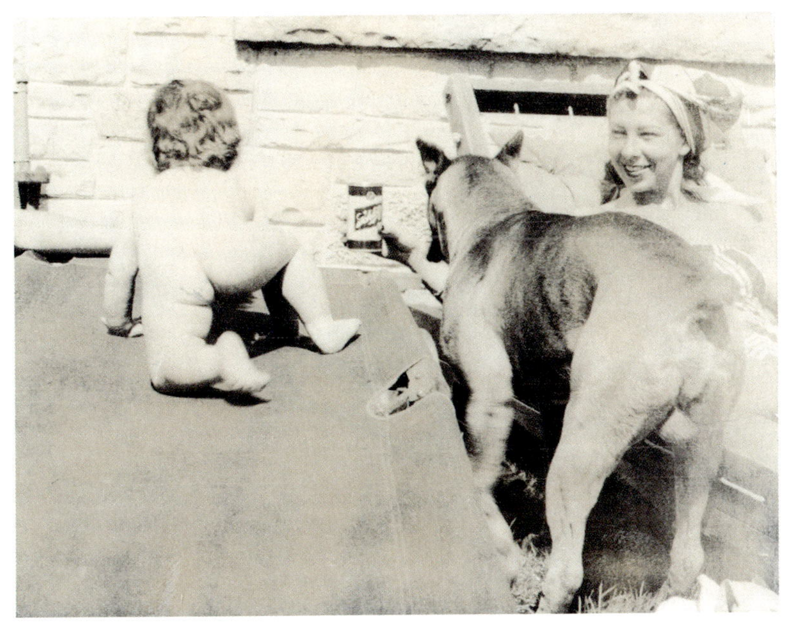

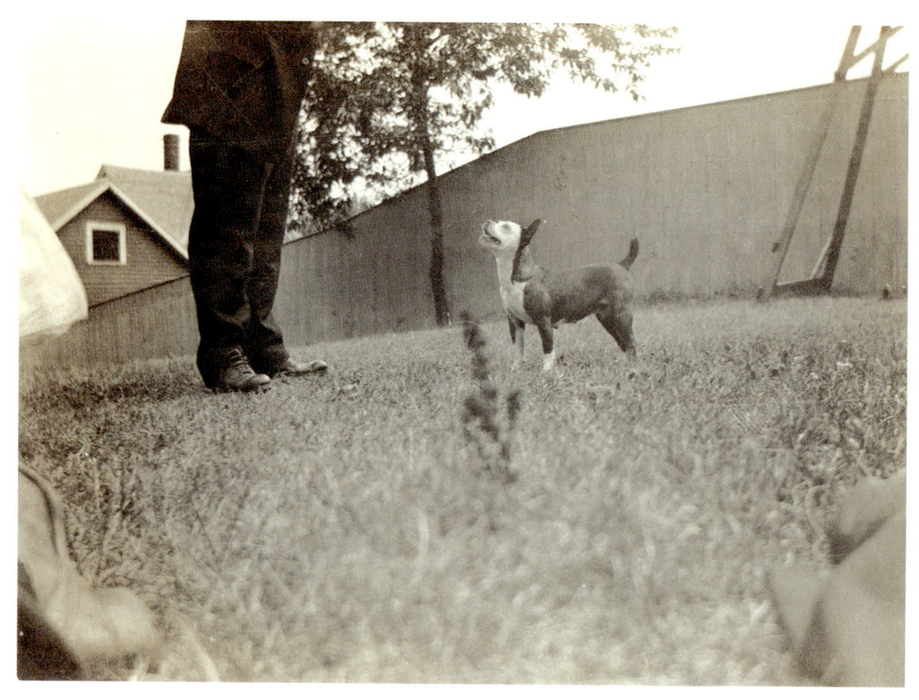

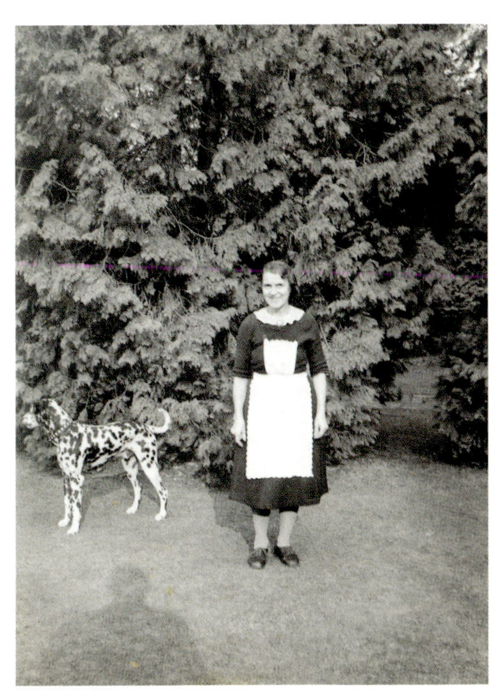

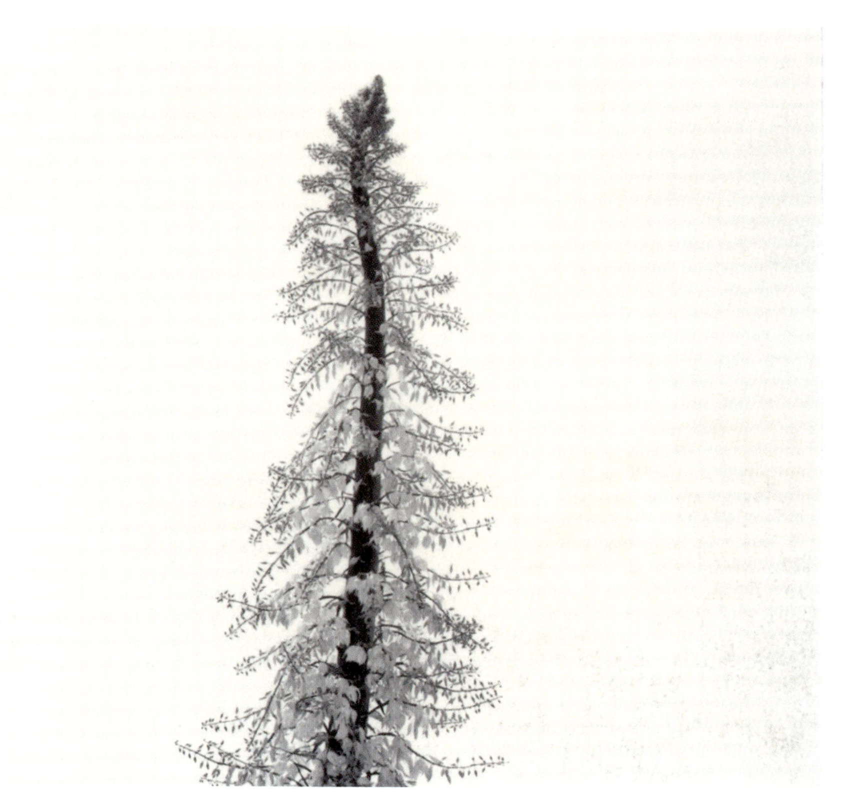

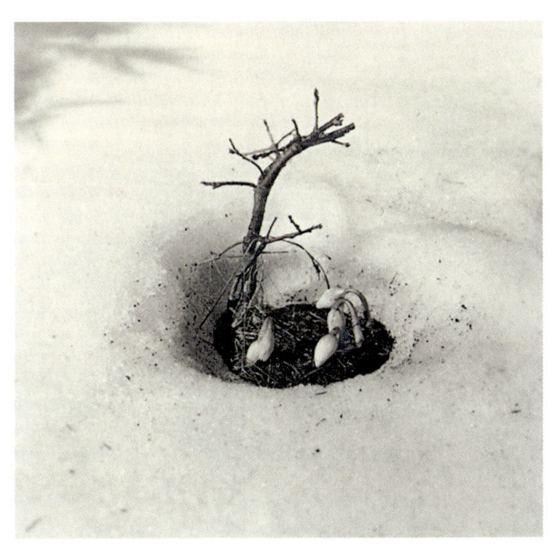

10)

Sports Sport

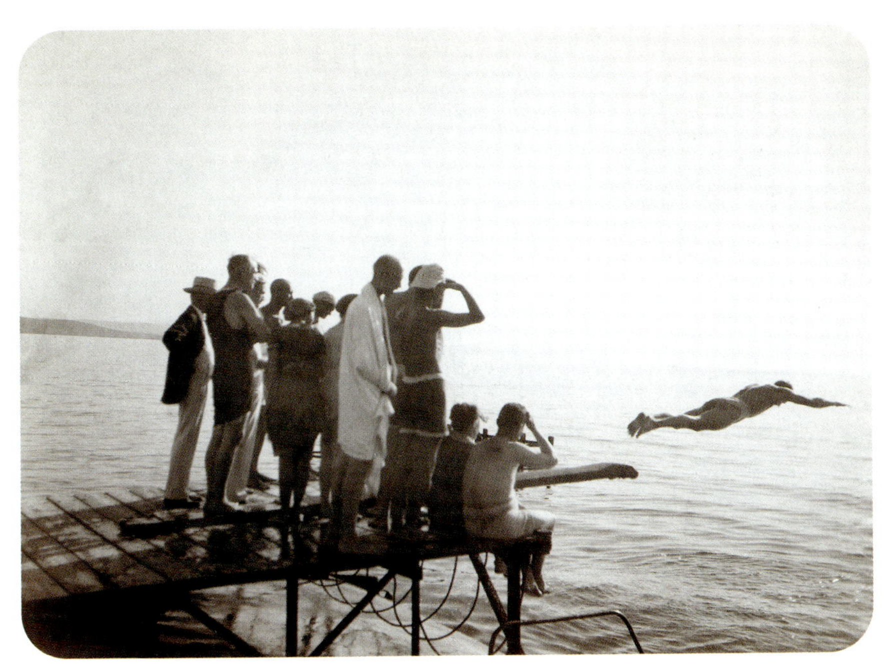

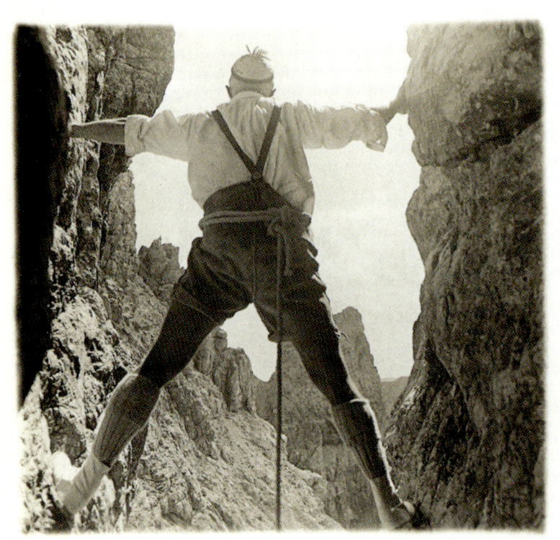
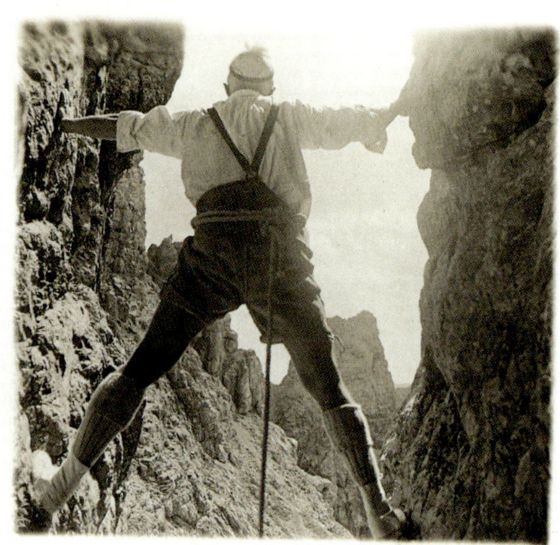

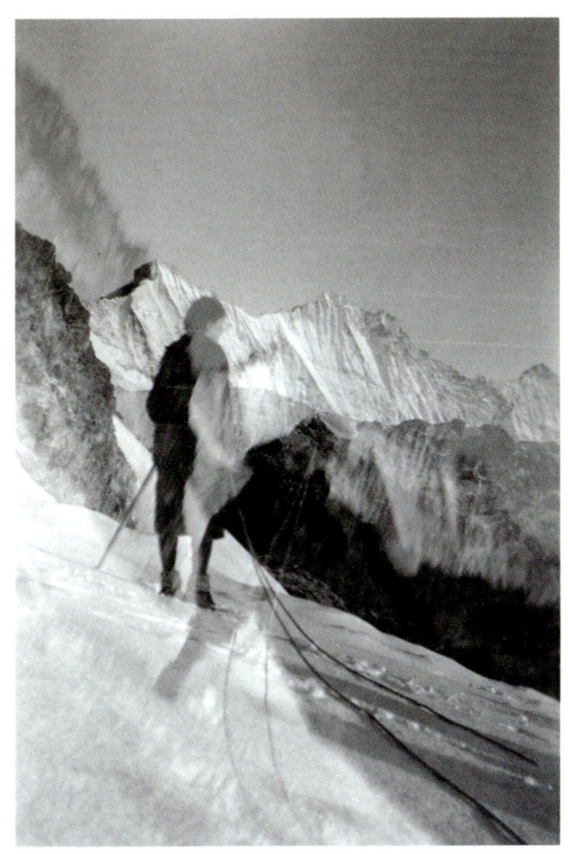

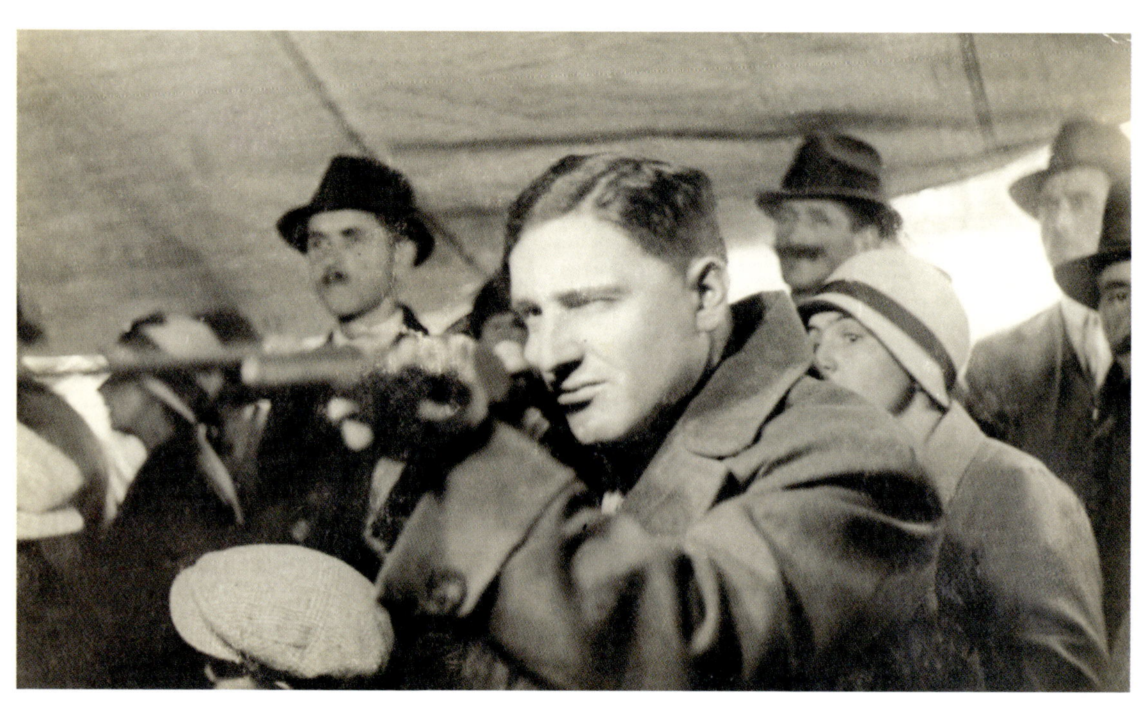

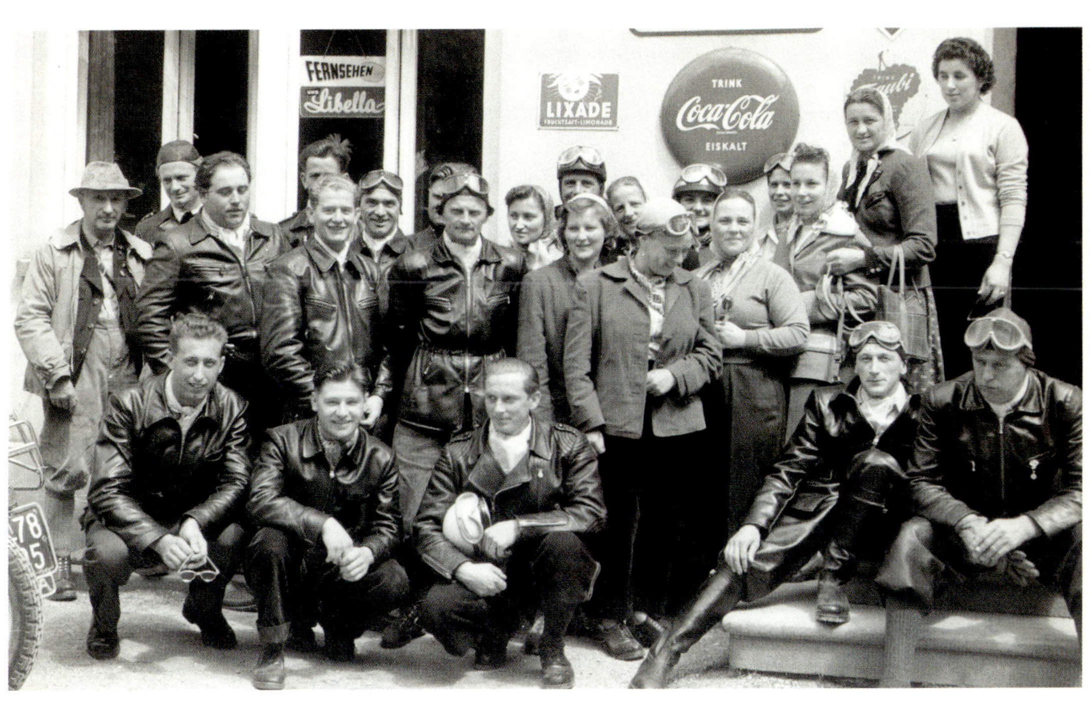
FERNSEHEN
Libella
LIXADE
TRINK
Coca-Cola
EISKALT

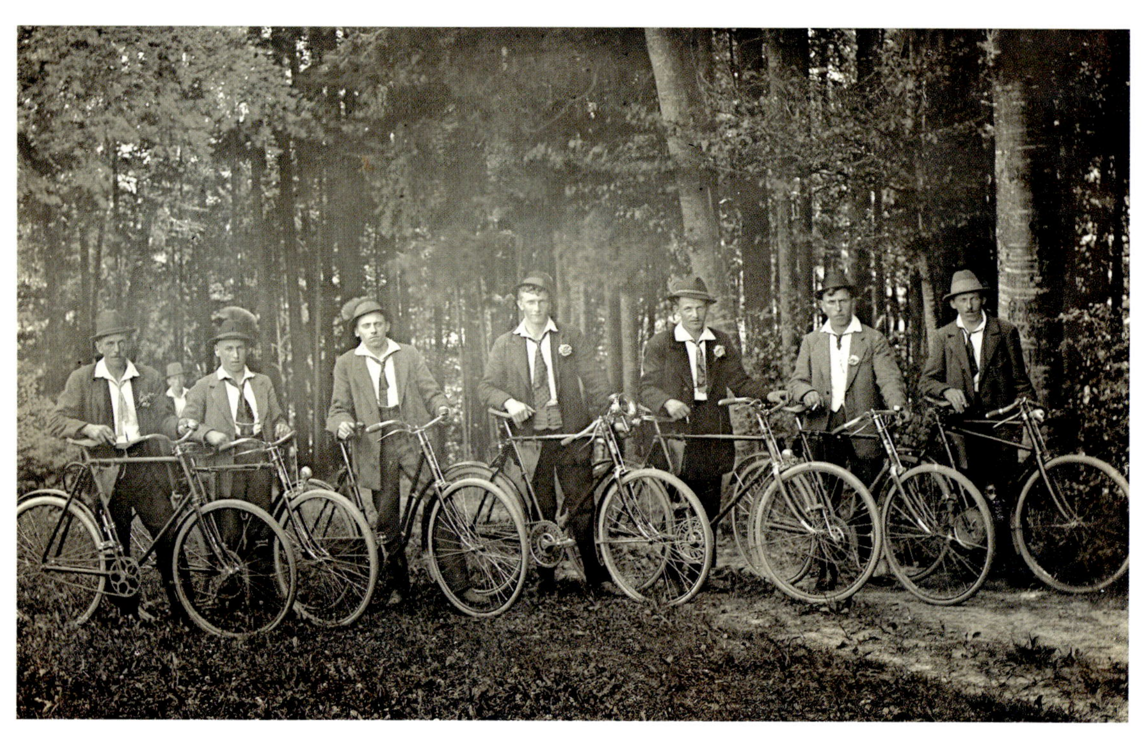

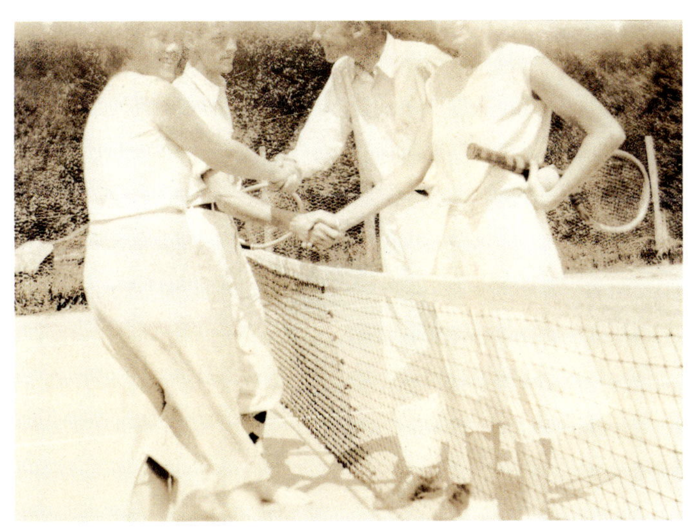

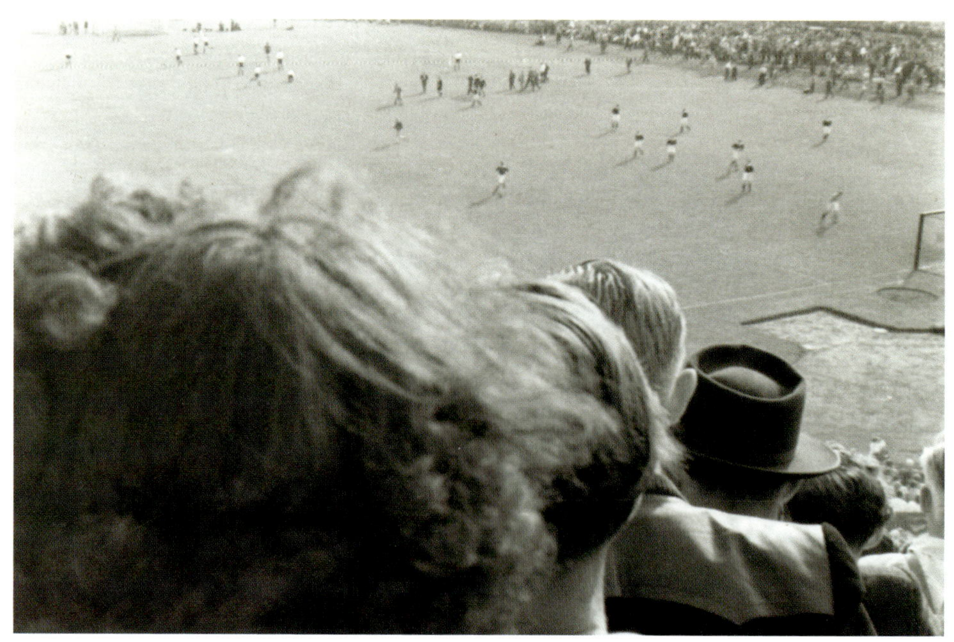

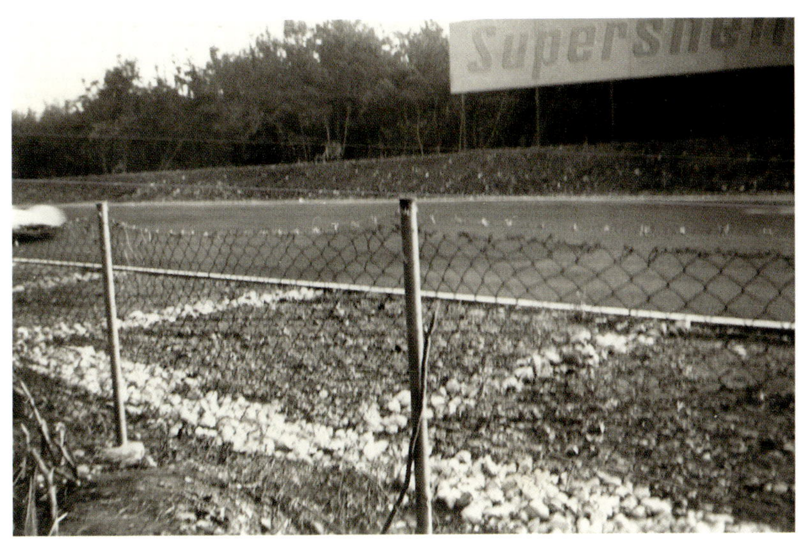
Supersh

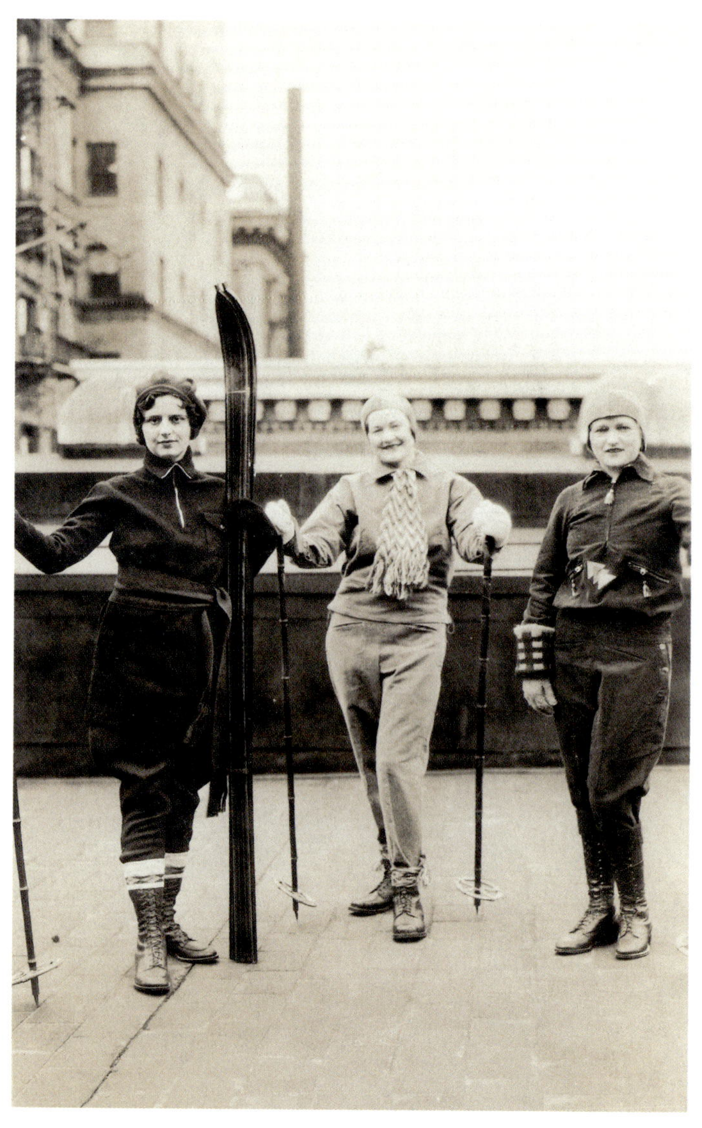

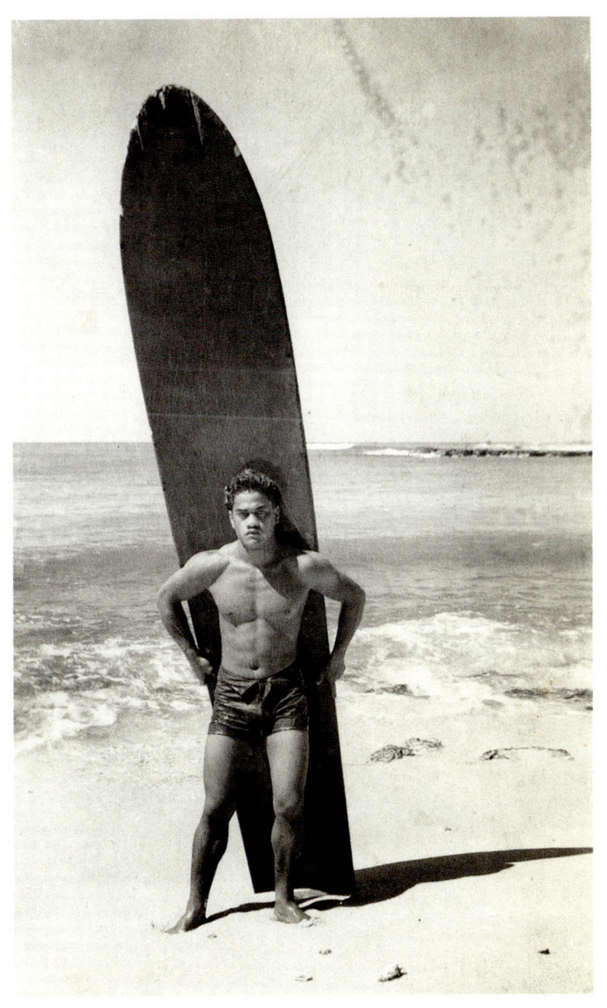

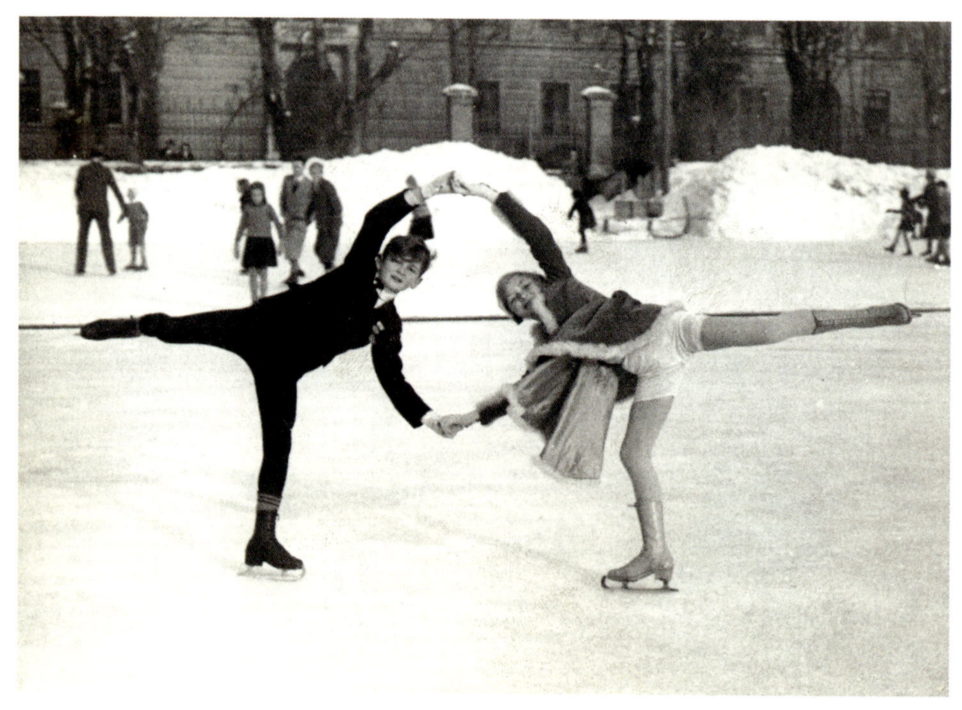

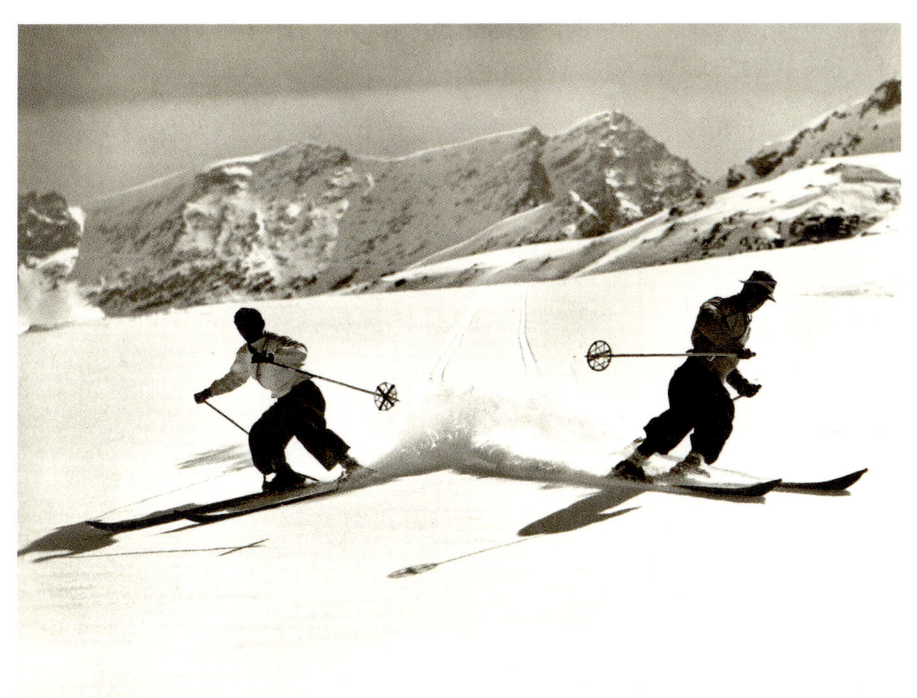

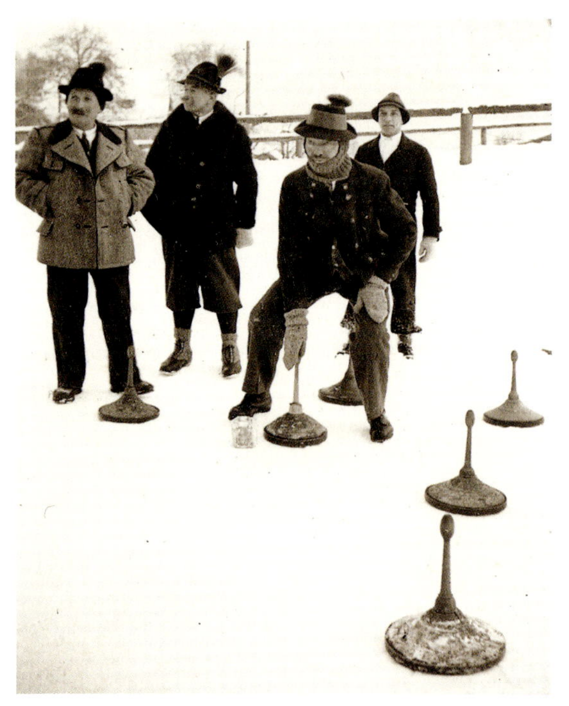

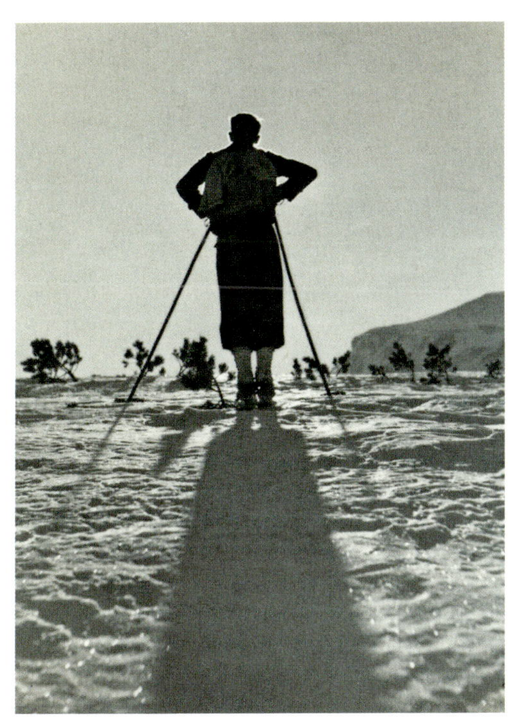

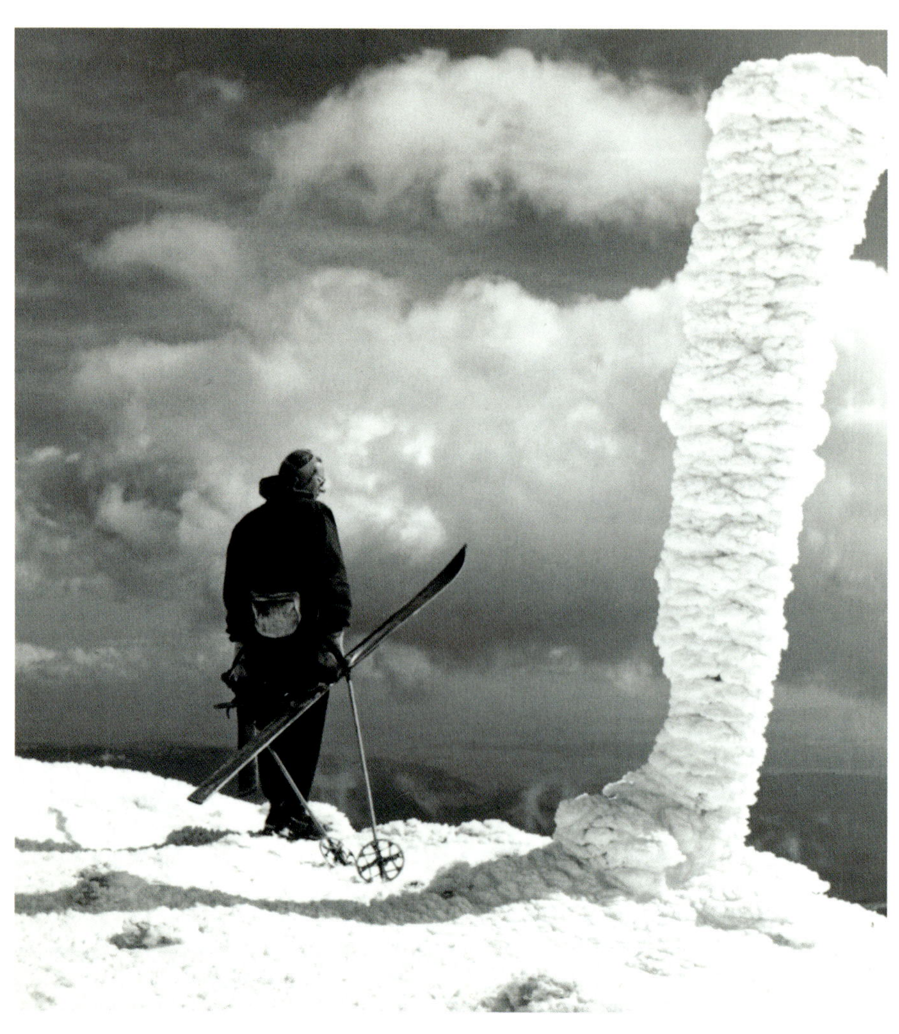

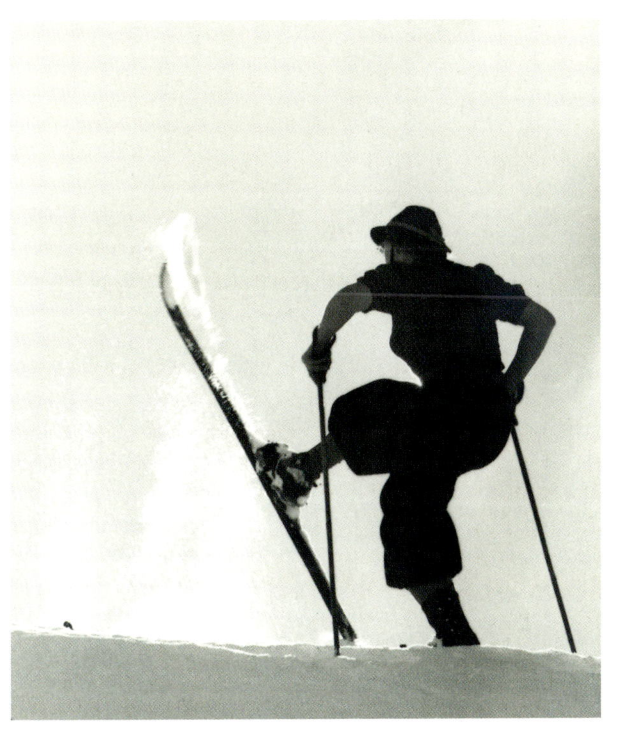

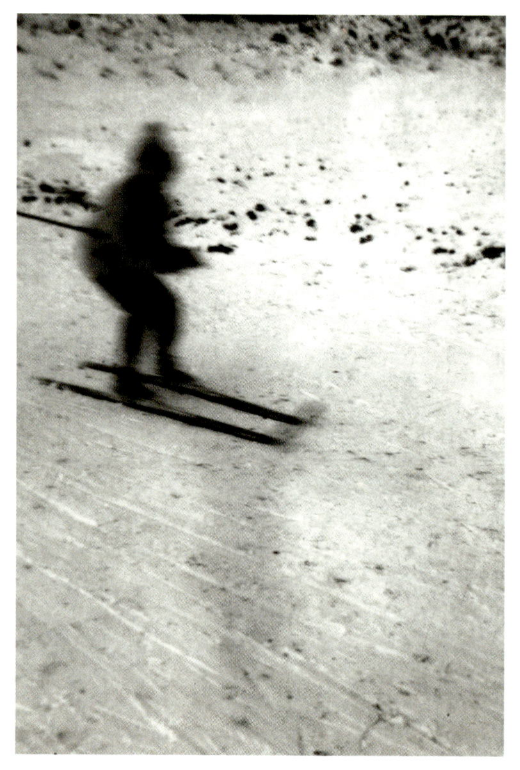

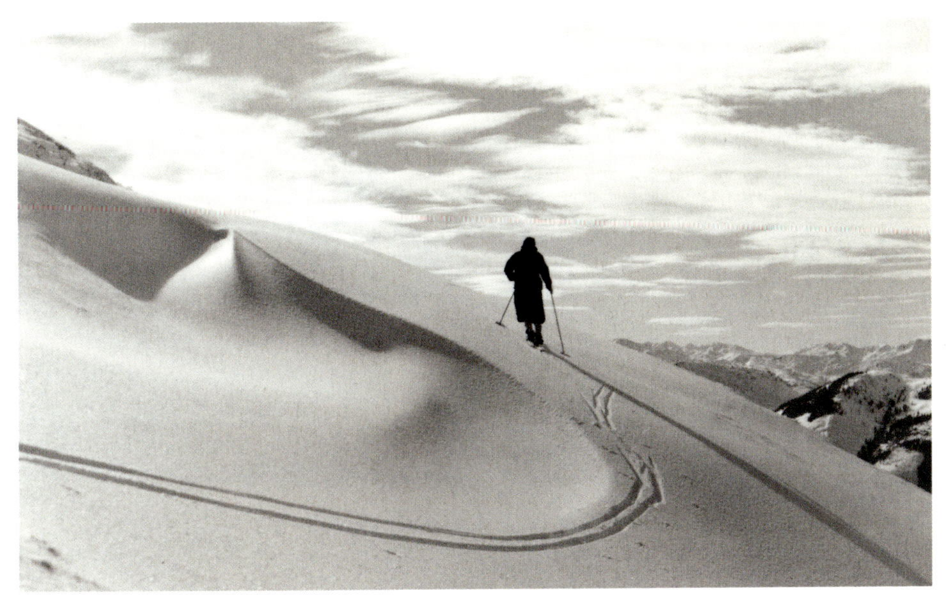

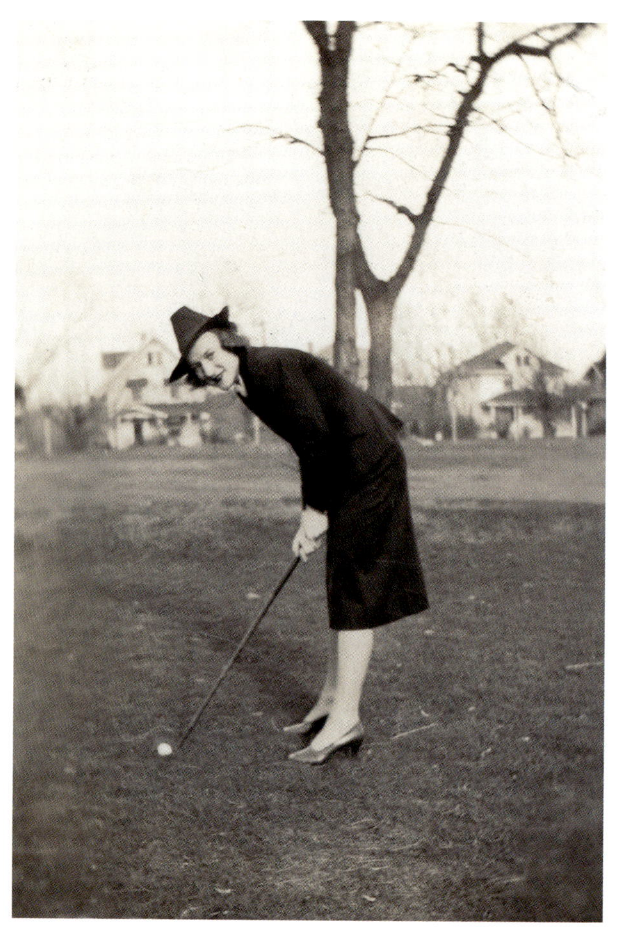

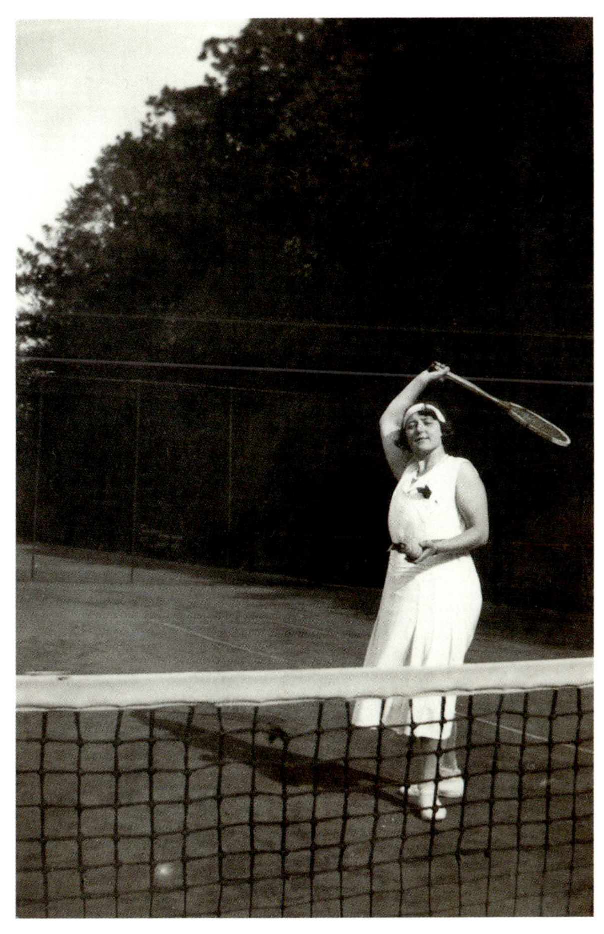

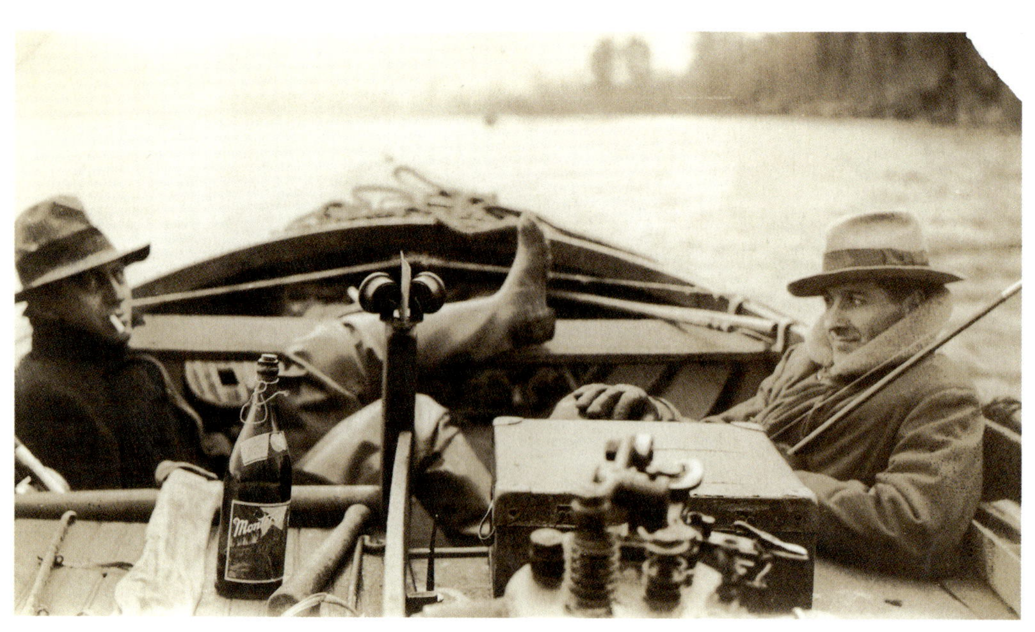

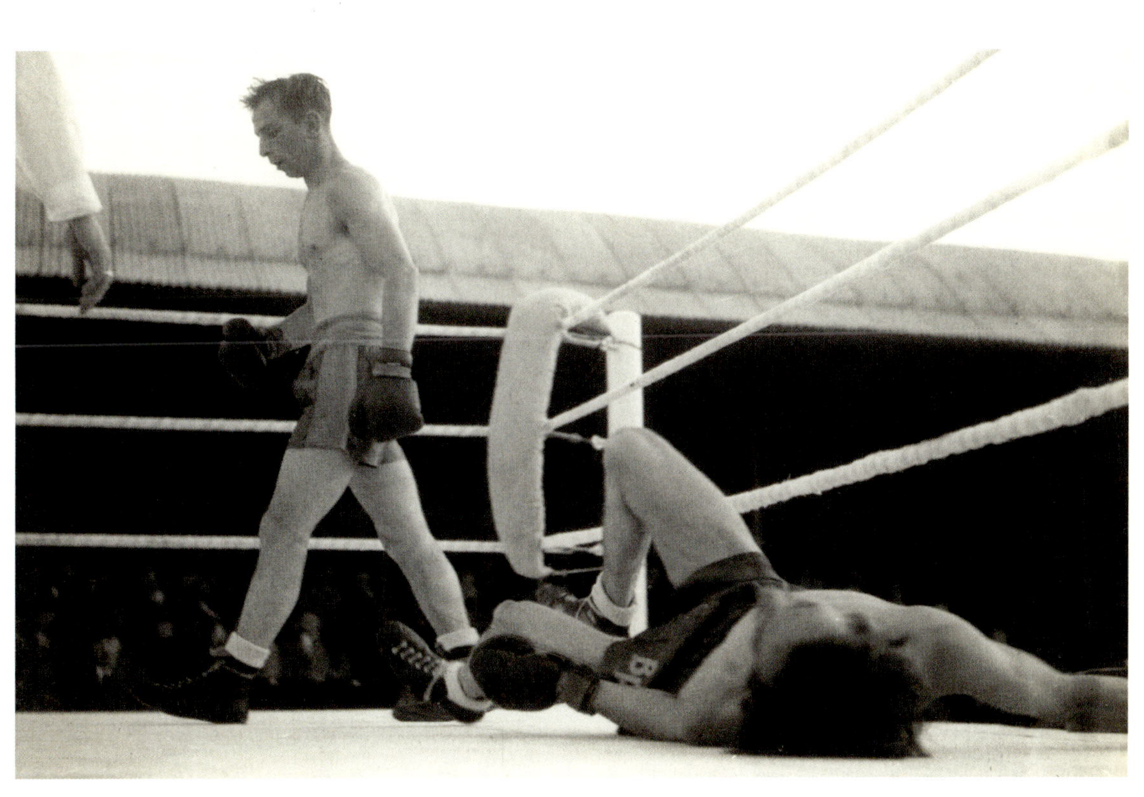

11)

Travels Reisen

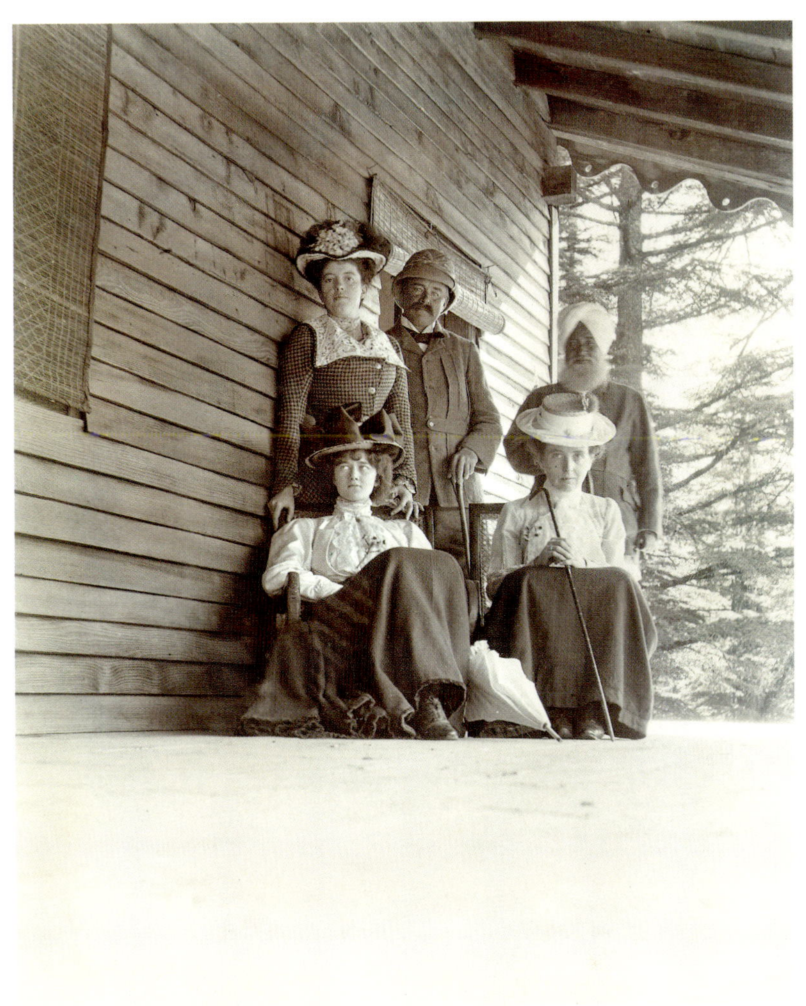

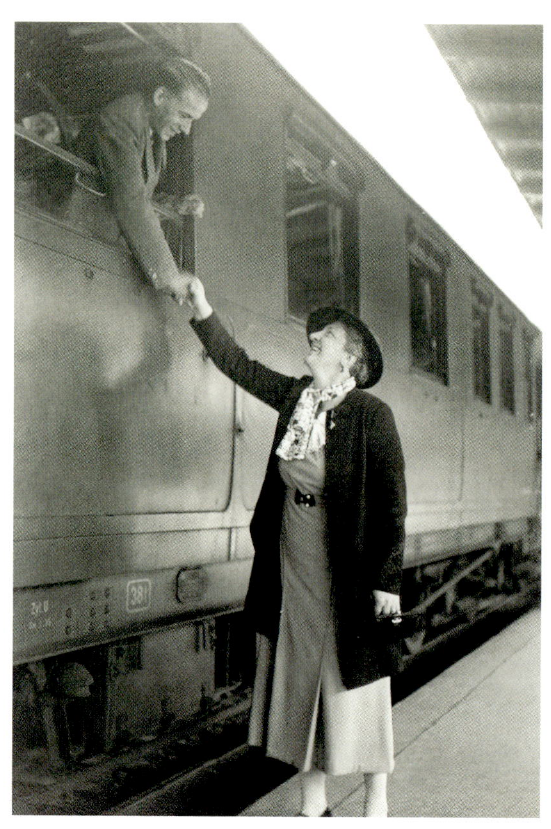

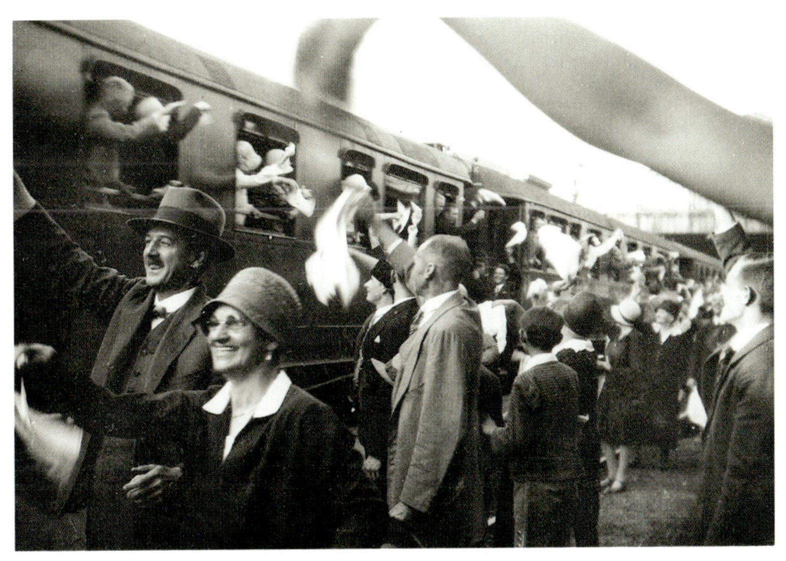

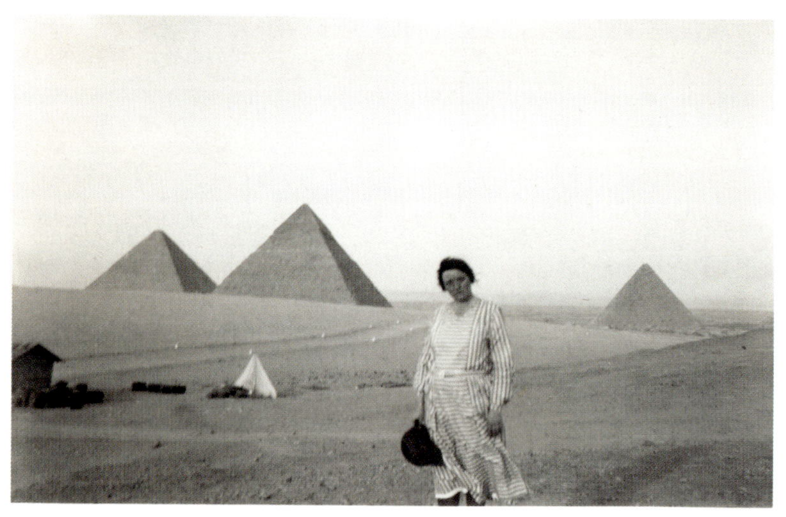

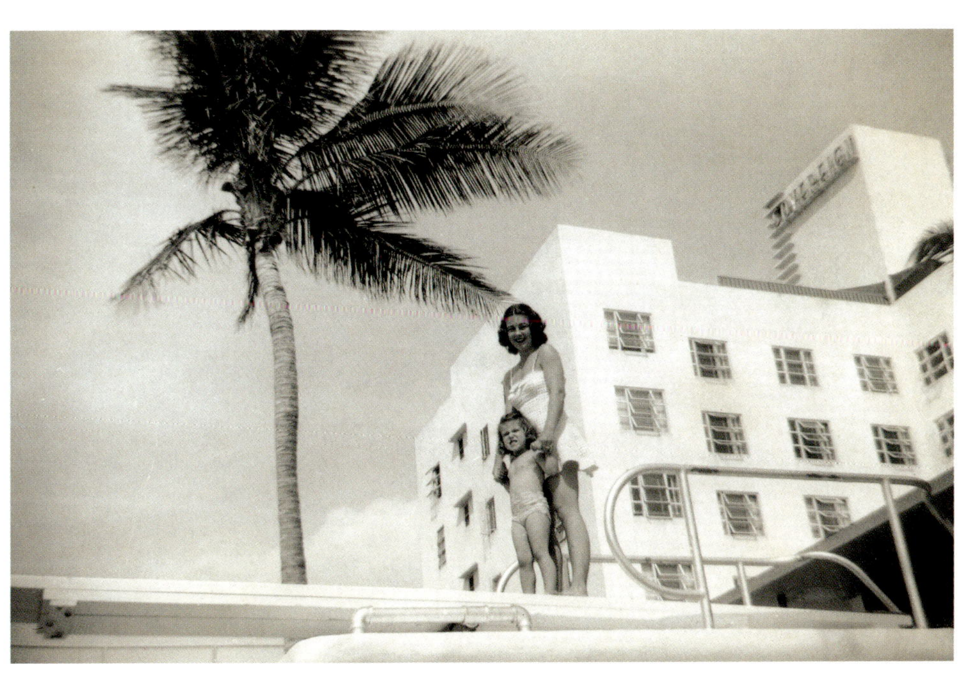

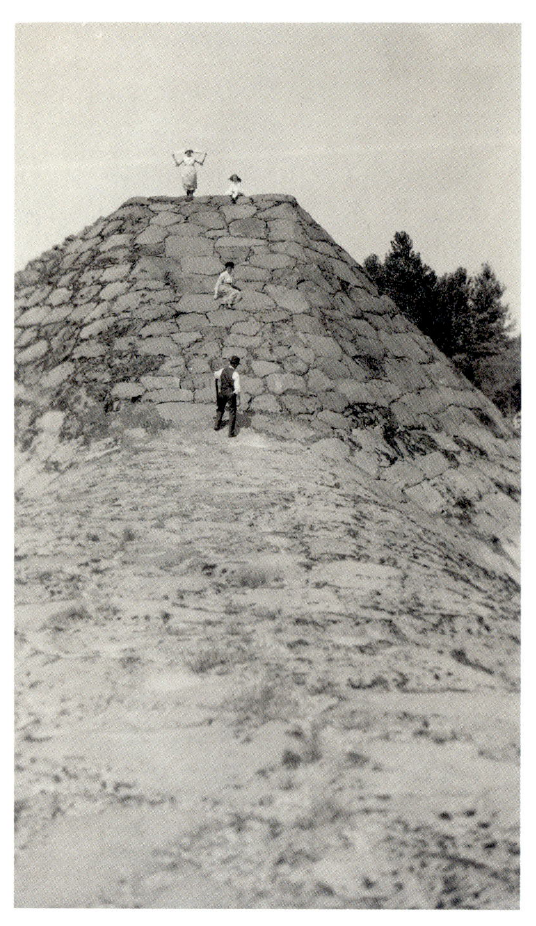

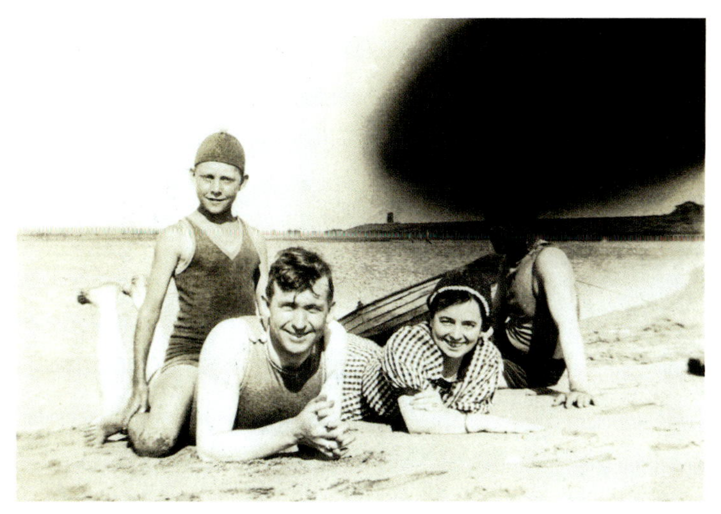

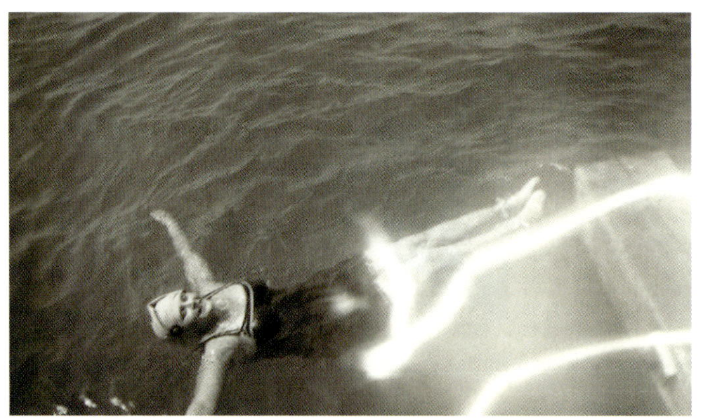

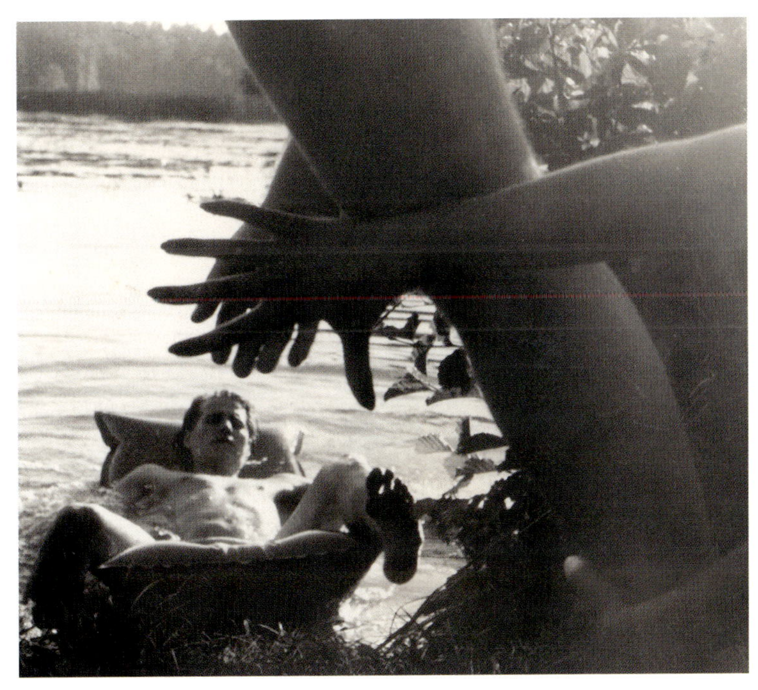

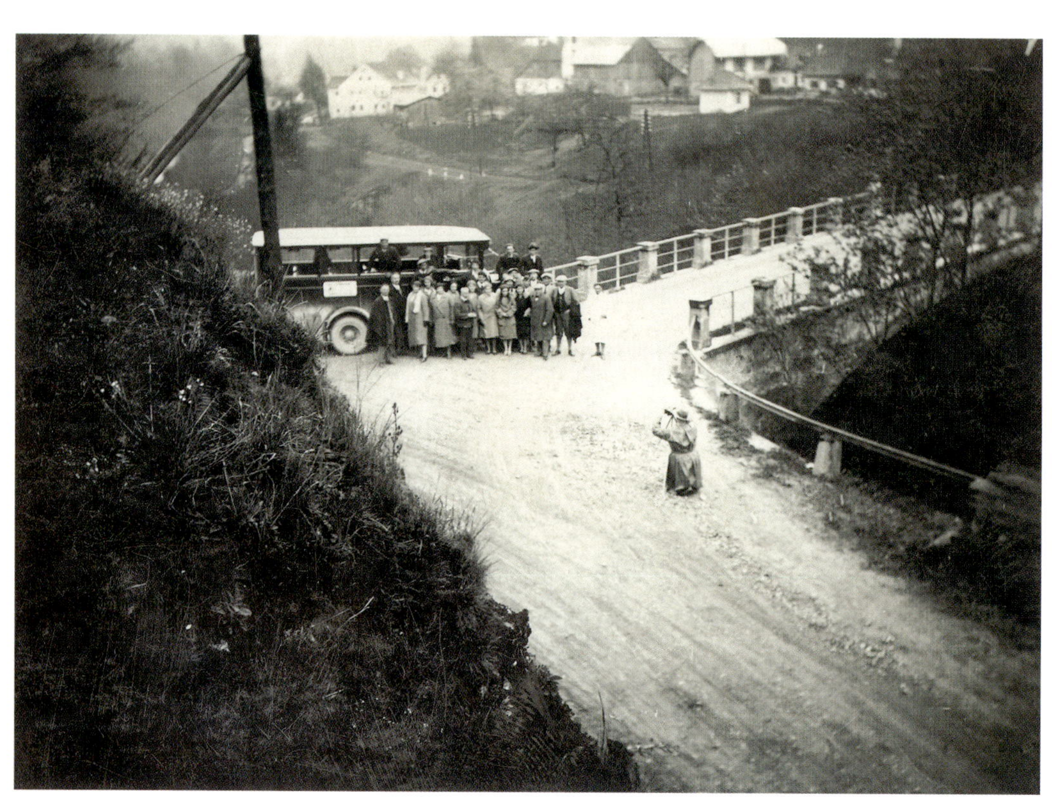

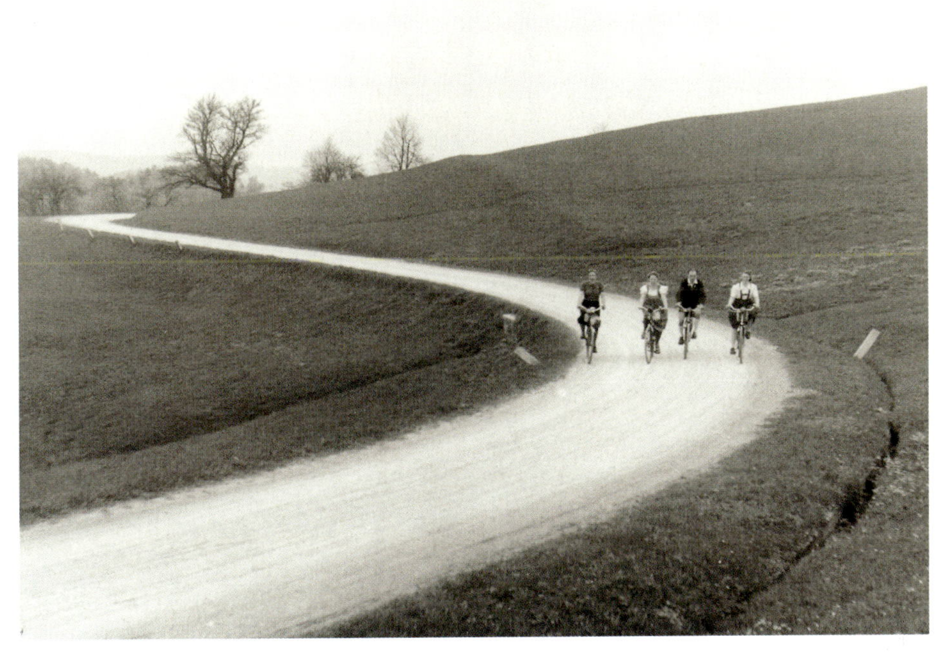

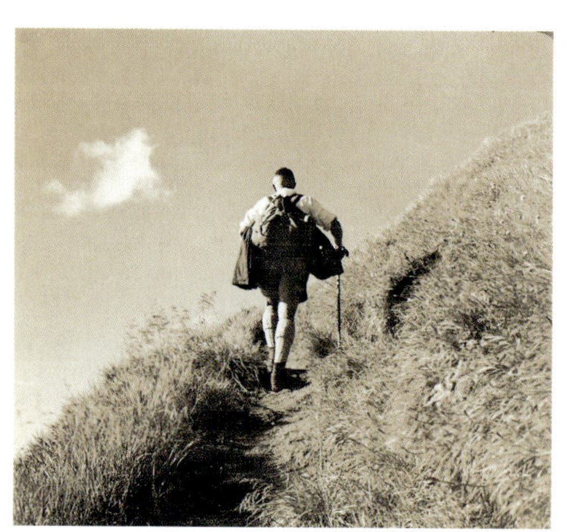
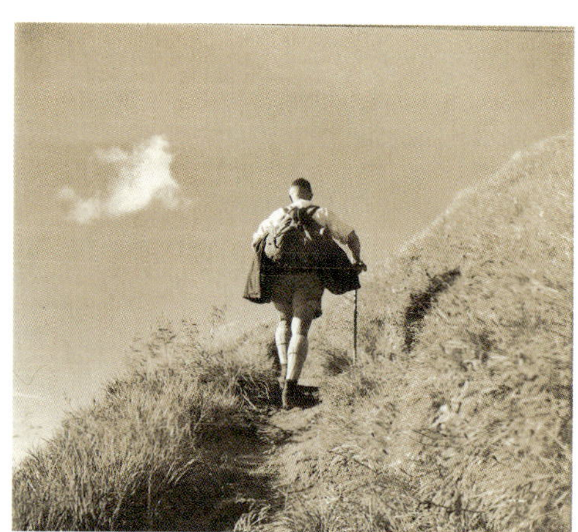

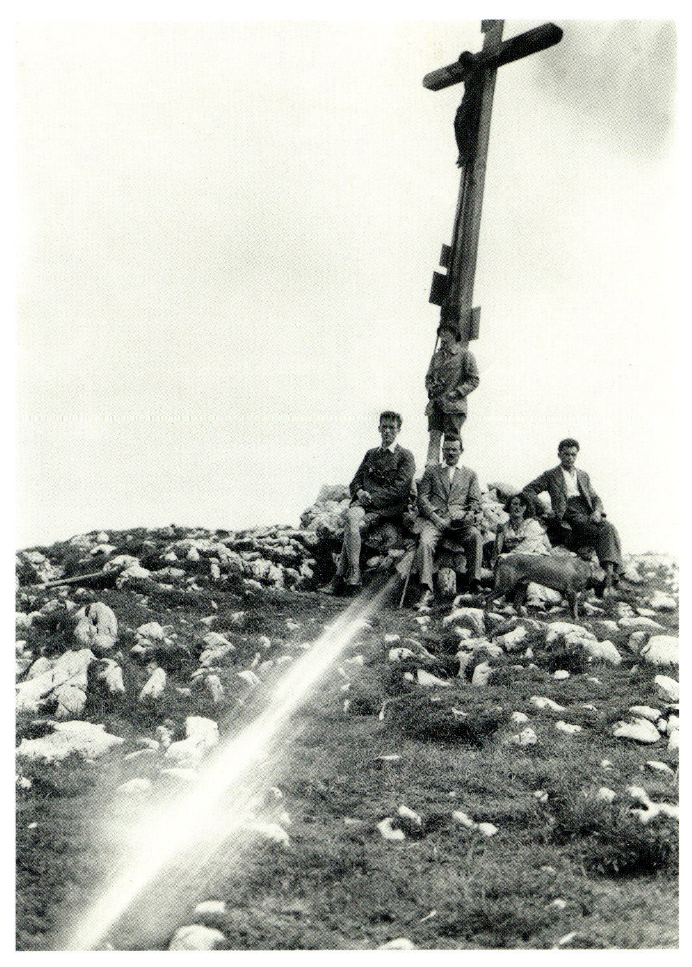

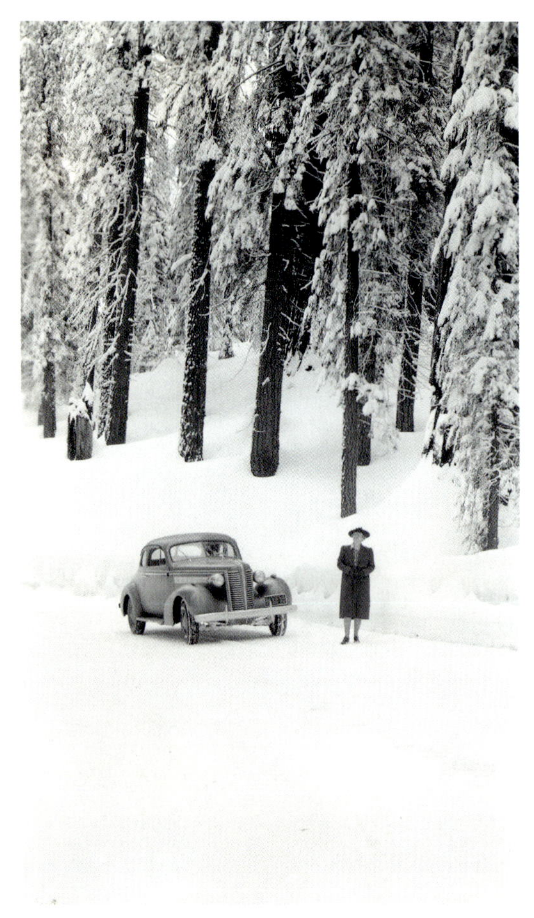

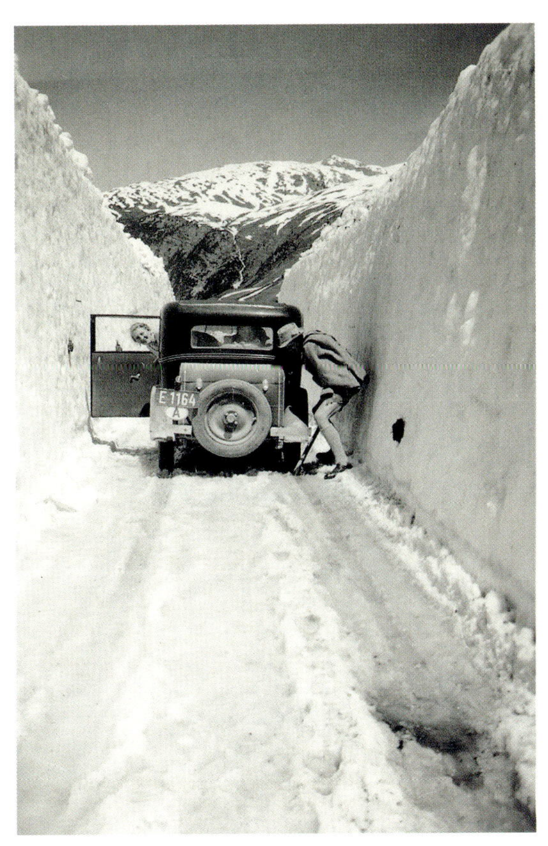
E 1164
A

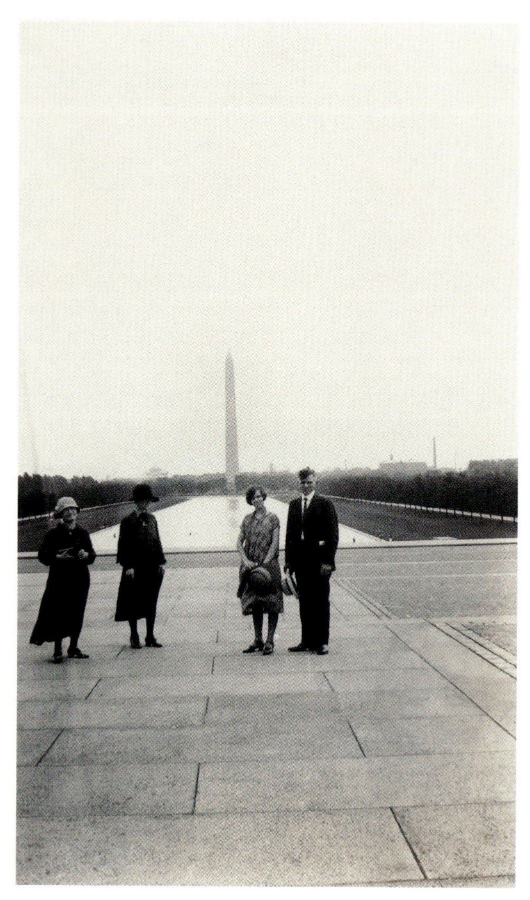

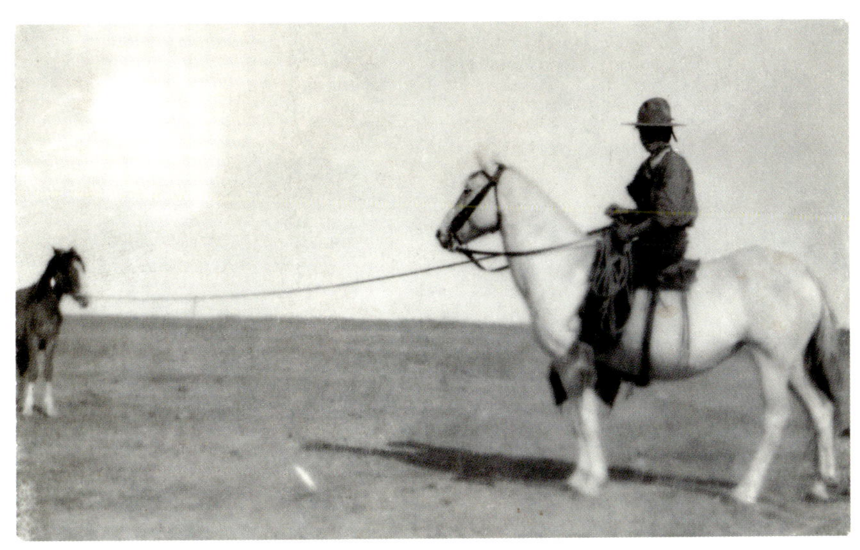

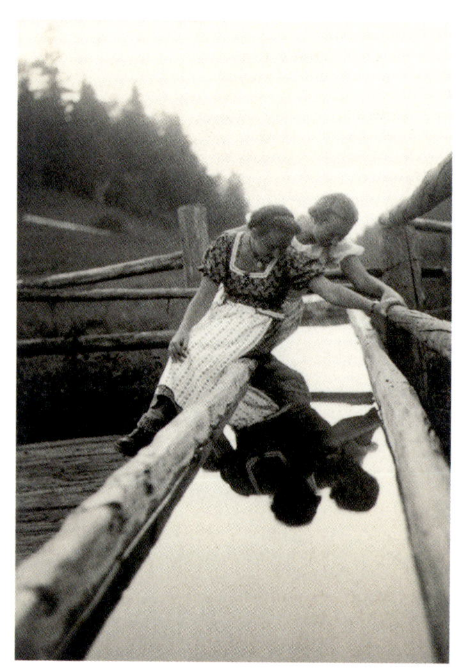

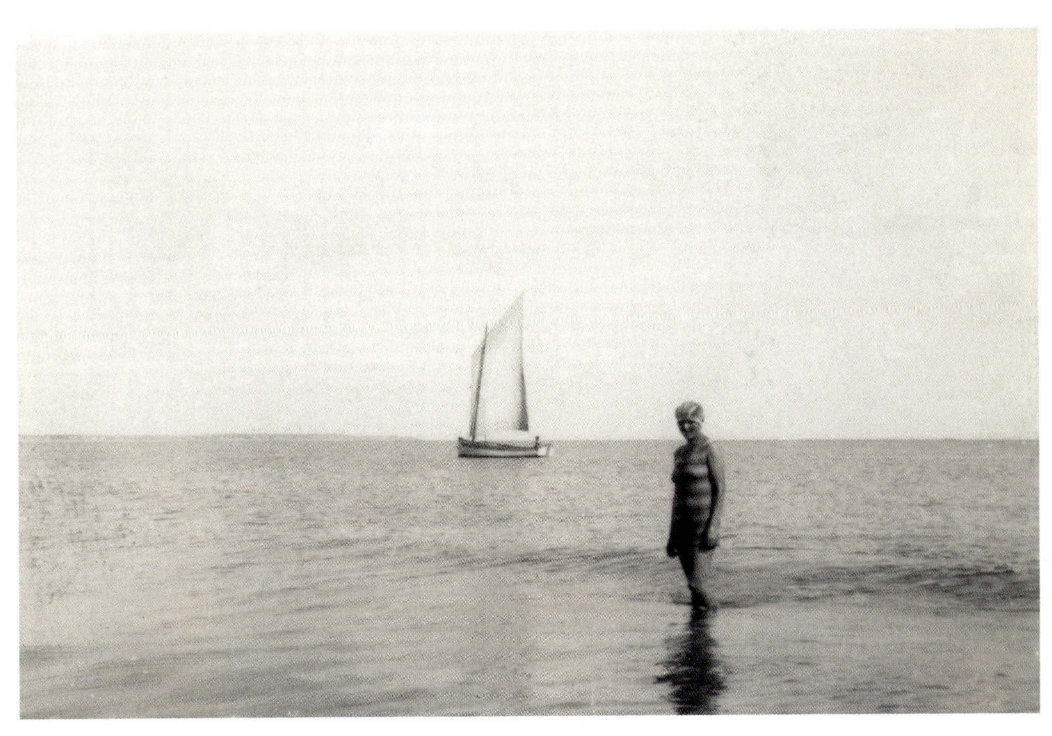

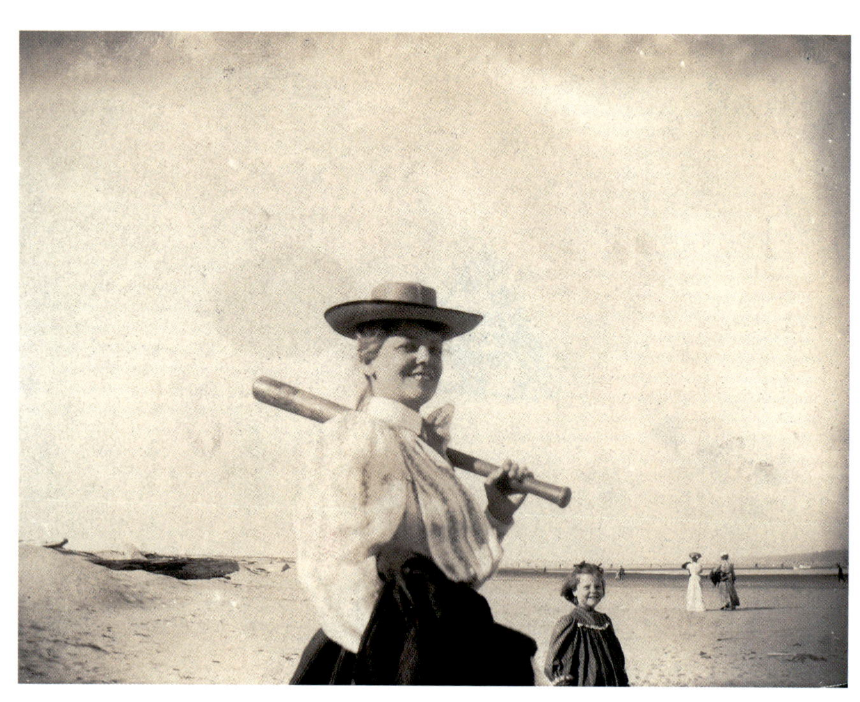

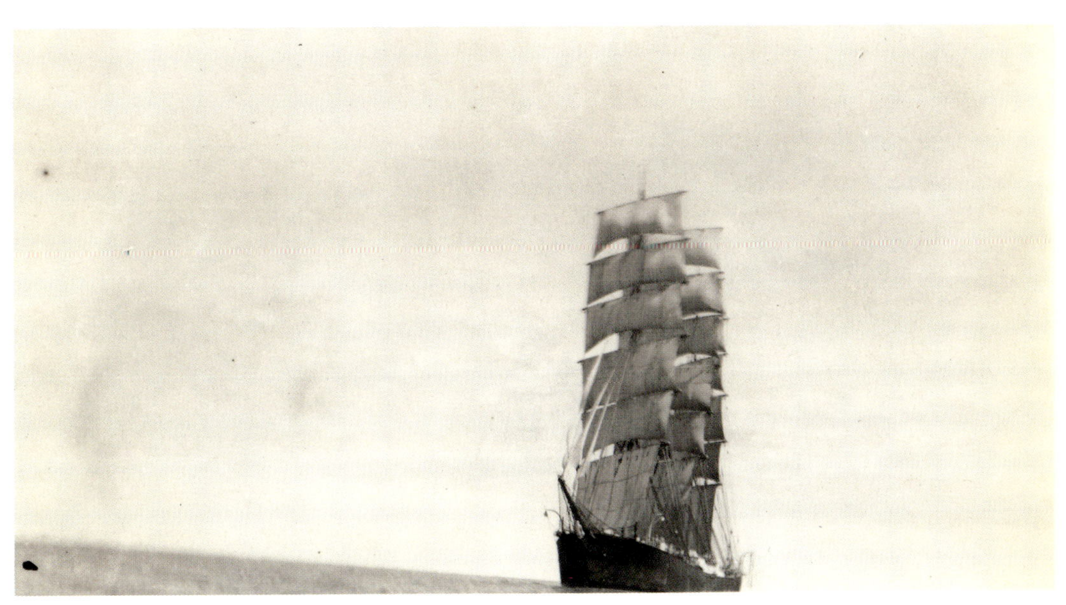

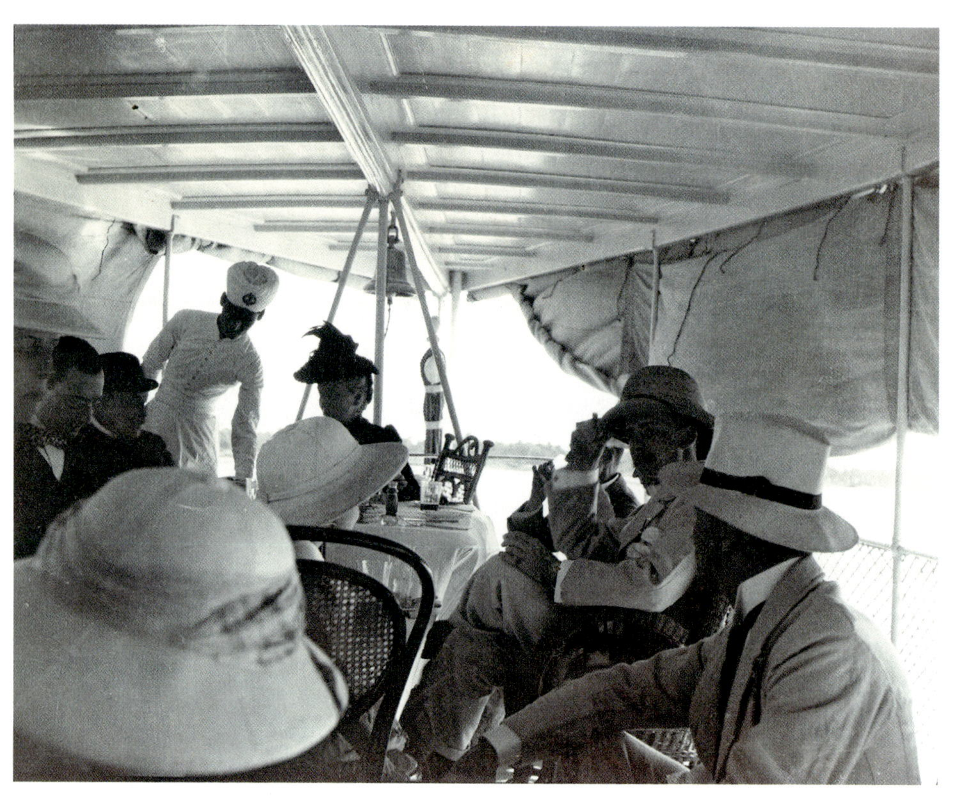

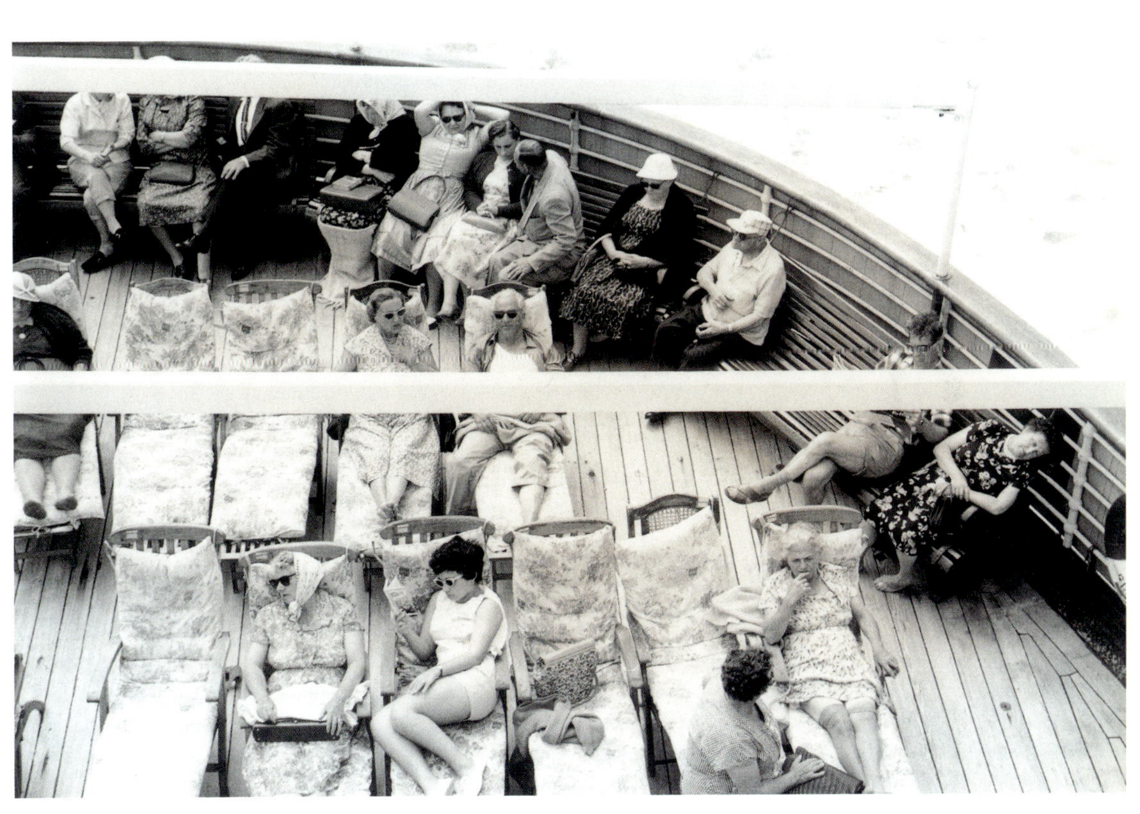

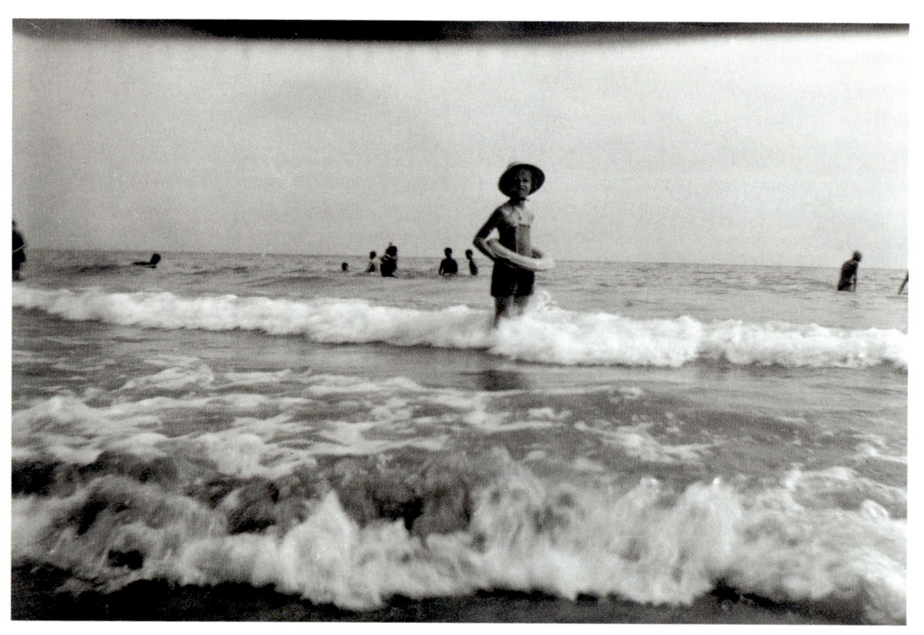

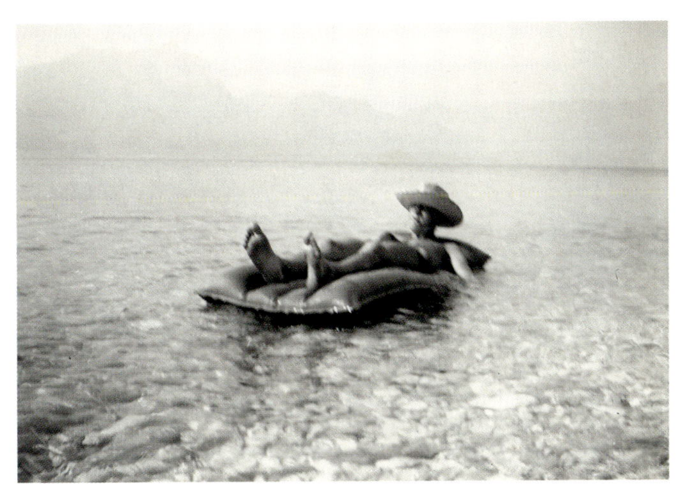

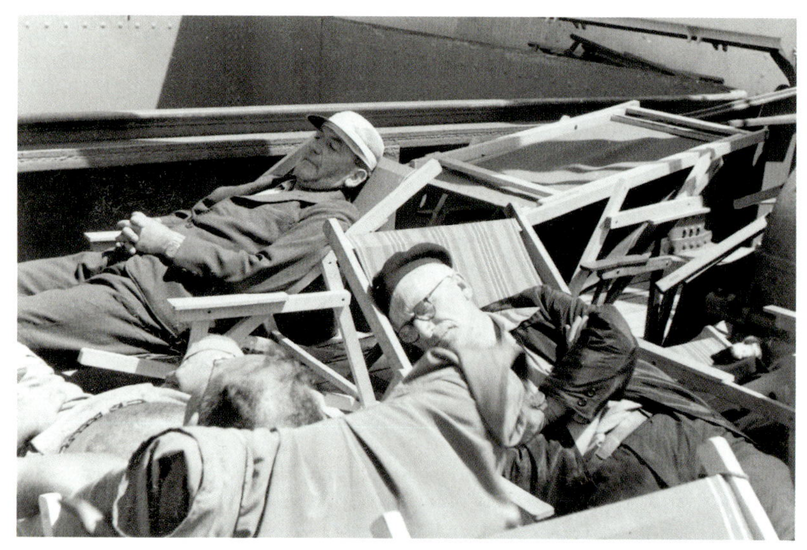

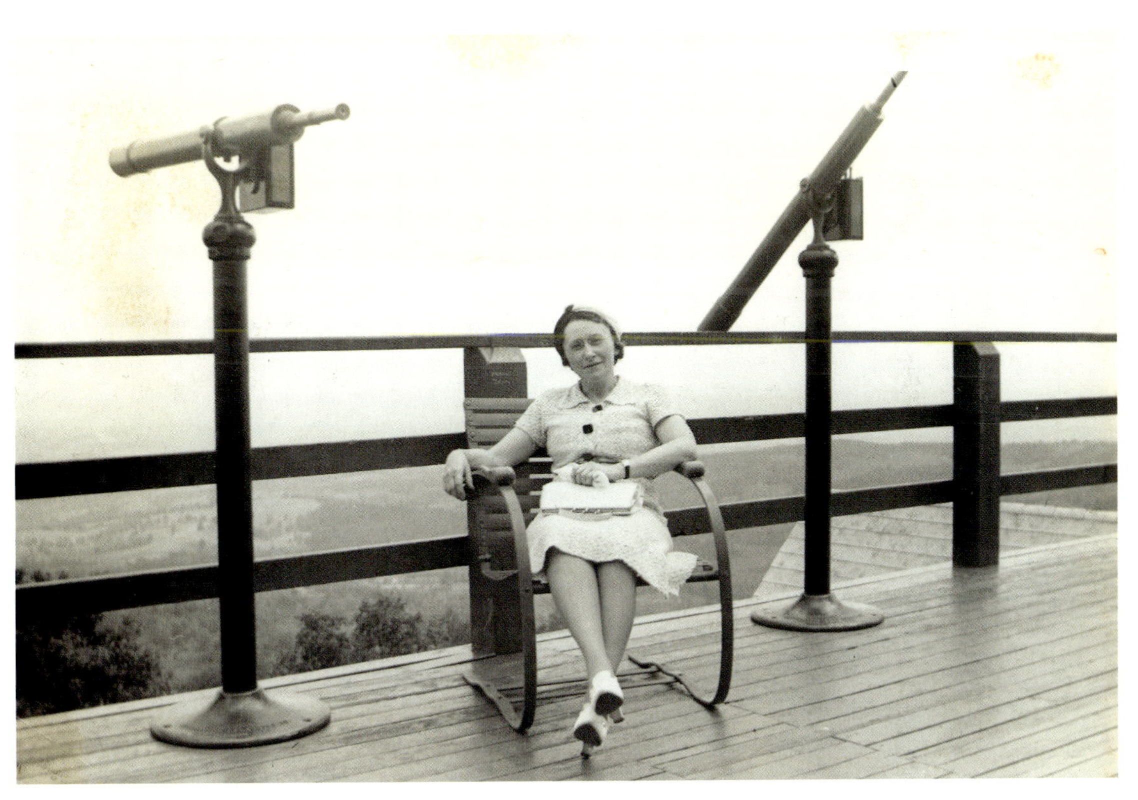

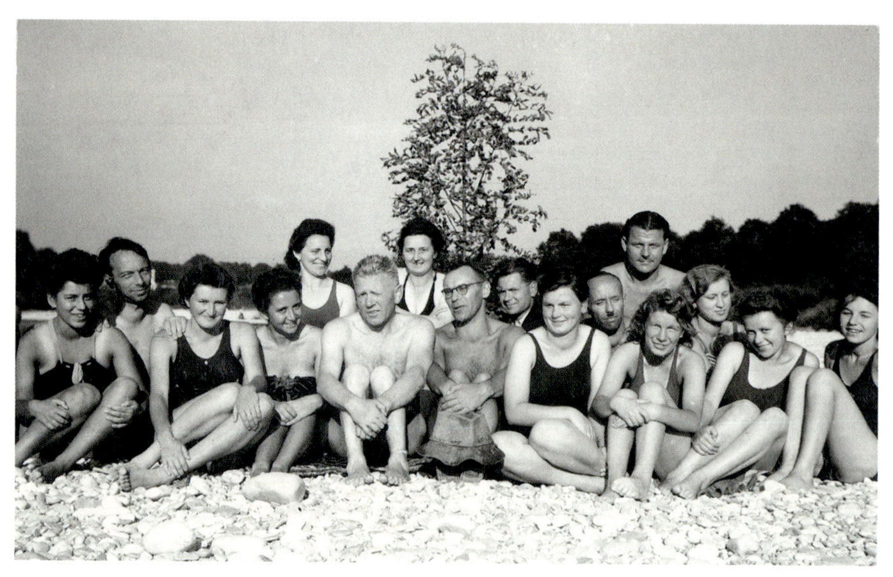

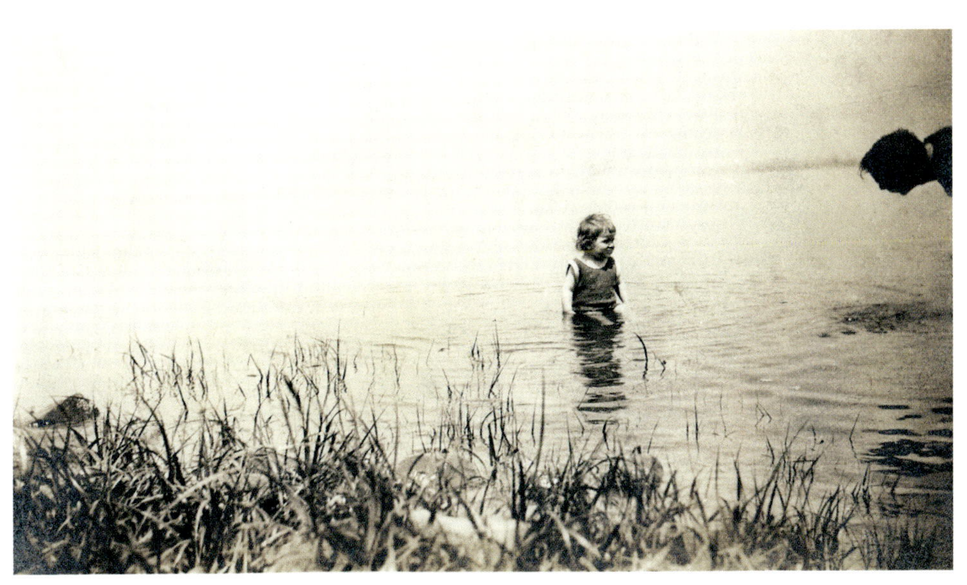

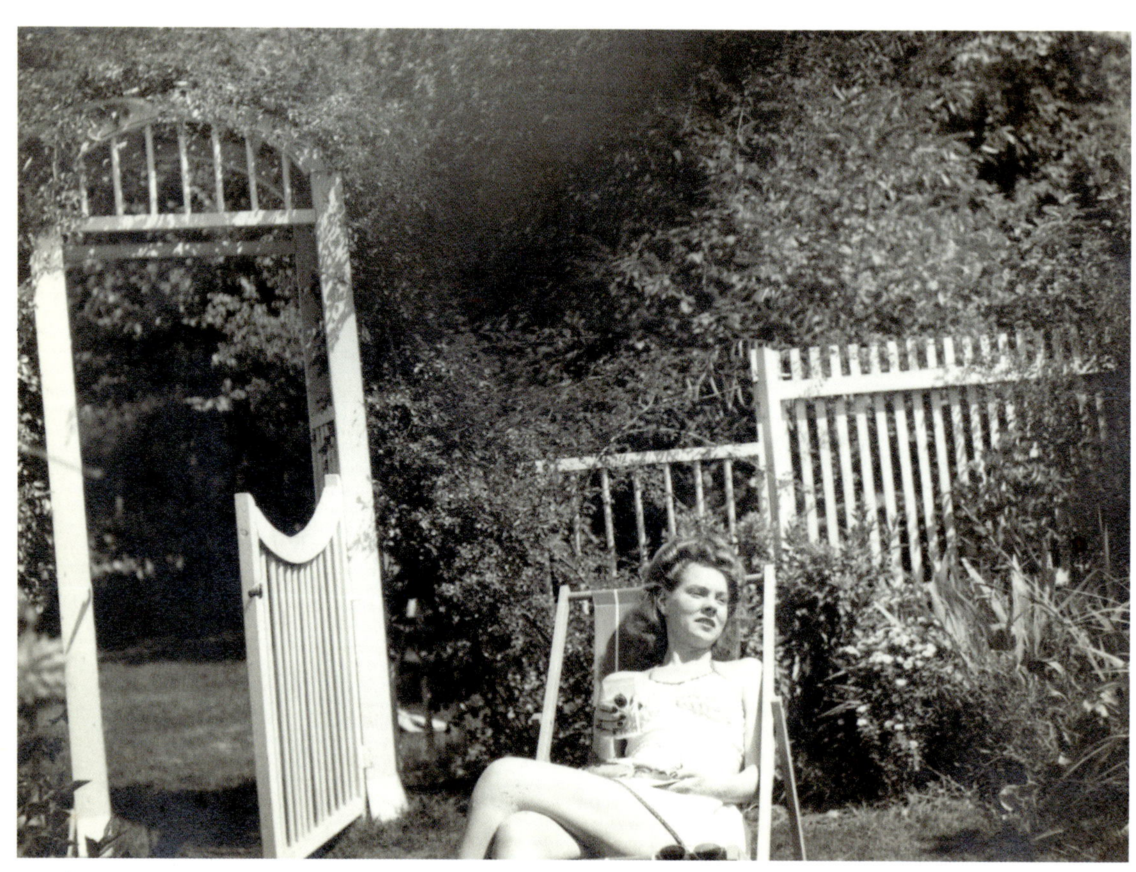

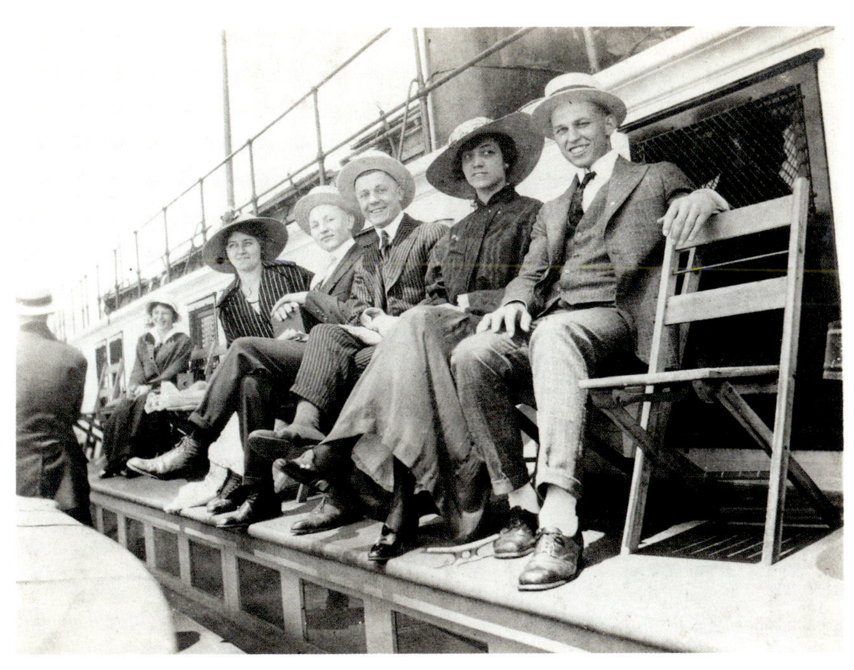

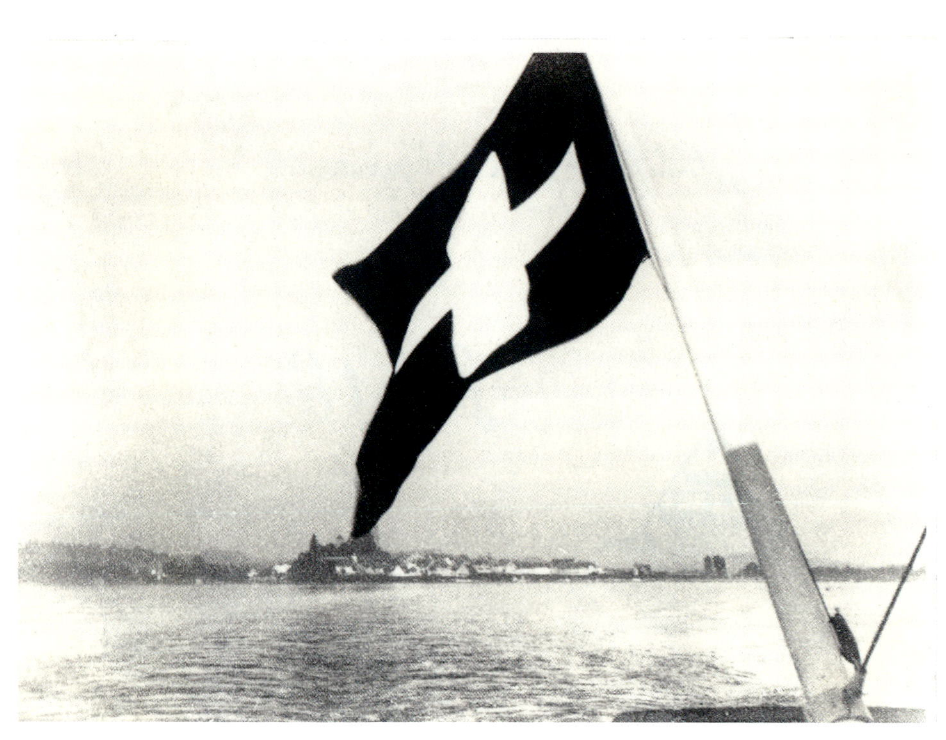

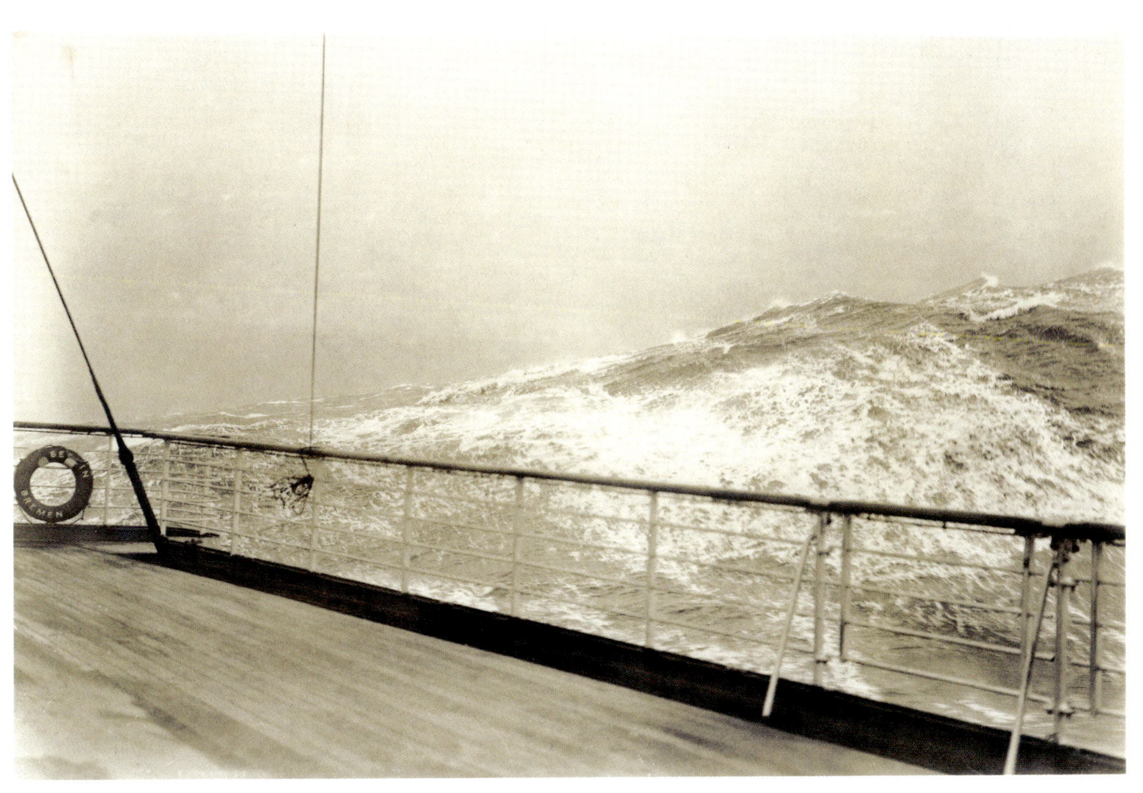

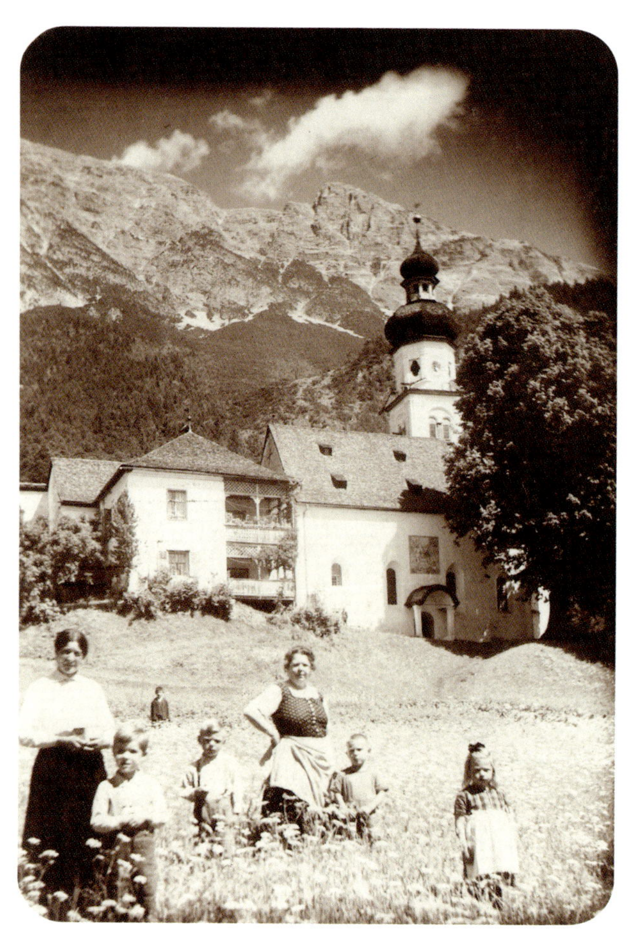

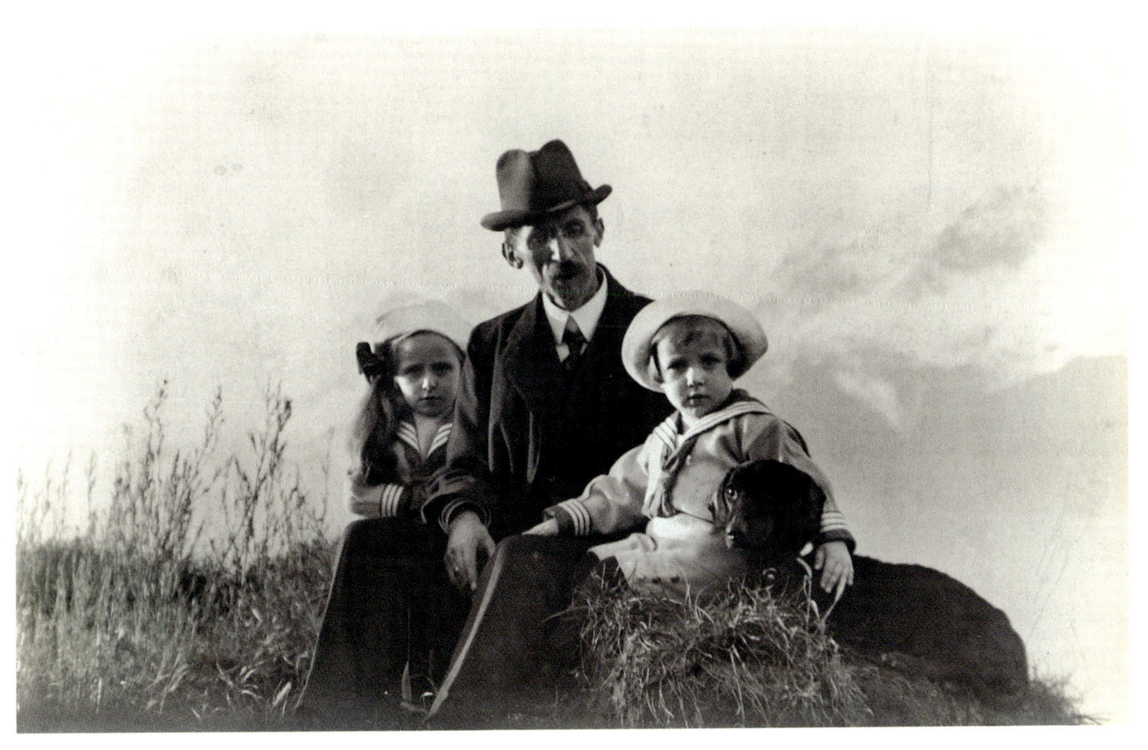

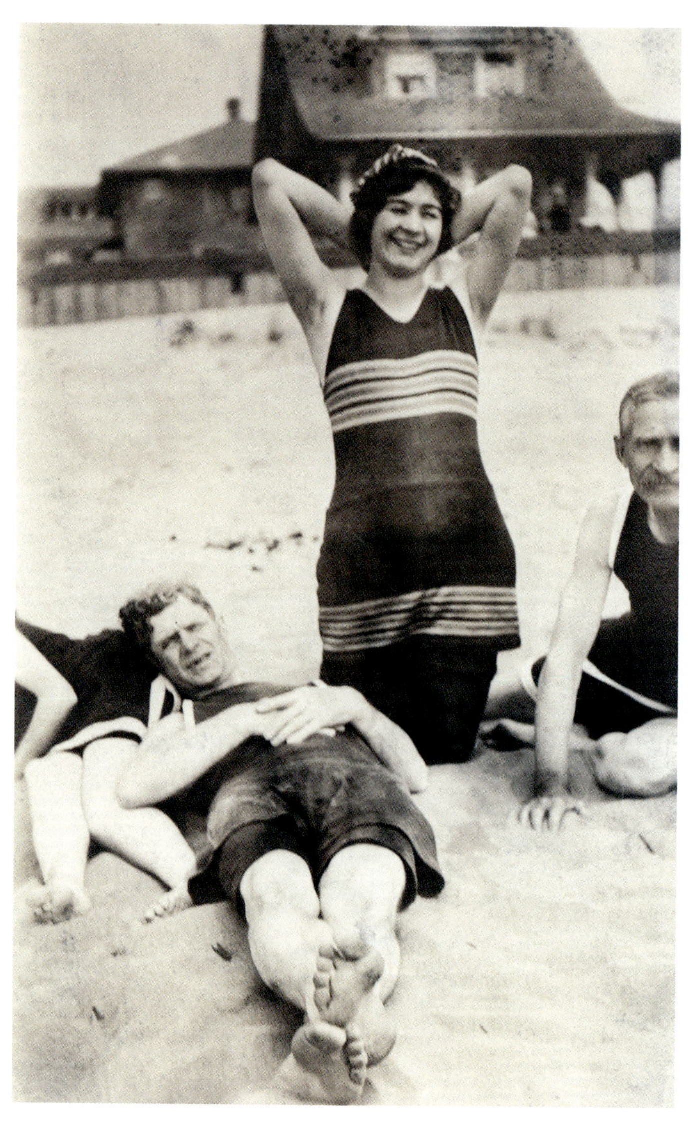

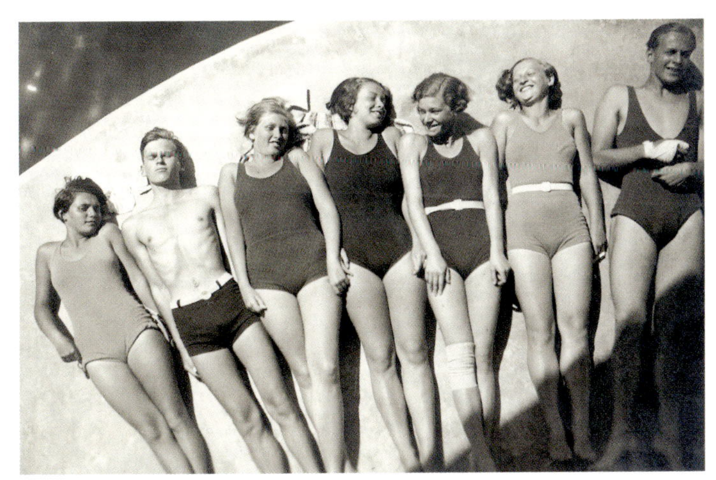

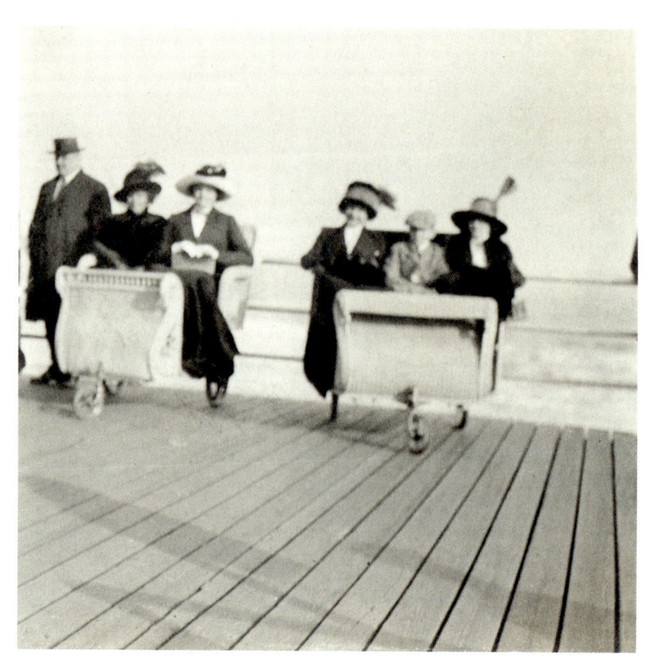

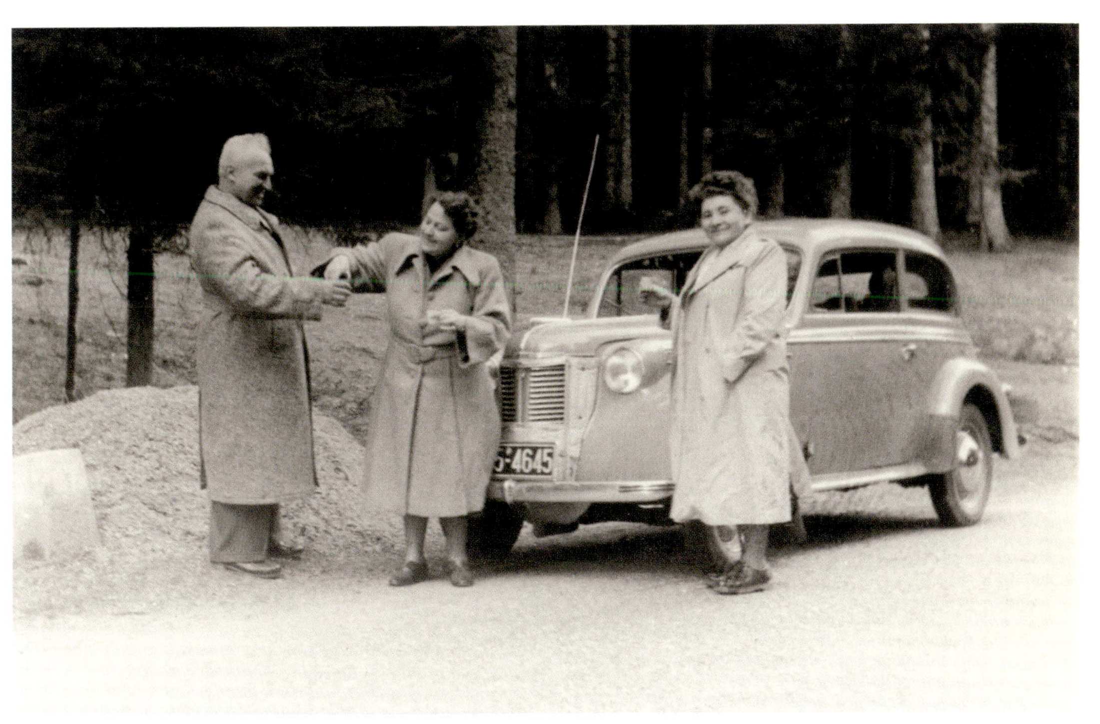
4645

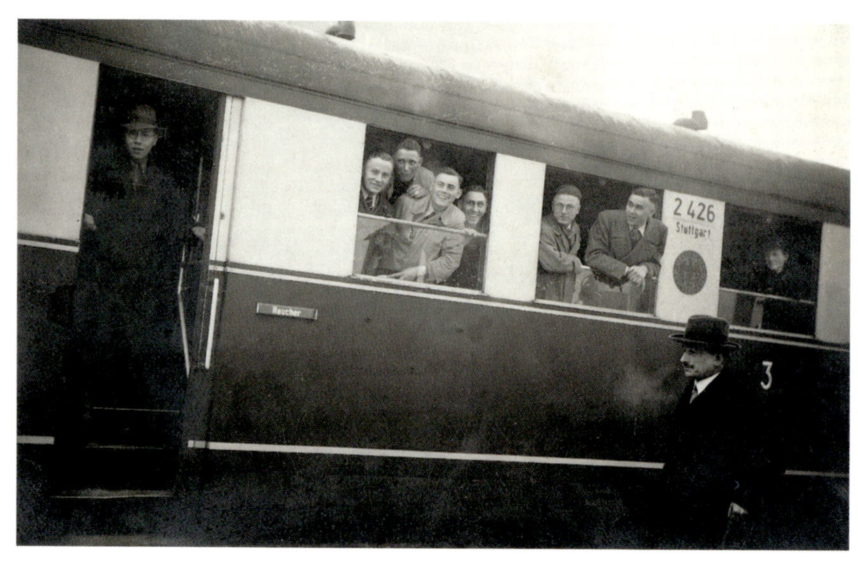
2 426
Stuttgart
3

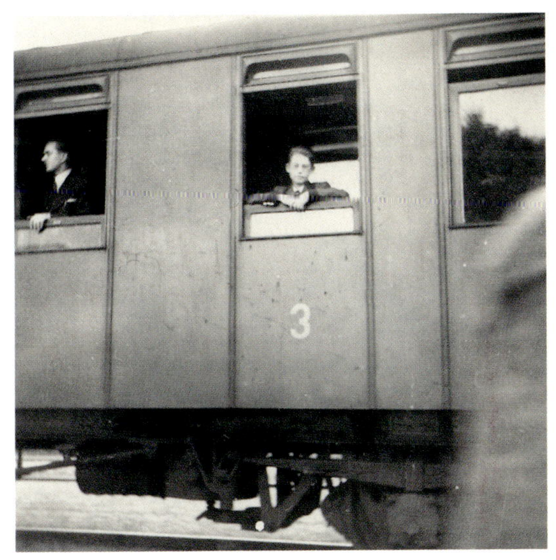

12)

Transportation Verkehrsmittel

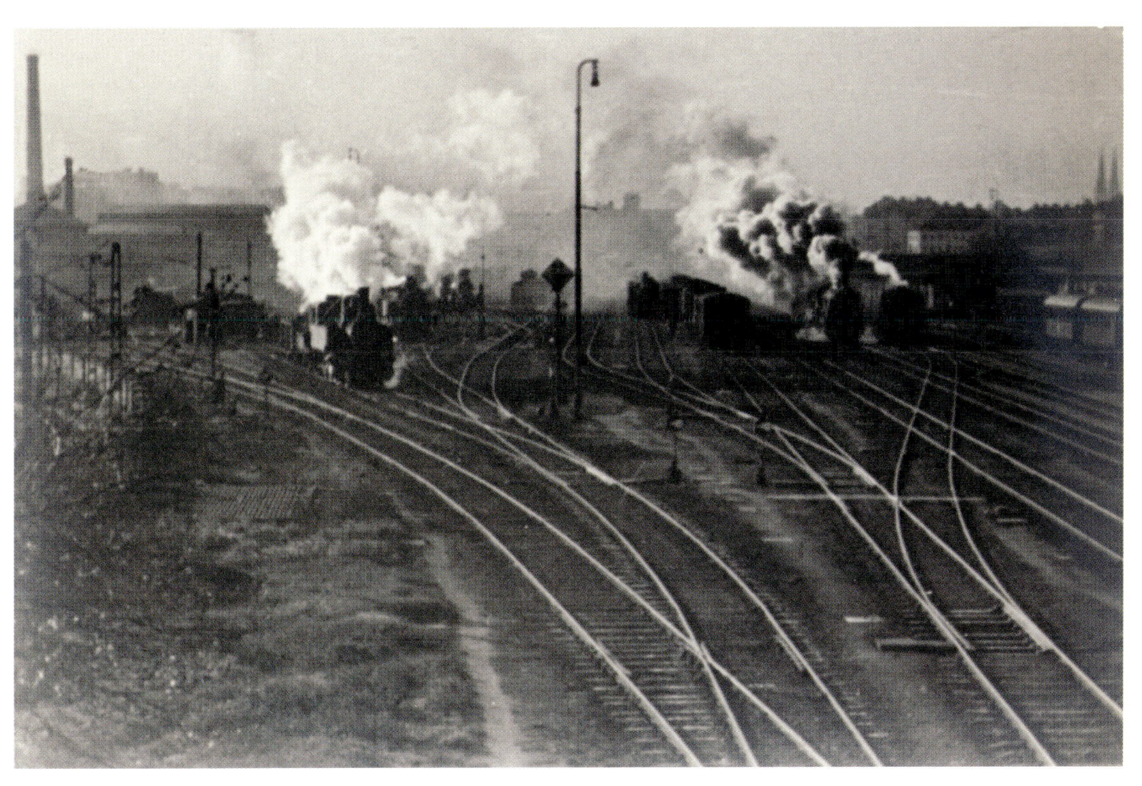

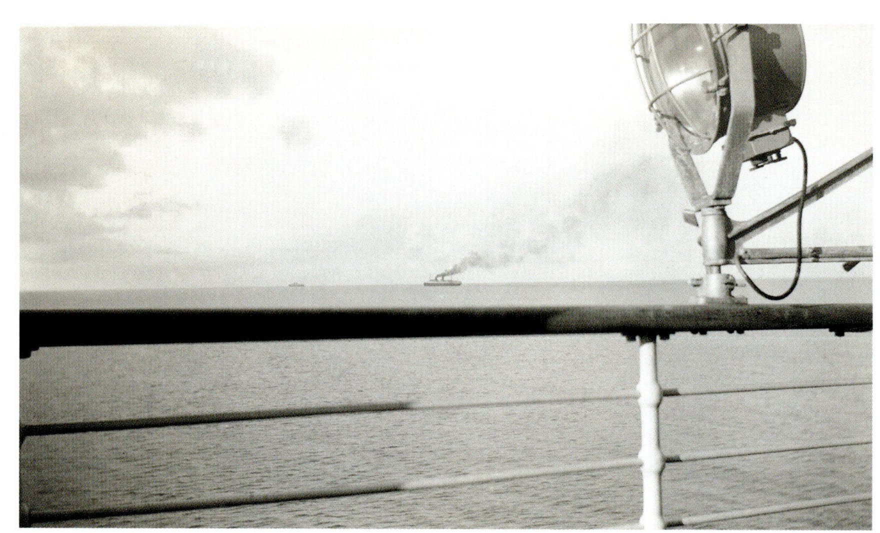

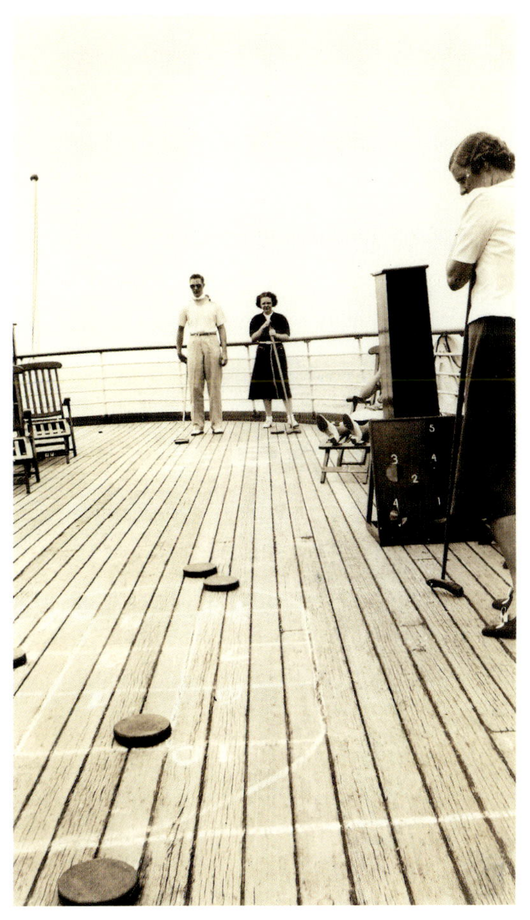

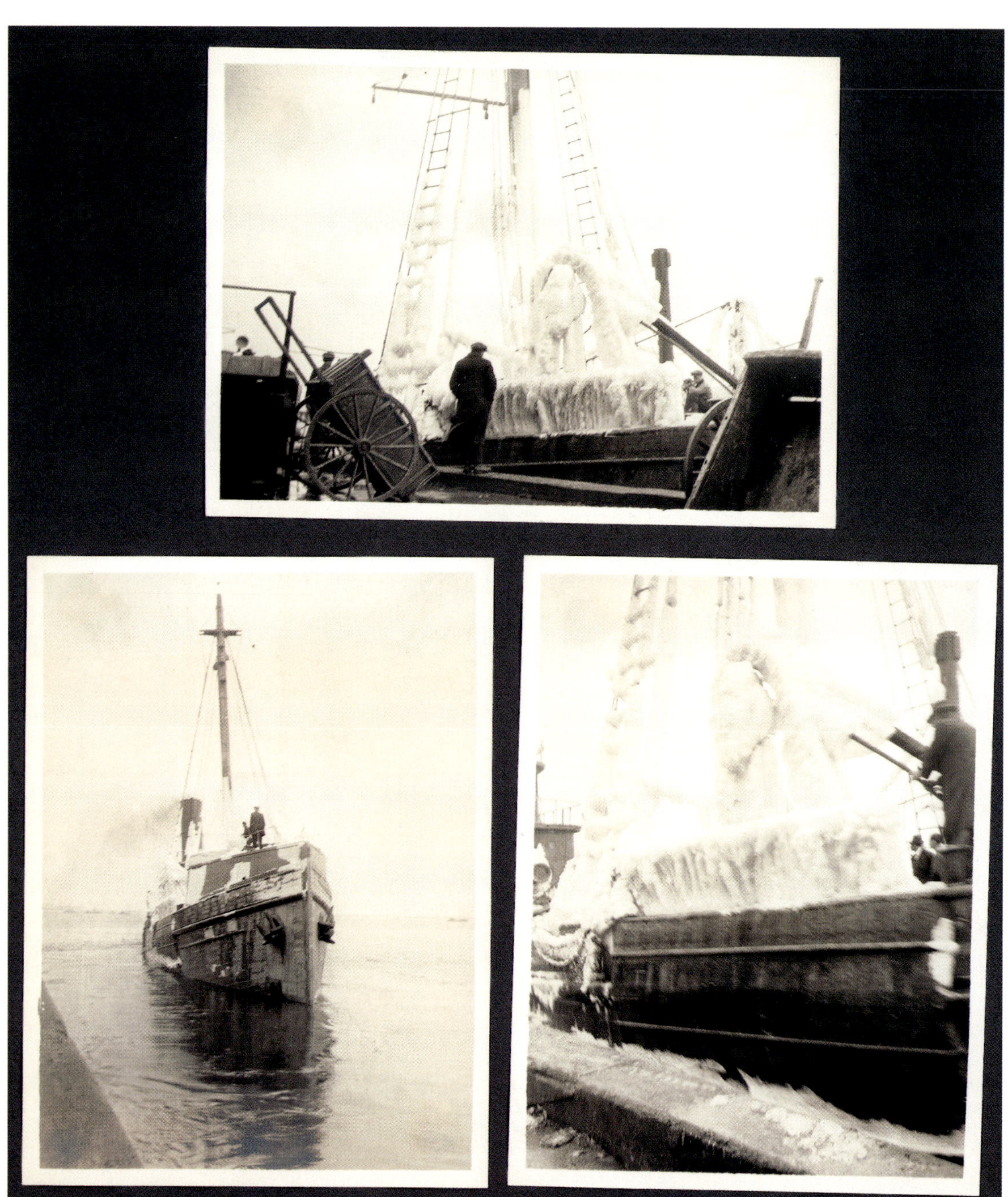

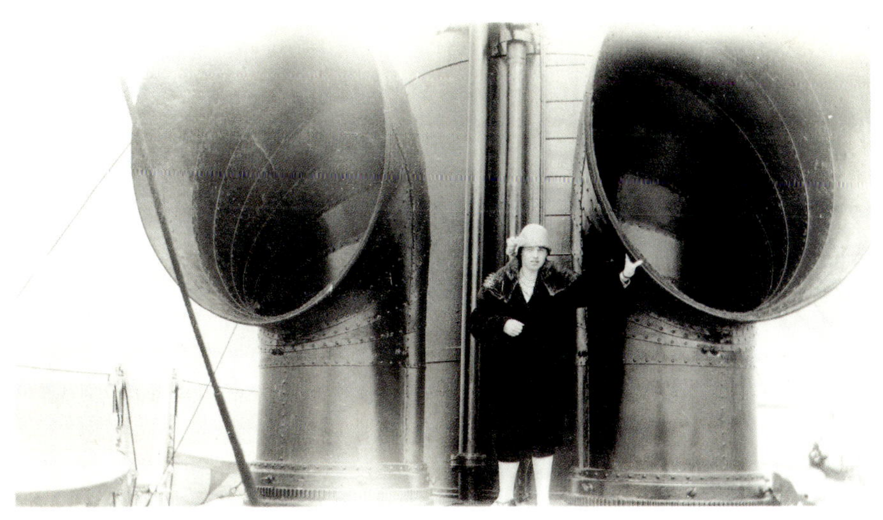

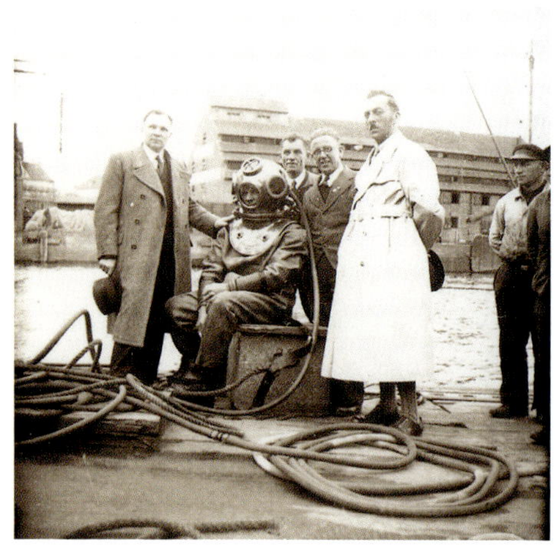

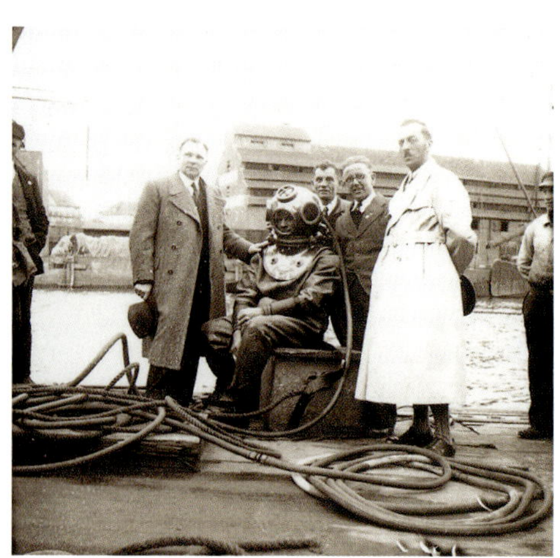

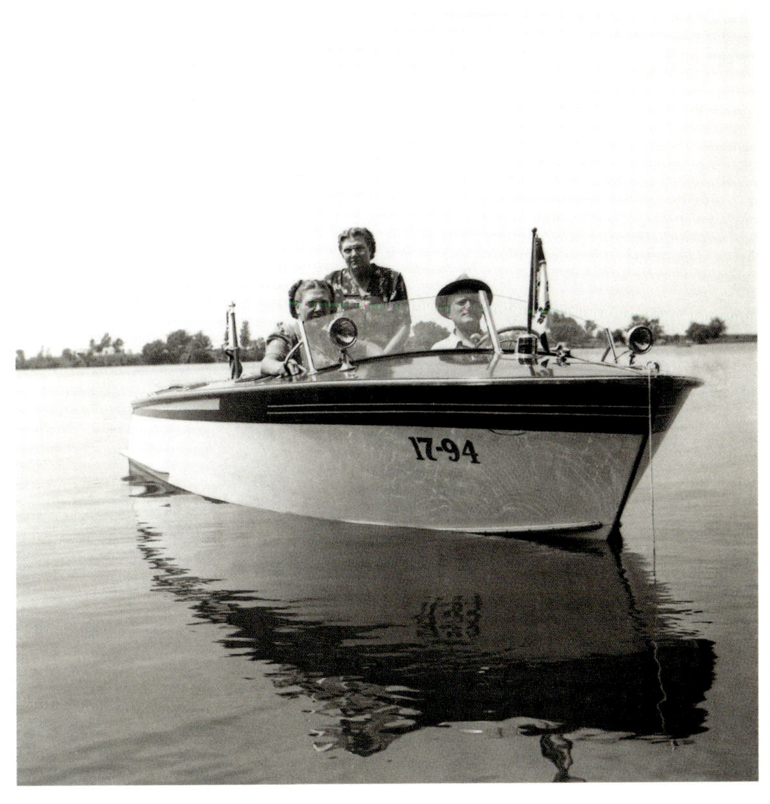
17-94

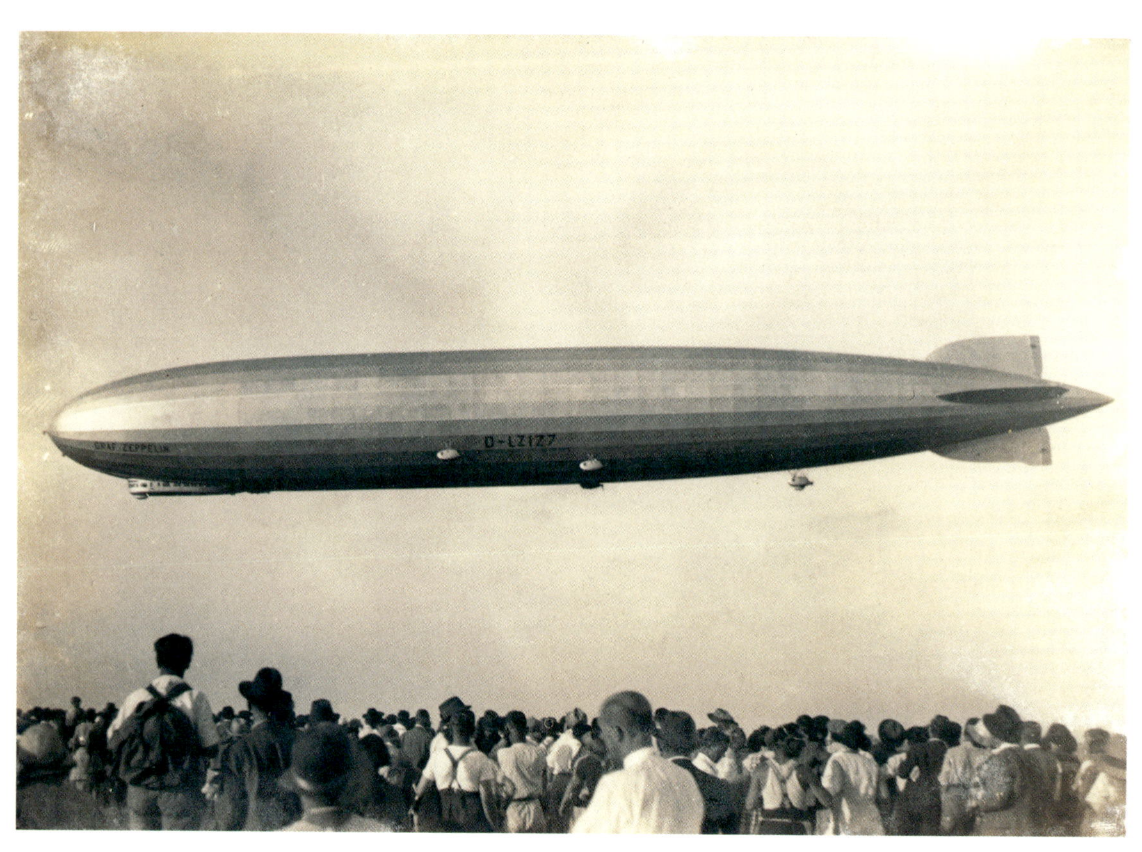
GRAF ZEPPELIN
D-LZ127

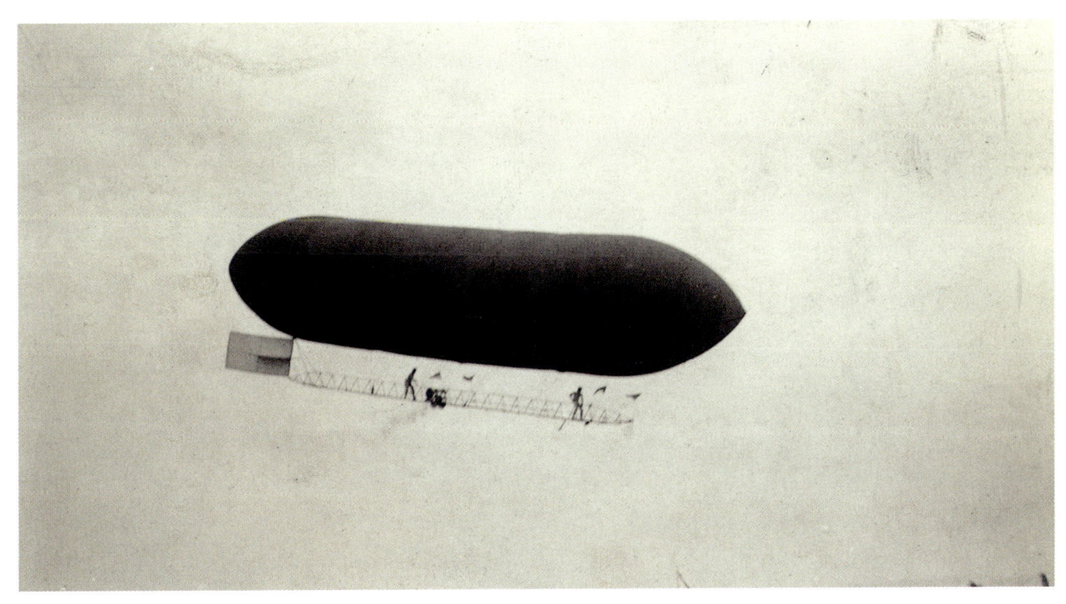

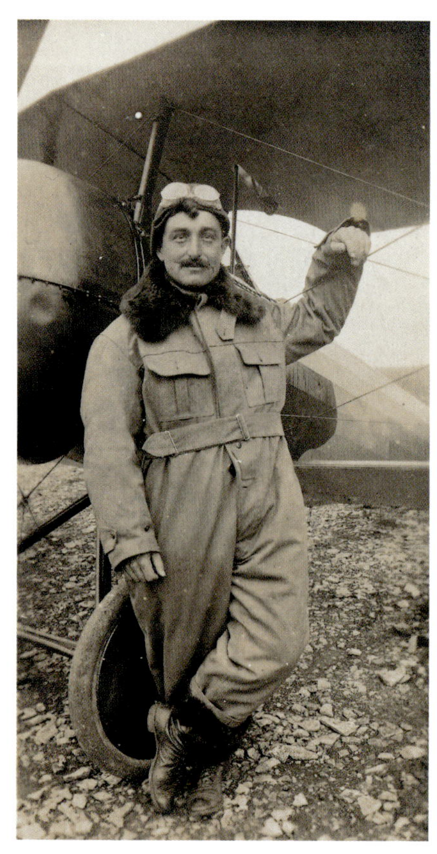

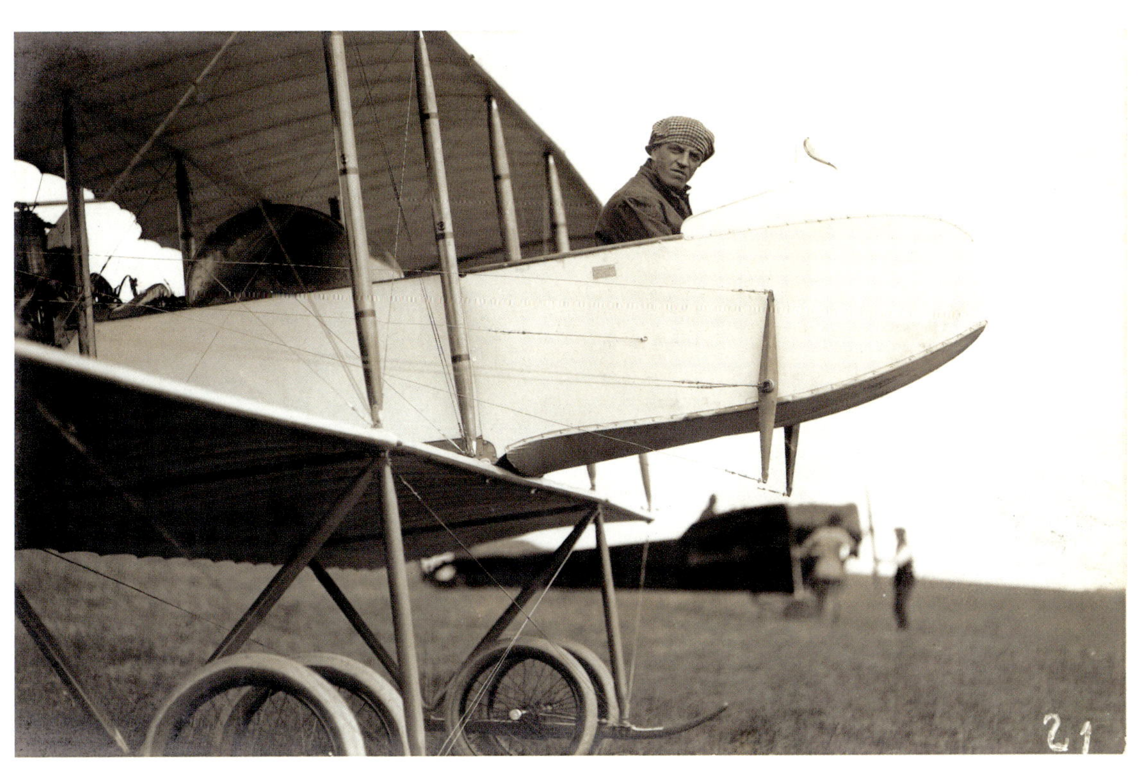
21

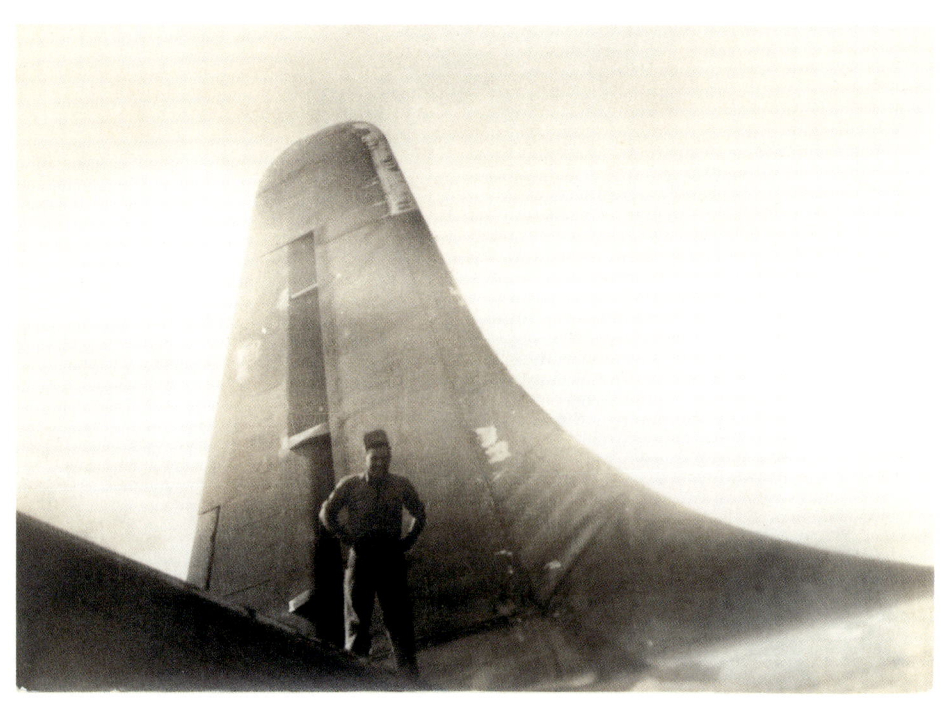

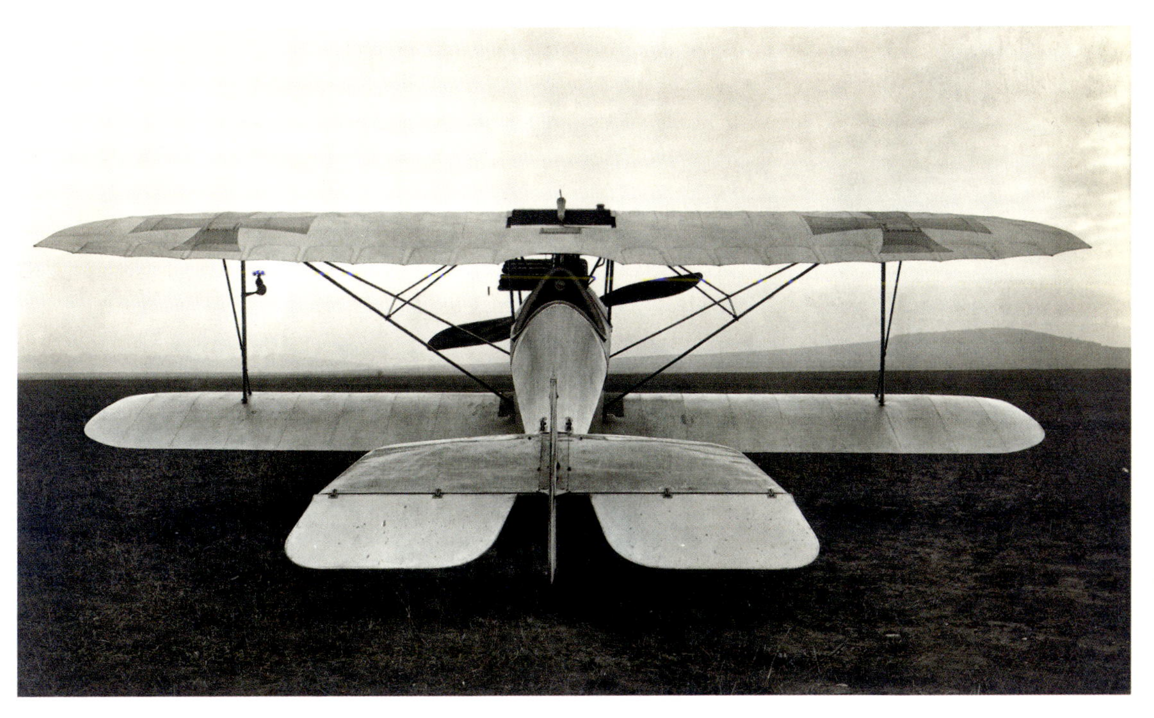

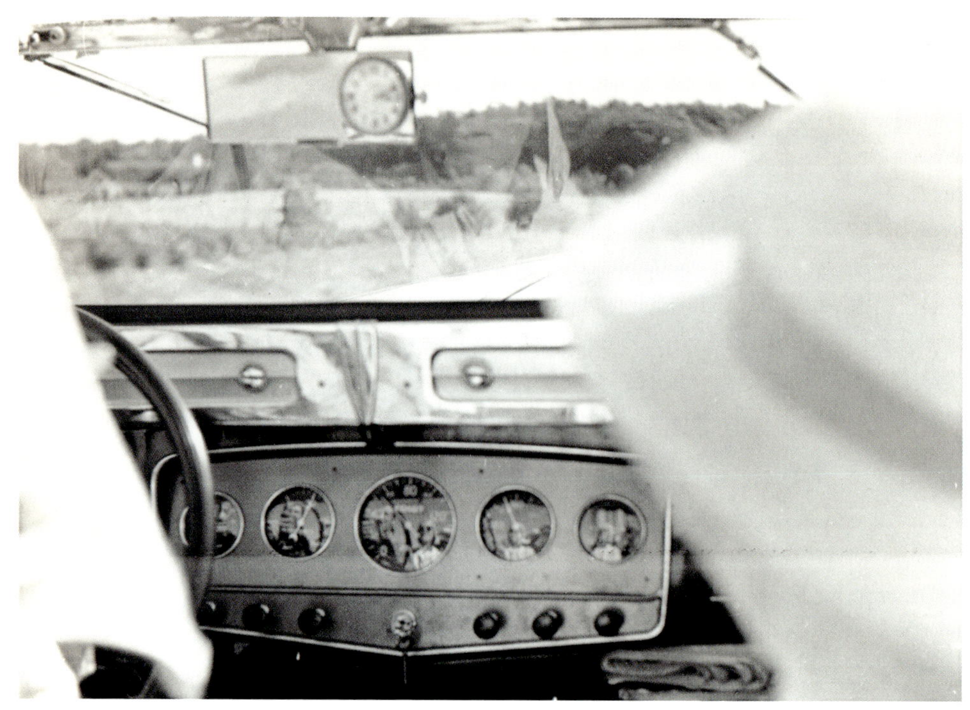

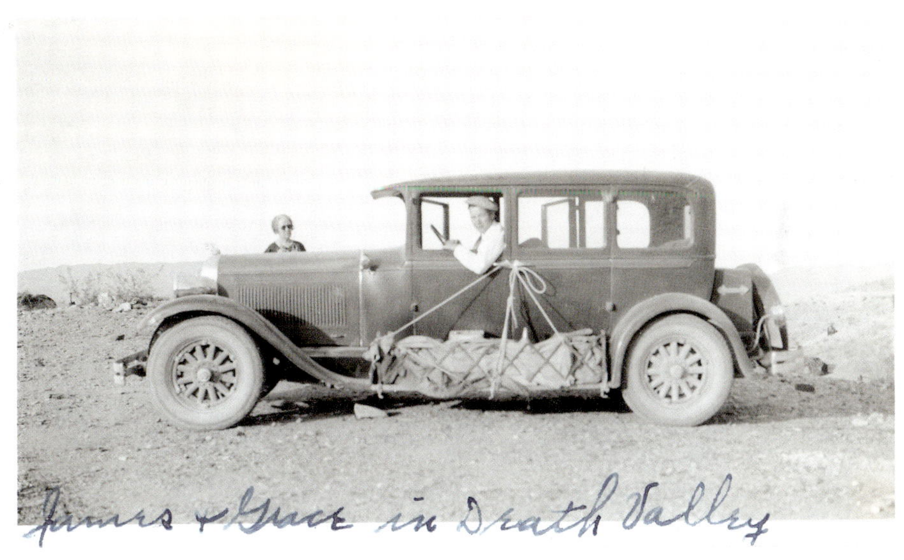
James + Grace in Death Valley

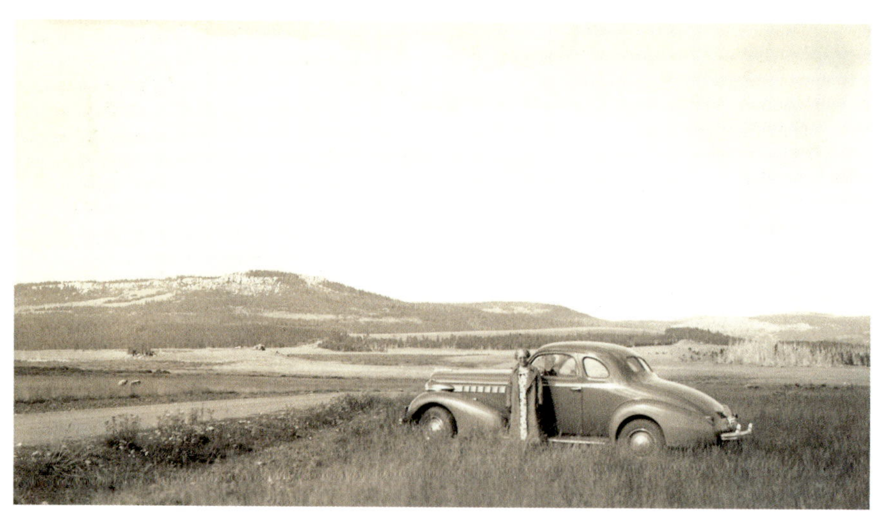

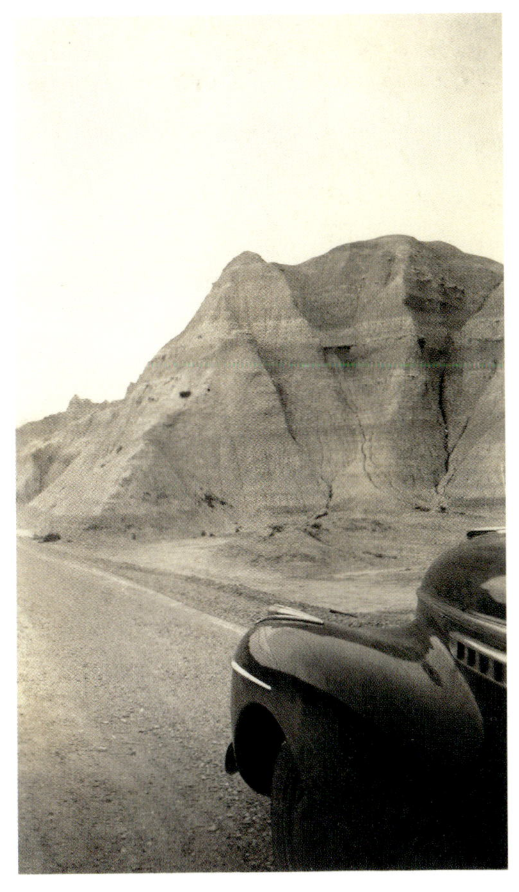

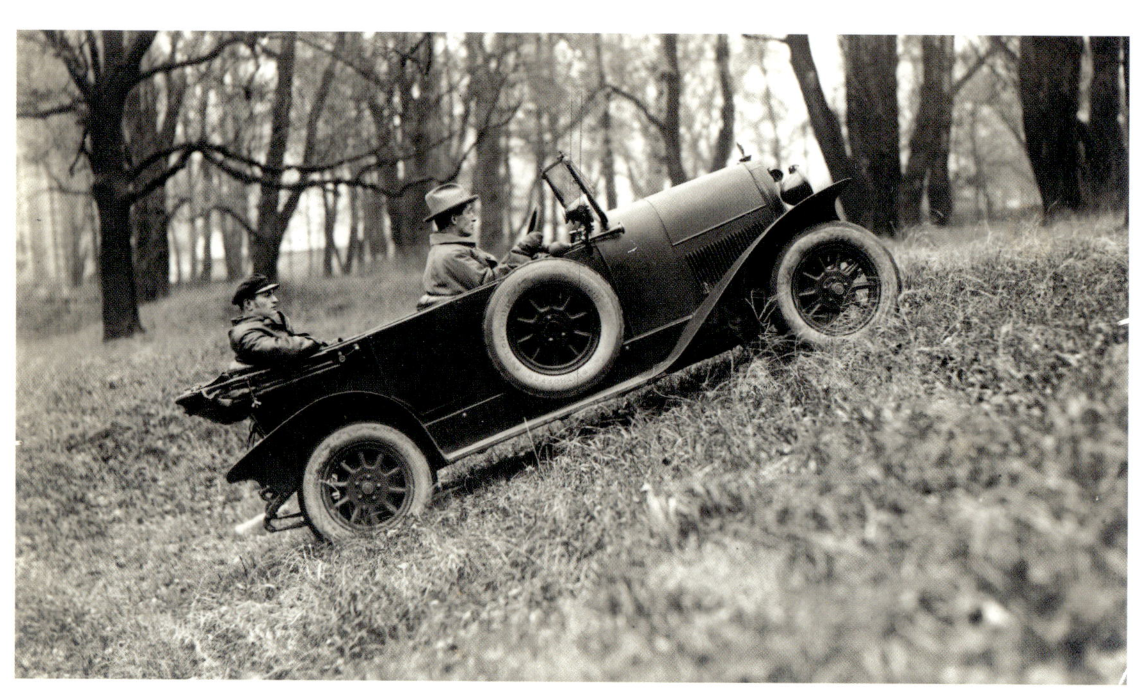

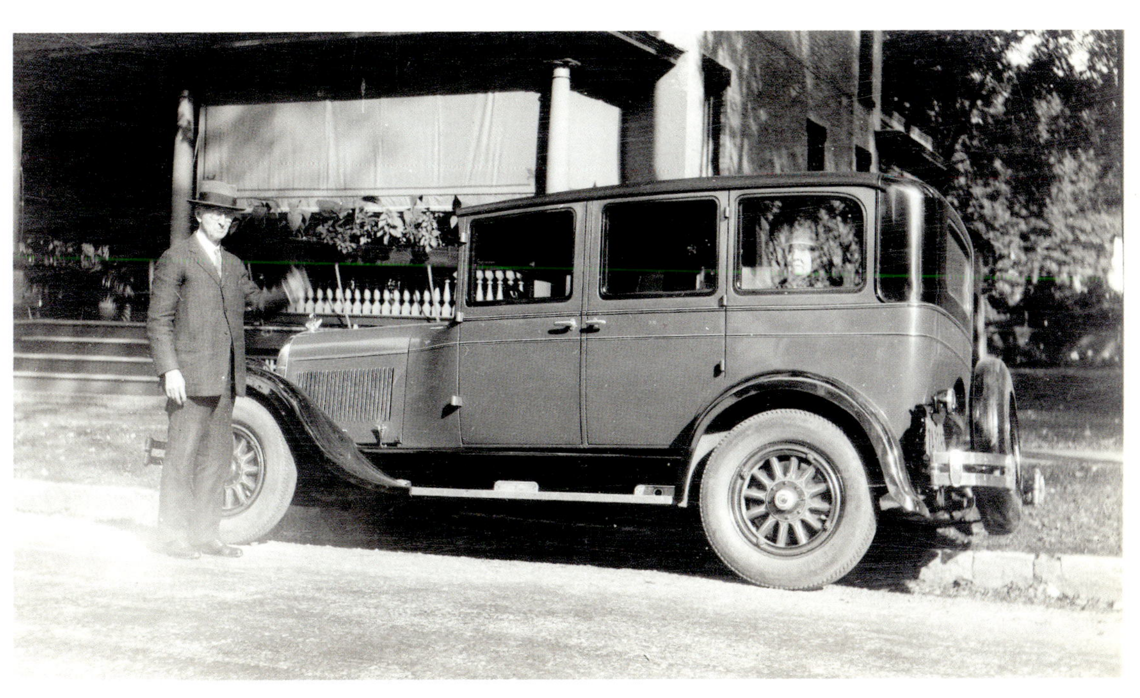

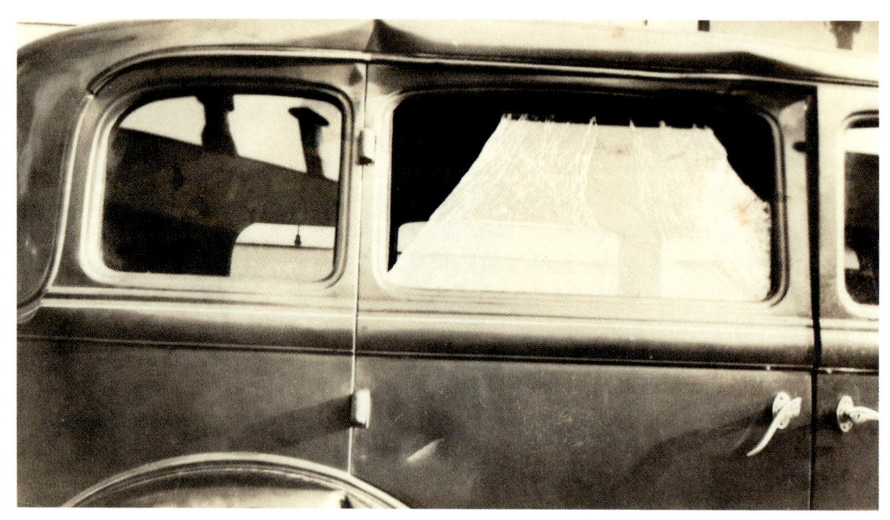

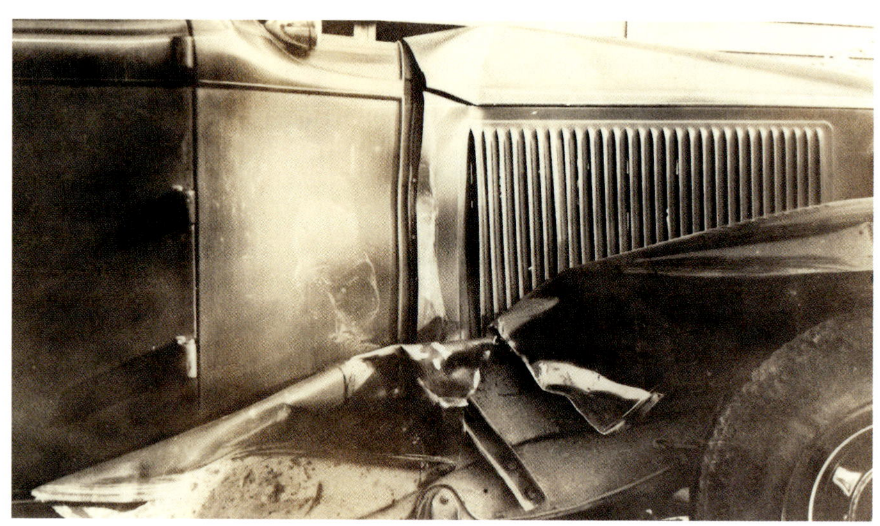

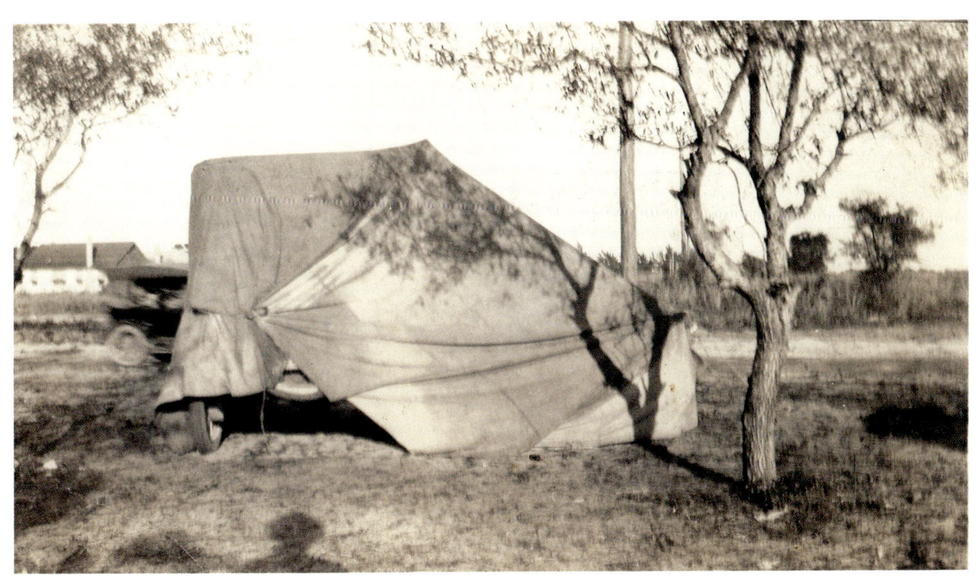

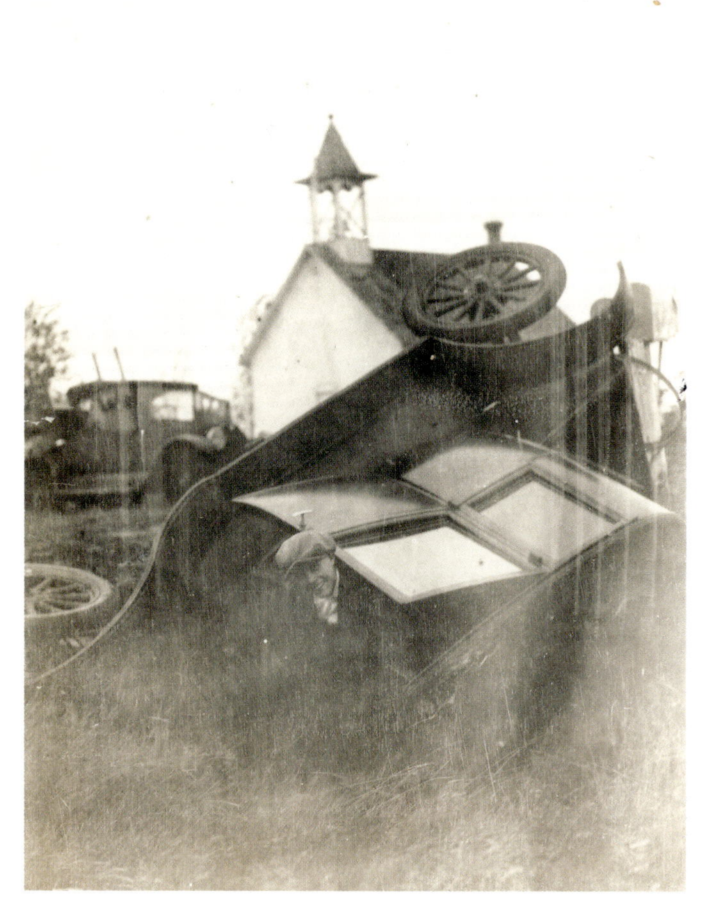

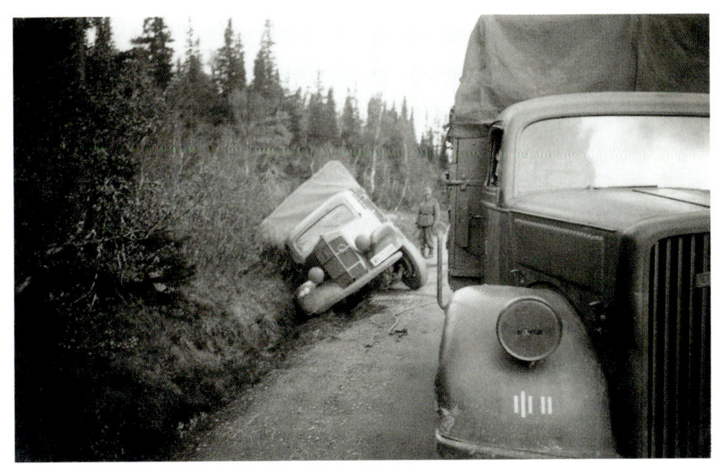

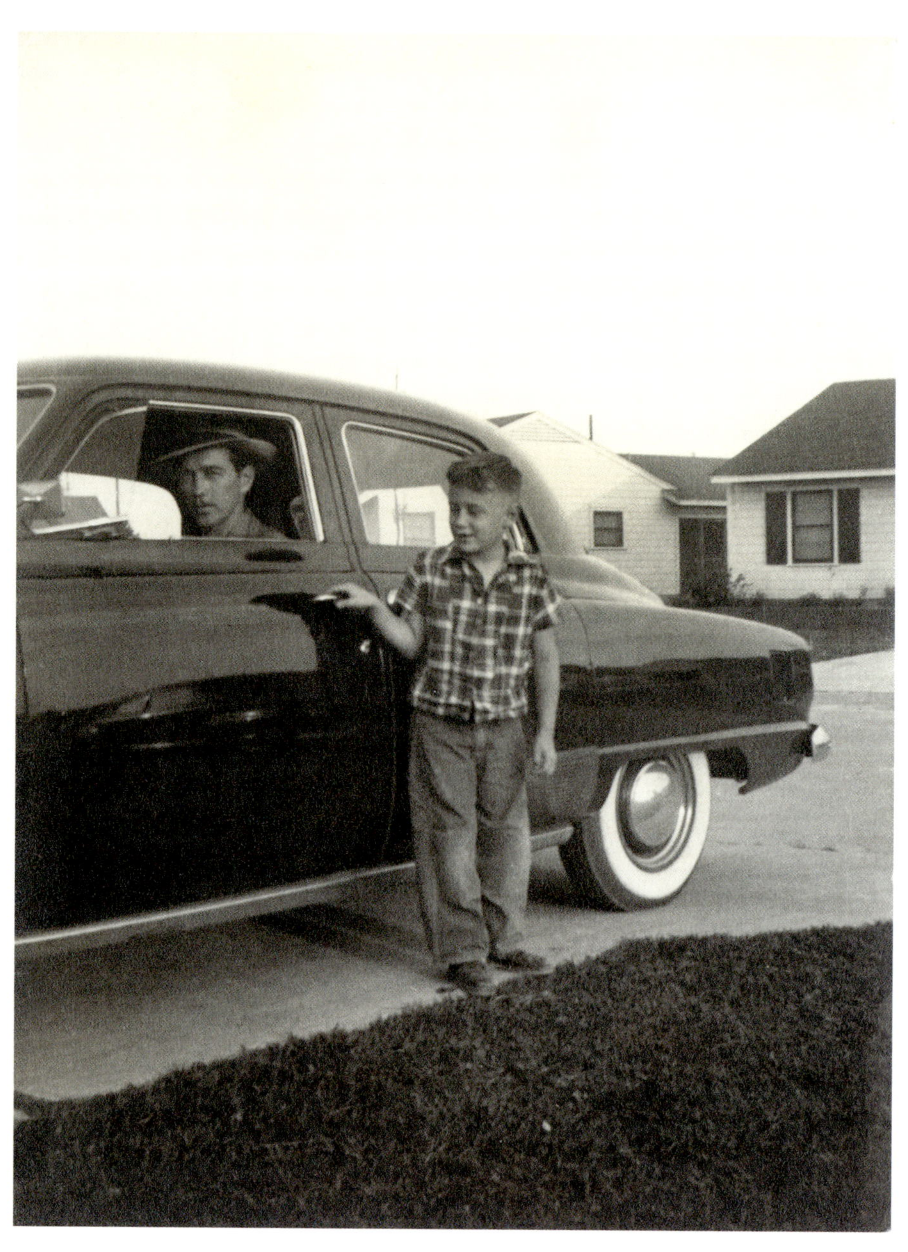

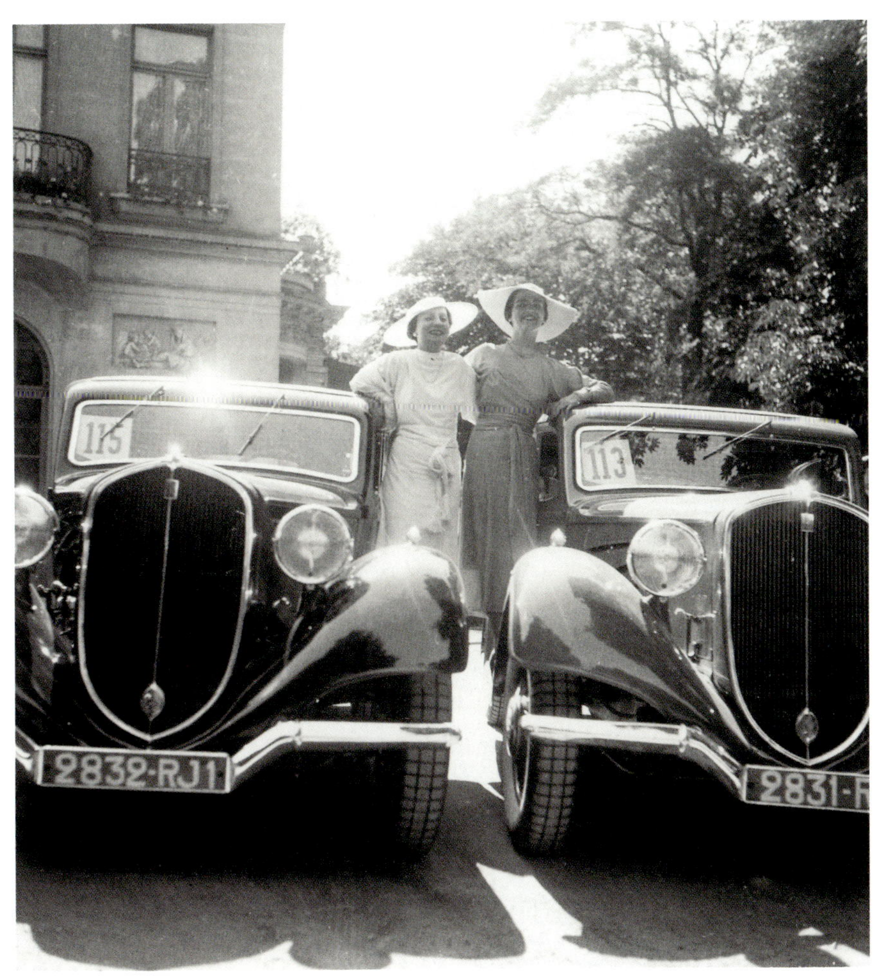
115
113
2832-RJ1
2831-R

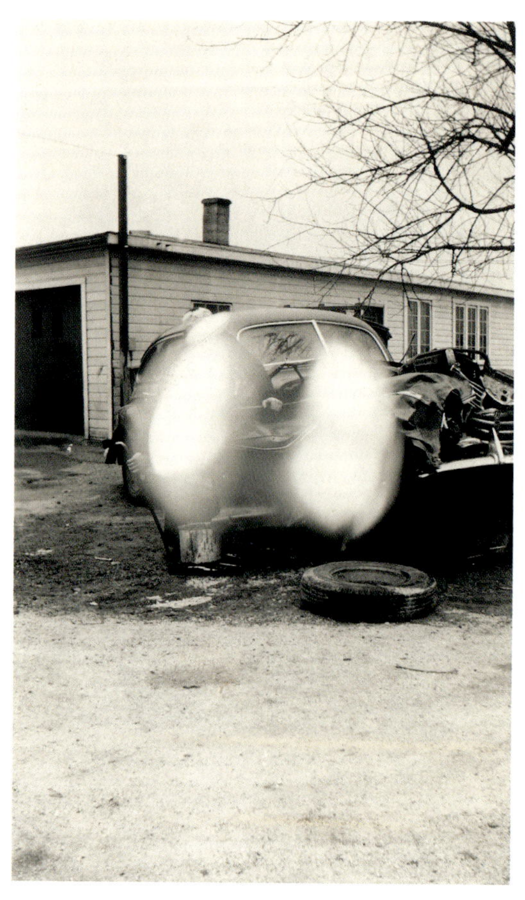

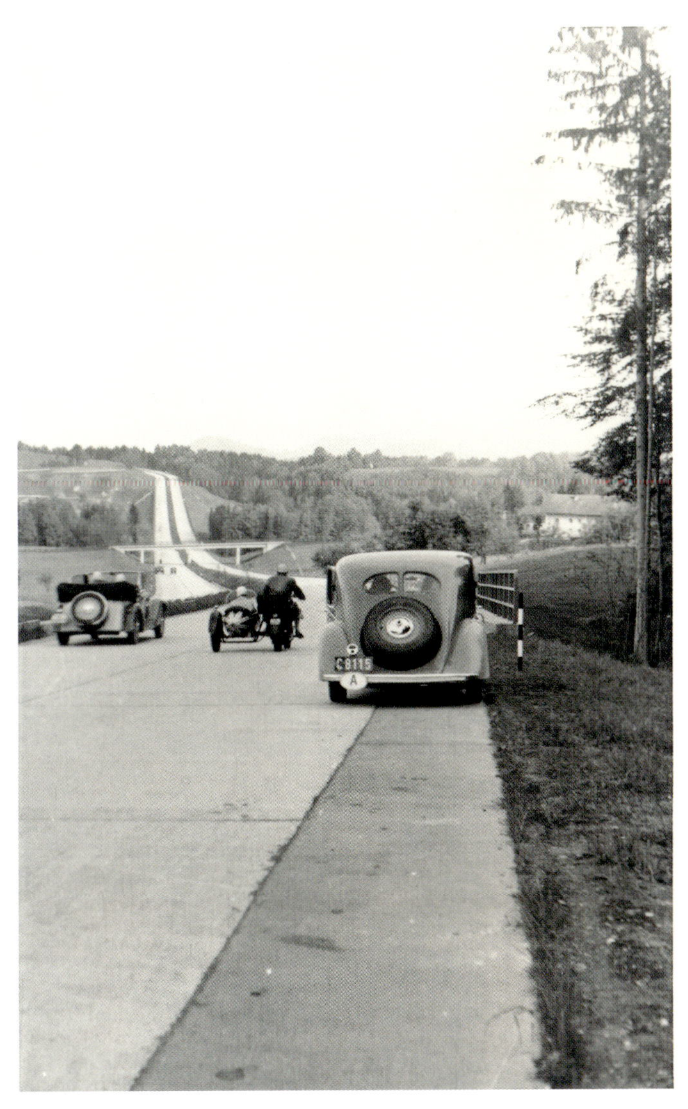
C8115
A

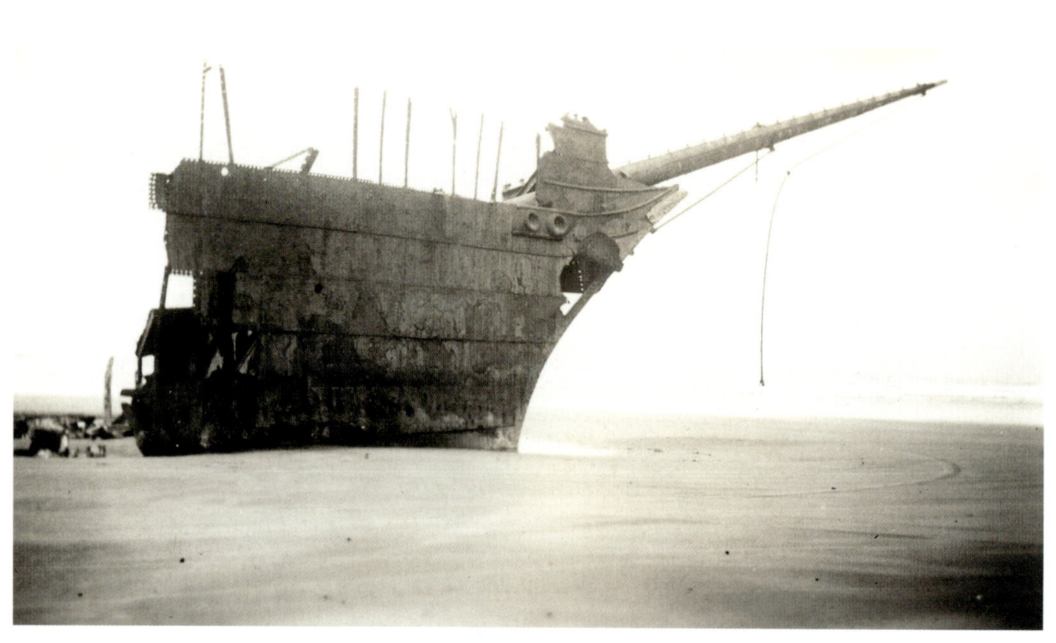

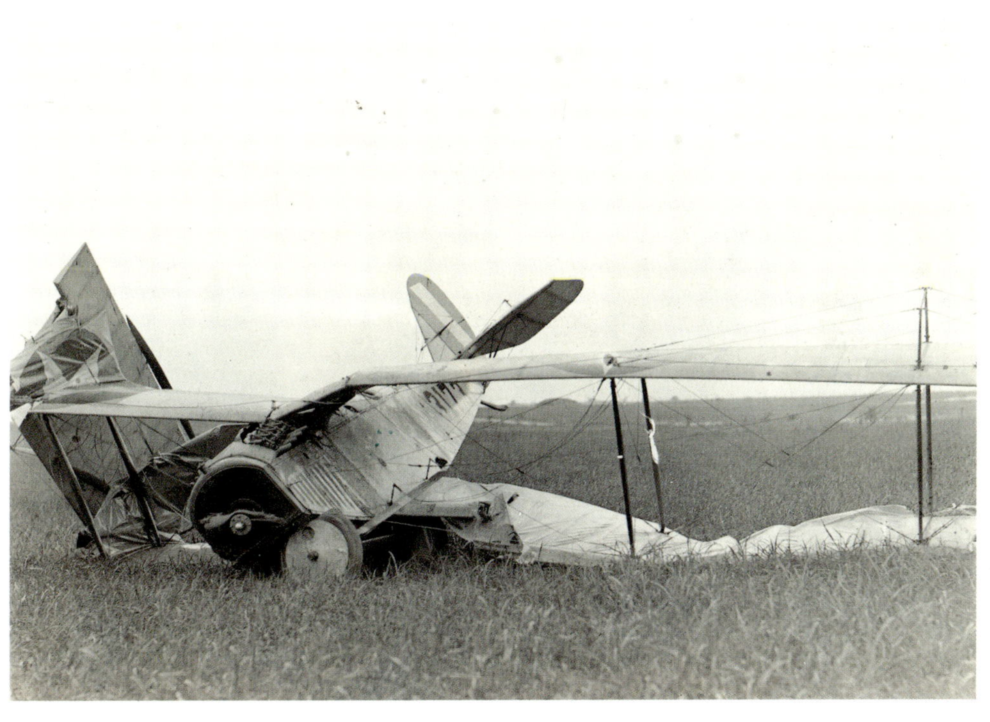

13)

Big Town—Small Town   Großstadt – Kleinstadt

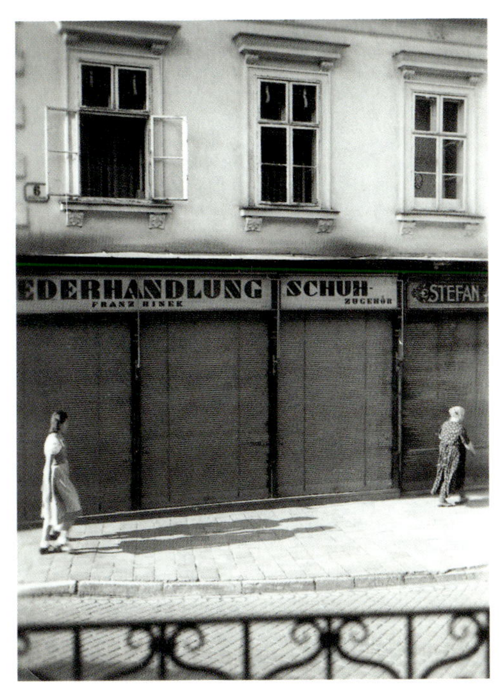
6
EDERHANDLUNG
FRANZ RINEK
SCHUH-
ZUGEHÖR
STEFAN

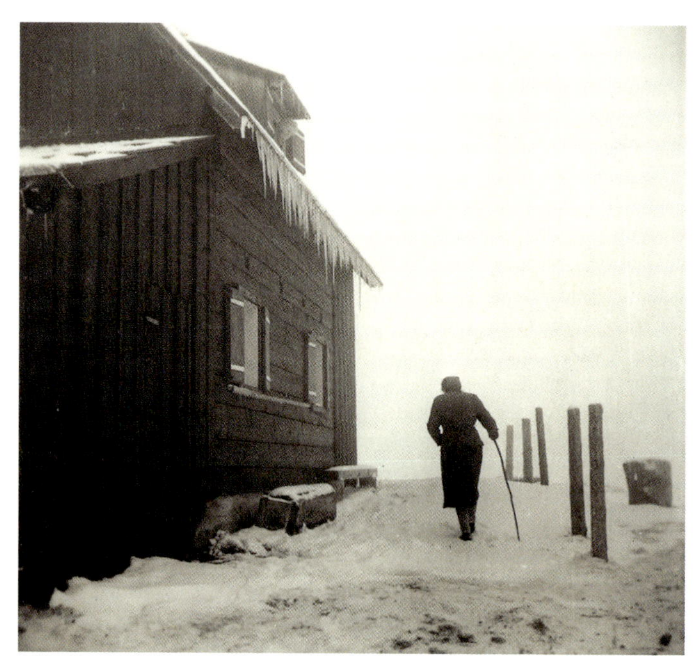

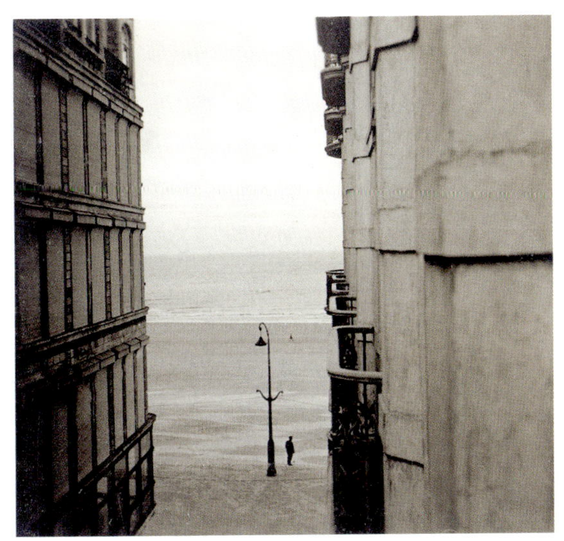

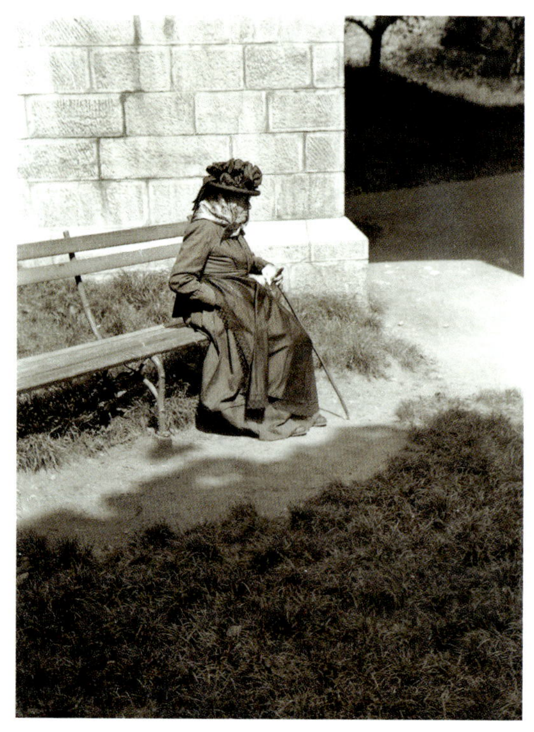

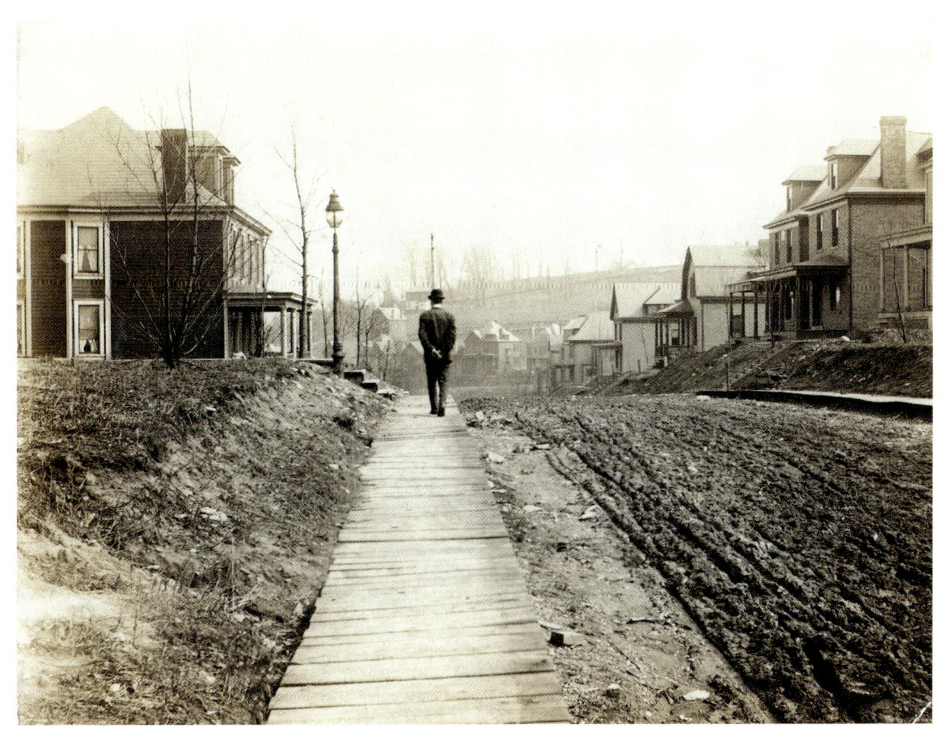

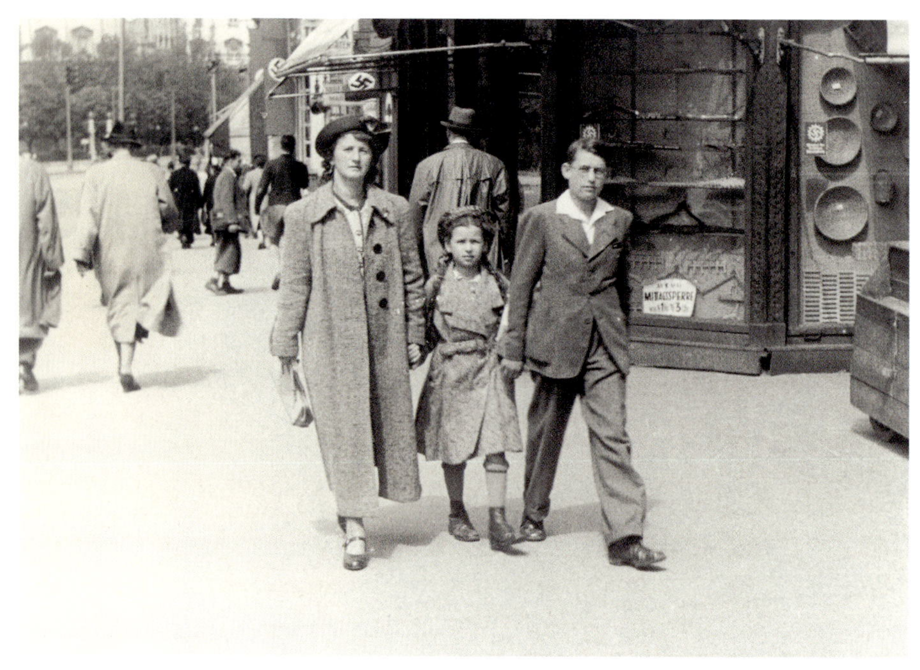

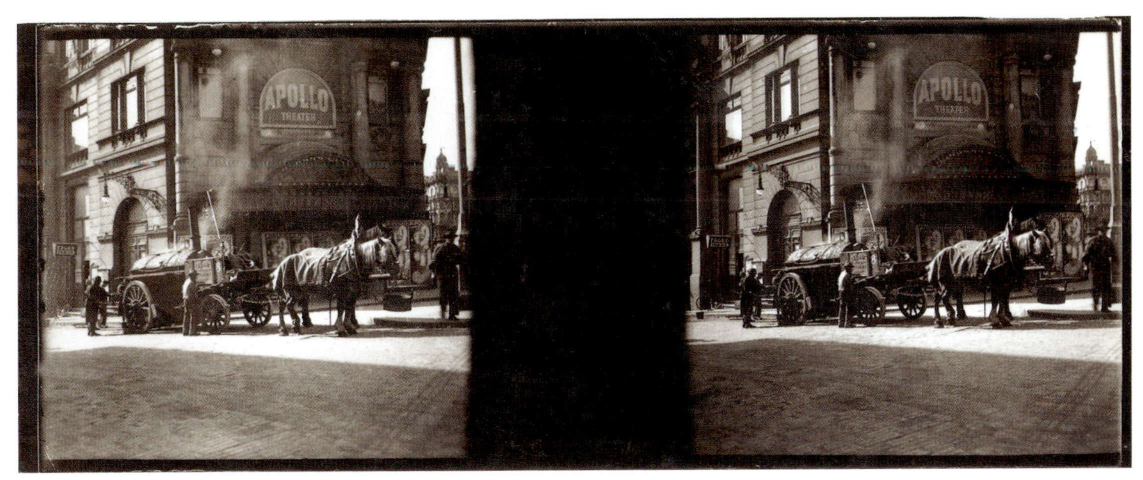
APOLLO
THEATER

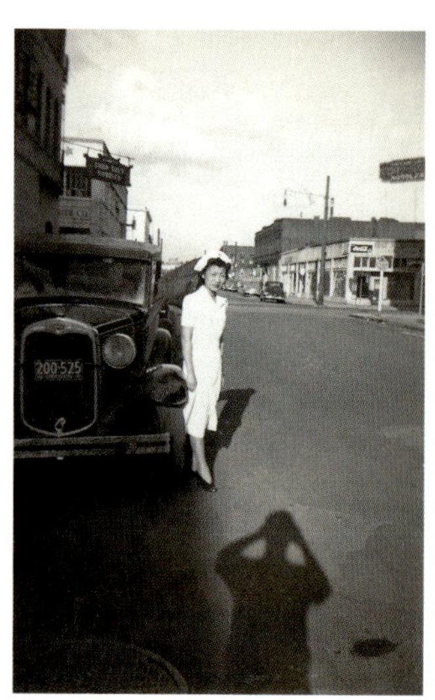
200-525
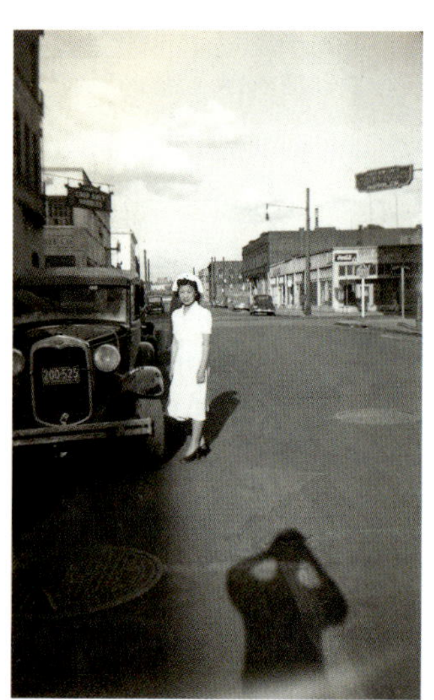
200-525

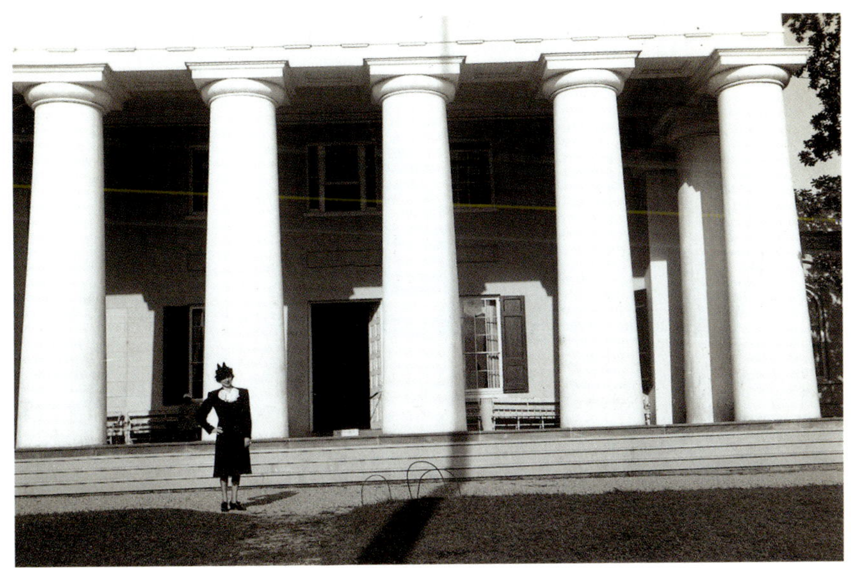

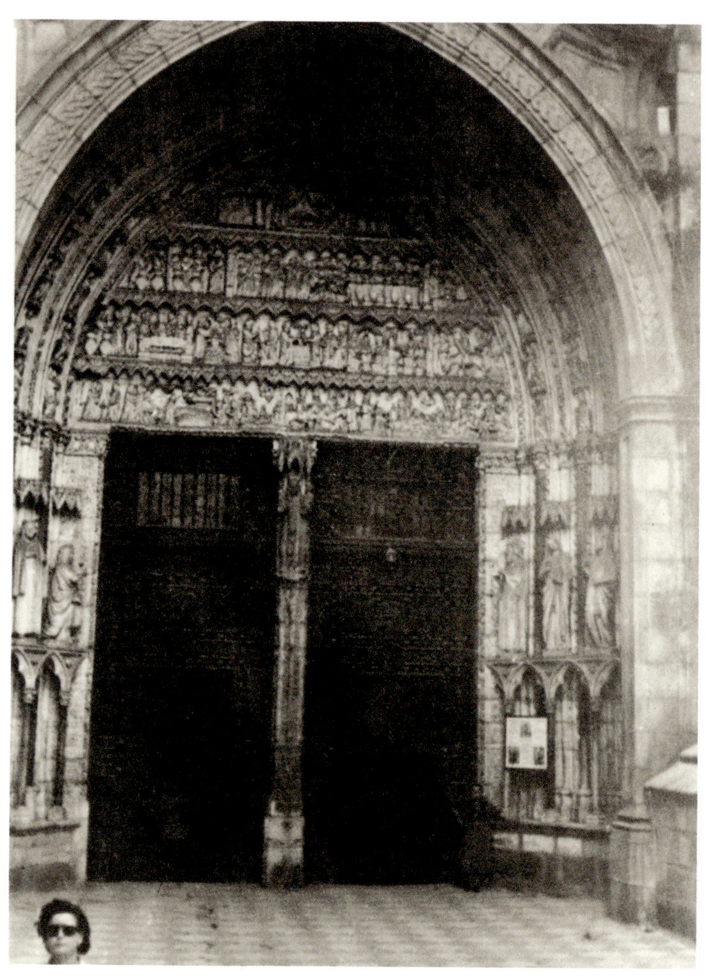

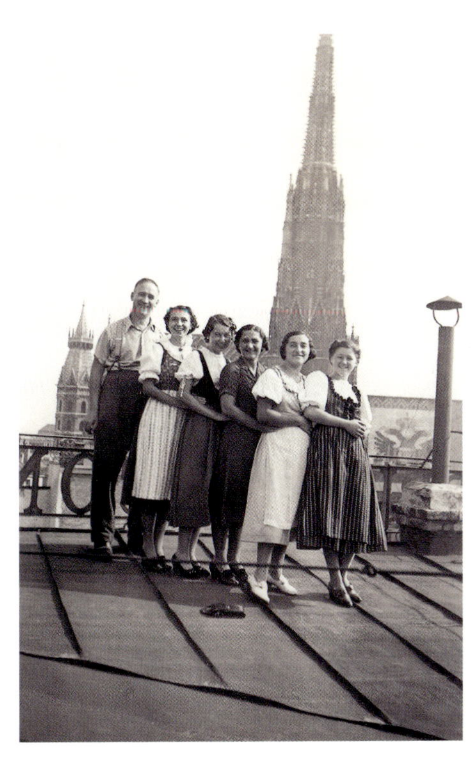

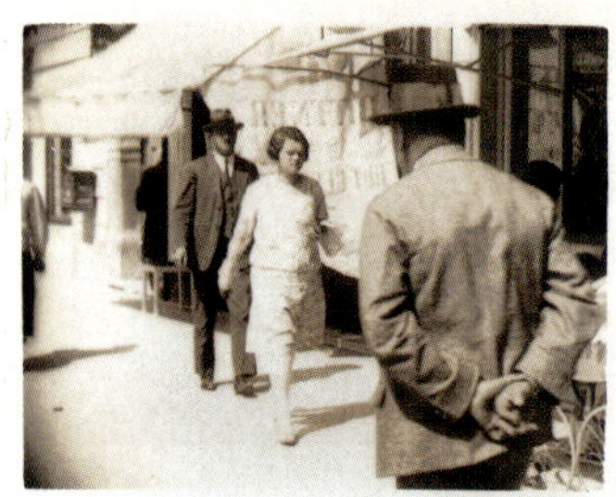

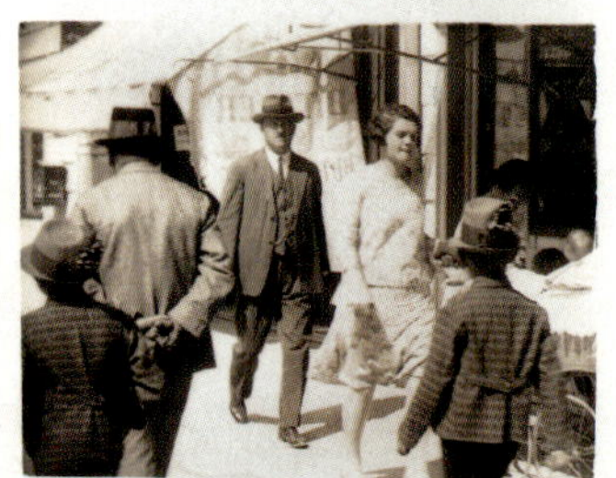

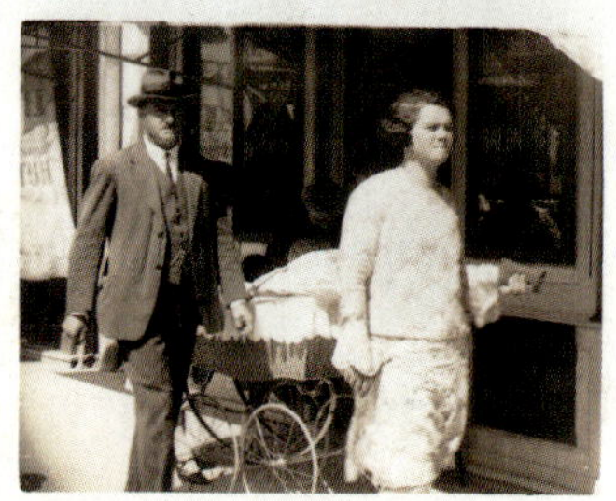

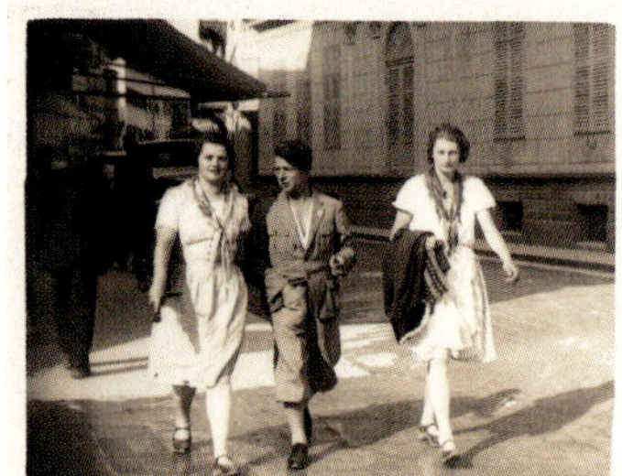

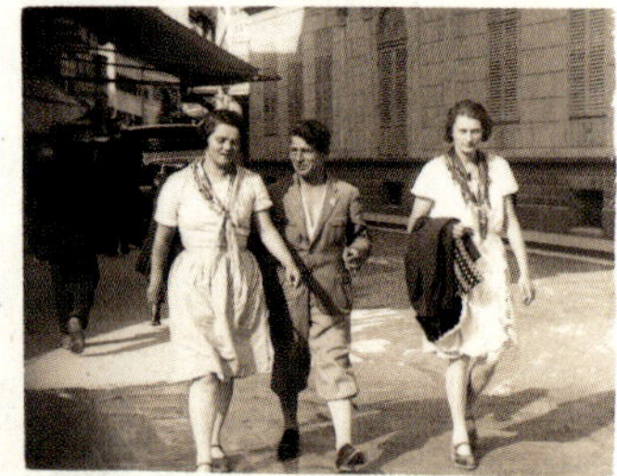

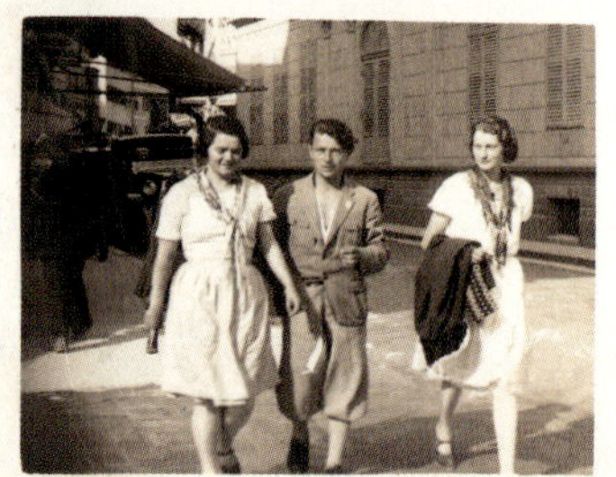

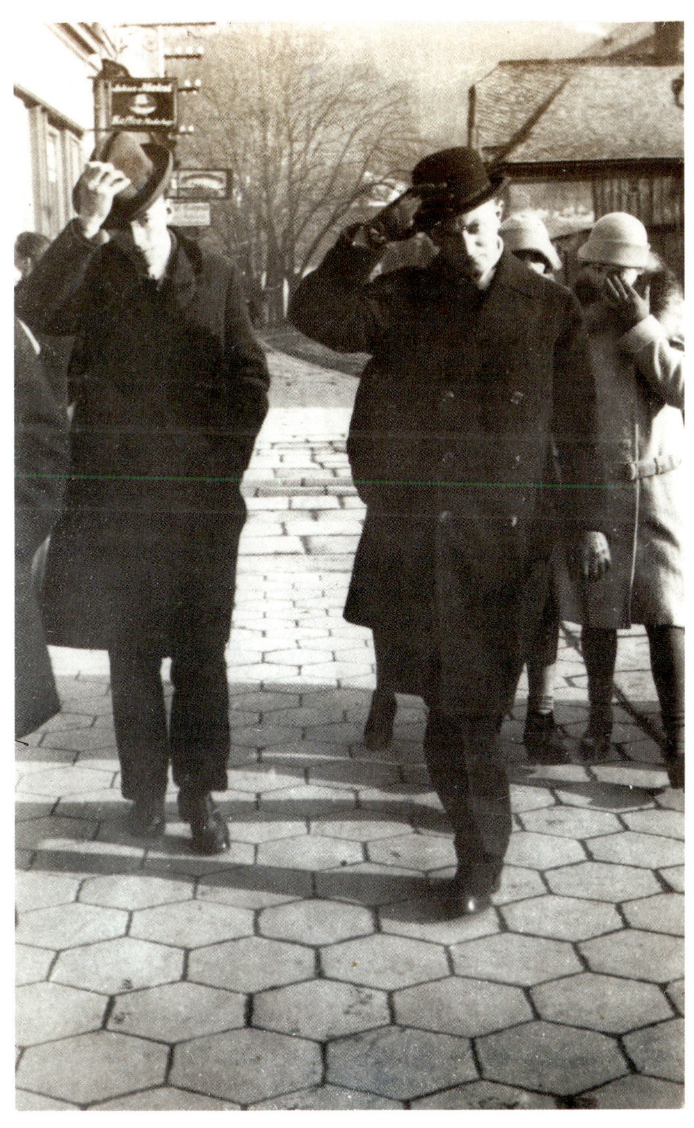

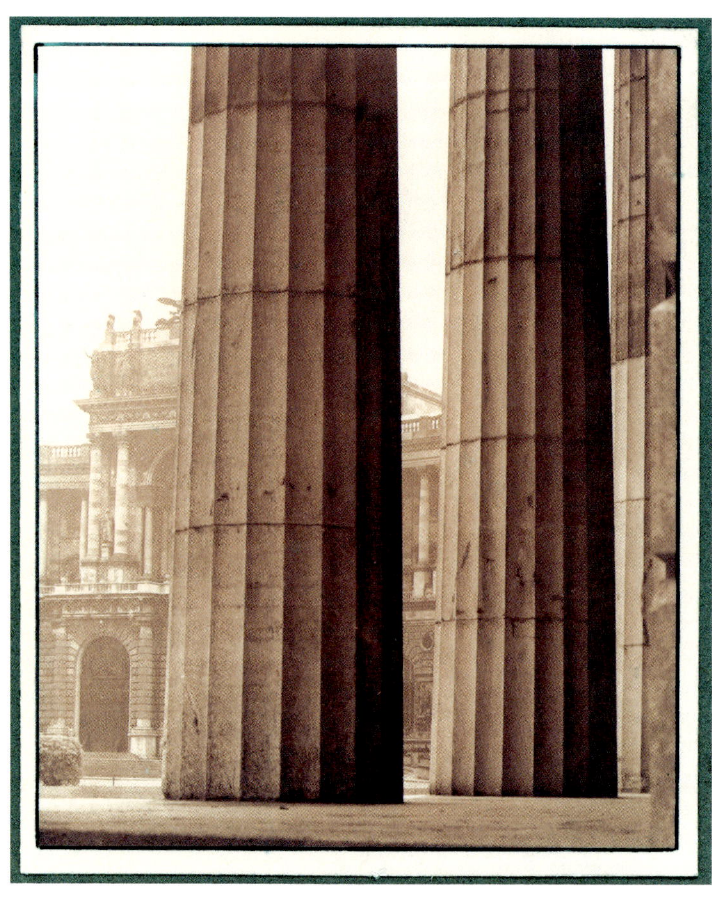

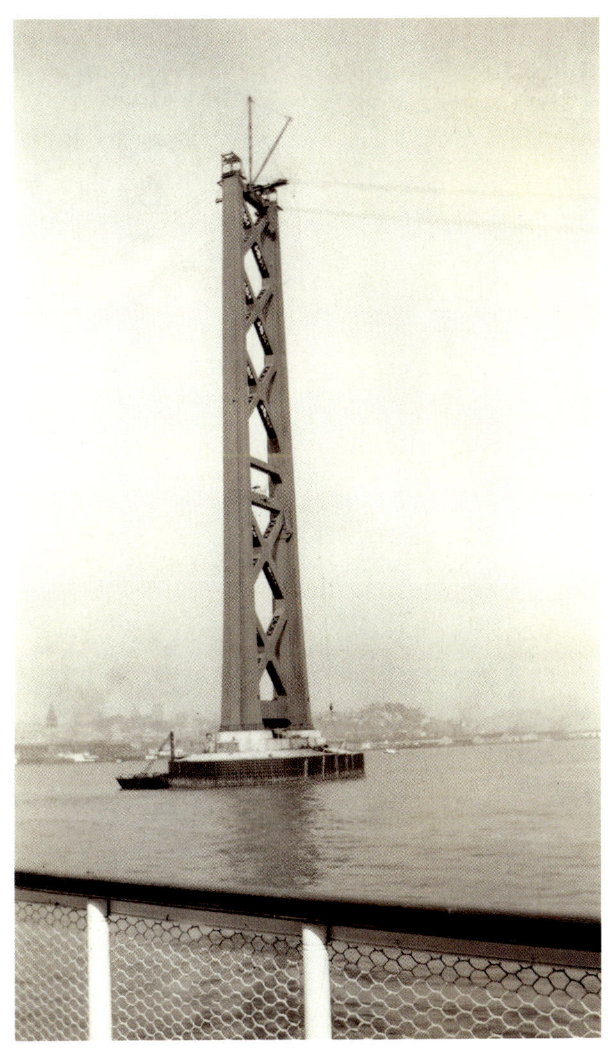

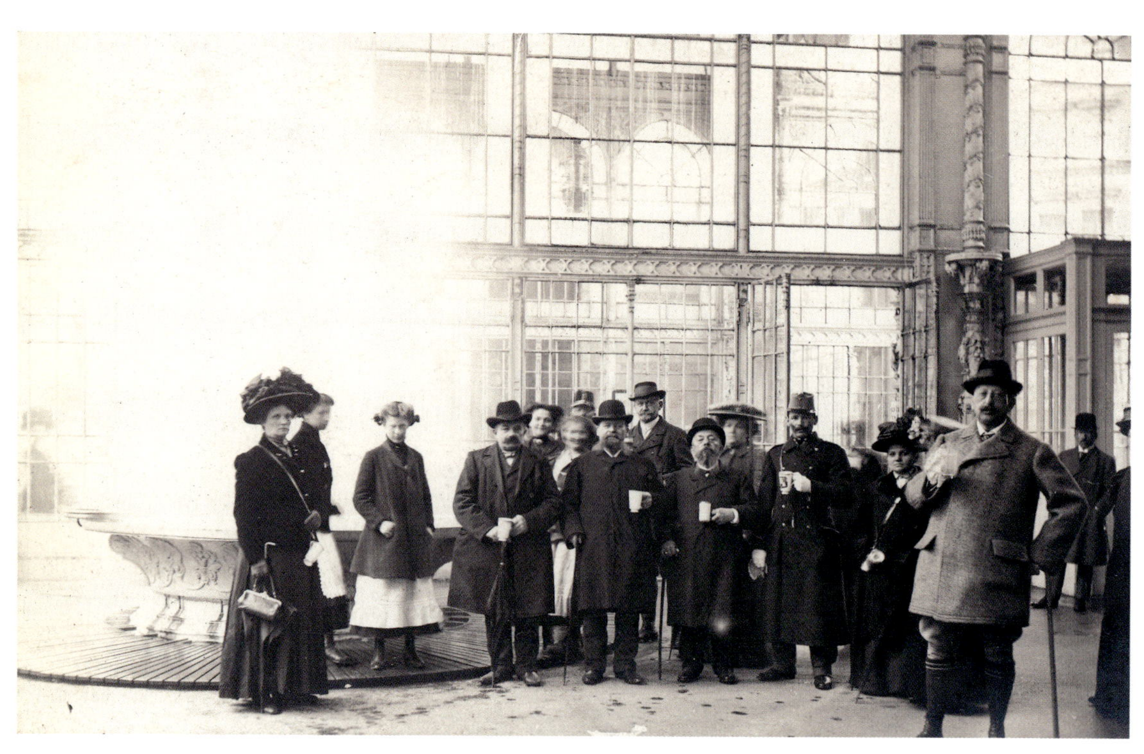

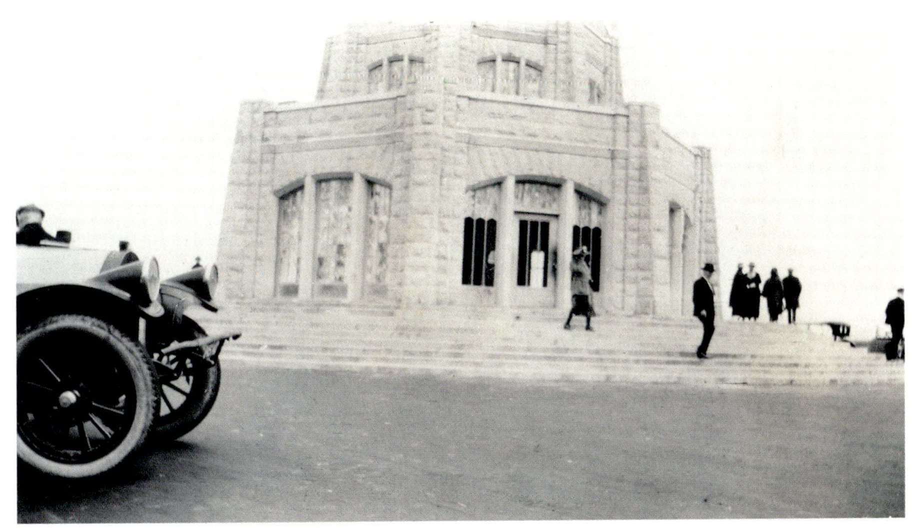

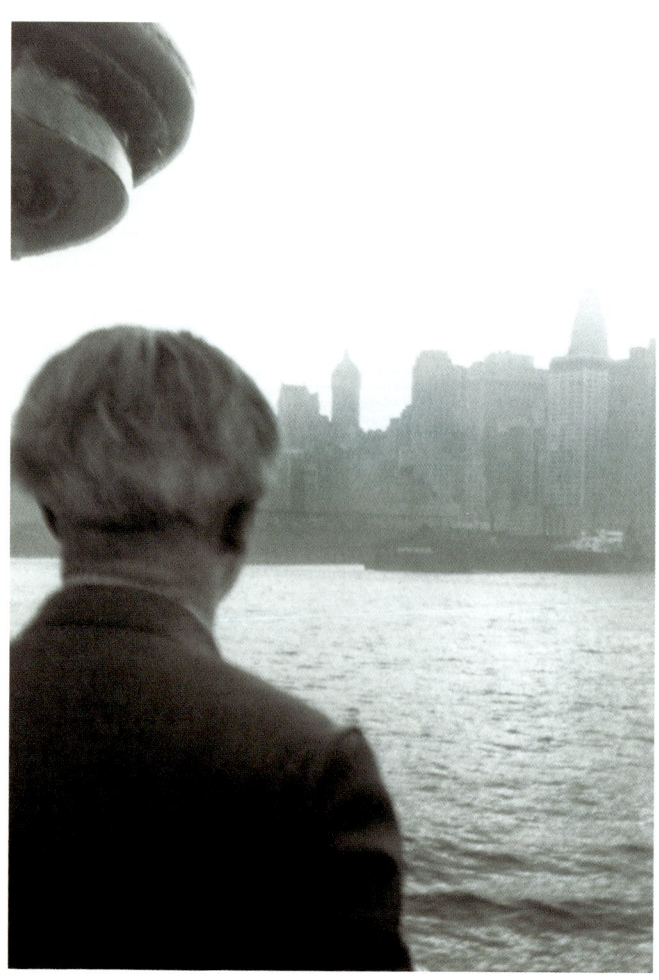

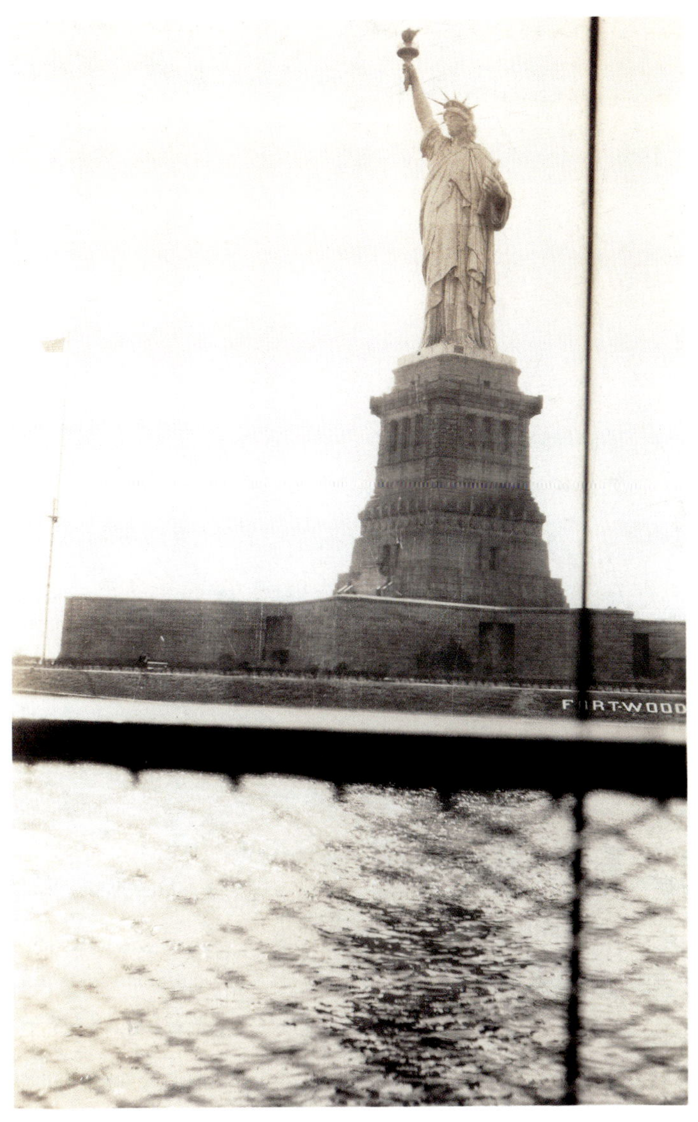

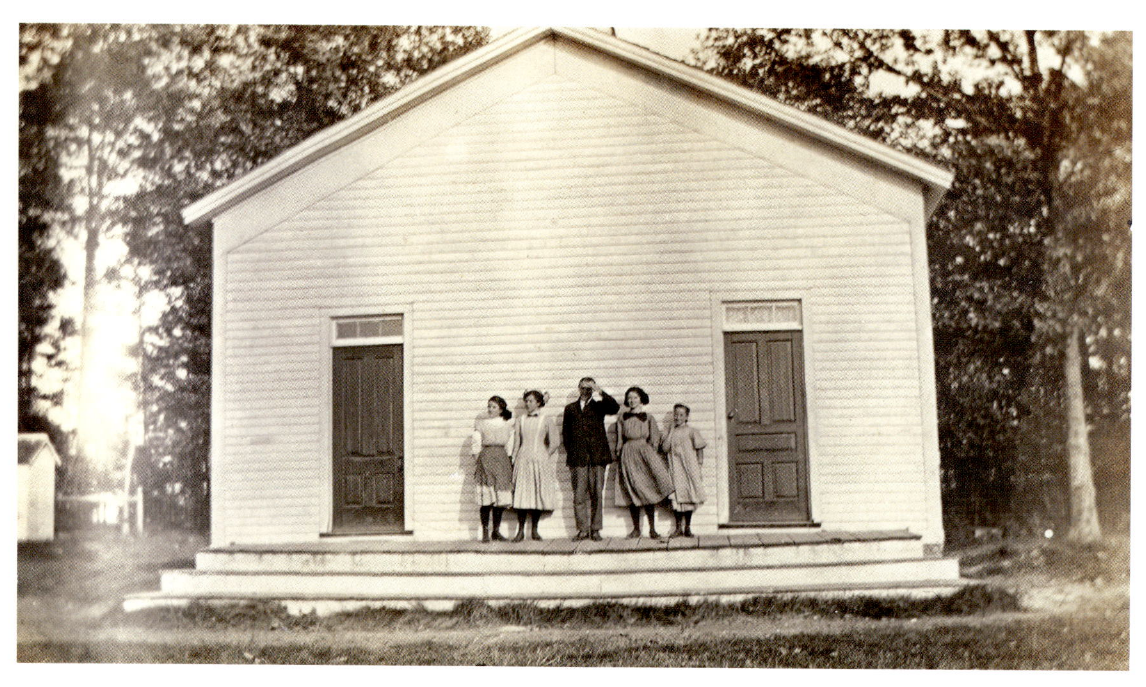

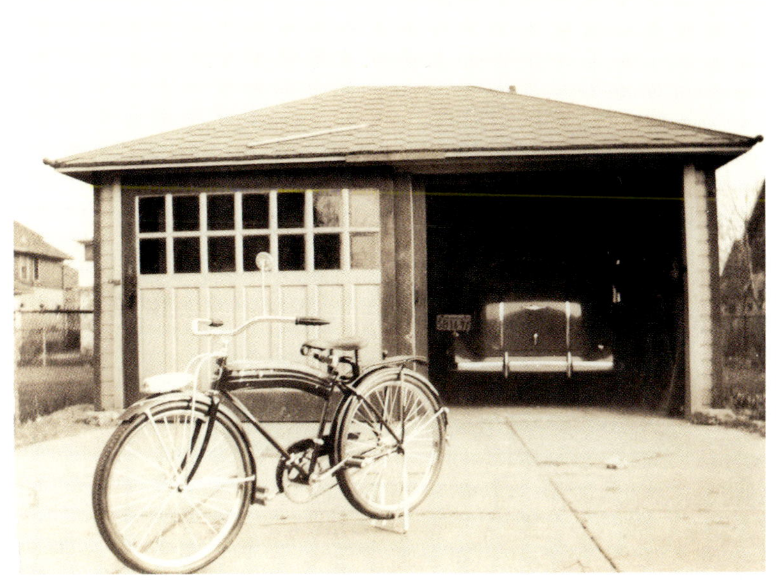

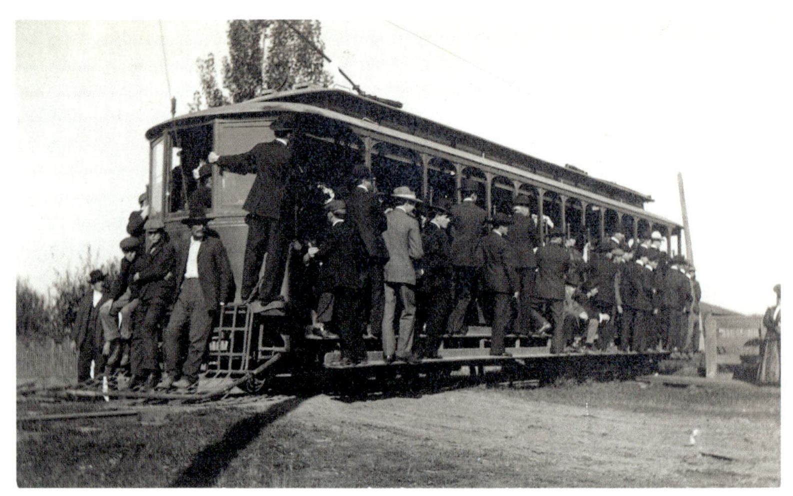

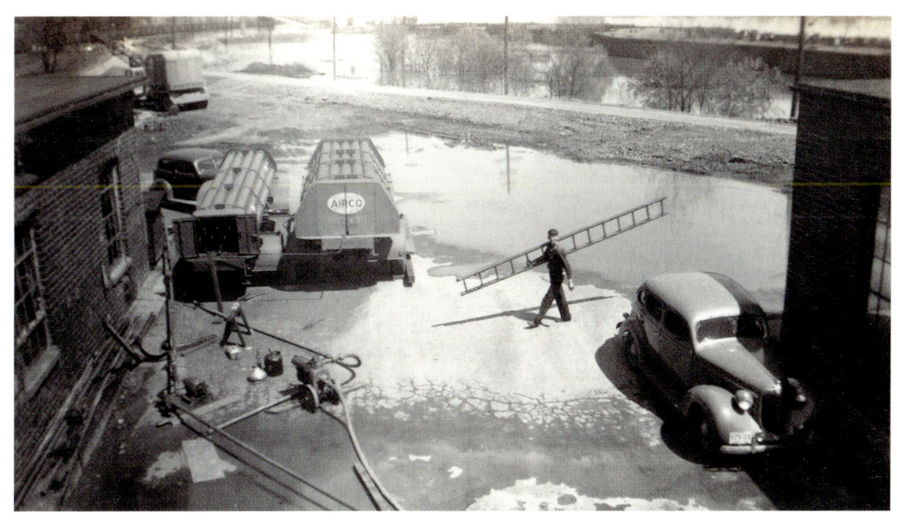
AIRCO

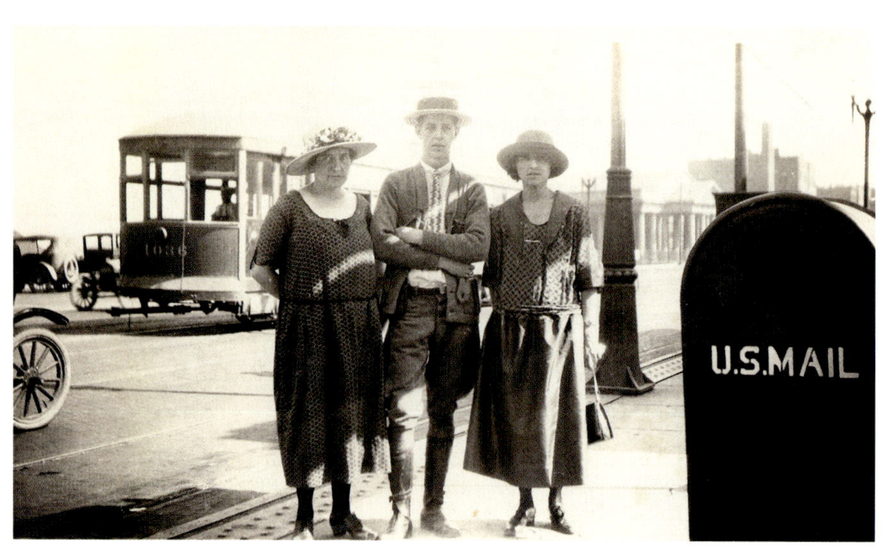
U.S.MAIL

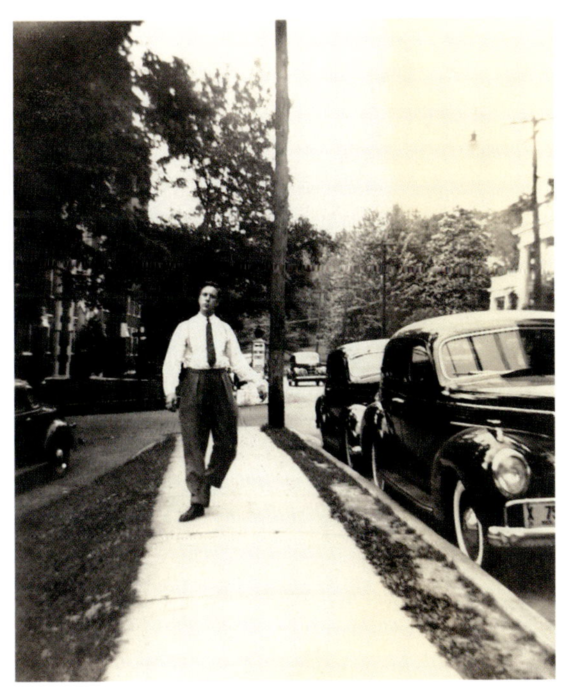

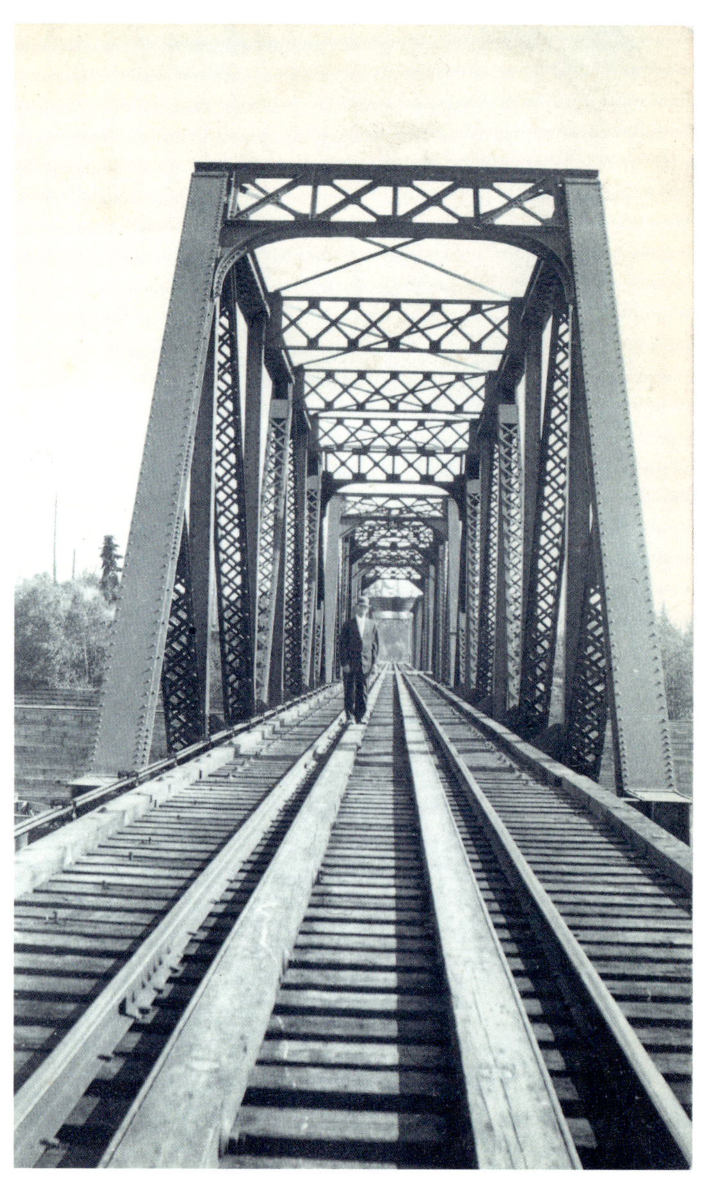

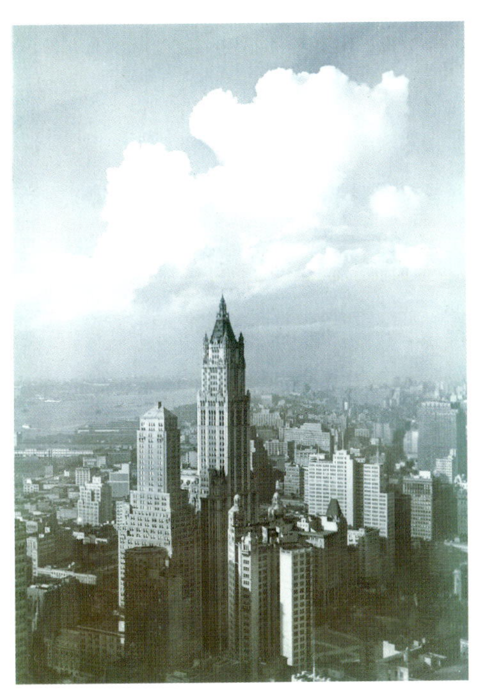

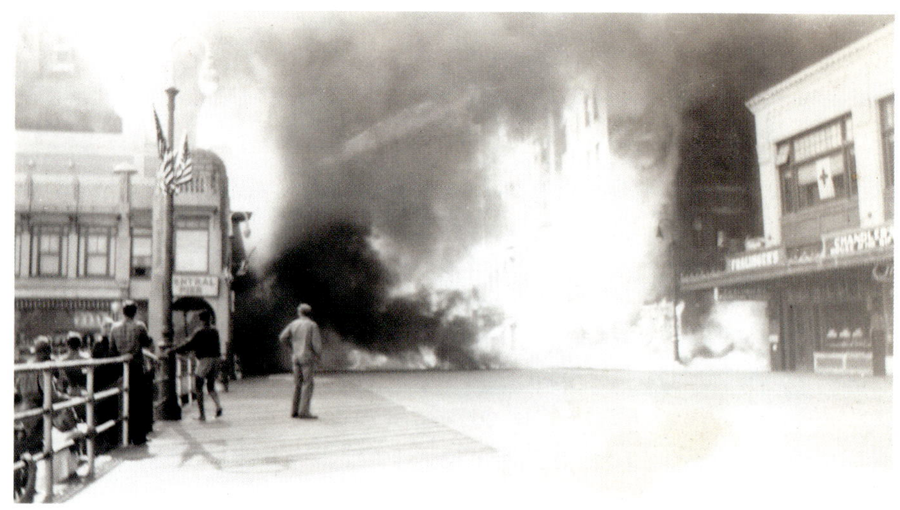

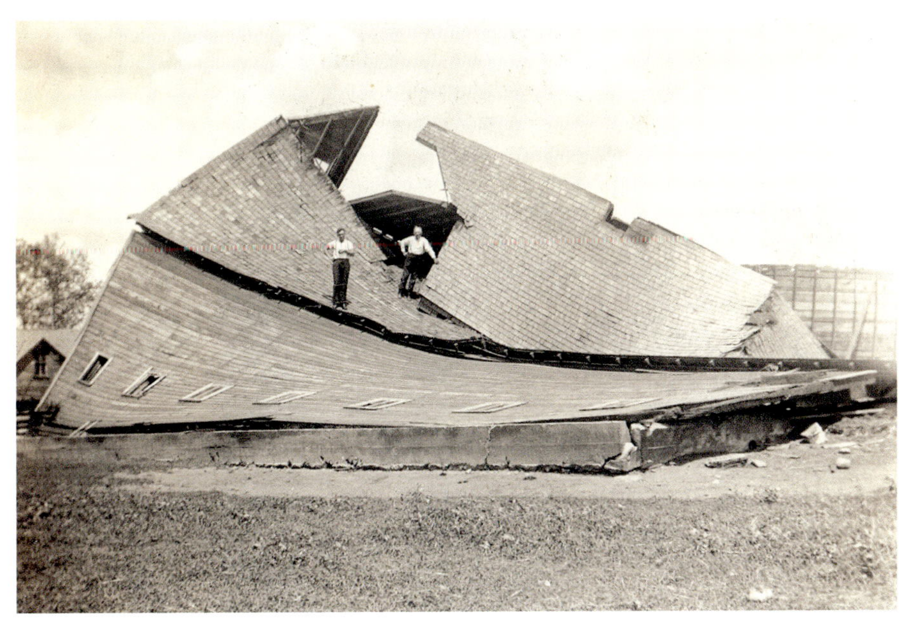

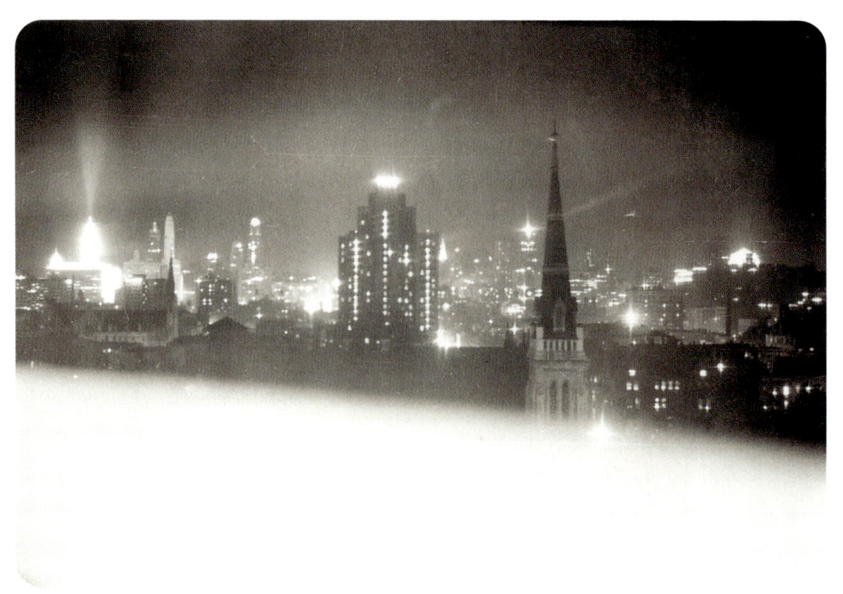

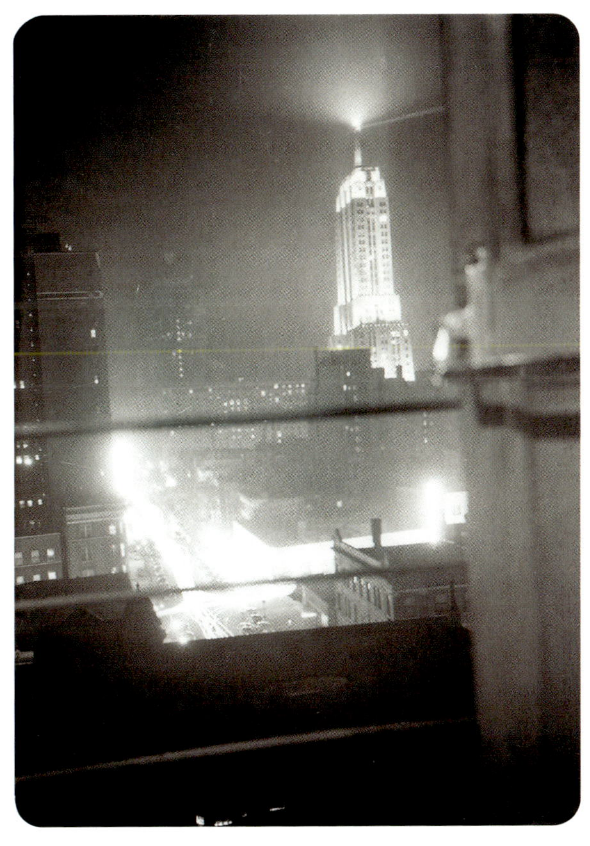

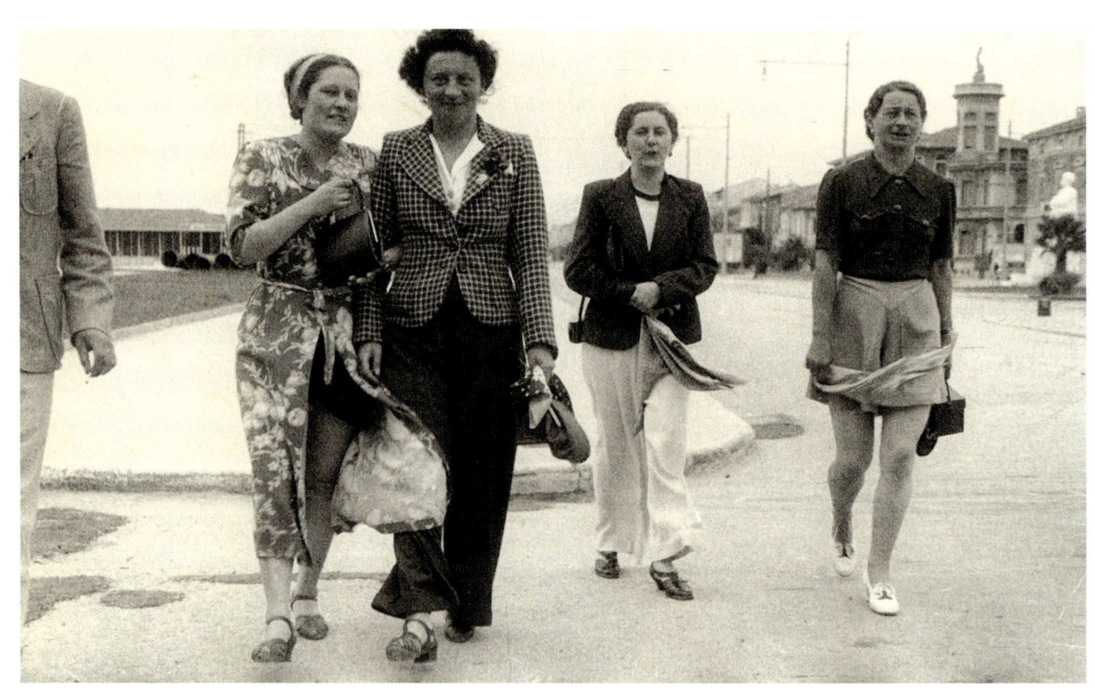

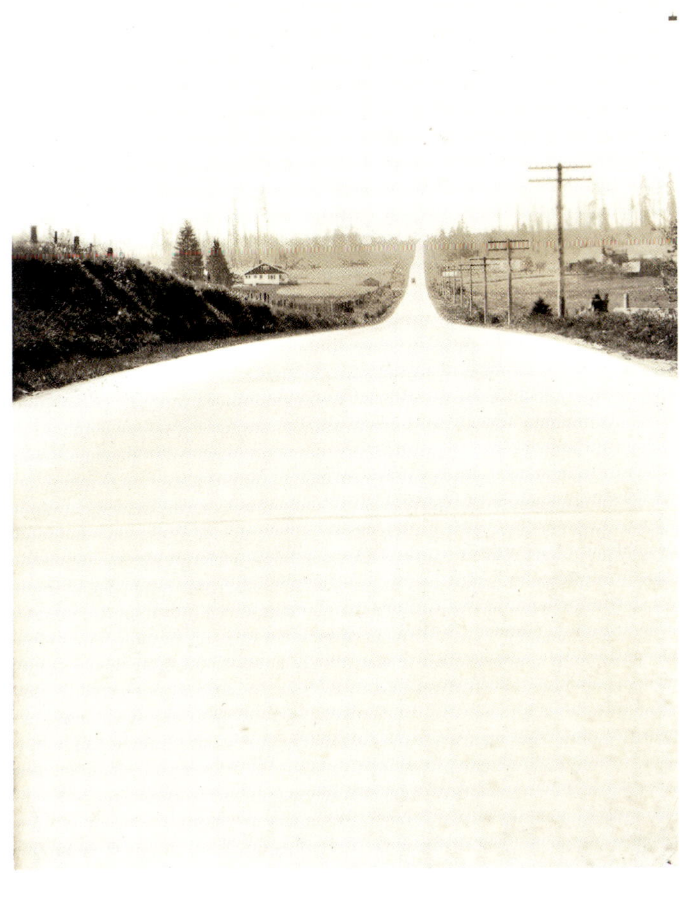

14)

At Work Bei der Arbeit

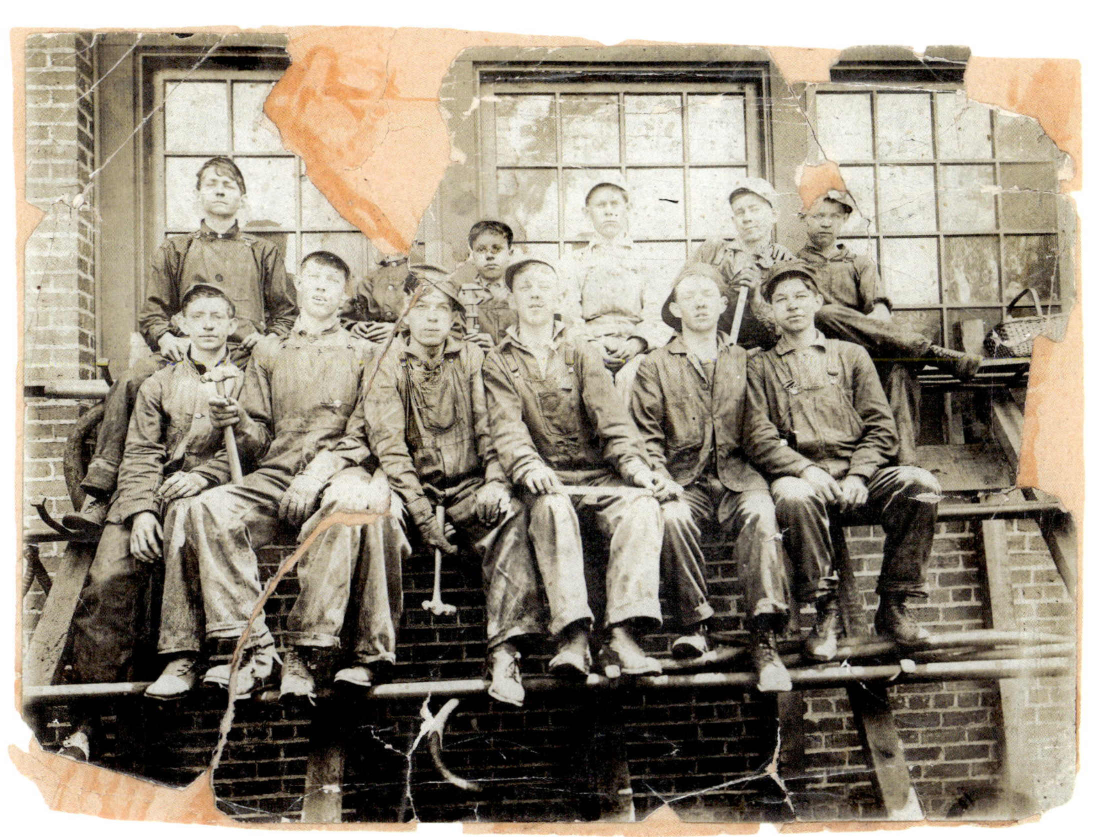

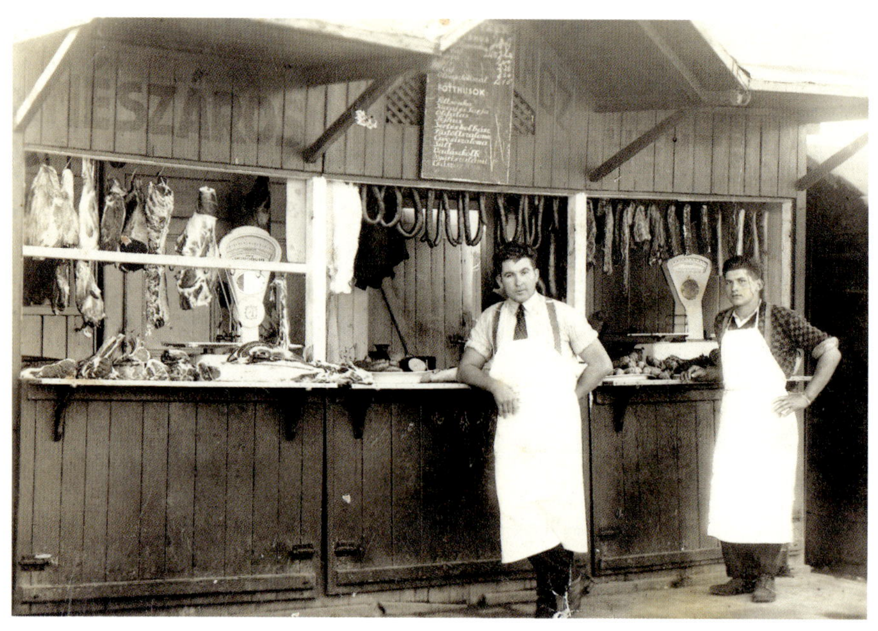

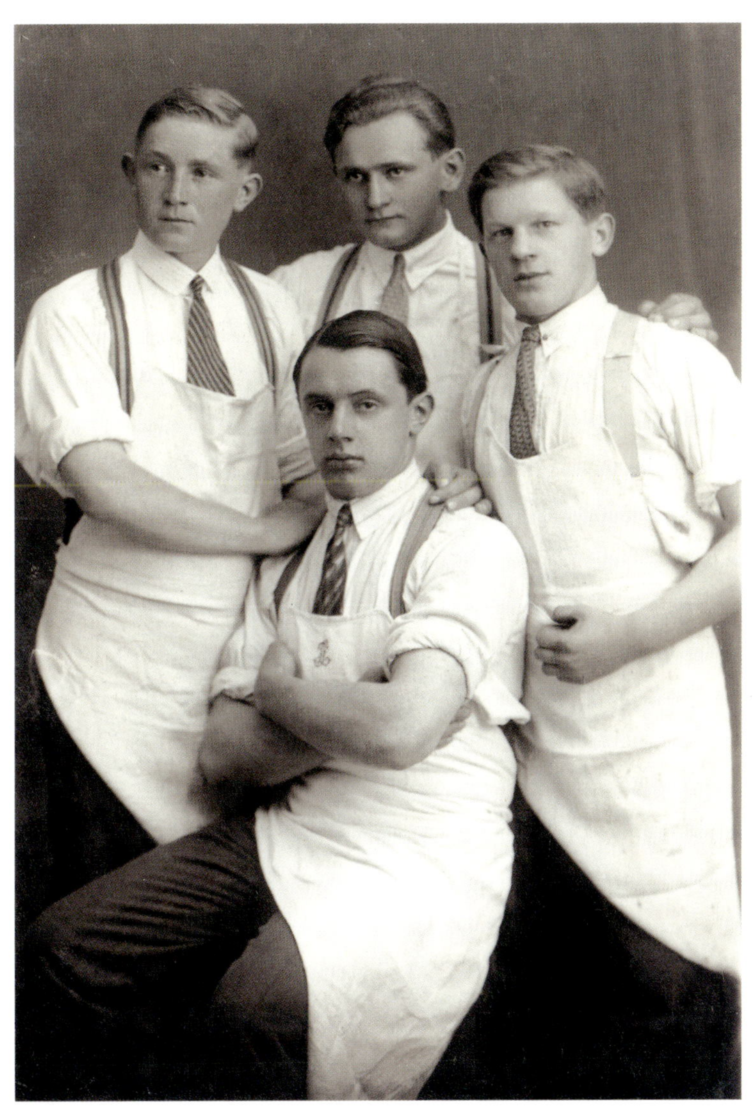

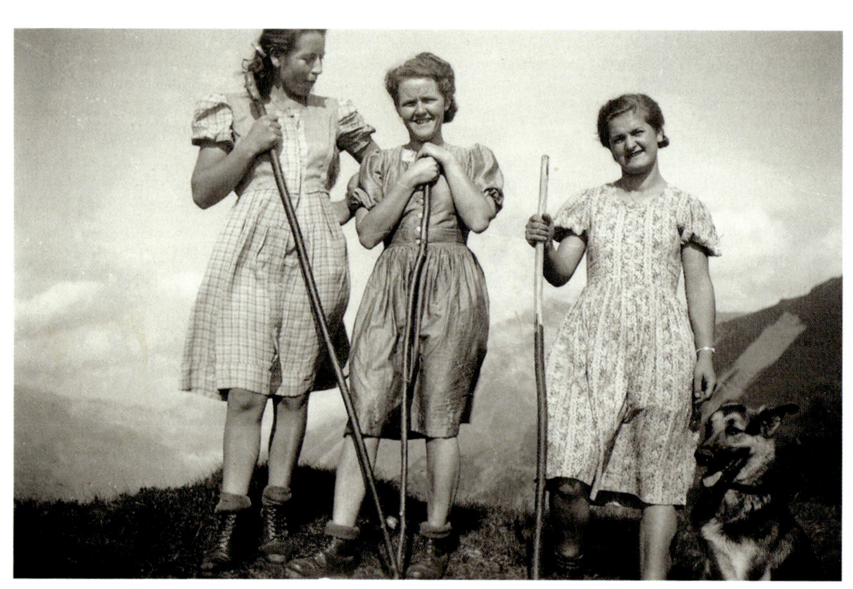

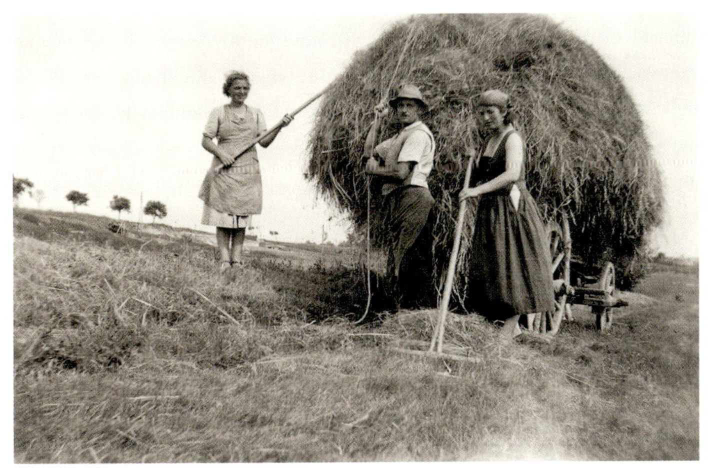

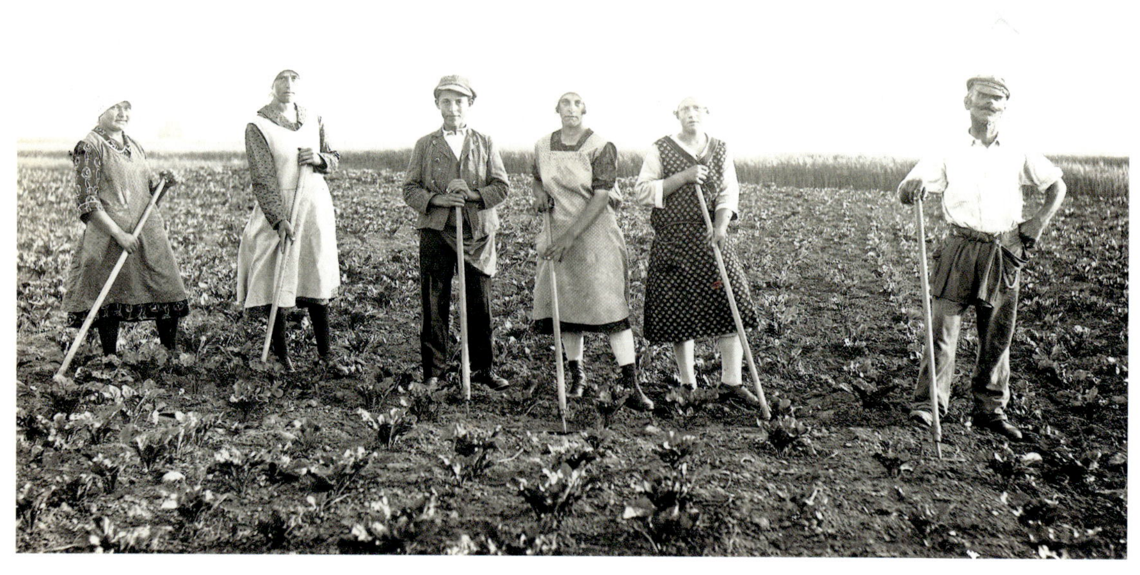

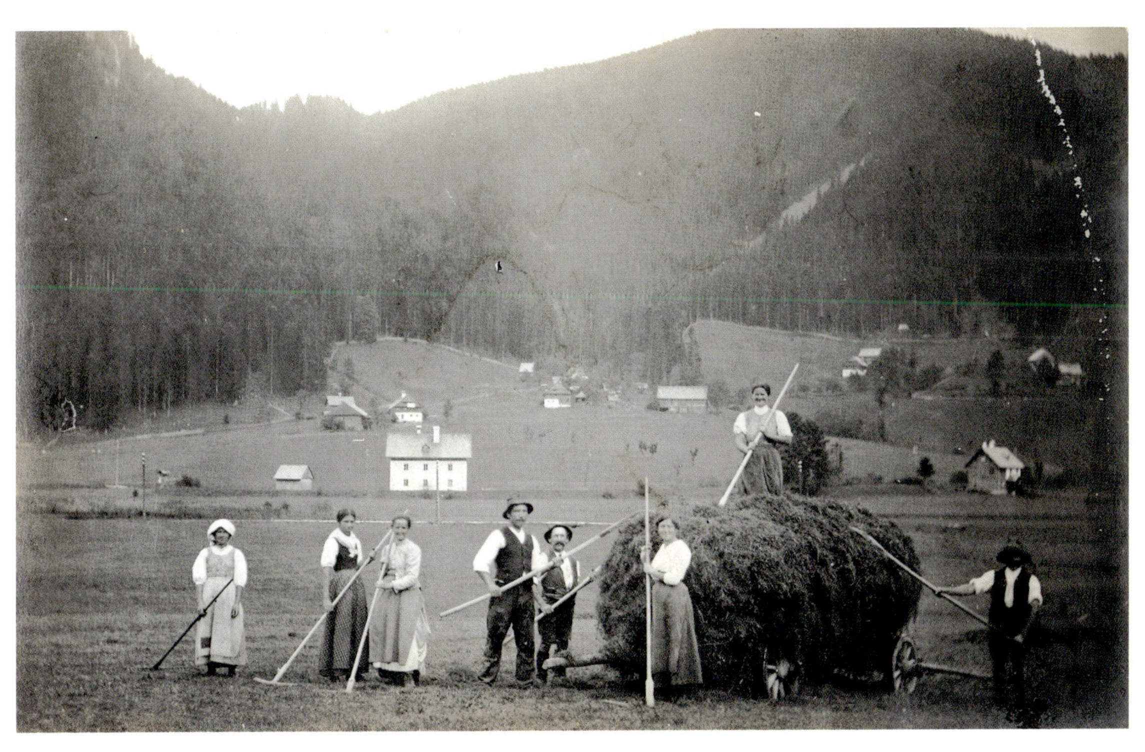

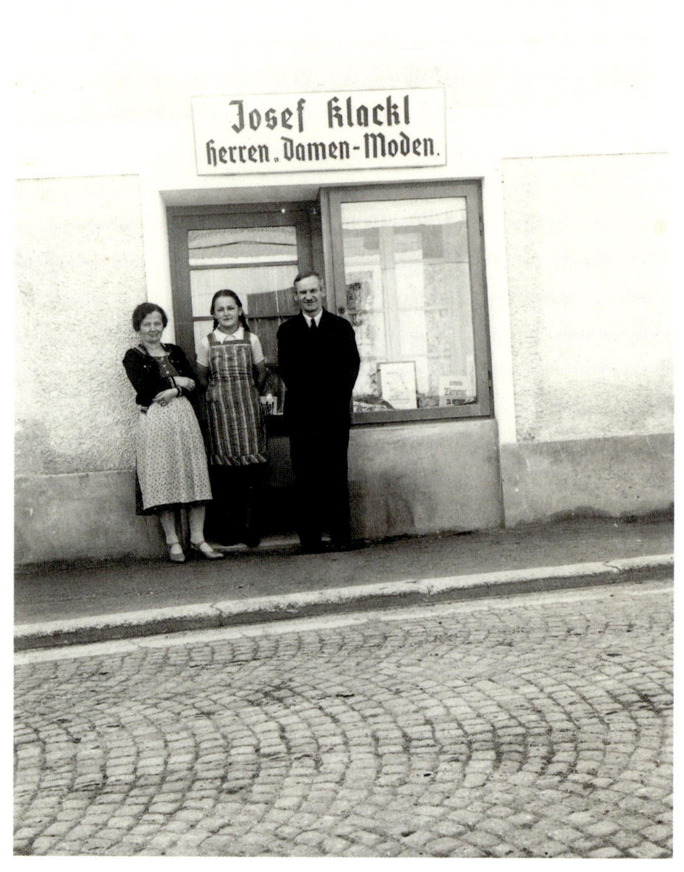
Josef Klackl
Herren u. Damen-Moden.

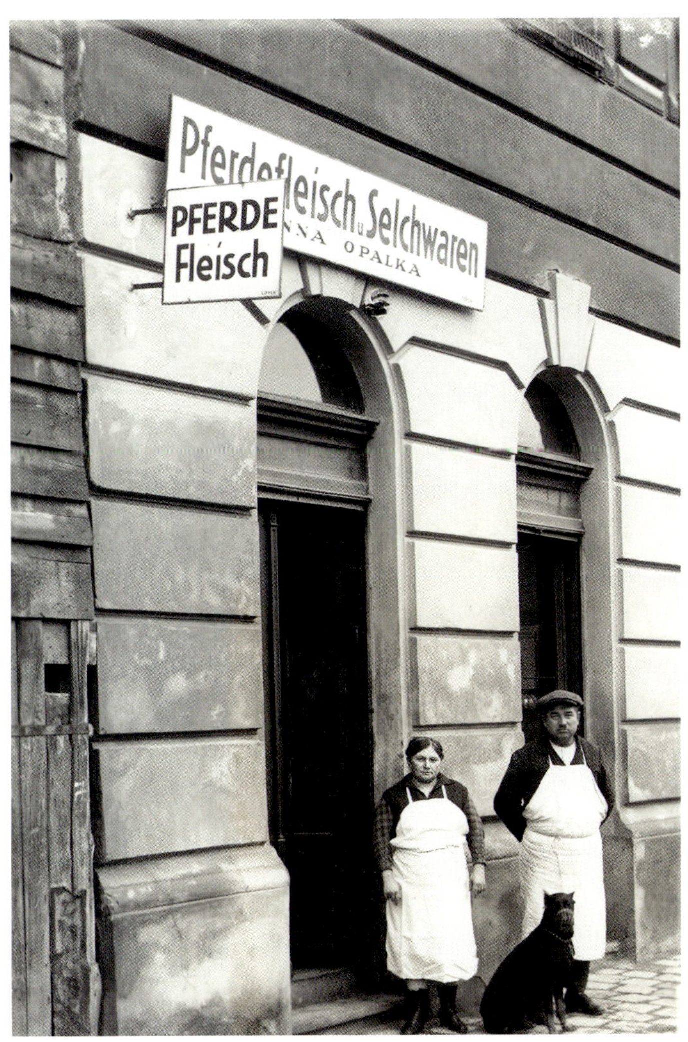
Pferdefleisch u. Selchwaren
NNA OPALKA
PFERDE
Fleisch

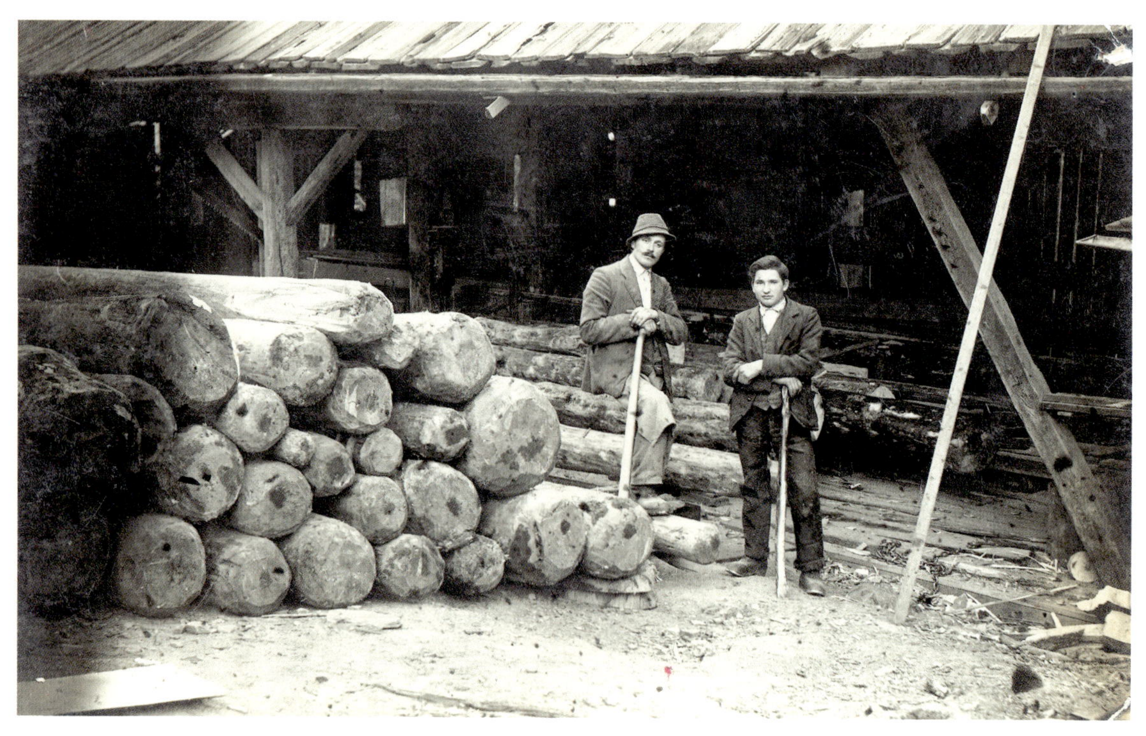

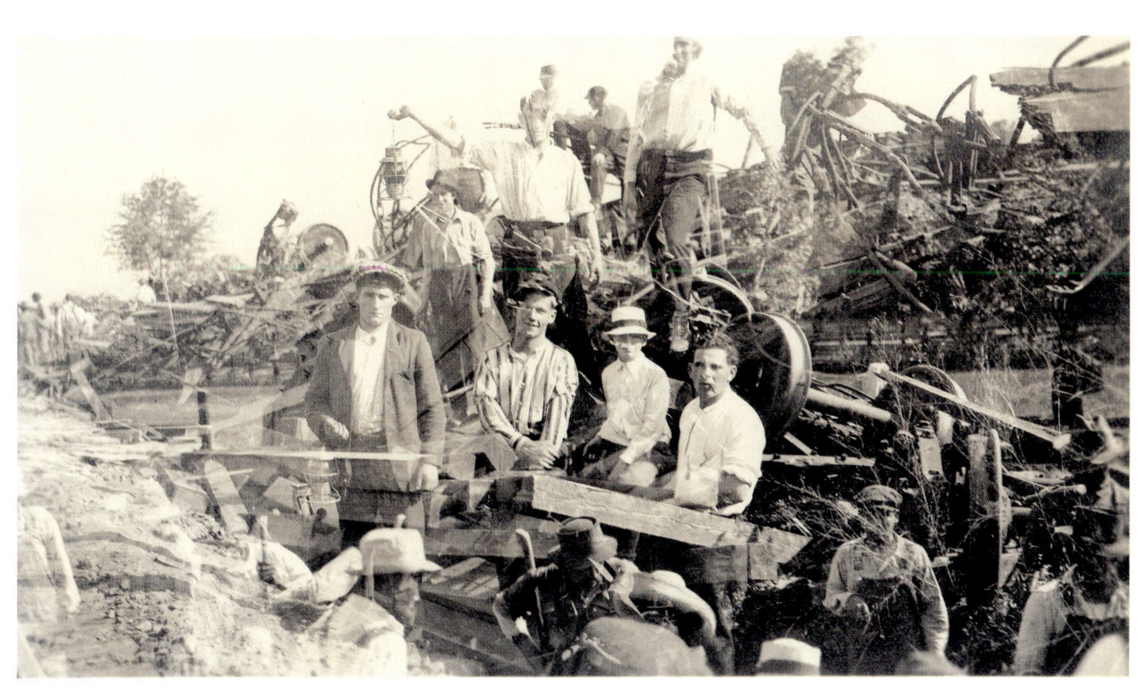

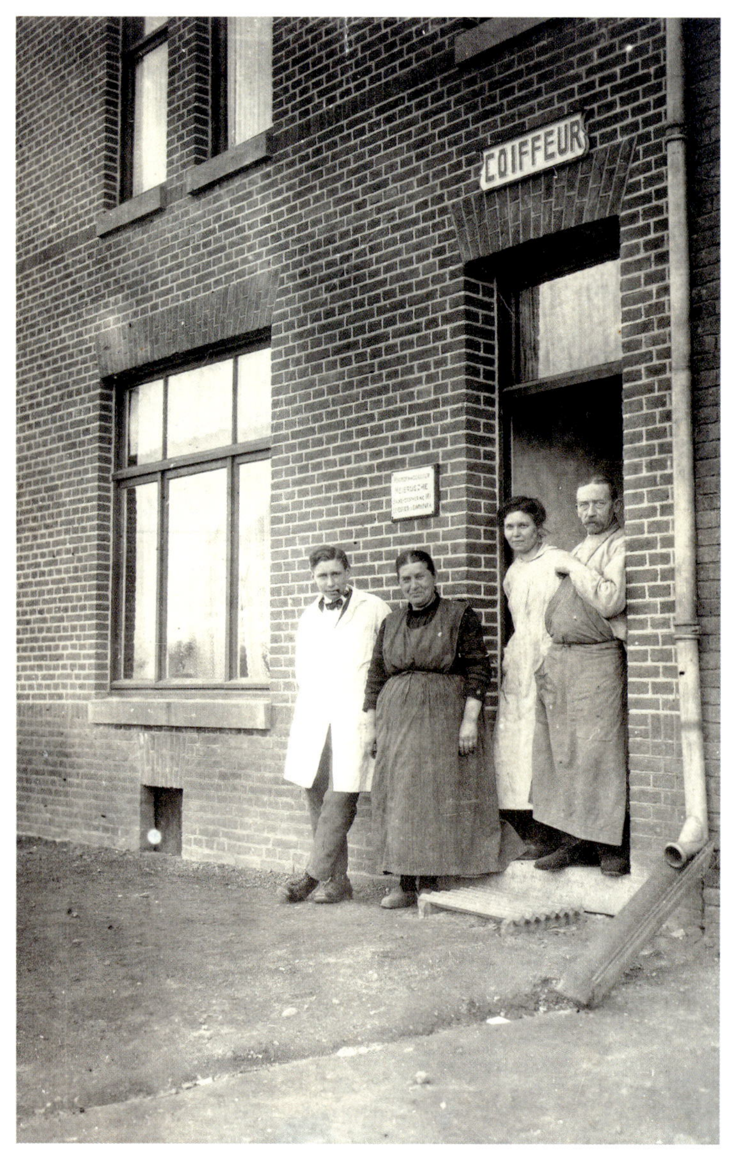
COIFFEUR

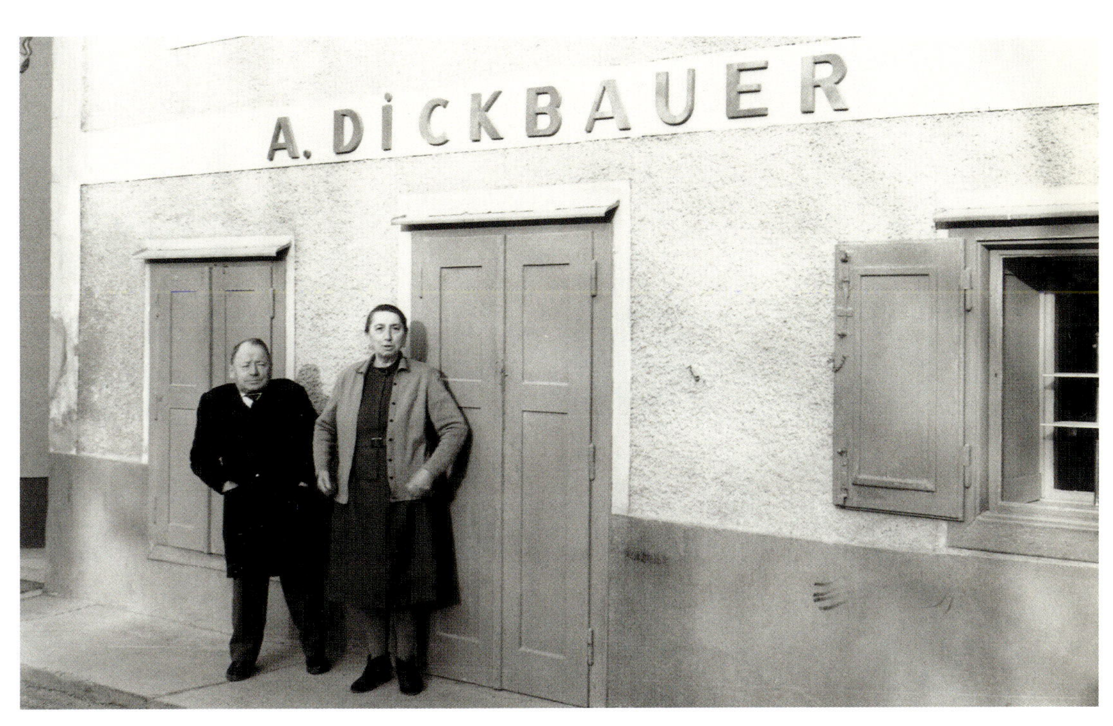
A. DICKBAUER

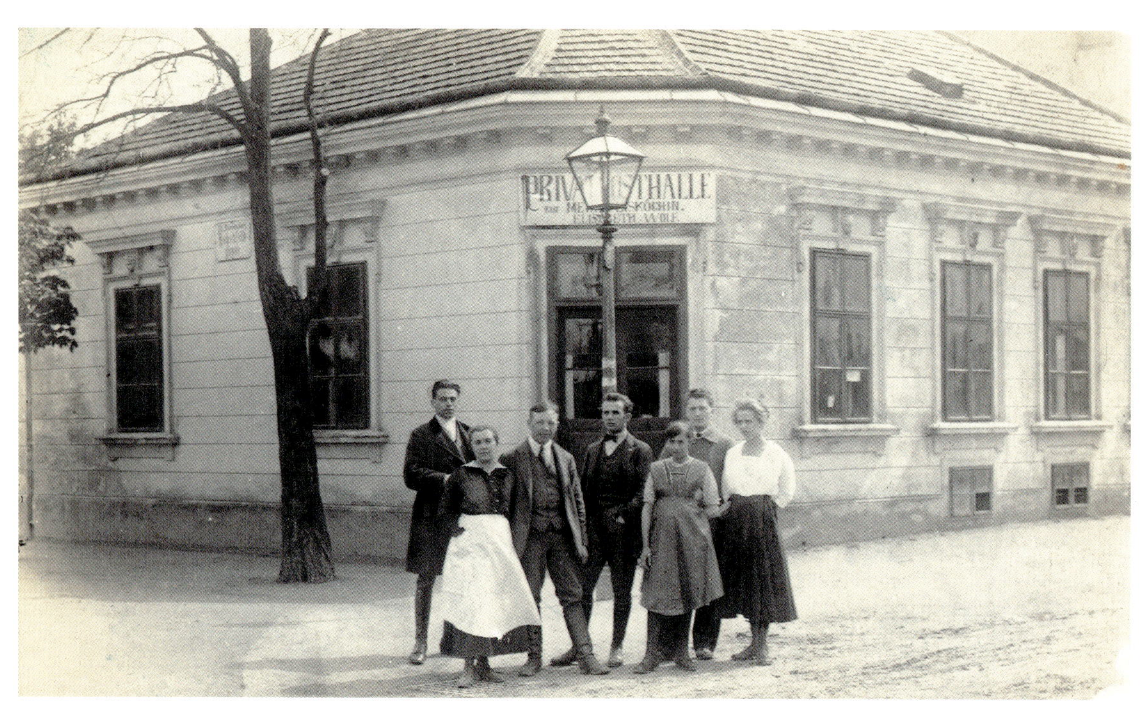

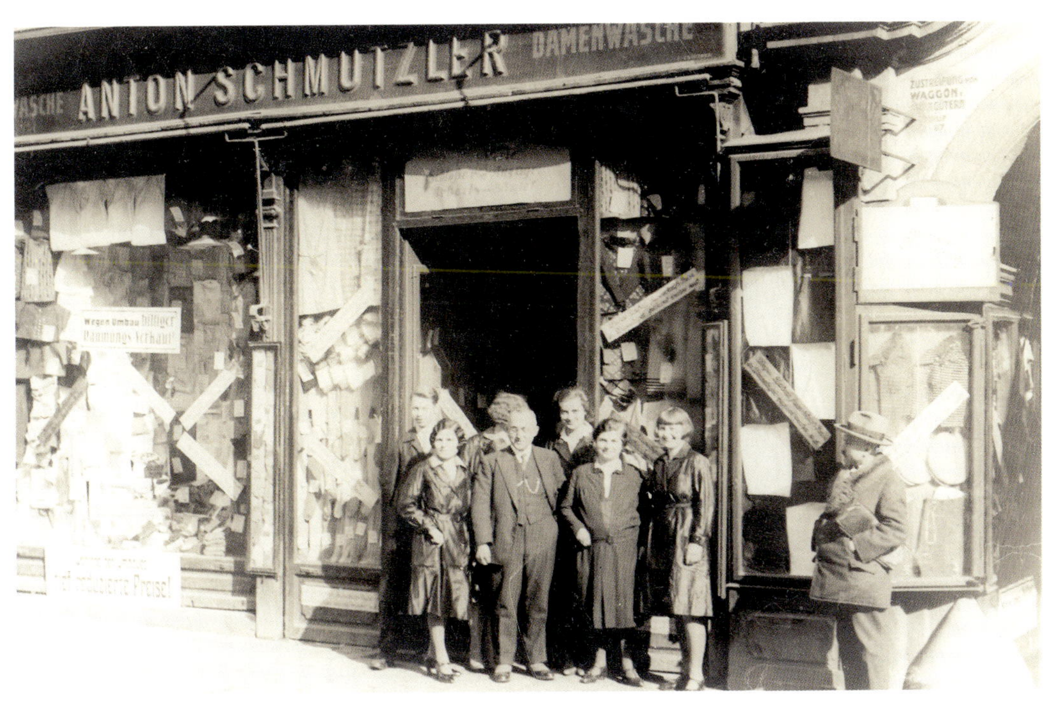

ANTON SCHMUTZLER
DAMENWASCHE
Wegen Umbau billiger
Räumungs-Verkauf!
Preise!
WAGGON

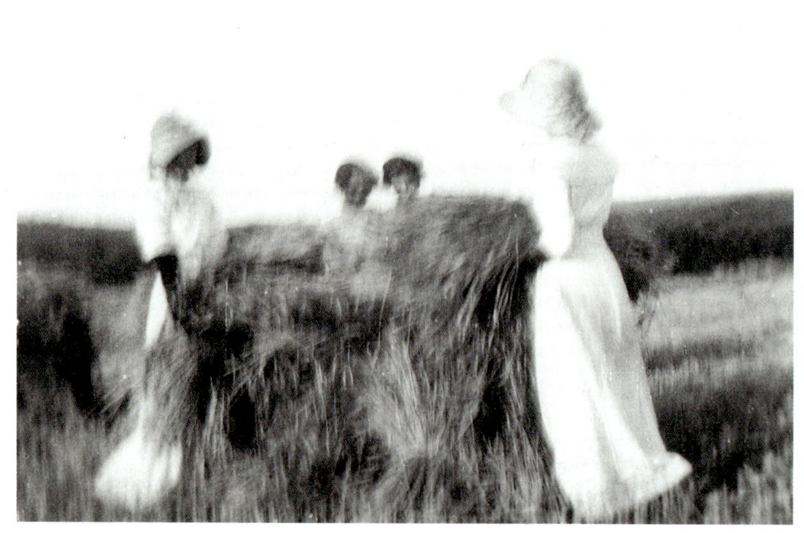

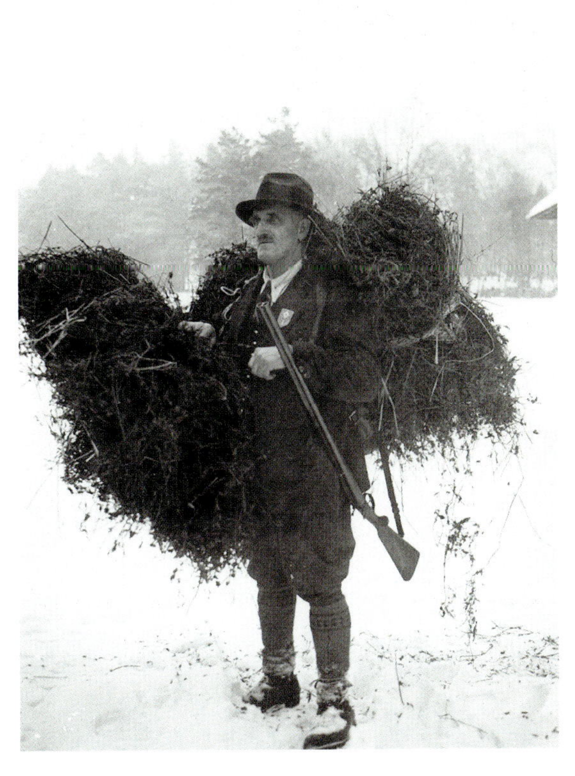

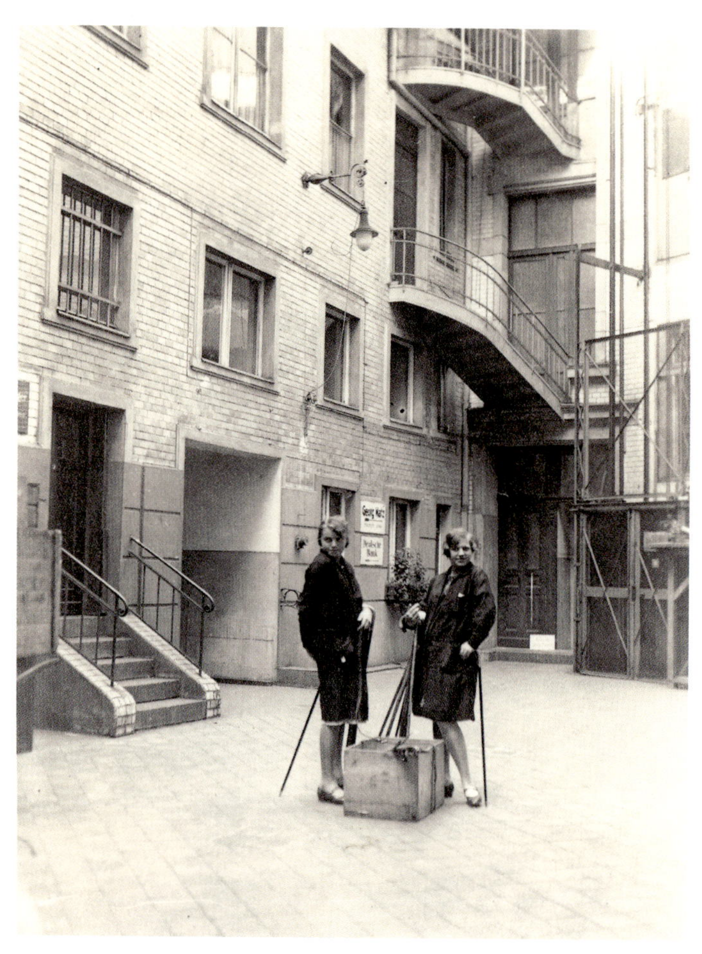

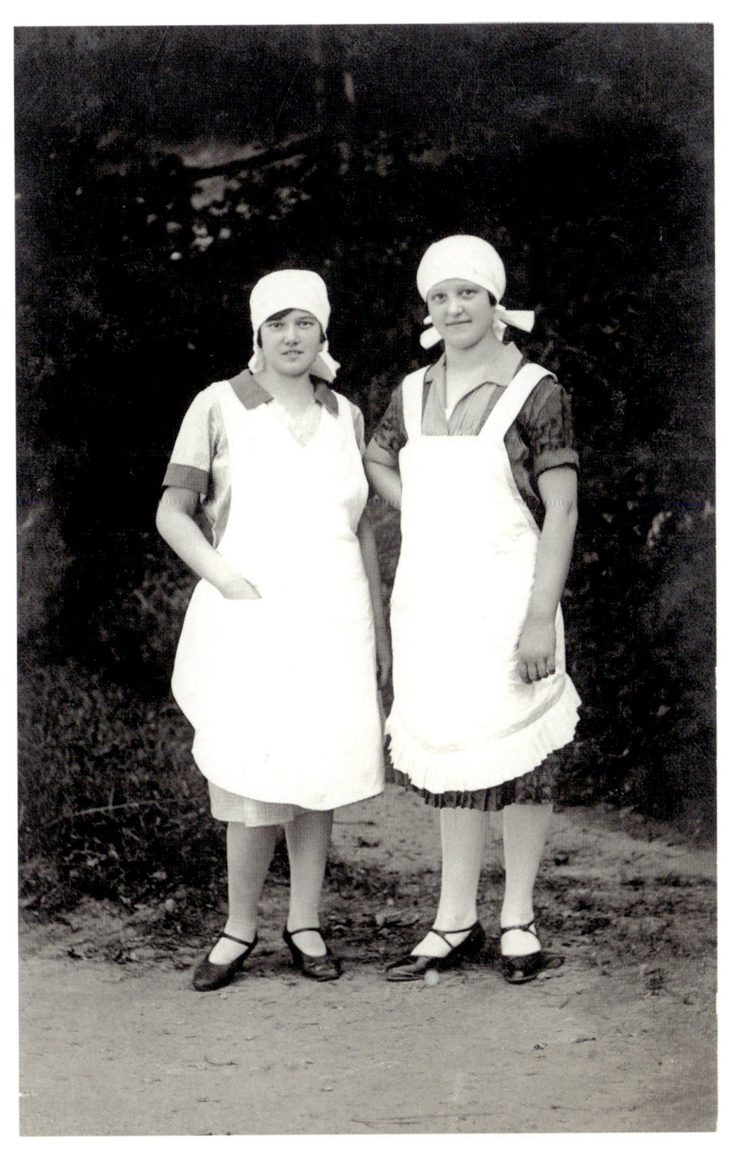

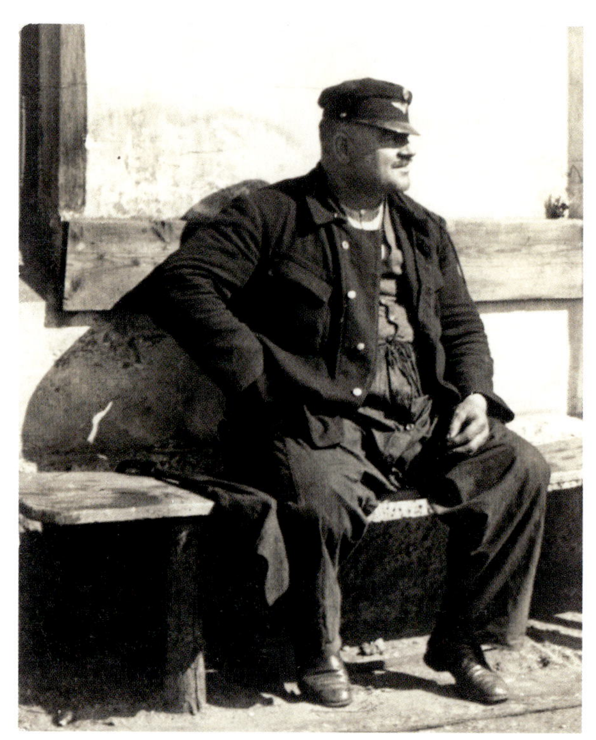

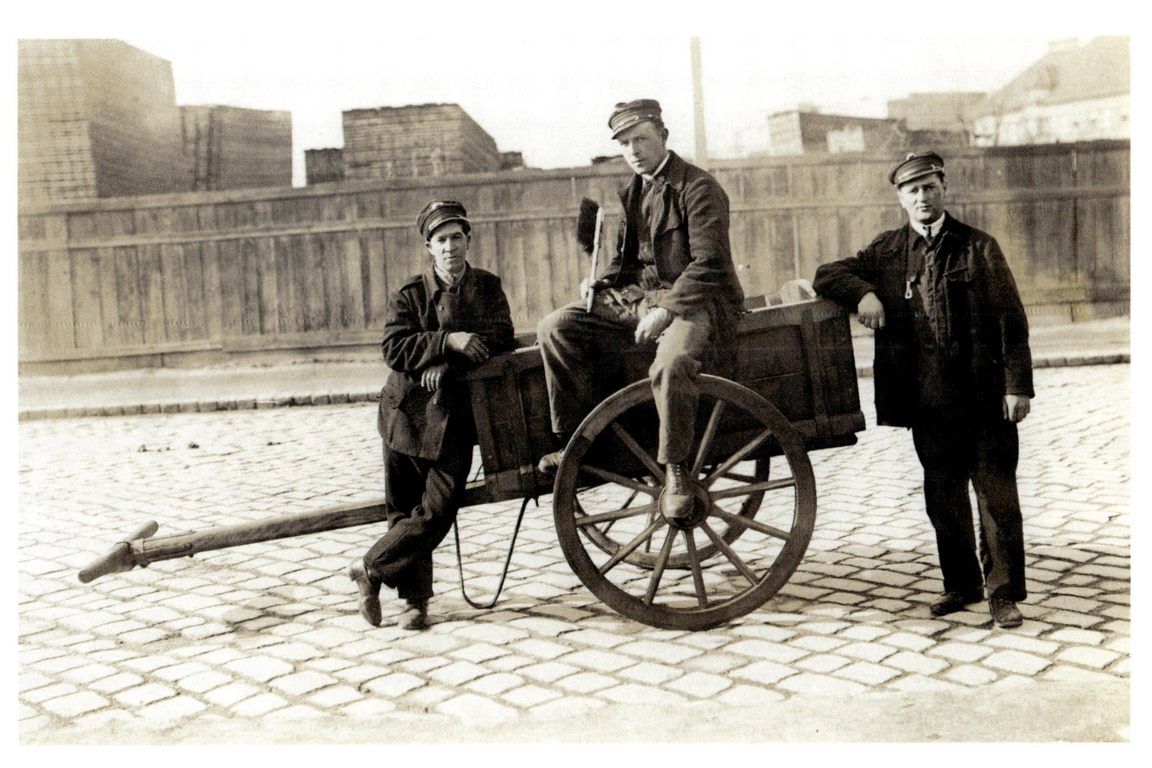

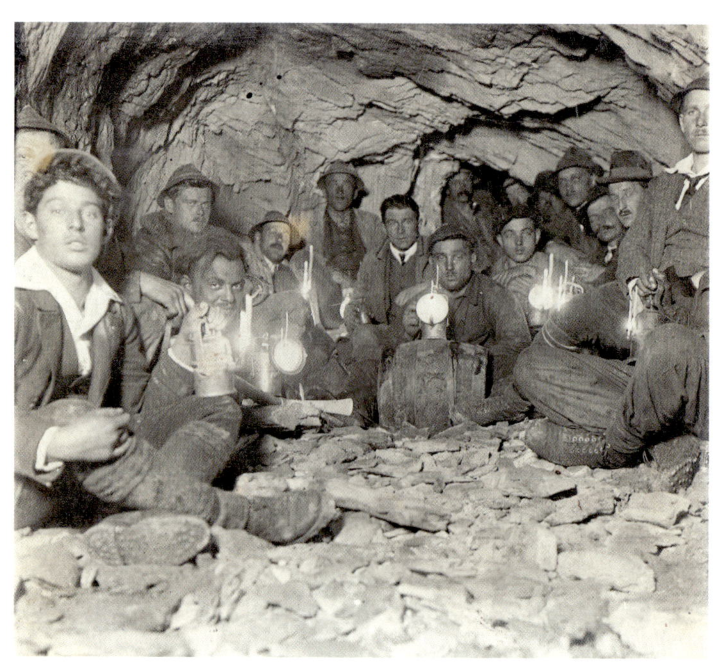

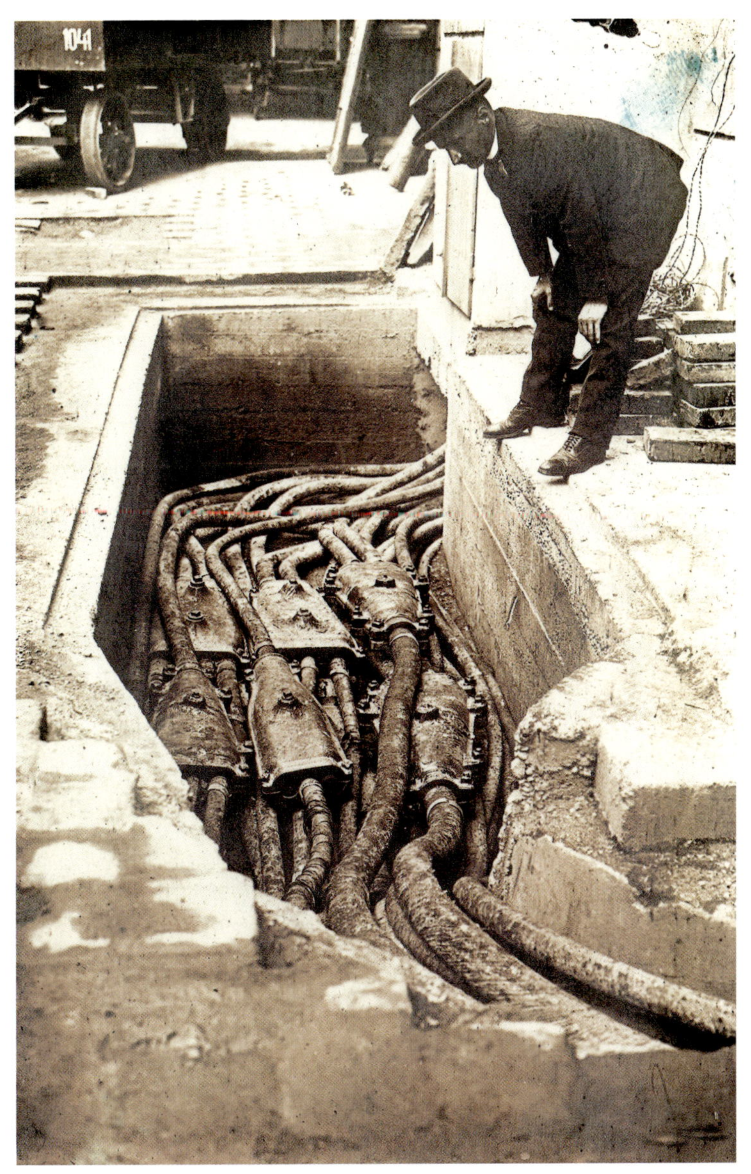
1041

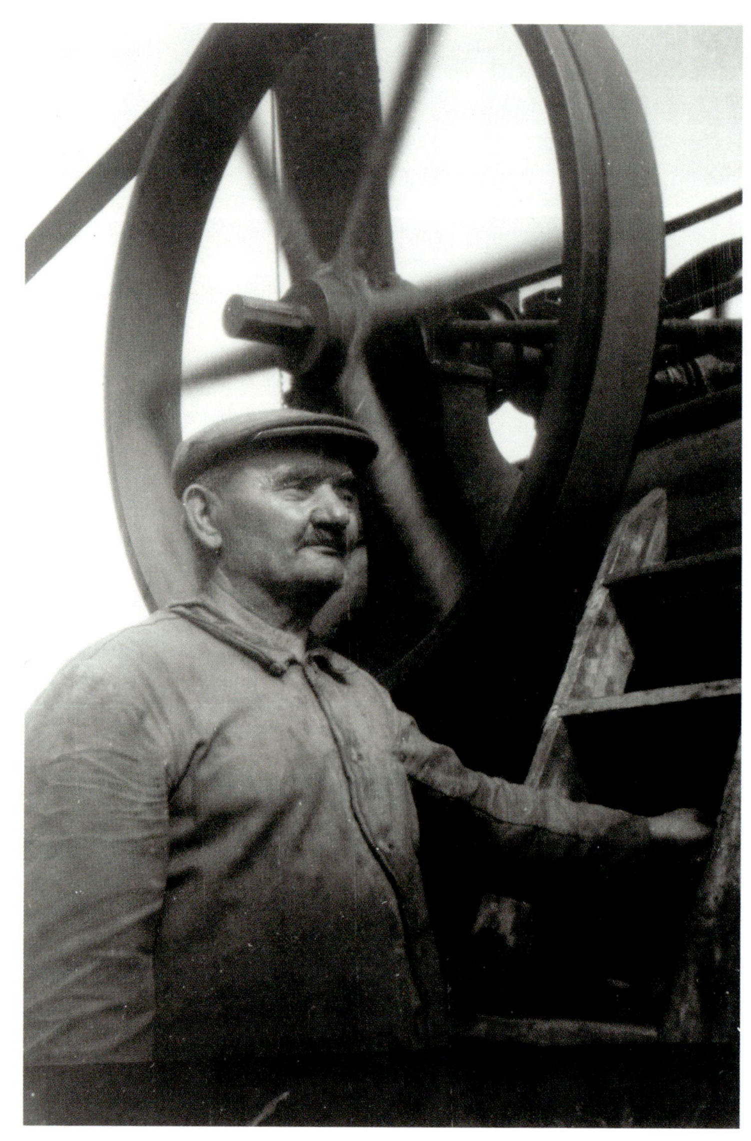

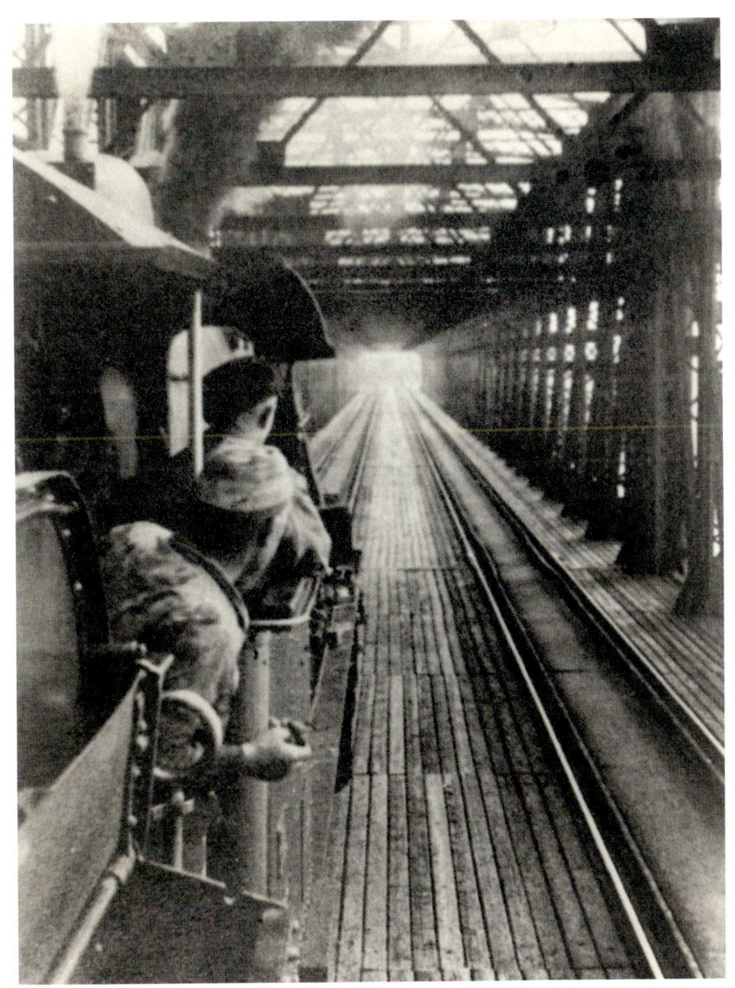

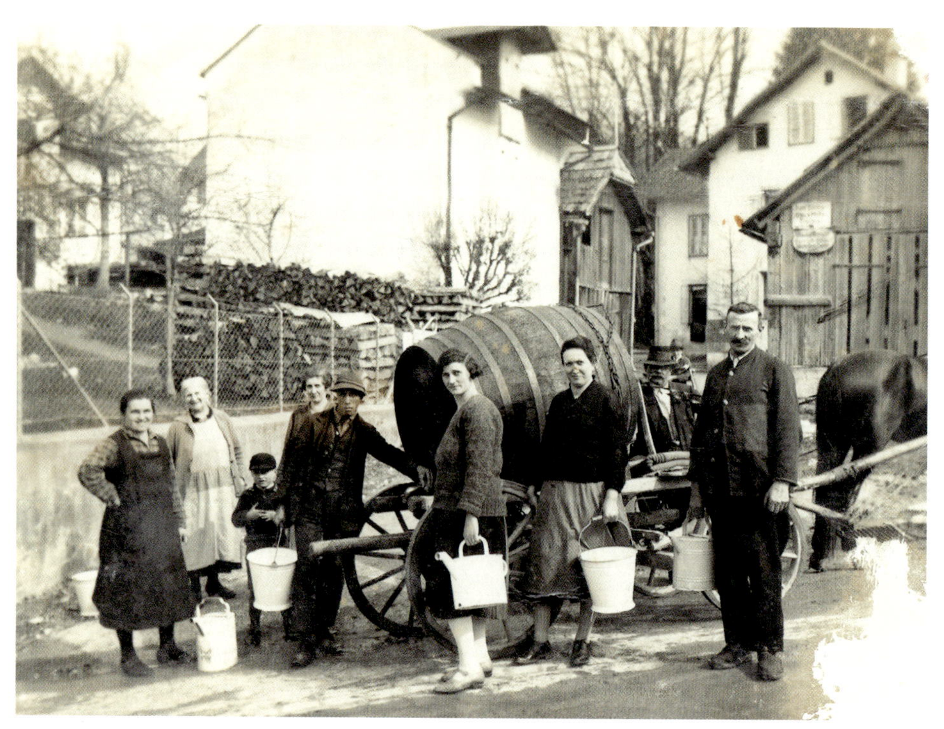

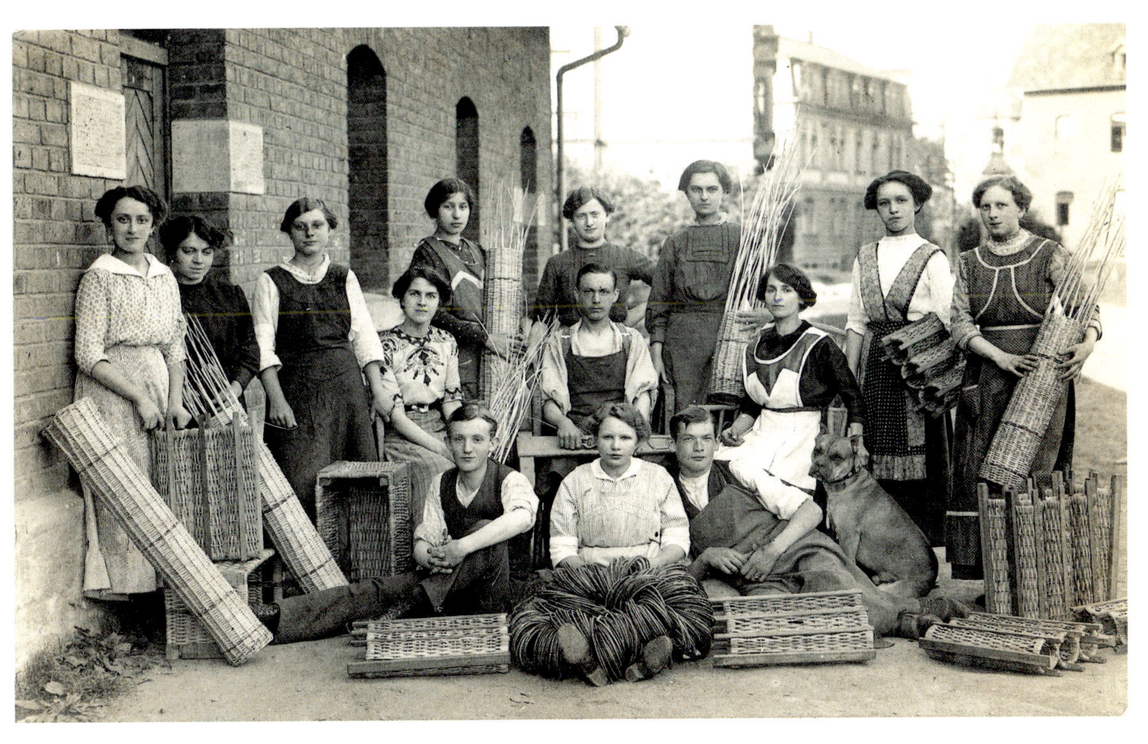

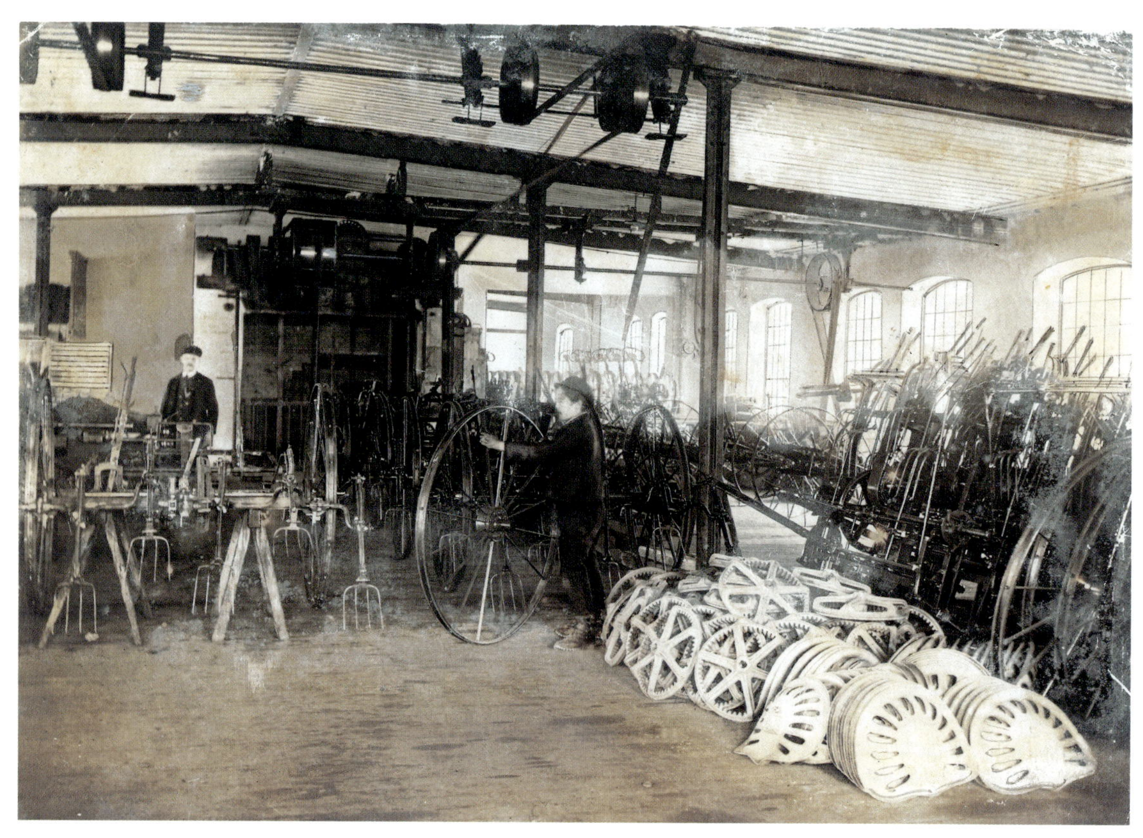

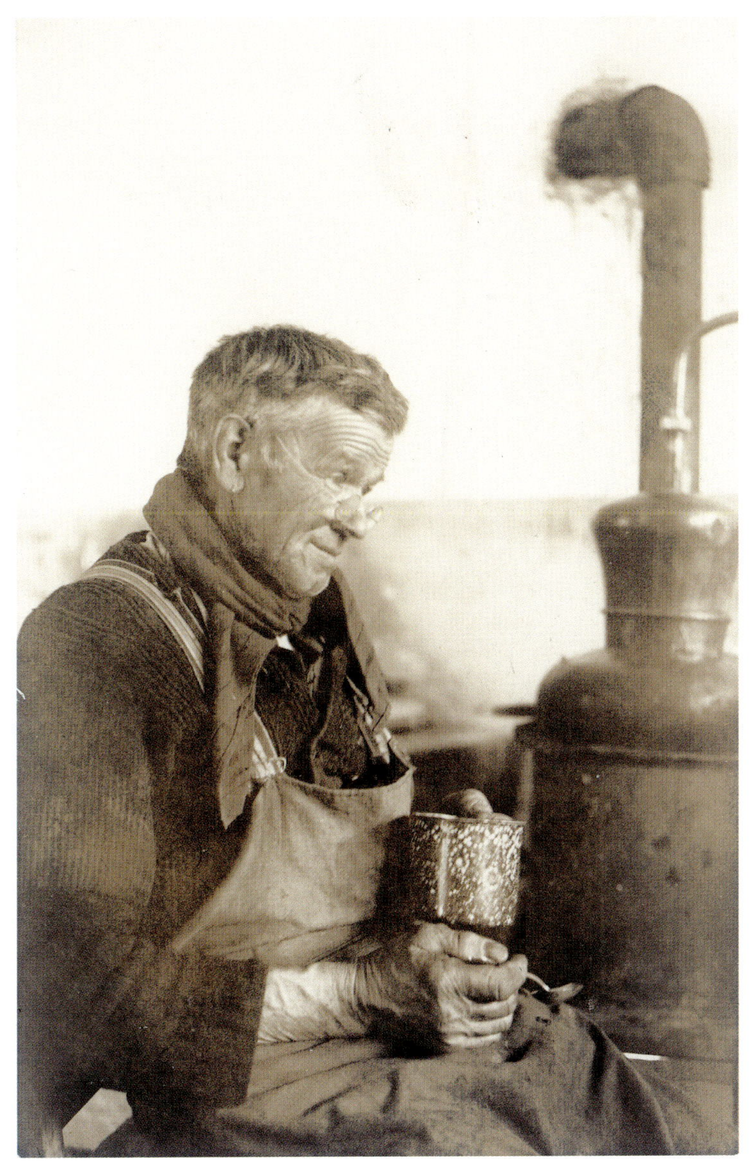

15)

War Krieg

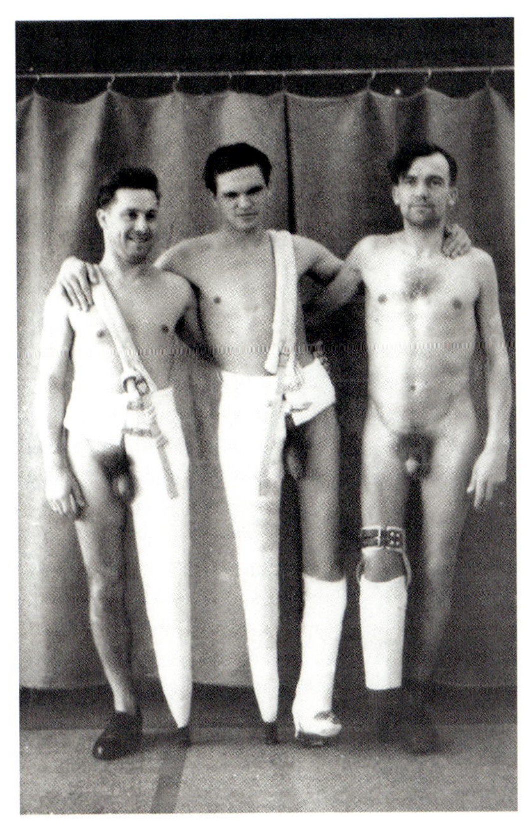

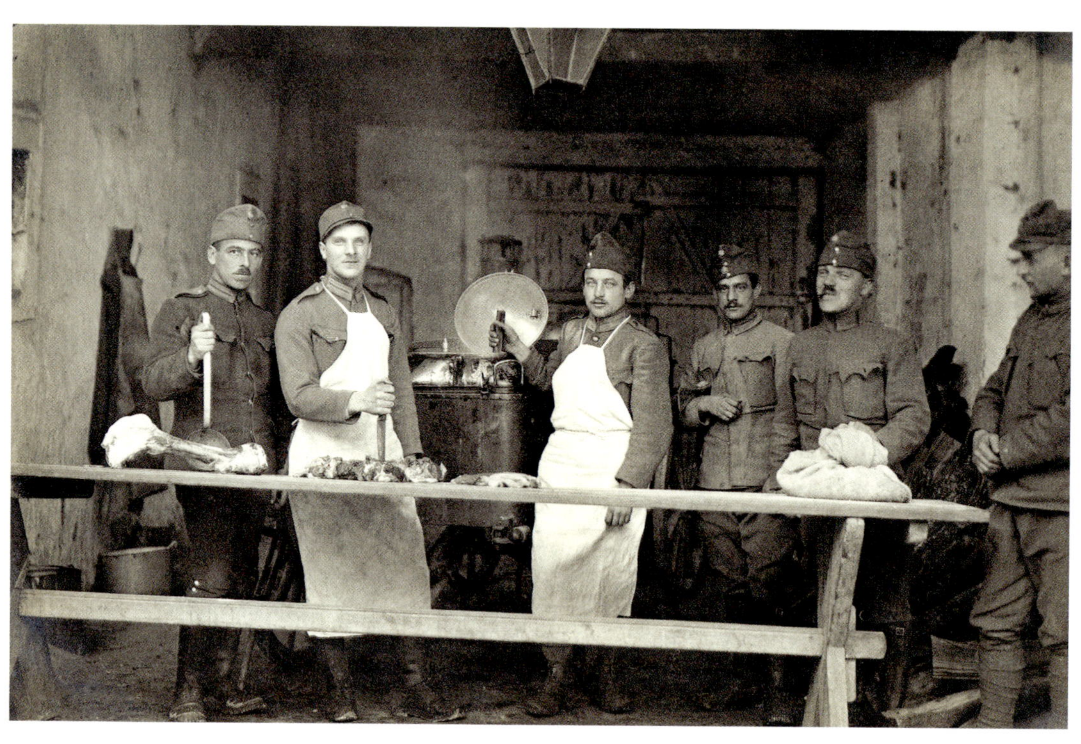

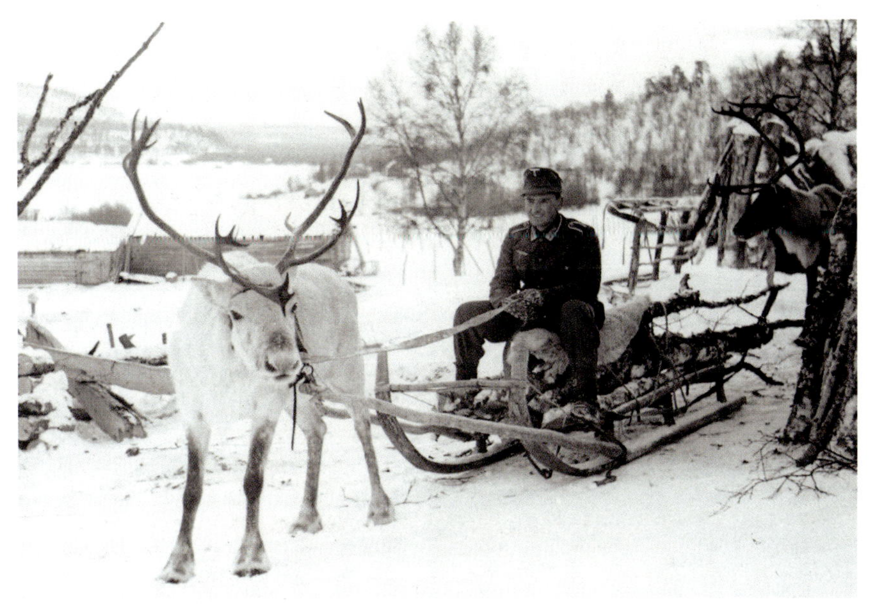

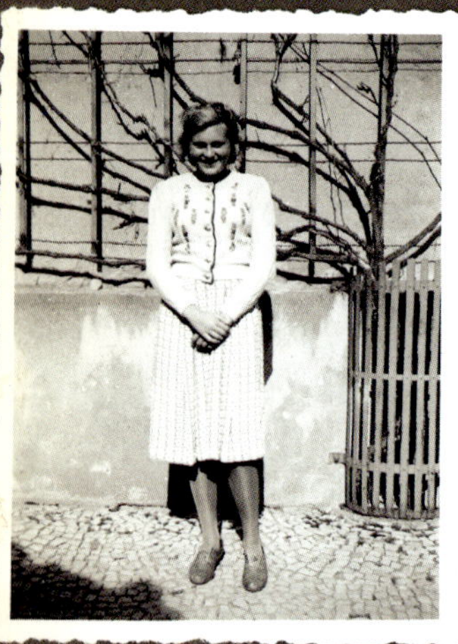

Giesela

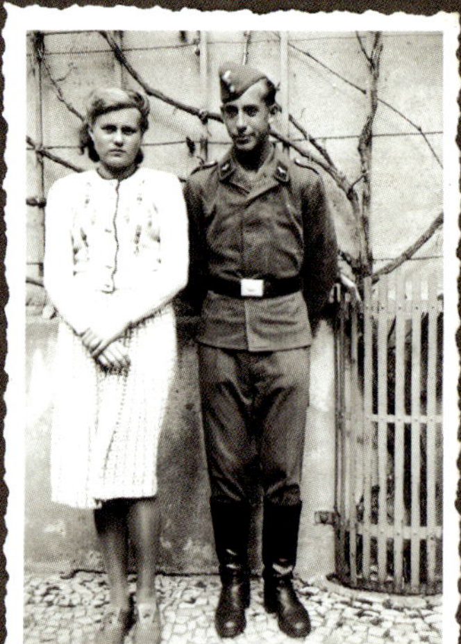

Giesela und Werner

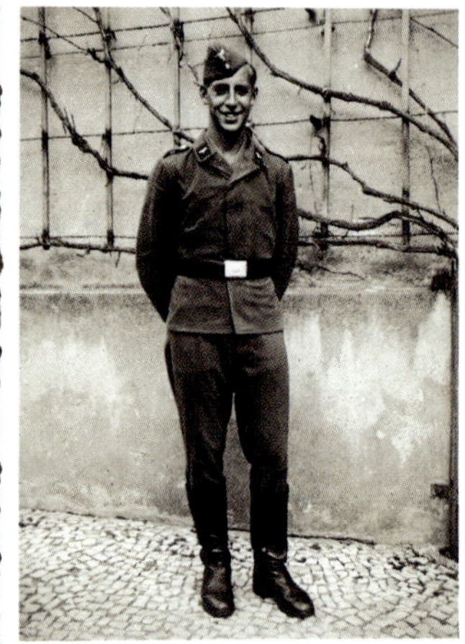

Werner

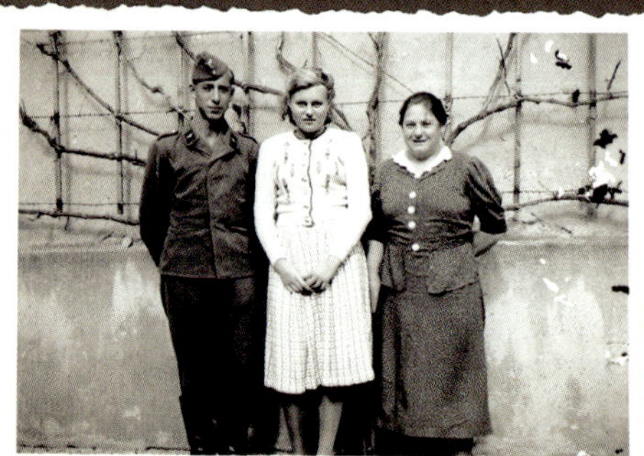

Werner - Giesela - Tante Meta

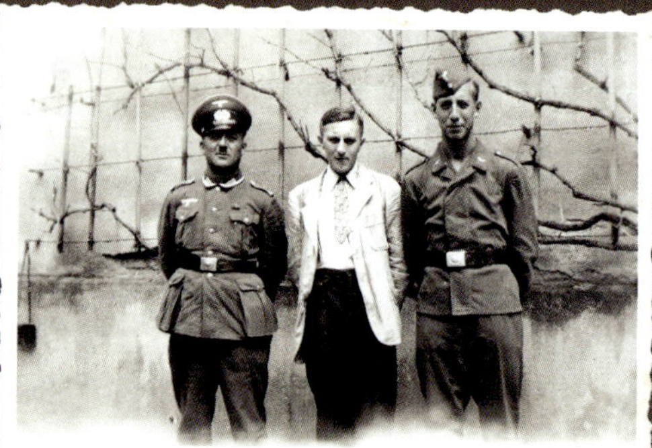

Onkel Paul - Walter - Werner

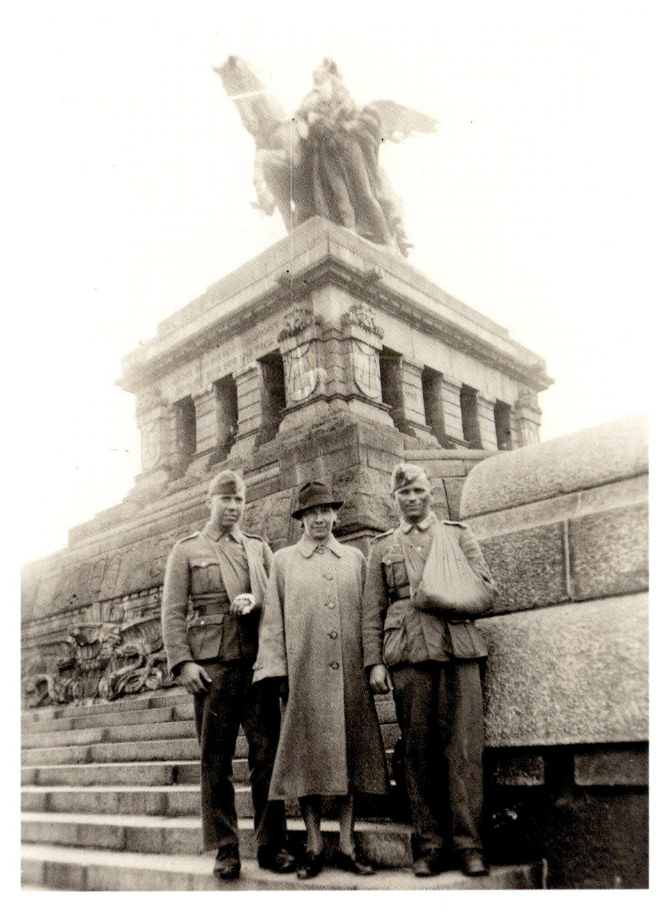

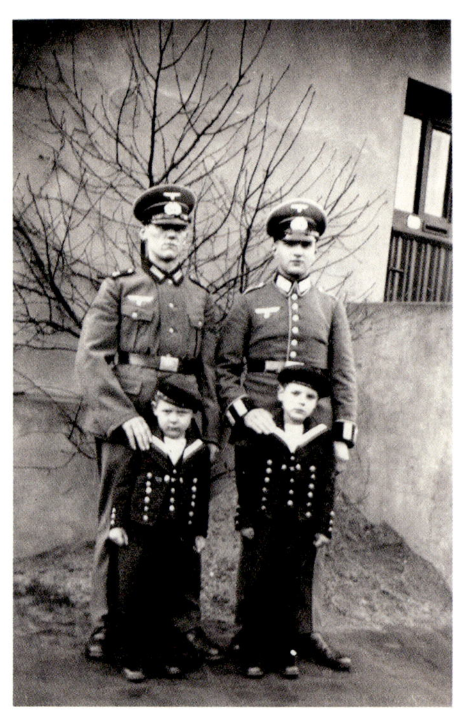

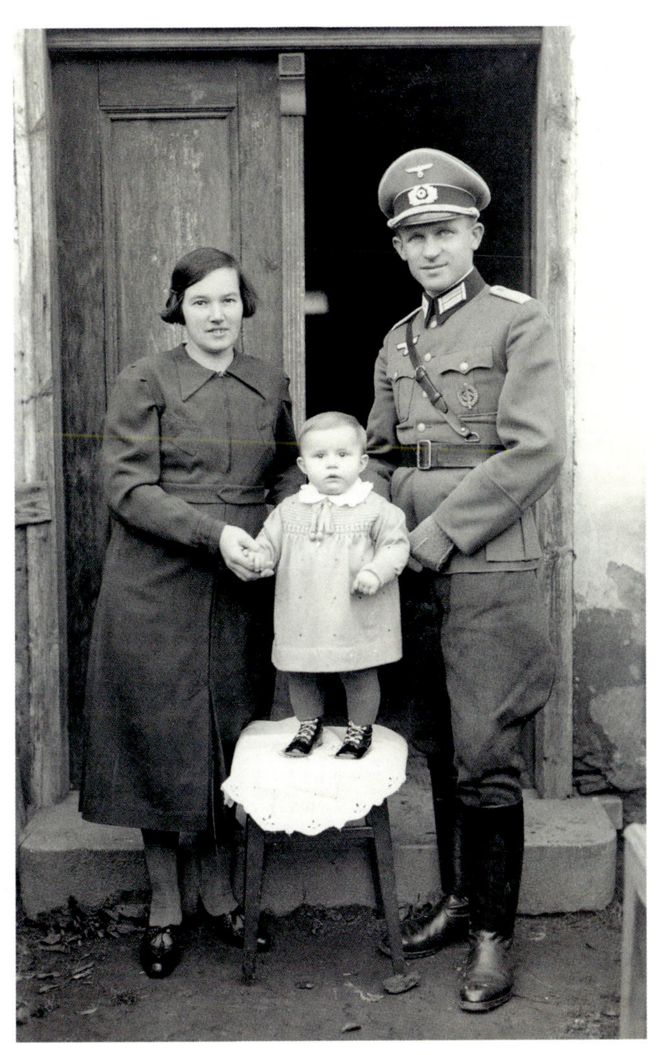

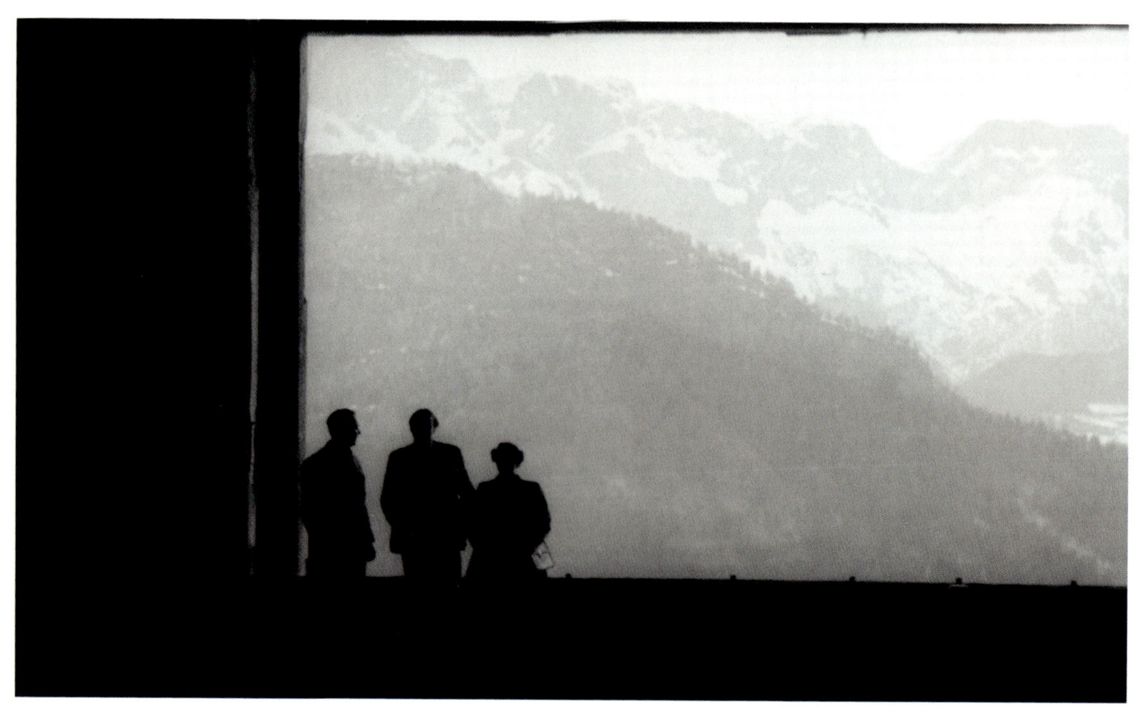

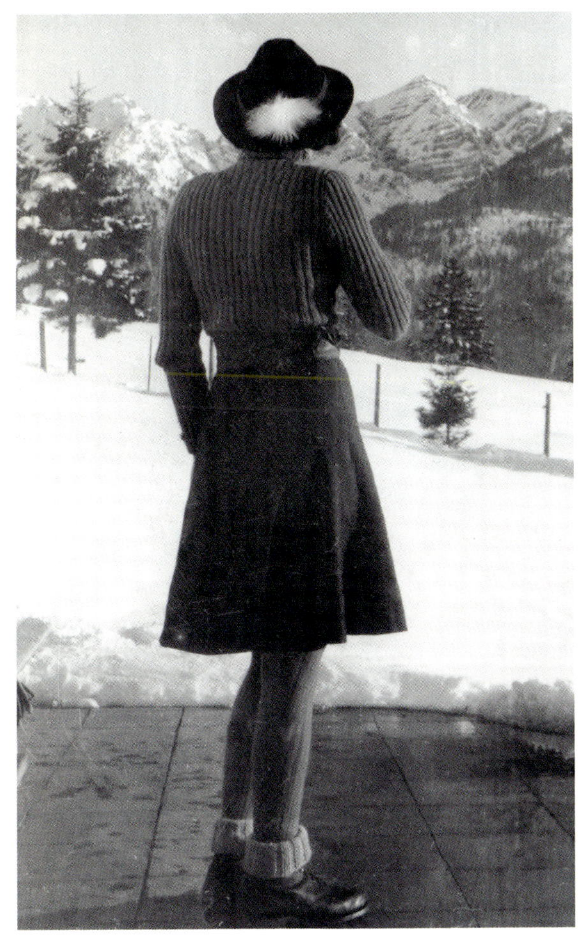

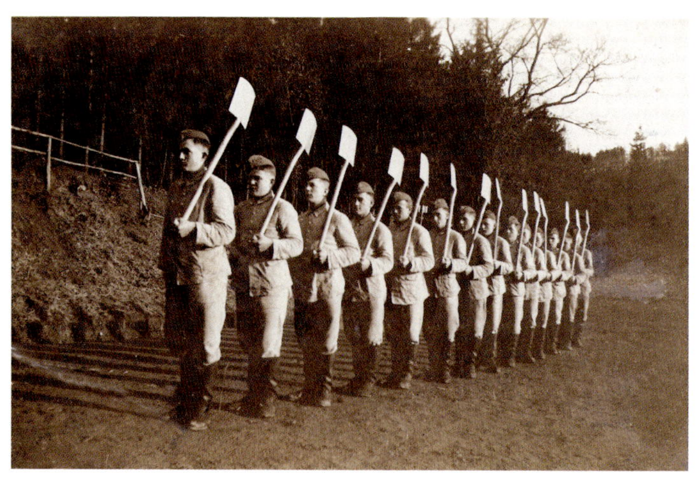

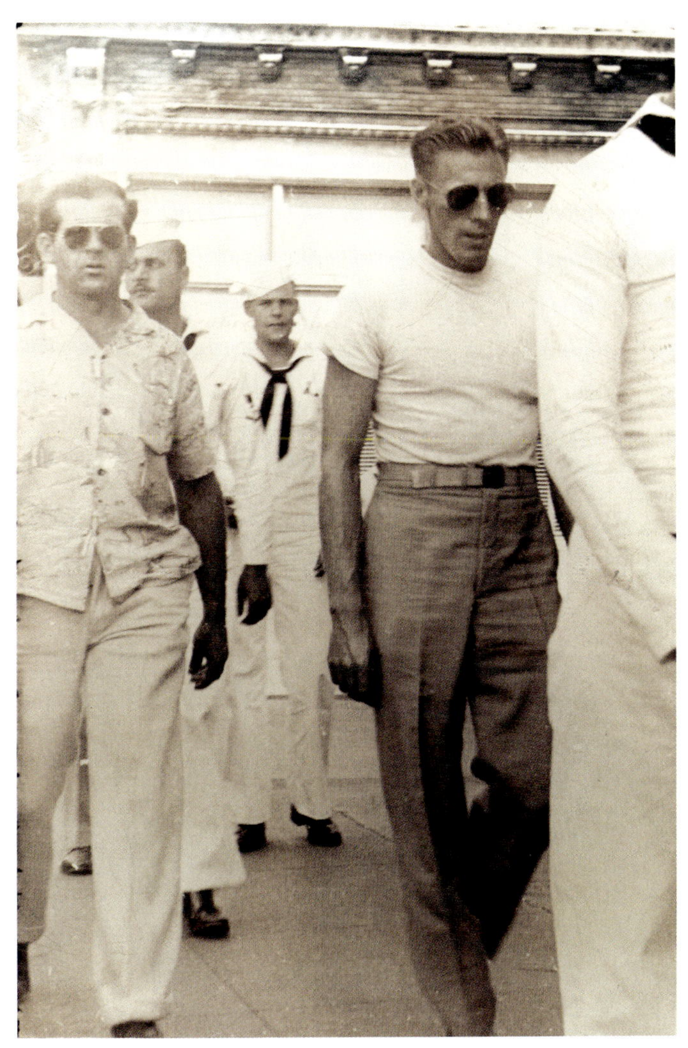

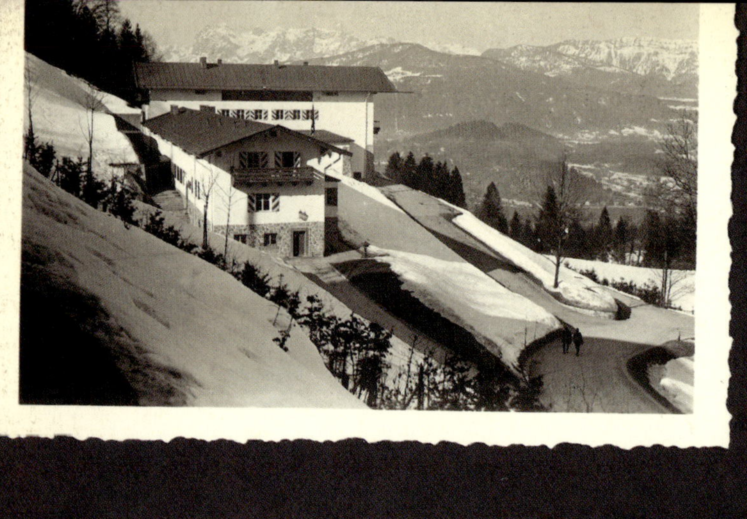

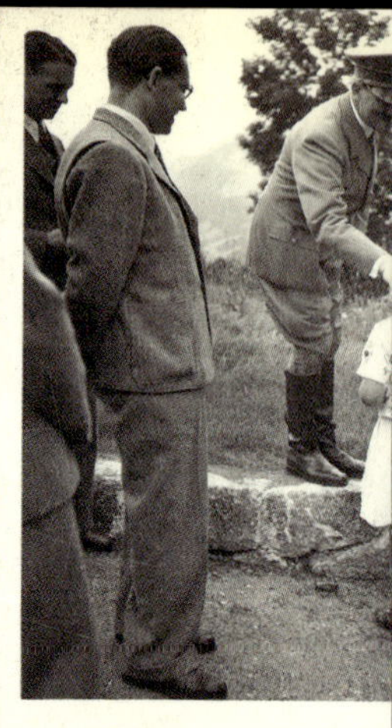

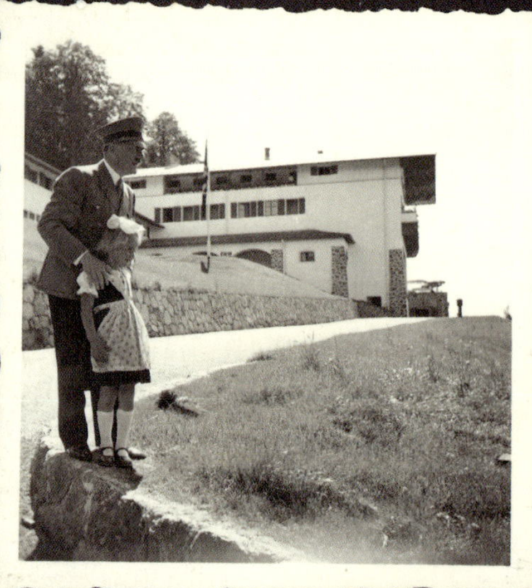

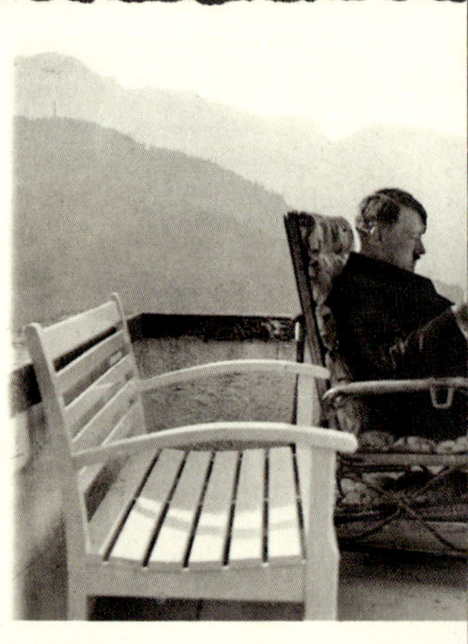

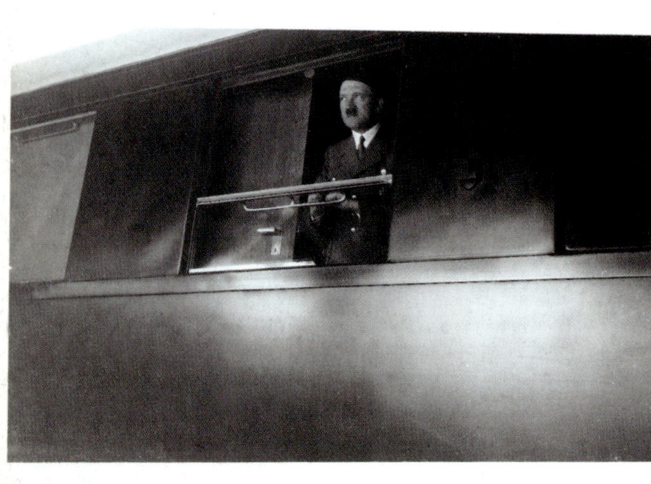

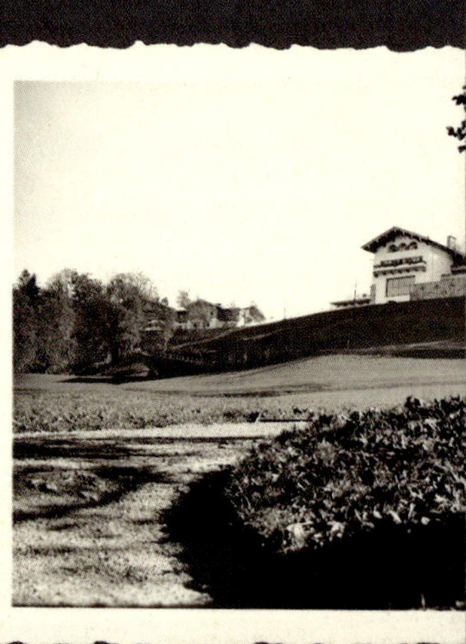

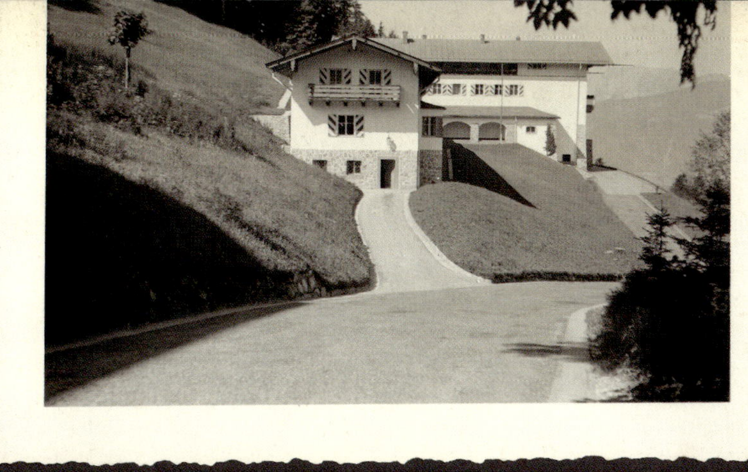

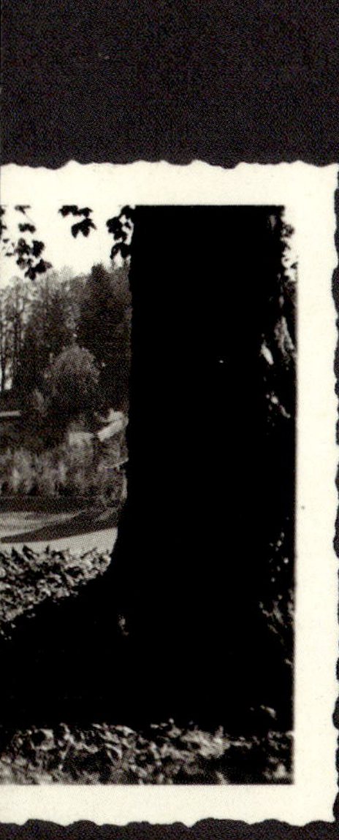

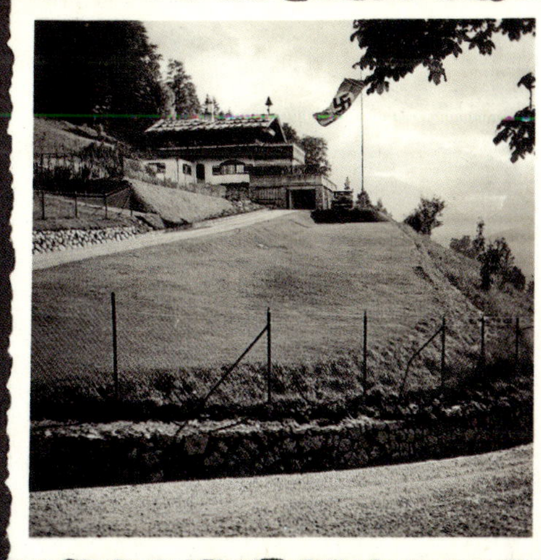

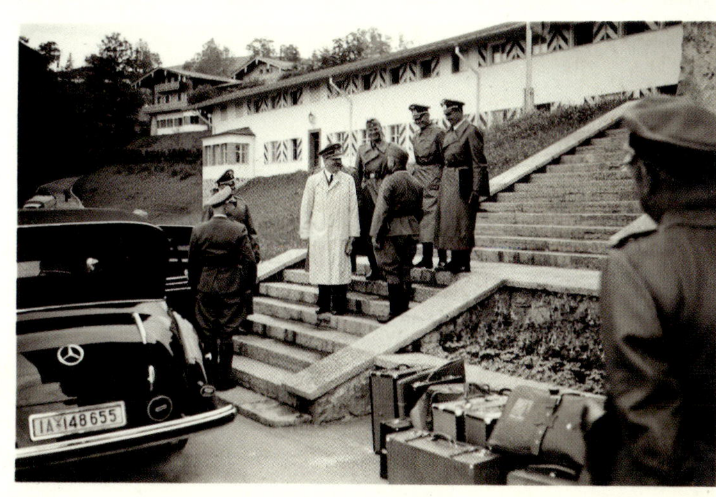
IA 148655

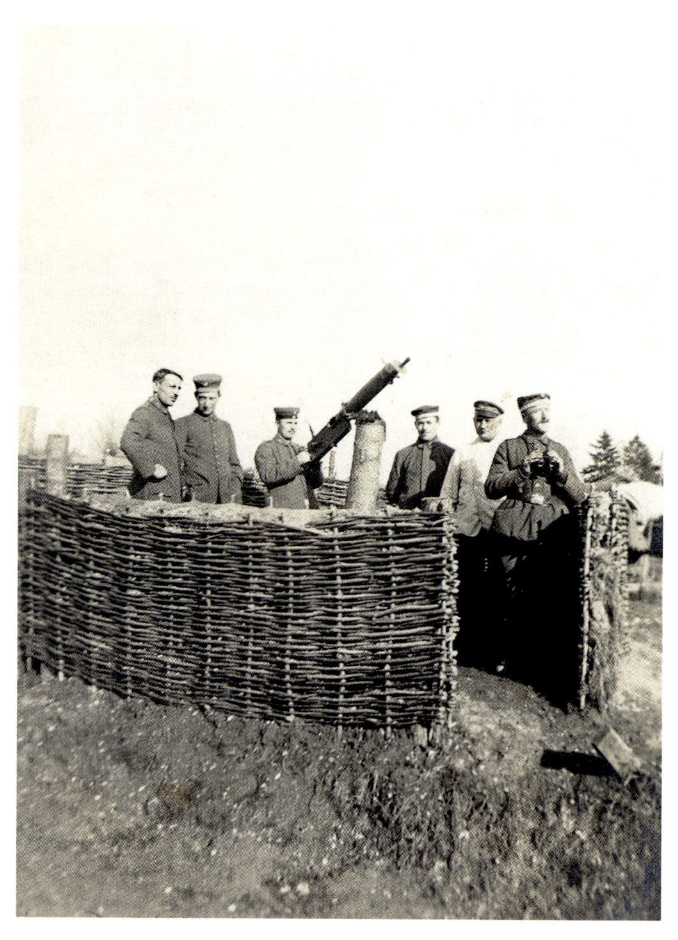

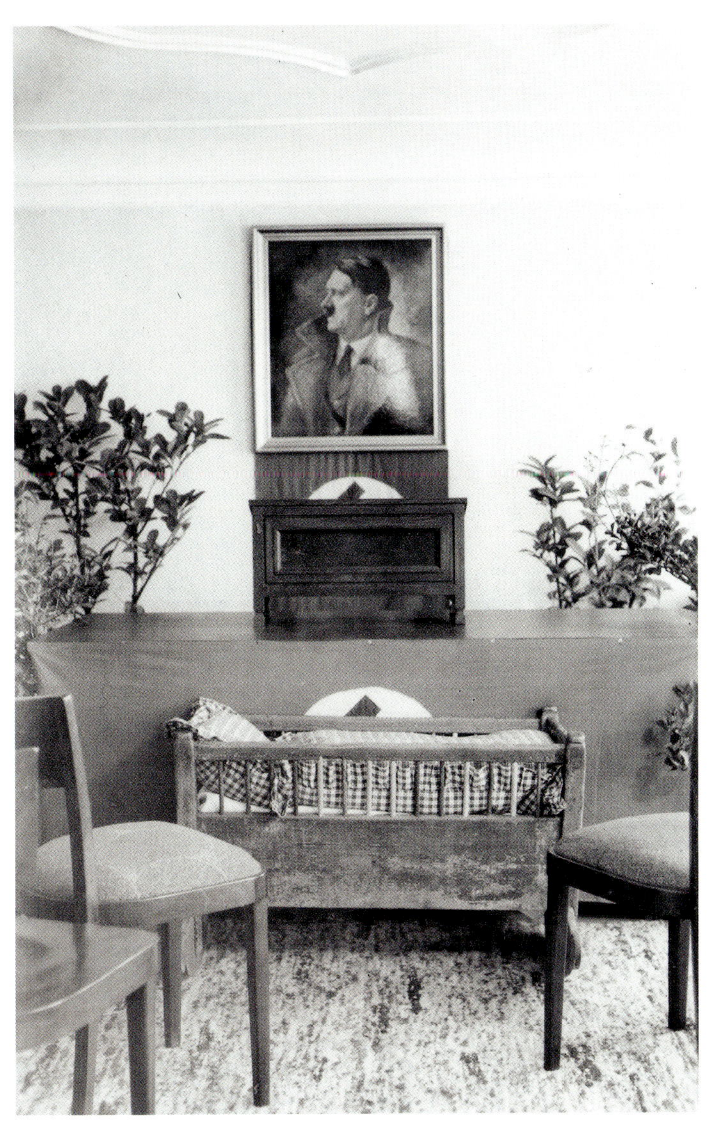

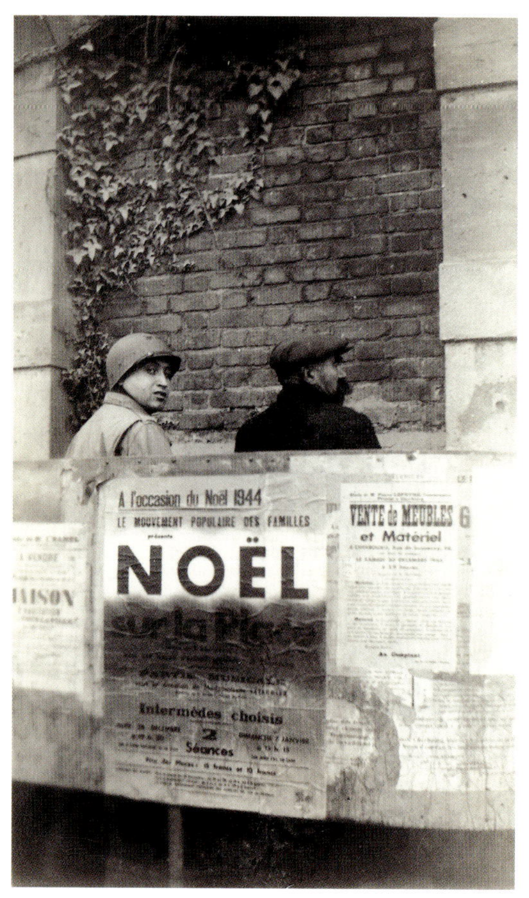
A l'occasion du Noël 1944
LE MOUVEMENT POPULAIRE DES FAMILLES
présente
NOËL
Intermèdes choisis
2
Séances
VENTE de MEUBLES
et Matériel

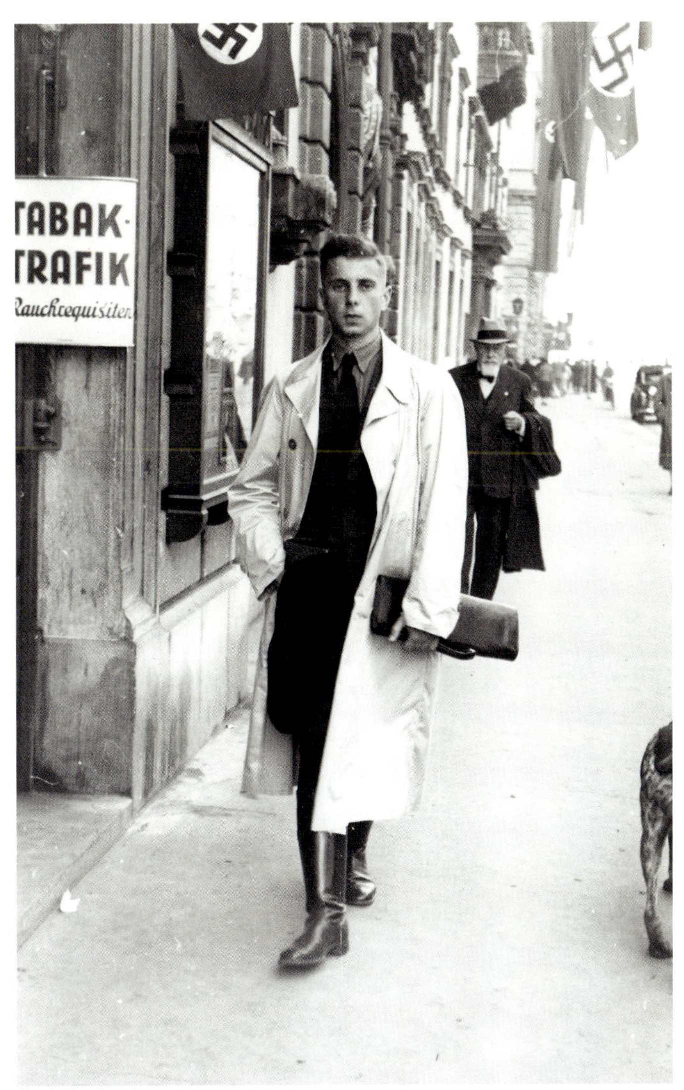
TABAK-
TRAFIK
Rauchrequisiten

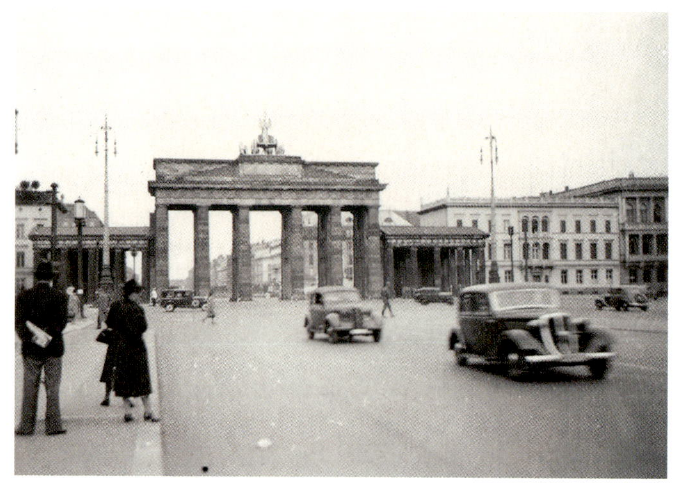

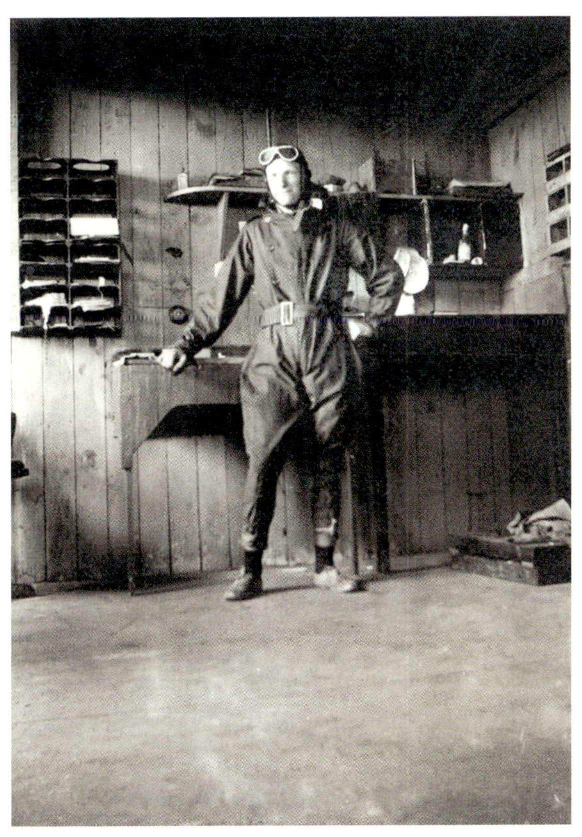

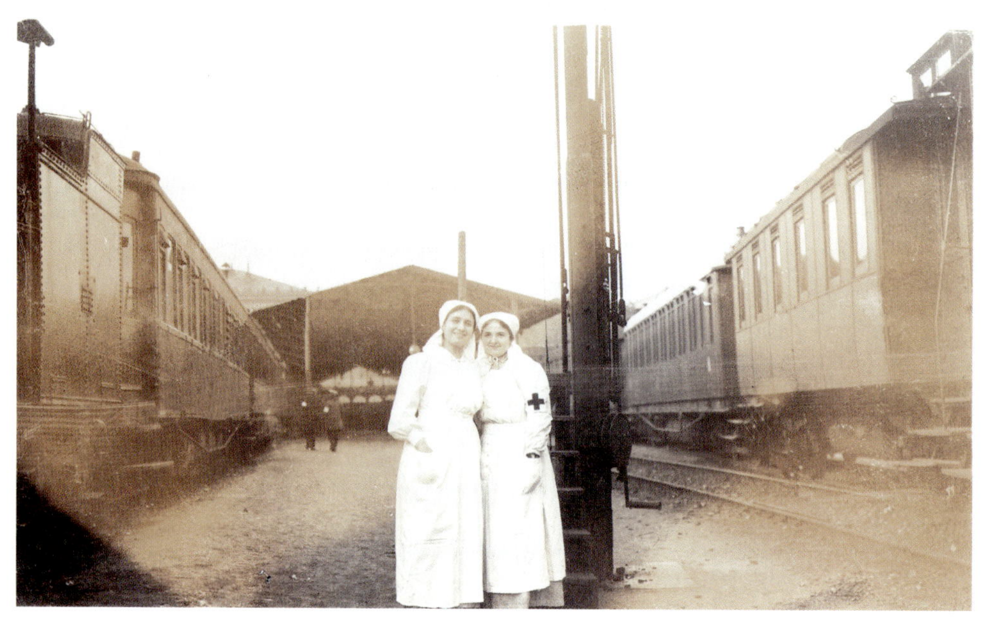

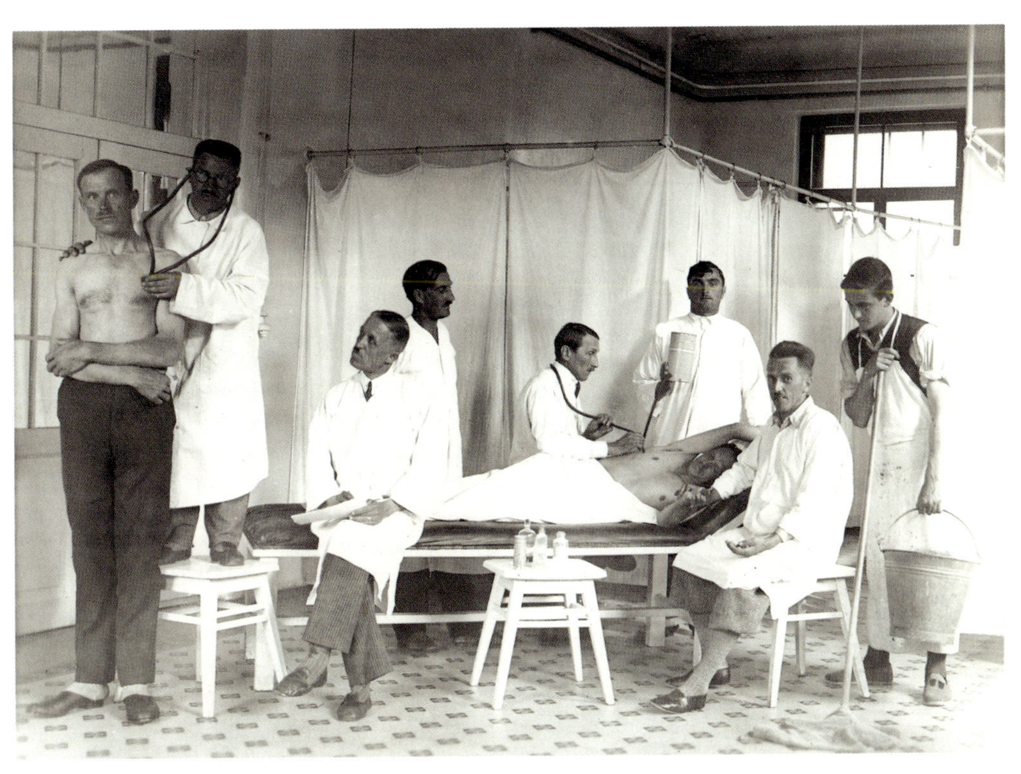

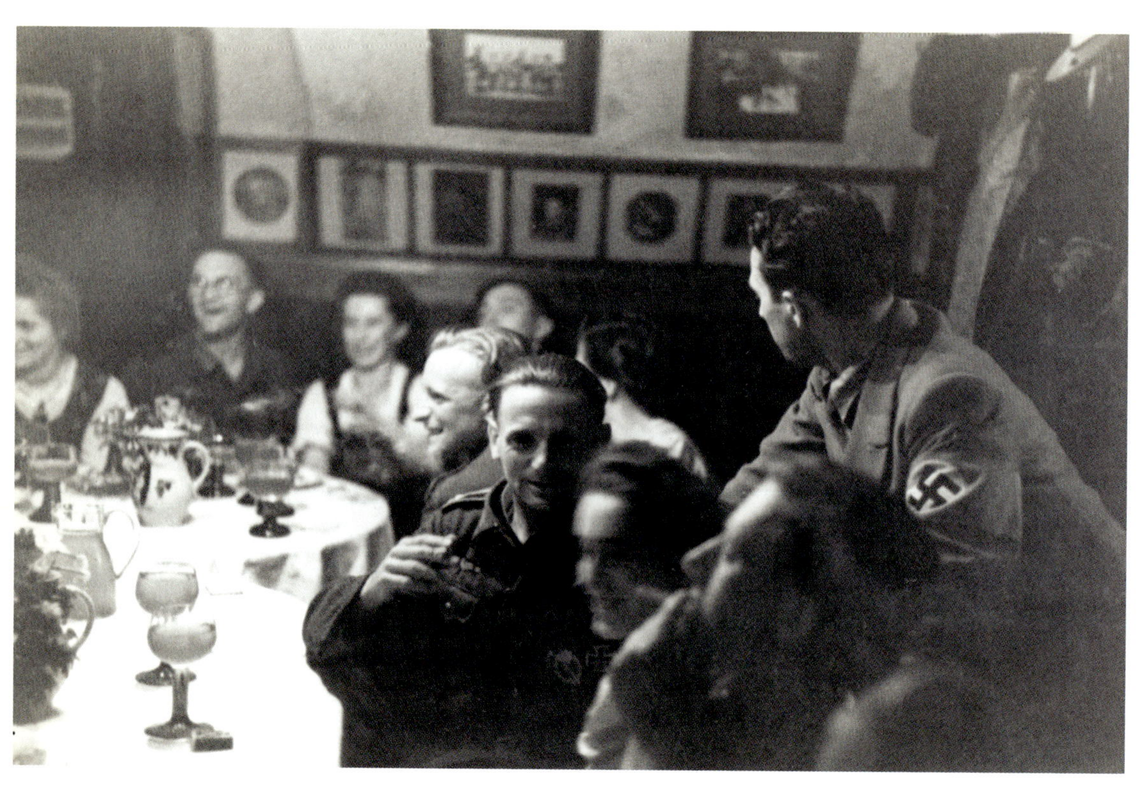

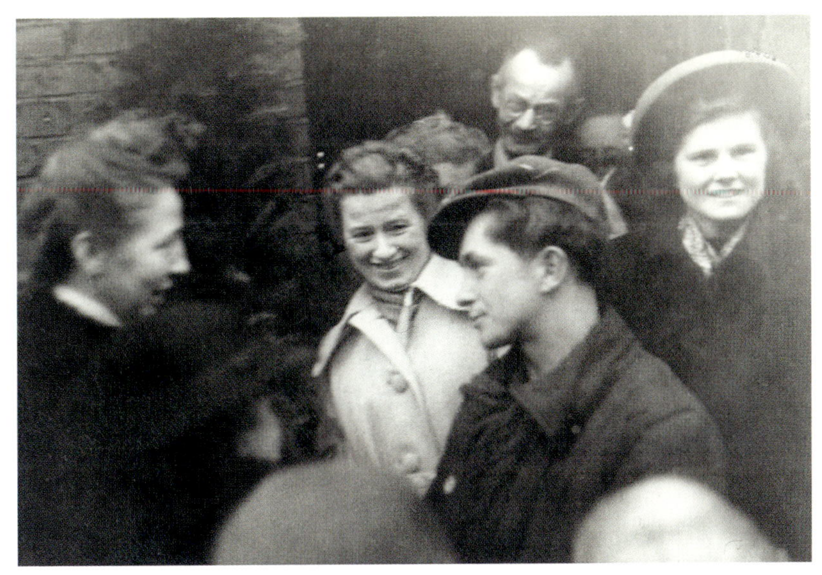

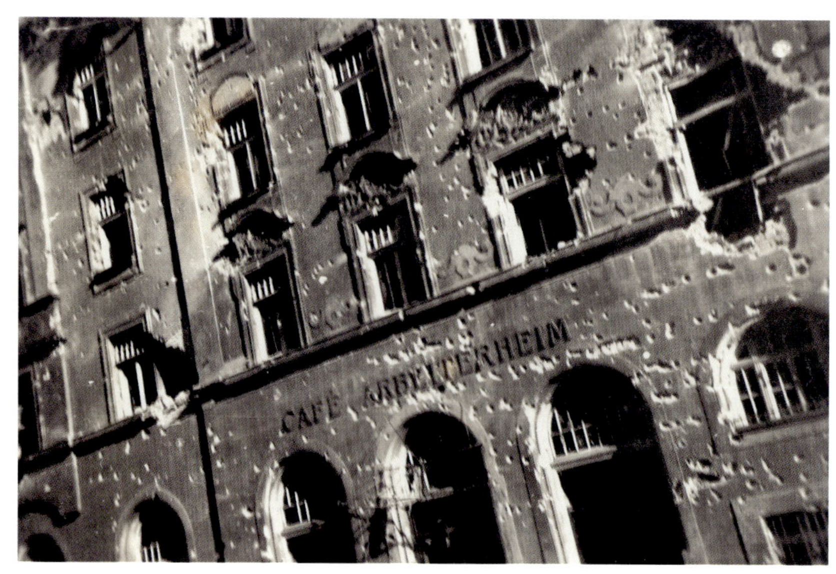
CAFE ARBEITERHEIM

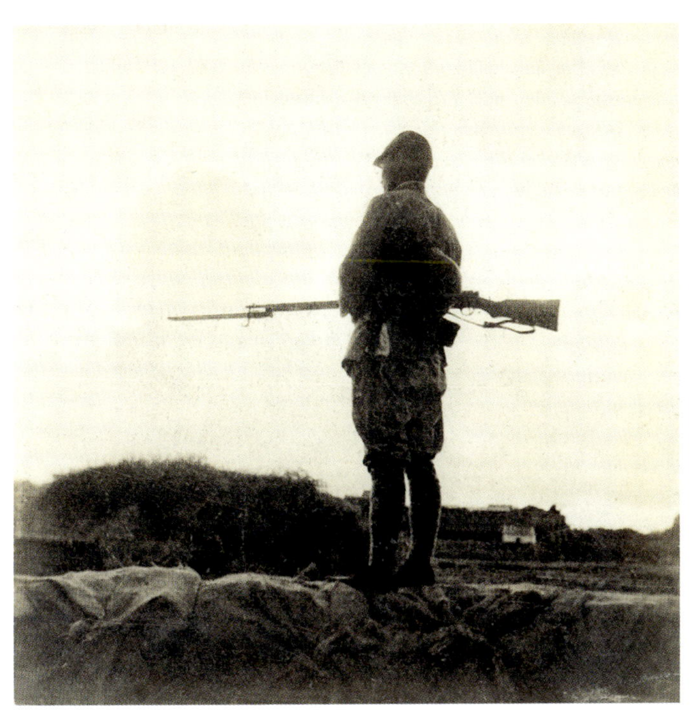

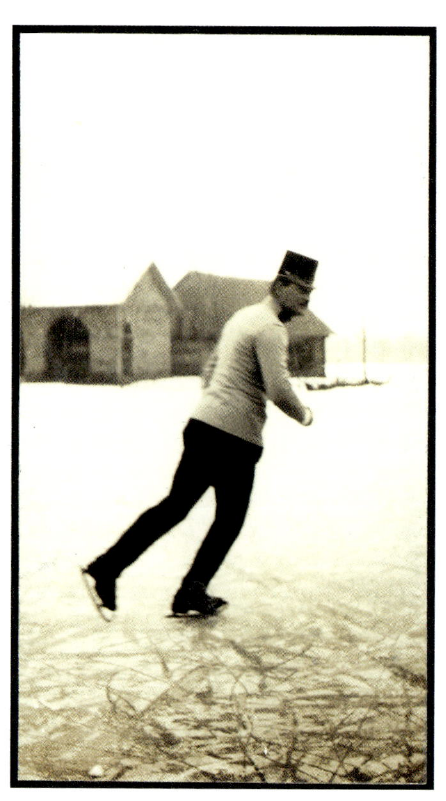

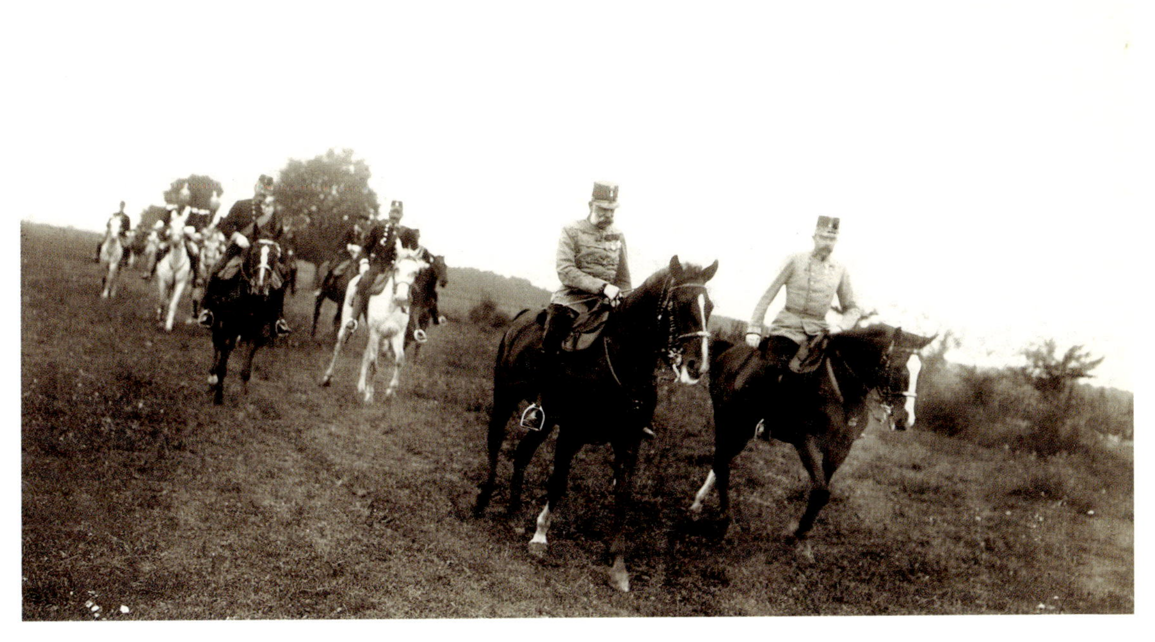

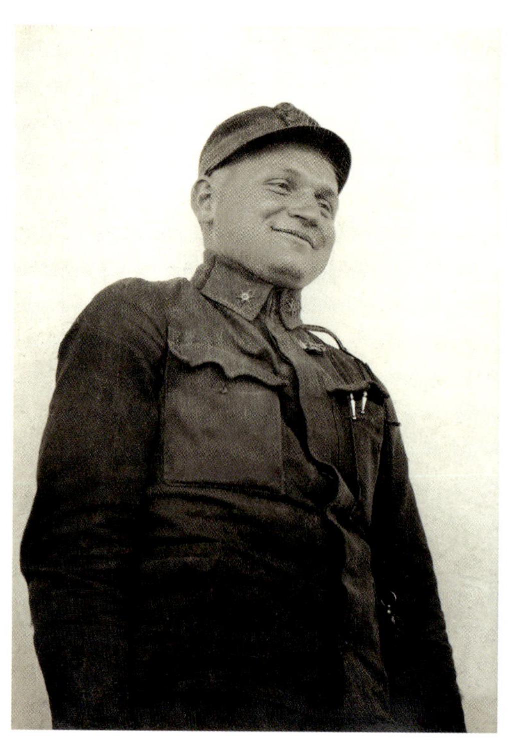

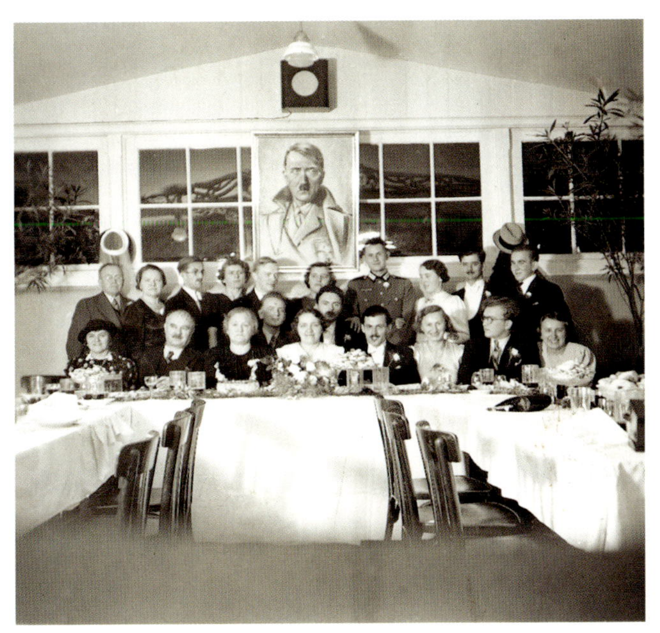

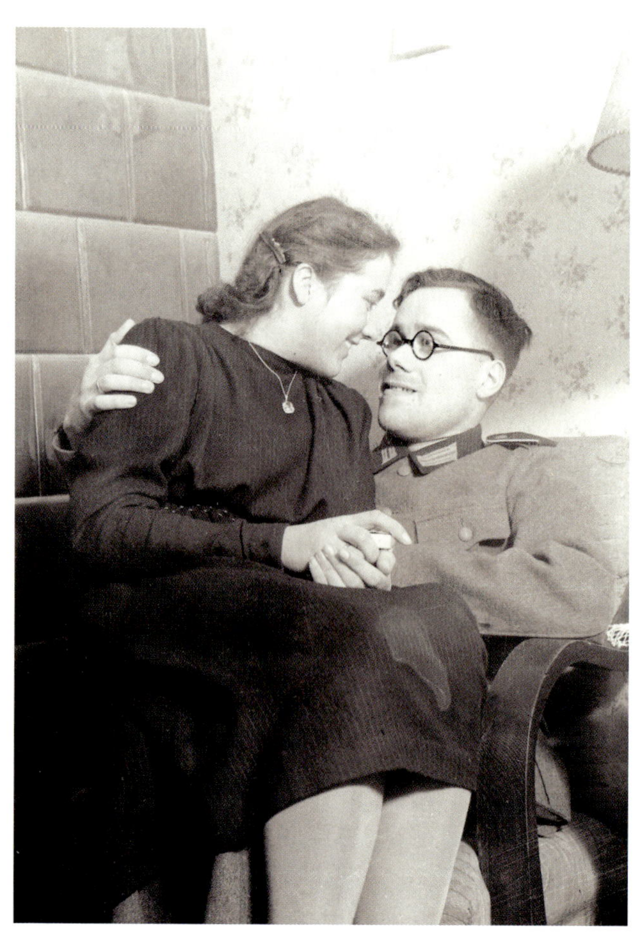

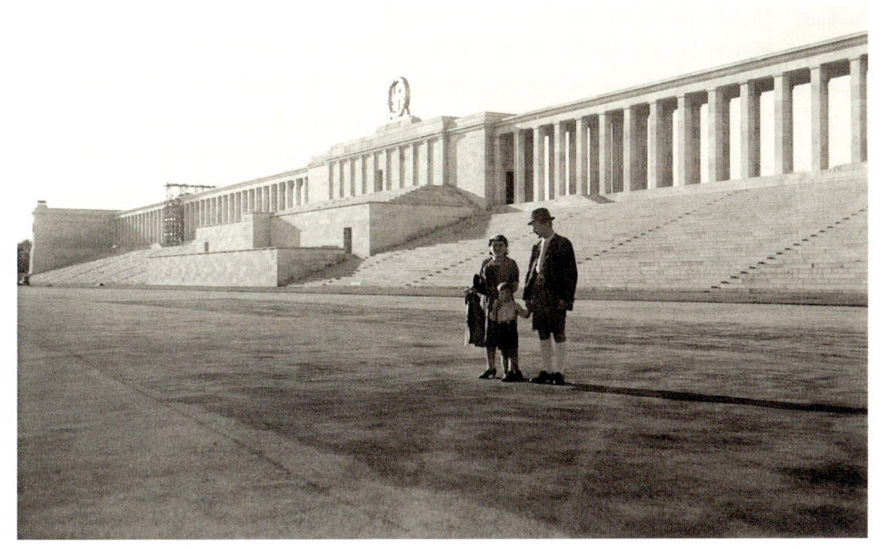

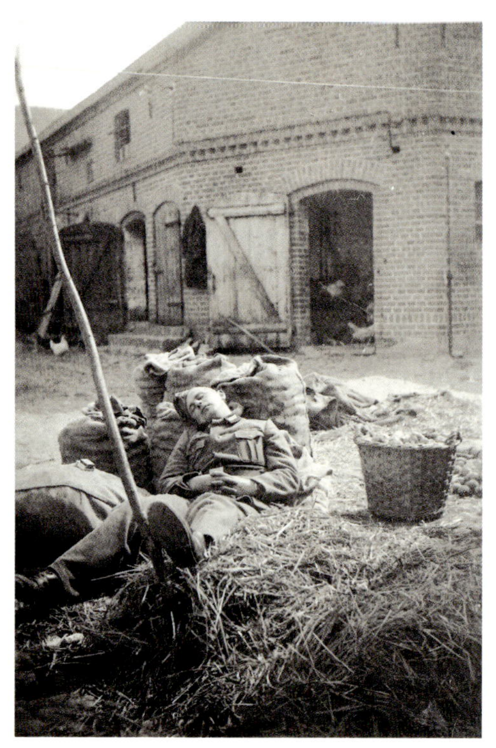

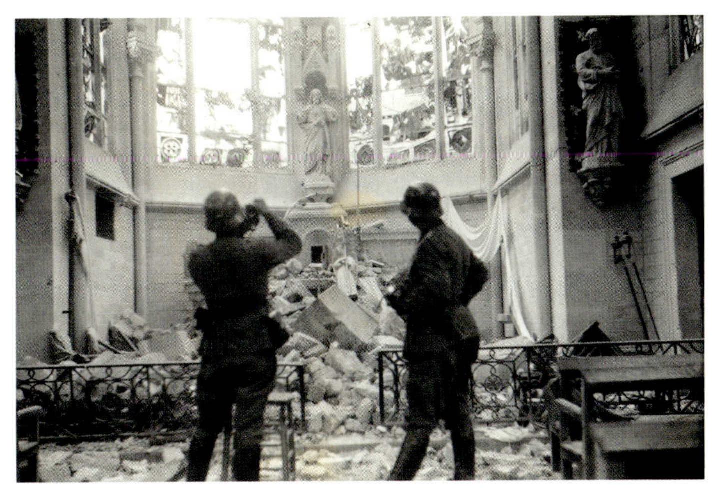

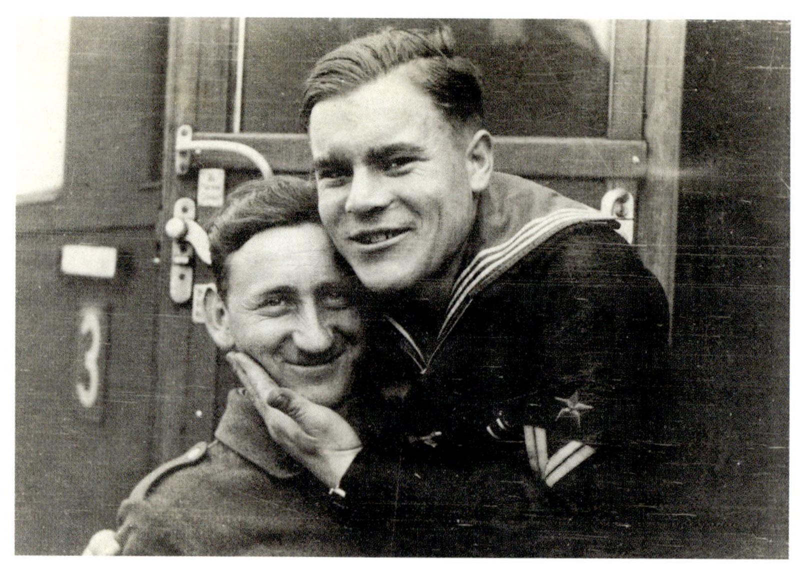
3

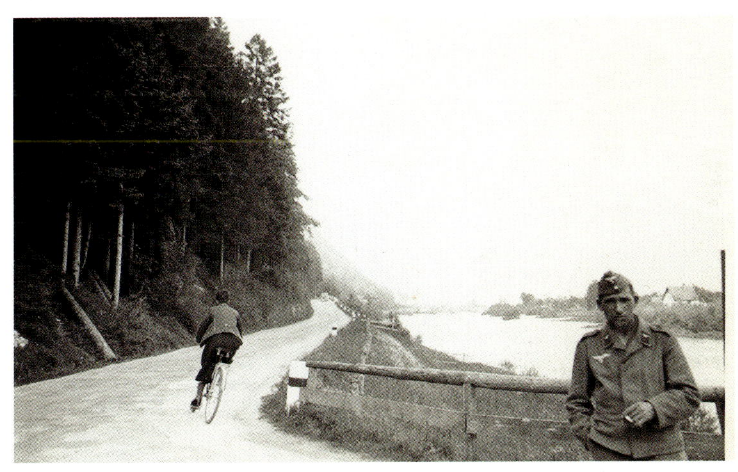

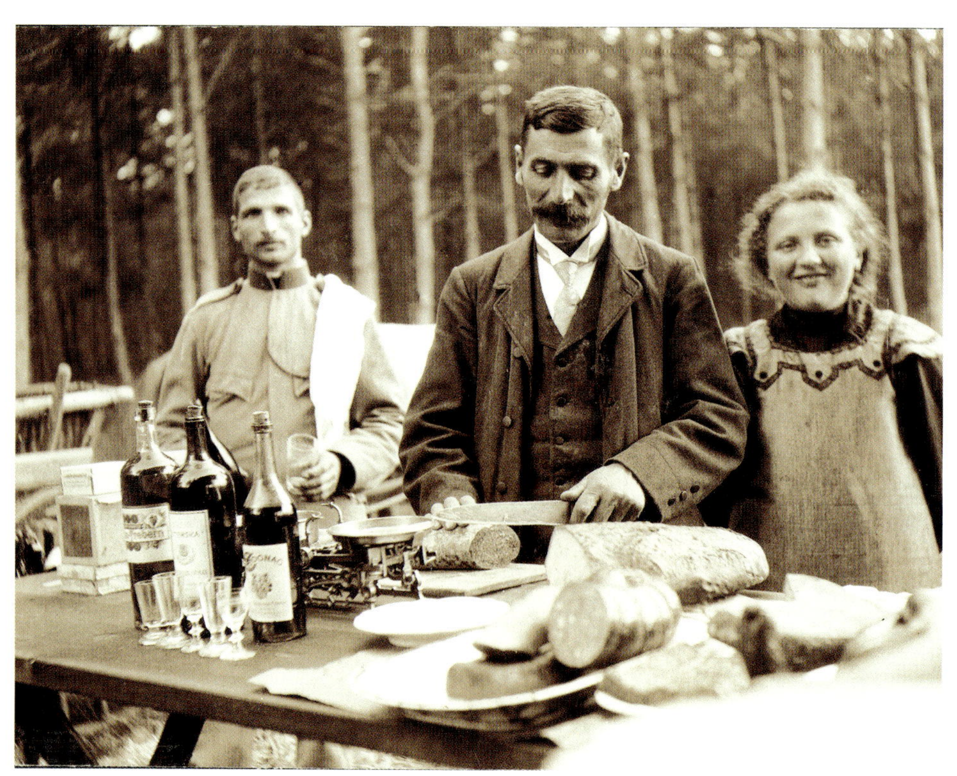

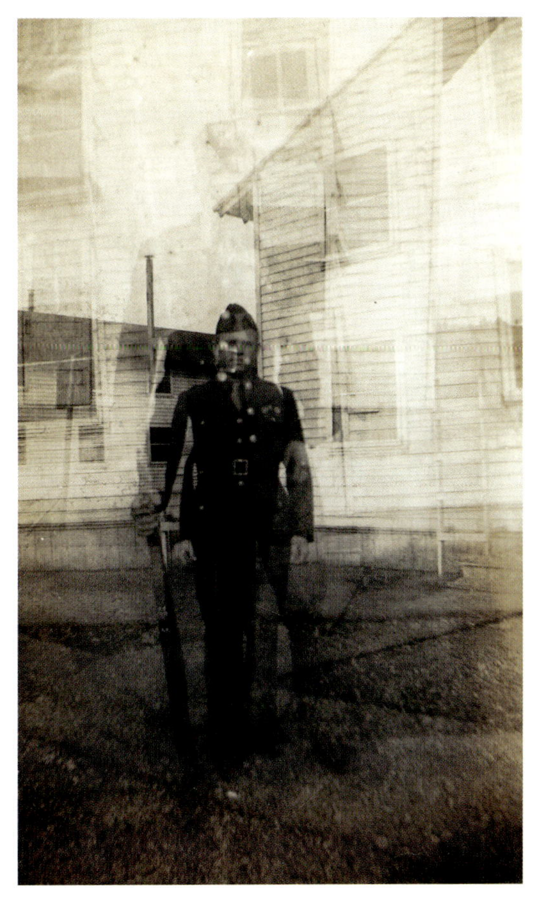

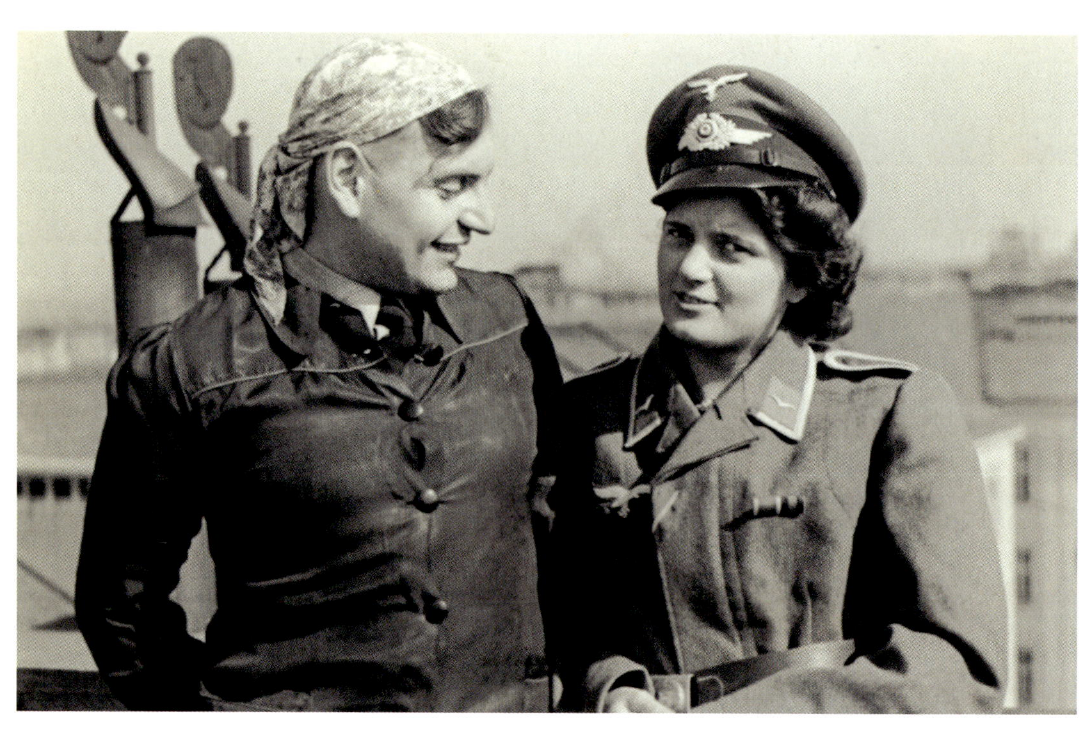

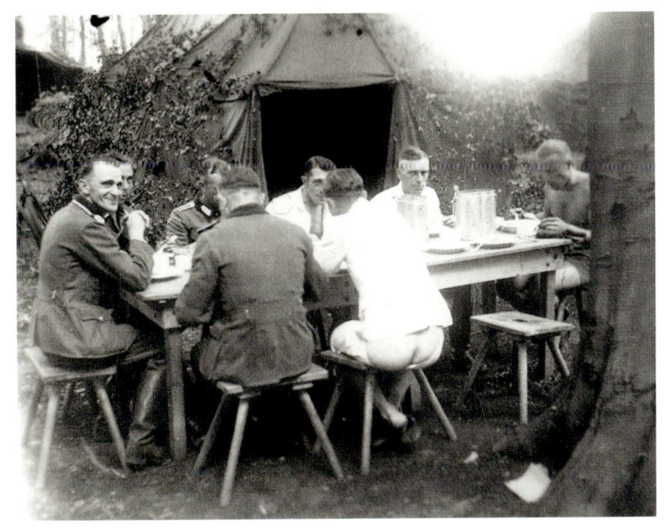

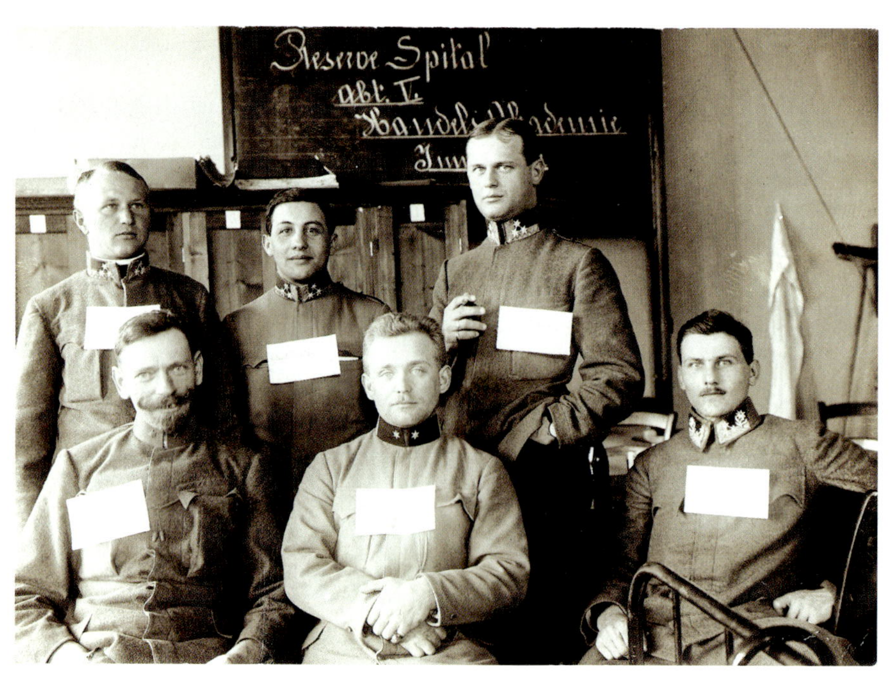
Reserve Spital
Abt. V.

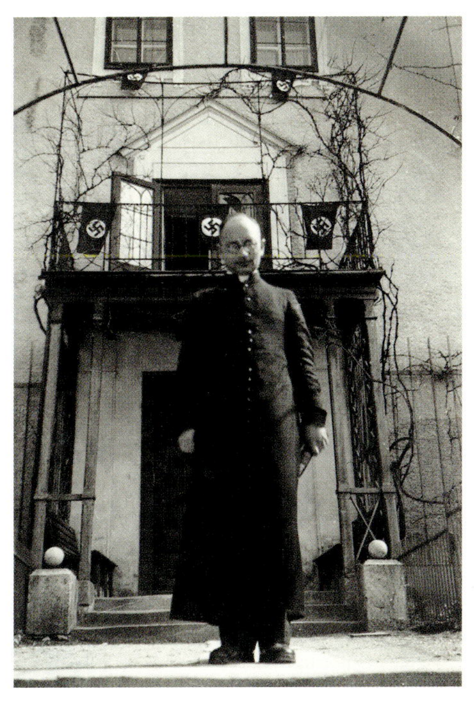

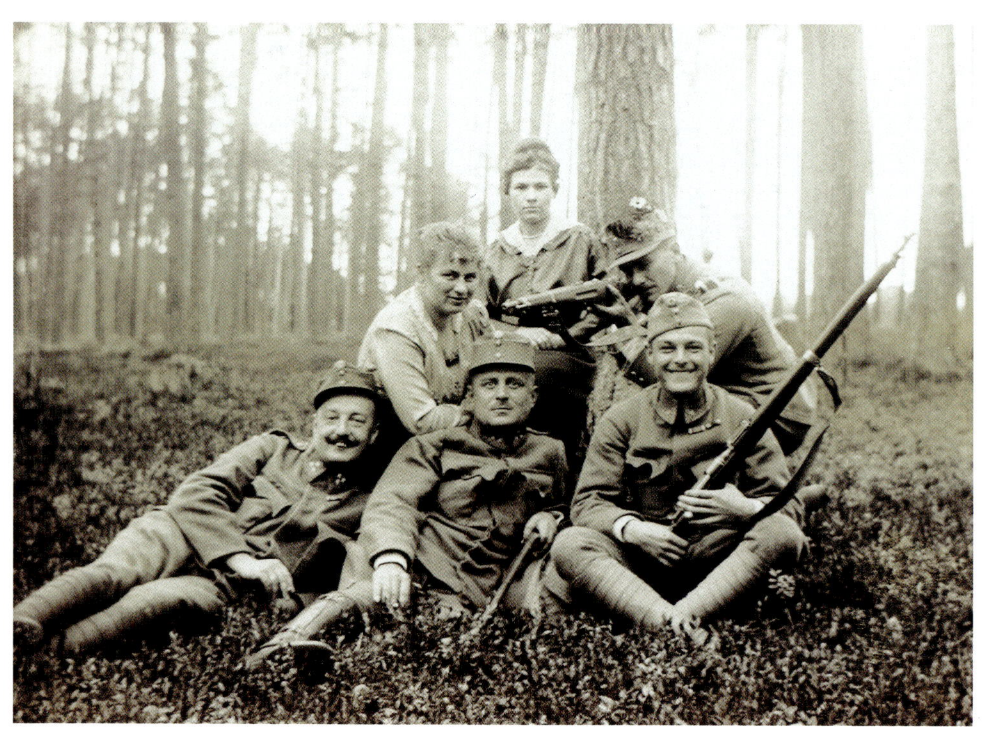

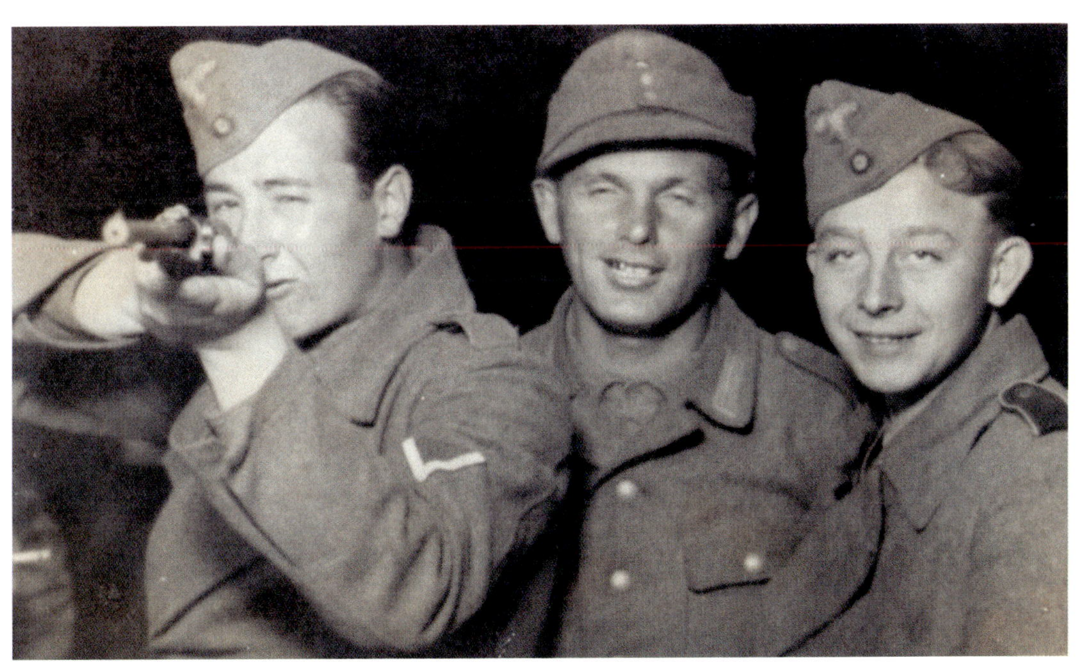

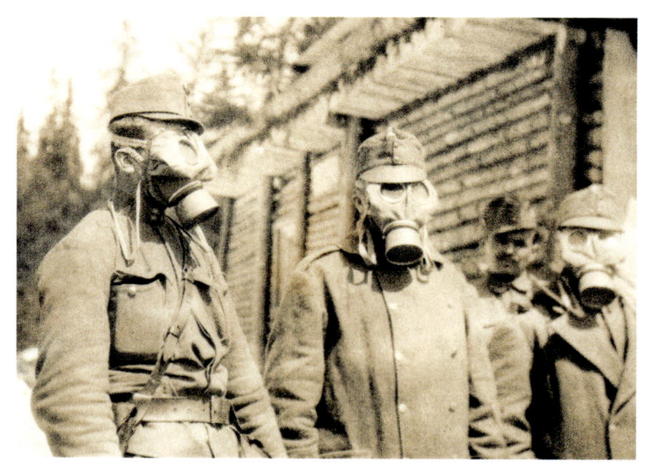

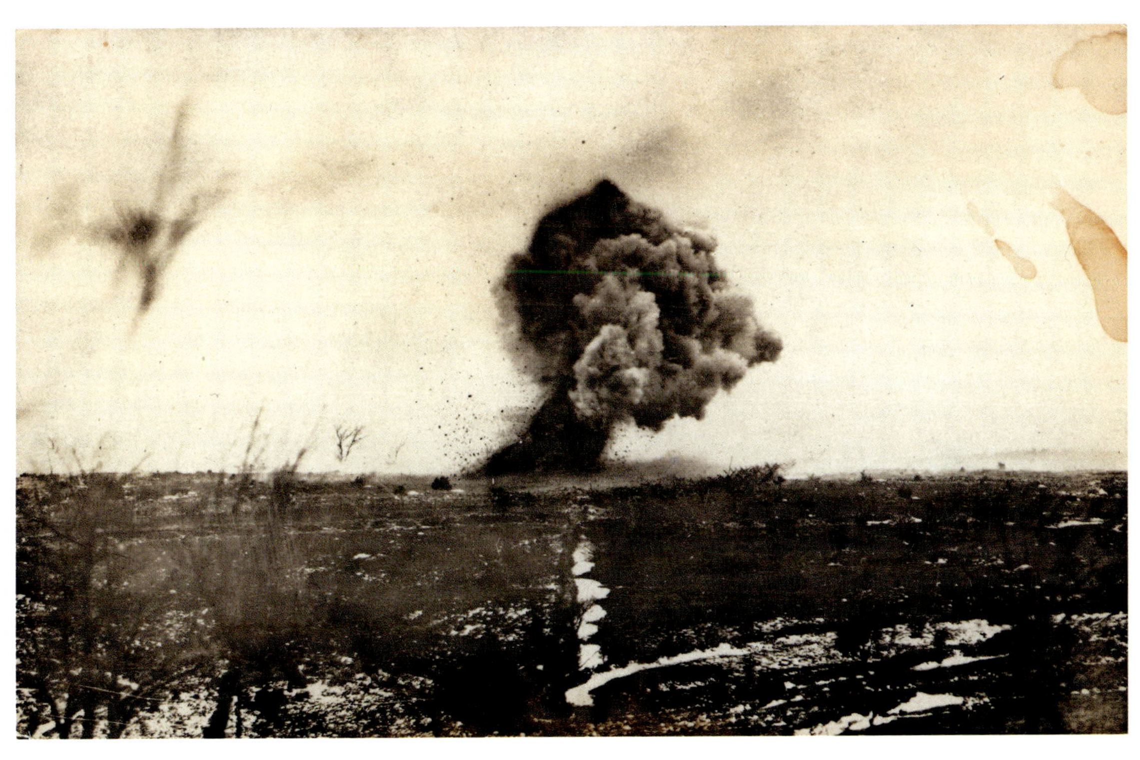

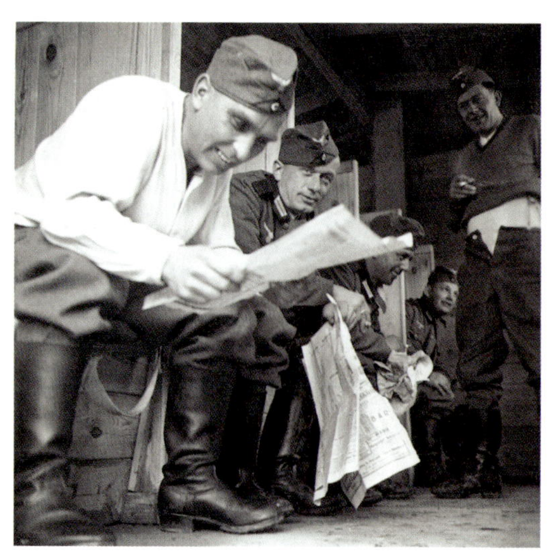

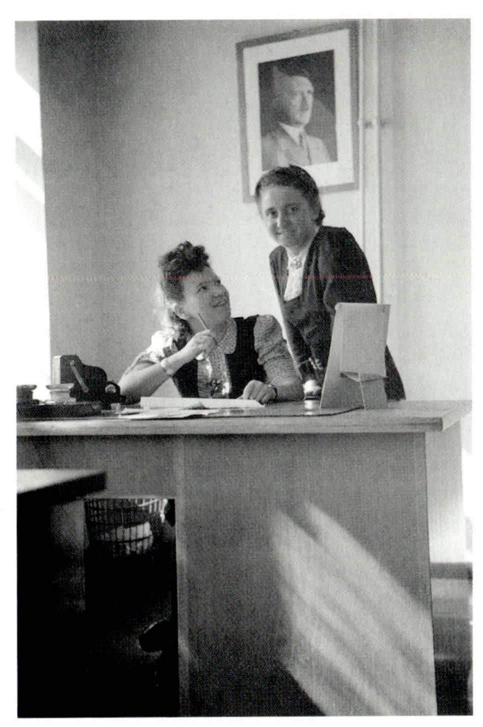

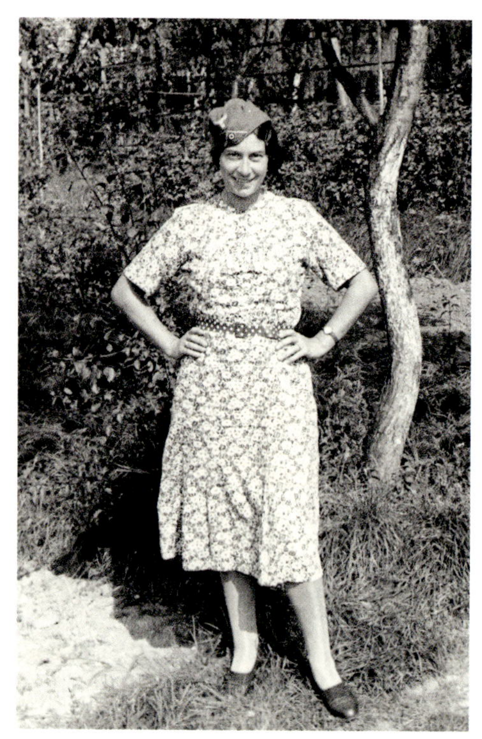

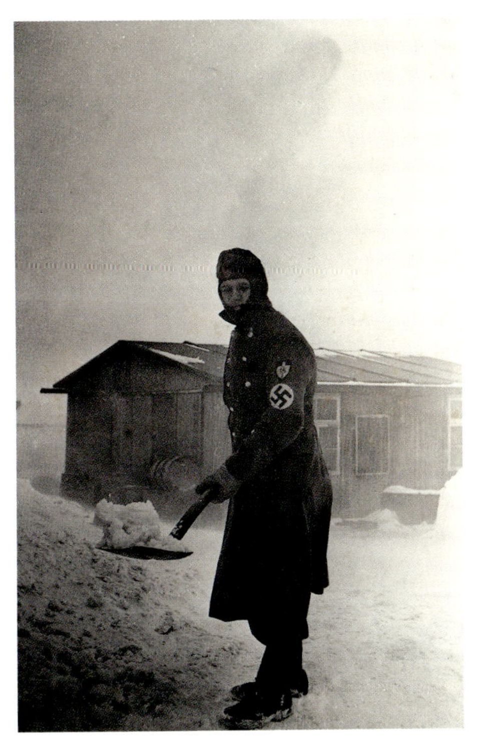

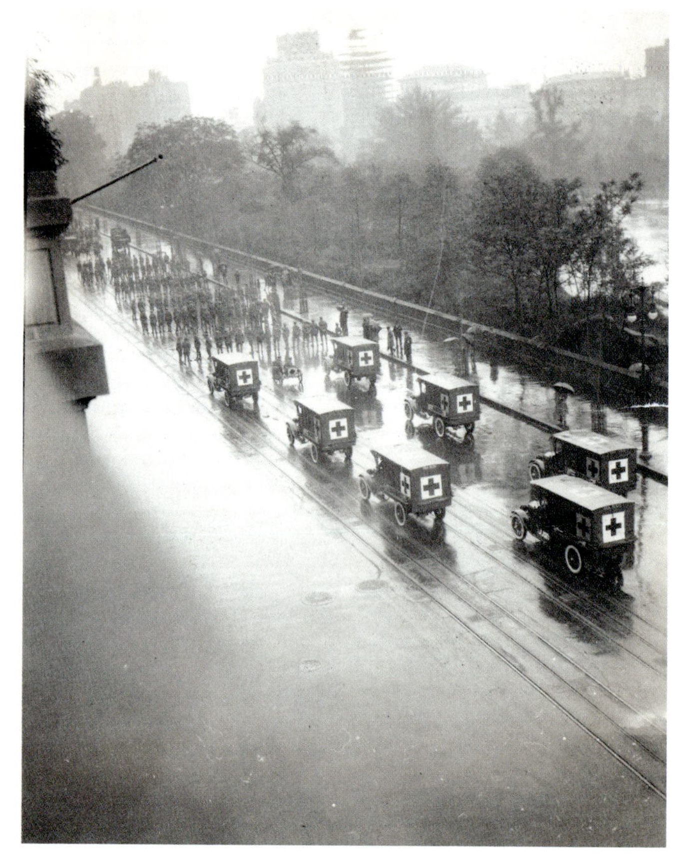

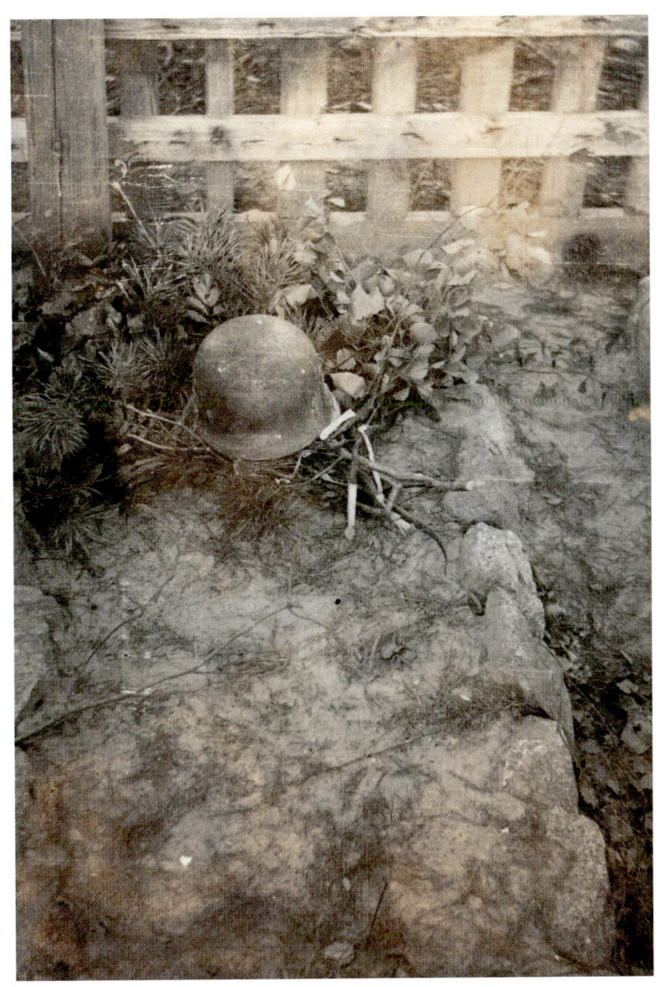

16)

Artistic Photography Künstlerische Fotografie

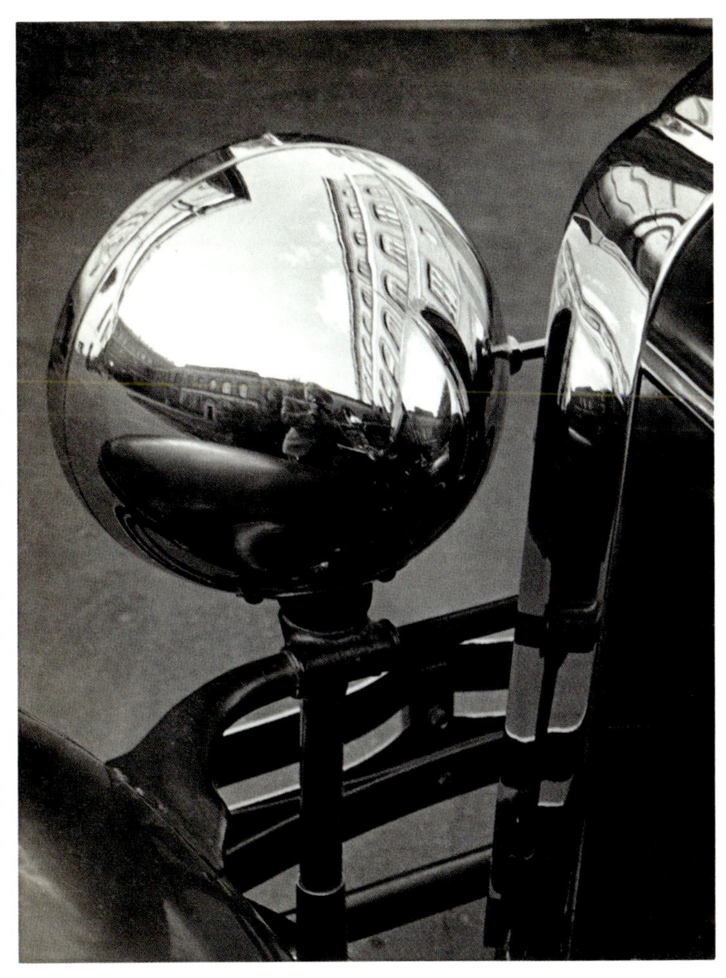

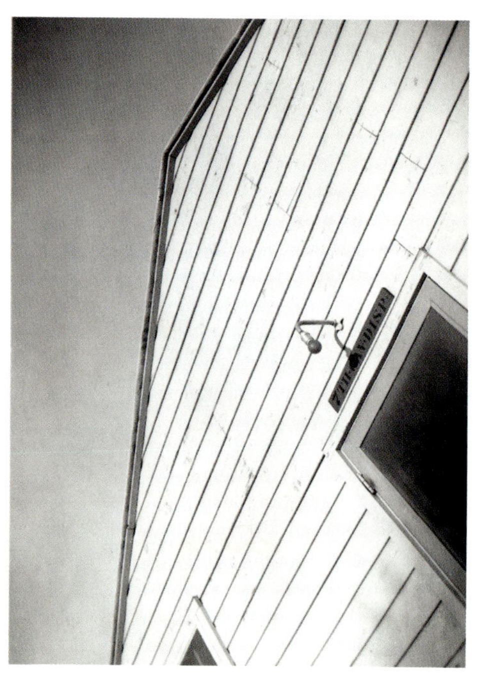

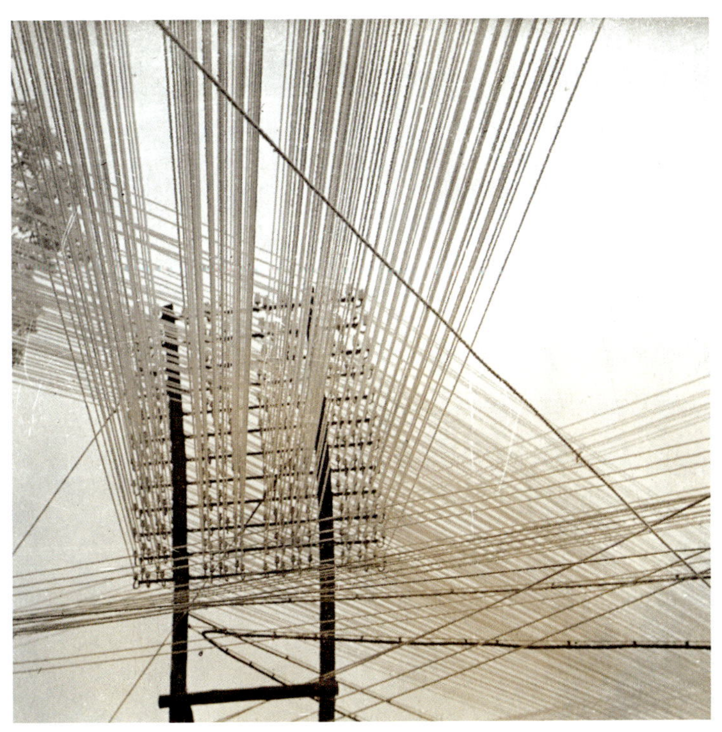

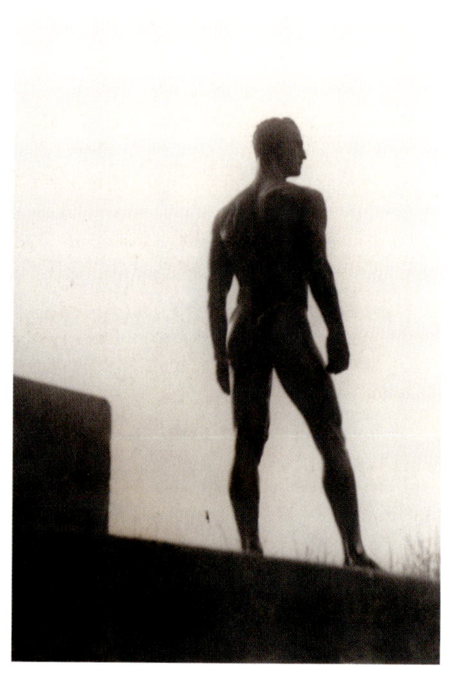

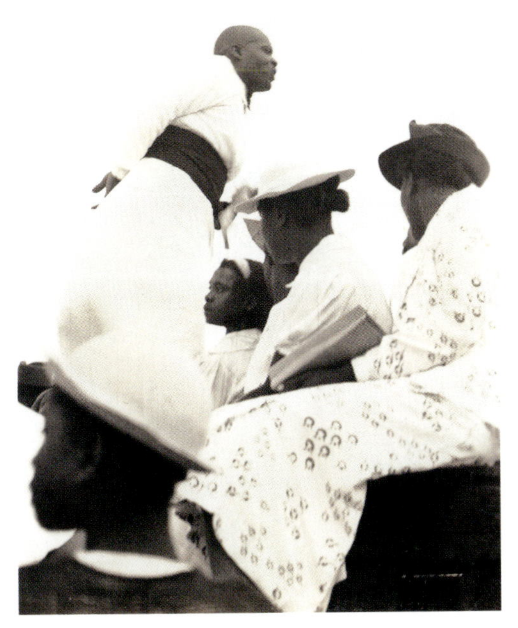

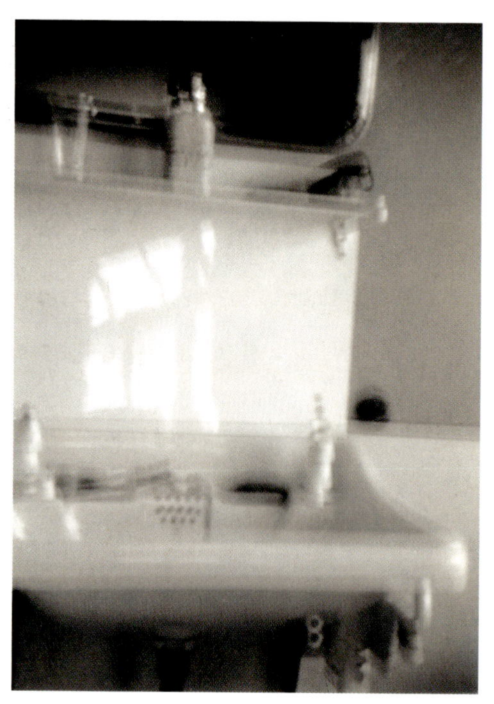

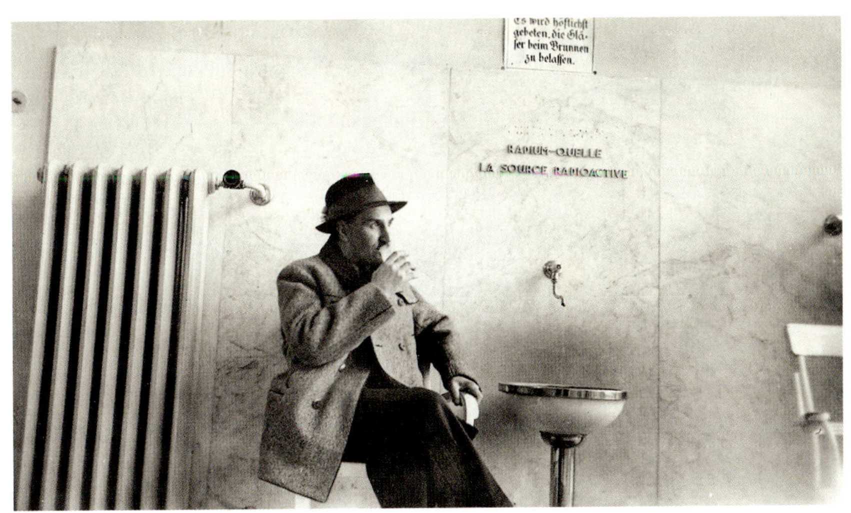
Es wird höflichst
gebeten, die Glä-
ser beim Brunnen
zu belassen.
RADIUM-QUELLE
LA SOURCE RADIOACTIVE

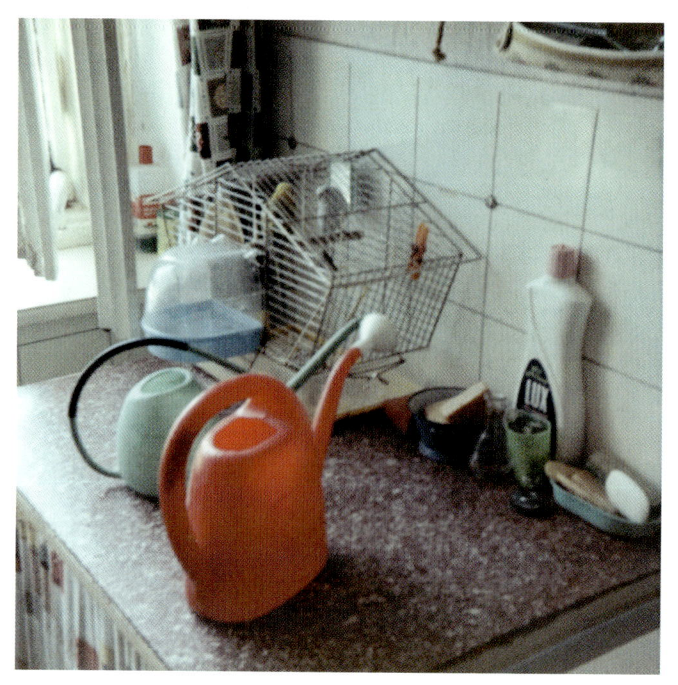
LUX

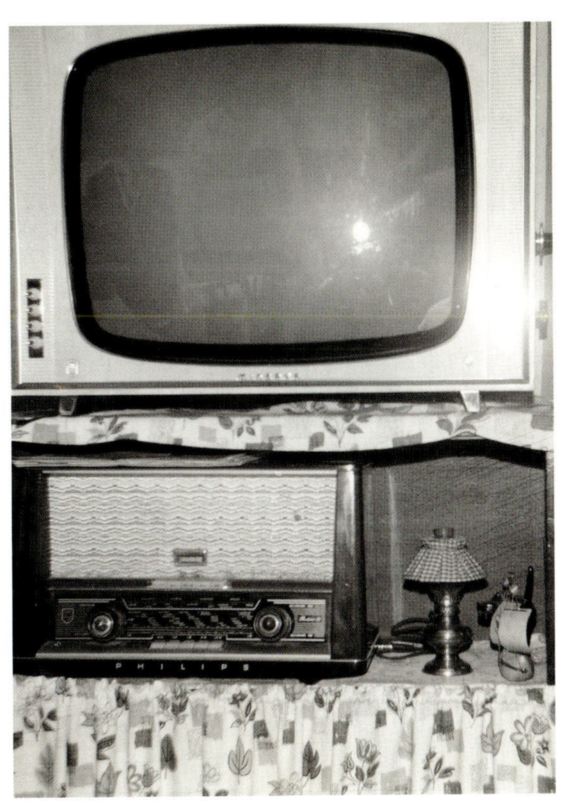
PHILIPS

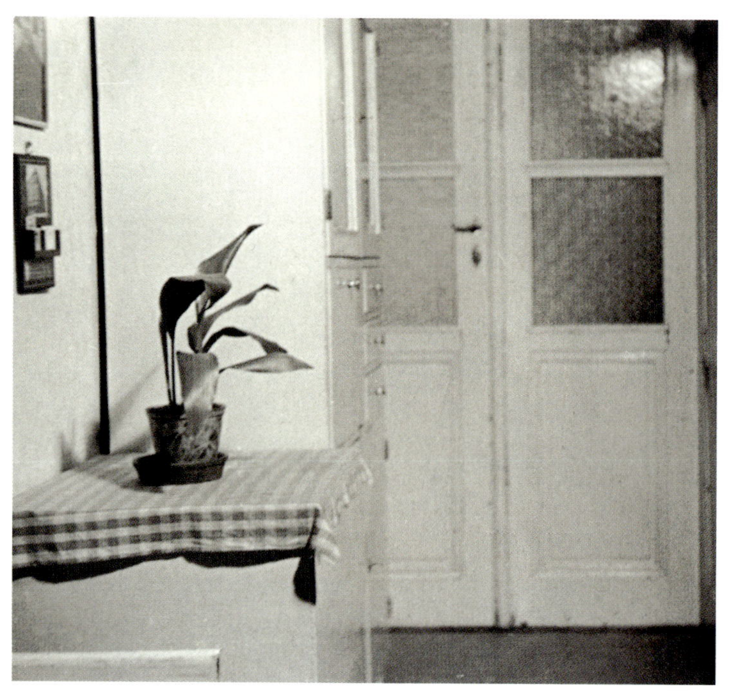

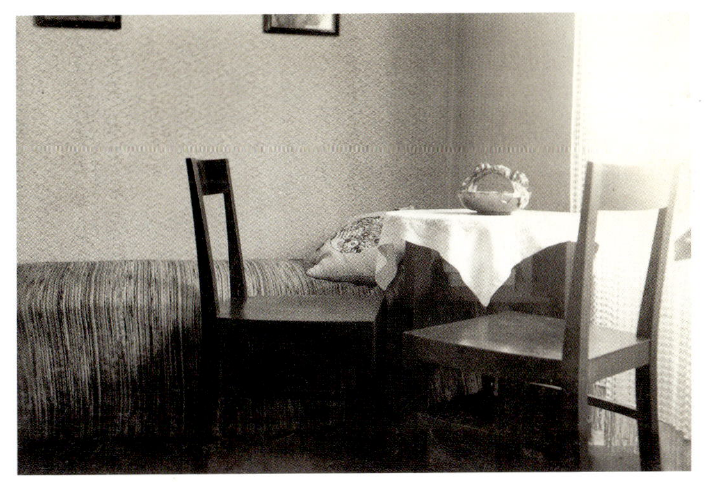

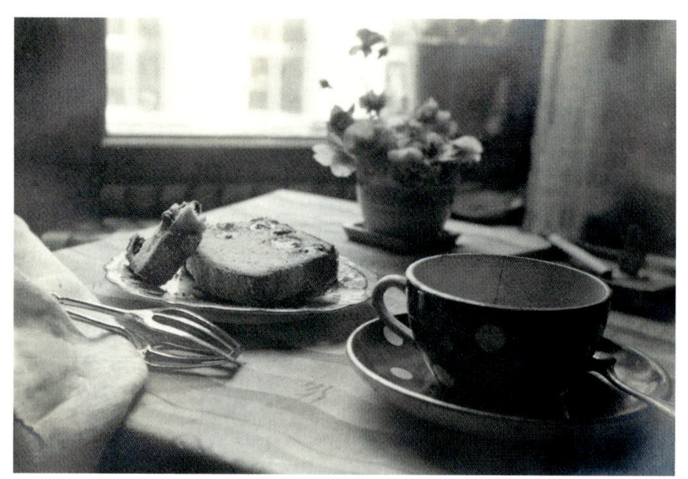

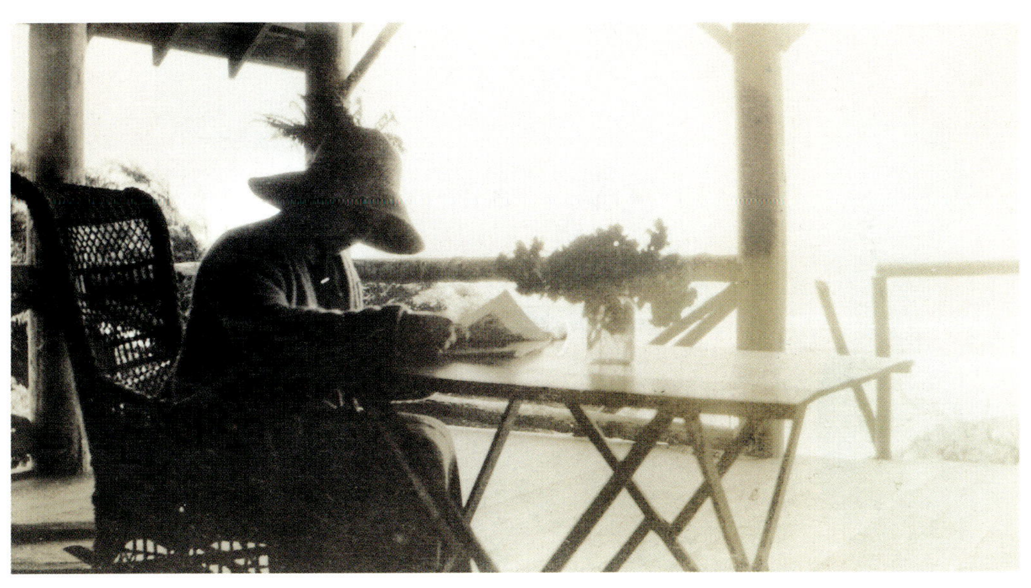

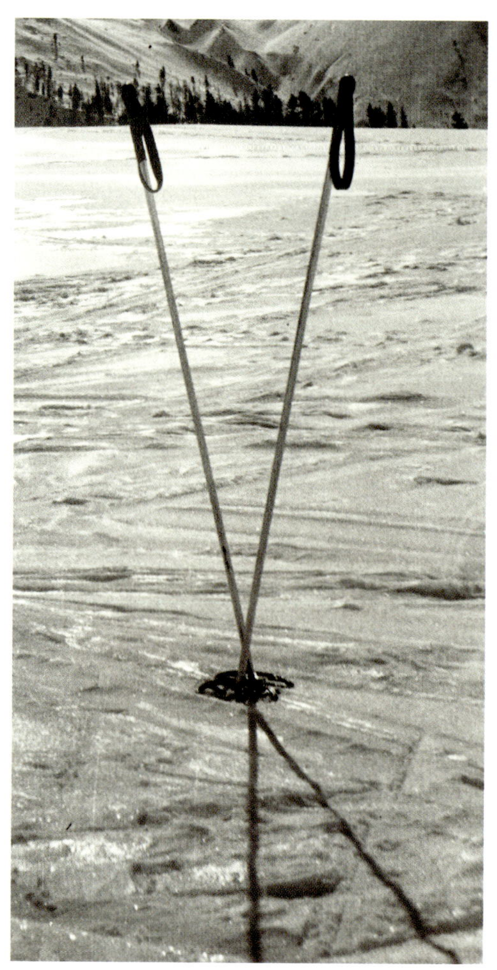

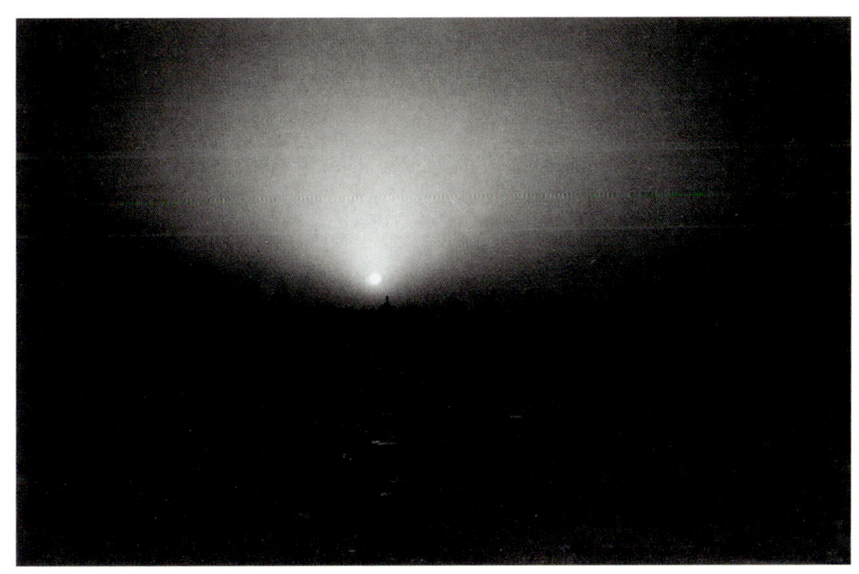

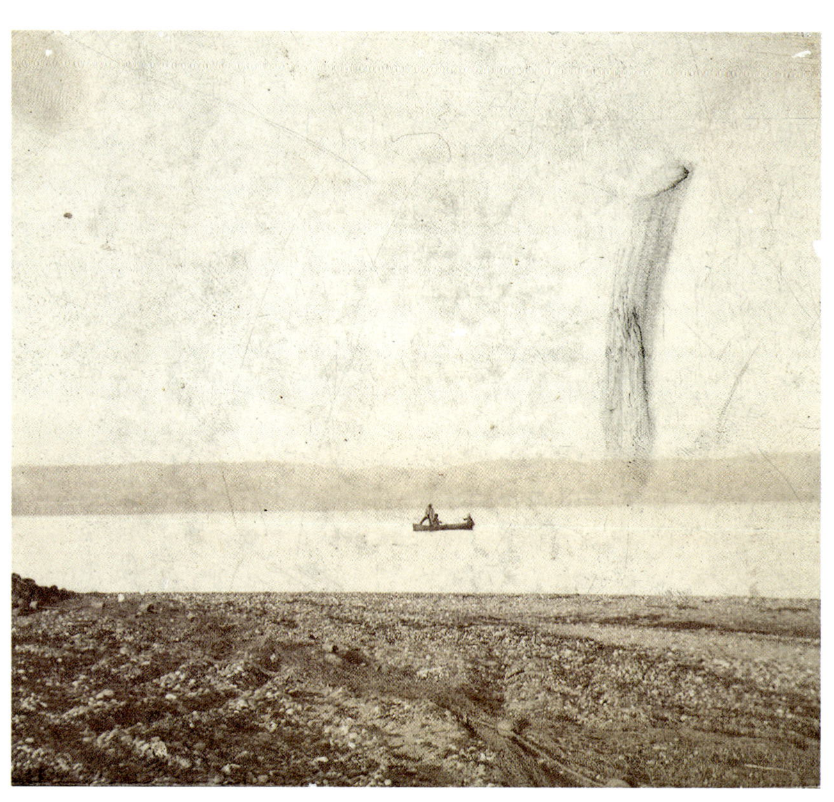

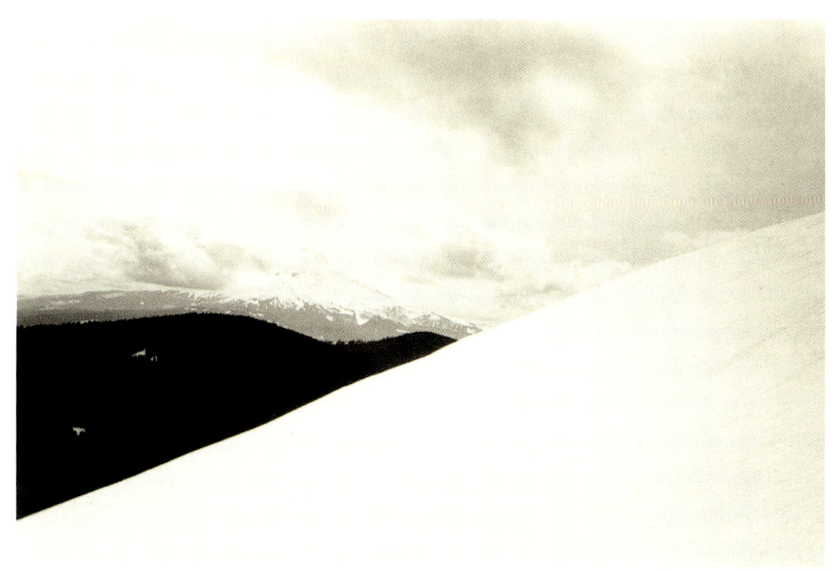

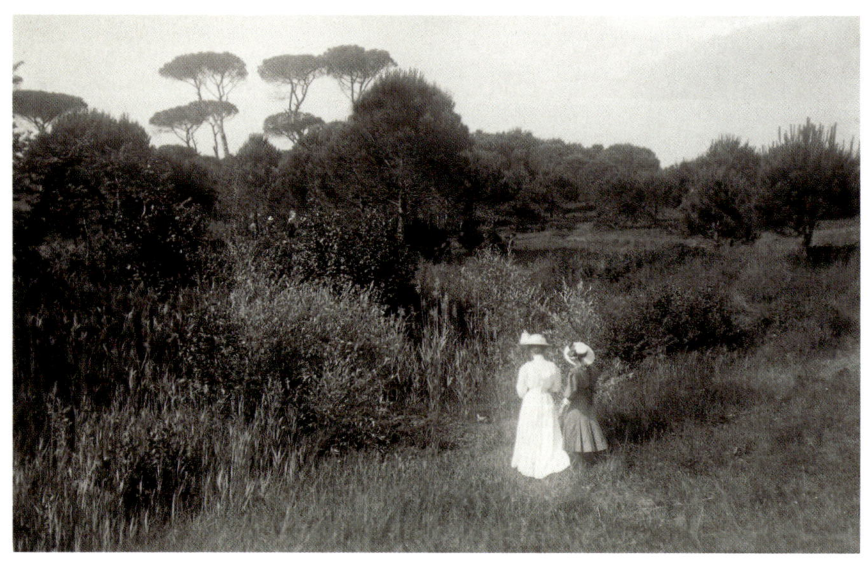

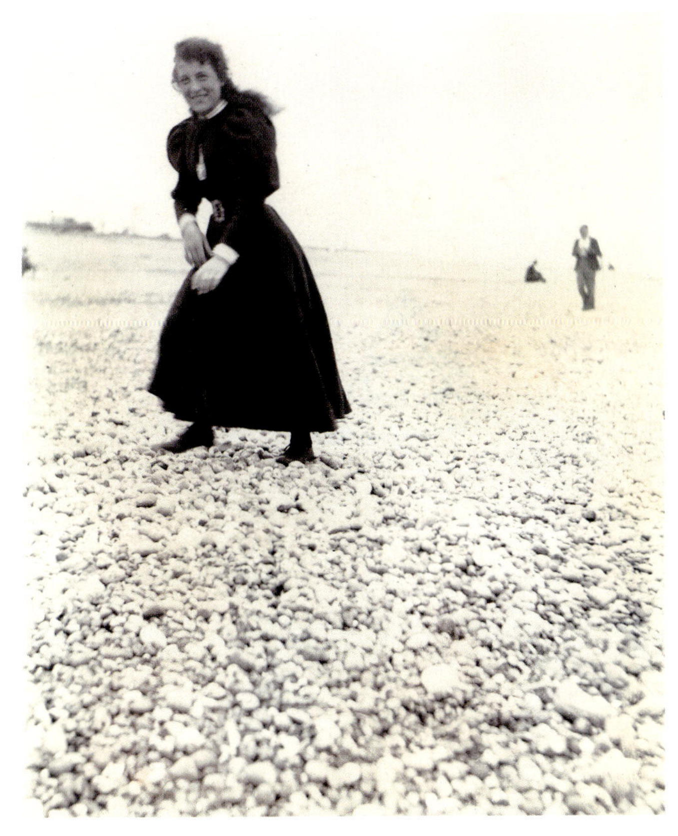

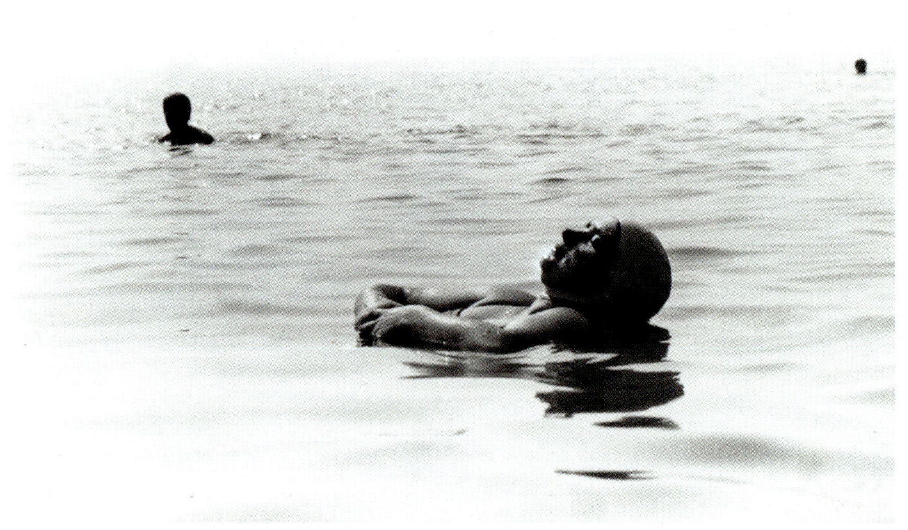

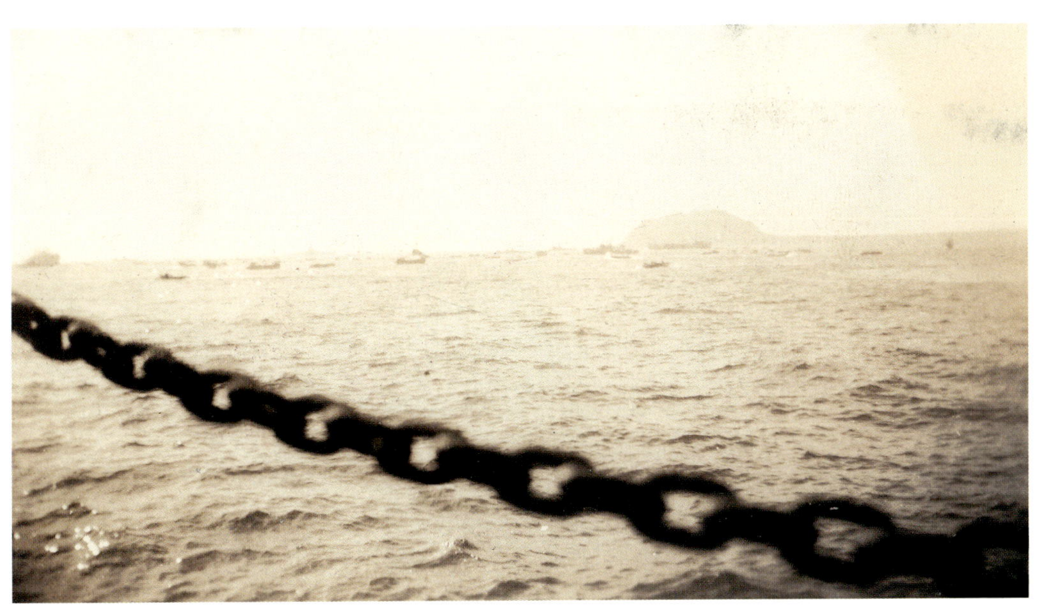

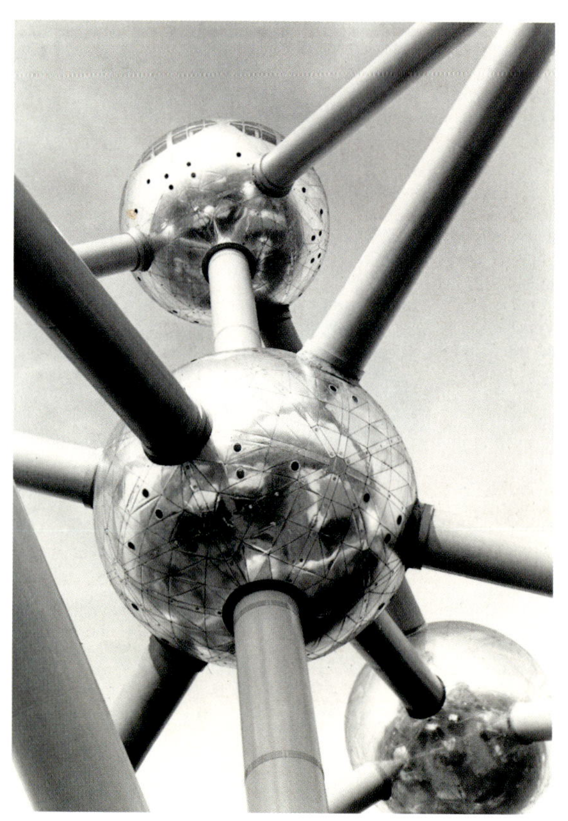

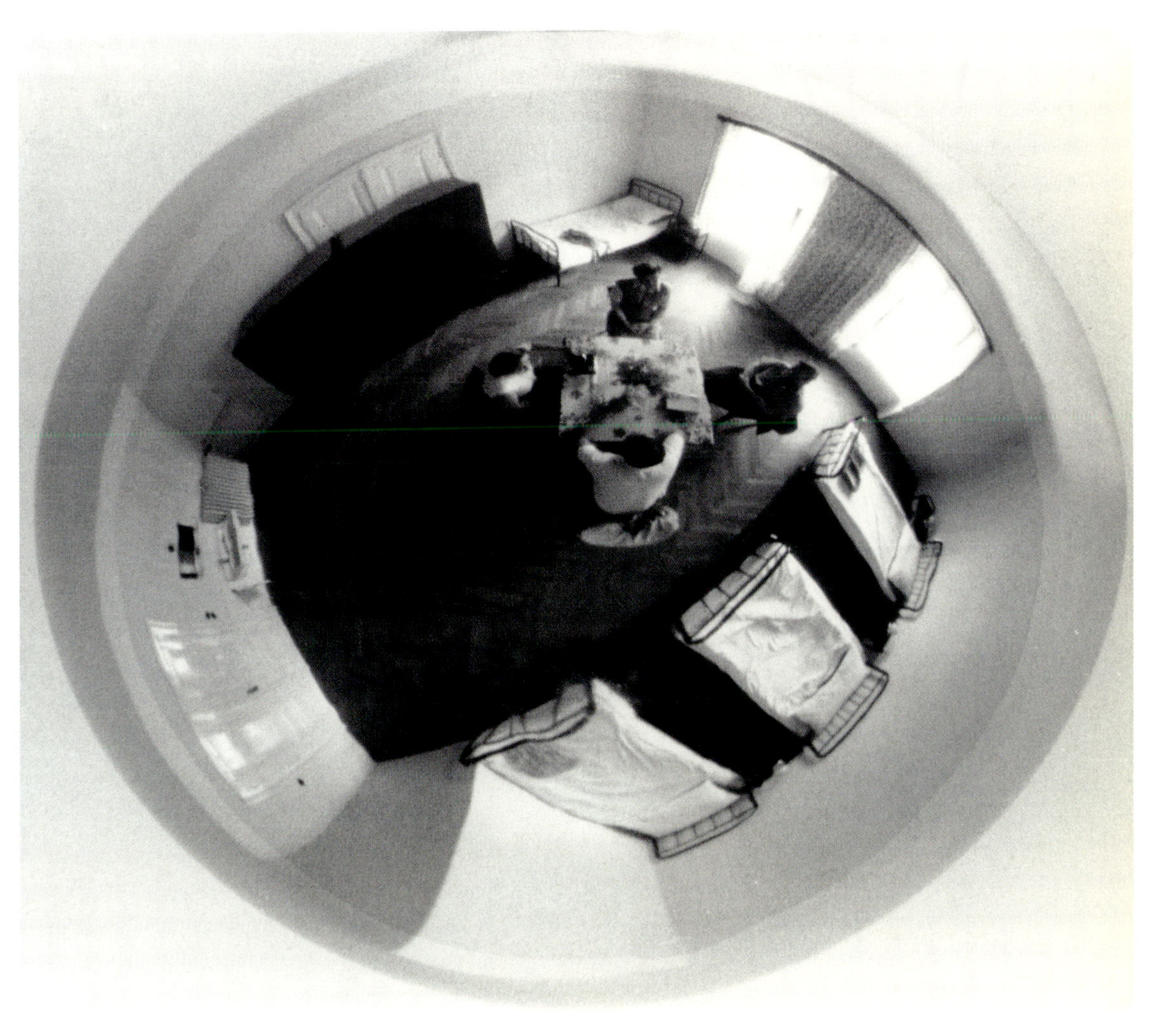

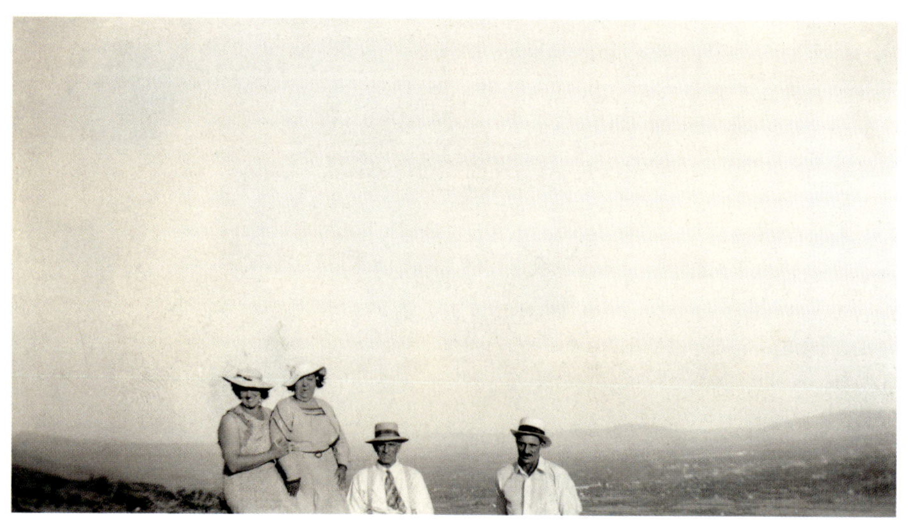

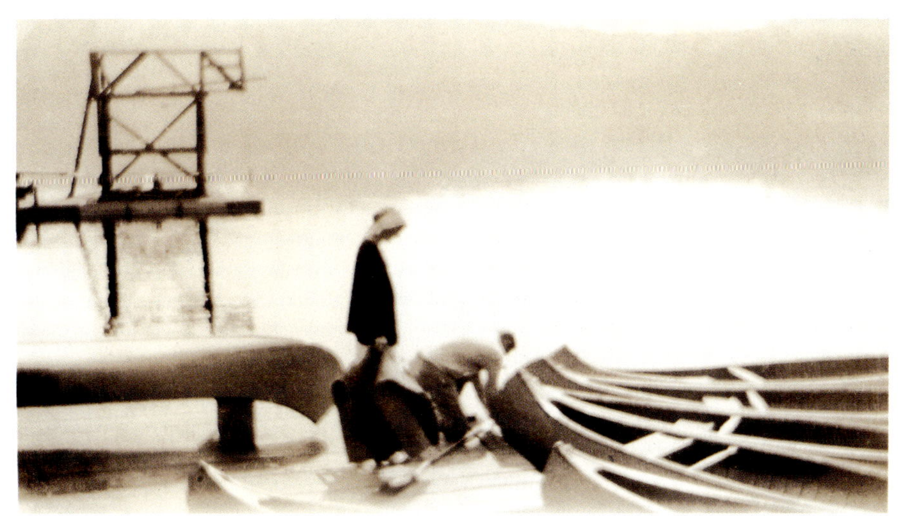

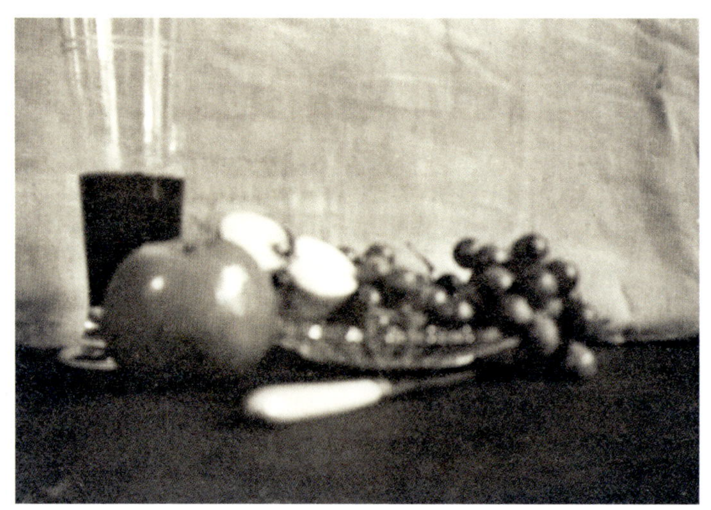

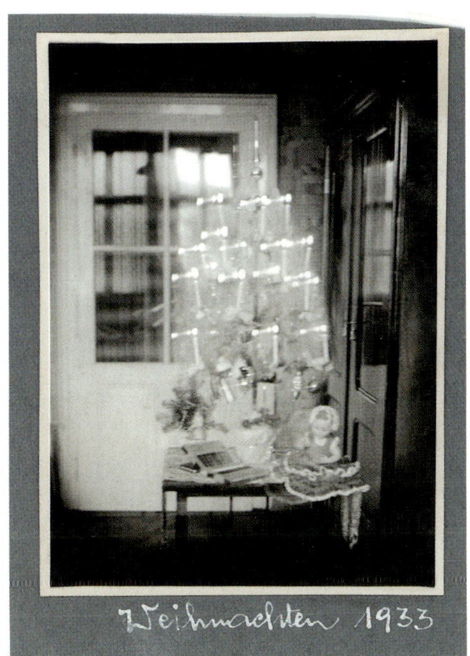
Weihnachten 1933

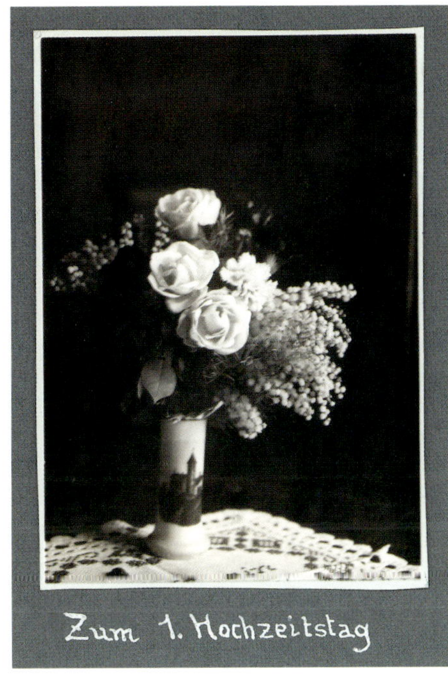
Zum 1. Hochzeitstag

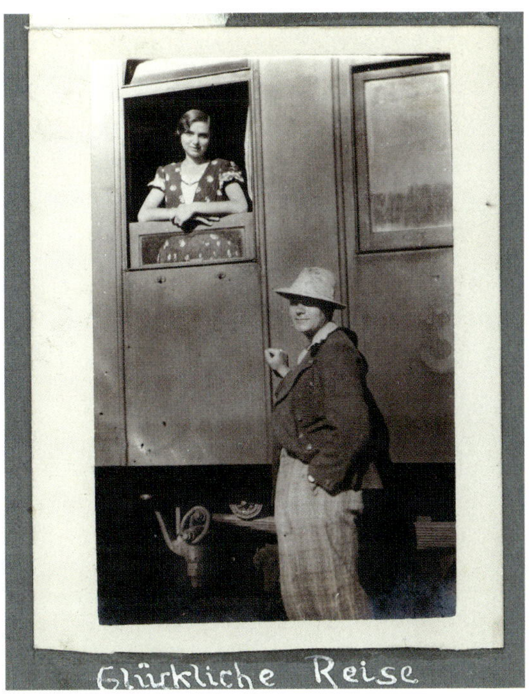
Glückliche Reise

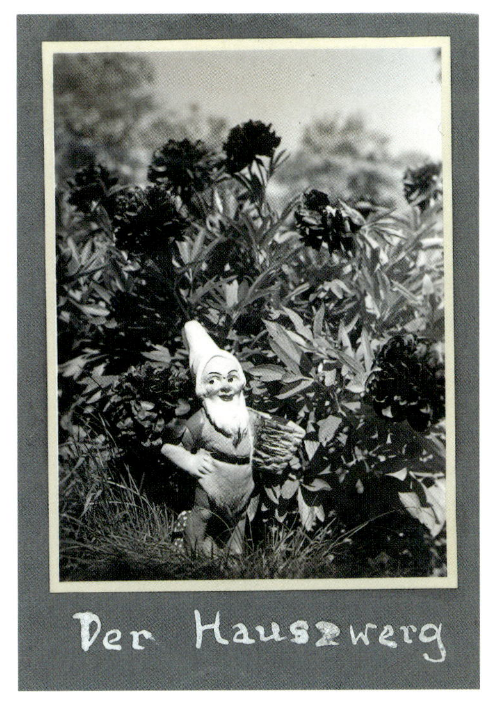
Der Hauszwerg

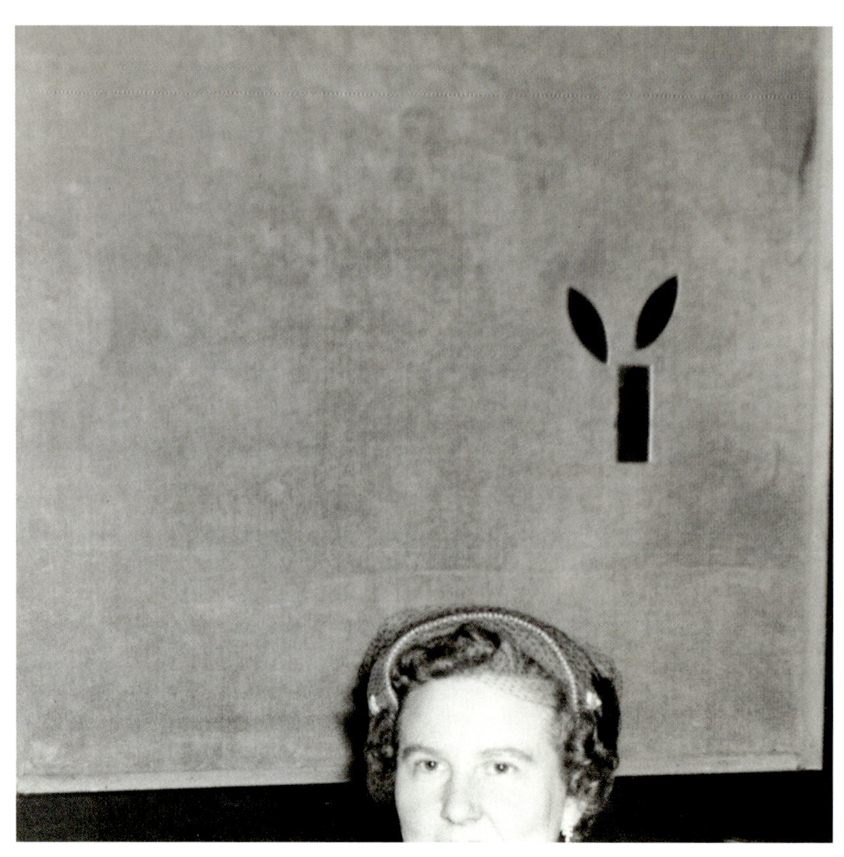

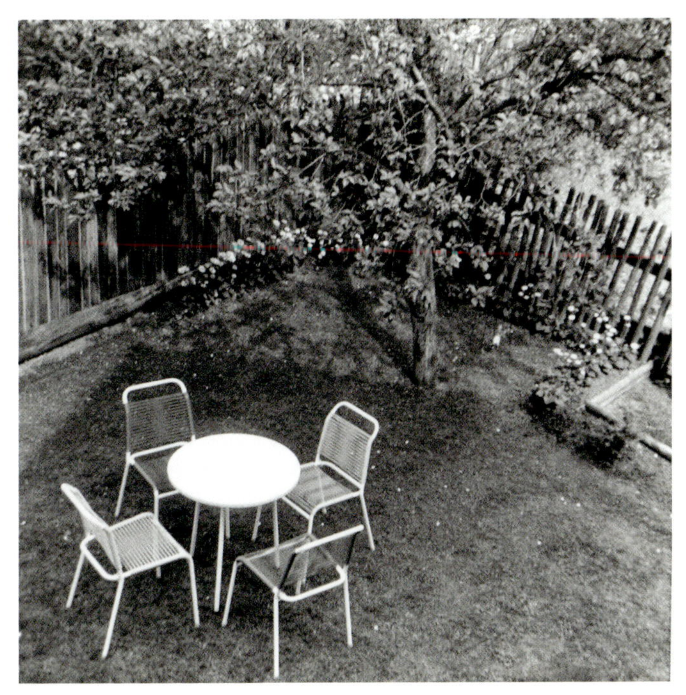

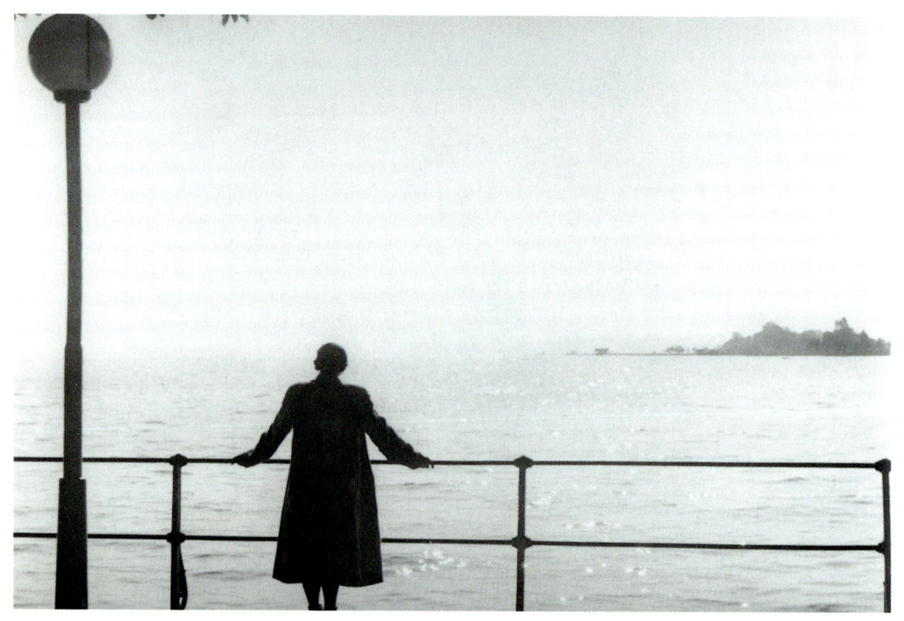

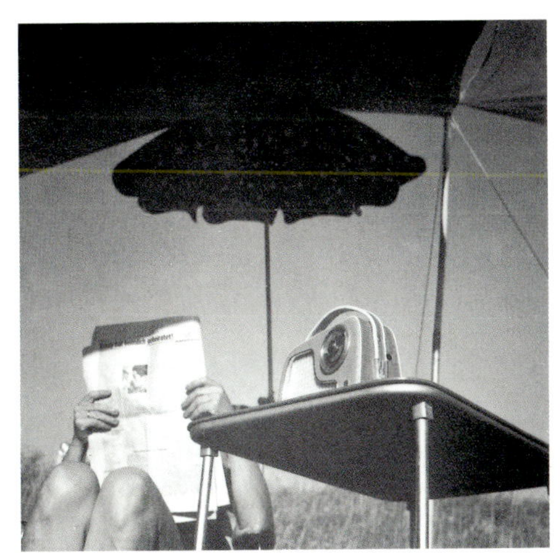

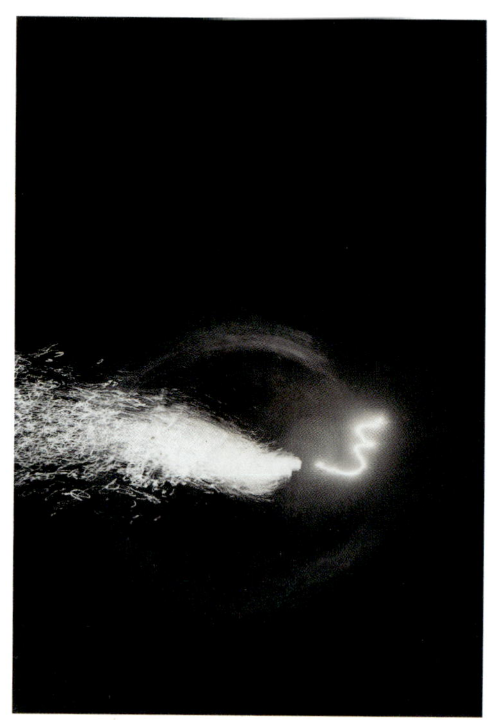

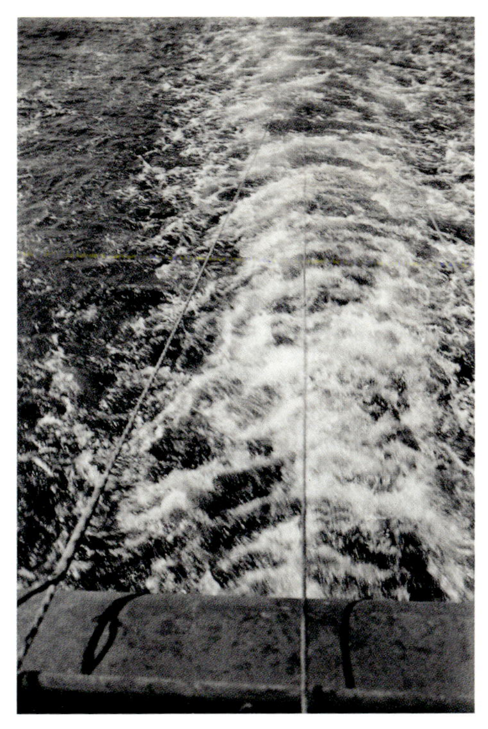

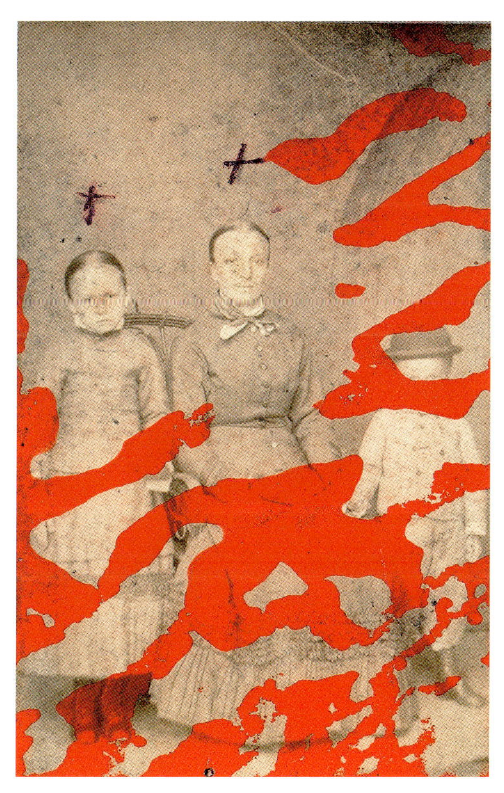

17)

Photographers Fotografen

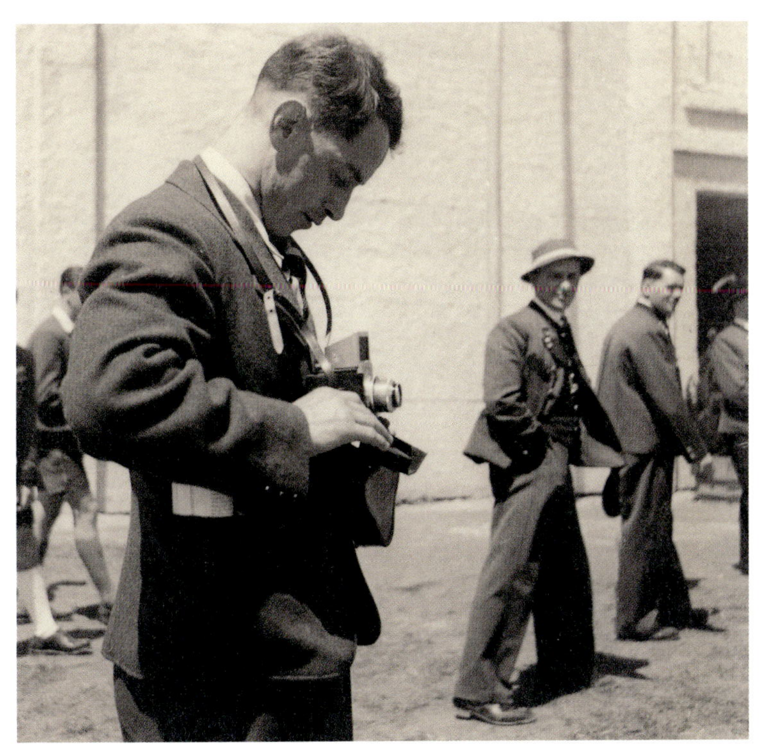

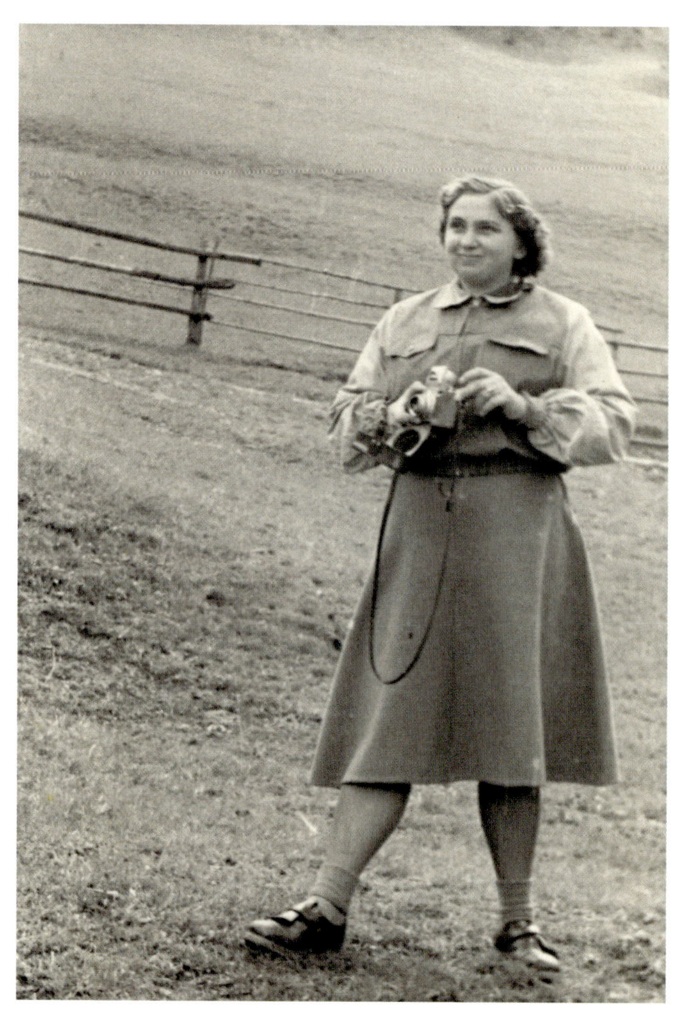

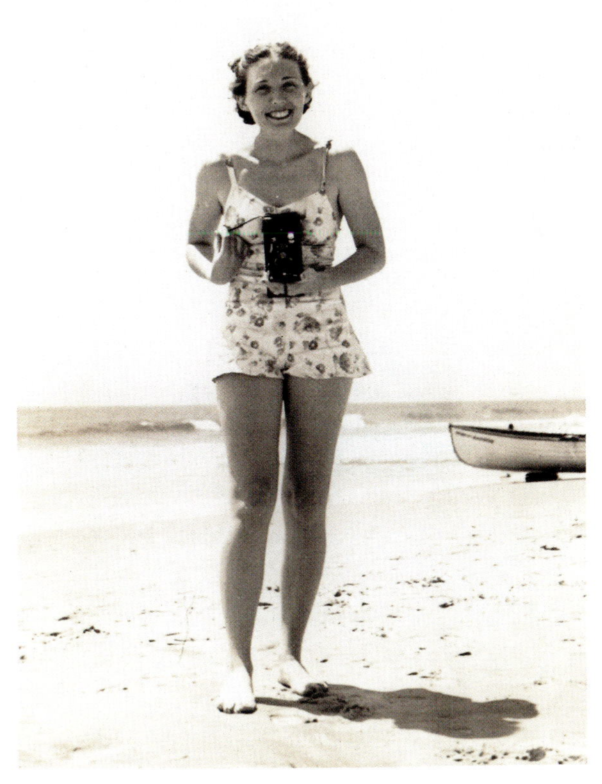

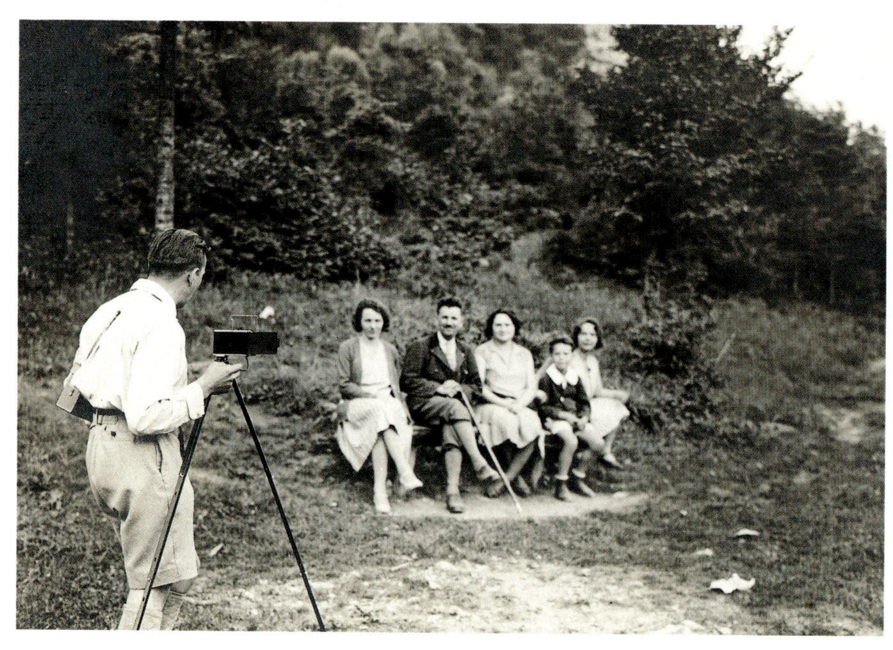

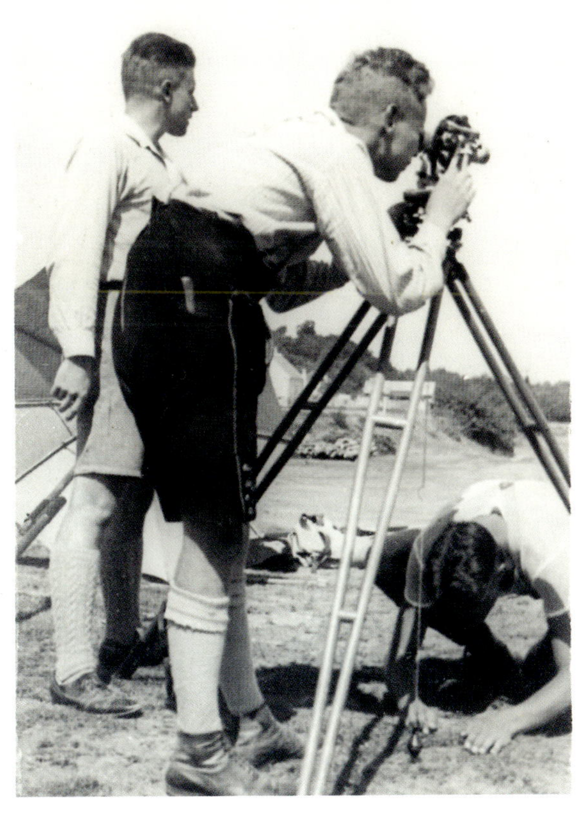

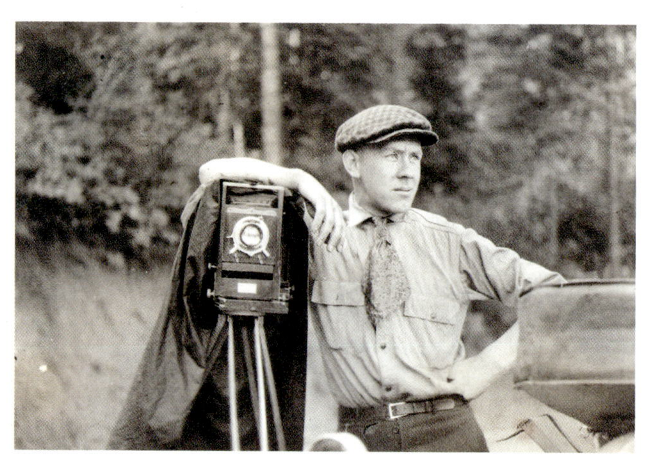

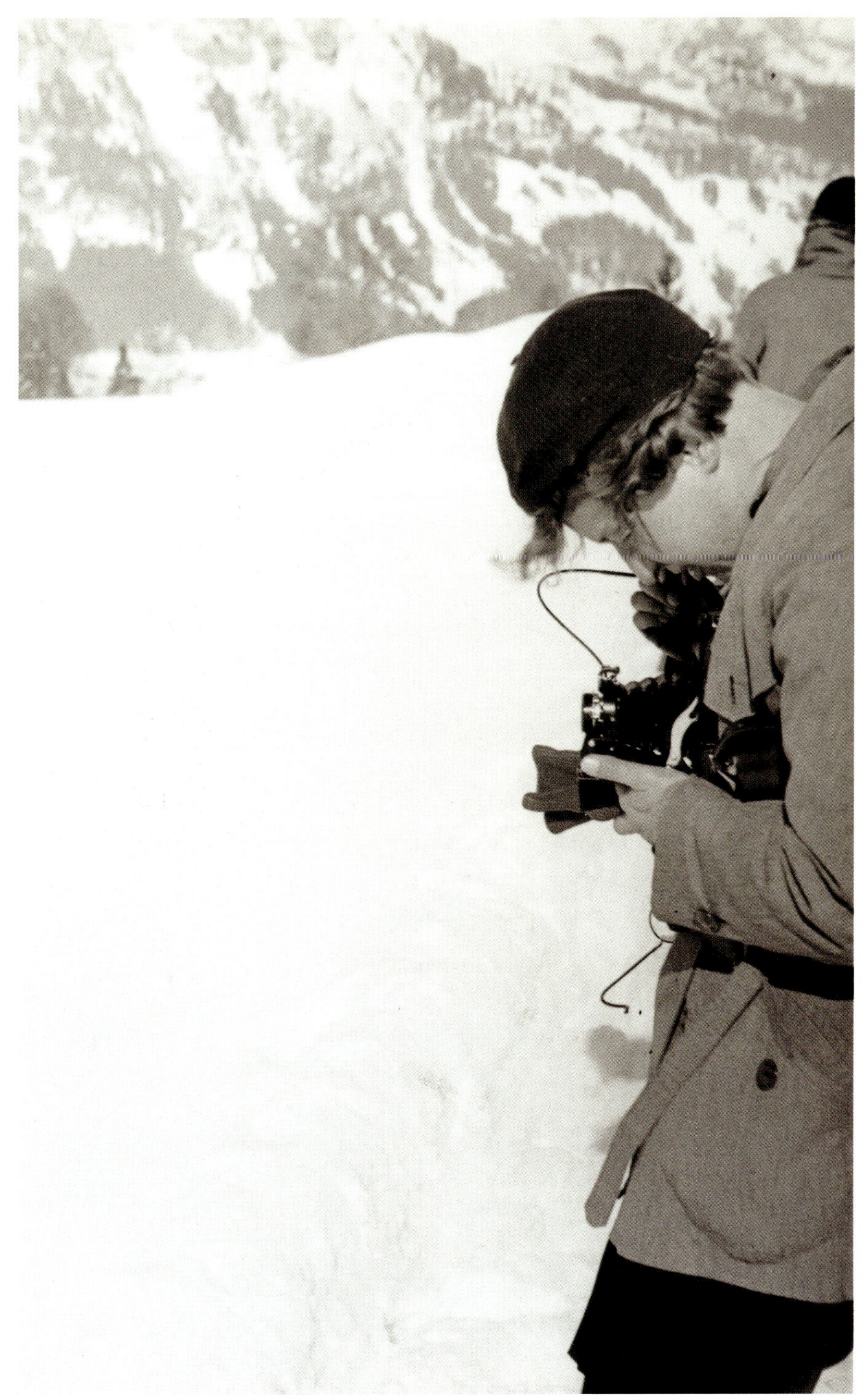

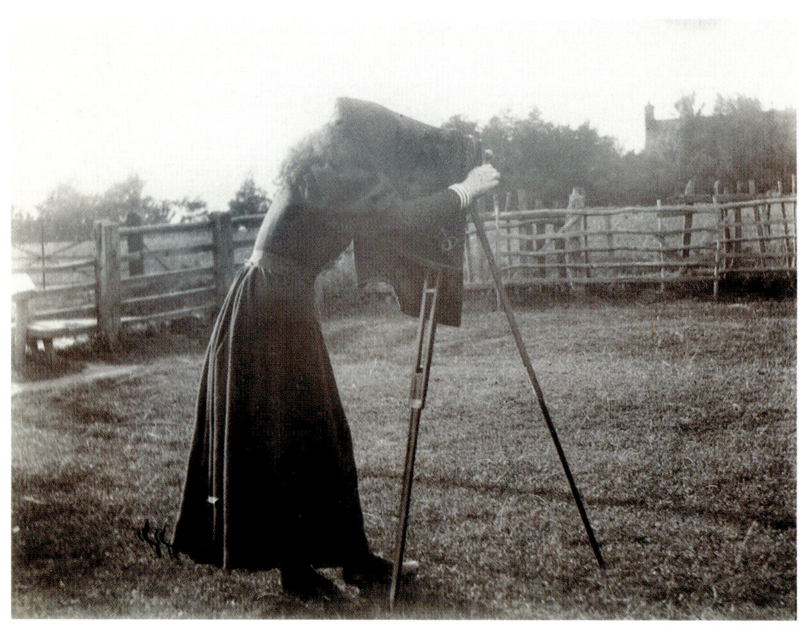

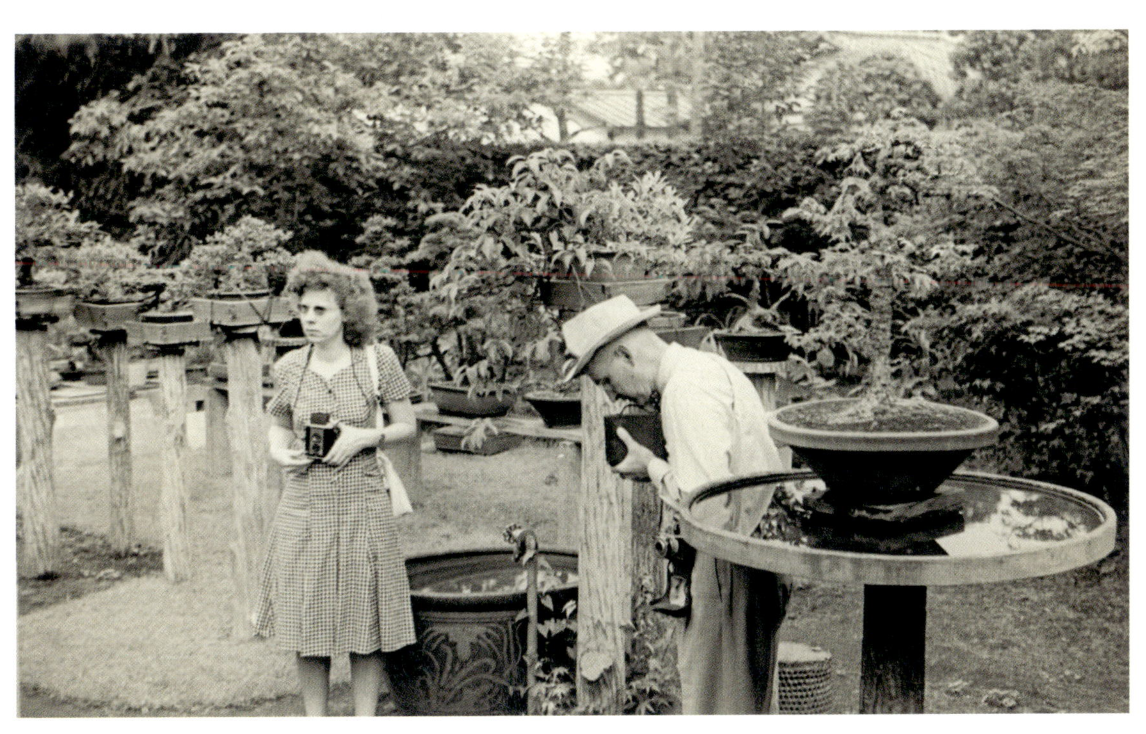

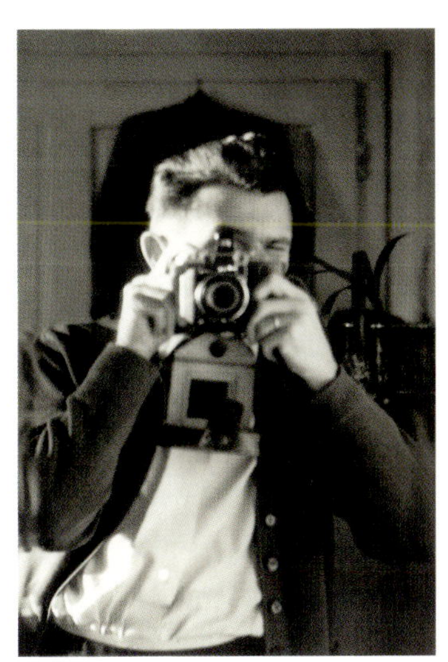

List of Works Verzeichnis der Werke

All photographs are vintage prints. The images are 10 to 25 per cent larger or smaller than the original print. Album pages are shown in the original state.
CST: Censor stamp

1) Moments Augenblicke

Snapshot – shot from rifle, USA, 1920s
3.8 x 6 cm
p. 21

"9.6.1946 – 'Na' der Plafond Inzersdorf," Vienna, Austria, 1946
8 x 5.5 cm
p. 22

USA, 1950s
CST: Ansco, 7.5 x 7.5 cm
p. 23

USA, 1960s
Kodak color, 7 x 8.5 cm
p. 24

Florence, Italy, 1910s
10.5 x 6 cm
p. 25

"Julienpass, 2200 m, Schweiz 1955," Switzerland, 1955
Agfa Bovira, 9.5 x 6.6 cm
p. 26

"California 1934773," USA, 1928
CST: 119, 12 x 7 cm
p. 27

Bavaria, Germany, 1932
Double exposure, 5 x 8 cm
p. 28

Austria, c. 1938
CST: 3711, 8.5 x 5.5 cm
p. 29

Serbia, c. 1915
7.7 x 9.5 cm
p. 30

"2. März 1934 – St. Anton," Austria, 1934
Agfa Lupex, 8.5 x 6 cm
p. 31

Halloween, USA, 1930s
5.7 x 10 cm
p. 32

Dead fish on a model of an aeroplane, USA, 1938
5 x 7.5 cm
p. 33

"Kitty was sick and we were dressed," USA, 1938
Velox; CST: 348, 6 x 10.5 cm
p. 34

Germany, 1950s
5.5 x 8 cm
p. 35

USA, c. 1918
Postcard imprint, 6 x 10.5 cm
p. 36

USA, 1934
10 x 6 cm
p. 37

"Much love from Billy," Great Britain, 1920s
26 x 19 cm
p. 38

USA, c. 1935
6 x 4 cm
p. 39

Germany, 1940s
Brovira, 6 x 9 cm
p. 40

USA, c. 1925
Velox; incidence of light, 11.5 x 7.5 cm
p. 41

"Dec. 25, 1937," USA, 1937
Double exposure, 5.5 x 8 cm
p. 42

Germany, c. 1951
CST: 259X; double exposure, 7.5 x 11 cm
p. 43

USA, c. 1925
10.5 x 9 cm
p. 44

USA, 1920s
5.7 x 10 cm
p. 45

USA, 1910s
CST: 3; double exposure, 10 x 5.7 cm
p. 46

Connecticut, USA, 1938
Stamp: This print is certified by photo finishing institute / Dec. 5, 1938, 6 x 10.5 cm
p. 47

Australia, 1950s
CST: 25, 10.5 x 5.8 cm
p. 48

France, c. 1955
4.5 x 5.5 cm
p. 49

Spain, 1950s
CST: 66, 5.1 x 8 cm
p. 50

USA, 1950s
CST: 527 E, 10.5 x 6 cm
p. 51

Netherlands ?, c. 1945
CST: 8927, 5.7 x 10 cm
p. 52

Monaco, 1920s
10.5 x 6 cm
p. 53

"My Dorothy," USA, 1934
5.7 x 10 cm
p. 54

Germany, 1918
Leonar, 6.5 x 11 cm
p. 55

Germany, 1924
Print from glass plate negative, 9 x 12 cm
p. 56

Germany, 1924
Print from glass plate negative, 9 x 12 cm
p. 57

Charlie Chaplin, Los Angeles, USA, 1915
Album page
pp. 58/59

"Wenn man mit straffgespannter Keilhose stürzt, Kitzbühel 1941," Austria, c. 1941
7.5 x 7 cm
p. 60

USA, 1920s
9 x 7.5 cm
p. 61

Germany, 1931
Double exposure, 8 x 5 cm
p. 62

Rax, Austria, 31. 12. 1936
10.7 x 8 cm
p. 63

Four umbrellas, seven pairs of legs, USA, 1910s
9 x 3.5 cm
p. 64

"Savage," USA, 1920
10 x 6 cm
p. 65

Switzerland, 1950s
6.5 x 9.7 cm
p. 66

Spain, 1940s
7 x 10 cm
p. 67

"Frastanz," Vorarlberg, Austria, 1955
Agfa Lupex; CST: 641, 8 x 5.3 cm
p. 68

Austria, 1930s
Cardboard; reflection, 8.5 x 6 cm
p. 69

USA, 1930s
CST: 240S, 6 x 10.5 cm
p. 70

France, 1945
8 x 5.6 cm
p. 71

Germany, 1951, Incidence of light, 5.5 x 5.5 cm
p. 72

Otto von Habsburg, Bavaria, Germany, 1950s
CST: 61, 9 x 6 cm
p. 73

Germany, 1950s
Leonar-C 710, 6.5 x 10 cm
p. 74

France, 1960s
7.5 x 10.6 cm
p. 75

USA, 1920s
Stamp: Lo! Birm., May; CST: 36; double exposure, 5.8 x 10.5 cm
p. 76

USA, 1930s
Double exposure, 5.8 x 13.5 cm
p. 77

"Home Gene," USA, 1950s
5 x 7.5 cm
p. 78

Germany, 1940s
Velox, 4.8 x 8 cm
p. 79

2) Women Frauen

"Am Strand, Sommer 1937," Germany, 1937
7 x 9 cm
p. 81

Germany, 1937
Velox, 5.5 x 8 cm
p. 82

"Kate, Anna," USA, 1904
10 x 7.5 cm
p. 83

"Sylvester 55," Germany, 1955
11 x 9 cm
p. 84

USA, c. 1925
7.5 x 10 cm
p. 85

Bavaria, Germany, 1950s
7.5 x 10.5 cm
p. 86

"Chapel," USA, 1960s
CST: 829 A; double exposure, 6 x 10.5 cm
p. 87

Hungary, 1940s
CST: 862, 5 x 8 cm
p. 88

"Annie S..., Mary Ms, Vera, Anna," USA, 1916
Cyanoatype; blueprint, 11.5 x 9 cm
p. 89

"Grundelsee," Austria, 1951
9.5 x 8 cm
p. 90

"Atlantic City, N.J.," USA, 1902
Cyanotype, 8 x 8 cm
p. 91

Liezen, Austria, 1950s
Agfa Lupex, 4.8 x 5.5 cm
p. 92

"Luzy Effe," USA, 1920s
7.5 x 5.5 cm
p. 93

Salzburg, Austria, 1910s
13 x 8 cm
p. 94

Potatoe planting, Austria, 1945
Leonar, 8 x 5.5 cm
p. 95

Haus Dachsteinblick, Austria, 1960s
Leonar IF 267, 8 x 8 cm
p. 96

Czechoslovakia, 1940s
6 x 9 cm
p. 97

3) Men Männer

Austria, 1950s
Baryta paper, 16 x 11 cm
p. 99

Germany, 1950s
5.5 x 7.8 cm
p. 100

Rom, Italy, c. 1909
7 x 10 cm
p. 101

USA, c. 1947
9.4 x 6.8 cm
p. 102

USA, 1920s
CST: 68, 7.6 x 13.5 cm
p. 103

Belgium, 1950s
12.5 x 16.5 cm
p. 104

Germany, 1960s
CST: 68, 6 x 9.5 cm
p. 105

USA, 1940s
Double exposure, 7.5 x 5.4 cm
p. 106

"Eating Hot Dogs on the beach – 8 May, Venice, LA," USA, 1921
CST: 195, 13.5 x 7.5 cm
p. 107

"Picnic Peninsula Park," USA, 1914
13.5 x 8 cm
p. 108

"Waikiki, Hawaii," USA, 1944
CST: 30, 6 x 10.4 cm
p. 109

Linz, Austria, 1925
13.5 x 9 cm
p. 110

Germany, 1924
On the negative: 12, 12 x 7 cm
p. 111

Germany, 1946
CST: M 186, 6 x 9.5 cm
p. 112

Great Britain, 1920s
8 x 12 cm
p. 113

USA, 1930s
5 x 8 cm
p. 115

4) Posing Posen

Marilyn Monroe, USA, c. 1949
7 x 11 cm
p. 117

"Am Strand," Austria, 1937
Agfa Lupex; CST: 763, 8.5 x 5.5 cm
p. 118

Spain, 1948
Leonar, 6.5 x 8 cm
p. 119

"Das Bild ist...," Austria, c. 1905
Postcard paper, 8 x 10 cm
p. 120

"Ruth on Veranda, Kyle's Cottages, May 1950," USA, 1950
11.4 x 8.5 cm
p. 121

"27.8.40," Austria, 1940
Agfa Lupex, 5.4 x 5.5 cm
p. 122

Austria, 1950
Agfa Lupex; CST 727,
5.3 x 5.3 cm
p. 123

USA, c. 1905
10.7 x 7 cm
p. 124

"Oregon," USA, 1920s
9.5 x 14.7 cm
p. 125

"My Ohio Catch," USA, 1920
13 x 8 cm
p. 126

Netherlands, 1940s
5.5 x 7.5 cm
p. 127

"Mexico," Mexico, 1930
Stamp: AM Photo 72,
8.1 x 11.1 cm
p. 128

Spain, 1930s
12 x 7 cm
p. 129

USA, c. 1925
5 x 7.5 cm
p. 130

USA, April 1939
Stamp: Ray's Photo
Service, 323, 6.4 x 10.1 cm
p. 131

"Maria 40," USA, 1951
5 x 7.5 cm
p. 132

"Auf der Hotelterrasse 'Villa
Ana' 31.8.1937," Italy, 1937
5.3 x 8.5 cm
p. 133

USA, 1920
6 x 10.5 cm
p. 134

Berchtesgaden, Germany,
1931
15 x 17 cm
p. 135

"Feber 1957," Germany,
c. 1957
6.6 x 9.4 cm
p. 136

Germany, c. 1938
6 x 8 cm
p. 137

"Betty, 5/48," USA, 1948
10.4 x 7.5 cm
p. 138

USA, 1920s
8.1 x 5.6 cm
p. 139

"um 1950," Austria, 1950
6.4 x 9.6 cm
p. 140

"Karin im Töchterheim,"
Germany, 1935
Leonar, 5.6 x 8.5 cm
p. 141

"Sommer," Germany, c. 1941
Agfa Lupex, 4.5 x 7.1 cm
p. 142

"Jones Beach 21. 7. 40,"
USA, 1940
CST: 129, 5 x 8 cm
p. 143

"Four sisters: A rest period on
the way home from Ford
Knox, KY," USA, 1950s
CST: BK 66, 8 x 14 cm
p. 144

Germany, 1960s
7.6 x 12.8 cm
p. 145

USA, 1934
6 x 10.5 cm
p. 146

USA, 1934
CST: 785 U, 7.4 x 11.4 cm
p. 147

USA, 1940
Stamp: July 5, 1940 Ray's
Photoshop 573 W, 10.5 x 6 cm
p. 148

Austria, 1947
Agfa, 8 x 11.5 cm
p. 149

Madame Ruthild Skrein,
Juan-le-Pins, France, 1948
Color print, 8.5 x 5.5 cm
p. 151

5) **Kids** Kinder

Austria, c. 1929
11 x 8.1 cm
p. 153

"25. 7. geboren, 13. 8 .
getauft," Germany, 1916
8.5 x 13.5 cm
p. 154

"April 58," Germany, 1958
Postcard imprint, 6 x 8 cm
p. 155

Austria, 1930s
Stereo, 12.3 x 5.5 cm
p. 156

Austria, c. 1931
CST: 421, 6 x 9.5 cm
p. 157

"Helen taken at Bearer –
Oregon," USA, 1910
8 x 14 cm
p. 158

Blind child, blind doll, USA,
1931
Postcard imprint, 7.5 x 10 cm
p. 159

School class 1941, 3rd year,
Austria, 1941
5.5 x 8 cm
p. 161

USA, 1940s
6 x 10.5 cm
p. 162

"Girls with the parasol you
sent," USA, 1920s
6 x 10 cm
p. 163

USA, 1902
Laminated on cardboard,
11.5 x 9 cm
p. 164

c. 1925
10.5 x 8 cm
p. 165

Germany, c. 1949
8 x 13 cm
p. 166

Switzerland, 1960s
CST: 17; 2 photographs,
6 x 10 cm each
p. 167

Above: Grandchildren; below:
Grandmothers, Oregon, USA,
c. 1955
10.7 x 7.5; 12.5 x 7 cm
p. 168

USA, c. 1952
11 x 7.5 cm
p. 169

"Juni 1956," Austria, 1956
9.5 x 6.5 cm
p. 170

"März 1957," Austria, 1957
9.5 x 6.5 cm
p. 171

Germany, 1940
Stamp: 24. Mrz. 1940,
8 x 12 cm
p. 172

USA, August 1959
CST: 048 A, 7.5 x 7.5 cm
p. 173

"9.3.56," Los Angeles,
USA, 1956
CST: 052 A, 13.1 x 7.8 cm
p. 174

"3.3.40," Jugoslavia, 1940
16.8 x 12 cm
p. 175

"Eadit Healt 5 weeks old,
June 1920," USA, 1920
10.5 x 6 cm
p. 176

"November 7 Months, 1939,"
USA, 1939
10 x 6.1 cm
p. 177

Austria, 1940s
Stereo; 2 photographs,
5.5 x 5.5 cm each
p. 178

Dacoma, Canada, 1927
Velox; CST 44; Stamp: Finish
French Drug, 6 x 10.5 cm
p. 179

"Mai 1929," Switzerland, 1929
Stereo, 12 x 5.5 cm
p. 180

"Peperl 9 Monate alt," Austria, 1921
Snowflake added by touch-up, 8 x 12.5 cm
p. 181

Austria, 1949
8.1 x 11 cm
p. 182

1950s
5.5 x 8 cm
p. 183

USA, 1930s
CST: 65, 7.5 x 13.5 cm
p. 184

USA, c. 1927
Velox, 5 x 8 cm
p. 185

Vienna, Austria, 1950s
Agfa Brovira, 11.5 x 15.5 cm
p. 186

"June 1952," USA, 1952
6.5 x 10 cm
p. 187

6) Together Beisammen

Germany, 1937
10 x 7.5 cm
p. 189

USA, 1940
CST: 27 II, 9 x 11.5 cm
p. 190

USA, 1953
Kodak Velox 330, 6.5 x 10 cm
p. 191

1950
7.5 x 7.5 cm
p. 192

Austria, 1960s
7.8 x 5.5 cm
p. 193

"Gerda Traunsee," Austria, 1936
10.5 x 8 cm
p. 194

Austria, 1950s
Album page: 2 photographs, 8.5 x 5.5 cm each
p. 195

Germany, 1900s
11 x 8.1 cm
p. 196

"Weihnachten 1954," Austria, 1954
Postcard imprint, 11 x 8 cm
p. 197

Germany, 1939
Agfa Brovira, 7.8 x 3.5 cm
p. 198

"Jannie," Princeton, A.W.Y.S. Motor Corps, USA, 1941
16.5 x 11.5 cm
p. 199

France, 1920s
10.4 x 7.5 cm
p. 200

Austria, 1940s
10.5 x 8 cm
p. 201

Switzerland, c. 1948
16.7 x 12 cm
p. 202

France, 1950s
7 x 10.5 cm
p. 203

Germany, c. 1895
13.5 x 9 cm
p. 204

USA, 1900s
13.5 x 7.5 cm
p. 205

Germany, 1952
CST: H659, 6 x 9 cm
p. 206

"Boy! How we like us –," USA. May 1933
CST: 107, 6 x 10.5 cm
p. 207

Arizona, USA, 1910s
10 x 6 cm
p. 208

Bavaria, Germany, 1918
Postcard paper, 11 x 8.5 cm
p. 209

Germany, 1930s
Postcard imprint; 2 photographs,11 x 8 cm each
pp. 210/211

"ich – Deutsch Prof m Mann – Schulkollegen," Germany, 1954
11.5 x 7.5 cm
p. 212

Germany, 1907
Postcard imprint, on the negative: 762.17/6, 8 x 13 cm
p. 213

Germany, 1938
Velox, 5.5 x 5.5 cm
p. 214

Austria, 1960s
5.4 x 9.5 cm
p. 215

7) Love Liebe

Austria, 1938
Agfa Lupex, 5.5 x 8.5 cm
p. 217

USA, 1940s
8 x 6 cm
p. 218

"Sylvester 55," Austria, 1955
11 x 8 cm
p. 219

Great Britain, 1906
10.7 x 8 cm
p. 220

Germany, 1941
5.5 x 5.5 cm
p. 221

"Lido Venedig 2. Mai 1964," Italy, 1964
Stamp: 5. 5. 64; Leonar 141 i., 10 x 7 cm
p. 222

Traun river, Bad Ischl, Austria, 1930s
Postcard imprint, 7 x 10 cm
p. 223

"August 1942," USA, 1942
CST: 000, 7 x 11 cm
p. 224

Germany, 1960s
6.5 x 9.5 cm
p. 225

USA, 1940s
7.5 x 13.5 cm
p. 226

"Oregon," USA, c. 1925
CST: 13, 6 x 10.5 cm
p. 227

Germany, 1960
8.4 x 7.5 cm
p. 229

8) Nudes Akte

USA, 1950s
9.5 x 6.5 cm
p. 231

c. 1946
5 x 7.5 cm
p. 232

1950s
6.1 x 9.5 cm
p. 233

Germany, 1960s
9 x 13.7 cm
p. 234

Germany, 1960s
9 x 15.5 cm
p. 235

France, 1950s
8 x 11 cm
p. 236

France, 1950s
11.5 x 9 cm
p. 237

Germany, c. 1947
5 x 8 cm
p. 238

Paris, France, c. 1932
9.5 x 10.5 cm
p. 239

USA, 1960s
6.5 x 9.5 cm
p. 240

1920s
9.5 x 14 cm
p. 241

Germany, 1950s
Agfa Portriga Rapid, 8 x 12 cm
p. 242

Spain, 1920s
4.4 x 5 cm
p. 243

World War II – Brothel,
France, c. 1942
10.4 x 7.5 cm
p. 244

1930s
7.5 x 12.5 cm
p. 245

USA, 1940s
7.5 x 5.7 cm
p. 246

1940s
7 x 6 cm
p. 247

Pennsylvania, camera club – outdoor session, USA, 1940s
6.5 x 9.5 cm
p. 248

1950s
7.5 x 10.5 cm
p. 249

Germany, c. 1955
Agfa Color, 7 x 11 cm
p. 250

Germany, 1962
Agfa Color; CST: 0000,
11.5 x 8 cm
p. 251

1950s
Postcard imprint; CST: 5876,
12.5 x 8.7 cm
p. 252

Austria, 1950s
13 x 8 cm
p. 253

Cheesecake, USA, 1950s
11 x 8.5 cm
p. 254

USA, 1940s
8 x 5 cm
p. 255

1950s
5.5 x 7.7 cm
p. 256

USA, 1950s
7.5 x 11.5 cm
p. 257

9) Nature Natur

USA, c. 1959
7.5 x 10 cm
p. 259

"Töchterheim, Hannis Plüschhund," Dresden, Germany, 1937
5.5 x 5.3 cm
p. 260

Greece, 1940
5.5 x 5 cm
p. 261

Austria, 10. 7. 1945
Ridax, 5.5 x 8 cm
p. 262

Zug, Switzerland, c. 1928
7.5 x 9.7 cm
p. 263

"Zimmerfenster," Germany, 26. 6. 1940
5.5 x 5.5 cm
p. 264

Iris blossom, Austria, c. 1915
5.5 x 5.3 cm
p. 265

Austria, 1914
Contact print, 5.5 x 5 cm
p. 266

"Indianer," Austria, 1941
5.5 x 7 cm
p. 267

Mexico, 1933
8 x 7.5 cm
p. 268

USA, 1900s
8.5 x 8 cm
p. 269

Scotland, Great Britain, 1930
17.6 x 12.5 cm
p. 270

Germany, 1907
Laminated on cardboard,
15 x 10.5 cm
p. 271

USA, 1939
Stamp: 20 Feb. 1939,
5.7 x 10.5 cm
p. 272

Germany, c. 1935
Agfa Brovira, 9 x 6.4 cm
p. 273

"Kennwort: Korsar 1026," Austria, 1950
11.8 x 12 cm
p. 274

Italy, 1901
7.8 x 10.7 cm
p. 275

Austria, 1950
Agfa Brovira, 10.7 x 7.5 cm
p. 276

USA, 1950s
4.7 x 7.5 cm
p. 277

Russian cemetery, Burgenland, Austria, 1932
5.4 x 8.4 cm
p. 278

"Harbach (im Regen)," Austria, 1940
Contact print, 5.4 x 5.2 cm
p. 279

Austria, 1915
Oil print, 8 x 10 cm
p. 280

Alaska, USA, 1931
5.7 x 10.5 cm
p. 281

"Hund, Lux," Germany, c. 1945
5.3 x 5.5 cm
p. 282

USA, 1930s
7 x 6 cm
p. 283

USA, 1930s
10.3 x 7.8 cm
p. 284

Germany, 1932
Velox; CST 1778, 5.5 x 7.5 cm
p. 285

Italy, 1960s
8.5 x 7.4 cm
p. 286

Mont Blanc, Switzerland, 1930s
Agfa Lupex, 3.8 x 3.7 cm
p. 287

10) Sports Sport

Salzkammergut, Austria, 1925
9.8 x 7 cm
p. 289

Switzerland, 1930
Stereo, 12.1 x 5 cm
p. 290

"Beim Aufstieg... ," Switzerland, 1930s
Double exposure, 5 x 8 cm
p. 291

"Herbstduld," Munich Beer Festival, Munich, Germany, 1930
Imprint: Wellington,
13.5 x 8 cm
p. 292

"Frühlingsfahrt 1957," Austria, 1957
Postcard imprint,
13.5 x 8.5 cm
p. 293

Upper Austria, Austria, 1925
13.7 x 8.5 cm
p. 294

USA, c. 1925
8 x 6 cm
p. 295

"Österr. – Schottland 27. 5. 51 Stadion Wien," Austria, 1951
CST 61-0, 9.4 x 6.3 cm
p. 296

"Autorennen von Monza 11. 9. 55 – Sieger Fangio," Italy, 1955
8 x 5.5 cm
p. 297

Portland, USA, 1930s
CST: 11, 8 x 14 cm
p. 298

"Waikiki, Hawaiian Islands," USA, 1944
5.8 x 10 cm
p. 299

"Der Engel," Tyrol, Austria, 1933
11 x 8 cm
p. 300

"Lieber Sohn ...," Austria, 1930
Postcard imprint, 10.5 x 8 cm
p. 301

Styria, Austria, c. 1955
5 x 6.5 cm
p. 302

"Rax," Austria, 1936
5.5 x 8 cm
p. 303

Schneeberg, Austria, 1941
Print from glass plate negative, 9 x 10 cm
p. 304

Kitzbühel, Austria, 1939
Agfa, 7 x 8.8 cm
p. 305

Germany, 1960
Agfa; CST 605, 5.5 x 9 cm
p. 306

Kitzbühel, Austria, 1939
Agfa, 11 x 7.3 cm
p. 307

USA, 1940
6.1 x 4.1 cm
p. 308

Karlsbad, Czechoslovakia, 1925
5 x 8 cm
p. 309

Great Britain, 1930s
7 x 12 cm
p. 310

"Out for the count in 7 rounds," Great Britain, c. 1949
12.8 x 8.5 cm
p. 311

11) Travels Reisen

1907
9 x 12 cm
p. 313

"Innsbruck 5.10.1935," Austria, 1935
5.5 x 8 cm
p. 314

"Pommern 1929," Germany, 1929
7 x 5 cm
p. 315

"Mai 1932, Ägypten, Gizeh, Pyramiden," Egypt, 1932
CST: 546, 8.5 x 5.5 cm
p. 316

"March 1951, Cuba," Havana, Cuba, 1951
11 x 7.5 cm
p. 317

Trip, USA, 1930s
4.4 x 10.7 cm
p. 318

USA, 1930s
CST: 452, 7.5 x 5.5 cm
p. 319

Austria, 1920s
Incidence of light on the negative before shooting, 3.5 x 5.8 cm
p. 320

Austria, c. 1955
7 x 6.5 cm
p. 321

Switzerland, 1937
11.3 x 8 cm
p. 322

Germany, 1942
10.5 x 7.5 cm
p. 323

Germany, 1930
Stereo, 12.5 x 5 cm
p. 324

Austria, 1940
Contact print, 8 x 11.3 cm
p. 325

Canada, 1930s
Stamp: Doria Photo Tone 18, 6 x 10.5 cm
p. 326

"Von Zürs, Pfingsten 30," Austria, 1930
Agfa Lupex; CST: EL 64 A, 5 x 7.8 cm
p. 327

"Lincoln Monument, in distance Washington Monument, Washington. D.C.," USA, c. 1932
6 x 10.5 cm
p. 328

"May-15-1911," Arizona, USA, 1911
Postcard paper, 8.4 x 5 cm
p. 329

"8.8.37," Austria, 1937
Agfa, 4.5 x 6.8 cm
p. 330

Italy, 1905
12.5 x 8.5 cm
p. 331

USA, c. 1912
9.8 x 7.8 cm
p. 332

Cape Horn, Argentina, c. 1905
12.4 x 6.8 cm
p. 333

On the Nile, Egypt, 1910s
11.7 x 9.5 cm
p. 334

1950s
13.8 x 9.5 cm
p. 335

"San Remo, Juli 1938," Italy, 1938
11.7 x 5.8 cm
p. 336

"Kinder ist das Lebe schön – einmal richtig baden gehen," Austria, 1956
8 x 5.5 cm
p. 337

"Don Camillo und Peppone – An Bord der 'Victoria', 27. Juli 1953," Spain, 1953
9.5 x 6 cm
p. 338

USA, c. 1948
CST: 770 G, 13 x 8.5 cm
p. 339

Germany, 1942
8 x 5 cm
p. 340

Germany, 1921
10.5 x 6 cm
p. 341

Germany, 1940s
13 x 10 cm
p. 342

USA, 1913
10 x 7.5 cm
p. 343

"Zürich – Dampfschiffahrt nach Rapperswill," Switzerland, 1930s
11 x 8 cm
p. 344

Bremen–Berlin, Atlantic, 1930s
15 x 11.4 cm
p. 345

Austria, 1920s
Postcard paper, 7.5 x 11 cm
p. 346

Walter Grundmann with Lumpi and Susi, Germany, 1929
13 x 8.5 cm
p. 347

USA, 1920s
8 x 13 cm
p. 348

Czechoslovakia, 1940s
Stamp: Fotohaus Potrykiowicz, 8 x 5.5 cm
p. 349

USA, 1930s
CST: 279, 7 x 7.5 cm
p. 350

"Osterfahrt Schwarzwald," Germany, 1950
Postcard imprint, 13.7 x 8 cm
p. 351

Germany, 1935
Agfa Lupex, 8 x 5.3 cm
p. 352

"Deine 1. Fahrt allein 3. Oktober 1937," Germany, 1937
5 x 5.5 cm
p. 353

12) Transportation
Verkehr

Germany, 1936
17 x 11 cm
p. 355

"'Roma-Britannic' leaving St. George," c. 1938
10 x 5.5 cm
p. 356

Ocean, 1930s
CST: 012E, 6 x 10.7 cm
p. 357

"Pacific Ocean, Washington State –1915," USA, 1915
Album page: 3 photographs, 18 x 21 cm
p. 358

Great Britain, 1920s
10 x 6 cm
p. 359

1920s
Stereo, 11.5 x 4.8 cm
p. 360

USA, 1950s
9 x 9.5 cm
p. 361

"Luftschiff Graf Zeppelin LZ 127, in Wien, 12. Iuli 1931," Austria, 1931
17.3 x 12.5 cm
p. 362

"Renner's Lenkballon 'Estaric' Puch-Motor, Graz," Austria, c. 1902–05
12.5 x 7 cm
p. 363

Italy, 1910s
Postcard imprint, 4.7 x 9.7 cm
p. 364

France, c. 1908
On the negative: 21, 13.5 x 9 cm
p. 365

World War II, France, c. 1940
10.8 x 8.3 cm
p. 366

German air force, Germany, c. 1914
16.3 x 10 cm
p. 367

Canada, 1930s
11.3 x 8 cm
p. 368

In Death Valley, USA, c. 1929
10.5 x 6 cm
p. 369

"Big Horn Mountains," Oregon, USA, 1940s
10 x 5.5 cm
p. 370

USA, 1940s
CST: 18, 5.7 x 10 cm
p. 371

France, 1920s
16.7 x 10 cm
p. 372

Explosion, USA, 1944
CST: Oct. 4, 1944 – 881L, 10.5 x 6 cm
p. 373

Photographs for insurance company, USA, 1920s
2 photgraphs, 10 x 6 cm each
p. 374

"The 'Peter Ardsle' near Warrenton," USA, 1920s
10.5 x 6.2 cm
p. 375

Traffic accident, USA, c. 1915
CST: E5, 7.8 x 13 cm
p. 376

"Zwischen Brekvaselv und Melingsmo," 1942
Mimosa synotype, 8.2 x 5.7 cm
p. 377

USA, 1950s
12.3 x 17 cm
p. 378

"Lancia, Av. Foch 115, 113," France, 1940s
11.5 x 12.5 cm
p. 379

"Idaho," USA, c. 1952
CST: 449, 6 x 10.5 cm
p. 380

"Pfingsten 1937 Reichsautobahn," Germany, 1937
Agfa, 7.7 x 12.6 cm
p. 381

"West Palm Beach," USA, 1920s
11.5 x 6.5 cm
p. 382

"Could be Bobby's 1st plane," USA, c. 1919
11.5 x 8.5 cm
p. 383

13) Big Town – Small Town
Großstadt – Kleinstadt

One woman – two shadows, Austria, 1950s
CST: A 1805, 3.7 x 5.5 cm
p. 385

Austria, 1941
5.3 x 5 cm
p. 386

Nice ?, France, c. 1935
Agfa Lupex, 5.5 x 5.5 cm
p. 387

Germany, 1900s
5.4 x 8.1 cm
p. 388

"Clinton at ...," USA, 1910s
10.4 x 8 cm
p. 389

Austria, c. 1938
10.5 x 7.7 cm
p. 390

"Apollotheater," Vienna, Austria, 1920s
Stereo, 11 x 4.5 cm
p. 391

China Town, San Francisco ?, USA, 1940s
2 photographs, 3.5 x 6 cm each
p. 392

USA, c. 1935
CST: 412 F, 8.1 x 5.6 cm
p. 393

"Toledo, Kathedrale, Tor," Spain, 1950s
6 x 8 cm
p. 394

"August 1938," Vienna, Austria, 1938
CST: 438, 5 x 8.5 cm
p. 395

Germany, c. 1938
CST: 810; serial shooting with Arriflex film camera; 3 photographs, 6.5 x 17 cm
p. 396

Germany, c. 1938
Serial shooting with Arriflex film camera; 3 photographs, 6.5 x 17 cm
p. 396

"Nr. 47," Germany, 1928
CST: 33508, 8 x 13 cm
p. 397

Castle gate, Vienna, Austria, c. 1913
Oil print, 7.5 x 9.5 cm
p. 398

Golden Gate Bridge pillar, San Francisco, USA
CST: 373 C, 6 x 10.5 cm
p. 399

Drinking cure, Karlsbad ?, Czechoslovakia, 1906
13.7 x 8.5 cm
p. 400

Public building, c. 1925
10.5 x 6 cm
p. 401

"1959, May," New York, USA, 1959
7.5 x 11 cm
p. 402

USA, 1931
CST: 1125, 8 x 13 cm
p. 403

USA, c. 1918
Postcard imprint; on the negative: Bentler Albio, 13.3 x 8.3 cm
p. 404

USA, 1939
CST: May 6, 1939, 5, 8.5 x 6 cm
p. 405

"Interurban," USA, 1920s
8.7 x 5.5 cm
p. 406

USA, 1934
Stamp: Portsmouth, Ohio, App 20, 1934, 273, 10.5 x 6 cm
p. 407

USA, 1920s
10.4 x 6 cm
p. 408

USA, 1940s
CST: C05, 5 x 6 cm
p. 409

USA, 1929
Cyanotype, 8 x 13.7 cm
p. 410

Lower Manhattan, New York, USA, 1930s
Cyanotype, 5 x 8 cm
p. 411

"This picture was taken at Ogden, Utah," USA, 1944
CST: 12, 6 x 10 cm
p. 412

"For Carlsons...,"
Photographs for insurance company after hurricane, USA, 1955
7.5 x 5 cm
p. 413

"Chicago Dec. 1941 Oakst. Room 706," USA, 1941
CST: 654 Y, 8 x 5.5 cm
p. 414

"Chicago Dec. 1941 Oakst. Room 706," USA, 1941
CST: 654 Y, 5.3 x 7.8 cm
p. 415

Italy, 1950s
Ferrania, 13 x 7.6 cm
p. 416

"Northwest Perspective," USA, 1910s
7.7 x 13 cm
p. 417

14) At Work
Bei der Arbeit

Fragment, 1910s
20.7 x 15.2 cm
p. 419

Meszaros, Hungary, 1919
10.4 x 7.3 cm
p. 420

Germany, 1920s
8.5 x 13.5 cm
p. 421

Germany, 1950s
Agfa, 7.5 x 5 cm
p. 422

Bavaria, Germany, 1940s
7 x 5.5 cm
p. 423

"1928. II. 30," Hungary, 1928
13.6 x 8.5 cm
p. 424

Austria, 1922
13.5 x 9 cm
p. 425

Josef Klackl, Herren–Damenmoden, Austria, 1947
7.8 x 10.3 cm
p. 426

"Zum Andenken Tante, Onkel und Mira," Horse meat, Austria, November 1930
Postcard imprint, 7.8 x 12.4 cm
p. 427

Italy, 1940s
12.8 x 8 cm
p. 428

USA, 1920s
Double exposure, 13.3 x 7.5 cm
p. 429

Coiffeur, Eindhoven, Netherlands, 1920
Postcard imprint, 8.5 x 13.5 cm
p. 430

A. Dickbauer, Austria, 1948
Agfa; CST 627, 13 x 8 cm
p. 431

Inn, Austria, c. 1913
Postcard imprint, 12.3 x 8 cm
p. 432

Ladies' lingerie, clearance sale, 1930
Postcard imprint, 11.8 x 8 cm
p. 433

"We choked wheat till nearly Sunday June 14," USA, 1914
7.5 x 5 cm
p. 434

"St. Magdalene, Wildfütterung," Austria, 1940
Velox, 5 x 8 cm
p. 435

"Oktober 1929 Umzug," Germany, 1929
7.8 x 11 cm
p. 436

Czechoslovakia, 1931
Postcard imprint, 8 x 13 cm
p. 437

Germany, 1920
6.3 x 8 cm
p. 438

Austria, c. 1905
Postcard imprint, 13.5 x 8.5 cm
p. 439

Germany, 1910
Postcard imprint, 8.3 x 7.5 cm
p. 440

Austria, 1910s
Postcard imprint, 8.3 x 13.5 cm
p. 441

Germany, 1940
8.4 x 13 cm
p. 442

Poland, 1930
Postcard imprint, 8 x 11 cm
p. 443

Austria, 1940s
10.5 x 8 cm
p. 444

"Zum Andenken an das Kriegsjahr," Austria, 1914–15
Postcard imprint, 13.5 x 8.5 cm
p. 445

Italy, 1900s
15.5 x 11.5 cm
p. 446

Germany, 1910
Postcard imprint, 8.5 x 13.5 cm
p. 447

15) War Krieg

Military hospital, Germany, c. 1943
4.5 x 7.7 cm
p. 449

Field kitchen, Austria, 1916
Stamp: Vergrößerungsanstalt, 13.3 x 8.6 cm
p. 450

"Rentiergespann", Norway, 1940–41
8 x 6 cm
p. 451

Germany, c. 1942
Album page: 5 photographs, 22 x 18 cm
p. 452

"7. 5. 42, Kaiser-Wilhelm-Denkmal," Germany, 1942
8 x 11 cm
p. 453

Home leave, Germany, 1943
5 x 8 cm
p. 454

"Irmi 15 1/2 M.! 12. 11. 39," Germany, 1939
7.5 x 12 cm
p. 455

"Obersalzberg, Hitlers Aussichtsfenster, nach Bombardierung," Berchtesgaden, Germany, 1948
13 x 8 cm
p. 456

Eva Braun, Obersalzberg, Berchtesgaden, Germany, c. 1940
Postcard paper, 7.7 x 12.5 cm
p. 457

Reichs labor service, Germany, c. 1937
8 x 5.5 cm
p. 458

Pearl Harbor, Hawaii, USA, c. 1940
CST: 14030; stamp: Movieland – Honolulu..., 7.7 x 12 cm
p. 459

Adolf Hitler – album page assembled by a domestic servant in Obersalzberg, Berchtesgaden, Germany
Album page: 9 photographs, 31 x 22 cm
pp. 460/461

Presumably Adolf Hitler as private – positional battle in French-Flanders, France, 1917
7.7 x 11.3 cm
p. 462

Hidden swastika, Austria, c. 1940
Postcard paper, 8 x 13 cm
p. 463

"France, Dec. 1944. Pfc Cohen and an unidentified Frenchman relieving themselves simultaneously at one of those practical and not gaudy open-air French latrines," France, 1944
CST: 836 D, 5.8 x 10.4 cm
p. 464

Tabacco factory, Austria, 1938
Postcard imprint, 7.7 x 12.7 cm
p. 465

Brandenburger Tor, Berlin, Germany, 1940s
Agfa Lupex, 5.5 x 4 cm
p. 466

"Myself just after a loop," USA, c. 1929
5.4 x 7.8 cm
p. 467

"Ostbahnhof," Vienna, Austria, c. 1915
12.5 x 8 cm
p. 468

Medical examination for military service, Austria, 1913
10.5 x 8 cm
p. 469

Germany, c. 1942
14 x 9.5 cm
p. 470

Home comer from Russia, Germany, 1947
9.3 x 6.5 cm
p. 471

"Bürgerkrieg – Café Arbeiterheim ," Vienna, Austria, 1934
7.5 x 5.4 cm
p. 472

"Jap on sentry duty," New Guinea, 1942
5 x 5 cm
p. 473

Austria, c. 1914
6 x 11.3 cm
p. 474

Kaiser Franz Joseph I. and heir to the throne Franz Ferdinand: Emperor's manoeuvre, Austria, c. 1905
13.2 x 7.7 cm
p. 475

Austria, c. 1914
6 x 8.5 cm
p. 476

"Na památku nasi manje ...," Germany, c. 1936
5.4 x 5.4 cm
p. 477

Austria, 1941
7.5 x 11 cm
p. 478

"Nürnberg," Germany, 1939
8.4 x 5.5 cm
p. 479

"Poltnitz," heading for Polsnepz, Czechoslovakia, 1939
5.5 x 8.5 cm
p. 480

Poland, c. 1939
CST: A 567, 7.7 x 5.3 cm
p. 481

Germany, 1939
8.5 x 7 cm
p. 482

Germany, c. 1940
CST: 478, 8.4 x 5.5 cm
p. 483

Field provision, Serbia, c. 1915
11.3 x 9 cm
p. 484

USA, 1944
CST: 681; double exposure, 6 x 10.5 cm
p. 485

"Dach der Trostkaserne Mai 1943," Vienna, Austria, 1943
Postcard paper, 12.7 x 8 cm
p. 486

Front in the Balkans, Serbia, c. 1942
Lupex; CST: 660, 5.5 x 4.5 cm
p. 487

"Weltkrieg 1914/16," hospital of the reserves, Austria, 1914–16
10 x 7.5 cm
p. 488

Priest and swastika, Austria, c. 1938
Lupex, 5.4 x 8 cm
p. 489

"Chotrjow, 2. 6. 18," Galicia (presumably), 1918
11 x 8 cm
p. 490

"Kölner Junge u. Pauli, Italien, Modena," Italy, 1944
12.7 x 7.5 cm
p. 491

Presumably German soldiers, France, c. 1918
7.5 x 5.5 cm
p. 492

"38 cm Granat Piave," Piave front, Italy, 1915
13.5 x 8.4 cm
p. 493

"Idyll," Russland, c. 1943
Leonar; CST: 641, 5.4 x 5.4 cm
p. 494

Germany, 1942
CST: 2306, 5.4 x 8.5 cm
p. 495

Germany, 1941
Leonar, 5.4 x 8.5 cm
p. 496

Russland, c. 1943
Velox, 5 x 8 cm
p. 497

"Decoration day parade in rain," USA, c. 1919
7.3 x 10.1 cm
p. 498

Russland, c. 1943
7.8 x 11.5 cm
p. 499

16) Artistic Photography
Künstlerische Fotografie

France, 1930s
8.3 x 11.3 cm
p. 501

1943
CST: 228, 5 x 7.7 cm
p. 502

"Friedensdrähte nach allen Richtungen," Brest-Litowsk, Poland, c. 1916
9.3 x 10.4 cm
p. 503

Germany, 1940s
5 x 8.5 cm
p. 504

"Holy Rollers," Bahamas, USA, c. 1915
6 x 10.5 cm
p. 505

"Badezimmer," Switzerland, 1937
5.5 x 8 cm
p. 506

"Joachimstal Sudetengau März 39"
Czechoslovakia, then Germany, 1939
Agfa Lupex, 7 x 4 cm
p. 507

Austria, 1960
Kodakcolor, 7.5 x 7.5 cm
p. 508

Germany, 1959
Agfa, 6.5 x 9.5 cm
p. 509

"Unser Vorzimmer," Austria, 1946
Postcard imprint, 11.5 x 8 cm
p. 510

Italy, 1940s
8 x 5.5 cm
p. 511

Germany, 1933
5.5 x 8 cm
p. 512

"Beach cabin, Merchant Beach," USA, 1914
10.4 x 6.1 cm
p. 513

Switzerland, 1950s
5.5 x 11 cm
p. 514

Norway, 1952
CST 606, 8.3 x 5.5 cm
p. 515

USA, 1880s
Albumen print, 7.5 x 7 cm
p. 516

Austria, 1920
7.8 x 5.5 cm
p. 517

Italy, 1900s
10 x 6.5 cm
p. 518

Oregon, USA, c. 1918
7.5 x 9.5 cm
p. 519

"1954 Lido in V.," Venice, Italy, 1954
9.5 x 6.4 cm
p. 520

USA, 1920s
10 x 6.5 cm
p. 521

Atomium, landmark of the world fair in Brussels, Belgium, 1958
6.4 x 9.5 cm
p. 522

Reflection in the ceiling light, Germany, 1949
18 x 16.4 cm
p. 523

USA, 1930
Velox, 10.5 x 6 cm
p. 524

USA, 1920s
CST: 27, 10.5 x 6 cm
p. 525

"Oktober 1932, Linz," Austria, 1932
7 x 5 cm
p. 526

Germany, 1933
Album page: 4 photographs, 5 x 8 cm each
p. 527

USA, 1951
9.5 x 9.7 cm
p. 528

1969
CST: 230A, 7.5 x 8 cm
p. 529

View of the Swabian Sea, Germany, 1924
7.8 x 5.5 cm
p. 530

Germany, 1950
Contact print, 4.8 x 5 cm
p. 531

Blast furnace smelting, Germany, c. 1946
Agfa Lupex; CST: 612, 5.5 x 8.3 cm
p. 532

Minesweeper, Atlantic Ocean, 1943
Agfa Lupex, 5.3 x 8 cm
p. 533

Model for tombstone picture, corroded by enamel chemicals, Germany, 1880s
Salt paper on cardboard, 5.7 x 9.5 cm
p. 535

17) Photographers
Fotografen

Austria, 1950
Agfa Brovira, 8.5 x 8.5 cm
p. 537

"April 1951," Germany, 1951
7.5 x 11.5 cm
p. 538

USA, 1930s
6.5 x 10 cm
p. 539

Austria, 1940s
10.5 x 7.5 cm
p. 540

"Zeiss Schätzmikroskop," Germany, 1940s
5.4 x 8 cm
p. 541

"Portland," professional photographer, USA, 1930s
7.5 x 5 cm
p. 542

"Vor dem Schuß beim Almwirtshaus, 1/30 –6'3, 1936. II. 1300," Austria, 1936
7.5 x 12.5 cm
p. 543

Czechoslovakia, 1910s
9.5 x 7.5 cm
p. 544

USA, 1950s
13 x 8 cm
p. 545

"Warte Wohnung," Germany, 1959
5 x 7.5 cm
p. 547

Selected Bibliography Ausgewählte Bibliografie

Walter Benjamin. *Das Kunstwerk im Zeitalter seiner technischen Reduzierbarkeit.* Frankfurt/Main 1975

The Blackbook Photography. New York 2003

Marianne Brandt. *Fotografien am Bauhaus.* Ostfildern-Ruit 2003

Marcelo Brodsky, *Buena memoria/Good Memory,* Ostfildern-Ruit 2003

Brian Coe, Paul Gates. *The Snapshot Photograph: The Rise of Popular Photography, 1888–1939.* London 1977

Tacita Dean. *Floh.* Göttingen 2001

Bodo van Dewitz. *Agfa Foto-Historama Köln.* Braunschweig 1988

Disderi. *L'Art de la photographie.* Paris 1862

Ute Eskildsen. *Ein Bilderbuch. Die fotografische Sammlung im Museum Folkwang.* Göttingen 2003

Monika Faber. *Das Auge und der Apparat. Die Fotosammlung der Albertina.* Ostfildern-Ruit 2003

Hans-Peter Feldmann. *Voyeur.* Köln 1997

Vilém Flusser. *Für eine Philosophie der Fotografie.* 5th ed., Göttingen 2000

Das Fotomuseum im Münchner Stadtmuseum. Heidelberg1991

Peter Galassi. *American Photography 1890–1965 from The Museum of Modern Art, New York.* New York 1995

Alice Rose George. *Here is New York, a Democracy of Photographs.* Zürich 2002

Georg Grosz. *Das Auge des Künstlers. Photographien, New York 1932.* Weingarten 2002

Roger Handy. *Summer Vacation/Found Photographs.* Santa Barbara 2002

Ulrike Hick. *Geschichte der optischen Medien.* Munich 1999

Julia Hirsh. *Family Photographs: Content, Meaning and Effect.* New York 1981

Donald Hoffmann. *Visuelle Intelligenz.* Munich 2003

Teresa Hubbard, Alexander Birchler. *Scene.* Zürich 1998

Gottfried Jäger. *Die Kunst der abstrakten Fotografie.* Stuttgart 2002

Peter Jenny. *Bildkonzepte.* Mainz 2000

Rudolf Kicken. "Photographie als Sammlerobjekt." In: *Fotografie,* no. 5, 1978

Guido Knopp. *100 Jahre. Die großen Bilder des 20. Jahrhunderts.* Munich 1999

Rolf H. Krauss. *Walter Benjamin und der neue Blick auf die Photographie.* Ostfildern-Ruit 1998

Ellen Maas. *Die goldenen Jahre der Photoalben. Fundgrube und Spiegel von gestern.* Cologne 1977

Douglas R. Nickel. *Snapshots: The Photography of Everyday Life, 1888 to the Present.* San Francisco 1998

Ulrich Pohlmann. "Die vergessenen Fotomuseen." In: *Fotogeschichte,* no. 35, 1990, pp. 14–21

Els Rijper. *The American Invention of Our World 1943–1959.* New York 2002

Rolf Sachsse. *Die Erziehung zum Wegsehen.* Dresden 2003

August Sander. *Menschen des 20. Jahrhunderts.* Berlin 1929

Marjen Schmidt. *Fotografien in Museen, Archiven und Sammlungen.* Munich 1994

Mark Silber. *The Family Album.* Boston 1973

Christian Skrein. *68.* Vienna 2001

Urs Stahel, Giorgio Wolfensberger. *Industriebild.* Zürich 1994

Timm Starl. *Knipser. Die Bildgeschichte der privaten Fotografie in Deutschland und Österreich von 1880 bis 1980.* Munich 1995

Edward Steichen. *The Family of Man.* New York 1955

Otto Steinert (ed.). *Subjektive Fotografie. Ein Bildband moderner europäischer Fotografie.* Bonn 1952

Alfred Stieglitz. *Stieglitz on Photography. His Selected Essays and Notes.* New York 2000

William Henry Fox Talbot. *The Pencil of Nature.* London 1844 (reprint: Budapest 1998)

Urs Tillmanns. *Fotolexikon.* Schaffhausen 1991

Colin Jacobson (ed.). *Underexposed. Pictures can lie and liars use pictures.* London 2002

Jac G. Ferwerda. *The World of 3-D: a Practical Guide to Stereo Photography.* Amsterdam 1990

Jeff Wall. *Szenarien im Bildraum der Wirklichkeit. Essays und Interviews.* Dresden 1997

Thomas Wather. *Other Pictures.* Santa Fe 2000

Acknowledgements Dank

We would like to thank all photographers whose pictures were used for this publication. For their great support we like to thank the following persons without whom this project would not have been possible: Dank an alle Fotografen, deren Bilder für diese Publikation verwendet wurden. Für ihre hilfreiche Unterstützung danken für den folgenden Personen, ohne die dieses umfangreiche Projekt nicht möglich gewesen wäre:

Carl Aigner, St. Pölten
Günther Andorfer, Seewalchen
Jack Banning, New York
Peter Baum, Linz
Thomas Bell, Portland
Hendrik Berinson, Berlin
Bärbel Bernsdorfer, Deutschlandsberg
Adam Boxer, New York
Christian Brandstätter, Vienna
Nicki Brandstätter, Vienna
Monika Brücher-Bernsköper, Paris
Barbara Brunner, Anif
Heike Curtze, Vienna-Berlin
Gerhard Dietrich, Cologne
Lui Dimanche, Vienna
Christian Dürkheim, London
Michael Etter, Berlin
Michael Fairley, Seattle
Elisabeth Ginthör, Vienna
Albrecht Habsburg-Lothringen, Salzburg
Richie Hart, New York
Markus Hartmann, Stuttgart
Claudia Hell, Großgmain
William Helter, Naples, Florida
Rosi Jantz, Vienna
Mattheus Jiszda, Vienna
P. and E. Kaindl, St. Gilgen
Martina Kandeler-Fritsch, Vienna
Rudolf Kicken, Berlin
Alfred Kohlhammer, Klosterneuburg
Manfred Kostal, Vienna
Gerhard Makinger, Salzburg
Michael Maslan, Seattle
Jan Mathias, Los Angeles
Patrick Meier, Paris
Maria Neuhardt, Salzburg
Traudl Neuhardt, Salzburg
Birgit C. Orlich, Salzburg
Paola de Polo Saibanti, Florence
Willy Puchner, Vienna
Gabi Reich, Stainz
Markus Schaden, Cologne
Maria Schlupp-Denzel, Marco Island
Dietrich Schneider-Henn, Munich
Helfried Seemann, Vienna
Ruthild Skrein, Vienna
Alexander Skrein, Vienna
Horst Stassny, Linz
Jo C. Tartt, Washington D.C.
Stefan Vargha, Salzburg
Ludwig Vavrovsky, Salzburg
David Winter, New York
Margit Zuckriegel, Salzburg

I dedicate this book to
Daniela, Raoul, Maximilian
and to Maria

This catalogue is published in conjunction with the exhibition
Snapshots – The Eye of the Century
MAK – Österreichisches Museum für Angewandte Kunst, Vienna: March 24 until May 23, 2004
Nederlands Foto Museum, Rotterdam: June 26 until September 13, 2004
Museum für Angewandte Kunst, Cologne: September 29 until November 28, 2004
Deutsches Historisches Museum, Berlin: 2006

Diese Publikation erscheint anlässlich der Ausstellungstournee
Snapshots – The Eye of the Century
MAK – Österreichisches Museum für Angewandte Kunst, Wien: 24. März bis 23. Mai 2004
Nederlands Foto Museum, Rotterdam: 26. Juni bis 13. September 2004
Museum für Angewandte Kunst, Köln: 29. September bis 28. November 2004
Deutsches Historisches Museum, Berlin: 2006

Editor Herausgeber: Christian Skrein
Text coordination Textkoordination: Birgit C. Orlich
Catalogue conception Katalogkonzeption: Daniela Bell-Skrein
Catalogue assistance Katalogassistenz: Rosi Jantz
Copy-editing Lektorat: Karin Osbahr, Tas Skorupa
Translations Übersetzungen: Alfons Rutigliano, Marlene Müller-Haas
Graphic Design Grafische Gestaltung: Daniela Bell-Skrein, Christine Müller, Andreas Platzgummer
Reproductions Reproduktionen: Pixelstrom, Vienna Wien
Gesamtherstellung Printed by: Dr. Cantz'sche Druckerei, Ostfildern-Ruit

All images are owned by Christian Skrein Photo Collection.
Christian Skrein is represented by:
IMAGNO brandstätter images
Würthgasse 14
1190 Wien
Austria
T +43 / 1 / 369 1 369-0
F +43 / 1 / 369 1 369-20
Email: office@imagno.com
Website : www.imagno.com

Published by Erschienen im
Hatje Cantz Verlag
Senefelderstr. 12
73760 Ostfildern-Ruit
Deutschland / Germany
Tel. +49 / 7 11 / 4 40 50
Fax +49 / 7 11 / 4 40 52 20
www.hatjecantz.de

Hatje Cantz books are available internationally at selected bookstores and from the following distribution partners:

USA/North America – D.A.P., Distributed Art Publishers, New York, www.artbook.com
France – Interart, Paris, interart.paris@wanadoo.fr
UK – Art Books International, London, sales@art-bks.com
Belgium – Exhibitions International, Leuven, www.exhibitionsinternational.be
Australia – Towerbooks, French Forest (Sydney), towerbks@zipworld.com.au

For Asia, Japan, South America, and Africa, as well as for general questions, please contact Hatje Cantz directly at sales@hatjecantz.de, or visit our homepage www.hatjecantz.com for further information.

ISBN 3-7757-1396-4
Printed in Germany

EXHIBITION AUSSTELLUNG

Artistic concept Künstlerische Konzeption: Christian Skrein
Exhibition design Ausstellungsgestaltung: Peter Noever, Christian Skrein
Curator Kurator: Rüdiger Andorfer, MAK Wien
Exhibition assistance Ausstellungsassistenz: Rosi Jantz